Contemporary Moral Issues

Fourth Edition

Contemporary Moral Issues

Fourth Edition

Wesley Cragg
George R. Gardiner Professor of Business Ethics
York University

Christine M. Koggel
Department of Philosophy
Bryn Mawr College

McGraw-Hill Ryerson Limited

Toronto Montreal New York Auckland Bogotá Caracas
Lisbon London Madrid Mexico Milan New Delhi
San Juan Singapore Sydney Tokyo

McGraw-Hill
Ryerson Limited

A Subsidiary of The McGraw-Hill Companies

CONTEMPORARY MORAL ISSUES
Fourth Edition

Copyright © 1997, 1992, 1987, 1983 McGraw-Hill Ryerson Limited, a Subsidiary of The McGraw-Hill Companies. All rights reserved. No part of this publication may be reproduced or transmitted in any form or by any means, or stored in a data base or retrieval system, without the prior written permission of McGraw-Hill Ryerson Limited, or in the case of photocopying or other reprographic copying, a licence from CANCOPY (the Canadian Copyright Licensing Agency), 6 Adelaide Street East, Suite 900, Toronto, Ontario, M5C 1H6.

Any request for photocopying, recording, or taping of any part of this publication shall be directed in writing to CANCOPY.

ISBN: 0-07-552784-7

1 2 3 4 5 6 7 8 9 10 BG 6 5 4 3 2 1 0 9 8 7

Printed and bound in Canada

Care has been taken to trace ownership of copyright material contained in this text. The publishers will gladly take any information that will enable them to rectify any reference or credit in subsequent editions.

Editor-in-Chief: Dave Ward
Developmental Editor: Laurie Graham
Production Editor: Heather Lange
Production Co-ordinator: Nicla Dattolico
Interior and Cover Design: Dianna Little
Cover Image: Todd Davidson/The Image Bank
Typesetter: McGraphics Desktop Publishing Ltd.
Printer: Best Book Manufacturers

Canadian Cataloguing in Publication Data

Main entry under title:

Contemporary moral issues

4th ed.
ISBN 0-07-552784-7

1. Social ethics. I. Cragg, Wesley. II. Koggel, Christine M.

HN110.Z9M66 1997   170   C96-932099-X

In memory of my father,
Arthur R. Cragg
(WC)

For my parents
(CMK)

Table of Contents

Chapter 3: Capital Punishment 110

Chapter 4: Pornography 178

Chapter 5: Discrimination 224

Chapter 6: Affirmative Action 294

Preface to the Fourth Edition

The first edition of *Contemporary Moral Issues* was published in 1983. A comparison of the contents of that edition and the subsequent second and third editions with this fourth edition illustrates how dramatically the social landscape has changed in Canada over the intervening period. The chapters on abortion and pornography illustrate this well. New chapters on discrimination, affirmative action, and poverty are further evidence, were any needed. The justifiability of nuclear deterrence is no longer actively debated. It is true that nuclear weapons remain in large numbers. However, where they are concerned, the focus of debate has shifted to problems of their disposal. The war in the Persian Gulf supported by the United Nations has faded from public discussion, though the problems that caused it remain largely unresolved. Concern with war as an instrument of international politics has been displaced with concern for civil conflicts around the world and the vast displacement of people. Events in Rwanda and the former Yugoslavia have become potent symbols of this. As a result, the chapters on nuclear deterrence (second edition) and war (third edition) have been replaced by a chapter on poverty and the duty of those who are well off to alleviate suffering and poverty both locally and globally.

Change in the moral issues landscape has not been universal, however. The law with respect to euthanasia has not changed in spite of high-profile legal challenges not dissimilar to those mounted by Henry Morgentaler in the 1970s and 1980s. The capital punishment debate has returned to the fourth edition. It is an issue that will not die in spite of the fact that the last execution in Canada took place more than thirty years ago. There have been significant changes in the legal status of aboriginal peoples resulting from the Constitution Act of 1982 and subsequent judicial interpretation of its provisions. Nevertheless, the material position of First Nations peoples has not changed substantially since 1983 and few significant land claim settlements have occurred.

This edition brings a significant editorial change that should be noted. There is in this edition a new chapter entitled "Tools and Theories," which replaces the chapter on "Philosophy and the Resolution of Moral Issues." This change represents a decision to deal more directly with moral theory and its role in the resolution of moral issues and has been motivated by several considerations. First, a chapter on theory is a standard feature of most moral issues texts and was widely requested by users and non-users alike. Secondly, for better or worse, philosophical discussion of moral issues is now firmly entrenched in the philosophical community. This was not so obviously the case in 1983, at which time there was considerable debate about what philosophy had to contribute to the resolution of moral issues. This debate goes on. However, its texture has changed in significant ways. Today it is moral theory and its role in the resolution of concrete moral problems that is widely debated. The chapter on theory is designed to provide needed background support in understanding those authors included in this anthology who appeal directly to moral theories in developing their positions. As in previous editions, the chapter dealing with theory is placed at the end. The new theory chapter is not intended to change the structure adopted in all editions of *Contemporary Moral Issues*, but to provide support for those instructors for whom an introduction to moral theory is a standard feature of their approach to applied ethics.

Over the past two decades the range of topics and the literature in applied ethics has grown exponentially. Many of these recent contributions reflect a diversity of perspectives, some of which present challenges to traditional accounts of morality and have implications for the way in which particular moral issues are discussed. To give one example, those defending an ethic of care argue that conditions of inequality experienced by members of traditionally disadvantaged groups shape an understanding of social relations and moral responsibilities that is less centred on individuals and individual rights than traditional western accounts of morality. An account of the social and political contexts within which people interact and have rights is then taken to be relevant to a discussion of the morality of particular practices. This fourth edition attempts to ensure a balanced representation of points of view by exploring some of the implications for moral issues by taking different perspectives into account.

There are people whose advice and support were invaluable throughout the process of preparing this edition. Our developmental editor, Laurie Graham, attended to the details throughout and played a significant role in bringing this collection together. In the course of working on the fourth edition, we received several reviews, all of which were extremely useful during the process of making revisions, selecting new material, creating new chapters, thinking through the structure of each chapter, and putting the book together as a whole. Our thanks go to the following reviewers: Nathan Brett, Dalhousie University; Leo Groarke, Wilfrid Laurier University; John P.F. Lang, Kwantlen University College; Ronald MacDonald, University of New Brunswick; Robert Murray, University of Toronto and Ryerson Polytechnic University; and Jan Narveson, University of Waterloo. We would also like to thank those who were involved in the production process. Special thanks go to the Manager of Editorial Services, Susan Calvert, and to our copy-editor, Heather Lange, whose keen editorial eye has made this a much cleaner text than it would otherwise be.

In addition, Wesley Cragg would like to welcome Christine Koggel as a partner and co-editor of the fourth edition. Christine brings to the fourth edition a wealth of knowledge, fresh perspectives, and clear commitment to editorial quality. For her part, Christine Koggel is delighted to have had the opportunity to work with Wesley Cragg on this fourth edition. She has used *Contemporary Moral Issues* as a text in moral issues courses for more than a decade and has watched each new edition add strengths to an already successful publication. She is pleased to have contributed to a project that is so important. She would also like to thank Janet Andison Stewart, whose reference skills in tracking down publications on short notice proved to be invaluable, Mary Cragg, who always accommodated our sometimes impossible schedules and provided a good working environment, and Andrew Brook, whose constant support and insights into various aspects of the project were always appreciated.

After all is said and done, the purpose of *Contemporary Moral Issues* remains unchanged. Its goal has been to provide a reasonably priced, balanced introduction to the issues that are currently attracting the interest and concern of thoughtful observers of the Canadian scene. We hope our colleagues and readers will find the results of our work to be useful both as an introduction and as a pedagogical tool.

Wesley Cragg
Christine Koggel
February 1997

Chapter 1

Euthanasia

Introduction

Rules play a central role in our lives as human beings. They govern much of what we do and how we do it. One reason for the existence of rules is to provide an environment in which individuals can grow and mature without threat to their personal existence. Hence, some of our most important rules are designed to protect the lives of human beings and assure access to needed support and assistance. Rules prohibiting murder are one example. Not surprisingly, rules whose purpose is the protection of human life play a central role in discussions of the morality of euthanasia.

Protection of life, however, is not the only concern at stake. Two others are of particular relevance. First, suffering is a common feature of the human condition and one that human beings almost invariably try to avoid. Many people think that, both collectively and as individuals, we have an obligation to help each other alleviate suffering wherever we can and offer relief if it is available. Second, as moral agents we are assumed capable of thinking through moral problems and deciding how we ought to act. It is sometimes argued that the special significance of being human lies in just this capability. Does it follow that, as autonomous moral agents, we ought to be allowed the freedom to act on our own assessments of what, morally speaking, is required of us in any given situation? The answer here is no. If there were no restrictions on my freedom to act on my assessment of what is required, the result might well be that your freedom to act as you think right would be seriously reduced or eliminated. This limitation is sometimes expressed by saying that respect for persons as moral agents requires that each person be given as much freedom to act on his or her moral beliefs (or lack of them) as is compatible with others having an equal degree of freedom to do the same.

We now have three principles to consider: the *protection-of-life principle,* the *avoidance-of-suffering principle,* and the *moral-autonomy principle.* If the first of these principles was the only one that inspired our respect, euthanasia would not generate any moral problems: it would simply be wrong in all cases. If the avoidance-of-suffering principle was the only one of the three principles worthy of respect, again euthanasia would generate no moral problems. Euthanasia would be morally acceptable if ending someone's life was the only effective way of ending that person's suffering. Finally, if the moral-autonomy principle was the only operative, we might well conclude that it was morally acceptable to respect someone's request to terminate his life if we believed that in arriving at his request, he was acting as an autonomous moral agent.

In fact, all three principles are widely regarded as worthy of respect. Situations do arise, however, in which it would appear that all three cannot be applied. Should that happen, we are faced with a decision. Which of these principles should have priority?

Background Considerations

Societies rooted in the Judeo-Christian tradition have, in the past, thought euthanasia immoral. This attitude reflects the view that human life is sacred and that rules protecting human life should override all other considerations. But should this traditional view continue to command respect? Have medical advances in the twentieth century rendered it obsolete?

The Current Situation

In recent years, the morality of euthanasia has been subjected to increasing scrutiny, largely because of remarkable developments in medical science. Many life-threatening diseases have been conquered, smallpox being but one example. People are often now rescued from serious illness where death would once have been inevitable. Accidents that might once have caused death are no longer fatal. At the same time, our society has made funds available for social and medical services that allow most of us to benefit from these medical advances.

Paradoxically, however, there is another side to this picture. Modern medicine can rescue seriously ill or injured persons from death. But it is not always capable of restoring the capacity to enjoy the life that has been prolonged. Thus, the elderly can frequently be cured of illness, disease, or injury (pneumonia, for example) which in the past might well have resulted in death. But should the cure be effected if the person in question is senile? Children born with serious handicaps that once would have hastened death can be saved using modern medical techniques. But should they be saved if the alternative to death is a life plagued with pain, or one handicapped by mental retardation or serious physical disability?

Three cases in recent years highlight the intensity and significance of the debate these developments have generated. In Montreal, Nancy B., who was paralyzed from the neck down by a neurological disease and dependent on a respirator to breathe, was allowed by the court to direct that her respirator be unplugged. The courts ruled in her case that to unplug the respirator was not contrary to the criminal code prohibiting anyone from causing or assisting in the death of another person. Rather, it constituted the exercise of the right of any patient to direct her own treatment. The case of Sue Rodriguez, described in the first reading, resulted in a split decision in which the Supreme Court upheld the law prohibiting assisted suicide. Finally, Austin Bastable, who was suffering from advanced multiple sclerosis, carried out a public campaign to change the law. In the end, he crossed the border and committed suicide with the help of Dr. Kevorkian, who is a forceful advocate of the legalization of assisted suicide in the United States.

Situations of the kind just described have led people in two directions. Some argue that protection of life is the fundamental and overriding obligation of any society. People who take this view tend to emphasize the dangers of expanding the role of the physician to include decisions to end human life and focus on the importance of palliative care as a morally preferable alternative. Others argue, on the other hand, that the traditional view of euthanasia is no longer adequate. In their view, where continued existence has become intolerable through suffering or has lost its meaning because of mental degeneration or retardation, euthanasia is not immoral. Some would go even further. They would argue that members of the medical profession have an obligation to end the lives of those whose suffering has become intolerable or whose capacity to enjoy life has ended.

The view that euthanasia is sometimes justified is frequently defended by appealing to the avoidance of suffering principle. However, the moral autonomy principle has also found a place in current debates. There is a deeply entrenched view in our society that each person should be left free to act on his or her own assessment of what is required in particular situations unless there are strong reasons to the contrary. Applied to the euthanasia debate, this view would seem to imply that both individually and collectively we should respect peoples' decisions to end their lives unless ending their lives will harm others.

The Moral Dimension

There are three types of situations in which the problem of euthanasia arises. First, a person may decide that his or her life has become intolerable and request that it be ended as an act of mercy. The request may be direct. Or it may be communicated in a "living will," a document in which a person indicates that treatment is not to be attempted if, for example, he or she has suffered serious brain damage or serious and irreversible physical disability. Euthanasia that is performed in response to a "direct" request is said to be voluntary.

The problem of euthanasia can also arise in situations where someone is believed to be suffering in an intolerable or pointless way but, because of his or her condition, cannot direct how to be treated. If euthanasia is administered under these conditions it is nonvoluntary. The assumption is that it is not contrary to the presumed wishes of the person in question. Nevertheless, it is not voluntary because it has not been explicitly requested.

Finally, it is sometimes argued that euthanasia is justified, on occasion, even when the "victim" does not concur, or might not concur, or might reasonably be expected not to concur. We might describe this third possibility as coercive euthanasia. Infanticide in cases where a child is seriously deformed or retarded (thalidomide babies, for example) *may* be an example of coercive euthanasia depending on why the action is taken. The Nazi practice of putting mentally defective, ill, old, and other "socially useless" persons to death is another example of coercive euthanasia.

Discussions of euthanasia, then, give rise to three questions. Is voluntary euthanasia ever justified? Is nonvoluntary euthanasia ever justified? Is coercive euthanasia ever justified?

A final distinction should be noted. Some participants in the debate argue that it is important to differentiate between active and passive euthanasia, a distinction that is in- tended to mark the difference between actively intervening to end a person's life (by administering an injection, for example) and simply not treating a person who has been injured or is ill, knowing that without treatment the person will likely die. Assessing the merits of this distinction is also an essential step in evaluating the morality of euthanasia.

The Readings

The readings begin with the case of Sue Rodriguez, a woman suffering from Lou Gehrig's disease, who petitioned the courts to set aside the criminal law prohibition against euthana- sia and assisted suicide. Noting that suicide is not illegal, she argued that in prohibiting assisted suicide, the law discriminated against those like herself who were so physically disabled that they were unable to end their lives without assistance. This case was eventually decided in the Supreme Court of Canada. The Chief Justice at the time, Judge Lamer, argued in a dissenting view that the law was discriminatory and should be struck down. The effect of his judgement would among other things have been to allow Sue Rodriguez the right to an assisted suicide. His judgement sets out the parameters of a euthanasia law that in his view would adequately balance the protection of life and the moral autonomy principles around which so much of the euthanasia debate turns. The majority of the court, however, disagreed with Judge Lamer. In a judgement representing that majority view, Judge Sopinka argues that Criminal Code provisions prohibiting assisted suicide do not constitute unjustifiable discrimination against those unable to end their own lives.

In the second reading, Colin Harrison, who was at the time the article was written a practising West Coast physician, defends what is the official view of the Canadian Medical Association; namely, that euthanasia should not be legalized in Canada. For both Judge Sopinka and Colin Harrison, the protection of life principle is argued to have moral priority.

The third reading shifts focus dramatically. In contrast to Colin Harrison, James Rachels challenges the moral significance of the distinction between active and passive euthanasia. If it is acceptable as a way of relieving suffering to let nature take its course where medical intervention could prolong life, then it is equally acceptable, he argues, to intervene to end life where the goal is to ease suffering. Patrick Nowell-Smith, too, argues in support of the legalization of euthanasia. His argument emphasizes the avoidance of suffering and the moral autonomy principles.

In the last reading, E.W. Keyserlingk examines the assumption that, in the final analysis, we must choose whether priority should be given to the protection of life or the avoidance of suffering. He counters this assumption by arguing that these two principles (he calls them the sanctity of life and the quality of life principles) are not in conflict. In his view, commitment to the sanctity of life entails a deep concern for quality of life. This leads him to reject Rachels's view that there is no morally relevant difference between passive and active euthanasia. Passive euthanasia may sometimes be justified, he concludes. But active euthanasia is always morally wrong.

RODRIGUEZ V. BRITISH COLUMBIA (ATTORNEY GENERAL), 1993

Mr. Justice A. Lamer

I. Facts

The facts of this case are straightforward and well known. Sue Rodriguez is a 42-year-old woman living in British Columbia. She is married and the mother of an 8½-year-old son. Ms. Rodriguez suffers from amyotrophic lateral sclerosis (ALS), which is widely known as Lou Gehrig's disease; her life expectancy is between 2 and 14 months but her condition is rapidly deteriorating. Very soon she will lose the ability to swallow, speak, walk and move her body without assistance. Thereafter she will lose the capacity to breathe without a respirator, to eat without a gastrotomy and will eventually become confined to a bed.

Ms. Rodriguez knows of her condition, the trajectory of her illness and the inevitability of how her life will end; her wish is to control the circumstances, timing and manner of her death. She does not wish to die so long as she still has the capacity to enjoy life. However, by the time she no longer is able to enjoy life, she will be physically unable to terminate her life without assistance. Ms. Rodriguez seeks an order which will allow a qualified medical practitioner to set up technological means by which she might, by her own hand, at the time of her choosing, end her life.

Ms. Rodriguez applied to the Supreme Court of British Columbia for an order that s. 241(*b*) of the *Criminal Code*, R.S.C., 1985, c. C-46, be declared invalid, pursuant to s. 24(1) of the *Canadian Charter of Rights and Freedoms*, on the ground that it violates her rights under ss. 7, 12 and 15(1) of the *Charter*, and was therefore, to the extent it prohibits a terminally ill person from committing "physician-assisted" suicide, of no force and effect. . . .

241. Every one who

(*a*) counsels a person to commit suicide, or

(*b*) aids or abets a person to commit suicide,

whether suicide ensues or not, is guilty of an indictable offence and liable to imprisonment for a term not exceeding fourteen years.

The relevant sections of the Charter are as follows:

1. The *Canadian Charter of Rights and Freedoms* guarantees the rights and freedoms set out in it subject only to such reasonable limits prescribed by law as can be demonstrably justified in a free and democratic society.

7. Everyone has the right to life, liberty and security of the person and the right not to be deprived thereof except in accordance with the principles of fundamental justice.

12. Everyone has the right not to be subjected to any cruel and unusual treatment or punishment.

15. (1) Every individual is equal before and under the law and has the right to the equal protection and equal benefit of the law without discrimination and, in particular, without discrimination based on race, national or ethnic origin, colour, religion, sex, age or mental or physical disability. . . .

The principal fear is that the decriminalization of assisted suicide will increase the risk of persons with physical disabilities being manipulated by others. This "slippery slope" argument appeared to be the central justification behind the Law Reform Commission of Canada's recommendation not to repeal this provision. The Commission stated the following in its Working Paper 28, *Euthanasia, Aiding Suicide and Cessation of Treatment* (1892), at p. 46:

> The principal consideration in terms of legislative policy, and the deciding one for the Commission, remains that of possible abuses. There is, first of all, a real danger that the procedure developed to allow the death of those who are a burden to themselves may be gradually diverted from its original purpose and eventually used as well to eliminate those who are a burden to others or to society. There is also the constant danger that the subject's consent to euthanasia may not really be a perfectly free and voluntary act.

While I share a deep concern over the subtle and overt pressures that may be brought to bear on such persons if assisted suicide is decriminalized, even in limited circumstances, I do not think legislation that deprives a disadvantaged group of the right to equality can be justified solely on such speculative grounds, no matter how well intentioned. Similar dangers to the ones outlined above have surrounded the decriminalization of attempted suicide as well. It is impossible to know the degree of pressure or intimidation a physically able person may have been under when deciding to commit suicide. The truth is that we simply do not and cannot know the range of implications that allowing some form of assisted suicide will have for persons with physical disabilities. What we do know and cannot ignore is the anguish of those in the position of Ms. Rodriguez. Respecting the consent of those in her position may necessarily imply running the risk that the consent will have been obtained improperly. The proper role of the legal system in these circumstances is to provide safeguards to ensure that the consent in question is as independent and informed as is reasonably possible.

The fear of a "slippery slope" cannot, in my view, justify the over-inclusive reach of the *Criminal Code* to encompass not only people who may be vulnerable to the pressure of others but also persons with no evidence of vulnerability, and, in the case of the appellant, persons where there is positive evidence of freely determined consent. Sue Rodriguez is and will remain mentally competent. She has testified at trial to the fact that she alone, in consultation with her physicians, wishes to control the decision-making regarding the timing and circumstances of her death. I see no reason to disbelieve her, nor has the Crown suggested that she is being wrongfully influenced by anyone. Ms. Rodriguez has also emphasized that she remains and wishes to remain free *not* to avail herself of the opportunity to end her own life should that be her eventual choice. The issue here is whether Parliament is justified in denying her the ability to make this choice lawfully, as could any physically able person.

While s. 241(*b*) restricts the equality rights of all those people who are physically unable to commit suicide without assistance, the choice for a mentally competent but physically disabled person who additionally suffers from a terminal illness is, I think, different from the choice of an individual whose disability is not life-threatening; in other words, for Ms. Rodriguez, tragically, the choice is not whether to live as she is or to die, but rather when and how to experience a death that is inexorably impending. I do not, however, by observing this distinction, mean to suggest that the terminally ill are immune from vulnerability, or that they are less likely to be influenced by the intervention of others whatever their motives. Indeed, there is substantial evidence that people in this position may be susceptible to certain types of vulnerability that others are not. Further, it should not be assumed that a person with a physical disability who chooses suicide is doing so only as a result of the incapacity. It must be acknowledged that mentally competent people who commit suicide do so for a wide variety of motives, irrespective of their physical condition or life expectancy.

The law, in its present form, takes no account of the particular risks and interests that may be at issue in these differing contexts. The Law Reform Commission used the distinction between these differing contexts to justify its recommendation not to decriminalize assisted suicide in the Working Paper 28, *supra*, at pp. 53-54:

> . . . the prohibition in section 224 is not restricted solely to the case of the terminally ill patient, for whom we can only have sympathy, or solely to his physician or a member of his family who helps him to put an end to his suffering. The section is

more general and applies to a variety of situations for which it is much more difficult to feel sympathy. Consider, for example, a recent incident, that of inciting to mass suicide. What of the person who takes advantage of another's depressed state to encourage him to commit suicide, for his own financial benefit? What of the person who, knowing an adolescent's suicidal tendencies, provides him with large enough quantities of drugs to kill him? The "accomplice" in these cases cannot be considered morally blameless. Nor can one conclude that the criminal law should not punish such conduct. To decriminalize *completely* the act of aiding, abetting or counselling suicide would therefore not be a valid legislative policy [Emphasis added.]

I agree with the importance of distinguishing between the situation where a person who is aided in his or her decision to commit suicide and the situation where the decision itself is a product of someone else's influence. However, I fail to see how preventing against abuse in one context must result in denying self-determination in another. I remain unpersuaded by the government's apparent contention that it is not possible to design legislation that is somewhere in between complete decriminalization and absolute prohibition. . . .

To summarize, then, I would make a constitutional exemption available to Ms. Rodriguez, and others, on the following conditions:

(1) the constitutional exemption may only be sought by way of application to a superior court;

(2) the applicant must be certified by a treating physician and independent psychiatrist, in the manner and at the time suggested by McEachern C.J., to be competent to make the decision to end her own life, and the physicians must certify that the applicant's decision has been made freely and voluntarily, and at least one of the physicians must be present with the applicant at the time the applicant commits assisted suicide;

(3) the physicians must also certify:
   (i) that the applicant is or will become physically incapable of committing suicide unassisted, and (ii) that they have informed him or her, and that he or she understands, that he or she has a continuing right to change his or her mind about terminating his or her life;

(4) notice and access must be given to the Regional Coroner at the time and in the manner described by McEachern C.J.;

(5) the applicant must be examined daily by one of the certifying physicians at the time and in the manner outlined by McEachern C.J.;

(6) the constitutional exemption will expire according to the time limits set by McEachern C.J.; and

(7) the act causing the death of the applicant must be that of the applicant him- or herself, and not of anyone else.

I wish to emphasize that these conditions have been tailored to the particular circumstances of Ms. Rodriguez. While they may be used as guidelines for future petitioners in a similar position, each application must be considered in its own context.

VI. <u>Disposition</u>

I would answer the constitutional questions as follows:

1. Does s. 241(b) of the *Criminal Code* of Canada infringe or deny, in whole or in part, the rights and freedoms guaranteed by ss. 7, 12 and 15(1) of the *Canadian Charter of Rights and Freedoms*?

<u>Answer</u>: Yes.

2. If so, is it justified by s. 1 of the *Canadian Charter of Rights and Freedoms* and therefore not inconsistent with the *Constitution Act, 1982*?

<u>Answer</u>: No.

I would therefore allow the appeal, with costs to the appellant against the Attorneys General of British Columbia and Canada, and declare s. 241(*b*) to be of no force or effect, on the condition that the effect of this declaration be suspended for one year from the date of this judgment. During that one-year suspension period, a constitutional exemption from s. 241(*b*) may be granted by superior court on application, on the terms and in accordance with the conditions set out above. In the case of Ms. Rodriguez, in light of the factual record before this Court, it is not necessary for her to make application to a superior court. As long as she satisfies the conditions outlined above, she is granted the constitutional exemption and may proceed as she wishes.

DATED AT OTTAWA this 4th day of August 1993

· · ·

SOPINKA J. — I have read the reasons of the Chief Justice and those of McLachlin J. herein. The result of the reasons of my colleagues is that all persons who by reason of disability are unable to commit suicide have a right under the *Canadian Charter of Rights and Freedoms* to be free from government interference in procuring the assistance of others to take their life. They are entitled to a constitutional exemption from the operation of s. 241 of the *Criminal Code*, R.S.C., 1985, c. C-46, which prohibits the giving of assistance to commit suicide (hereinafter referred to as "assisted suicide"). The exemption would apply during the period that this Court's order would be suspended and thereafter Parliament could only replace the legislation subject to this right. I must respectfully disagree with the conclusion reached by my colleagues and with their reasons. In my view, nothing in the *Charter* mandates this result which raises the following serious concerns:

1. It recognizes a constitutional right to legally assisted suicide beyond that of any country in the western world, beyond any serious proposal for reform in the western world and

beyond the claim made in this very case. The apparent reason for the expansion beyond the claim in this case is that restriction of the right to the terminally ill could not be justified under s. 15.

2. It fails to provide the safeguards which are required either under the Dutch guidelines or the recent proposals for reform in the states of Washington and California which were defeated by voters in those states principally because comparable and even more stringent safeguards were considered inadequate.

3. The conditions imposed are vague and in some respects unenforceable. While the proposals in California were criticized for failure to specify the type of physician who is authorized to assist and the Dutch guidelines specify the treating physician, the conditions imposed by my colleagues do not require that the person assisting be a physician or impose any restriction in this regard. Since much of the medical profession is opposed to being involved in assisting suicide because it is antithetical to their role as healers of the sick, many doctors will refuse to assist, leaving open the potential for the growth of a macabre specialty in this area reminiscent of Dr. Kevorkian and his suicide machine.

4. To add to the uncertainty of the conditions, they are to serve merely as guidelines, leaving it to individual judges to decide upon application whether to grant or withhold the right to commit suicide. In the case of the appellant, the remedy proposed by the Chief Justice, concurred in by McLachlin J., would not require such an application. She alone is to decide that the conditions or guidelines are complied with. Any judicial review of this decision would only occur if she were to commit suicide and a charge were laid against the person who assisted her. The reasons of McLachlin J. remove any requirement to monitor the choice made by the appellant to commit suicide so that the act might occur after the last expression of the desire to commit suicide is stale-dated.

I have concluded that the conclusion of my colleagues cannot be supported under the provisions of the *Charter*. Reliance was placed on ss. 7, 12 and 15 and I will examine each in turn.

I. Section 7

The most substantial issue in this appeal is whether s. 241(*b*) infringes s. 7 in that it inhibits the appellant in controlling the timing and manner of her death. I conclude that while the section impinges on the security interest of the appellant, any resulting deprivation is not contrary to the principles of fundamental justice. I would come to the same conclusion with respect to any liberty interest which may be involved.

Section 7 of the *Charter* provides as follows:

7. Everyone has the right to life, liberty and security of the person and the right not to be deprived thereof except in accordance with the principles of fundamental justice.

The appellant argues that, by prohibiting anyone from assisting her to end her life when her illness has rendered her incapable of terminating her life without such assistance, by threat of criminal sanction, s. 241(*b*) deprives her of both her liberty and her security of the person. The appellant asserts that her application is based upon (a) the right to live her remaining life with the inherent dignity of a human person, (b) the right to control what happens to her body while she is living, and (c) the right to be free from governmental interference in making fundamental personal decisions concerning the terminal stages of her life. The first two of these asserted rights can be seen to invoke both liberty and security of the person; the latter is more closely associated with only the liberty interest.

(a) *Life, Liberty and Security of the Person*

The appellant seeks a remedy which would assure her some control over the time and manner of her death. While she supports her claim on the ground that her liberty and security of the person interests are engaged, a consideration of these interests cannot be divorced from the sanctity of life, which is one of the three *Charter* values protected by s. 7.

None of these values prevail a priori over the others. All must be taken into account in determining the content of the principles of fundamental justice and there is no basis for imposing a greater burden on the propounder of one value as against that imposed on another. . . .

I find more merit in the argument that security of the person, by its nature, cannot encompass a right to take action that will end one's life as security of the person is intrinsically concerned with the well-being of the living person. This argument focuses on the generally held and deeply rooted belief in our society that human life is sacred or inviolable (which terms I use in the non-religious sense described by Dworkin (*Life's Dominion: An Argument About Abortion, Euthanasia, and Individual Freedom* (1993)) to mean that human life is seen to have a deep intrinsic value of its own). As members of a society based upon respect for the intrinsic value of human life and on the inherent dignity of every human being, can we incorporate within the Constitution which embodies our most fundamental values a right to terminate one's own life in any circumstances? This question in turn evokes other queries of fundamental importance such as the degree to which our conception of the sanctity of life includes notions of quality of life as well.

Sanctity of life, as we will see, has been understood historically as excluding freedom of choice in the self-infliction of death and certainly in the involvement of others in carrying out that choice. At the very least, no new consensus has emerged in society opposing the right of the state to regulate the involvement of others in exercising power over individuals ending their lives.

The appellant suggests that for the terminally ill, the choice is one of time and manner of death rather than death itself since the latter is inevitable.

I disagree. Rather it is one of choosing death instead of allowing natural forces to run their course. The time and precise manner of death remain unknown until death actually occurs. There can be no certainty in forecasting the precise circumstances of a death. Death is, for all mortals, inevitable. Even when death appears imminent, seeking to control the manner and timing of one's death constitutes a conscious choice of death over life. It follows that life as a value is engaged even in the case of the terminally ill who seek to choose death over life. . . .

In this case, it is not disputed that in general s. 241(*b*) is valid and desirable legislation which fulfils the government's objectives of preserving life and protecting the vulnerable.

The complaint is that the legislation is over-inclusive because it does not exclude from the reach of the prohibition those in the situation of the appellant who are terminally ill, mentally competent, but cannot commit suicide on their own. It is also argued that the extension of the prohibition to the appellant is arbitrary and unfair as suicide itself is not unlawful, and the common law allows a physician to withhold or withdraw life-saving or life-maintaining treatment on the patient's instructions and to administer palliative care which has the effect of hastening death. The issue is whether, given this legal context, the existence of a criminal prohibition on assisting suicide for one in the appellant's situation is contrary to principles of fundamental justice.

Discerning the principles of fundamental justice with which deprivation of life, liberty or security of the person must accord, in order to withstand constitutional scrutiny, is not an easy task. A mere common law rule does not suffice to constitute a principle of fundamental justice, rather, as the term implies, principles upon which there is some consensus that they are vital or fundamental to our societal notion of justice are required. Principles of fundamental justice must not, however, be so broad as to be no more than vague generalizations about what our society considers to be ethical or moral. They must be capable of being identified with some precision and applied to situations in a manner which yields an understandable result. They must also, in my view, be legal principles. The now familiar words of Lamer J. in *Re B.C. Motor Vehicle Act*, [1985] 2 S.C.R. 486, at pp. 512-13, are as follows:

> Consequently, the principles of fundamental justice are to be found in the basic tenets and principles, not only of our judicial process, but also of the other components of our legal system.

> . . . the proper approach to the determination of the principles of fundamental justice is quite simply one in which, as Professor L. Tremblay has written, "future growth will be based on historical roots". . . .

> Whether any given principle may be said to be a principle of fundamental justice within the meaning of s. 7 will rest upon an analysis of the nature, sources, *rationale* and essential role of that principle within the judicial process and in our legal system, as it evolves.

This Court has often stated that in discerning the principles of fundamental justice governing a particular case, it is helpful to look at the common law and legislative history of the offence in question (*Re B.C. Motor Vehicle Act and Morgentaler, supra*, and *R. v. Swain*, [1991] 1 S.C.R. 933). It is not sufficient, however, merely to conduct a historical review and conclude that because neither Parliament nor the various medical associations had ever expressed a view that assisted suicide should be decriminalized, that to prohibit it could not be said to be contrary to the principles of fundamental justice. Such an approach would be problematic for two reasons. First, a strictly historical analysis will always lead to the conclusion in a case such as this that the deprivation is in accordance with fundamental justice as the legislation will not have kept pace with advances in medical technology. Second, such reasoning is somewhat circular, in that it relies on the continuing existence of the prohibition to find the prohibition to be fundamentally just.

The way to resolve these problems is not to avoid the historical analysis, but to make sure that one is looking not just at the existence of the practice itself (i.e., the continued criminalization of assisted suicide) but at the rationale behind that practice and the principles which underlie it.

The appellant asserts that it is a principle of fundamental justice that the human dignity and autonomy of individuals be respected, and that to subject her to needless suffering in this manner is to rob her of her dignity. The importance of the concept of human dignity in our society was enunciated by Cory J. (dissenting, Lamer C.J. concurring) in *Kindler v. Canada (Minister of Justice)*, [1991] 2 S.C.R. 779, at p. 813. Respect for human dignity underlies many of the rights and freedoms in the *Charter.*

That respect for human dignity is one of the underlying principles upon which our society is based is unquestioned. I have difficulty, however, in characterizing this in itself as a principle of fundamental justice within the meaning of s. 7. While respect for human dignity is the genesis for many principles of fundamental justice, not every law that fails to accord such respect runs afoul of these principles. To state that "respect for human dignity and autonomy" is a principle of fundamental justice, then, is essentially to state that the deprivation of the appellant's security of the person is contrary to principles of fundamental justice because it deprives her of security of the person. This interpretation would equate security of the person with a principle of fundamental justice and render the latter redundant. . . .

The issue here, then, can be characterized as being whether the blanket prohibition on assisted suicide is arbitrary or unfair in that it is unrelated to the state's interest in protecting the vulnerable, and that it lacks a foundation in the legal tradition and societal beliefs which are said to be represented by the prohibition.

Section 241(*b*) has as its purpose the protection of the vulnerable who might be induced in moments of weakness to commit suicide. This purpose is grounded in the state interest in protecting life and reflects the policy of the state that human life should not be depreciated by allowing life to be taken. This policy finds expression not only in the provisions of our *Criminal Code* which prohibit murder and other violent acts against others notwithstanding the consent of the victim, but also in the policy against capital punishment and, until its repeal, attempted suicide. This is not only a policy of the state, however, but is part of our fundamental conception of the sanctity of human life. The Law Reform Commission expressed this philosophy appropriately in its Working Paper 28, *Euthanasia, Aiding Suicide and Cessation of Treatment* (1982), at p. 36:

> Preservation of human life is acknowledged to be a fundamental value of our society. Historically, our criminal law has changed very little on this point. Generally speaking, it sanctions the principle of the sanctity of human life. Over the years, however, law has come to temper the apparent absolutism of the principle, to delineate its intrinsic limitations and to define its true dimensions.

As is noted in the above passage, the principle of sanctity of life is no longer seen to require that all human life be preserved at all costs. Rather, it has come to be understood, at least by some, as encompassing quality of life considerations, and to be subject to certain limitations and qualifications reflective of personal autonomy and dignity. . . .

(iv) <u>Conclusion on Principles of Fundamental Justice</u>

What the preceding review demonstrates is that Canada and other Western democracies recognize and apply the principle of the sanctity of life as a general principle which is subject to limited and narrow exceptions in situations in which notions of personal autonomy and dignity must prevail. However, these same societies continue to draw distinctions between passive and active forms of intervention in the dying process, and with very few exceptions, prohibit assisted suicide in situations akin to that of the appellant. The task then becomes to identify the rationales upon which these distinctions are based and to determine whether they are constitutionally supportable.

The distinction between withdrawing treatment upon a patient's request, such as occurred in the *Nancy B.* case, on the one hand, and assisted suicide on the other has been criticized as resting on a legal fiction — that is, the distinction between active and passive forms of treatment. The criticism is based on the fact that the withdrawal of life supportive measures is done with the knowledge that death will ensue, just as is assisting suicide, and that death does in fact ensue as a result of the action taken. See, for example, the *Harvard Law Review* note "Physician-Assisted Suicide and the Right to Die with Assistance" (1992), 105 *Harv. L. Rev.* 2021, at pp. 2030-31.

Other commentators, however, uphold the distinction on the basis that in the case of withdrawal of treatment, the death is "natural" — the artificial forces of medical technology which have kept the patient alive are removed and nature takes its course. In the case of assisted suicide or euthanasia, however, the course of nature is interrupted, and death results *directly* from the human action taken (E. W. Keyserlingk, *Sanctity of Life or Quality of Life in the Context of Ethics, Medicine and Law* (1979), a study paper for the Law Reform Commission of Canada's Protection of Life Series). The Law Reform Commission calls this distinction "fundamental" (at p. 19 of the Working Paper 28).

Whether or not one agrees that the active vs. passive distinction is maintainable, however, the fact remains that under our common law, the physician has no choice but to accept the patient's instructions to discontinue treatment. To continue to treat the patient when the patient has withdrawn consent to that treatment constitutes battery (*Ciarlariello and Nancy B., supra*). The doctor is therefore not required to make a choice which will result in the patient's death as he would be if he chose to assist a suicide or to perform active euthanasia.

The fact that doctors may deliver palliative care to terminally ill patients without fear of sanction, it is argued, attenuates to an even greater degree any legitimate distinction which can be drawn between assisted suicide and what are currently acceptable forms of medical treatment. The administration of drugs designed for pain control in dosages which the physician knows will hasten death constitutes active contribution to death by any standard. However, the distinction drawn here is one based upon intention — in the case of palliative care the intention is to ease pain, which has the effect of hastening death, while in the case of assisted suicide, the intention is undeniably to cause death. The Law Reform Commission, although it recommended the continued criminal prohibition of both euthanasia and assisted suicide, stated, at p. 70 of the Working Paper, that a doctor should never refuse palliative care to a terminally ill person only because it may hasten death. In my view, distinctions based upon intent are important, and in fact form the basis of our criminal law. While factually the distinction may, at times, be difficult to draw, legally it is clear. The fact that in some cases, the third party will, under the guise of palliative care, commit euthanasia or assist in suicide and go unsanctioned due to the difficulty of proof cannot be said to render the existence of the prohibition fundamentally unjust.

The principles of fundamental justice cannot be created for the occasion to reflect the court's dislike or distaste of a particular statute. While the principles of fundamental justice are concerned with more than process, reference must be made to principles which are "fundamental" in the sense that they would have general acceptance among reasonable people. From the review that I have conducted above, I am unable to discern anything approaching unanimity with respect to the issue before us. Regardless of one's personal views as to whether the distinctions drawn between withdrawal of treatment and palliative care, on the one hand, and assisted suicide on the other are practically compelling, the fact remains that these distinctions are maintained and can be persuasively defended. To the extent that there is a consensus, it is that human life must be respected and we must be careful not to undermine the institutions that protect it.

This consensus finds legal expression in our legal system which prohibits capital punishment. This prohibition is supported, in part, on the basis that allowing the state to kill will cheapen the value of human life and thus the state will serve in a sense as a role model for individuals in society. The prohibition against assisted suicide serves a similar purpose. In upholding the respect for life, it may discourage those who consider that life is unbearable at a particular moment, or who perceive themselves to be a burden upon others, from committing suicide. To permit a physician to lawfully participate in taking life would send a signal that there are circumstances in which the state approves of suicide.

I also place some significance in the fact that the official position of various medical associations is against decriminalizing assisted suicide (Canadian Medical Association, British Medical Association, Council of Ethical and Judicial Affairs of the American Medical Association, World Medical Association and the American Nurses Association). Given the concerns about abuse that have been expressed and the great difficulty in creating appropriate safeguards to prevent these, it can not be said that the blanket prohibition on assisted suicide is arbitrary or unfair, or that it is not reflective of fundamental values at play in our society. I am thus unable to find that any principle of fundamental justice is violated by s. 241(*b*). . . .

EUTHANASIA, MEDICINE, AND THE LAW

Colin P. Harrison

It should be no surprise that the legalization of abortion was followed rapidly by a growing interest in euthanasia. The devaluation of humanity at one end of the life span has enabled us already to dispose of a large number of problem humans, albeit with no foreseeable end in sight at the moment. It promises to be equally fruitful at the other end of the span. But the debate often illuminates the great confusion that exists between euthanasia and sound medical practice. Between mercy killing, on the one hand, and the inexcusable prolongation of death and suffering, on the other, lies the sound medical care of the dying patient. Though this is part of the normal practice of medicine, it is separated off because the prudential judgments involved are altered by the loss of hope and failure of the therapeutic process. To it, Ramsay[1] has applied the term "agathanasia," which means good death without the implication of killing. This enables the physician to escape between the horns of the apparent dilemma "euthanasia or not." This service required great courage, a courage that must be based on a clear understanding of the issues involved — a courage to discontinue treatment that no longer affects the patient's disease, and to use pain-relieving measures in adequate amount. These are matters of sound medical practice, not of positive and negative

Reprinted by permission of Patricia M. Harrison.

euthanasia. Without that courage on the part of the physician, the patient will suffer inordinately, and the situation may well arise in which the physician who is afraid to use drugs in adequate amount lest his dying patient die will use an overdose to ensure his death. That would be folly, but in this day of confusion not an unlikely folly.

By virtue of the content of medical education, the expertise of the physician relates to health and disease, not to life and death, however much these may become entwined. The physician is obliged to recognize realistically the limits of his expertise and to treat the patient secundum artem, whatever effect that might have on the length of life of the dying patient. It is not the physician's right to decide when the patients should die, and the law must not be allowed to make it otherwise. Both "life" and "death" are indefinable realities, and while we can identify what is positively alive and what is positively dead, we cannot identify the point at which the one merges into the other. The physician is not obliged to keep the patient alive (or preserve him from decomposition) or to kill him, but to treat his terminal illness as best he can. He must not presume to be able to weigh the value of continued life against death for the practical reason that he has not the faintest idea of what is means to be dead and because, from the philosophic point of view, there is no element common to being and non-being by which the one can be valued against the other. If the physician pushes the patient through death's door he does so without knowing what is on the other side. That is a denial of responsibility.

During the last decades we have resolutely denied the reality of death, and the word "death" has been considered obscene — as was the word "sex" in Victorian times. We are recovering from this delusion, but its effect has been that the care of the dying patient has not kept pace with the rest of medical care. There is no growing interest in the care of the dying, but there is a great deal to be learned and many changes to be made. That knowledge and those changes will not eventuate if medicine embarks on euthanasia, for then it will be infinitely simpler to kill the patient than to care for him. The earlier he is killed, the more pain he is spared, the easier it is on the physician and relatives, and the less the cost of hospitalization. Why keep the patient alive when there are so many advantages in killing him? Surely that is a philosophical question and there is now no unifying philosophy of medicine.

As the emphasis of medical care has changed from the sick to the healthy, it has changed from the personal to the impersonal, from the concrete and real to the putative, from a holistic to a fragmented discipline. At the same time, the ratio of academics to practising physicians has increased and there have been changes in medical practice and medical ethics that have subverted the traditional philosophy of medicine. In addition, there is a covert tension between the academic and the practising physician who, because their points of view are basically opposed, compete with each other for the authorship of the philosophy of modern medicine. It is a competition that goes badly for the practising physician and for the patient. If this philosophy is elaborated by the practising physician it will embody the values he sees in medicine and it has some hope of being concrete, real, holistic and people-oriented. Medicine might then remain the servant — and medicine can be free only so long as it is the servant, for the state will not cast covetous eyes on its position of servitude. But if this philosophy is elaborated by the academic it will become health-centred and medicine will grow in power and become a tyrant, then be rapidly deposed by the state. The World Health Organization has defined "health" as a *petitio principii*, susceptible of almost any interpretation. Health is more than health; it is a pristine order of well-being such as might have existed only in the Garden of Eden before the Fall. This mutual well-being is a mystery of faith, known only to the élite. It is not man without disease, it is man without sin; and man who was once said to have been created in the image and likeness of God is to be recreated in the current idiom of well-being. The logical extension of this idea of health is unlimited and there is nothing that cannot be imposed in its name. So it is that in the name of the same health, we assault the unborn child of one woman because she does not want it and at the same time we assault the pregnant, anemic Jehovah's Witness with a blood transfusion for the sake of her child. There is no logical nexus between the two but it does not really matter, for we are not practising medicine, we are exercising power. If health is to be measured in terms of mutual well-being, what more certain and efficient mechanism can be found than the killing of those who are interfering with that well-being?

In theory, the killing of the fetus was legalized for the sake of health but, practically, it can be used for any end that might be subsumed under the title of "happiness." It is not, however, the happiness of the one aborted, but of everybody else. So it is likely to be with mercy killing if that be legalized, and this despite the fact that there is a great deal of human sympathy in the euthanasia movement. It is the killing and not the mercy that appeals as the answer to our social problems. For there are real social advantages in killing:

1. It terminates the patient's suffering.
2. It reduces the strain on the family and the physician.
3. It makes the death convenient: if the physician is to kill the patient, he must do it at some specific time.
4. It speeds up the turnover of beds for patients with terminal illnesses.
5. It has a benevolent effect on the statistics of human morbidity.
6. It reduces the cost of terminal illness.

The suffering patient may well ask for death, but it is relief from suffering, mental and physical, that he seeks. He does not know what death is; how, then, can he desire it? As Kübler-Ross[2] has pointed out, the patient can come to terms with his own death and become resigned to it, and in the resignation overcome the fear. But he can only desire surcease from suffering. That surcease the physician should try to give from all that is available to him. It is possible that some physicians, out of sympathy, sometimes practise mercy killing, but it is no easy matter to disentangle the motive of mercy from the practical considerations already listed. Granted that it is mercy killing, all of the effects mentioned above still occur, so that the sympathy of the physician at the personal level becomes transformed into the benefits of killing at the social level. That is the real danger of legal euthanasia.

It is important to recognize the part played by emotion in the ethical equation. It explains why an act occurred and it absolves the agent from ethical condemnation. But it does not make the act ethical. Emotion is a psychological force that tends to bring the act about; it is not a rational judgment. Finally, the human sympathy of the physician is personal and not transformable into a social mechanism such that it can be represented in law. The fact is that the law can legalize the killing but it cannot possibly ensure the mercy. But perhaps what is really wanted is the right to kill off our elderly and ailing human burdens as we presently kill off our prenatal ones. That at least would be consistent, but it would open a floodgate that would be impossible to close.

NOTES

1. Ramsay, P., quoted in Byrne, P.M. and Stogre, M.J. "Agathanasia and the Care of the Dying," *Can Med Assoc J.* 112: 1396 (1975).
2. Kübler-Ross, E., *On Death and Dying* (New York: Macmillan, 1969).

QUESTIONS

1. Colin Harrison argues that abortion leads to euthanasia. What reasons does he give for this view? Are those reasons sound?
2. Harrison lists six "real social advantages" in legalizing euthanasia. Which, if any, of these advantages provide morally acceptable grounds for euthanasia?
3. Identify what Harrison considers to be "the real danger of legal euthanasia" and evaluate the seriousness of that danger from a moral point of view.
4. Evaluate Harrison's view of the medical alternative to euthanasia.

ACTIVE AND PASSIVE EUTHANASIA

James Rachels

The distinction between active and passive euthanasia is thought to be crucial for medical ethics. The idea is that it is permissible, at least in some cases, to withhold treatment and allow a patient to die, but it is never permissible to take any direct action designed to kill the patient. This doctrine seems to be accepted by most doctors, and it is endorsed in a statement adopted by the House of Delegates of the American Medical Association on 4 December 1973:

> The intentional termination of the life of one human being by another — mercy killing — is contrary to that for which the medical profession stands and is contrary to the policy of the American Medical Association.
>
> The cessation of the employment of extraordinary means to prolong the life of the body when there is irrefutable evidence that biological death is imminent is the decision of the patient and/or his immediate family. The advice and judgement of the physician should be freely available to the patient and/or his immediate family.

However, a strong case can be made against this doctrine. In what follows I will set out some of the relevant arguments, and urge doctors to reconsider their views on this matter.

To begin with a familiar type of situation, a patient who is dying of incurable cancer of the throat is in terrible pain, which can no longer be satisfactorily alleviated. He is certain to die within a few days, even if present treatment is continued, but he does not want to go on living for those days since the pain is unbearable. So he asks the doctor for an end to it, and his family joins in the request.

Suppose the doctor agrees to withhold treatment, as the conventional doctrine says he may. The justification for his doing so is that the patient is in terrible agony, and since he is going to die anyway, it would be wrong to prolong his suffering needlessly. But now notice this. If one simply withholds treatment, it may take the patient longer to die, and so he may suffer more than he would if more direct action were taken and a lethal injection given. This fact provides strong reason for thinking that, once the initial decision not to prolong his

From The New England Journal of Medicine, *vol. 292, no. 2 (9 January 1975), pp. 78–80. Copyright 1975 Massachusetts Medical Society. Reprinted by permission of* The New England Journal of Medicine.

agony has been made, active euthanasia is actually preferable to passive euthanasia, rather than the reverse. To say otherwise is to endorse the option that leads to more suffering rather than less, and is contrary to the humanitarian impulse that prompts the decision not to prolong his life in the first place.

Part of my point is that the process of being 'allowed to die' can be relatively slow and painful, whereas being given a lethal injection is relatively quick and painless. Let me give a different sort of example. In the United States about one in 600 babies is born with Down's syndrome. Most of these babies are otherwise healthy — that is, with only the usual pediatric care, they will proceed to an otherwise normal infancy. Some, however, are born with congenital defects such as intestinal obstructions that require operations if they are to live. Sometimes, the parents and the doctor will decide not to operate, and let the infant die. Anthony Shaw describes what happens then:

> When surgery is denied [the doctor] must try to keep the infant from suffering while natural forces sap the baby's life away. As a surgeon whose natural inclination is to use the scalpel to fight off death, standing by and watching a salvageable baby die is the most emotionally exhausting experience I know. It is easy at a conference, in a theoretical discussion to decide that such infants should be allowed to die. It is altogether different to stand by in the nursery and watch as dehydration and infection wither a tiny being over hours and days. This is a terrible ordeal for me and the hospital staff — much more so than for the parents who never set foot in the nursery.[1]

I can understand why some people are opposed to all euthanasia, and insist that such infants must be allowed to live. I think I can also understand why other people favour destroying these babies quickly and painlessly. But why should anyone favour letting 'dehydration and infection wither a tiny being over hours and days'? The doctrine that says a baby may be allowed to dehydrate and wither, but may not be given an injection that would end its life without suffering, seems so patently cruel as to require no further refutation. The strong language is not intended to offend, but only to put the point in the clearest possible way.

My second argument is that the conventional doctrine leads to decisions concerning life and death made on irrelevant grounds.

Consider again the case of the infants with Down's syndrome who need operations for congenital defects unrelated to the syndrome to live. Sometimes, there is no operation, and the baby dies, but when there is no such defect, the baby lives on. Now, an operation such as that to remove an intestinal obstruction is not prohibitively difficult. The reason why such operations are not performed in these cases is, clearly, that the child has Down's syndrome and the parents and the doctor judge that because of that fact it is better for the child to die.

But notice that this situation is absurd, no matter what view one takes of the lives and potentials of such babies. If the life of such an infant is worth preserving what does it matter if it needs a simple operation? Or, if one thinks it better that such a baby should not live on, what difference does it make that it happens to have an unobstructed intestinal tract? In either case, the matter of life and death is being decided on irrelevant grounds. It is the Down's syndrome, and not the intestines, that is the issue. The matter should be decided, if at all, on that basis, and not be allowed to depend on the essentially irrelevant question of whether the intestinal tract is blocked.

What makes this situation possible, of course, is the idea that when there is an intestinal blockage, one can 'let the baby die', but when there is no such defect there is nothing that can be done, for one must not 'kill' it. The fact that this idea leads to such results as deciding life or death on irrelevant grounds is another good reason why the doctrine would be rejected.

One reason why so many people think that there is an important moral difference between active and passive euthanasia is that they think killing someone is morally worse than letting someone die. But is it? Is killing, in itself, worse than letting die? To investigate this issue, two cases may be considered that are exactly alike except that one involves killing whereas the other involves letting someone die. Then, it can be asked whether this difference makes any difference to the moral assessments. It is important that the cases be exactly alike, except for this one difference, since otherwise one cannot be confident that it is this difference and not some other that accounts for any variation in the assessments of the two cases. So, let us consider this pair of cases:

In the first, Smith stands to gain a large inheritance if anything should happen to his six-year-old cousin. One evening while the child is taking his bath, Smith sneaks into the bathroom and drowns the child, and then arranges things so that it will look like an accident.

In the second, Jones also stands to gain if anything should happen to his six-year-old cousin. Like Smith, Jones sneaks in planning to drown the child in his bath. However, just as he enters the bathroom Jones sees the child slip and hit his head, and fall face down in the water. Jones is delighted; he stands by, ready to push the child's head back under if it is necessary, but it is not necessary. With only a little thrashing about, the child drowns all by himself, 'accidentally', as Jones watches and does nothing.

Now Smith killed the child, whereas Jones 'merely' let the child die. That is the only difference between them. Did either man behave better, from a moral point of view? If the difference between killing and letting die were in itself a morally important matter, one should say that Jones's behaviour was less reprehensible than Smith's. But does one really want to say that? I think not. In the first place, both men acted from the same motive, personal gain, and both had exactly the same end in view when they acted. It may be inferred from Smith's conduct that he is a bad man, although that judgement may be withdrawn or modified if certain further facts are learned about him — for example, that he is mentally deranged. But would not the very same thing be inferred about Jones from his conduct? And would not the same further considerations also be relevant to any modification of this judgement? Moreover, suppose Jones pleaded, in his own defence, 'After all, I didn't do anything except just stand there and watch the child drown. I didn't kill him; I only let him die.' Again, if letting die were in itself less bad than killing, this defence should have at least some weight. But it does not. Such a 'defence' can only be regarded as a grotesque perversion of moral reasoning. Morally speaking, it is no defence at all.

Now, it may be pointed out, quite properly, that the cases of euthanasia with which doctors are concerned are not like this at all. They do not involve personal gain or the destruction of normal healthy children. Doctors are concerned only with cases in which the patient's life is of no further use to him, or in which the patient's life has become or will soon become a terrible burden. However, the point is the same in these cases: the bare difference between killing and letting die does not, in itself, make a moral difference. If a doctor lets a patient die, for humane reasons, he is in the same moral position as if he had given the patient a lethal injection for humane reasons. If his decision was wrong — if, for example, the patient's illness was in fact curable — the decision would be equally regrettable no matter which method was used to carry it out. And if the doctor's decision was the right one, the method used is not in itself important.

The AMA policy statement isolates the crucial issue very well; the crucial issue is 'the intentional termination of the life of one human being by another'. But after identifying this issue, and forbidding 'mercy killing', the statement goes on to deny that the cessation of treatment is the intentional termination of a life. This is where the mistake comes in, for what is the cessation of treatment, in these circumstances, if it is not 'the intentional termination of the life of one human being by another'? Of course it is exactly that, and if it were not, there would be no point to it.

Many people will find this judgement hard to accept. One reason, I think, is that it is very easy to conflate the question of whether killing is, in itself, worse than letting die, with the very different question of whether most actual cases of killing are more reprehensible than most actual cases of letting die. Most actual cases of killing are clearly terrible (think, for example, of all the murders reported in the newspapers), and one hears of such cases every day. On the other hand, one hardly ever hears of a case of letting die, except for the actions of doctors who are motivated by humanitarian reasons. So one learns to think of killing in a much worse light than of letting die. But this does not mean that there is something about killing that makes it in itself worse than letting die, for it is not the bare difference between killing and letting die that makes the difference in these cases. Rather, the other factors — the murderer's motive of personal gain, for example, contrasted with the doctor's humanitarian motivation — account for different reactions to the different cases.

I have argued that killing is not in itself any worse than letting die; if my contention is right, it follows that active euthanasia is not any worse than passive euthanasia. What arguments can be given on the other side? The most common, I believe, is the following:

The important difference between active and passive euthanasia is that, in passive euthanasia, the doctor does not do anything to bring about the patient's death. The doctor does nothing, and the patient dies of whatever ills already afflict him. In active euthanasia, however, the doctor does something to bring about the patient's death: he kills him. The doctor who gives the patient with cancer a lethal injection has himself caused his patient's death; whereas if he merely ceases treatment, the cancer is the cause of the death.

A number of points need to be made here. The first is that it is not exactly correct to say that in passive euthanasia the doctor does nothing, for he does do one thing that is very important: he lets the patient die. 'Letting someone die' is certainly different, in some respects, from other types of action — mainly in that it is a kind of action that one may perform by way of not performing certain other actions. For example, one may let a patient die by way of not giving medication, just as one may insult someone by way of not shaking his hand. But for any purpose of moral assessment, it is a type of action none the less. The decision to let a patient die is subject to moral appraisal in the same way that a decision to kill him would be subject to moral appraisal: it may be assessed as wise or unwise, compassionate or sadistic, right or wrong. If a doctor deliberately let a patient die who was suffering from a routinely curable illness, the doctor would certainly be to blame for what he had done, just as he would be to blame if he had needlessly killed the patient. Charges against him would then be appropriate. If so, it would be no defence at all for him to insist that he didn't 'do anything'. He would have done something very serious indeed, for he let his patient die.

Fixing the cause of death may be very important from a legal point of view, for it may determine whether criminal charges are brought against the doctor. But I do not think that this notion can be used to show a moral difference between active and passive euthanasia. The reason why it is considered bad to be the cause of someone's death is that death is regarded as a great evil — and so it is. However, if it has been decided that euthanasia — even passive euthanasia — is desirable in a given case, it has also been decided that in this instance death is no greater an evil than the patient's continued existence. And if this is true, the usual reason for not wanting to be the cause of someone's death simply does not apply.

Finally, doctors may think that all of this is only of academic interest — the sort of thing that philosophers may worry about but that has no practical bearing on their own work. After all, doctors must be concerned about the legal consequences of what they do, and active euthanasia is clearly forbidden by the law. But even so, doctors should also be concerned with the fact that the law is forcing upon them a moral doctrine that may be indefensible, and has a considerable effect on their practices. Of course, most doctors are not now in the position of being coerced in this matter, for they do not regard themselves as merely going along with what the law requires. Rather, in statements such as the AMA policy statement that I have quoted, they are endorsing this doctrine as a central point of medical ethics. In that statement, active euthanasia is condemned not merely as illegal but as 'contrary to that for which the medical profession stands', whereas passive euthanasia is approved. However, the preceding considerations suggest that there is really no moral difference between the two, considered in themselves (there may be important moral differences in some cases in their *consequences*, but, as I pointed out, these differences may make active euthanasia, and not passive euthanasia, the morally preferable option). So, whereas doctors may have to discriminate between active and passive euthanasia to satisfy the law, they should not do any more than that. In particular, they should not give the distinction any added authority and weight by writing it into official statements of medical ethics.

NOTES

1. Shaw, Anthony, "Doctor, Do We Have a Choice?" *The New York Times Magazine*, 30 January 1972, p. 54.

QUESTIONS

1. Rachels argues that in some cases to simply withhold treatment rather than provide a lethal injection is to "endorse the option that leads to more suffering rather than less and is contrary to the humanitarian impulse that prompts the decision not to prolong life in the first place." How would Sopinka, Harrison, or Keyserlingk, whose contribution concludes the readings in this chapter, respond to Rachels's claim in light of the arguments they offer to support their view that euthanasia should not be legalized?

2. Rachels suggests that if it is morally acceptable not to operate on a Down's syndrome baby, thus ensuring that it will die of dehydration and starvation, it must also be morally acceptable to give such a baby a lethal injection. Is he right about this? Is it morally acceptable to treat Down's syndrome children in this way? Is this an example of the slippery slope that concerns those opposed to euthanasia like Sopinka, Harrison, and Keyserlingk?

3. Does Rachels's comparison of the man who drowns a child and a man who allows a child to drown without intervening to save its life show that where euthanasia is concerned there is no morally relevant difference between active and passive euthanasia?

4. Rachels offers the following argument: most people would agree that a doctor who lets a patient die if it is within his or her power to provide a medical remedy is just as culpable, morally speaking, as a doctor who actively intervenes to kill a patient. On pain of inconsistency, these same people should therefore accept that "letting die" has the same moral quality for a doctor as killing. Is this a sound argument? How would you propose to assess its validity?

THE RIGHT TO DIE

Patrick Nowell-Smith

Do we have a right to die at a time and in a manner of our own choice? That this question is being more and more urgently asked is due to two changes, one technological and one social, that have occurred in our lifetime. Modern medical technology has virtually eliminated the main killer diseases of the past; in particular the introduction of antibiotics has made possible the prevention and cure of pneumonia, a disease that used to be called "the dying man's friend." Human beings can be kept biologically alive, though unconscious, almost indefinitely.

As for the social change, before the First World War there could hardly have been an adult who had never watched over a parent, baby, child, neighbour, or friend and seen him die. In short, death was familiar. And *accepted*. Sad, to be sure; often very sad indeed. But it was nonetheless accepted as part of the natural order of things, talked about openly, and frequently dealt with in literature. All that has changed. Apart from those professionally concerned, few of us have ever seen a corpse unless it was laid out for viewing. Most of us will die in an institution. Death has replaced sex as the unmentionable topic.

Euthanasia is commonly divided into "active" (killing) and "passive" (letting die), a distinction that will be challenged later. It is also divided into "voluntary" (at the request or with the consent of the person) and "involuntary" (without such consent). The legal position in the United Kingdom is simple. Before 1961 suicide had always been a common law crime, and aiding suicide was therefore automatically a crime as well. But when, in 1961, the crime of suicide was abolished, a new statutory offence of *aiding* suicide was introduced, except in Scotland. Active euthanasia was always treated as murder, and still is. So much for the law on paper, which is pretty much the same in all common law jurisdictions.

However, this severity toward mercy killing and aiding suicide is in practice greatly mitigated by the wide powers of sentencing which our legal system accords to judges, especially when the issue is one of passive rather than active euthanasia. If a doctor allows a grossly deformed baby to die, he will be discharged if he can show that his decision not to treat the baby was standard medical practice; and there are many cases which are not even prosecuted. In cases of active euthanasia judges almost always impose a very light sentence or no sentence at all, when the motive was clearly compassion.

Since the methods most of us would choose to commit suicide require the illegal co-operation of others, it is clear that we have at best a very restricted *legal* right to die at a time and in a manner of our own choice. Whether or not we have a *moral* right which ought to be reflected in the law depends on the type of moral theory we take as a starting-point. On a theory which starts from the concept of individual rights, we have a right to do anything we like provided there are no good reasons for prohibiting what we want to do — for example that it infringes on the equal right of another. The countervailing reasons can be divided into the religious, the moral, and the practical.

Of the religious reasons little need be said. It is argued that we are not the absolute owners of our own lives, but hold them in trust from a God who gave them to us, so that the times of our dying should be chosen, not by us, but by God. But whatever the theoretical merits of this argument, it would be wrong to base any prohibition solely on the grounds that others have a religious objection to what someone proposes to do.

The main categories of moral theories are the *right-based* and the *utilitarian*. For a rights theorist, the right to life, the right not to be killed, is the most fundamental of all rights. When rights are listed, it always comes first, for the very good reason that to deprive someone of life is to deprive him at one blow of all his rights, of all possibility of earthly enjoyment. But if we grant, as no doubt we all do, that everyone has a right to life, it follows at once that we have a right to choose to die. For it is a feature of all rights that they can be invoked or not *at the option of the right-holder*. If you owe me ten dollars, I have a right to demand and get ten dollars from you. But I have no *duty* to demand repayment; I may, if I choose, waive my right — in this example forgive the debt. Similarly, the correlative of my right to life is your duty not to kill me; but I can release you from this duty by requesting you to kill me or giving my consent. To deny this is to confuse the right to life with the duty, if there is one, to go on living.

In special circumstances there may be such a duty. For example, if a person is the only breadwinner of a family and has no life insurance, it may well be his duty to struggle on against his desire to die. For some few of us, perhaps, some larger loyalty, even the national interest, might require us to forego our right to die. But such considerations are rare and not likely to figure in the type of case that leads people to advocate a more liberal law on euthanasia. Their concern is for people who, either from incurable disease or from extreme old age, are unlikely to be able to contribute substantially to the good of others.

A large majority of the people who join voluntary euthanasia societies are people in their sixties and seventies who are still enjoying life but do not like what they see in front of them in a society in which more than three-quarters of us will die in institutions. They ask for the various guides to self-deliverance issued by some of these societies not because they want to use the information now, but because they want the security of knowing that, in the words of John Donne, the keys of their prison house are in their own hands. The following letter sent to the Canadian society Dying with Dignity is typical.

I am seventy-nine years of age, in relatively vigorous health and constantly amused with life while it lasts. But I saw my mother and my father, years apart, in the same chronic care hospital suffering helplessly for months when they might have been quietly released; and this makes me dread a similar fate unless the law is changed so that one can choose, if still able, to slip away in dignity from the inhumane methods many hospitals employ today to keep one from dying a natural death.

Inevitably some people will be sad when a person dies; but that sadness will come to them anyway, and it should be lessened rather than increased by the thought that the person they loved died as he wished to die.

But what if no one is willing to kill me or to help me die? What then becomes of my right to choose death? This objection can be met by pointing out that the right to life and its corollary, the right to die, are only *negative* rights. My right to life imposes on you a duty not to kill me without my consent, but it imposes on you no duty to keep me alive (though, for other reasons, you may have such a duty). The same is true of the right to die. Supporters of voluntary euthanasia are not asking for "death on demand." They are not asking that anyone be saddled with a duty to kill a person who asks for death. They assert only that neither a person who asks for help in dying nor a person who gives that help is committing a moral wrong, and they claim that this moral position should be reflected in our criminal law.

If we look at the question from the point of view of utilitarianism, we get the same result. The utilitarian judges the morality of an action by assessing the good and the evil consequences, for the agent and all others concerned, of either doing something or not doing it. Obviously such calculations are not easy; but they are not always impossible. *Ex hypothesi*, a person who asks for death has come to the conclusion that, for him, dying is better than staying alive. He may be mistaken; but often this is very unlikely, and in any case he is the best judge of his own interests. As for the interests of others, his choice of death will be morally right so long as the benefit for them of his remaining alive is less than the burden on them and on him.

Let us now turn to the practical arguments, according to which, even if the moral admissibility of voluntary euthanasia were conceded, proposals to change the law would run into insuperable difficulties. First, it is argued that no proposal to change the law has any chance of success unless it has the support of the medical profession, which, it is said, it will never have. "Doctors vary in their approach to passive euthanasia but the profession condemns legalised active voluntary euthanasia."[1] Nevertheless, there are some British physicians who practise active voluntary euthanasia, but it is difficult to find out just how many there are. Since such an admission would, under present British law, be a confession of murder, it is understandable that they do not openly admit it.

On the other hand, voluntary active euthanasia is now practised openly in Holland, where there are between 5000 and 6000 cases a year.[2] The procedure starts with an application by the patient. A team is then formed consisting of a doctor and a nurse, a pastor if the patient asks for one, and others as appropriate.[3] The team discusses the application with the patient, and then either grants or refuses it. Some years ago, Dr. Pieter Admiraal, a leading proponent of the practice, was convicted of aiding suicide, but was discharged on the grounds that his actions had been medically necessary. "What made Dr. Admiraal's actions acceptable were (1) the patient's voluntary and spontaneous requests, (2) the rational and 'durable' nature of the requests, (3) the presence of unacceptable and 'endless' suffering, and (4) Dr. Admiraal's consultation with his colleagues."[4] If the consensus of medical opinion could change in the course of a few years in Holland, it could change in other countries too.

The second type of practical objection comes from lawyers, who, like doctors, are on the whole opposed to active euthanasia and the assistance of suicide. In 1984 the Law Reform Commission of Canada's report *Euthanasia, Suicide, and Cessation of Treatment* recommended that the law on active euthanasia and aiding suicide should not be changed. One of its arguments for this conservative stance was that the law in action is much less severe than the law on paper:

> Our legal system has internal mechanisms which offset the apparent harshness of the law. It is possible that in *some* circumstances the accused would be allowed to plead guilty to a lesser charge. . . . Finally in *truly exceptional circumstances*, the authorities already have it within their discretion to decide not to prosecute.[5]

But this is cold comfort indeed, since the circumstances in which people wish to die are, even now, not "truly exceptional"; and as the population ages and the power of medical technology increases such circumstances are likely to become even more common.

Many doctors and paramedics would like to put an end to suffering they know to be hopeless; but they are law-abiding people, and they have a special need to be careful of their reputations. That they are less inclined than they used to be to follow their humane inclinations is due to fear of possible prosecution and of malpractice suits if they do not pull out all the stops to keep a patient alive. It is not fair to say to them, as the Commission in effect does, "What you are doing is against the law, but we *may* turn a blind eye."

The Commission's second argument was that any relaxation of the law could lead to mistakes and to serious abuses. This is a weighty argument, and it will be considered later; but it is surprising that the Commission did not consider the possibility of building safeguards against abuse into a more liberal law. Perhaps the reason for this omission was that it relied most heavily on its third argument: that relaxation of the law would be "morally unacceptable to the majority of the Canadian people."[6] This, however, is not a moral question, but a question of empirical fact, and the Commission should surely have produced some evidence to support its view. But not only did it cite no evidence; it ignored such evidence as there was. In 1968, the Canadian Institute for Public Opinion (the Gallup Poll) had asked the following narrowly worded question:

> When a person has an incurable disease that causes great suffering, do you or do you not think that competent doctors should be allowed by law to end the patient's life through mercy-killing, if the patient has made a formal request in writing?

Forty-five percent of the firm answers were yes, 43 no. In 1974 the proportion was 55 to 35 percent. By 1978 the favourable replies outnumbered the unfavourable by more than two to one, and this result was repeated in 1984. In Britain a similar 1969 survey showed 51 percent in favour of active voluntary euthanasia. By 1976 the fraction had increased to 69 percent; in 1985 it was 72 percent. In the United States, though the proportion of favourable replies was lower, the trend was similar. In 1973 the Harris Poll showed only 37 percent in favour; by 1985 the figure had reached 61 percent.[7]

This disparity between legal and popular thinking is also shown by the many cases in which even newspapers of a generally conservative complexion have criticized a court decision. One example must suffice. In December 1984 an 84-year-old lady who had many reasons for ending her life tried to commit suicide by taking a lethal drug. She had a legal right to do so; but, fearful that the attempt might not succeed, she asked a friend, Mrs. Charlotte Hough, to sit with her and to place a plastic bag over her head after she had lost consciousness. Mrs. Hough did so and reported her action to the police. Initially she was charged with murder, but because of the uncertainty as to whether the death was due to the drug or to the plastic bag, the charge was reduced to attempted murder. She pleaded guilty, and was sentenced to nine months' imprisonment, a sentence upheld on appeal.[8] The judge said that although he had the greatest sympathy for Mrs. Hough, a prison sentence was necessary to uphold the law. On this *The Sunday Times* commented:

What is often morally right in this sensitive area remains legally incorrect because, as a nation, we tend to sweep discussion of death under the carpet. In 1976 Baroness Wootton introduced a bill into the House of Lords which would have brought a modicum of good sense and regulation to the subject of euthanasia. But it was not supported. As a result, uncounted numbers of people kept alive by medical science, often die without dignity. . . . Mrs. Hough's crime was compassion and it served to underline once more the need for better legislation governing voluntary euthanasia and the dangers of being without it. People should be allowed to die on their own terms and, as Barbara Wootton once wrote, "not those of nature's cruelty or doctors' ingenuity."[9]

The third type of objection arises from the possibility that mistakes will be made and abuses will occur. It would be a pity, it is said, if someone were to choose death when a cure for his condition was just around the corner. As it stands, this objection is based on a misunderstanding of the nature of biomedical research. The time that elapses between someone's thinking of a new drug or a new application of a known drug and its actual availability is to be measured, not in weeks or months, but in years. So, if there is really a new treatment likely to be available soon, that fact will be known. The patient should be told what the treatment can do for him now or in the near future and left to choose whether or not to hang on and hope for the best. New cures apart, it is true that people whose case seemed hopeless have recovered to lead meaningful lives; so it may well be true that some of those who chose to die would also have recovered. But, from the nature of the case, we can never know whether a person who choses to die would have recovered, and since cases of unexpected recovery are rare, it must be presumed that in most cases they would not.

The possibility that a more liberal law might be abused is a much more serious objection. How can we be sure that when a patient chooses death the choice is *fully voluntary*? Obviously this opens one of the most notorious cans of worms in the history of philosophy. Aristotle defined a voluntary action as one not taken under compulsion or due to ignorance,[10] and no one has been able to improve significantly on that definition. But this raises the problem of what counts as compulsion. Subtle pressures which would not amount to coercion in law might be put on old people to sign their own death warrants, for example, by greedy heirs who want to inherit sooner rather than later; and even if there is little to inherit, family members might want to get the old person off their backs. Senility, even without the aid of high technology, can last quite a time and people who need constant care can be a great nuisance. It is also tempting for family members to insinuate that the old person really has a duty to get out of the way.

A more liberal law to mitigate the uncertainties and inhumanity of our current laws is urgently needed; but the problem of devising adequate safeguards is one, not for philosophers, but for lawyers. For the law has great experience of dealing with problems of coercion and constraint in other areas. The validity of a contract may depend on whether the parties freely consented to its terms; and in many crimes the guilt of the accused depends on whether or not he intended of his own free will to commit the crime. So we might insist that possible sources of coercion be fully investigated, that the would-be suicide has been fully informed of the options, and that his will has been expressed several times over a stipulated period. Under the Dutch system the most serious abuses — coercion and fraud — are all but eliminated since active voluntary euthanasia is practised openly, only in hospitals, and after consultations so wide that there can be no reasonable doubt that the patient's request is uncoerced, considered, and durable.

Passive euthanasia (letting die), whether voluntary or not, is now generally accepted except by the more fervent right-to-life groups. But, while most religious leaders, doctors, and lawyers consider it morally acceptable, they still regard active euthanasia as morally wrong. Their morality can be summed up in Clough's often-quoted words, "Thou shalt not kill, but needst not strive/Officiously to keep alive." But what, if any, is the difference?

There is certainly a conceptual difference between killing and letting die. A life-guard who holds a child's head under water till he drowns certainly kills the child; a lifeguard who sits on the bank watching the child drown as certainly does not. He lets the child die. But is there any *morally relevant* difference between these two cases? Is not the lifeguard in the second case just as culpable, just as responsible for the death of the child as the lifeguard in the first? The law has long accepted the principle that acts of omission can be just as criminal as acts of commission, and popular morality accepts that they can be just as reprehensible.

If a baby is born with Tay-Sachs disease or anencephalic, it is routine practice to prescribe "nursing care only" and when the baby dies this is thought of as a merciful dispensation of Providence. But in this sort of case the physician intentionally causes death, for all that he causes it, not by action but by refraining from taking action. So there is no moral superiority of passive over active euthanasia here, and if the former is allowed to be morally permissible (as it generally is), the latter is also permissible. In fact, if there is any moral superiority here at all, it lies with active euthanasia, since, assuming the baby to be conscious, its suffering will be shorter. On this point the conventional moral position seems to be simply confused.

The fundamental principle of medical ethics has always been that a physician should act in the best interest of his patient, and this principle has been reaffirmed by two eminent bodies, the World Medical Assembly[11] and the United States President's Commission for the Study of Ethical Problems in Medicine and Biomedical and Behavioral Research.[12] Both of these bodies advocate passive euthanasia as often preferable to the use of "extraordinary" measures to keep a person alive. What neither of them asks, however, is whether letting someone die, even with the best possible care while dying, is really better for that person than giving him a quicker release.

The question of what is in a person's best interests is not an easy one to answer and the World Medical Assembly did not try to answer it. But the President's Commission did.

> In its report *Deciding to Forego Life-sustaining Treatment* the Commission says that all patients have an interest in well-being and that, in addition to this, normal adult or competent patients also have an interest in self-determination. . . . In other words, seriously disabled infants should, according to the Commission, not have their lives sustained if their lives are likely to contain more suffering and frustrated desires than happiness and satisfactions.[13]

In line with the Commission's thinking, the United States Surgeon General recommended that an infant who cannot be nourished orally "should not be put on hyperalimentation for a year and a half . . . but should be provided with a bed and food by mouth knowing that it was not going to be nutritious" and thus allowed to die.[14] But once it has been decided that it is better for the baby to die than to be kept alive by extraordinary means, would it not be in his best interests to die quickly rather than slowly and perhaps painfully?

> In one recently publicized case, an 85-year-old patient starved himself to death over a 47-day period. But who would seriously want to suggest that it is in the patient's best

interests to be dehydrated and starved to death? It appears that the World Medical Assembly and the American President's Commission would.[15]

If there is no moral difference between passive and active euthanasia, it is illogical to accept the former and reject the later; and if there is a moral difference *in favour of* active euthanasia, current medical practice is immoral as well.

In the case, not of an infant, but of a competent patient who, in addition to an interest in general well-being, has an interest in self-determination, the inconsistency of the Commission's position is even more glaring, since it says that a competent person's interest in and right to self-determination is paramount.

> Competent patients should be allowed to die when, from their point of view, life in a distressing or seriously debilitating condition is no longer worthwhile. Different patients will decide differently under similar circumstances. These goals and values ought to be respected. Hence, the Commission says, "no uniform, objective determination can be adequate — whether defined by society or by health care professionals."
>
> No objective determination can be adequate, the Commission states, because normal adult persons have an overriding interest in self-determination, that is, in the exercise of their "capacity to form, revise, and pursue his or her own plans for life." It is self-determination, the Commission suggests, which gives persons an element of worth and dignity.[16]

But if the right to self-determination really has the paramount status which the Commission accords to it, it must surely extend to include a right to die at a time and in a manner of one's own choice.

Postscript

I have argued that changes in the law of common law jurisdictions are urgent, that such changes will not occur without the support of the medical profession, and that, to judge from the polls, public opinion is more liberal on these issues. But opinion polls are notoriously unreliable, because the respondents are often unaware of the complexities of the issues underlying the questions put. Other evidence suggests that the public is, on the whole, indifferent. For example, though it is growing fast, the total membership of the 27 right-to-die societies that exist in 17 countries remains very small.

What we need to bring about is a change in our whole society's attitude toward death and dying. Instead of sweeping it under the carpet, we must learn again to accept it as our forefathers did, as not only the inevitable, but the natural end to earthly life. My own ideal death is that of Socrates, who took poison and died discussing the immortality of the soul with his friends. To be sure, his reason for choosing to die was that he had been condemned to death by the law of his country, which he felt bound to obey. But change that story a little: Socrates is growing old; he can no longer handle his stonemason's tools with his old skill, and worst of all, he can no longer match his friends in philosophic discussion. Life has no more that he values to offer him. So he accepts death, not knowing what is to come, having enjoyed life to the end.

NOTES

1. *Handbook of Medical Ethics* (British Medical Association, 1980), p. 31.
2. John Dawson, "An open and gentle death," *News Review* (British Medical Association), Vol. 12, No. 1 (January 1986), p. 22.
3. Pieter V. Admiraal, "Active voluntary euthanasia," *Newsletter* (Voluntary Euthanasia Society, London), No. 24 (May 1985).
4. Dawson, *op. cit.*, p. 23.
5. Law Reform Commission of Canada, *Euthanasia, Suicide, and Cessation of Treatment* (Ottawa, 1984). Emphasis added.
6. *Ibid.*
7. *Newsletter* (Voluntary Euthanasia Society, London), No. 24 (May 1985), p. 5.
8. *Ibid.*, No. 23, pp. 1-2.
9. *The Sunday Times* (London), December 16, 1984.
10. Aristotle, *Nicomachean Ethics*, III, 1110a.
11. "Statement on terminal illness and boxing, October 1983," *Medical Journal of Australia*, Vol. 141 (1984), p. 549. I am indebted for this and the following references to Dr. Helga Kuhse of the Centre for Human Bioethics, Monash University, Australia.
12. *Deciding to Forego Life-sustaining Treatment* (Washington: U.S. Government Printing Office, 1983).
13. Helga Kuhse, "Euthanasia — again," *Medical Journal of Australia*, Vol. 142 (1985), p. 612.
14. Quoted by Peter Singer and Helga Kuhse, "The future of Baby Doe," *New York Review of Books*, No. 31 (1984), pp. 17–22.
15. Kuhse, *op. cit.*, p. 611.
16. *Ibid.*, p. 612.

QUESTIONS

1. Does the commitment of our society to religious freedom imply, as Patrick Nowell-Smith suggests, that religious objections to euthanasia should not be allowed to influence the debate on the legalization of euthanasia?
2. Let us grant that all human beings have a right to life. Does it follow, as Nowell-Smith suggests, that everyone has a right to waive his or her right to go on living and ask that his or her life be ended?
3. A recurring theme in the discussion of euthanasia is the problem of preventing the abuse of legislation allowing euthanasia under specified conditions. Are the concerns of Colin P. Harrison in this regard adequately dealt with by Nowell-Smith?

SANCTITY OF LIFE AND QUALITY OF LIFE — ARE THEY COMPATIBLE?

E.W. Keyserlingk

Especially in the context of discussion and debates about euthanasia, the expression "quality of life" tends to incur either enthusiastic support or total rejection. Consideration of a patient's quality of life (hereafter QOL) as a criterion for decision-making in a life-and-death context tends to evoke from both its supporters and its opponents general agreement on two counts:

Reprinted by permission of the author.

i. QOL considerations inevitably and essentially involve entirely subjective (not objective) judgments, and the assigning of only relative (not absolute) value to the lives of others. For QOL supporters that is to be applauded; for others, it makes QOL considerations at best highly suspect.

ii. Since (both sides claim) the sanctity-of-life principle (hereafter SOL) obliges the conviction that all lives are of equal and absolute value, based upon their inherent sacredness as opposed to their state of health, therefore QOL and SOL must be mutually exclusive. Much said and written on the subject states or implies that there are only these two irreconcilable sides, and no middle ground between them. To espouse SOL is to reject QOL and vice versa, and never the twain shall meet.

Consider, for example, the following not untypical approval by a proponent of QOL:

The traditional Western ethic has always placed great emphasis on the intrinsic worth and equal value of every human life regardless of its stage or condition. . . . This traditional ethic is still clearly dominant, but there is much to suggest that it is being eroded at its core and may eventually be abandoned . . . there is a quite new emphasis on something which is beginning to be called the quality of life. . . . It will become necessary and acceptable to place relative rather than absolute values on such things as human lives, the use of scarce resources and the various elements that are to make up the quality of life or of living that is to be sought.[1]

Or consider the following and equally typical disapproval by an opponent of QOL:

The quality-of-life ethic puts the emphasis on the type of life being lived not upon the fact of life. . . . What the life means to someone is what is important. Keeping this in mind, it is not inappropriate to say that some lives are of *greater value than others*, that the condition or meaning of life does have much to do with the justification for terminating that life. The sanctity of life ethic defends two propositions: 1. That human life is sacred by the very fact of its existence; its value does not depend upon a certain condition or perfection of that life. 2. That, therefore, all human lives are of *equal value*; all have the same right to life. The quality-of-life ethic finds neither of these two propositions acceptable.[2]

But must the "quality-of-life" ethic necessarily find those two propositions unacceptable? Must we, in fact, choose between the "traditional Western ethic" (SOL) and a "quite new emphasis" (QOL)? Are SOL and QOL as incompatible, opposed, and mutually exclusive as both spokespersons just cited assume? Have the meanings, context, and implications for medical decision-making been sufficiently explored and articulated to justify the sort of polarization indicated? Our own answer to all these questions is in the negative, and it will be the task of this paper to argue that case.

The double-barrelled thesis we will sketch and define is, first of all, that the sanctity-of-life principle is not as absolute and rigid in its maintenance of life as is often claimed or assumed. At the same time, the quality-of-life concept need not involve attaching only relative or subjective value to human life. Briefly stated, SOL and QOL may, and even should, be seen and used as compatible and complementary standards and, in a very real sense, respect for the sanctity of life includes attending to the quality of life.

At issue is more than just semantics and subjective interpretations of the terms in question. Obviously, one could peremptorily assign to both SOL and QOL meanings that would *make* them compatible and complementary, whatever violence is thereby done to roots, traditions, or common usage. But apart from the dishonesty and pretension inherent in such a semantic fiat, why create when discovery will do? In other words, on careful examination of the roots and tradition behind the SOL principle, in philosophy and theology and reflected in sound medical practice, one discovers that there are no grounds for the view that that principle demands that human life must always be "aggressively" maintained, no matter what the damage or prospects for recovery. As for those quality-of-life factors, the manner in which they influence sound medical decision-making in actual practice established that QOL need not essentially mean anything different from what is meant by more readily acceptable terminology, such as "ordinary-extraordinary treatment."

At issue here as well is more than just an interesting academic debate. It would be no great accomplishment simply to establish the compatibility and complementarity of SOL and QOL if the outcome did not have important and practical implications for medical decision-making and attitudes toward human lives. But it is arguable that there are indeed such implications for decisions to support or not support life. Let us suggest two at this point. On the one hand, a respect for the sanctity of human life that includes concern for the quality of that life escapes the sort of simplistic medical decisions that pretend that complex, multi-dimensional, and difficult cases can be solved by the application of one simplistic, rigid, and unqualified standard. While comforting, easier, and righteousness-inducing for the one or ones making the decision or policy, black-and-white standards applied to mostly gray problems can be detrimental to the particular benefits, rights, and needs of the patient in question. To that extent, simplistic interpretations and applications of the SOL principle can be decision-avoiding rather than decision-making tools.

But on the other hand, decisions to support or not support life based on the particular patient's conditions and prognosis (that is, on that patient's quality of life) are less likely to be reduced to another party's subjective values and biases if they are tested by and restrained by the more general principle of the sanctity of life. More on this below.

We should note that the sort of decision-making we have in mind is that involving decisions made *by others* (doctors, families, agents, courts, etc.) for patients who, because of age and/or disability, are unable to make them for themselves. These second-or third-party decisions, made without knowing the wishes and preferences of the patient (or defective newborn) are the ones that always risk the imposition of someone else's wishes and values, and hence the ones that require some limiting and guiding principles and policies. Decisions made by *competent* patients for themselves are another matter. Ethical, legal, and medical stances should, and increasingly do, affirm that competent patients should have the right to make their own judgments about their remaining quality of life, and accept or refuse further treatment whether death results and whether others consider that decision foolish and disrespectful of the sanctity of that person's life.

Let us consider first the SOL principle itself. It is often assumed that it is more or less equivalent to "vitalism." "Vitalism" is the view that maintains that, where there is human life, even mere metabolism and vital processes, whether fetal, deformed, suffering, brain-dead, or dying life, and no matter how damaged it is, it would be wrong not to preserve it by any means possible and for as long as possible. If this is the meaning chosen for SOL, then of course SOL and QOL would be incompatible, opposed, and mutually exclusive.

But a careful study of both the Biblical/theological roots and more recent philosophical analyses of the SOL principle suggest another and better meaning and choice. Those Biblical/theological roots of the principle clearly emphasize, on the one hand, that human life is to be respected, and never to be taken, altered or left unprotected without justifying reasons, because only God has full dominion over it, and not humans. But on the other hand, those same traditions, as well as more recent theologies, insist that God has "deputized" to and shared with humans some of this dominion, some of this control over life, extending even to responsible decision-making in matters of life and death.[3] To accept that God-given responsibility is not "playing god" but *being* human." In effect, from the theological perspective, responsible decision-making even in life-and-death contexts finds its basis and starting point in Genesis 1:28: ". . . Fulfill the earth and subdue it; and have dominion over the fish of the sea and over the birds of the air and over every living thing that moves upon the earth." It would be a form of cowardice and abdication of responsibility to hide behind a vitalistic understanding of a principle that (like all general principles) is too vague and indeterminate to solve complex ethical problems all by itself. One physician put it this way:

> When it comes to many of the social problems of medicine . . . doctors retreat behind the cliché that they won't play God. This type of intellectual cowardice, this mental retreat, is irrational. It lacks logic completely, because through the nature of his work, a doctor is constantly intruding himself into the work of the Deity. Does he wait for God to show His decision by making some outward manifestation before he undertakes a Caesarean section, orders a transfusion, or performs a risk-fraught open-heart operation?[4]

Many recent analyses from the perspective of moral philosophy emphasize essentially the same points about the SOL principle, leaving out, of course, the element of divine creation and dominion. One the one hand, human life is worthy of respect, wonder, and protection. A philosopher posited a "secular" interpretation and affirmation of the SOL principle:

> The chief feature of the proto-religious "natural metaphysic" is the affirmation that life is sacred. It is believed to be sacred not because it is a manifestation of a transcendent creator from whom life comes: it is believed to be sacred because it is life. The idea of sacredness is generated by the primordial experience of being alive, or experiencing the elemental sensations of vitality and the elemental fear of its extinction. Man stands in awe before his own vitality, the vitality of his lineage and his species. The sense of awe is the attribution and therefore the acknowledgment of sanctity . . . if the sanctity of life goes then nothing else would be sacred.[5]

But on the other hand, it cannot be made to answer all questions in advance about *how* life is to be best respected in all circumstances; it cannot carry by itself the whole moral load of ethical decisions. Largely for that reason, some philosophers conclude that the SOL principle is at best meaningless.[6] We do not agree. Its value and role emerge only if we remind ourselves of the role of principles — that of testing moral rules.[7]

Two kinds of evaluation are involved at the "ought" level of life. One involves *facts* (what is), the other involves *rules* (what ought to be done or not done). Sometimes (and increasingly in our times) in the light of new facts, such as evolving perceptions and new scientific knowledge or possibilities, a rule becomes open to reconsideration. But how shall that rule or a new rule be tested, evaluated? What parameters and limits should it respect? It is precisely the role of general principles like SOL to answer those questions. It is *not* its function to prohibit new rules, or to preclude the difficult and sensitive task of weighing competing needs, rights, and benefits, or to insist that we should not attempt to evolve and rephrase our old rules in the light of new facts.

To questions such as, "Would it be a good rule that abortions be performed in certain circumstances?" or, "Would it be a good rule that life-supporting treatment be ceased in certain circumstances?" the SOL principle replies, "Would the proposed rule respect and protect the human life in question and indirectly all human life, or would it degrade and threaten the life in question and indirectly all human life?"

Thus the sanctity-of-life principle itself leads us inescapably to face such questions as: What *is* human life? What are its normative signs? What are the qualities or properties of human life that demand our respect for and preservations of that life? In other words, the SOL principle itself leads us inescapably to QOL concerns. One can emphatically agree that human life is "sacred" but what is human life? What makes this a question at all, and an increasingly urgent and difficult one, are precisely the new facts we cannot ignore in the form of both new knowledge about how life does begin, continue, and end, as well as availability of new medical technology to control how life *could* begin, continue, and end. In the biomedical context, as in any other, knowledge and technology are not value-neutral. Depending upon how human life and human benefit are defined, they can be used beneficially or harmfully.

Because our increasingly sophisticated technology can now arrest and prolong the dying process at any level of life from near fullness to merely biological, "quality" choices related to that technology cannot be avoided as they may have been in a simpler age. Now, in more and more cases not to choose is to choose. Not to make choices on reasoned and moral bases is to risk that those choices will be made by bureaucrats or technicians, and to the detriment of both the individual patient under consideration and, ultimately, all patients. If decision-making norms are not anchored in careful ethical analyses and choices about what we mean by and value about human life, then those norms will focus on the sort of quality-of-life criteria such as usefulness or burden to others, and social worth.

It is precisely at this point that the sanctity-of-life principle performs its limiting and testing function. It urges us to exclude from life-and-death decision-making (about factually or legally incompetent patients) all considerations of social worth and usefulness to others, and insists that the only valid norm is benefit to the patient in question, not burden or benefit to others.

This norm, in turn, makes it arguable that in decisions to initiate, continue, or cease "aggressive" medical treatment for patients who are incompetent and seriously or terminally ill or for seriously defective newborns, those are two justifiable *quality-of-life* concerns: the patients' (or newborns') actual and potential capacity to experience or relate; and the intensity, protraction, and susceptibility to control of their pain and suffering. The first concern would appear to matter if one grants that the capacity to experience and relate to the world around us is the essence of human life. The second concern assumes what is, in fact, medical experience, namely that there are still some cases of excruciating and intractable pain, despite the existence of sophisticated palliative and painkilling techniques.

One could therefore formulate, as a quality-of-life rule, perfectly consistent with the sanctity of life, the following: if, despite aggressive treatment, there is not and cannot be restored a minimal capacity to experience or relate, or if the level of pain and suffering will be prolonged, excruciating, and intractable, then a decision to cease or not initiate treatment is justified and perhaps even obligatory. In other words, for irreversibly comatose adults, for example, or for some defective newborns with severe spina bifida and a host of complications for whom the prognosis is a life of excruciating suffering, the most beneficial decision (for them), the one most respectful of the sanctity of their lives, may well be ceasing to support those lives.

What then of the "equal-lives" argument? Does not the use of quality-of-life language imply that there is an *inequality* between lives and the degree of protection they therefore merit? Some think so, as the following indicates:

> Can one really use a condition-of-life criterion and still insist that every life is of equal value regardless of condition? . . . does not one statement cancel out the other in the actual ethical climate in which today's debate is taking place?[8]

But surely it depends upon what is meant by and should be meant by human life. Increasingly, in a medical context it appears necessary to distinguish between what could be called "human biological life" and "human personal life" if one is to determine the human life the support of which the sanctity-of-life principle has in mind. Clearly there can be no human personal life, a life capable of enjoying, relating, communicating, and so forth, unless there is also human biological life. But increasingly, thanks in large part to new medical techniques and life-support systems, there can be human *biological* life without any significant human *personal* life. Both sorts of life are "human" — after all, even anencephalic newborns or irreversibly brain-dead adults were born of humans, but the human life the support of which the sanctity-of-life principle promotes is surely human personal life.

Insofar as humans are essentially relating, communicating, experiencing beings, mere human biological or metabolic life is not a good in itself, but a condition for the capacities of the human person. If human life essentially means "personal life," then there is no inconsistency or inequality in deciding that not all lives should be supported. All persons are of equal value no matter what their condition. But not all lives in the biological sense are equally of value to the individual person concerned. We want life for what can be done with it, because it is at least minimally bearable, enjoyable, and worthwhile, not for what it is in itself. As has been rightly observed.

> It always seems to be assumed that life, or whatever quality, is the most priceless of possessions. Physicians often assume that patients would always prefer life, no matter how handicapped, to death. The opposite is often the case.[9]

All lives are not equal if "equal" means that all lives are to be treated and supported identically no matter how different their condition. What is to be avoided is unjust discrimination in treatment and support. But inequality of treatment need not be unjust. Injustice and inequality are avoided if decisions focus on what is of benefit to the particular patient's quality of life.

Respect for both the sanctity of life and the condition or quality of that life could guard against either of two extremes — on the one hand considering all human lives as good in themselves, equally meaningful and equally to be supported no matter what, and on the other hand, ascribing *no* meaning, value, or support to lives that are handicapped or burdensome.

One can only be enormously impressed by the compassionate and heroic care extended to seriously defective newborns and infants, as well as irreversibly comatose or terminally ill adults by parents, families, and staff of institutions. Undoubtedly such experiences and the people they care for are extremely meaningful to those who provide the care, and they are provided with unique opportunities for extending and learning compassion, love, fidelity. Those who care find meaning and purpose:

> Someone in the institution was capable of relating closely to every child, and at every bedside as we made rounds there would be a staff member who could tell us the child's history. . . . Severe hydrocephalics and markedly obtunded neurologically damaged children were called by name and regarded as individuals. Their disease and related irascibility was understood, explained away, and assuaged by acts of comfort.[10]

That observation leads us to add an important qualification to what has been said thus far about QOL. It is this: a newborn's or adult patient's quality of life or condition is not always a static reality and can sometimes be considerably improved not only by strictly medical treatment but by the love, compassion, and persistence of those who surround that newborn or adult. For that reason, quality-of-life rules or criteria indicated earlier should be expanded in this manner: if and when a reliable diagnosis and prognosis can be made, including a reliable assessment of how *both* loving care as well as (presently or likely to be available) medical techniques and treatments may improve the patient's condition, ability to function, or level of pain, then and only then are we in a position to make ethical decisions to allow or not allow others to die.

Yet such rounds in such institutions can also raise two nagging suspicions. One is that in *some* of these cases (no doubt a minority), if decisions had been made soon after birth or later not to treat or support life aggressively, decisions based on the sorts of quality-of-life criteria indicated above, they may well have been decisions for the benefit of those children. The second suspicion is that *sometimes* we do not make such decisions partially at least because we, the healthy, derive meaning, purpose, and satisfaction from experiences that can have no such positive features for those children. To a certain extent, we may be deriving our satisfaction and meaning at *their* expense.

But the other extreme is just as, if not more, worrying: the tendency to ascribe no meaning or value to those who are handicapped and to cherish and support people not for what they are but for what they can do or make and only if they are not very burdensome to us. Such a stance is encouraged by proposals of what could be called criteria for "optimal" human life, standards and tests that give higher marks and more attention (including life support) to those who are brighter, have more self-control, need less help. One finds this tendency reflected not only in the context of life-and-death decision-making, but also, for example, in those who ask sperm banks for the product of donors with high IQs. In both cases there is a distasteful and distorted exaggeration of rationality and a disdain for human "imperfections."

Typical of this stance is the moral philosopher Joseph Fletcher, who proposed fifteen criteria as indicators of "human" or "person," with particular stress on rationality. He is both arbitrary and demanding when he decrees, for example, that, "Any individual of the species homo sapiens who falls below the IQ 40 mark in a Standford-Binet test . . . is questionably a person; below the 20 mark not a person."[11]

Should such a criterion ever become normative, many of the mentally retarded and senile now receiving care and able to function, albeit at a minimal level, would be excluded from care and support. There is a flavour of reductionism and elitism to such proposals that make them inconsistent with respect for the sanctity of life.

The attempt by Judeo-Christian tradition to seek a balance between two unacceptable extremes has been well described:

> In the past the Judeo-Christian tradition has attempted to walk a balanced middle path between medical vitalism (that preserves life at any cost) and medical pessimism (that kills when life seems frustrating, burdensome, "useless"). Both of these extremes root in an identical idolatry of life — an attitude that, at least by inference, views death as an unmitigated, absolute evil, and life as the absolute good. The middle course that has structured Judeo-Christian attitudes is that life is indeed a basic and precious good, but a good to be preserved precisely as the condition of other values. It is these other values and possibilities that found the duty to preserve physical life and also dictate the limits of this duty. In other words, life is a relative good, and the duty to preserve it a limited one.[12]

It is sometimes argued that the more traditional "ordinary-extraordinary-means" tradition and language is a better alternative to the use of quality-of-life criteria because the former is more likely to focus on objective considerations. Leonard Weber, for example, claims that, "The focus on means is a constant reminder that we should not decide who should live or die on the basis of the worth of someone's life."[13] Paul Ramsey notes that:

> The terms "ordinary/extraordinary," however cumbersome, opaque and unilluminating, directed the attention . . . to *objective* considerations in the patient's condition and in the armamentarium of medicine's remedies.[14]

But arguments that QOL criteria are necessarily more likely to result in subjective decisions about the "worth" of the lives of others than the means criteria are not convincing. The ordinary-extraordinary-means distinction is notoriously ambiguous, and in any case cannot really escape consideration of the quality or condition of the patient in question. Does it mean that "usual" treatments are morally obligatory, while "unusual" treatments are not? Hardly — if so, no change in medical policy or practice would ever occur. Does it mean that "useful" treatments are morally obligatory, while "useless" treatments are not? This would seem the more reasonable and justified meaning of the distinction, but useful in what respect? Useful to save life? But if so, at what level of function? Useful to provide comfort rather than prolong life? And is "usefulness" the only justifiable consideration? What about questions of costs, indignity, and so forth involved in the medical means being considered?

For all these reasons various alternatives to the ordinary-extraordinary-treatment distinction have been proposed, some of which focus much more directly on quality-of-life considerations yet attempt to guard against the imposition of someone else's subjective values. An example is the "reasonable/unreasonable-treatment" distinction proposed by Robert Veatch:

> A reasonable person would find a refusal unreasonable (and treatment thus morally required) if the treatment is useful in *treating a patient's condition* (though not necessarily lifesaving) and at the same time does not give rise to any significant *patient-*

centred objections based on physical or mental burden; familial, social, or economic concern; or religious belief [emphasis added].[15]

One may conclude that in the final analysis what matters most is where the lines are drawn, not what particular terminology is used. In our view, behind the "ordinary-extraordinary-means" language inescapably lie judgments about burdens, handicaps, damage, prognoses, and degrees of same — in other words, quality-of-life considerations. What will ultimately provide the needed protection and objectivity for a patient unable to make a decision is not the particular language and terminology used, but that the decision is tested in the light of the sanctity of that person's life and made for that person's benefit, not the benefit of others.

Two final points merit brief consideration. The first has to do with active euthanasia, the second with the care of the dying.

If it is sometimes justifiable for quality-of-life reasons and consistent with the sanctity-of-life principle not to initiate or continue supporting life, does the not-continuing extend beyond allowing-to-die to active euthanasia or killing? Moral arguments in favor of active euthanasia generally fall within one or two lines of reasoning. The first is that, because the motive can be benevolent in both cases, there is no moral difference between allowing to die (or passive euthanasia) and active euthanasia; if the former is sometimes justified, so is the latter. The second is that, even if there are moral and other differences between them, it is nevertheless sometimes justifiable to kill. We disagree on both counts.

Regarding the first line or argument, one may agree that the motives in both cases may be the same — that the patient, friend, or relative in question will die as soon as possible so that, for example, his or her intense and intractable suffering will cease. But motives alone do not determine morality. There are other considerations as well, among them the methods used and the nature of duties owed. For example, a physician may not always have a duty to provide life-saving treatment. In fact, a physician may have a duty *not* to provide it faced with a patient's refusal, or faced with the knowledge that it would impose too heavy a burden on the patient. In such cases the cause of death is the illness that it is no longer reasonable or merciful to fight. In our view it is misleading to label such decisions "passive" or "negative" euthanasia — they are not euthanasia and not the "cause" of anything, but rather good medical decisions based on evidence that curing is no longer possible. But a physician may, and we think does, have a duty not to kill, not to be the cause of death. In practice, physicians understand and insist upon the difference. This moral difference between acting (killing) and not-acting (allowing to die) has been well expressed.

> Acting seems to start with a presumption against it: e.g., killing is *prima facie* wrong. Not-acting starts without any such presumption, and it is only by establishing a duty to act that we show that not-acting is wrong. Killing needs to be justified; not saving life does not.[16]

What then of the second line of argument? Even if there is a moral difference, is active euthanasia in fact sometimes justifiable? We think not. What makes the morality of active euthanasia attractive is, of course, that there are indeed individual cases in which it would indeed appear to be more humane not simply to allow to die but to actively hasten death. But it should not be necessary to argue or prove that this is not so to establish that a general policy against active (even voluntary) euthanasia, one allowing no exceptions, is nevertheless the policy most consistent with the sanctity of human life. Not to kill in some instances is tragic for those individual cases; there is no point in denying that.

But the greater tragedy may well be that of following our natural sympathies and actually killing. Apart from religious arguments against it, there are a number of others that merit attention. One is the argument from medical fallibility. At least sometimes, to kill would preclude the chance for life in the event of prognostic error. Another is the serious harm such a change in moral and legal policy would do to the trust required in patient-physician relationship. A third is the wedge argument — to allow killing, even by exception, may well prove to be the thin edge of the wedge, sooner or later putting all life in a more precarious position. After all, rules against killing are not isolated from other rules and attitudes promoting respect for life. To disturb and qualify the rules against killing would seem inevitably to weaken the whole web of rules and attitudes that foster that respect.

What, finally, of allowing to die itself? If it is sometimes justified, once that decision has been made do we have no further duties toward the person concerned? By no means. There remains the continuing obligation to provide for the newborn's or patient's care and comfort. The obligation to aggressively prolong life may well cease, but allowing to die with care never does. The duty to provide care and comfort applies whether life-prolonging treatment continues or not, no matter how damaged the patient's condition or quality of life. The SOL principle surely calls for at least the same respect and consideration for dying human life as for healthy human life. And if greater need should elicit greater care and concern, then those who are irreversibly and seriously ill or dying deserve most care of all. In this regard the growing skills in pain control and palliative care reflect the growing awareness of medicine: that while it is *sometimes* about curing, it is *always* about caring; though the former goal sometimes becomes unrealizable, the latter always is. The art of medicine is, in large part, the art of knowing when to stop trying to cure and how to continue caring.

NOTES

1. Editorial, *California Medicine*, September, 1970, pp. 67–68.
2. Weber, Leonard J., *Who Shall Live?* (New York: Paulist Press, 1976), pp. 41–42.
3. Among these theologians are, for example, Dietrick Bonhoeffer, Karl Rahner, Johannes Metz, Harvey Cox, Rudolf Bultmann, Teilhard de Chardin and many others. See for example Johannes Metz, *Theology of the World* (New York: The Seabury Press, 1972).
4. Guttmacher, Alan F., "The United States Medical Profession and Family Planning," in Bernard Berelson (ed.), *Family Planning and Population Problems* (Chicago: University of Chicago Press, 1966), p. 458.
5. Shils, Edward, "The Sanctity of Life," in Edward H. Labby (ed.), *Life or Death: Ethics and Options* (Seattle: University of Washington Press, 1968), pp. 12–13.
6. For example K. Danner Clouser, "The Sanctity of Life: An Analysis of a Concept," (1973) 78 *Annals of Internal Medicine*, pp. 120–21.
7. On the role of abstract principles see Henry David Aiken, *Reason and Conduct* (New York: Alfred A. Knopf, 1962). See especially ch. 4, "Levels of Moral Discourse."
8. Weber, Leonard J., *Who Shall Live?* (New York: Paulist Press, 1976), p. 83.
9. Gellman, Derek, (1975) 52 *Dimensions in Health Services*, p. 23.
10. Diamond, Eugene F., M.D., "Quality vs. Sanctity of Life in the Nursery," (1976) 135 *America*, p. 397.
11. Fletcher, Joseph, "Indicators of Humanhood: A Tentative Profile of Man," (1972) 2 *Hastings Center Report*, p. 1.
12. McCormick, Richard, "To Save or Let Die," (1974) 229 *Journal of the American Medical Association*, p. 174.

13. Weber, Leonard, op. cit. supra (note 8), p. 85.
14. Ramsey, Paul, "Euthanasia and Dying Well Enough," (1977) 44 *Linacre Quarterly*, p. 44.
15. Veatch, Robert, *Death, Dying and the Biological Revolution* (New Haven: Yale University Press, 1976), p. 112.
16. Fitzgerald, P.J., "Acting and Refraining," (1967) 27 *Analysis*, p. 136. See also T.L. Beauchamp, "A Reply to Rachels on Active and Passive Euthanasia," *Social Ethics* (McGraw-Hill, 1977), pp. 67–74. For the opposite view see James Rachels, "Active and Passive Euthanasia," (1975) 292 *The New England Journal of Medicine*, pp. 78–80.

QUESTIONS

1. Is Keyserlingk right in thinking that the sanctity of life principle and the quality of life principle are compatible?
2. What does Keyserlingk think distinguishes active and passive euthanasia? Compare his position in this regard with that of Rachels. In light of the discussion in this chapter, how would you evaluate the relative merits of these two positions?
3. Based on his distinction between curing and caring, how would Keyserlingk respond to Rachels's Down's syndrome child example?

SUGGESTIONS FOR FURTHER READING

- Ronald Dworkin, *Life's Dominion: An Argument About Abortion, Euthanasia and Individual Freedom* (New York: Knopf, 1993). In this book, Ronald Dworkin describes the recent history of the abortion and euthanasia controversies in the United States and elsewhere. He argues that in the end, respect for human dignity requires respect for human freedom and freedom of choice both with regard to abortion and euthanasia.
- John Chandler, "Killing and Letting Die — Putting the Debate in Context," *Australasian Journal of Philosophy*, Vol. 68, No. 4 (December, 1990). The author argues that this distinction rests in part on a wider set of moral beliefs within which it plays a part.
- R.C.A. Hunter, "Euthanasia, A Paper for Discussion by Psychiatrists," *Canadian Journal of Psychiatry*, Vol. 25, No. 5 (August, 1980). Hunter asks, "What are the problems posed for psychiatry by euthanasia?" Tentative answers are offered, and the author concludes by suggesting that there is no case in his experience for active euthanasia. However, judicious (conservative) use of passive euthanasia is in some cases warranted.
- E.W. Keyserlingk, *Sanctity of Life or Quality of Life in the Context of Ethics, Medicine and Law*. This is a report prepared as a background study for the Law Reform Commission of Canada. The report studies the notions of "sanctity of life" and "quality of life" in depth and goes on to make a series of proposals. Although the focus of the Commission work is law reform, this report is primarily ethical in nature.
- E-H.W. Kluge, *The Practice of Death* (New Haven: Yale University Press, 1975). This book examines the morality of abortion, infanticide, and euthanasia. The author comes to the view that abortion in the early months of pregnancy is morally acceptable. But, following the development of "the constitutional capabilities for rational symbolic thought and self-awareness, a person exists." This occurs between the fourth and sixth months of pregnancy, after which time abortion is murder. It follows that infanticide, too, is the killing of a person and therefore murder. Euthanasia is, however, acceptable in certain

specified situations. Michael Tooley offers a sustained critical evaluation of Kluge's thesis in "The Practice of Death," *Canadian Journal of Philosophy*, Vol. 6, No. 2, June 1976.

- Marvin Kohl, ed., *Beneficent Euthanasia* (Buffalo: Prometheus Books, 1975). This book contains an excellent collection of articles on the subject of euthanasia viewed from many perspectives — religious and secular, pro and con.

- Marvin Kohl, ed., *Infanticide and the Value of Life* (Buffalo: Prometheus Books, 1978). Again, an excellent collection of articles representing a variety of perspectives on the subject of infanticide.

- John Ladd, ed., *Ethical Issues Relating to Life and Death* (Oxford: Oxford University Press, 1979). This volume includes articles by a number of notable authors and takes up many of the issues touched on in the first two chapters of this book.

- Douglas Walton, "Splitting the Difference: Killing and Letting Die," *Dialogue*, Vol. 20, No. 1, 1981. Is there a morally relevant distinction between killing and letting die? Some have argued that there is and some have argued equally strongly that there is not. In this article, Walton explores the distinction. In particular, he examines the position of James Rachels, an American author who has written extensively in defence of euthanasia and who concludes that there is no distinction to be made between active and passive euthanasia that is morally relevant.

- John Woods, *Engineered Death: Abortion, Suicide, Euthanasia and Senecide* (Ottawa: University of Ottawa Press, 1978). Adopting a secular, liberal perspective, the author finds himself directed (to his own surprise, given current liberal views on these subjects) toward the conclusion that abortion is rarely permissible but euthanasia frequently is.

Chapter 2

Abortion

Introduction

Abortion is a complex moral issue involving important questions about procreative choice, status of the unborn, welfare of children, responsibilities of fathers, involvement of the medical profession, and interests of the state. All of these dimensions bring into sharp relief each of the principles of protection-of-life, avoidance-of-suffering, and moral autonomy introduced in the last chapter.

With the development of reliable methods of birth control, having children has become widely viewed as a matter of choice and not a matter of necessity or obligation. But birth control is not always used; neither is it always effective. Advancements in medical science have resulted in the development of relatively safe abortion procedures. Many people now believe that if having children is really a matter of choice, the terminating of a pregnancy by abortion should, like the use of birth control, be a matter of choice.

Why might a woman choose to have an abortion? Sometimes the procedure is therapeutic. For example, the pregnancy might have become a threat to the life or health of the mother; it might be the result of rape or incest; or the mother may fear that she will be unable to cope with a child. Sometimes the reason may centre on the child. It may simply be unwanted by the mother, or the parents and doctors may have concluded that there is a substantial risk the child will be born with severe mental or physical disabilities. Finally, abortion may be requested for what might be called reasons of convenience. Either the pregnancy or parenthood may conflict with the lifestyle of one or the other parent. Or amniocentesis may indicate that the child that has been conceived is not of the desired sex. While not exhaustive, this list and grouping of reasons provides a starting point for assessing the relevance of the principles of moral autonomy and avoidance-of-suffering to the issue of abortion.

The life and welfare of a woman seeking to terminate an unwanted pregnancy are clearly central to a discussion of the morality of abortion. But there is a second life involved. It is a long-held view in our society that protecting human life is a central, morally obligatory task. We do not, as a rule, leave those whose lives are in danger to fend for themselves. It is also true that extending such protection to *all* human beings, regardless of such things as race, religion, colour, or disability has been a difficult and frequently unsuccessful struggle. The abortion debate, because of the problem of determining the point in human development at which someone acquires the status of an equal member of the community, with the rights and protections that confers, evokes echoes of the age-old struggle for human rights. One reason that has been given for opposing abortion is that the welfare of many "marginal" (disabled, sick, or rejected) individuals might well be jeopardized by widespread access to and use of abortion procedures.

So far, our discussion highlights what many see as the central aspect of the abortion debate: the conflict between a woman's right to choose and the right to life of the fetus. If the interests of a mother are in conflict with those of the child she is carrying, whose interest should prevail? As is reflected in some of the readings, many take the task of explicating and settling whose rights are primary and in what contexts to be central to resolving the abortion debate. But there are also reasons for seeing abortion not simply as a matter of individual rights, but as a social issue that raises questions about societal responsibilities for the welfare of others.

All societies are inevitably involved in the creation of rules about procreation, child nurture, and child rearing. In our society this concern takes the form of providing medical and other facilities for the care of women who are pregnant. Further, we have laws that govern the treatment of both mother and child before and after birth. Caring for children may not be the sole prerogative of the biological parents, but the law presumes this to be their responsibility unless they demonstrate otherwise. However, barring further technological developments, only women can bear children. Moreover, in our society, women continue to be responsible for most of the child-rearing activities. As we will see in the readings, some take these factors about women's roles to be relevant to a discussion of abortion. More recent concerns raised by New Reproductive Technologies in the areas of surrogate motherhood, in vitro fertilization, frozen embryos, et cetera, provide additional reasons for seeing the relevance of social and political factors for issues of human reproduction more generally. Modern technological advances provide good examples of how the current discussion of abortion has been broadened to issues other than those of the status of the fetus and the mother's right to choose.

Background Considerations

To a considerable degree, abortion as we usually encounter it today is a phenomenon made possible by advances in modern medicine. There are, of course, records of abortions and attempted abortions going back to the beginning of recorded time. However, it is only in this century that medical science has developed to the point where an abortion, properly performed in the first 12 weeks of pregnancy, poses little risk to the life or health of the person seeking the abortion.

There is another side to the story, however. The knowledge that allows for relatively safe abortions has also provided the basis for remarkable developments in the field of fetal medicine. Sophisticated techniques exist for diagnosing genetic and other disorders; blood transfusions are possible; and fetal surgery both inside and outside the womb is now a reality.

Thus, modern medicine has become a means for enhancing the quality of life of a child by intervening to correct problems prior to birth. But it has also become both a means for providing information that may well lead to a request for abortion and a means for procuring that abortion with a minimum of risk.

The Current Situation

It is worth reminding ourselves that the legal status of abortion in Canada has changed quite dramatically in the last few years. Since those changes stem directly from social, political, and moral debate, knowledge of them is essential to a balanced understanding of the issue.

Prior to 1969, abortion was prohibited by the Canadian Criminal Code. In 1969, the code was amended to allow for therapeutic abortions approved by a hospital committee comprising three doctors. Hospitals were permitted but not required to perform approved abortions.

It is generally agreed that the drafters of the 1969 law were seeking a middle ground between those who were of the view that continuing a pregnancy was a private matter to be resolved by women faced with unwanted pregnancies in accordance with values of their own choosing and those who believed that abortion was a form of murder. Perhaps not surprisingly, therefore, the law was from its inception the subject of controversy. Some thought it too restrictive and unfair in its application. Others thought it too lenient because it seemed to allow abortion on demand, at least in large urban settings.

Shortly after the new law came into effect, Dr. Henry Morgentaler challenged its moral and legal validity by setting up a private abortion clinic in Montreal and performing abortions in apparent contravention of the new law. He was subsequently charged with performing an illegal abortion and found not guilty by a jury. The verdict was subsequently overturned on appeal, and a verdict of guilt put in its place. That verdict was appealed to the Supreme Court of Canada, which in 1973 confirmed it and the 1969 law.

In 1982, Canada found itself with a new Constitution, an important part of which was a Charter of Rights. This was a significant new development and in the view of the law's opponents justified a new legal challenge. That challenge was once again mounted by Dr. Morgentaler, who opened a private abortion clinic in Toronto and performed abortions in apparent defiance of the Criminal Code. Dr. Morgentaler was once again charged under the Criminal Code. Once again, a jury returned a verdict of not guilty. Both the trial and the verdict were very controversial for a variety of reasons. On appeal, the Ontario Supreme Court concluded that the 1969 law was consistent with the new Charter of Rights and ordered a new trial. A majority of the Supreme Court of Canada disagreed. Some of the reasons are set out in the readings that follow. The resulting judgement ruled that the 1969 law was contrary to the Charter, and therefore unconstitutional.

Faced with this decision, the government of Canada undertook to draft a new law. When the law was presented to Parliament, however, it failed to gain the necessary majority. Hence, for the moment at least, the criminal law is no longer an obstacle in the path of women seeking an abortion. However, the procedure remains controversial. Various public opinion polls suggest that a majority of Canadians do not regard abortion as a purely private matter and believe that it should be controlled in some fashion by legislation. Furthermore, right to life groups have continued to lobby for laws that would protect human life from conception onward.

In practice, abortion is not uniformly available throughout the country. Some hospitals refuse to permit the procedure. Others are reluctant to give it a high priority in light of other demands on their facilities. Some provinces, Quebec for example, have facilitated access to abortion by recognizing and encouraging the creation of abortion clinics. Other provinces have been more reluctant to take this step and have resisted the creation of clinics for this purpose. All of these factors indicate that the topic continues to be actively debated in our society.

In terms of the law, our society is now faced with three options. The first is to leave things as they now are. A second option is to attempt to define in law the reasons for which abortion should be allowed, prohibiting it in all other cases. For example, Parliament might seek to prohibit abortion except in carefully defined extenuating circumstances. A third option is to determine a point in gestation after which abortion should be prohibited.

The Moral Dimension

The abortion issue, like a number of the issues to be examined in later chapters, raises two closely related but distinct groups of questions. First, what is the morality of abortion? Is abortion ever morally justified? If so, under what conditions? The second set of issues is concerned with whether access to abortion should be regulated by law. Should we prohibit by law abortions that the community believes are not morally justified? Much of our law reflects our moral values. Yet not everything we judge to be immoral is unlawful. For example, most of us would probably agree that, as a rule, promises should not be broken. Yet the law enforces only some promises and not others. Reasons for enforcing by law some moral values and not others will be explored in later chapters.

For the discussion of abortion, as well as for the discussion of a number of other issues raised in later chapters, it is important that these be seen as distinct groups of questions. We prize our right to form our own moral assessments and to act on those assessments. Laws created to control human behaviour circumscribe individual liberty. Thus, limiting the freedom of individuals by creating laws is a moral issue in itself. Paradoxically, failing to limit freedom of choice can also limit the freedom of individuals. This is one of the reasons the creation of laws restricting individual liberty is sometimes a moral imperative. This paradox can be illustrated by the problem of abortion. The freedom to choose for oneself to have an abortion is a very significant one to many people. But the freedom accorded to adults in this area has a direct impact on the freedom of the child, as yet unborn, to grow and mature as he or she will if the pregnancy is not terminated.

Let us consider here simply whether abortion is ever morally justified. One way of approaching this question is to evaluate the types of reasons given above that lead to a desire for an abortion. Is abortion ever justified for therapeutic reasons? If so, when is it justified, and why? Similar questions can be asked of the second and third kinds of reasons. And as these questions are answered, a view of the morality of abortion will begin to emerge.

An unavoidable problem in the discussion of human development concerns the point at which we become members of the human community, with all the protection its system of rules is designed to ensure. Is an unborn child a person? The question might, at first glance, seem a simple one. Unfortunately, in this case, first glances are deceptive. Human development from conception to birth is gradual; there are no sudden qualitative changes clearly signalling that the unborn child is now a member of the human community. Indeed, even birth, though traumatic, generates no significant, sharp, qualitative changes in a child. And so we are left with a clear dilemma. Do the moral and legal rules generated by the human community to offer a social environment in which human development can continue through childhood to adulthood extend to those who are not yet born? And, perhaps more importantly, should those rules be so extended?

There are other dimensions to be considered as well. As we have seen, an abortion may be requested because the parents of the unborn child have discovered that their child, if born, will be disabled in some way, and have concluded that, from the child's own point of view, it is better that it should not be born. Approaching abortion from this point of view creates serious moral tensions, similar in many respects to those raised by euthanasia. Those concerned with the morality of abortion are faced with the challenge of resolving those tensions.

The involvement of the medical profession is unavoidable, and this dimension raises another set of questions. Do doctors have moral obligations to unborn children similar in nature to their obligations to other patients? If undertaking an abortion, does the doctor have a moral obligation to use techniques most likely to result in a live birth? Or does the mother have a moral right to decide, where a live birth is possible, that it will or will not occur? Whose decisions about the life of the fetus should prevail in those cases where modern technology allows doctors to use clinically "dead" mothers as incubators for fetuses that are not yet viable?

Lastly, there is a dimension that explores the idea that social and political factors are relevant to an examination of the morality of abortion. Although women's roles are changing in our society, they continue to have primary responsibility for the caring and rearing of children. Does this factor provide an additional argument for respecting women's deliberations and decisions regarding abortion? Is there a sense in which engagement in child-rearing activities gives women a different or privileged way of reasoning through moral dilemmas such as abortion? If so, how does this thinking about abortion differ from questions about the status of the fetus that have framed the traditional debate on abortion? Does a consideration of social and political factors help us understand fathers' responsibilities for child care? We will see that this last set of questions introduces some of the issues relevant to the later chapters on discrimination and affirmative action.

The Readings

The first set of readings set out the legal background to current discussions of abortion in Canada: extracts from Madam Justice Wilson's judgement in the Morgentaler case supporting the majority view that the 1969 Criminal Code provisions were in conflict with sections of the Canadian Charter of Rights and Freedoms, and extracts from Justice McIntyre's dissenting judgement arguing that the abortion law was a legitimate use of legislative power and not in conflict with the Charter.

The Supreme Court judgement written by Madam Justice Bertha Wilson rests in large measure on a distinction between private and public morality. That distinction was first made by John Stuart Mill, an eighteenth-century philosopher whose ideas have influenced modern thinking in a number of significant ways (his seminal ideas on Utilitarianism are included in the Tools and Theories chapter). It is important because it provides a criterion for determining those areas of social life with which the law has a legitimate concern and those areas that are properly regarded as private and beyond the law's reach. The idea that morality can be divided into a public and a private sphere is one of the central themes in several chapters and is subjected to critical analysis by a number of contributors to this book. It is particularly important in discussions of pornography and the issues it raises.

The next group of readings present various positions on the issue of the morality of abortion. Sheila and George Grant argue that by virtue of the fact that the fetus has his or her unique genetic code from the moment of conception onwards, moral and legal rules designed to protect human life should be extended to the unborn. They claim that abortion undermines respect for human life and our willingness as a society to extend that respect to the very young and the old, those who are severely disabled, and those who are in some way seriously stigmatized.

In the next reading, Judith Jarvis Thomson grants the premise that the fetus is a human being from conception onwards, but she then argues that it does not follow from this that abortion is morally wrong. By imagining cases analogous to that of the mother and fetus in which the two principles of protection-of-life and moral autonomy come into conflict, Thomson appeals to the reader's sense that terminating a life may not be always morally wrong. In many cases, she argues, the mother's right to decide what happens in and to her body overrides the right to life of the fetus.

The reading by Jane English brings us back to the question of the status of the fetus and occupies the middle ground between the two positions presented thus far. While English rejects the conservative view that a fetus is a person from the moment of conception, she also takes issue with the liberal view that abortion is a purely private matter regardless of the development of a fetus. She argues that early in pregnancy a human fetus is not sufficiently well developed to be properly described as a person. Hence, early abortions are not morally objectionable. In the later stages of pregnancy, however, a human fetus is a person and abortion does generate legitimate moral worries.

The final two articles examine feminist perspectives on the issue of abortion. Celia Wolf-Devine summarizes arguments presented by those feminists who defend the idea that women have a distinctive "feminine voice" that reasons about moral problems in terms of our interconnectedness with others and our responsibilities to care for others. This approach, represented in the Tools and Theories chapter by Annette Baier, moves the focus from the task of determining individual rights and settling conflicting rights to the social and political contexts within which relationships are formed and responsibilities are created. The idea that our embeddedness in social relations is relevant to the identification, examination, and analysis of moral issues is another recurring theme in this book and is particularly evident in the chapters on discrimination, affirmative action, aboriginal rights, and poverty.

In the context of a discussion of the issue of abortion, however, Wolf-Devine locates a tension in a feminist defence of abortion that appears to support individual choice at the same time as it emphasizes our responsibilities to care for others. The reading by Susan Sherwin, "Abortion Through a Feminist Ethics Lens," addresses some of Wolf-Devine's concerns. Sherwin distinguishes between feminist and nonfeminist approaches to abortion. She defends a feminist approach that differs from that which Wolf-Devine targets. Sherwin argues that the issue of abortion cannot be properly understood unless it is placed in the context of the lives of women and the kinds of inequalities they continue to experience. In that context, she argues, the value of a human fetus can be properly determined and the justifiability of abortion defended.

DR. HENRY MORGENTALER V. HER MAJESTY THE QUEEN, 1988

[The 1988 judgement of the Supreme Court of Canada]

Madam Justice Bertha Wilson

The Right to Liberty

. . .

The *Charter* is predicated on a particular conception of the place of the individual in society. An individual is not a totally independent entity disconnected from the society in

Excerpts from the 1988 judgement of the Supreme Court of Canada. Reproduced by permission of Supply and Services Canada, 1996.

which he or she lives. Neither, however, is the individual a mere cog in an impersonal machine in which his or her values, goals and aspirations are subordinated to those of the collectivity. The individual is a bit of both. The *Charter* reflects this reality by leaving a wide range of activities and decisions open to legitimate government control while at the same time placing limits on the proper scope of that control. Thus, the rights guaranteed in the *Charter* erect around each individual, metaphorically speaking, an invisible fence over which the state will not be allowed to trespass. The role of the courts is to map out, piece by piece, the parameters of the fence.

The *Charter* and the right to individual liberty guaranteed under it are inextricably tied to the concept of human dignity. Professor Neil MacCormick,* *Legal Right and Social Democracy: Essays in Legal and Political Philosophy*, speaks of liberty as "a condition of human self-respect and of that contentment which resides in the ability to pursue one's own conception of a full and rewarding life" (p. 39). He says at p. 41:

> To be able to decide what to do and how to do it, to carry out one's own decisions and accept their consequences, seems to me essential to one's self-respect as a human being, and essential to the possibility of that contentment. Such self-respect and contentment are in my judgment fundamental goods for human beings, the worth of life itself being on condition of having or striving for them. If a person were deliberately denied the opportunity of self-respect and that contentment, he would suffer deprivation of his essential humanity.

Dickson C.J. in *R. v. Big M Drug Mart Ltd.* makes the same point at p. 346:

> It should also be noted, however, that an emphasis on individual conscience and individual judgment also lies at the heart of our democratic political tradition. The ability of each citizen to make free and informed decisions is the absolute prerequisite for the legitimacy, acceptability, and efficacy of our system of self-government. It is because of the centrality of the rights associated with freedom of individual conscience both to basic beliefs about human worth and dignity and to a free and democratic political system that American jurisprudence has emphasize the primary or "firstness" of the First Amendment. It is this same centrality that in my view underlies their designation in the *Canadian Charter of Rights and Freedoms* as "fundamental." They are the *sine qua non* of the political tradition underlying the *Charter*.

It was further amplified in Dickson C.J.'s discussion of *Charter* interpretation in *R. v. Oakes*, [1986] 1 S.C.R. 103, at p. 136:

> A second contextual element of interpretation of s. 1 is provided by the words "free and democratic society." Inclusion of these words as the final standard of justification for limits on rights and freedoms refers the Court to the very purpose for which the *Charter* was originally entrenched in the Constitution: Canadian society is to be free and democratic. The Court must be guided by the values and principles essential to a free and democratic society which I believe embody, to name but a few, respect for the inherent dignity of the human person, commitment to social justice and equality,

---

* *Regius Professor of Public Law and the Law of Nature and Nations, University of Edinburgh.*

accommodation of a wide variety of beliefs, respect for cultural and group identity, and faith in social and political institutions which enhance the participation of individuals and groups in society. The underlying values and principles of a free and democratic society are the genesis of the rights and freedoms guaranteed by the *Charter* and the ultimate standard against which a limit on a right or freedom must be shown, despite its effect, to be reasonable and demonstrably justified.

The idea of human dignity finds expression in almost every right and freedom guaranteed in the *Charter*. Individuals are afforded the right to choose their own religion and their own philosophy of life, the right to choose with whom they will associate and how they will express themselves, the right to choose where they will live and what occupation they will pursue. These are all examples of the basic theory underlying the *Charter*, namely that the state will respect choices made by individuals and, to the greatest extent possible, will avoid subordinating these choices to any one conception of the good life.

Thus, an aspect of the respect for human dignity on which the *Charter* is founded is the right to make fundamental personal decisions without interference from the state. This right is a critical component of the right to liberty. Liberty, as was noted in *Singh*, is a phrase capable of a broad range of meaning. In my view, this right, properly construed, grants the individual a degree of autonomy in making decisions of fundamental personal importance. . . .

The question then becomes whether the decision of a woman to terminate her pregnancy falls within this class of protected decisions. I have no doubt that it does. This decision is one that will have profound psychological, economic and social consequences for the pregnant woman. The circumstances giving rise to it can be complex and varied and there may be, and usually are, powerful considerations militating in opposite directions. It is a decision that deeply reflects the way the woman thinks about herself and her relationship to others and to society at large. It is not just a medical decision; it is a profound social and ethical one, as well. Her response to it will be the response of the whole person.

It is probably impossible for a man to respond, even imaginatively, to such a dilemma not just because it is outside the realm of his personal experience (although this is, of course, the case) but because he can relate to it only by objectifying it, thereby eliminating the subjective elements of the female psyche which are at the heart of the dilemma. As Noreen Burrows* has pointed out in her essay on "International Law and Human Rights: the Case of Women's Rights," in *Human Rights: From Rhetoric to Reality*, the history of the struggle for human rights from the eighteenth century on has been the history of men struggling to assert their dignity and common humanity against an overbearing state apparatus. The more recent struggle for women's rights has been a struggle to eliminate discrimination, to achieve a place for women in a man's world, to develop a set of legislative reforms in order to place women in the same position as men (pp. 81–82). It has not been a struggle to define the rights of women in relation to their special place in the societal structure and in relation to the biological distinction between the two sexes. Thus, women's needs and aspirations are only now being translated into protected rights. The right to reproduce or not to reproduce, which is an issue in this case, is one such right and is properly perceived as an integral part of modern woman's struggle to assert *her* dignity and worth as a human being.

---

* *Lecturer in European Law, University of Glasgow.*

Given then that the right to liberty guaranteed by s. 7 of the *Charter* gives a woman the right to decide for herself whether or not to terminate her pregnancy, does s. 251 of the *Criminal Code* violate this right? Clearly it does. The purpose of the section is to take the decision away from the woman and give it to a committee. Furthermore, as the Chief Justice correctly points out, the committee bases its decision on "criteria entirely unrelated to [the pregnant woman's] priorities and aspirations." The fact that the decision whether a woman will be allowed to terminate her pregnancy is in the hands of a committee is just as great a violation of the woman's right to personal autonomy in decisions of an intimate and private nature as it would be if a committee were established to decide whether a woman should be allowed to continue her pregnancy. Both these arrangements violate the woman's right to liberty by deciding for her something that she has the right to decide for herself. . . .

Re: Section 2(a)

In my view, the deprivation of the s. 7 right with which we are concerned in this case offends s. 2(*a*) of the *Charter*. I say this because I believe that the decision whether or not to terminate a pregnancy is essentially a moral decision, a matter of conscience. I do not think there is or can be any dispute about that. The question is: Whose conscience? Is the conscience of the woman to be paramount or the conscience of the state? I believe, for the reasons I gave in discussing the right to liberty, that in a free and democratic society it must be the conscience of the individual. Indeed, s. 2(*a*) makes it clear that this freedom belongs to "everyone," *i.e.*, to each of us individually. . . .

In *R. v. Big M Drug Mart Ltd., supra*, Dickson C.J. made some very insightful comments about the nature of the right enshrined in s. 2(*a*) of the *Charter* at pp. 345–47:

> Beginning, however, with the Independent faction within the Parliamentary party during the Commonwealth or Interregnum, many, even among those who shared the basic beliefs of the ascendant religion, came to voice opposition to the use of the State's coercive power to secure obedience to religious precepts and to extirpate nonconforming beliefs. The basis of this opposition was no longer simply a conviction that the State was enforcing the wrong set of beliefs and practices but rather the perception that belief itself was not amenable to compulsion. Attempts to compel belief or practice denied the reality of individual conscience and dishonoured the God that had planted it in His creatures. It is from these antecedents that the concepts of freedom of religion and freedom of conscience became associated, to form, as they do in s. 2(*a*) of our *Charter*, the single integrated concept of "freedom of conscience and religion."
>
> What unites enunciated freedoms in the American First Amendment, in s. 2(*a*) of the *Charter* and in the provisions of other human rights documents in which they are associated, *is the notion of the centrality of individual conscience and the inappropriateness of governmental intervention to compel or to constrain its manifestation.* [my emphasis] In *Hunter v. Southam Inc., supra*, the purpose of the *Charter* was identified, at p. 155, as "the unremitting protection of individual rights and liberties." It is easy to see the relationship between respect for individual conscience and the valuation of human dignity that motivates such unremitting protection.
>
> It should also be noted, however, that an emphasis on individual conscience and individual judgment also lies at the heart of our democratic political tradition. The ability of each citizen to make free and informed decisions is the absolute prerequisite

for the legitimacy, acceptability, and efficacy of our system of self-government. [my emphasis] It is because of the centrality of the rights associated with freedom of individual conscience both to basic beliefs about human worth and dignity and to a free and democratic political system that American jurisprudence has emphasized the primacy or "firstness" of the First Amendment. It is this same centrality that in my view underlies their designation in the Canadian Charter of Rights and Freedoms as "fundamental." They are the sine qua non of the political tradition underlying the Charter.

Viewed in this context, the purpose of freedom of conscience and religion becomes clear. *The values that underlie our political and philosophic traditions demand that every individual be free to hold and to manifest whatever beliefs and opinions his or her conscience dictates, provided inter alia only that such manifestations do not injure his or her neighbours or their parallel rights to hold and manifest beliefs and opinions of their own.* [my emphasis] Religious belief and practice are historically prototypical and, in many ways, paradigmatic of conscientiously held beliefs and manifestations and are therefore protected by the *Charter.* Equally protected, and for the same reasons, are expressions and manifestations of religious non-belief and refusals to participate in religious practice. It may perhaps be that freedom of conscience and religion extends beyond these principles to prohibit other sorts of governmental involvement in matters having to do with religion. For the present case it is sufficient in my opinion to say that whatever else freedom of conscience and religion may mean, it must at the very least mean this: government may not coerce individuals to affirm a specific religious belief or to manifest a specific religious practice for a sectarian purpose. I leave to another case the degree, if any, to which the government may, to achieve a vital interest or objective, engage in coercive action which s. 2(*a*) might otherwise prohibit.

The Chief Justice sees religious belief and practice as the paradigmatic example of conscientiously held beliefs and manifestations and as such protected by the *Charter.* But I do not think he is saying that a personal morality which is not founded in religion is outside the protection of s. 2(*a*). Certainly, it would be my view that conscientious beliefs which are not religiously motivated are equally protected by freedom of conscience in s. 2(*a*). In so saying I am not unmindful of the fact that the *Charter* opens with an affirmation that "Canada is founded upon principles that recognize the supremacy of God. . . ." But I am also mindful that the values entrenched in the *Charter* are those which characterize a free and democratic society.

As is pointed out by Professor C.E.M. Joad*: *Guide to the Philosophy of Morals and Politics*, the role of the state in a democracy is to establish the background conditions under which individual citizens may pursue the ethical values which in their view underlie the good life. He states at p. 801:

For the welfare of the state is nothing apart from the good of the citizens who compose it. It is no doubt true that a State whose citizens are compelled to go right is more efficient than one whose citizens are free to go wrong. But what then? To sacrifice freedom in the interests of efficiency is to sacrifice what confers upon

---

* *Then Head of Department of Philosophy and Psychology, Birkbeck College, University of London.*

human beings their humanity. It is no doubt easy to govern a flock of sheep; but there is no credit in the governing, and, if the sheep were born as men, no virtue in the sheep.

Professor Joad further emphasizes at p. 803 that individuals in a democratic society can never be treated "merely as means to ends beyond themselves" because:

> To the right of the individual to be treated as an end, which entails his right to the full development and expression of his personality, all other rights and claims must, the democrat holds, be subordinated. I do not know how this principle is to be defended any more than I can frame a defence for the principles of democracy and liberty.

Professor Joad stresses that the essence of a democracy is its recognition of the fact that the state is made for man and not man for the state (p. 805). He firmly rejects the notion that science provides a basis for subordinating the individual to the state. He says at pp. 805–6:

> Human beings, it is said, are important only in so far as they fit into a biological scheme or assist in the furtherance of the evolutionary process. Thus each generation of women must accept as its sole function the production of children who will constitute the next generation who, in their turn, will devote their lives and sacrifice their inclinations to the task of producing a further generation, and so on ad infinitum. This is the doctrine of eternal sacrifice — "jam yesterday, jam tomorrow, but never jam today." For, it may be asked, to what end should generations be produced, unless the individuals who compose them are valued in and for themselves, are, in fact, ends in themselves? There is no escape from the doctrine of the perpetual recurrence of generations who have value only in so far as they produce more generations, the perpetual subordination of citizens who have value only in so far as they promote the interests of the State to which they are subordinated, except in the individualist doctrine, which is also the Christian doctrine, that the individual is an end in himself.

It seems to me, therefore, that in a free and democratic society "freedom of conscience and religion" should be broadly construed to extend to conscientiously held beliefs, whether grounded in religion or in a secular morality. Indeed, as a matter of statutory interpretation, "conscience" and "religion" should not be treated as tautologous if capable of independent, although related, meaning. Accordingly, for the state to take sides on the issue of abortion, as it does in the impugned legislation by making it a criminal offence for the pregnant woman to exercise one of her options, is not only to endorse but also to enforce, on pain of a further loss of liberty through actual imprisonment, one conscientiously held view at the expense of another. It is to deny freedom of conscience to some, to treat them as means to an end, to deprive them, as Professor MacCormick puts it, of their "essential humanity." Can this comport with fundamental justice? Was Blackmun J. not correct when he said in *Thornburgh, supra,* at p. 2185:

> A woman's right to make that choice freely is fundamental. Any other result . . . would protect inadequately a central part of the sphere of liberty that our law guarantees equally to all.

Legislation which violates freedom of conscience in this manner cannot, in my view, be in accordance with the principles of fundamental justice within the meaning of s. 7. . . .

Re: Section 1

In my view, the primary objective of the impugned legislation must be seen as the protection of the foetus. It undoubtedly has other ancillary objectives, such as the protection of the life and health of pregnant women, but I believe that the main objective advanced to justify a restriction on the pregnant woman's s. 7 right is the protection of the foetus. I think this is a perfectly valid legislative objective.

Miss Wein submitted on behalf of the Crown that the Court of Appeal was correct in concluding that "the situation respecting a woman's right to control her own person becomes more complex when she becomes pregnant, and that some statutory control may be appropriate." I agree. I think s. 1 of the *Charter* authorizes reasonable limits to be put upon the woman's right having regard to the fact of the developing foetus within her body. The question is: At what point in the pregnancy does the protection of the foetus become such a pressing and substantial concern as to outweigh the fundamental right of the woman to decide whether or not to carry the foetus to term? At what point does the state's interest in the protection of the foetus become "compelling" and justify state intervention in what is otherwise a matter of purely personal and private concern?

In *Roe v. Wade, supra*, the United States Supreme Court held that the state's interest became compelling when the foetus became viable, *i.e.*, when it could exist outside the body of the mother. As Miss Wein pointed out, no particular justification was advanced by the Court for this selection of viability as the relevant criterion. The Court expressly avoided the question as to when human life begins. Blackmun J. stated at p. 159:

> We need not resolve the difficult question of when life begins. When those in the respective disciplines of medicine, philosophy, and theology are unable to arrive at any consensus, the judiciary, at this point in the development of man's knowledge, is not in a position to speculate as to the answer.

He referred, therefore, to the developing foetus as "potential life" and to the state's interest as "the protection of potential life."

Miss Wein submitted that it was likewise not necessary for the Court in this case to decide when human life begins although she acknowledged that the value to be placed on "potential life" was significant in assessing the importance of the legislative objective sought to be achieved by s. 251. It would be my view, and I think it is consistent with the position taken by the United States Supreme Court in *Roe v. Wade*, that the value to be placed on the foetus as potential life is directly related to the stage of its development during gestation. The undeveloped foetus starts out as a newly fertilized ovum; the fully developed foetus emerges ultimately as an infant. A developmental progression takes place in between these two extremes and, in my opinion, this progression has a direct bearing on the value of the foetus as potential life. It is a fact of human experience that a miscarriage or spontaneous abortion of the foetus at six months is attended by far greater sorrow and sense of loss than a miscarriage or spontaneous abortion at six days or even six weeks. This is not, of course, to deny that the foetus is potential life from the moment of conception. Indeed, I agree with the observation of O'Connor J. dissenting in *City of Akron v. Akron Center for Reproductive Health, Inc., supra*, at p. 461 (referred to by my colleague Beetz J. in his reasons) that the foetus is potential life from the moment of conception. It is simply to say that in balancing the state's interest in the protection of the foetus as potential life under s. 1 of the *Charter* against the right of the pregnant woman under s. 7 greater weight should be given to the state's interest in the later stages of pregnancy than in the earlier. The foetus should accordingly, for purposes of s. 1, be viewed in differential and developmental terms: see Sumner*: *Abortion and Moral Theory*, pp. 125–28.

As Professor Sumner points out, both traditional approaches to abortion, the so-called "liberal" and "conservative" approaches, fail to take account of the essentially developmental nature of the gestation process. A developmental view of the foetus, on the other hand, supports a permissive approach to abortion in the early stages of pregnancy and a restrictive approach in the later stages. In the early stages the woman's autonomy would be absolute; her decision, reached in consultation with her physician, not to carry the foetus to term would be conclusive. The state would have no business inquiring into her reasons. Her reasons for having an abortion would, however, be the proper subject of inquiry at the later stages of her pregnancy when the state's compelling interest in the protection of the foetus would justify it in prescribing conditions. The precise point in the development of the foetus at which the state's interest in its protection becomes "compelling" I leave to the informed judgment of the legislature, which is in a position to receive guidance on the subject from all the relevant disciplines. It seems to me, however, that it might fall somewhere in the second trimester. Indeed, according to Professor Sumner (p. 159), a differential abortion policy with a time limit in the second trimester is already in operation in the United States, Great Britain, France, Italy, Sweden, the Soviet Union, China, India, Japan and most of the countries of Eastern Europe although the time limits vary in these countries from the beginning to the end of the second trimester (*cf.* Isaacs, Stephen L., "Reproductive Rights 1983: An International Survey" [1982–83], 14 *Columbia Human Rights Law Review* 311, with respect to France and Italy).

Section 251 of the *Criminal Code* takes the decision away from the woman at *all* stages of her pregnancy. It is a complete denial of the woman's constitutionally protected right under s. 7, not merely a limitation on it. . . . It cannot be saved under section 1 (of the *Charter*).

Mr. Justice Wm. R. McIntyre

The Right to Abortion and s. 7 of the Charter

The judgment of my colleague, Wilson J., is based upon the proposition that a pregnant woman has a right, under s. 7 of the *Charter*, to have an abortion. The same concept underlies the judgment of the Chief Justice. He reached the conclusion that a law which forces a woman to carry a foetus to term, unless certain criteria are met which are unrelated to her own priorities and aspirations, impairs the security of her person. That, in his view, is the effect of s. 251 of the *Criminal Code*. He has not said in specific terms that the pregnant woman has the right to an abortion, whether therapeutic or otherwise. In my view, however, his whole position depends for its validity upon that proposition, and that interference with the right constitutes an infringement of her right to security of the person. It is said that a law which forces a woman to carry a foetus to term unless she meets certain criteria unrelated to her own priorities and aspirations interferes with security of her person. If

---

* *Professor of Philosophy, University of Toronto.*

compelling a woman to complete her pregnancy interferes with security of her person, it can only be because the concept of security of her person includes a right not to be compelled to carry the child to completion of her pregnancy. This, then, is simply to say that she has a right to have an abortion. It follows, then, that if no such right can be shown, it cannot be said that security of her person has been infringed by state action or otherwise. . . .

It cannot be said that the history, traditions and underlying philosophies of our society would support the proposition that a right to abortion could be implied in the *Charter*. The history of the legal approach to this question, reflective of public policy, was conveniently canvassed in the Ontario Court of Appeal in this case in these terms, at pp. 364–66:

History of the Law of Abortion
The history of the law of abortion is of some importance. At common law procuring an abortion before quickening was not a criminal offence. Quickening occurred when the pregnant woman could feel the foetus move in her womb. It was a misdemeanour to procure an abortion after quickening: *Blackstone's Commentaries on the Laws of England*, Book 1, pp. 129–30. The law of criminal abortion was first codified in England in *Lord Ellenborough's Act* 1803 (U.K.), c. 58. That Act made procuring an abortion of a quick foetus a capital offence and provided lesser penalties for abortion before quickening. After the *Offences Against the Person Act*, 1861 (U.K.), c. 100, s. 58, no differentiation in penalty was made in England on the basis of the stage of foetal development. The offence was a felony and the maximum penalty life imprisonment. The *Infant Life (Preservation) Act*, 1929 (U.K.), c. 34, gave greater protection to a viable foetus by creating the offence of child destruction where a child capable of being born alive was caused to die except in good faith to preserve the life of the mother. In *R. v. Bourne*, [1939] 1 K.B. 687, the prohibition against abortion both at common law and by statute was held to be subject to the common law defence based upon the necessity of saving the mother's life.

The earliest statutory prohibition in Canada against attempting to procure an abortion is to be found in "An Act respecting Offences against the Person," 1869 (Can.), c. 20, ss. 59 and 60. The Act was based on *Lord Ellenborough's Act* and the *Offences Against the Person Act*, 1861. The provisions relating to abortion were included in the Canadian *Criminal Code* in 1892 (1892 [Can.], c. 29, ss. 272 to 274), and with slight changes were included in the Codes of 1906 (R.S.C. 1906, c. 146, ss. 303 to 306); 1927 (R.S.C. 1927, c. 36, ss. 303 to 306) and 1954 (1953-54 (Can.), c. 51, ss. 237 and 238).

Section 251(1) made it clear that Parliament regarded procuring an abortion as a very serious crime for which there was a maximum sentence of imprisonment for life.

In 1969, Parliament alleviated the situation by the addition to s. 251 of ss. (4), (5), (6) and (7) as exculpatory provisions by 1968–69, c. 38, s. 18. These subsections provided that it was not a criminal act to procure an abortion where the continuation of the pregnancy would or would be likely to endanger the life or health of a female person.

. . . By defining criminal conduct more narrowly, these amendments reflected the contemporary view that abortion is not always socially undesirable behaviour.

As the Court of Appeal said, the amendments to the *Criminal Code* which imported s. 251 are indicative of a changing view on this question, but it is not possible to erect upon the words of s. 251 a constitutional right to abortion.

. . . I would conclude that, save for the provisions of the *Criminal Code*, which permit abortion where the life or health of the woman is at risk, no right of abortion can be found in Canadian law, custom or tradition, and that the *Charter*, including s. 7, creates no further right. Accordingly, it is my view that s. 251 of the *Code* does not in its terms violate s. 7 of the *Charter*.

ABORTION AND RIGHTS

Sheila and George Grant

We are often told these days that the rights of women require the freedom to obtain abortions as part of the liberty and privacy proper to every individual. When the argument for easy abortion is made on the basis of rights, it clearly rests on the weighing of the rights of some against the rights of others. The right of a woman to have an abortion can only be made law by denying to another member of our species the right to exist. The right of women to freedom, privacy, and other good things is put higher than the right of the foetus to continued existence.

Behind this conflict of rights, there is unveiled in the debate about abortion an even more fundamental question about rights themselves. What is it about human beings that makes it proper that we should have any rights at all? Because of this the abortion issue involves all modern societies (Canadian included) in basic questions of political principle.

These questions of principle were brought out into the open for Americans in 1973, when the Supreme Court of that country made it law that no legislation can be passed which prevents women from receiving abortions during the first six months of pregnancy. In laying down the reasons for that decision, the judges spoke as if they were basing it on the supremacy of rights in a democratic society. But to settle the case in terms of rights, the judges said that the mother has all the rights, and that the foetus has none. Because they make this distinction, the very principle of rights is made dubious in the following way: In negating all rights to the foetuses, the court says something negative about what they are, namely that they are such as to warrant no right to continued existence. The foetus is of the same species as the mother, and unless violent action is taken, will be a citizen in a few months. We are inevitably turned back onto the fundamental question of principle: What is it about the mother (or any human being) that makes it proper that she should have rights? Because in the laws about abortion one is forced back to the stark comparison between the rights of members of the same species (our own), the foundations of the principles behind rights are unveiled inescapably. What is it about our species that gives us rights beyond those of dogs or cattle? In discussing our laws about abortion, these fundamental issues can no longer be avoided.

The legal and political system, which was the noblest achievement of the English-speaking societies, came forth from our long tradition of free institutions and Common Law, which was itself produced and sustained by centuries of Christian belief. Ruthlessness in law and politics was limited by a system of legal and political rights which guarded the individual from the abuses of arbitrary power, by both the state and other individuals. The building of this system has depended on the struggle and courage of many, and was

Reprinted by permission of Sheila Grant and the late George Grant.

fundamentally founded on the Biblical assumption that human beings are more than accidental conglomerations of matter. For this reason, everybody should be properly protected
by carefully defined rights. Those who advocate easy abortion in the name of women's
rights are at the same time unwittingly undermining the very basis of rights. The view of
human beings they are implying destroys any reason why any of us should have rights. This
does not portend well for the continuing health of our freedoms.

In the modern era we have seen our basic political assumptions radically denied by Nazi
and Communist regimes. Terrible programs of persecution have been carried out by these
regimes, not only against their political opponents, but against whole races and against
whole classes of people, such as the aged and unprotected young. Where the doctrine of
rights has been denied (above all the right to existence) whole groups of individuals have
been left completely unprotected. The first stage in the establishment of all modern totali-
tarianism has been the explicit destruction of religion in the name of some pseudo-scientific
ideology. And with the destruction of Western religion has always gone the undermining of
political and legal rights.

The talk about rights by those who work for abortion on demand has a sinister tone to it.
What will be demanded next: the denial of the rights of the less economically privileged
who cannot defend themselves? Our system of legal and political rights is the crown of our
heritage, and it is being undermined. The denial of any right to existence for the foetus has
already been declared officially in the United States. There is no mention of it in our
Charter. Are we going to let it happen in Canada, and open the gates to all the consequences
of tyranny which will follow?

The validity of this argument must stand or fall primarily on the assertion that the foetus is a
living member of our own species. It is a fact, accepted by all scientists, that the individual
has his or her unique genetic code from conception onwards. He or she is therefore not
simply part of the mother's body. Even the blood type may be different. After 18 days a
heart beats; at three and a half weeks there are already the beginnings of eyes, spinal cord,
nervous system, thyroid glands, lungs, stomach, liver, kidney, and intestines; at six weeks
brain waves can be detected. It is not necessary to elaborate on the further development. It
can be found in any textbook of embryology.

It would be difficult to find anyone who would deny that a foetus is a member of our
species. Why is this not a possible basis for some agreement between those who differ so
much as to the nature of the foetus? There is no disagreement until we try to give a name to
our species. The usual one is "human beings." At these words the chasm suddenly opens
between those favouring easy abortion and those against it. Immediate polarization takes
place, with one side insisting that the unborn are not really human, and the others that there
is nothing else they can be. The reason for this total disagreement is the fact that the word
"human" has two meanings. To understand this ambiguity is the first step to any clear
thinking about the abortion controversy.

In the Oxford dictionary the adjective "human" is first defined in the generic sense: "of
or belonging to a man," the name of our species, covering all of its members. Then a
secondary meaning is given: "having the qualities or attributes proper to a man."[1] With the
word "proper" evaluation has crept in. This meaning is retained in the word "humane" (the
older spelling of human), which now means "characterized by such behaviour or disposition towards others as befits a man." The generic sense of human, which applies to all our
species, is specialized into meanings which are qualitative, and only apply to members of

our species at their best. Words do not hold their meanings in water-tight compartments. We often use "human" in such contexts as "human values," "inhuman cruelty," "what properly befits a human being," or even "a very human person," where the word means much more than belonging to the human race, and suggests the characteristics of men and women at their maturest and noblest. Obviously such a meaning is as inappropriate for the foetus as for the infant.

Further definitions of the word are practically a free-for-all. Joseph Fletcher, a well-known proponent of abortion and euthanasia, gives a whole list of the characteristics by which life may be recognized as "human."[2] Included is "self-awareness," "a sense of time," "self-control," "capability of relating to others," "the ability to communicate," "a concern for others," "control over existence," and "a balance of rationality and feeling." (A bit unnerving when one looks at oneself!) This is an example of the word "human" being used qualitatively, and then identified with the generic sense. This is not just confusion, but a deadly double-talk, for Fletcher makes no secret of what can be done to those who fail to meet his criteria. Astonishingly, Fletcher is still taught to student doctors in bioethics classes. It is no accident that he is a member of the board of directors of the Euthanasia Education Council. The criteria for humanity work equally destructively at the beginning or at the end of life.

Similarly, the word "person" can mean an individual of our species; but can also connote a mature man or woman, capable of "personal relationships," "personal integrity," and so on. In these contexts it is almost identical with the specialized uses of "human."[3] So if, with these associations of quality in mind, we return to the naming of ourselves as "human beings," we are able to exclude the foetus from being thought of as human. We may also have no difficulty in excluding other categories of mankind that do not measure up to our view of what is "truly human" in the fullest and most meaningful sense.

A confusion is also found in the use of the word "life." "The foetus may be alive in a biological sense," we are told, "but human, no." It is implied that to talk of our species in terms of biological life is to talk on a very low level indeed. In fact, "biological life" is a misleading tautology. There is no such thing in nature as a living organism that has merely "biological life." It must belong to some species, even if it is only an amoeba. If the foetus is alive, yet is not human, what is it? No woman has yet given birth to a cat.[4]

There is another kind of double-talk about life that has a place in a United States Supreme Court decision.[5] After viability (a date varying according to the sophistication of our current supportive techniques), a foetus becomes legally recognizable as "potential life." Presumably "potential" must mean "capable of, but not yet possessing." By this vague phrase, do they mean that the foetus is not alive? If not alive, do they mean it is dead? Even the United States Supreme Court must know the difference between a living foetus and a dead one. There is no halfway. Beings with only "potential" life do not suck their thumbs in the womb in preparation for sucking the breast. It makes perfect sense to say that we all have potential not yet fulfilled, or even that we are all potentially dead, but it does not make sense to say the foetus is "potential life."

It is best to be suspicious of such phrases as "potential life," "person in the whole sense," "human in the full sense of the word." They are used to confuse what is being done in abortion. The primary, or generic, sense of "human" cannot be denied to the foetus. What a dog begets is canine; what we beget is human. Nor do we need the word "person" to defend the right of the foetus to continue developing. We do not tell the fireman not to bother rescuing the infant trapped in the burning house because that infant is not yet "a person in the fullest sense of the word."

In our day, the struggle for rights has often been effective. It now runs counter to the temper of our society to challenge the claims of personal freedom. In our society, men and women are grasping toward an understanding that would preclude violence against one another. The noble attempt to eliminate capital punishment is a good example. The fight for civil rights in the United States has won great victories, however incomplete. Women are struggling courageously for their proper equality. What of children? In the preamble to the United Nations Declaration of the Rights of a Child (November 29, 1959), it is stated that the Declaration is necessary "because the child, by reason of his physical and mental immaturity, needs special safeguards and care, including legal protection before as well as after birth." There is pressure now for this sentence to be omitted from the declaration. It is ironic that at the time of many compassionate victories there has arisen a new category of the unprotected. Despite the tradition of rights in which we were nurtured, the unborn child in the United States has been deprived of the right to exist, and the pressure to deny this right to unborn children in Canada is mounting. Strangely enough, the unborn still have some rights: they can inherit under a will, they can even be recognized as plaintiffs in a lawsuit. Recently it has been suggested that they have a right not to be born with alcoholic syndrome. But for the individuals who can be put to death at the will of the very person who brought them into existence, such rights as these are rather a bad joke.

Some distinctions must be made here between the legal situation in Canada and in the States. In January 1973, the United States Supreme Court made its declaration in *Roe v. Wade*. It affirmed a new right, nowhere mentioned in their constitution but "felt" to be "intended."[6] No legislation can infringe the right of a woman to procure the termination of her pregnancy. For the first six months of pregnancy, no reason at all need be given for the killing of the developing child. After that time, though still declared not to be a "person in the whole sense," the unborn child is recognized as "potential life." A little red tape is required, after six months, to abort the foetus; namely, one doctor must declare it necessary for the mother's health, "health" in the widest possible sense of the word, that of "well-being."

Canada's position is different. The law grants no "right to abortion." Abortion is still on the Criminal Code as a punishable offence; but an exception is made to the general prohibition in the case of danger to the life or health of the mother. An abortion may be performed, anytime during pregnancy, on the recommendation of one doctor, ratified by a hospital committee of three doctors. The committee does not need to see the woman. The numbers of ratifications done in a short time are very large. A disinclination toward bearing a child is usually interpreted as a danger to mental health. In 1980, according to Statistics Canada, 65,751 legal abortions were performed, and the number increases each year, although the medical necessity of abortion decreases. It is obvious that convenience, rather than danger, is already the usual criterion. Yet there is mounting pressure today for still easier laws. The only possible extension would be abortion on demand, which already *de facto* exists in many parts of Canada, for example Ontario and British Columbia.

What has happened to our belief in rights that, in the name of a lesser right, the primary one — the right to life — can be denied to members of our own species? Not only is the woman's own right to life affirmed, but it includes her right to freedom and privacy, and well-being, and all sorts of other good things. Yet she herself, her own unique, unrepeatable self, was once growing in her mother's womb. What magic has occurred with the passage of time that gives her all these rights, and denies any to her unborn child?

Light can be thrown on this denial of rights by looking at a familiar quotation: "We hold these truths to be self-evident; that all men are created equal, that they are endowed by their

Creator with inalienable rights, that among these rights are life . . . that to secure these rights, governments are instituted among men." Fine, ringing words, but no longer self-evident. Our world has changed. Many believe that we are accidental beings in a world that came into being through chance. In such a situation the very foundations of the doctrine of rights have been eroded. All men are not created equal; they are not created at all. But in that case, why are they equal? Justice can become a privilege society grants to some of its people, if they are the right age, and sufficiently like most other people. One can foresee a time when before one can qualify for rights, a kind of means test may be used: "Are you human in the fullest sense of the word?" "Are you still enjoying quality of life?" And here is the crunch: as the foetus loses out, so will the weak, the aged, the infirm, the unproductive. If we come to believe that we are nothing but accidents, rights will no longer be given in the very nature of our legal system. The most powerful among us will then decide who is to have rights and who is not.

The effect of this undermining of our political tradition is often sugar-coated by talk about "quality of life." The phrase "quality of life" has a high-minded ring about it. Like the slogan "every child a wanted child" it is impossible to be against it. Of course it is better for children to be wanted rather than rejected, and for lives to have a high quality rather than a low one. But let us remember for what purpose these slogans are now mainly used. They are used negatively, and with terrible, destructive implications. Every child should be a wanted child, so destroy those that do not seem to be wanted. Only quality of life deserves our respect, not life itself. So we deny rights to those who do not measure up.

When "quality of life" is urged for constructive purposes, it is indeed a compassionate approach to human suffering; but when it is used to downgrade some lives as expendable, because of their absence of quality, its proper use is perverted. It can then justify "selective abortion," or getting rid of the defective. Although our law makes no provision for "selective abortion," it is already widely practised in Canada, and is the purpose of the well-known test, amniocentesis, that identifies certain defects in the foetus. It is wonderful when medicine can eliminate certain diseases, but it is not at all the same thing to eliminate the patients suffering from them. Once we take the cost-benefit approach, and start grading the right to life in terms of quality, our criteria exclude more and more groups from human status. What will we be willing to do to these groups?

The most pressing warning of how far the destruction of rights could go in the Western world took place in Nazi Germany. We in the English-speaking world would like to think of this as a monstrous happening that was defeated, and stopped, and that has no relation to ourselves. But if we look at some of the basic programs carried out by the Nazis against their own people, we may find that, whatever our revulsions, our society seems to be moving away from the clear principles that would condemn these practices.

We are not referring to abortion, but to the Nazi program of euthanasia of the insane and the incurable that was extended, in 1943, to include children orphaned by the war. These children were put to death in the gas chambers along with the incurable and the insane. The country was thus relieved of the burden of those who could not care for themselves. The techniques of the gas chambers and the crematoria were used first for such people, then extended to the Jews, the Gypsies, and political opponents. Hitler had to keep these programs as secret as possible. Largely through the courage of Bishop Galen, the programs became known to the public, and evoked great horror among the German people, even though they were living in a totalitarian state.

We, of course, do not live in a totalitarian regime, and we do not yet kill our mentally ill. Nevertheless we are moving toward ways of thought that could be used to justify such actions. We are starting to arrogate to ourselves the power to decide not only who should live, but who really wants to live. Despite all the evidence that retarded people, or the very old, are frequently as happy and as unhappy as other people, we are coming to know better. They may seem happy, but if they were normal, they would agree that as defective or old they are really better off dead.

If this sounds unjustifiably alarmist, it is well to remember the figures of abortions since the law was amended in 1969. In 1970, according to Statistics Canada, there were 11,152 legal abortions in Canada; in 1980 there were 65,751.* Certainly the rare medical necessities have not increased, for medical techniques have improved. The situation is clearly self-accelerating. If women know they never need bear children they have conceived, they are less and less likely to face the initial inconveniences. We have moved fast in a few years toward the point where, in the name of convenience, we say that a woman has an absolute right to an abortion and an unborn child has no right to existence. Such an absolute denial of rights to unborn children has moved Canada down the road to a society where the sanctity of the individual is openly denied, and where the idea of rights may gradually disappear. The end of this road is tyranny — a tyranny in which legal protection will be based upon power. This erosion of rights will be smooth, for when tyranny comes in North America, it will come cosily and on cats' feet. It will come in the name of the cost-benefit analysis of human life, sugared over with liberal rhetoric about quality of life.**

NOTES

1. The word "man" is used here to include both men and women. This old way of speech now seems discriminatory and should be avoided.
2. Fletcher, Joseph, "Indicators of Humanhood: A Tentative Profile of Man," *Hastings Centre Report*, 1972, pp. 1–4.
3. The Dred Scott Decision in 1856 by the American Supreme Court rules that although Negroes were human beings, they were not "persons" in the eyes of the law. The Fourteenth Amendment to their constitution was enacted specifically to overturn this, and interpreted "person" as including all living human beings.
4. The National Council of Women is evidently not quite sure about this. In 1967 it presented a resolution to a Parliamentary Committee in which abortion was defined as the "premature expulsion of the mammalian foetus." It is impossible to meet a mammal pure and simple — one meets a mouse, dog, human being, and so on.
5. *Roe v. Wade*, p. 48.
6. Justice Blackmun spoke for the majority: "We feel the Right is located in the Fourteenth Amendment's concept of personal liberty." *Roe v. Wade*, pp. 37–38.

QUESTIONS

1. Does the liberalizing of abortion laws lead to the liberalizing of laws that prohibit euthanasia?

---

* The statistics for therapeutic abortions performed in hospitals from 1970 to 1993 (the most recent figures available to the editors) are as follows: 1970, 11,200; 1975, 49,390; 1985, 62,740; 1990, 71,222; 1993, 72,530. Note that these figures do not include therapeutic abortions performed in clinics or in the United States.

** The law in Canada has of course changed since this article was written in the mid-1980s in the direction the authors warn of toward the end of this paragraph. The details of those changes are set out elsewhere. (The editors.)

2. If we deny to unborn children the right to life, are we undermining the right to life of other members of the human race?
3. Have the Grants provided convincing arguments for the view that a human being is a person from the moment of conception forward?

A DEFENSE OF ABORTION

Judith Jarvis Thomson

Most opposition to abortion relies on the premise that the fetus is a human being, a person, from the moment of conception. The premise is argued for, but, as I think, not well. Take, for example, the most common argument. We are asked to notice that the development of a human being from conception through birth into childhood is continuous; then it is said that to draw a line, to choose a point in this development and say "before this point the thing is not a person, after this point it is a person" is to make an arbitrary choice, a choice for which in the nature of things no good reason can be given. It is concluded that the fetus is, or anyway that we had better say it is, a person from the moment of conception. But this conclusion does not follow. Similar things might be said about the development of an acorn into an oak tree, and it does not follow that acorns are oak trees, or that we had better say they are. Arguments of this form are sometimes called "slippery slope arguments" — the phrase is perhaps self-explanatory — and it is dismaying that opponents of abortion rely on them so heavily and uncritically.

I am inclined to agree, however, that the prospects for "drawing a line" in the development of the fetus look dim. I am inclined to think also that we shall probably have to agree that the fetus has already become a human person well before birth. Indeed, it comes as a surprise when one first learns how early in its life it begins to acquire human characteristics. By the tenth week, for example, it already has a face, arms and legs, fingers and toes; it has internal organs, and brain activity is detectable. On the other hand, I think that the premise is false, that the fetus is not a person from the moment of conception. A newly fertilized ovum, a newly implanted clump of cells, is no more a person than an acorn is an oak tree. But I shall not discuss any of this. For it seems to me to be of great interest to ask what happens if, for the sake of argument, we allow the premise. How, precisely, are we supposed to get from there to the conclusion that abortion is morally impermissible? Opponents of abortion commonly spend most of their time establishing that the fetus is a person, and hardly any time explaining the step from there to the impermissibility of abortion. Perhaps they think the step too simple and obvious to require much comment. Or perhaps instead they are simply being economical in argument. Many of those who defend abortion rely on the premise that the fetus is not a person, but only a bit of tissue that will become a person at birth; and why pay out more arguments than you have to? Whatever the explanation, I suggest that the step they take is neither easy nor obvious, that it calls for closer examination than it is commonly given, and that when we do give it this closer examination we shall feel inclined to reject it.

From Philosophy & Public Affairs, *v. 1, no. 1 (Fall 1971), pp. 47–66. Copyright 1971 by Princeton University Press. Reprinted by permission of Princeton University Press.*

I propose, then, that we grant that the fetus is a person from the moment of conception. How does the argument go from here? Something like this, I take it. Every person has a right to life. So the fetus has a right to life. No doubt the mother has a right to decide what shall happen in and to her body; everyone would grant that. But surely a person's right to life is stronger and more stringent than the mother's right to decide what happens in and to her body, and so outweighs it. So the fetus may not be killed; an abortion may not be performed.

It sounds plausible. But now let me ask you to imagine this. You wake up in the morning and find yourself back to back in bed with an unconscious violinist. A famous unconscious violinist. He has been found to have a fatal kidney ailment, and the Society of Music Lovers has canvassed all the available medical records and found that you alone have the right blood type to help. They have therefore kidnapped you, and last night the violinist's circulatory system was plugged into yours, so that your kidneys can be used to extract poisons from his blood as well as your own. The director of the hospital now tells you, "Look, we're sorry the Society of Music Lovers did this to you — we would never have permitted it if we had known. But still, they did it, and the violinist now is plugged into you. To unplug you would be to kill him. But never mind, it's only for nine months. By then he will have recovered from his ailment, and can safely be unplugged from you." Is it morally incumbent on you to accede to this situation? No doubt it would be very nice of you if you did, a great kindness. But do you *have* to accede to it? What if it were not nine months, but nine years? Or longer still? What if the director of the hospital says, "Tough luck, I agree, but you've now got to stay in bed, with the violinist plugged into you, for the rest of your life. Because remember this. All persons have a right to life, and violinists are persons. Granted you have a right to decide what happens in and to your body, but a person's right to life outweighs your right to decide what happens in and to your body. So you cannot ever be unplugged from him." I imagine you would regard this as outrageous, which suggests that something really is wrong with that plausible sounding argument I mentioned a moment ago.

In this case, of course, you were kidnapped; you didn't volunteer for the operation that plugged the violinist into your kidneys. Can those who oppose abortion on the ground I mentioned make an exception for a pregnancy due to rape? Certainly. They can say that persons have a right to life only if they didn't come into existence because of rape; or they can say that all persons have a right to life, but that some have less of a right to life than others, in particular, that those who came into existence because of rape have less. But these statements have a rather unpleasant sound. Surely the question of whether you have a right to life at all, or how much of it you have, shouldn't turn on the question of whether or not you are the product of a rape. And in fact the people who oppose abortion on the ground I mentioned do not make this distinction, and hence do not make an exception in case of rape.

Nor do they make an exception for a case in which the mother has to spend the nine months of her pregnancy in bed. They would agree that would be a great pity, and hard on the mother; but all the same, all persons have a right to life, the fetus is a person, and so on. I suspect, in fact, that they would not make an exception for a case in which, miraculously enough, the pregnancy went on for nine years, or even the rest of the mother's life.

Some won't even make an exception for a case in which continuation of the pregnancy is likely to shorten the mother's life; they regard abortion as impermissible even to save the mother's life. Such cases are nowadays very rare, and many opponents of abortion do not accept this extreme view. All the same, it is a good place to begin: a number of points of interest come out in respect to it.

1. Let us call the view that abortion is impermissible even to save the mother's life "the extreme view." I want to suggest first that it does not issue from the argument I mentioned earlier without the addition of some fairly powerful premises. Suppose a woman has become pregnant, and now learns that she has a cardiac condition such that she will die if she carries the baby to term. What may be done for her? The fetus, being a person, has a right to life, but as the mother is a person too, so has she a right to life. Presumably they have an equal right to life. How is it supposed to come out that an abortion may not be performed? If mother and child have an equal right to life, shouldn't we perhaps flip a coin? Or should we add to the mother's right to life her right to decide what happens in and to her body, which everybody seems to be ready to grant — the sum of her rights now outweighing the fetus' right to life?

The most familiar argument here is the following. We are told that performing the abortion would be directly killing the child, whereas doing nothing would not be killing the mother, but only letting her die. Moreover, in killing the child, one would be killing an innocent person, for the child has committed no crime, and is not aiming at his mother's death. And then there are a variety of ways in which this might be continued. (1) But as directly killing an innocent person is always and absolutely impermissible, an abortion may not be performed. Or, (2) as directly killing an innocent person is murder, and murder is always and absolutely impermissible, an abortion may not be performed. Or, (3) as one's duty to refrain from directly killing an innocent person is more stringent than one's duty to keep a person from dying, an abortion may not be performed. Or, (4) if one's only options are directly killing an innocent person or letting a person die, one must prefer letting the person die, and thus an abortion may not be performed.

Some people seem to have thought that these are not further premises which must be added if the conclusion is to be reached, but that they follow from the very fact that an innocent person has a right to life. But this seems to me to be a mistake, and perhaps the simplest way to show this is to bring out that while we must certainly grant that innocent persons have a right to life, the theses in (1) through (4) are all false. Take (2), for example. If directly killing an innocent person is murder, and thus is impermissible, then the mother's directly killing the innocent person inside her is murder, and thus is impermissible. But it cannot seriously be thought to be murder if the mother performs an abortion on herself to save her life. It cannot seriously be said that she *must* refrain, that she *must* sit passively by and wait for her death. Let us look again at the case of you and the violinist. There you are, in bed with the violinist, and the director of the hospital says to you, "It's all most distressing, and I deeply sympathize, but you see this is putting an additional strain on your kidneys, and you'll be dead within the month. But you *have* to stay where you are all the same. Because unplugging you would be directly killing an innocent violinist, and that's murder, and that's impermissible." If anything in the world is true, it is that you do not commit murder, you do not do what is impermissible, if you reach around to your back and unplug yourself from that violinist to save your life.

The main focus of attention in writings on abortion has been on what a third party may or may not do in answer to a request from a woman for an abortion. This is in a way understandable. Things being as they are, there isn't much a woman can safely do to abort herself. So the question asked is what a third party may do, and what the mother may do, if it is mentioned at all, is deduced, almost as an afterthought, from what it is concluded that third parties may do. But it seems to me that to treat the matter in this way is to refuse to grant to the mother that very status of person which is so firmly insisted on for the fetus. For we cannot simply read off what a person may do from what a third party may do. Suppose you find yourself trapped in a tiny house with a growing child. I mean a very tiny house, and a rapidly growing child — you are already up against the wall of the house and in a few minutes you'll be crushed to death. The child on the other hand won't be crushed to death; if nothing is done to stop him from growing he'll be hurt, but in the end he'll simply burst open the house and walk out a free man. Now I could well understand it if a bystander were to say, "There's nothing we can do for you. We cannot choose between your life and his, we cannot be the ones to decide who is to live, we cannot intervene." But it cannot be concluded that you too can do nothing, that you cannot attack it to save your life. However innocent the child may be, you do not have to wait passively while it crushes you to death. Perhaps a pregnant woman is vaguely felt to have the status of house, to which we don't allow the right of self-defense. But if the woman houses the child, it should be remembered that she is a person who houses it.

I should perhaps stop to say explicitly that I am not claiming that people have a right to do anything whatever to save their lives. I think, rather, that there limits to the right of self-defense. If someone threatens you with death unless you torture someone else to death, I think you have not the right, even to save your life, to do so. But the case under consideration here is very different. In our case there are only two people involved, one whose life is threatened, and one who threatens it. Both are innocent: the one who is threatened is not threatened because of any fault, the one who threatens does not threaten because of any fault. For this reason we may feel that we bystanders cannot intervene. But the person threatened can.

In sum, a woman surely can defend her life against the threat to it posed by the unborn child, even if doing so involves its death. And this shows not merely that the theses in (1) through (4) are false; it shows also that the extreme view of abortion is false, and so we need not canvass any other possible ways of arriving at it from the argument I mentioned at the outset.

2. The extreme view could of course be weakened to say that while abortion is permissible to save the mother's life, it may not be performed by a third party, but only by the mother herself. But this cannot be right either. For what we have to keep in mind is that the mother and the unborn child are not like two tenants in a small house which has, by an unfortunate mistake, been rented to both: the mother *owns* the house. The fact that she does adds to the offensiveness of deducing that the mother can do nothing from the supposition that third parties can do nothing. But it does more than this: it casts a bright light on the supposition that third parties can do nothing. Certainly it lets us see that a third party who says "I cannot choose between you" is fooling himself if he thinks this is impartiality. If Jones has found and fastened on a certain coat, which he needs to keep him from freezing, but which Smith also needs to keep him from freezing, then it is not impartiality that says "I cannot chose between you" when Smith owns the coat. Women have said again and again "This body is *my* body!" and they have reason to feel angry, reason to feel that it has been like shouting into the wind. Smith, after all, is hardly likely to bless us if we say to him, "Of course it's your coat; anybody would grant that it is. But no one may choose between you and Jones who is to have it."

We should really ask what it is that says "no one may choose" in the face of the fact that the body that houses the child is the mother's body. It may be simply a failure to appreciate this fact. But it may be something more interesting, namely the sense that one has a right to refuse to lay hands on people, even where it would be just and fair to do so, even where justice seems to require that somebody do so. This justice might call for somebody to get Smith's coat back from Jones and yet you have a right to refuse to be the one to lay hands on Jones, a right to refuse to do physical violence to him. This, I think, must be granted. But then what should be said is not "no one may choose," but only "I cannot choose," and indeed not even this, but "I will not *act*," leaving it open that somebody else can or should, and in particular that anyone in a position of authority, with the job of securing people's rights, both can and should. So this is no difficulty. I have not been arguing that any given third party must accede to the mother's request that he perform an abortion to save her life, but only that he may.

I suppose that in some views of human life the mother's body is only on loan to her, the loan not being one which gives her any prior claim to it. One who held this view might well think it impartiality to say "I cannot choose." But I shall simply ignore this possibility. My own view is that if a human being has any just, prior claim to anything at all, he has a just, prior claim to his own body. And perhaps this needn't be argued for here anyway, since, as I mentioned, the arguments against abortion we are looking at do grant that the woman has a right to decide what happens in and to her body.

But although they do grant it, I have tried to show that they do not take seriously what is done in granting it. I suggest the same thing will reappear even more clearly when we turn away from cases in which the mother's life is at stake, and attend, as I propose we now do, to the vastly more common cases in which a woman wants an abortion for some less weighty reason than preserving her own life.

3. Where the mother's life is not at stake, the argument I mentioned at the outset seems to have a much stronger pull. "Everyone has a right to life, so the unborn person has a right to life." And isn't the child's right to life weightier than anything other than the mother's own right to life, which she might put forward as ground for an abortion?

This argument treats the right to life as if it were unproblematic. It is not, and this seems to me to be precisely the source of the mistake.

For we should now, at long last, ask what it comes to, to have a right to life. In some views having a right to life includes having a right to be given at least the bare minimum one needs for continued life. But suppose that what in fact is the bare minimum a man needs for continued life is something he has no right at all to be given? If I am sick unto death, and the only thing that will save my life is the touch of Henry Fonda's cool hand on my fevered brow, then all the same, I have no right to be given the touch of Henry Fonda's cool hand on my fevered brow. It would be frightfully nice of him to fly in from the West Coast to provide it. It would be less nice, though no doubt well meant, if my friends flew out to the West Coast and carried Henry Fonda back with them. But I have no right at all against anybody that he should do this for me. Or again, to return to the story I told earlier, the fact that for continued life that violinist needs the continued use of your kidneys does not establish that he has a right to be given the continued use of your kidneys. He certainly has no right against you that you should give him continued use of your kidneys. For nobody has any right to use your kidneys unless you give him such a right; and nobody has the right against you that you shall give him this right — if you do allow him to go on using your kidneys, this is a kindness on your part, and not something he can claim from you as his due. Nor has he any right against anybody else that *they* should give him continued use of your kidneys. Certainly he had no right against the Society of Music Lovers that they should plug him into you in the first place. And if you now start to unplug yourself, having learned that you will otherwise have to spend nine years in bed with him, there is nobody in the world who must try to prevent you, in order to see to it that he is given something he has a right to be given.

Some people are rather stricter about the right to life. In their view, it does not include the right to be given anything, but amounts to, and only to, the right not to be killed by anybody. But here a related difficulty arises. If everybody is to refrain from killing that violinist, then everybody must refrain from doing a great many different sorts of things. Everybody must refrain from slitting his throat, everybody must refrain from shooting him — and everybody must refrain from unplugging you from him. But does he have a right against everybody that they shall refrain from unplugging you from him? To refrain from doing this is to allow him to continue to use your kidneys. It could be argued that he has a right against us that we should allow him to continue to use your kidneys. That is, while he had no right against us that we should give him the use of your kidneys, it might be argued that he anyway has a right against us that we shall not now intervene and deprive him of the use of your kidneys. I shall come back to third-party interventions later. But certainly the violinist has no right against you that *you* shall allow him to continue to use your kidneys. As I said, if you do allow him to use them, it is a kindness on your part, and not something you owe him.

The difficulty I point to here is not peculiar to the right to life. It reappears in connection with all the other natural rights; and it is something which an adequate account of rights must deal with. For present purposes it is enough just to draw attention to it. But I would stress that I am not arguing that people do not have a right to life — quite to the contrary, it seems to me that the primary control we must place on the acceptability of an account of rights is that it should turn out in that account to be a truth that all persons have a right to life. I am arguing only that having a right to life does not guarantee having either a right to be given the use of or a right to be allowed continued use of another person's body — even if one needs it for life itself. So the right to life will not serve the opponents of abortion in the very simple and clear way in which they seem to have thought it would.

4. There is another way to bring out the difficulty. In the most ordinary sort of case, to deprive someone of what he has a right to is to treat him unjustly. Suppose a boy and his brother are jointly given a box of chocolates for Christmas. If the older boy takes the box and refuses to give his brother any of the chocolates, he is unjust to him, for the brother has been given a right to half of them. But suppose that, having learned that otherwise it means nine years in bed with that violinist, you unplug yourself from him. You surely are not being unjust to him, for you gave him no right to use your kidneys, and no one else can have given him any such right. But we have to notice that in unplugging yourself, you are killing him; and violinists, like everybody else, have a right to life, and thus in the view we were considering just now, the right not to be killed. So here you do what he supposedly has a right you shall not do, but you do not act unjustly to him in doing it.

The emendation which may be made at this point is this: the right to life consists not in the right not to be killed, but rather in the right not to be killed unjustly. This runs a risk of circularity, but never mind: it would enable us to square the fact that the violinist has a right to life with the fact that you do not act unjustly toward him in unplugging yourself, thereby killing him. For if you do not kill him unjustly, you do not violate his right to life, and so it is no wonder you do him no injustice.

But if this emendation is accepted, the gap in the argument against abortion stares us plainly in the face: it is by no means enough to show that the fetus is a person, and to remind us that all persons have a right to life — we need to be shown also that killing the fetus violates its right to life, i.e., that abortion is unjust killing. And is it?

I suppose we may take it as a datum that in a case of pregnancy due to rape the mother has not given the unborn person a right to the use of her body for food and shelter. Indeed, in what pregnancy could it be supposed that the mother has given the unborn person such a right? It is not as if there were unborn persons drifting about the world, to whom a woman who wants a child says "I invite you in."

But it might be argued that there are other ways one can have acquired a right to the use of another person's body than by having been invited to use it by that person. Suppose a woman voluntarily indulges in intercourse, knowing of the chance it will issue in pregnancy, and then she does become pregnant; is she not in part responsible for the presence, in fact the very existence, of the unborn person inside her? No doubt she did not invite it in. But doesn't her partial responsibility for its being there itself give it a right to the use of her body? If so, then her aborting it would be more like the boy's taking away the chocolates, and less like your unplugging yourself from the violinist — doing so would be depriving it of what it does have a right to, and thus would be doing it an injustice.

And then, too, it might be asked whether or not she can kill it even to save her own life: If she voluntarily called it into existence, how can she now kill it, even in self-defense?

The first thing to be said about this is that it is something new. Opponents of abortion have been so concerned to make out the independence of the fetus, in order to establish that it has a right to life, just as its mother does, that they have tended to overlook the possible support they might gain from making out that the fetus is *dependent* on the mother, in order to establish that she has a special kind of responsibility for it, a responsibility that gives it rights against her which are not possessed by any independent person — such as an ailing violinist who is a stranger to her.

On the other hand, this argument would give the unborn person a right to its mother's body only if her pregnancy resulted from a voluntary act, undertaken in full knowledge of the chance a pregnancy might result from it. It would leave out entirely the unborn person whose existence is due to rape. Pending the availability of some further argument, then, we would be left with the conclusion that unborn persons whose existence is due to rape have no right to the use of their mother's bodies, and thus that aborting them is not depriving them of anything they have a right to and hence is not unjust killing.

And we should also notice that it is not at all plain that this argument really does go even as far as it purports to. For there are cases and cases, and the details make a difference. If the room is stuffy, and I therefore open a window to air it, and a burglar climbs in, it would be absurd to say, "Ah, now he can stay, she's given him a right to the use of her house — for she is partially responsible for his presence there, having voluntarily done what enabled him to get in, in full knowledge that there are such things as burglars, and that burglars burgle." It would be still more absurd to say this if I had had bars installed outside my windows, precisely to prevent burglars from getting in, and a burglar got in only because of a defect in the bars. It remains equally absurd if we imagine it is not a burglar who climbs in, but an innocent person who blunders or falls in. Again, suppose it were like this: people-seeds drift about in the air like pollen, and if you open your windows, one may drift in and take root in your carpets or upholstery. You don't want children, so you fix up your windows with fine mesh screens, the very best you can buy. As can happen, however, and on very, very rare occasions does happen, one of the screens is defective; and a seed drifts in and takes root. Does the person-plant who now develops have a right to the use of your house? Surely not — despite the fact that you voluntarily opened your windows, you knowingly kept carpets and upholstered furniture, and you knew that screens were sometimes defective. Someone may argue that you are responsible for its rooting, that it does have a right to your house, because after all you *could* have lived out your life with bare floors and furniture, or with sealed windows and doors. But this won't do — for by the same token anyone can avoid a pregnancy due to rape by having a hysterectomy, or anyway by never leaving home without a (reliable!) army.

It seems to me that the argument we are looking at can establish at most that there are *some* cases in which the unborn person has a right to the use of its mother's body, and therefore *some* cases in which abortion is unjust killing. There is room for much discussion and argument as to precisely which, if any. But I think we should sidestep this issue and leave it open, for at any rate the argument certainly does not establish that all abortion is unjust killing.

5. There is room for yet another argument here, however. We surely must all grant that there may be cases in which it would be morally indecent to detach a person from your body at the cost of his life. Suppose you learn that what the violinist needs is not nine years of your life, but only one hour: all you need do to save his life is to spend one hour in that bed with him. Suppose also that letting him use your kidneys for that one hour would not affect your health in the slightest. Admittedly you were kidnapped. Admittedly you did not give anyone permission to plug him into you. Nevertheless it seems to me plain you *ought* to allow him to use your kidneys for that hour — it would be indecent to refuse.

Again, suppose pregnancy lasted only an hour, and constituted no threat to life or health. And suppose that a woman becomes pregnant as a result of rape. Admittedly she did not voluntarily do anything to bring about the existence of a child. Admittedly she did nothing at all which would give the unborn person a right to the use of her body. All the same it might well be said, as in the newly emended violinist story, that she *ought* to allow it to remain for that hour — that it would be indecent in her to refuse.

Now some people are inclined to use the term "right" in such a way that it follows from the fact that you ought to allow a person to use your body for the hour he needs, that he has a right to use your body for the hour he needs, even though he has not been given that right by any person or act. They may say that it follows also that if you refuse, you act unjustly toward him. This use of the term is perhaps so common that it cannot be called wrong; nevertheless it seems to me to be an unfortunate loosening of what we would do better to keep a tight rein on. Suppose that box of chocolates I mentioned earlier had not been given to both boys jointly, but was given only to the older boy. There he sits, stolidly eating his way through the box, his small brother watching enviously. Here we are likely to say "You ought not to be so mean. You ought to give your brother some of those chocolates." My own view is that it just does not follow from the truth of this that the brother has any right to any of the chocolates. If the boy refuses to give his brother any, he is greedy, stingy, callous — but not unjust. I suppose that the people I have in mind will say it does follow that the brother has a right to some of the chocolates, and thus that the boy does act unjustly if he refuses to give his brother any. But the effect of saying this is to obscure what we should keep distinct, namely the difference between the boy's refusal in this case and the boy's refusal in the earlier case, in which the box was given to both boys jointly, and in which the small brother thus had what was from any point of view clear title to half.

A further objection to so using the term "right" that from the fact that A ought to do a thing for B, it follows that B has a right against A that A do it for him, is that it is going to make the question of whether or not a man has a right to a thing turn on how easy it is to provide him with it; and this seems not merely unfortunate, but morally unacceptable. Take the case of Henry Fonda again. I said earlier that I had no right to the touch of his cool hand on my fevered brow, even though I needed it to save my life. I said it would be frightfully nice of him to fly in from the West Coast to provide me with it, but that I had no right against him that he should do so. But suppose he isn't on the West Coast. Suppose he has only to walk across the room, place a hand briefly on my brow — and lo, my life is saved. Then surely he ought to do it, it would be indecent to refuse. Is it to be said "Ah, well, it follows that in this case she has a right to the touch of his hand on her brow, and so it would be an injustice in him to refuse"? So that I have a right to it when it is easy for him to provide it, though no right when it's hard? It's rather a shocking idea that anyone's rights should fade away and disappear as it gets harder and harder to accord them to him.

So my own view is that even though you ought to let the violinist use your kidneys for the one hour he needs, we should not conclude that he has a right to do so — we should say that if you refuse, you are, like the boy who owns all the chocolates and will give none away, self-centered and callous, indecent in fact, but not unjust. And similarly, that even supposing a case in which a woman pregnant due to rape ought to allow the unborn person to use her body for the hour he needs, we should not conclude that he has a right to do so; we should conclude that she is self-centered, callous, indecent, but not unjust, if she refuses. The complaints are no less grave; they are just different. However, there is no need to insist on this point. If anyone does wish to deduce "he has a right" from "you ought," then all the same he must surely grant that there are cases in which it is not morally required of you that you allow that violinist to use your kidneys, and in which he does not have a right to use them, and in which you do not do him an injustice if you refuse. And so also for mother and unborn child. Except in such cases as the unborn person has a right to demand it — and we were leaving open the possibility that there may be such cases — nobody is morally *required* to make large sacrifices, of health, of all other interests and concerns, of all other duties and commitments, for nine years, or even for nine months, in order to keep another person alive.

6. We have in fact to distinguish between two kinds of Samaritan: the Good Samaritan and what we might call the Minimally Decent Samaritan. The story of the Good Samaritan, you will remember, goes like this:

> A certain man went down from Jerusalem to Jericho, and fell among thieves, which stripped him of his raiment, and wounded him, and departed, leaving him half dead.
>
> And by chance there came down a certain priest that way; and when he saw him, he passed by on the other side.
>
> And likewise a Levite, when he was at the place, came and looked on him, and passed by on the other side.
>
> But a certain Samaritan, as he journeyed, came where he was; and when he saw him he had compassion on him.
>
> And went to him, and bound up his wounds, pouring in oil and wine, and set him on his own beast, and brought him to an inn, and took care of him.
>
> And on the morrow, when he departed, he took out two pence, and gave them to the host, and said unto him, "Take care of him; and whatsoever thou spendest more, when I come again, I will repay thee."
>
> (Luke 10:30–35)

The Good Samaritan went out of his way, at some cost to himself, to help one in need of it. We are not told what the options were, that is, whether or not the priest and the Levite could have helped by doing less than the Good Samaritan did, but assuming they could have, then the fact they did nothing at all shows they were not even Minimally Decent Samaritans, not because they were not Samaritans, but because they were not even minimally decent.

These things are a matter of degree, of course, but there is a difference, and it comes out perhaps most clearly in the story of Kitty Genovese, who, as you will remember, was murdered while thirty-eight people watched or listened, and did nothing at all to help her. A Good Samaritan would have rushed out to give direct assistance against the murderer. Or perhaps we had better allow that it would have been a Splendid Samaritan who did this, on the ground that it would have involved a risk of death for himself. But the thirty-eight not only did not do this, they did not even trouble to pick up a phone to call the police. Minimally Decent Samaritanism would call for doing at least that, and their not having done it was monstrous.

After telling the story of the Good Samaritan, Jesus said "Go, and do thou likewise." Perhaps he meant that we are morally required to act as the Good Samaritan did. Perhaps he was urging people to do more than is morally required of them. At all events it seems plain that it was not morally required of any of the thirty-eight that he rush out to give direct assistance at the risk of his own life, and that it is not morally required of anyone that he give long stretches of his life — nine years or nine months — to sustaining the life of a person who has no special right (we were leaving open the possibility of this) to demand it.

Indeed, with one rather striking class of exceptions, no one in any country in the world is *legally* required to do anywhere near as much as this for anyone else. The class of exceptions is obvious. My main concern here is not the state of the law in respect to abortion, but it is worth drawing attention to the fact that in no state in this country is any man compelled by law to be even a Minimally Decent Samaritan to any person; there is no law under which charges could be brought against the thirty-eight who stood by while Kitty Genovese died. By contrast, in most states in this country women are compelled by law to be not merely Minimally Decent Samaritans, but Good Samaritans to unborn persons inside them. This doesn't by itself settle anything one way or the other, because it may well be argued that there should be laws in this country — as there are in many European countries — compelling at least Minimally Decent Samaritanism. But it does show that there is a gross injustice in the existing state of the law. And it shows also that the groups currently working against liberalization of abortion laws, in fact working toward having it declared unconstitutional for a state to permit abortion, had better start working for the adoption of Good Samaritan laws generally, or earn the charge that they are acting in bad faith.

I should think, myself, that Minimally Decent Samaritan laws would be one thing, Good Samaritan laws quite another, and in fact highly improper. But we are not here concerned with the law. What we should ask is not whether anybody should be compelled by law to be a Good Samaritan, but whether we must accede to a situation in which somebody is being compelled — by nature, perhaps — to be a Good Samaritan. We have, in other words, to look now at third-party interventions. I have been arguing that no person is morally required to make large sacrifices to sustain the life of another who has no right to demand them, and this even where the sacrifices do not include life itself; we are not morally required to be Good Samaritans or anyway Very Good Samaritans to one another. But what if a man cannot extricate himself from such a situation? What if he appeals to us to extricate him? It seems to me plain that there are cases in which we can, cases in which a Good Samaritan would extricate him. There you are, you were kidnapped, and nine years in bed with that violinist lie ahead of you. You have your own life to lead. You are sorry, but you simply cannot see giving up so much of your life to the sustaining of his. You cannot extricate yourself, and ask us to do so. I should have thought that — in light of his having no right to the use of your body — it was obvious that we do not have to accede to your being forced to give up so much. We can do what you ask. There is no injustice to the violinist in our doing so.

7. Following the lead of the opponents of abortion, I have throughout been speaking of the fetus merely as a person, and what I have been asking is whether or not the argument we began with, which proceeds only from the fetus' being a person, really does establish its conclusion. I have argued that it does not.

But of course there are arguments and arguments, and it may be said that I have simply fastened on the wrong one. It may be said that what is important is not merely the fact that the fetus is a person, but that it is a person for whom the woman has a special kind of responsibility issuing from the fact that she is its mother. And it might be argued that all my analogies are therefore irrelevant — for you do not have that special kind of responsibility for that violinist, Henry Fonda does not have that special kind of responsibility for me. And our attention might be drawn to the fact that men and women both *are* compelled by law to provide support for their children.

I have in effect dealt (briefly) with this argument in section 4 above; but a (still briefer) recapitulation now may be in order. Surely we do not have any such "special responsibility" for a person unless we have assumed it, explicitly or implicitly. If a set of parents do not try to prevent pregnancy, do not obtain an abortion, and then at the time of birth of the child do not put it out for adoption, but rather take it home with them, then they have assumed responsibility for it, they have given it rights, and they cannot *now* withdraw support from it at the cost of its life because they now find it difficult to go on providing for it. But if they have taken all reasonable precautions against having a child, they do not simply by virtue of their biological relationship to the child who comes into existence have a special responsibility for it. They may wish to assume responsibility for it, or they may not wish to. And I am suggesting that if assuming responsibility for it would require large sacrifices, then they may refuse. A Good Samaritan would not refuse — or anyway, a Splendid Samaritan, if the sacrifices that had to be made were enormous. But then so would a Good Samaritan assume responsibility for that violinist; so would Fonda, if he is a Good Samaritan, fly in from the West Coast and assume responsibility for me.

8. My argument will be found unsatisfactory on two counts by many of those who want to regard abortion as morally permissible. First, while I do argue that abortion is not impermissible, I do not argue that it is always permissible. There may well be cases in which carrying the child to term requires only Minimally Decent Samaritanism of the mother, and this is a standard we must not fall below. I am inclined to think it a merit of my account precisely that it does *not* give a general yes or a general no. It allows for and supports our sense that, for example, a sick and desperately frightened fourteen-year-old schoolgirl, pregnant due to rape, may *of course* choose abortion, and that any law which rules this out is an insane law. And it also allows for and supports our sense that in other cases resort to abortion is even positively indecent. It would be indecent in the woman to request an abortion, and indecent in a doctor to perform it, if she is in her seventh month, and wants the abortion just to avoid the nuisance of postponing a trip abroad. The very fact that the arguments I have been drawing attention to treat all cases of abortion, or even all

cases of abortion in which the mother's life is not at stake, as morally on a par ought to have made them suspect at the outset.

Secondly, while I am arguing for the permissibility of abortion in some cases, I am not arguing for the right to secure the death of the unborn child. It is easy to confuse these two things in that up to a point in the life of the fetus it is not able to survive outside the mother's body; hence removing it from her body guarantees its death. But they are importantly different. I have argued that you are not morally required to spend nine months in bed, sustaining the life of that violinist; but to say this is by no means to say that if, when you unplug yourself, there is a miracle and he survives, you then have a right to turn round and slit his throat. You may detach yourself even if this costs him his life; you have no right to be guaranteed his death, by some other means, if unplugging yourself does not kill him. There are some people who will feel dissatisfied by this feature of my argument. A woman may be utterly devastated by the thought of a child, a bit of herself, put out for adoption and never seen or heard of again. She may therefore want not merely that the child be detached from her, but more, that it die. Some opponents of abortion are inclined to regard this as beneath contempt — thereby showing insensitivity to what is surely a powerful source of despair. All the same, I agree that the desire for the child's death is not one which anybody may gratify, should it turn out to be possible to detach the child alive.

At this place, however, it should be remembered that we have only been pretending throughout that the fetus is a human being from the moment of conception. A very early abortion is surely not the killing of a person, and so is not dealt with by anything I have said here.

QUESTIONS

1. Judith Jarvis Thomson begins by granting the premise that the fetus is a person from the moment of conception. How does she arrive at the conclusion that it does not follow from this premise that abortion is morally wrong?
2. Do you think the analogies that Thomson employs to reach her conclusion about the morality of abortion work? If not, what sorts of differences between the case of the fetus and that of the violinist, for example, would justify reaching a different conclusion for abortion? How would you answer the question about whether to unplug the violinist?
3. Thomson's basic argument is that "having a right to life does not guarantee having either a right to be given the use of or a right to be allowed continued use of another person's body — even if one needs it for life itself." Do you agree with Thomson's account of rights and the corresponding view that saving another's life is not a moral obligation but only good samaritanism on our part?
4. Does Thomson defend the mother's right to choose in all instances? If not, are the exceptions that Thomson allows consistent with her argument in defence of abortion?

ABORTION AND THE CONCEPT OF A PERSON*

Jane English

The abortion debate rages on. Yet the two most popular positions seem to be clearly mistaken. Conservatives maintain that a human life begins at conception and that therefore abortion must be wrong because it is murder. But not all killings of humans are murders. Most notably, self defense may justify even the killing of an innocent person.

Liberals, on the other hand, are just as mistaken in their argument that since a fetus does not become a person until birth, a woman may do whatever she pleases in and to her own body. First, you cannot do as you please with your own body if it affects other people adversely.[1] Second, if a fetus is not a person, that does not imply that you can do to it anything you wish. Animals, for example, are not persons, yet to kill or torture them for no reason at all is wrong.

At the center of the storm has been the issue of just when it is between ovulation and adulthood that a person appears on the scene. Conservatives draw the line at conception, liberals at birth. In this paper I first examine our concept of a person and conclude that no single criterion can capture the concept of a person and no sharp line can be drawn. Next I argue that if a fetus is a person, abortion is still justifiable in many cases; and if a fetus is not a person, killing it is still wrong in many cases. To a large extent, these two solutions are in agreement. I conclude that our concept of a person cannot and need not bear the weight that the abortion controversy has thrust upon it.

I

The several factions in the abortion argument have drawn battle lines around various proposed criteria for determining what is and what is not a person. For example, Mary Anne Warren[2] lists five features (capacities for reasoning, self-awareness, complex communication, etc.) as her criteria for personhood and argues for the permissibility of abortion because a fetus falls outside this concept. Baruch Brody[3] uses brain waves. Michael Tooley[4] picks having-a-concept-of-self as his criterion and concludes that infanticide and abortion are justifiable, while the killing of adult animals is not. On the other side, Paul Ramsey[5] claims a certain gene structure is the defining characteristic. John Noonan[6] prefers conceived-of-humans and presents counterexamples to various other candidate criteria. For instance, he argues against viability as the criterion because the newborn and infirm would then be non-persons, since they cannot live without the aid of others. He rejects any criterion that calls upon the sorts of sentiments a being can evoke in adults on the grounds that this would allow us to exclude other races as non-persons if we could just view them sufficiently unsentimentally.

These approaches are typical: foes of abortion propose sufficient conditions for personhood which fetuses satisfy, while friends of abortion counter with necessary conditions for personhood which fetuses lack. But these both presuppose that the concept of a person can be captured in a strait jacket of necessary and/or sufficient conditions.[7] Rather, "person" is a

From Canadian Journal of Philosophy, *vol. 5, no. 2 (October 1975), pp. 233–43. Reprinted by permission of the* Canadian Journal of Philosophy *and the Jane English Memorial Trust Fund.*

* *I am deeply indebted to Larry Crocker and Arthur Kuflik for their constructive comments.*

cluster of features, of which rationality, having a self-concept and being conceived of humans are only part.

What is typical of persons? Within our concept of a person we include, first, certain biological factors: descended from humans, having a certain genetic make-up, having a head, hands, arms, eyes, capable of locomotion, breathing, eating, sleeping. There are psychological factors: sentience, perception, having a concept of self and of one's own interests and desires, the ability to use tools, the ability to use language or symbol systems, the ability to joke, to be angry, to doubt. There are rationality factors: the ability to reason and draw conclusions, the ability to generalize and to learn from past experience, the ability to sacrifice present interests for greater gains in the future. There are social factors: the ability to work in groups and respond to peer pressures, the ability to recognize and con-sider as valuable the interests of others, seeing oneself as one among "other minds," the ability to sympathize, encourage, love, the ability to evoke from others the responses of sympathy, encouragement, love, the ability to work with others for mutual advantage. Then there are legal factors: being subject to the law and protected by it, having the ability to sue and enter contracts, being counted in the census, having a name and citizenship, the ability to own property, inherit, and so forth.

Now the point is not that this list is incomplete, or that you can find counterinstances to each of its points. People typically exhibit rationality, for instance, but someone who was irrational would not thereby fail to qualify as a person. On the other hand, something could exhibit the majority of these features and still fail to be a person, as an advanced robot might. There is no single core of necessary and sufficient features which we can draw upon with the assurance that they constitute what really makes a person; there are only features that are more or less typical.

This is not to say that no necessary or sufficient conditions can be given. Being alive is a necessary condition for being a person, and being a U.S. Senator is sufficient. But rather than falling inside a sufficient condition or outside a necessary one, a fetus lies in the penumbra region where our concept of a person is not so simple. For this reason I think a conclusive answer to the question whether a fetus is a person is unattainable.

Here we might note a family of simple fallacies that proceed by stating a necessary condition of personhood and showing that a fetus has that characteristic. This is a form of the fallacy of affirming the consequent. For example, some have mistakenly reasoned from the premise that a fetus is human (after all, it is a human fetus rather than, say, a canine fetus), to the conclusion that it is a human. Adding an equivocation on "being," we get the fallacious argument that since a fetus is something both living and human, it is a human being.

Nonetheless, it does seem clear that a fetus has very few of the above family of charac-teristics, whereas a newborn baby exhibits a much larger proportion of them — and a two-year-old has even more. Note that one traditional anti-abortion argument has centered on pointing out the many ways in which a fetus resembles a baby. They emphasize its develop-ment ("It already has ten fingers . . .") without mentioning its dissimilarities to adults (it still has gills and a tail). They also try to evoke the sort of sympathy on our part that we only feel toward other persons ("Never to laugh . . . or feel the sunshine?"). This all seems to be a relevant way to argue, since its purpose is to persuade us that a fetus satisfies so many of the important features on the list that it ought to be treated as a person. Also note that a fetus near the time of birth satisfies many more of these factors than a fetus in the early months of development. This could provide reason for making distinctions among the different stages of pregnancy, as the U.S. Supreme Court has done.[8]

Historically, the time at which a person has been said to come into existence has varied widely. Muslims date personhood from fourteen days after conception. Some medievals followed Aristotle in placing ensoulment at forty days after conception for a male fetus and eighty days for a female fetus.[9] In European common law since the seventeenth century, abortion was considered the killing of a person only after quickening, the time when a pregnant woman first feels the fetus move on its own. Nor is this variety of opinions surprising. Biologically, a human being develops gradually. We shouldn't expect there to be any specific time or sharp dividing point when a person appears on the scene.

For these reasons I believe our concept of a person is not sharp or decisive enough to bear the weight of a solution to the abortion controversy. To use it to solve the problem is to clarify *obscurum per obscurius.*

II

Next let us consider what follows if a fetus is a person after all. Judith Jarvis Thomson's landmark article, "A Defense of Abortion,"[10] correctly points out that some additional argumentation is needed at this point in the conservative argument to bridge the gap between the premise that a fetus is an innocent person and the conclusion that killing it is always wrong. To arrive at this conclusion, we would need the additional premise that killing an innocent person is always wrong. But killing an innocent person is sometimes permissible, most notably in self defense. Some examples may help draw out our intuitions or ordinary judgments about self defense.

Suppose a mad scientist, for instance, hypnotized innocent people to jump out of the bushes and attack innocent passers-by with knives. If you are so attacked, we agree you have a right to kill the attacker in self defense, if killing him is the only way to protect your life or to save yourself from serious injury. It does not seem to matter here that the attacker is not malicious but himself an innocent pawn, for your killing of him is not done in a spirit of retribution but only in self defense.

How severe an injury may you inflict in self defense? In part this depends upon the severity of the injury to be avoided: you may not shoot someone merely to avoid having your clothes torn. This might lead one to the mistaken conclusion that the defense may only equal the threatened injury in severity; that to avoid death you may kill, but to avoid a black eye you may only inflict a black eye or the equivalent. Rather, our laws and customs seem to say that you may create an injury somewhat, but not enormously, greater than the injury to be avoided. To fend off an attack whose outcome would be as serious as rape, a severe beating or the loss of a finger, you may shoot; to avoid having your clothes torn, you may blacken an eye.

Aside from this, the injury you may inflict should only be the minimum necessary to deter or incapacitate the attacker. Even if you know he intends to kill you, you are not justified in shooting him if you could equally well save yourself by the simple expedient of running away. Self defense is for the purpose of avoiding harms rather than equalizing harms.

Some cases of pregnancy present a parallel situation. Though the fetus is itself innocent, it may pose a threat to the pregnant woman's well-being, life prospects or health, mental or physical. If the pregnancy presents a slight threat to her interests, it seems self defense cannot justify abortion. But if the threat is on a par with a serious beating or the loss of a finger, she may kill the fetus that poses such a threat, even if it is an innocent person. If a lesser harm to the fetus could have the same defensive effect, killing it would not be justified. It is unfortunate that the only way to free the woman from the pregnancy entails the death of the fetus (except in very late stages of pregnancy). Thus a self defense model supports Thomson's point that the woman has a right only to be freed from the fetus, not a right to demand its death.[11]

The self defense model is most helpful when we take the pregnant women's point of view. In the pre-Thomson literature, abortion is often framed as a question for a third party: do you, a doctor, have a right to choose between the life of the woman and that of the fetus? Some have claimed that if you were a passer-by who witnessed a struggle between the innocent hypnotized attacker and his equally innocent victim, you would have no reason to kill either in defense of the other. They have concluded that the self defense model implies that a woman may attempt to abort herself, but that a doctor should not assist her. I think the position of the third party is somewhat more complex. We do feel some inclination to intervene on behalf of the victim rather than the attacker, other things equal. But if both parties are innocent, other factors come into consideration. You would rush to the aid of your husband whether he was attacker or attackee. If a hypnotized famous violinist were attacking a skid row bum, we would try to save the individual who is of more value to society. These considerations would tend to support abortion in some cases.

But suppose you are a frail senior citizen who wishes to avoid being knifed by one of these innocent hypnotics, so you have hired a bodyguard to accompany you. If you are attacked, it is clear we believe that the bodyguard, acting as your agent, has a right to kill the attacker to save you from a serious beating. Your rights of self defense are transferred to your agent. I suggest that we should similarly view the doctor as the pregnant woman's agent in carrying out a defense she is physically incapable of accomplishing herself.

Thanks to modern technology, the cases are rare in which a pregnancy poses as clear a threat to a woman's bodily health as an attacker brandishing a switchblade. How does self defense fare when more subtle, complex and long-range harms are involved?

To consider a somewhat fanciful example, suppose you are a highly trained surgeon when you are kidnapped by the hypnotic attacker. He says he does not intend to harm you but to take you back to the mad scientist who, it turns out, plans to hypnotize you to have a permanent mental block against all your knowledge of medicine. This would automatically destroy your career which would in turn have a serious adverse impact on your family, your personal relationships and your happiness. It seems to me that if the only way you can avoid this outcome is to shoot the innocent attacker, you are justified in so doing. You are defending yourself from a drastic injury to your life prospects. I think it is no exaggeration to claim that unwanted pregnancies (most obviously among teenagers) often have such adverse life-long consequences as the surgeon's loss of livelihood.

Several parallels arise between various views on abortion and the self defense model. Let's suppose further that these hypnotized attackers only operate at night, so that it is well known that they can be avoided completely by the considerable inconvenience of never leaving your house after dark. One view is that since you could stay home at night, therefore if you go out and are selected by one of these hypnotized people, you have no right to defend yourself. This parallels the view that abstinence is the only acceptable way to avoid pregnancy. Others might hold that you ought to take along some defense such as Mace which will deter the hypnotized person without killing him, but that if this defense fails, you are obliged to submit to the resulting injury, no matter how severe it is. This parallels the view that contraception is all right but abortion is always wrong, even in cases of contraceptive failure.

A third view is that you may kill the hypnotized person only if he will actually kill you, but not if he will only injure you. This is like the position that abortion is permissible only if it is required to save a woman's life. Finally we have the view that it is all right to kill the attacker, even if only to avoid a very slight inconvenience to yourself and even if you knowingly walked down the very street where all these incidents have been taking place without taking along any Mace or protective escort. If we assume that a fetus is a person, this is the analogue of the view that abortion is always justifiable, "on demand."

The self defense model allows us to see an important difference that exists between abortion and infanticide, even if a fetus is a person from conception. Many have argued that the only way to justify abortion without justifying infanticide would be to find some characteristic of personhood that is acquired at birth. Michael Tooley, for one, claims infanticide is justifiable because the really significant characteristics of person are acquired some time after birth. But all such approaches look to characteristics of the developing human and ignore the relation between the fetus and the woman. What if, after birth, the presence of an infant or the need to support it posed a grave threat to the woman's sanity or life prospects? She could escape this threat by the simple expedient of running away. So a solution that does not entail the death of the infant is available. Before birth, such solutions are not available because of the biological dependence of the fetus on the woman. Birth is the crucial point not because of any characteristics the fetus gains, but because after birth the woman can defend herself by a means less drastic than killing the infant. Hence self defense can be used to justify abortion without necessarily thereby justifying infanticide.

III

On the other hand, supposing a fetus is not after all a person, would abortion always be morally permissible? Some opponents of abortion seem worried that if a fetus is not a full-fledged person, then we are justified in treating it in any way at all. However, this does not follow. Non-persons do get some consideration in our moral code, though of course they do not have the same rights as persons have (and in general they do not have moral responsibilities), and though their interests may be overridden by the interests of persons. Still, we cannot just treat them in any way at all.

Treatment of animals is a case in point. It is wrong to torture dogs for fun or to kill wild birds for no reason at all. It is wrong Period, even though dogs and birds do not have the same rights persons do. However, few people think it is wrong to use dogs as experimental animals, causing them considerable suffering in some cases, provided that the resulting research will probably bring discoveries of great benefit to people. And most of us think it all right to kill birds for food or to protect our crops. People's rights are different from the consideration we give to animals, then, for it is wrong to experiment on people, even if others might later benefit a great deal as a result of their suffering. You might volunteer to be a subject, but this would be supererogatory; you certainly have a right to refuse to be a medical guinea pig.

But how do we decide what you may or may not do to non-persons? This is a difficult problem, one for which I believe no adequate account exists. You do not want to say, for instance, that torturing dogs is all right whenever the sum of its effects on people is good — when it doesn't warp the sensibilities of the torturer so much that he mistreats people. If that were the case, it would be all right to torture dogs if you did it in private, or if the torturer lived on a desert island or died soon afterward, so that his actions had no effect on people.

This is an inadequate account, because whatever moral consideration animals get, it has to be indefeasible, too. It will have to be a general proscription of certain actions, not merely a weighing of the impact on people on a case-by-case basis.

Rather, we need to distinguish two levels on which consequences of actions can be taken into account in moral reasoning. The traditional objections to Utilitarianism focus on the fact that it operates solely on the first level, taking all the consequences into account in particular cases only. Thus Utilitarianism is open to "desert island" and "lifeboat" counterexamples because these cases are rigged to make the consequences of actions severely limited.

Rawls' theory could be described as a teleological sort of theory, but with teleology operating on a higher level.[12] In choosing the principles to regulate society from the original position, his hypothetical choosers make their decision on the basis of the total consequences of various systems. Furthermore, they are constrained to choose a general set of rules which people can readily learn and apply. An ethical theory must operate by generating a set of sympathies and attitudes toward others which reinforces the functioning of that set of moral principles. Our prohibition against killing people operates by means of certain moral sentiments including sympathy, compassion and guilt. But if these attitudes are to form a coherent set, they carry us further: we tend to perform supererogatory actions, and we tend to feel similar compassion toward person-like non-persons.

It is crucial that psychological facts play a role here. Our psychological constitution makes it the case that for our ethical theory to work, it must prohibit certain treatment of non-persons which are significantly person-like. If our moral rules allowed people to treat some person-like non-persons in ways we do not want people to be treated, this would undermine the system of sympathies and attitudes that makes the ethical system work. For this reason, we would choose in the original position to make mistreatment of some sorts of animals wrong in general (not just wrong in the cases with public impact), even though animals are not themselves parties in the original position. Thus it makes sense that it is those animals whose appearance and behavior are most like those of people that get the most consideration in our moral scheme.

It is because of "coherence of attitudes," I think, that the similarity of a fetus to a baby is very significant. A fetus one week before birth is so much like a newborn baby in our psychological space that we cannot allow any cavalier treatment of the former while expecting full sympathy and nurturative support for the latter. Thus, I think that anti-abortion forces are indeed giving their strongest arguments when they point to the similarities between a fetus and a baby, and when they try to evoke our emotional attachment to and sympathy for the fetus. An early horror story from New York about nurses who were expected to alternate between caring for six-week premature infants and disposing of viable 24-week aborted fetuses is just that — a horror story. These beings are so much alike that no one can be asked to draw a distinction and treat them so very differently.

Remember, however, that in the early weeks after conception, a fetus is very much unlike a person. It is hard to develop these feelings for a set of genes which doesn't yet have a head, hands, beating heart, response to touch or the ability to move by itself. Thus it seems to me that the alleged "slippery slope" between conception and birth is not so very slippery. In the early stages of pregnancy, abortion can hardly be compared to murder for psychological reasons, but in the latest stages it is psychologically akin to murder.

Another source of similarity is the bodily continuity between fetus and adult. Bodies play a surprisingly central role in our attitudes toward persons. One has only to think of the philosophical literature on how far physical identity suffices for personal identity or Wittgenstein's remark that the best picture of the human soul is the human body. Even after death, when all agree the body is no longer a person, we still observe elaborate customs of respect for the human body; like people who torture dogs, necrophiliacs are not to be trusted with people.[13] So it is appropriate that we show respect to a fetus as the body continuous with the body of a person. This is a degree of resemblance to persons that animals cannot rival.

Michael Tooley also utilizes a parallel with animals. He claims that it is always permissible to drown newborn kittens and draws conclusions about infanticide.[14] But it is only permissible to drown kittens when their survival would cause some hardship. Perhaps it would be a burden to feed and house six more cats or to find other homes for them. The alternative of letting them starve produces even more suffering than the drowning. Since the kittens get their rights second hand, so to speak, *via* the need for coherence in our attitudes, their interests are often overridden by the interests of full-fledged persons. But if their survival would be no inconvenience to people at all, then it is wrong to drown them, *contra* Tooley.

Tooley's conclusions about abortion are wrong for the same reason. Even if a fetus is not a person, abortion is not always permissible, because of the resemblance of a fetus to a person. I agree with Thomson that it would be wrong for a woman who is seven months pregnant to have an abortion just to avoid having to postpone a trip to Europe. In the early months of pregnancy when the fetus hardly resembles a baby at all, then, abortion is permissible whenever it is in the interests of the pregnant woman or her family. The reasons would only need to outweigh the pain and inconvenience of the abortion itself. In the middle months, when the fetus comes to resemble a person, abortion would be justifiable only when the continuation of the pregnancy or the birth of the child would cause harms — physical, psychological, economic or social — to the woman. In the late months of pregnancy, even on our current assumption that a fetus is not a person, abortion seems to be wrong except to save a woman from significant injury or death.

The Supreme Court has recognized similar gradations in the alleged slippery slope stretching between conception and birth. To this point, the present paper has been a discussion of the moral status of abortion only, not its legal status. In view of the great physical, financial and sometimes psychological costs of abortion, perhaps the legal arrangement most compatible with the proposed moral solution would be the absence of restrictions, that is, so-called abortion "on demand."

So I conclude, first, that application of our concept of a person will not suffice to settle the abortion issue. After all, the biological development of a human being is gradual. Second, whether a fetus is a person or not, abortion is justifiable early in pregnancy to avoid modest harms and seldom justifiable late in pregnancy except to avoid significant injury or death.

NOTES

1. We also have paternalistic laws which keep us from harming our own bodies even when no one else is affected. Ironically, anti-abortion laws were originally designed to protect pregnant women from a dangerous but tempting procedure.
2. Mary Anne Warren, "On the Moral and Legal Status of Abortion," *Monist* 57 (1973), p. 55.
3. Baruch Brody, "Fetal Humanity and the Theory of Essentialism," in Robert Baker and Frederick Elliston (eds.), *Philosophy and Sex* (Buffalo, N.Y., 1975).

4. Michael Tooley, "Abortion and Infanticide," *Philosophy and Public Affairs* 2 (1971).

5. Paul Ramsey, "The Morality of Abortion," in James Rachels, ed., *Moral Problems* (New York, 1971).

6. John Noonan, "Abortion and the Catholic Church: a Summary History," *Natural Law Forum* 12 (1967), pp. 125–131.

7. Wittgenstein has argued against the possibility of so capturing the concept of a game. *Philosophical Investigations* (New York, 1958), pp. 66–71.

8. Not because the fetus is partly a person and so has some of the rights of persons, but rather because of the rights of person-like non-persons. This I discuss in part III below.

9. Aristotle himself was concerned, however, with the different question of when the soul takes form. For historical data, see Jimmye Kimmey, "How the Abortion Laws Happened," *Ms.* 1 (April, 1973), pp. 48ff and John Noonan, *loc. cit.*

10. J.J. Thomson, "A Defense of Abortion," *Philosophy and Public Affairs* 1 (1971).

11. *Ibid.*, p. 52.

12. John Rawls, *A Theory of Justice* (Cambridge, Mass., 1971), pp. 3–4.

13. On the other hand, if they can be trusted with people, then our moral customs are mistaken. It all depends on the facts of psychology.

14. *Op. cit.*, pp. 40, 60–61.

QUESTIONS

1. Why does Jane English think that the question "Is a fetus a person?" cannot be given an unambiguous answer? What reasons does she give for thinking that answering the question is not essential to determining the morality of abortion?

2. Can you extract from English's account her view of what it is to be a person? Building on her discussion, what is it to be a person? In your view, would having a clear and unambiguous answer to this question make a difference in determining the morality of abortion?

3. Do you think that English's discussion of Thomson's argument in Section II of her paper provides additional support for Thomson?

4. Are English's reasons for viewing abortion in the earlier stages of gestation as morally unproblematic sound? What reasons does she have for her view that abortion in the later stages of gestation is morally objectionable?

5. Is English correct in concluding from her own arguments that the law should not seek to prohibit abortion at any point in the gestational cycle?

ABORTION AND THE "FEMININE VOICE"

Celia Wolf-Devine

A growing number of feminists now seek to articulate the "feminine voice", to draw attention to women's special strengths, and to correct the systematic devaluation of these by our male-dominated society. Carol Gilligan's book, *In a Different Voice*, was especially important to the emergence of this strain of feminist thought. It was her intention to help women identify more positively with their own distinctive style of reasoning about ethics,

From Public Affairs Quarterly, *v. 3, no. 3 (July 1989), pp. 81–97. Reprinted by permission of Bowling Green State University.*

instead of feeling that there is something wrong with them because they do not think like men (as Kohlberg's and Freud's theories would imply). Inspired by her work, feminists such as Nel Noddings, Annette Baier, and the contributors to *Women and Moral Theory*,[1] have tried to articulate further the feminine voice in moral reasoning. Others such as Carol McMillan, Adrienne Rich, Sara Ruddick, and Nancy Harstock agree that women have distinct virtues, and argue that these need not be self-victimizing.[2] When properly transformed by a feminist consciousness, women's different characteristics can, they suggest, be productive of new social visions.

Similar work is also being done by feminists who try to correct for masculine bias in other areas such as our conception of human nature, the way we view the relationship between people and nature, and the kinds of paradigms we employ in thinking about society.[3]

Some of those engaged in this enterprise hold that women by *nature* possess certain valuable traits that men do not, but more frequently, they espouse the weaker position that, on the whole, the traits they label "feminine" are more common among women (for reasons which are at least partly cultural), but that they also can be found in men, and that they should be encouraged as good traits for a human being to have, regardless of sex.[4]

Virtually all of those feminists who are trying to reassert the value of the feminine voice, also express the sort of unqualified support for free access to abortion which has come to be regarded as a central tenet of feminist "orthodoxy." What I wish to argue in this paper is that: (1) abortion is, by their own accounts, clearly a masculine response to the problems posed by an unwanted pregnancy, and is thus highly problematic for those who seek to articulate and defend the "feminine voice" as the proper mode of moral response, and that (2) on the contrary the "feminine voice" as it has been articulated generates a strong presumption against abortion as a way of responding to an unwanted pregnancy.[5]

These conclusions, I believe, can be argued without relying on a precise determination of the moral status of the fetus. A case at least can be made that the fetus is a person since it is biologically a member of the human species and will, in time, develop normal human abilities. Whether the burden of proof rests on those who defend the personhood of the fetus, or on those who deny it, is a matter of moral methodology, and for that reason will depend in part on whether one adopts a masculine or feminine approach to moral issues.

I. Masculine Voice/Feminine Voice

A. Moral Reasoning

According to Gilligan, girls, being brought up by mothers, identify with them, while males must define themselves through separation from their mothers. As a result, girls have "a basis for empathy built into their primary definition of self in a way that boys do not."[6] Thus while masculinity is defined by separation and threatened by intimacy, femininity is defined through attachment and threatened by separation; girls come to understand themselves as imbedded within a network of personal relationships.

A second difference concerns attitudes toward general rules and principles. Boys tend to play in larger groups than girls, and become "increasingly fascinated with the legal elaboration of rules, and the development of fair procedures for adjudicating conflicts."[7] We thus find men conceiving of morality largely in terms of adjudicating fairly between the conflicting rights of self-assertive individuals.

Girls play in smaller groups, and accord a greater importance to relationships than to following rules. They are especially sensitive to the needs of the particular other, instead of emphasizing impartiality, which is more characteristic of the masculine perspective. They think of morality more in terms of having responsibilities for taking care of others, and place a high priority upon preserving the network of relationships which makes this possible. While the masculine justice perspective requires detachment, the feminine care perspective sees detachment and separation as themselves the moral problem.[8]

Inspired by Gilligan, many feminist philosophers have discovered a masculine bias in traditional ethical theories. Nel Noddings has written a book called *Caring: A Feminine Approach to Ethics*. Annette Baier has praised Hume for his emphasis on the role of the affections in ethics[9] and proposed that trust be taken as the central notion for ethical theory.[10] Christina Hoff Sommers has argued for giving a central role to special relationships in ethics.[11] And Virginia Held has suggested that the mother-child relationship be seen as paradigmatic of human relationships, instead of the economic relationship of buyer/seller (which she sees to be the ruling paradigm now).[12]

The feminine voice in ethics attends to the particular other, thinks in terms of responsibilities to care for others, is sensitive to our interconnectedness, and strives to preserve relationships. It contrasts with the masculine voice, which speaks in terms of justice and rights, stresses consistency and principles, and emphasizes the autonomy of the individual and impartiality in one's dealings with others.

B. Human Nature: Mind and Body

Feminist writers have also discovered a masculine bias in the way we think of mind and body and the relationship between them. A large number of feminists, for example, regard radical mind/body dualism as a masculine way of understanding human nature. Alison Jaggar, for example, criticizes what she calls "normative dualism" for being "male biased",[13] and defines "normative dualism" as "the belief that what is especially valuable about human beings is a particular 'mental' capacity, the capacity for rationality."[14]

Another critic of dualism is Rosemary Radford Reuther, a theologian. Her book *New Woman, New Earth* is an extended attack upon what she calls transcendent hierarchical dualism, which she regards as a "male ideology."[15] By "transcendent dualism" she means the view that consciousness is "transcendent to visible nature"[16] and that there is a sharp split between spirit and nature. In the attempt to deny our own mortality, our essential humanity is then identified with a "transcendent divine sphere beyond the matrix of coming to be and passing away."[17] In using the term "hierarchical," she means that the mental or spiritual component is taken to be superior to the physical. Thus "the relation of spirit and body is one of repression, subjugation and mastery."[18]

Dodson Gray, whose views resemble Reuther's, poetically contrasts the feminine attitude with the masculine one as follows:

> I see that life is not a line but a circle. Why do men imagine for themselves the illusory freedom of a soaring mind, so that the body of nature becomes a cage? 'Tis not true. To be human is to be circled in the cycles of nature, rooted in the processes that nurture us in life, breathing in and breathing out human life just as plants breathe in and out their photosynthesis.[19]

Feminists critical of traditional masculine ways of thinking about human nature also examine critically the conception of "reason" which has become engrained in our Western cultural heritage from the Greeks on. Genevieve Lloyd, for example, in *The Man of Reason:*

Male and Female in Western Philosophy,[20] suggests that the very notion of reason itself has been defined in part by the exclusion of the feminine. And if the thing which makes us distinctively human — namely our reason — is thought of as male, women and the things usually associated with them such as the body, emotion and nature, will be placed in an inferior position.

C. Our Relationship with Nature

Many feminists hold that mind-body dualism which sees mind as transcendent to and superior to the body, leads to the devaluation of both women and nature. For the transcendent mind is conceived as masculine, and women, the body and nature assigned an inferior and subservient status.[21] As Rosemary Radford Reuther puts it:

> The woman, the body and the world are the lower half of a dualism that must be declared posterior to, created by, subject to, and ultimately alien to the nature of (male) consciousness in whose image man made his God.[22]

Women are to be subject to men, and nature may be used by man in any way he chooses. Thus the male ideology of transcendent dualism sanctions unlimited technological manipulation of nature; nature is an alien object to be conquered.

Carolyn Merchant, in her book *The Death of Nature: Women, Ecology and the Scientific Revolution*,[23] focuses on the Cartesian version of dualism as particularly disastrous to our relationship with nature, and finds the roots of our present ecological crisis to lie in the 17th Century scientific revolution — itself based on Cartesian dualism and the mechanization of nature. According to Merchant, both feminism and the ecology movement are egalitarian movements which have a vision of our interconnectedness with each other and with nature.

Feminists who stress the deep affinities between feminism and the ecology movement are often called "ecofeminists." Stephanie Leland, radical feminist and co-editor of a recent collection of ecofeminist writings, has explained that:

> Ecology is universally defined as the study of the balance and interrelationship of all life on earth. The motivating force behind feminism is the expression of the feminine principle. As the essential impulse of the feminine principle is the striving towards balance and interrelationship, it follows that feminism and ecology are inextricably connected.[24]

The masculine urge is, she says, to "separate, discriminate and control," while the feminine impulse is "towards belonging, relationship and letting be."[25] The urge to discriminate leads, she thinks, to the need to dominate "in order to feel secure in the choice of a particular set of differences."[26] The feminine attitude springs from a more holistic view of the human person and sees us as imbedded in nature rather than standing over and above it. It entails a more egalitarian attitude, regarding the needs of other creatures as important and deserving of consideration. It seeks to "let be" rather than to control, and maintains a pervasive awareness of the interconnectedness of all things and the need to preserve this if all are to flourish.

Interconnectedness, which we found to be an important theme in feminist ethics, thus reappears in the writings of the ecofeminists as one of the central aspects of the feminine attitude toward nature.

D. Paradigms of Social Life

Feminists' descriptions of characteristically masculine and feminine paradigms of social life center around two different focusses. Those influenced by Gilligan tend to stress the contrast between individualism (which they take to be characteristic of the masculine "justice tradition") and the view of society as "a web of relationships sustained by a process of communication"[27] (which they take to characterize the feminine "care perspective"). According to them, the masculine paradigm sees society as a collection of self-assertive individuals seeking rules which will allow them to pursue their own goals without interfering with each other. The whole contractarian tradition from Locke and Hobbes through Rawls is thus seen as a masculine paradigm of social life; we are only connected to others and responsible to them through our own choice to relinquish part of our autonomy in favor of the state. The feminine care perspective guides us to think about societal problems in a different way. We are already imbedded in a network of relationships, and must never exploit or hurt the other. We must strive to preserve those relationships as much as possible without sacrificing the integrity of the self.

The ecofeminists, pacifist feminists, and those whose starting point is a rejection of dualism, tend to focus more on the contrast between viewing social relationships in terms of hierarchy, power, and domination (the masculine paradigm) and viewing them in a more egalitarian and nonviolent manner (the feminine one). Feminists taking this position range from the moderate ones who believe that masculine social thought tends to be more hierarchical than feminine thought, to the extreme radicals who believe males are irredeemably aggressive and dominating, and prone to violence in order to preserve their domination.

The more moderate characterization of masculine social thought would claim that men tend to prefer a clear structure of authority; they want to know who is in control and have a clear set of procedures or rules for resolving difficult cases. The more extreme view, common among ecofeminists and a large number of radical feminists, is that males seek to establish and maintain patriarchy (systematic domination by males) and use violence to maintain their control. These feminists thus see an affinity between feminism (which combats male violence against women) and the pacifist movement (which does so on a more global scale). Mary Daly, for example, holds that "the rulers of patriarchy — males with power — wage an unceasing war against life itself . . . female energy is essentially biophilic."[28] Another radical feminist, Sally Miller Gearhart, says that men possess the qualities of objectification, violence, and competitiveness, while women possess empathy, nurturance, and cooperation.[29] Thus the feminine virtues must prevail if we are to survive at all, and the entire hierarchical power structure must be replaced by "horizontal patterns of relationship."[30]

Women are thus viewed by the pacifist feminists as attuned in some special way to the values and attitudes underlying a pacifist commitment. Sara Ruddick, for example, believes that maternal practice, because it involves "preservative love" and nurtures growth, involves the kinds of virtues which, when put to work in the public domain, lead us in the direction of pacifism.[31]

II. Abortion

A person who had characteristically masculine traits, attitudes and values as defined above would very naturally choose abortion, and justify it ethically in the same way in which most feminists do. Conversely, a person manifesting feminine traits, attitudes and values would not make such a choice, or justify it in that way.

According to the ecofeminists, the masculine principle is insensitive to the interconnectedness of all life; it strives to discriminate, separate and control. It does not respect the natural cycles of nature, but objectifies it, and imposes its will upon it through unrestrained technological manipulation. Such a way of thinking would naturally lead to abortion. If the woman does not want to be pregnant, she has recourse to an operation involving highly sophisticated technology in order to defend her control of her body. This fits the characterization of the masculine principle perfectly.

Abortion is a separation — a severing of a life-preserving connection between the woman and the fetus. It thus fails to respect the interconnectedness of all life. Nor does it respect the natural cycles of nature. The mother and the developing child together form a delicately balanced ecosystem with the woman's entire hormonal system geared towards sustaining the pregnancy.[32] The abortionist forces the cervical muscles (which have become thick and hard in order to hold in the developing fetus) open and disrupts her hormonal system by removing it.

Abortion has something further in common with the behavior ecofeminists and pacifist feminists take to be characteristically masculine; it shows a willingness to use violence in order to maintain control. The fetus is destroyed by being pulled apart by suction, cut in pieces, or poisoned. It is not merely killed inadvertently as fish might be by toxic wastes, but it is deliberately targeted for destruction. Clearly this is not the expression of a "biophilic" attitude. This point was recently brought home to me by a Quaker woman who had reached the conclusion that the abortion she had had was contrary to her pacifist principles. She said, "we must seek peaceableness both within and without."

In terms of social thought, again, it is the masculine models which are most frequently employed in thinking about abortion. If masculine thought is naturally hierarchical and oriented toward power and control, then the interests of the fetus (who has no power) would naturally be suppressed in favor of the interests of the mother. But to the extent that feminist social thought is egalitarian, the question must be raised of why the mother's interests should prevail over the child's.

Feminist thought about abortion has, in addition, been deeply pervaded by the individualism which they so ardently criticize. The woman is supposed to have the sole authority to decide the outcome of the pregnancy. But what of her interconnectedness with the child and with others? Both she and the unborn child already exist within a network of relationships ranging from the closest ones — the father, grandparents, siblings, uncles and aunts, and so on — to ones with the broader society — including the mother's friends, employer, employees, potential adoptive parents, taxpayers who may be asked to fund the abortion or subsidize the child, and all the numerous other people affected by her choice. To dismiss this already existing network of relationships as irrelevant to the mother's decision is to manifest the sort of social atomism which feminist thinkers condemn as characteristically masculine.

Those feminists who are seeking to articulate the feminine voice in ethics also face a *prima facie* inconsistency between an ethics of care and abortion. Quite simply, abortion is a failure to care for one living being who exists in a particularly intimate relationship to oneself. If empathy, nurturance, and taking responsibility for caring for others are characteristic of the feminine voice, then abortion does not appear to be a feminine response to an unwanted pregnancy. If, as Gilligan says, "an ethic of care rests on the premise of non-violence—that no one should be hurt,"[33] then surely the feminine response to an unwanted pregnancy would be to try to find a solution which does not involve injury to anyone, including the unborn.

"Rights" have been invoked in the abortion controversy in a bewildering variety of ways, ranging from the "right to life" to the "right to control one's body." But clearly those who defend unrestricted access to abortion in terms of such things as the woman's right to privacy or her right to control her body are speaking the language of an ethics of justice rather than an ethics of care. For example, Judith Jarvis Thompson's widely read article "A Defense of Abortion"[34] treats the moral issue involved in abortion as a conflict between the rights of the fetus and the mother's rights over her own body. Mary Anne Warren also sees the issue in terms of a conflict of rights, but since the fetus does not meet her criteria for being a person, she weighs the woman's rights to "freedom, happiness and self-determination" against the rights of other people in the society who would like to see the fetus preserved for whatever reason.[35] And, insofar as she appeals to consciousness, reasoning, self-motivated activity, the capacity to communicate, and the presence of self-concepts and self-awareness as criteria of personhood, she relies on the kind of opposition between mind and nature criticized by many feminists as masculine. In particular, she is committed to what Jaggar calls "normative dualism" — the view that what is especially valuable about humans is their mental capacity for rational thought.

It is rather striking that feminists defending abortion lapse so quickly into speaking in the masculine voice. Is it because they feel they must do so in order to be heard in our male dominated society, or is it because no persuasive defense of abortion can be constructed from within the ethics of care tradition? We now consider several possible "feminine voice" defenses of abortion.

III. Possible Responses and Replies

Among the feminists seeking to articulate and defend the value of the feminine voice, very few have made any serious attempt to grapple with abortion. The writings of the ecofeminists and the pacifist feminists abound with impassioned defenses of such values as non-violence, a democratic attitude towards the needs of all living things, letting others be and nurturing them, and so on, existing side by side with impassioned defenses of "reproductive rights." They see denying women access to abortion as just another aspect of male domination and violence against women.

This will not do for several reasons. First, it is not true that males are the chief opponents of abortion. Many women are strongly opposed to it. The prolife movement at every level is largely composed of women. For example, as of May 1988, 38 of the state delegates to the National Right to Life Board of Directors were women, and only 13 were men. Indeed as Jean Bethke Elshtain has observed,[36] the pro-life movement has mobilized into political action an enormous number of women who were never politically active before. And a Gallup poll in 1981 found that 51% of women surveyed believed a person is present at conception, compared with only 33% of the men. The prolife movement, thus, can not be dismissed as representing male concerns and desires only. Granted, a pro-choice feminist could argue that women involved in the prolife movement suffer from "colonized minds", but this sort of argument clearly can be made to cut both directions. After all, many of the strongest supporters of "reproductive rights" have been men — ranging from the Supreme Court in *Roe v. Wade* to the Playboy Philosopher.

Secondly, terms like violence and domination are used far too loosely by those who condemn anti-abortion laws. If there are laws against wife abuse, does this mean that abusive husbands are being subjected to domination and violence? One does not exercise violence against someone merely by crossing his or her will, or even by crossing his or her will and backing this up by threats of legal retribution.

Finally, those who see violence and domination in laws against abortion, but not in abortion itself, generally fail to look at the nature of the act itself, and thus fail to judge that act in light of their professed values and principles. This is not surprising; abortion is a bloody and distressing thing to contemplate. But one cannot talk about it intelligently without being willing to look concretely at the act itself.

One line of thought is suggested by Gilligan, who holds that at the highest level of moral development, we must balance our responsibility to care for others against our need to care for ourselves. Perhaps we could, then, see the woman who has an abortion as still being caring and nurturing in that she is acting out of a legitimate care for herself. This is an implausible view of the actual feelings of women who undergo abortions. They may believe they are "doing something for themselves" in the sense of doing what they must do to safeguard their legitimate interests. But the operation is more naturally regarded as a violation of oneself than as a nurturing of oneself. This has been noted, even by feminists who support permissive abortion laws. For example, Carolyn Whitbeck speaks of "the unappealing prospect of having someone scraping away at one's core,"[37] and Adrienne Rich says that "Abortion is violence: a deep, desperate violence inflicted by a woman upon, first of all, herself."[38]

We here come up against the problem that a directive to care, to nurture, to take responsibility for others, and so on, provides a moral orientation, but leaves unanswered many important questions and hence provides little guidance in problem situations. What do we do when caring for one person involves being uncaring toward another? How widely must we extend our circle of care? Are some kinds of not caring worse than others? Is it caring to give someone what they want even though it may be bad for them?

Thinking in terms of preserving relationships suggests another possible "feminine" defense of abortion — namely that the woman is striving to preserve her interconnectedness with her family, husband, or boyfriend. Or perhaps she is concerned to strengthen her relationship with her other children by having enough time and resources to devote to their care. To simply tell a woman to preserve *all* her existing relationships is not the answer. Besides the fact that it may not be possible (women *do* sometimes have to sever relationships), it is not clear that it would be desirable even if it were possible. Attempting to preserve our existing relationships has conservative tendencies in several unfortunate ways. It fails to invite us to reflect critically on whether those relationships are good, healthy or worthy or preservation.[39] It also puts the unborn at a particular disadvantage, since the mother's relationship with him or her is just beginning, while her relationships with others have had time to develop. And not only the unborn, but any needy stranger who shows up at our door can be excluded on the grounds that caring for them would disrupt our existing pattern of relationships. Thus the care perspective could degenerate into a rationalization for a purely tribal morality; I take care of myself and my friends.

But how are decisions about severing relationships to be made? One possibility is suggested by Gilligan in a recent article. She looks at the network of connections within which the woman who is considering abortion finds herself entangled, and says "to ask what actions constitute care or are more caring directs attention to the parameters of connection and the *costs of detachment* . . . (emphasis added)."[40] Thus, the woman considering abortion, should reflect upon the comparative costs of severing various relationships. This method of decision, however, makes her vulnerable to emotional and psychological pressure from others, by encouraging her to sever whichever connection is easiest to break (the squeaky wheel principle).[41]

But perhaps we can lay out some guidelines (or, at least, rules of thumb) for making these difficult decisions. One way we might reason, from the point of view of the feminine voice, is that since preserving interconnectedness is good, we should prefer a short term estrangement to an irremediable severing of relationship. And we should choose an action which *may* cause an irremediable break in relationship over one which is certain to cause such a break. By either of these criteria, abortion is clearly to be avoided.[42]

Another consideration suggested by Gilligan's work is that since avoiding hurt to others (or non-violence) is integral to an ethics of care, severing a relationship where the other person will be only slightly hurt would be preferable to severing one where deep or lasting injury will be inflicted by our action. But on this criterion, again it would seem she should avoid abortion, since loss of life is clearly a graver harm than emotional distress.

Two other possible criteria which would also tell against abortion are: (1) that it is permissible to cut ties with someone who behaves unjustly and oppressively toward one, but not with someone who is innocent of any wrong against one, or (2) we have special obligations to our own offspring, and thus should not sever relationship with them.

Criteria can, perhaps, be found which would dictate severing relationship with the fetus rather than others, but it is hard to specify one which clearly reflects the feminine voice. Certainly the right to control one's body will not do. The claim that the unborn is not a person and therefore does not deserve moral consideration can be faulted on several grounds. First, if the feminine voice is one which accepts the interconnectedness of all life and strives to avoid harm to nature and to other species, then the non-personhood of the fetus (supposing it could be proved) would not imply that its needs can be discounted. And secondly, the entire debate over personhood has standardly been carried on very much in the masculine voice.[43] One feminist, Janice Raymond,[44] has suggested that the question of when life begins is a masculine one, and if this is a masculine question, it would seem that personhood, with its juridical connotations, would be also. It is not clear that the care perspective has the resources to resolve this issue. If it cannot, then, one cannot rely on the non-personhood of the fetus in constructing a "feminine voice" defense of abortion. A care perspective would at least seem to place the burden of proof on those who would restrict the scope of care, in this case to those that have been born.

It seems that the only way open to the person who seeks to defend abortion from the point of view of the feminine voice is to deny that a relationship (or at least any morally significant relationship) exists between the embryo/fetus and the mother. The question of how to tell when a relationship (or a morally significant relationship) exists is a deep and important one, which has, as yet, received insufficient attention from those who are trying to articulate the feminine voice in moral reasoning. The whole ecofeminist position relies on the assumption that our relationship with nature and with other species is a real and morally significant one. They, thus, have no basis at all for excluding the unborn from moral consideration.

There are those, however, who wish to define morally significant relationships more narrowly — thus effectively limiting our obligation to extend care. While many philosophers within the "justice tradition" (for example, Kant) have seen moral significance only where there is some impact upon rational beings, Nel Noddings, coming from the "care perspective" tries to limit our obligation to extend care in terms of the possibility of "completion" or "reciprocity" in a caring relationship.[45] Since she takes the mother-child relationship to be paradigmatic of caring, it comes as something of a surprise that she regards abortion as a permissible response to an unwanted pregnancy.[46]

There are, on Noddings' view, two different ways in which we may be bound, as caring persons, to extend our care to one for whom we do not already have the sort of feelings of love and affection which would lead us to do the caring action naturally. One is by virtue of being connected with our "inner circle" of caring (which is formed by natural relations of love and friendship) through "chains" of "personal or formal relations."[47] As an example of a person appropriately linked to the inner circle, she cites her daughter's fiancé. It would certainly *seem* that the embryo in one's womb would belong to one's "inner circle" (via natural caring), or at least be connected to it by a "formal relation" (that is, that of parenthood). But Noddings does not concede this. Who is part of my inner circle, and who is connected to it in such a way that I am obligated to extend care to him or her seems to be, for Noddings, largely a matter of my feelings toward the person and/or my choice to include him or her. Thus the mother *may* "confer sacredness" upon the "information speck"[48] in her womb, but need not if, for example, her relationship with the father is not a stable and loving one. During pregnancy "many women recognize the relation as established when the fetus begins to move about. It is not a question of when life begins, but of when relation begins."

But making the existence of a relation between the unborn and the mother a matter of her choice or feelings, seems to run contrary to one of the most central insights of the feminine perspective in moral reasoning — namely that we already *are* interconnected with others, and thus have responsibilities to them. The view that we are connected with others only when we choose to be or when we *feel* we are, presupposes the kind of individualism and social atomism which Noddings and other feminists criticize as masculine.

Noddings also claims that we sometimes are obligated to care for "the proximate stranger". She says:

> We cannot refuse obligation in human affairs by merely refusing to enter relation; we are, by virtue of our mutual humanity, already and perpetually in potential relation.[49]

Why, then, are we not obligated to extend care to the unborn? She gives two criteria for when we have an obligation to extend care: there must be "the existence of or potential for present relation" and the "dynamic potential for growth in relation, including the potential for increased reciprocity . . ." Animals are, she believes, excluded by this second criterion since their response is nearly static (unlike a human infant).

She regards the embryo/fetus as not having the potential for present relationships of caring and reciprocity, and thus as having no claim upon our care. As the fetus matures, he or she develops increasing potential for caring relationships, and thus our obligation increases also. There are problems with her position, however.

First of all, the only relationships which can be relevant to *my* obligation to extend care, for Noddings, must be relationships with *me*. Whatever the criteria for having a relationship are, it must be that at a given time, an entity either has a relationship with me or it does not. If it does not, it may either have no potential for a morally significant relationship with me (for example, my word processor), or it may have such potential in several ways: (1) The relationship may become actual at the will of one or both parties (for example, the stranger sitting next to me on the bus). (2) The relationship may become actual only after a change in relative spatial locations which will take time, and thus can occur only in the future (for example, walking several blocks to meet a new neighbor, or traveling to Tibet to meet a specific Tibetan). Or (3) The relationship may become actual only after some internal change occurs within the other (for example by waiting for a sleeping drug to wear off, for a deep but reversible coma to pass, or for the embryo to mature more fully) and thus can also happen only in the future.

In all three of these cases there is present now in the other the potential for relations of a caring and reciprocal sort. In cases (1) and (2) this is uncontroversial, but (3) requires some defense in the case of the unborn. The human embryo differs now from a rabbit embryo in that it possesses potential for these kinds of relationships although neither of them is presently able to enter into relationships of any sort.[50] That potential becomes actualized only over time, but it can become actualized only because it is there to be actualized (as it is not in the rabbit embryo).[51] Noddings fails to give any reason why the necessity for some internal change to occur in the other before relation can become actual has such moral importance that we are entitled to kill the other in case (3), but not in the others, especially since my refraining from killing it is a sufficient condition for the actualization of the embryo's potential for caring relationships. Her criterion as it stands would also seem to imply that we may kill persons in deep but predictably reversible comas.

Whichever strand of Noddings thought we choose, then, it is hard to see how the unborn can be excluded from being ones for whom we ought to care. If we focus on the narrow, tribal morality of "inner circles" and "chains," then an objective connection exists tying the unborn to the mother and other relatives. If we are to be open to the needy stranger because of the real potential for relationship and reciprocity, then we should be open to the unborn because he or she also has the real and present potential for a relationship of reciprocity and mutuality which comes with species membership.

Many feminists will object to my argument so far on the grounds that they do not, after all, consider abortion to be a *good* thing. They aren't pro-abortion in the sense that they encourage women to have abortions. They merely regard it as something which must be available as a kind of "grim option" — something a woman would choose only when the other alternatives are all immeasurably worse.[52]

First of all, the grim options view sounds very much like the "masculine voice" — we must grit our teeth, and do the distasteful but necessary deed (the more so where the deed involves killing).[53] Furthermore, it is in danger of collapsing into total subjectivism unless one is willing to specify some criteria for when an option is a genuinely grim one, beyond the agent's feeling that it is. What if she chooses to abort in order not to have to postpone her trip to Europe, or because she prefers sons to daughters? Surely these are not grim options no matter what she may say. Granted, the complicated circumstances surrounding her decision are best known to the woman herself. But this does not imply that no one is *ever* in a position to make judgments about whether her option is sufficiently grim to justify abortion. We do not generally concede that only the agent is in a position to judge the morality of his or her action.

Feminists standardly hold that absolutely no restrictions may be placed on a woman's right to choose abortion.[54] This position cannot be supported by the grim options argument. One who believes something is a grim option will be inclined to try to avoid or prevent it, and thus be willing, at least in principle, to place some restrictions on what counts as a grim option. Granted, practical problems exist about how such decisions are to be made and by whom. But someone who refuses in principle to allow any restrictions on women's right to abort, cannot in good faith claim that they regard abortion only as a grim option.

Some feminists will say: yes, feminine virtues are a good thing for any person to have, and yes, abortion is a characteristically masculine way of dealing with an unwanted pregnancy, but in the current state of things we live in a male dominated society, and we must be willing to use now weapons which, ideally, in a good, matriarchal society, we would not use.[55] But there are no indications that an ideal utopian society is just around the corner; thus we are condemned to a constant violation of our own deepest commitments. If the traits, values and attitudes characteristic of the "feminine voice" are asserted to be good ones, we ought to act according to them. And such values and attitudes simply do not lend support to either the choice of abortion as a way of dealing with an unwanted pregnancy in individual cases, or to the political demand for unrestricted[56] access to abortion which has become so entrenched in the feminist movement. Quite the contrary.[57]

NOTES

1. See Nel Noddings, *Caring: A Feminine Approach to Ethics* (Berkeley: University of California Press, 1984), Annette Baier, "What do Women Want in a Moral Theory?", *Nous*, vol. 19 (March, 1985), and "Hume, the Women's Moral Theorist?", in *Women and Moral Theory*, (eds.) Kittay and Meyers, (Minneapolis: University of Minnesota Press, 1987).
2. Carol McMillan, *Women, Reason and Nature*, (Princeton: Princeton University Press, 1982), Adrienne Rich, *Of Woman Born*, (N.Y.: Norton, 1976), Sara Ruddick, "Remarks on the Sexual Politics of Reason" in *Women and Moral Theory*, "Maternal Thinking" and "Preservative Love and Military Destruction: Some Reflections on Mothering and Peace" in Joyce Treblicot (ed.) *Mothering: Essays in Feminist Theory* (Totowa, N.J.: Rowman & Allanheld 1983), and Nancy Hartsock "The Feminist Standpoint" in *Discovering Reality*, Harding (ed.), (Boston: D. Reidel, 1983).
3. Among them are such writers as Rosemary Radford Reuther, Susan Griffin, Elizabeth Dodson Gray, Brian Easla, Sally Miller Gearhart, Carolyn Merchant, Genevieve Lloyd, the pacifist feminists, and a number of feminists involved in the ecology movement.
4. In this paper I shall use the terms "masculine" and "feminine" only in this weaker sense, which is agnostic about the existence of biologically based differences.
5. A strong presumption against abortion is not, of course, the same thing as an absolute ban on all abortions. I do not attempt here to resolve the really hard cases; it is not clear that the feminine voice (at least as it has been articulated so far) is sufficiently fine-grained to tell us exactly where to draw the line in such cases.
6. See Carol Gilligan, *In a Different Voice*, (Cambridge, MA: Harvard University Press, 1982), p. 8.
7. *Ibid.*, p. 10.
8. See Gilligan, "Moral Orientation and Moral Development" in *Women and Moral Theory*, p. 31.
9. Annette Baier, "Hume, the Woman's Moral Theorist?" in *Women and Moral Theory*, pp. 37–35.
10. "What do Women Want in a Moral Theory," *Nous*, vol. 19 (March, 1985), p. 53.
11. Christina Hoff Sommers, "Filial Morality" in *Women and Moral Theory*, pp. 69–84.
12. Virginia Held, "Feminism and Moral Theory", in *Women and Moral Theory*, pp. 111–128.
13. Alison Jaggar, *Feminist Politics and Human Nature*, (Totowa, N.J.: Rowman & Alanheld, 1983), p. 46.
14. *Ibid.*, p. 28.
15. Rosemary Radford Reuther, *New Woman, New Earth*, (New York: The Seabury Press, 1975), p. 195.
16. *Ibid.*, p. 188.
17. *Ibid.*, p. 195.
18. *Ibid.*, p. 189.
19. Elizabeth Dodson Gray, *Why the Green Nigger*, (Wellesley, MA: Round-table Press, 1979), p. 54.
20. Genevieve Lloyd, *The Man of Reason: Male and Female in Western Philosophy* (Minneapolis: University of Minnesota Press, 1984).
21. See, e.g. Rosemary Radford Reuther, *New Woman, New Earth*, Elizabeth Dodson Gray, *Why the Green Nigger* and Brian Easla, *Science and Sexual Oppression*, (London: Weidenfeld & Nicolson, 1981).

22. Reuther, *op. cit.*, p. 195.
23. Carolyn Merchant, *The Death of Nature: Women, Ecology and the Scientific Revolution* (San Francisco: Harper & Row, 1980).
24. Stephanie Leland and Leonie Caldecott, (eds.) *Reclaim the Earth: Women Speak out for Life on Earth* (London: The Women's Press, 1983), p. 72. For an overview of ecofeminist thought which focuses on the role of mind/body dualism, see Val Plumwood, "Ecofeminism: An Overview", *Australasian Journal of Philosophy*, Supplement to Vol. 64, (June, 1986), pp. 120–138.
25. Leland and Caldecott, *op. cit.*, p. 71.
26. *Ibid.*, p. 69.
27. Introduction to *Women and Moral Theory*, by Kittay and Meyers, p. 7.
28. Cited by Barbara Zanotti, "Patriarchy: A State of War", in *Reweaving the Web of Life*, Pam McAllister, (ed.), (Philadelphia: New Society Publishers, 1982), p. 17.
29. See, e.g., Sally Miller Gearhart, "The Future — if there is one — is Female" in *Reweaving the Web of Life*, p. 266.
30. *Ibid.*, p. 272.
31. See Sara Ruddick, "Remarks on the Sexual Politics of Reason".
32. I owe the idea of regarding mother and child as an ecosystem to a conversation with Leonie Caldecott, co-editor of *Reclaim the Earth*.
33. Gilligan, *op. cit.*, p. 174.
34. Judith Jarvis Thompson, "A Defense of Abortion," *Philosophy and Public Affairs*, vol. 1, (1971), pp. 47–66.
35. Mary Anne Warren, "On the Moral and Legal Status of Abortion", *The Monist*, vol. 57 (January, 1973), reprinted in Wasserstrom, *Today's Moral Problems*, (New York: Macmillan, 1985), p. 448.
36. Jean Bethke Elshtain, *Public Man, Private Woman*, (Princeton, NJ: Princeton University Press, 1981), p. 312.
37. Carolyn Whitbeck, "Women as People: Pregnancy and Personhood," in *Abortion and the Status of the Fetus*, W.B. Bondeson, et. al. (ed.), (Boston: D. Reidel Publishing Co., 1983), p. 252.
38. Rich, *op. cit.*, p. 269.
39. Joan Tronto makes this point in "Beyond Gender Differences to a Theory of Care", *Signs*, vol. 22 (Summer, 1987), p. 666.
40. Carol Gilligan "Moral Orientation and Moral Development" in *Women and Moral Theory*, p. 24.
41. This was evident in the reasoning of the women in Gilligan's case studies, many of whom had abortions in order to please or placate other significant persons in their lives.
42. Some post-abortion counsellors find the sense of irremediable break in relationship to be one of the most painful aspects of the post-abortion experience, and try to urge the woman to imaginatively re-create a relationship with the baby in order to be better able to complete the necessary grieving process. Conversation with Teresa Patterson, post abortion counselor at Crisis Pregnancy Center in Walnut Creek, California.
43. For an excellent "masculine voice" discussion of the personhood issues, see, e.g., Philip E. Devine, *The Ethics of Homicide*, (Ithaca, NY: Cornell University Press, 1978).
44. Janice Raymond, *The Transsexual Empire* (Boston: Beacon Press, 1979), p. 114.
45. It would seem that in using the term "obligation", Noddings is blurring the distinction between the masculine and feminine voice, since obligations imply rights. When she speaks of obligations to extend care, however, these are not absolute, but relative to the individual's choice of being a caring person as an ethical ideal. They are binding on us only as a result of our own prior choice, and our care is not something the other can claim as a matter of justice.
46. Nodding's discussion of abortion occurs on pp. 87–90 of *Caring: A Feminine Approach to Ethics, op. cit.*, and all quotes are from these pages unless otherwise noted.
47. *Ibid.*, p. 47.
48. It is inaccurate to call even the newly implanted zygote an "information speck". Unlike a blueprint or pattern of information, it is alive and growing.
49. I realize that Noddings would not be happy with the extent to which I lean on her use of the term "criteria", since she prefers to argue by autobiographical example. However, since moral intuitions about abortion vary so widely, this sort of argument is not effective here.
50. I omit here consideration of such difficult cases as severe genetic retardation.
51. The notion of potentiality I am relying on here is roughly an Aristotelian one.

52. Carolyn Whitbeck articulates a view of this sort in "Women as People: Pregnancy and Personhood", *op. cit.*

53. Granted, this sort of judgment is, at least in part, an impressionistic one. It is supported, however, by Gilligan's findings about the difference between boys and girls in their response to the "Heinz dilemma" (where the man is faced with a choice between allowing his wife to die or stealing an expensive drug from the druggist to save her). Although the females she studies do not all respond to the dilemma in the same way (e.g. Betty at first sounds more like Hobbes than like what has been characterized as the feminine voice — pp. 75–76), some recurring patterns which she singles out as representative of the feminine voice are: resisting being forced to accept either horn of the dilemma, seeing all those involved as in relationship with each other, viewing the dilemma in terms of conflicting responsibilities rather than rights, and seeking to avoid or minimize harm to anyone (see, e.g., Sarah p. 95). Since the abortion decision involves killing and not merely letting die, it would seem that the impetus to find a way through the horns of the dilemma would be, if anything, greater than in the Heinz dilemma.

54. For example, one feminist, Roberta Steinbach, argues that we must not restrict a woman's right to abort for reasons of sex selection *against females* because it might endanger our hard won "reproductive rights"! (See "Sex Selection: From Here to Fraternity" in Carol Gould (ed.) *Beyond Domination*, (Totowa, NJ: Rowman & Allanheld, 1984), p. 280.)

55. For example, Annette Baier regards trust as the central concept in a feminine ethics, but speaks of "the principled betrayal of the exploiter's trust" (Baier, "What do Women Want in a Moral Theory", p. 62).

56. Restrictions can take many forms, including laws against abortion, mandatory counselling which includes information about the facts of fetal development and encourages the woman to choose other options, obligatory waiting periods, legal requirements to notify (and/or obtain the consent of) the father, or in the case of a minor the girl's parents, etc. To defend the appropriateness of any particular sort of restrictions goes beyond the scope of this paper.

57. I wish to thank the following for reading and commenting on an earlier draft of this paper: Edith Black, Tony Celano, Phil Devine, James Nelson, Alan Soble, and Michael Wreen.

QUESTIONS

1. According to Celia Wolf-Devine, what are the differences between the "feminine" and "masculine" approaches to morality as outlined by theorists such as Carol Gilligan and Annette Baier?

2. In what ways does Thomson's defence of abortion fit what Wolf-Devine identifies as the "masculine" or "ethics of justice" approach to abortion?

3. Do you think there is a "feminine voice" that reasons in terms of our interconnectedness and values our responsibilities to care for others? Is Wolf-Devine correct in her claim that this "feminine voice" of an ethic of care is inconsistent with a feminist defence of abortion?

ABORTION THROUGH A FEMINIST ETHICS LENS

Susan Sherwin

Although abortion has long been an important issue in bioethics, the distinctive analysis of feminist ethics is generally overlooked in the discussion. Authors and readers commonly presume a familiarity with the feminist position and equate it with other liberal defenses of women's right to choose abortion; but feminist ethics yields a different analysis of the moral questions surrounding abortion from that usually offered by liberal abortion arguments.[1] Although feminists agree with some of the conclusions of nonfeminist arguments on abortion, they often disagree with the way the issues are formulated and with the reasoning that is offered in the mainstream literature.

Feminist reasoning in support of women's right to choose abortion is significantly different from the reasoning used by nonfeminist supporters of similar positions. For instance, most feminist accounts evaluate abortion policy within a broader framework, according to its place among the social institutions that support the subordination of women. In contrast, most nonfeminist discussions of abortion consider the moral or legal permissibility of abortion in isolation; they ignore (and thereby obscure) relevant connections with other social practices, including the ongoing power struggle within sexist societies over the control of women and their reproduction. Feminist arguments take into account the actual concerns that particular women attend to in their decision-making on abortion, such as the nature of a woman's feelings about her fetus, her relationships with her partner, other children she may have, and her various obligations to herself and others. In contrast, most nonfeminist discussions evaluate abortion decisions in their most abstract form (for example, questioning what sort of being a fetus is); from this perspective, specific questions of context are deemed irrelevant. In addition, nonfeminist arguments in support of choice about abortion are generally grounded in masculinist conceptions of freedom (such as privacy, individual choice, and individuals' property rights with respect to their own bodies), which do not meet the needs, interests, and intuitions of many of the women concerned.

Feminists also differ from nonfeminists in their conception of what is morally at issue with abortion. Nonfeminists focus exclusively on the morality and legality of performing abortions, whereas feminists insist that other issues, including the accessibility and delivery of abortion services, must also be addressed. Disputes about abortion arise even at the stage of defining the issue and setting the moral parameters for discussion. Although many nonfeminist bioethicists agree with feminists about which abortion policies should be supported, they tend to accept the proposals of the antifeminists as to what is morally at issue in developing that policy.

Thus although feminists welcome the support of nonfeminists in pursuing policies that grant women control over abortion decisions, they generally envision policies for this purpose that are very different from those considered by their nonfeminist sympathizers. Feminist ethicists promote a model for addressing the provision of abortion services different from the one conceived in traditional bioethical arguments. For example, Kathleen McDonnell urges feminists to develop an explicitly " 'feminist morality' of abortion. . . . At its root it would be characterized by the deep appreciations of the complexities of life, the

From No Longer Patient: Feminist Ethics and Health Care. *Philadelphia: Temple University Press, 1992. Reproduced by permission of Temple University Press.*

refusal to polarize and adopt simplistic formulas" (McDonnell 1984, 52). Here I propose one conception of the shape such an analysis should take.

Women and Abortion

The most obvious difference between feminist and nonfeminist approaches to abortion lies in the relative attention each gives in its analysis to the interests and experiences of women. Feminist analysis regards the effects of unwanted pregnancies on the lives of women individually and collectively as the central element in the moral examination of abortion; it is considered self-evident that the pregnant woman is the subject of principal concern in abortion decisions. In many nonfeminist accounts, however, not only is the pregnant woman not perceived as central, she is often rendered virtually invisible. Nonfeminist theorists, whether they support or oppose women's right to choose abortion, generally focus almost all their attention on the moral status of the fetus.[2]

In pursuing a distinctively feminist ethics, it is appropriate to begin with a look at the role of abortion in women's lives. The need for abortion can be very intense; no matter how appalling and dangerous the conditions, women from widely diverse cultures and historical periods have pursued abortions. No one denies that if abortion is not made legal, safe, and accessible in our society, women will seek out illegal and life-threatening abortions to terminate pregnancies they cannot accept. Antiabortion activists seem willing to accept this cost, although liberals definitely are not; feminists, who explicitly value women, judge the inevitable loss of women's lives that results from restrictive abortion policies to be a matter of fundamental concern.

Antiabortion campaigners imagine that women often make frivolous and irresponsible decisions about abortion, but feminists recognize that women have abortions for a wide variety of compelling reasons. Some women, for instance, find themselves seriously ill and incapacitated throughout pregnancy; they cannot continue in their jobs and may face insurmountable difficulties in fulfilling their responsibilities at home. Many employers and schools will not tolerate pregnancy in their employees or students, and not every woman is able to put her job, career, or studies on hold. Women of limited means may be unable to take adequate care of children they have already borne, and they may know that another mouth to feed will reduce their ability to provide for their existing children. Women who suffer from chronic disease, who believe themselves too young or too old to have children, or who are unable to maintain lasting relationships may recognize that they will not be able to care properly for a child when they face the decision. Some who are homeless, addicted to drugs, or diagnosed as carrying the AIDS virus may be unwilling to allow a child to enter the world with the handicaps that would result from the mother's condition. If the fetus is a result of rape or incest, then the psychological pain of carrying it may be unbearable, and the woman may recognize that her attitude to the child after birth will be tinged with bitterness. Some women learn that the fetuses that they carry have serious chromosomal anomalies and consider it best to prevent them from being born with a condition that is bound to cause them to suffer. Others, knowing the fathers to be brutal and violent, may be unwilling to subject a child to the beatings or incestuous attacks they anticipate; some may have no other realistic way to remove the child (or themselves) from the relationship.[3]

Finally, a woman may simply believe that bearing a child is incompatible with her life plans at the time. Continuing a pregnancy may have devastating repercussions throughout a woman's life. If the woman is young, then a pregnancy will likely reduce her chances of pursuing an education and hence limit her career and life opportunities: "The earlier a woman has a baby, it seems, the more likely she is to drop out of school; the less education she gets, the more likely she is to remain poorly paid, peripheral to the labor market, or unemployed, and the more children she will have" (Petchesky 1985, 150). In many circumstances, having a child will exacerbate the social and economic forces already stacked against a woman by virtue of her sex (and her race, class, age, sexual orientation, disabilities, and so forth). Access to abortion is necessary for many women if they are to escape the oppressive conditions of poverty.[4]

Whatever the specific reasons are for abortion, most feminists believe that the women concerned are in the best position to judge whether abortion is the appropriate response to a pregnancy. Because usually only the woman choosing abortion is properly situated to weigh all the relevant factors, most feminists resist attempts to offer general, abstract rules for determining when abortion is morally justified.[5] Women's personal deliberations about abortion involve contextually defined considerations that reflect their commitments to the needs and interests of everyone concerned, including themselves, the fetuses they carry, other members of their household, and so forth. Because no single formula is available for balancing these complex factors through all possible cases, it is vital that feminists insist on protecting each woman's right to come to her own conclusions and resist the attempts of other philosophers and moralists to set the agenda for these considerations. Feminists stress that women must be acknowledged as full moral agents, responsible for making moral decisions about their own pregnancies. Women may sometimes make mistakes in their moral judgments, but no one else can be assumed to have the authority to evaluate and overrule their judgments.[6]

Even without patriarchy, bearing a child would be a very important event in a woman's life, because it involves significant physical, emotional, social, and (usually) economic changes for her. The ability to exert control over the incidence, timing, and frequency of childbearing is often tied to a woman's ability to control most other things she values. Because we live in a patriarchal society, it is especially important to ensure that women have the authority to control their own reproduction.[7] Despite the diversity of opinion found among feminists on most other matters, most feminists agree that women must gain full control over their own reproductive lives if they are to free themselves from male dominance.[8]

Moreover, women's freedom to choose abortion is linked to their ability to control their own sexuality. Women's subordinate status often prevents them from refusing men sexual access to their bodies. If women cannot end the unwanted pregnancies that result from male sexual dominance, then their sexual vulnerability to particular men may increase, because caring for an(other) infant involves greater financial needs and reduced economic opportunities for women.[9] As a result, pregnancy often forces women to become dependent on particular men. Because a woman's dependence on a man is assumed to entail her continued sexual loyalty to him, restriction of abortion serves to commit women to remaining sexually accessible to particular men and thus helps to perpetuate the cycle of oppression.

In contrast to most nonfeminist accounts, feminist analyses of abortion direct attention to how women get pregnant. Those who reject abortion seem to believe that women can avoid unwanted pregnancies "simply" by avoiding sexual intercourse. These views show little appreciation for the power of sexual politics in a culture that oppresses women. Existing patterns of sexual dominance mean that women often have little control over their sexual lives. They may be subject to rape by their husbands, boyfriends, colleagues, employers, customers, fathers, brothers, uncles, and dates, as well as by strangers. Often the sexual coercion is not even recognized as such by the participants but is the price of continued "good will" — popularity, economic survival, peace, or simple acceptance. Many women have found themselves in circumstances where they do not feel free to refuse a man's demands for intercourse, either because he is holding a gun to her head or because he threatens to be emotionally hurt if she refuses (or both). Women are socialized to be compliant and accommodating, sensitive to the feelings of others, and frightened of physical power; men are socialized to take advantage of every opportunity to engage in sexual intercourse and to use sex to express dominance and power. Under such circumstances, it is difficult to argue that women could simply "choose" to avoid heterosexual activity if they wish to avoid pregnancy. Catharine MacKinnon neatly sums it up: "The logic by which women are supposed to consent to sex [is]: preclude the alternatives, then call the remaining option 'her choice'" (MacKinnon 1989, 192).

Furthermore, women cannot rely on birth control to avoid pregnancy. No form of contraception that is fully safe and reliable is available, other than sterilization; because women may wish only to avoid pregnancy temporarily, not permanently, sterilization is not always an acceptable choice. The pill and the IUD are the most effective contraceptive means offered, but both involve significant health hazards to women and are quite dangerous for some.[10] No woman should spend the thirty to forty years of her reproductive life on either form of birth control. Further, both have been associated with subsequent problems of involuntary infertility, so they are far from optimal for women who seek to control the timing of their pregnancies.

The safest form of birth control involves the use of barrier methods (condoms or diaphragms) in combination with spermicidal foams or jelly. But these methods also pose difficulties for women. They are sometimes socially awkward to use. Young women are discouraged from preparing for sexual activity that might never happen and are offered instead romantic models of spontaneous passion; few films or novels interrupt scenes of seduction for a partner to fetch contraceptives. Many women find their male partners unwilling to use barrier methods of contraception, and they often find themselves in no position to insist. Further, cost is a limiting factor for many women. Condoms and spermicides are expensive and are not covered under most health care plans.[11] Only one contraceptive option offers women safe and fully effective birth control: barrier methods with the backup option of abortion.[12]

From a feminist perspective, the central moral feature of pregnancy is that it takes place in women's bodies and has profound effects on women's lives. Gender-neutral accounts of pregnancy are not available; pregnancy is explicitly a condition associated with the female body.[13] Because only women experience a need for abortion, policies about abortion affect women uniquely. Therefore, it is important to consider how proposed policies on abortion fit into general patterns of oppression for women. Unlike nonfeminist accounts, feminist ethics demands that the effects of abortion policies on the oppression of women be of principal consideration in our ethical evaluations.

The Fetus

In contrast to feminist ethics, most nonfeminist analysts believe that the moral acceptability of abortion turns entirely on the question of the moral status of the fetus. Even those who support women's right to choose abortion tend to accept the premise of the antiabortion proponents that abortion can be tolerated only if we can first prove that the fetus lacks full personhood.[14] Opponents of abortion demand that we define the status of the fetus either as a being that is valued in the same way as other humans and hence is entitled not to be killed or as a being that lacks in all value. Rather than challenging the logic of this formulation, many defenders of abortion have concentrated on showing that the fetus is indeed without significant value (Tooley 1972, Warren 1973); others, such as L. W. Sumner (1981), offer a more subtle account that reflects the gradual development of fetuses and distinguishes between early fetal stages, where the relevant criterion for personhood is absent, and later stages, where it is present. Thus the debate often rages between abortion opponents, who describe the fetus as an "innocent," vulnerable, morally important, separate being whose life is threatened and who must be protected at all costs, and abortion supporters, who try to establish that fetuses are deficient in some critical respect and hence are outside the scope of the moral community. In both cases, however, the nature of the fetus as an independent being is said to determine the moral status of abortion.

The woman on whom the fetus depends for survival is considered as secondary (if she is considered at all) in these debates. The actual experiences and responsibilities of real women are not perceived as morally relevant to the debate, unless these women too, can be proved innocent by establishing that their pregnancies are a result of rape or incest.[15] In some contexts, women's role in gestation is literally reduced to that of "fetal containers"; the individual women disappear or are perceived simply as mechanical life-support systems.[16]

The current rhetoric against abortion stresses that the genetic makeup of the fetus is determined at conception and the genetic code is incontestably human. Lest there be any doubt about the humanity of the fetus, we are assailed with photographs of fetuses at various stages of development that demonstrate the early appearance of recognizably human characteristics, such as eyes, fingers, and toes. Modern ultrasound technology is used to obtain "baby's first picture" and stimulate bonding between pregnant women and their fetuses (Petchesky 1987). That the fetus in its early stages is microscopic, virtually indistinguishable to the untrained eye from fetuses of other species, and lacking in the capacities that make human life meaningful and valuable is not deemed relevant by the self-appointed defenders of the fetus. The antiabortion campaign is directed at evoking sympathetic attitudes toward a tiny, helpless being whose life is threatened by its own mother; the fetus is characterized as a being entangled in an adversarial relationship with the (presumably irresponsible) woman who carries it (Overall 1987). People are encouraged to identify with the "unborn child," not with the woman whose life is also at issue.

In the nonfeminist literature, both defenders and opponents of women's right to choose abortion agree that the difference between a late-term fetus and a newborn infant is "merely geographical" and cannot be considered morally significant. Daniel Callahan (1986), for instance, maintains a pro-choice stand but professes increasing uneasiness about this position in light of new medical and scientific developments that increase our knowledge of embryology and hasten the date of potential viability for fetuses; he insists that defenders of women's right to choose must come to terms with the question of the fetus and the effects of science on the fetus's prospects apart from the woman who carries it. Arguments that focus on the similarities between infants and fetuses, however, generally fail to acknowledge that a fetus inhabits a woman's body and is wholly dependent on her unique contribution to its maintenance, whereas a newborn is physically independent, although still in need of a lot of care.[17] One can only view the distinction between being in or out of a woman's womb as morally irrelevant if one discounts the perspective of the pregnant woman; feminists seem to be alone in recognizing the woman's perspective as morally important to the distinction.[18]

In antiabortion arguments, fetuses are identified as individuals; in our culture, which views the (abstract) individual as sacred, fetuses qua individuals are to be honored and preserved. Extraordinary claims are made to establish the individuality and moral agency of fetuses. At the same time, the women who carry these fetal individuals are viewed as passive hosts whose only significant role is to refrain from aborting or harming their fetuses. Because it is widely believed that a woman does not actually have to do anything to protect the life of her fetus, pregnancy is often considered (abstractly) to be a tolerable burden to protect the life of an individual so like us.[19]

Medicine has played its part in supporting these attitudes. Fetal medicine is a rapidly expanding specialty, and it is commonplace in professional medical journals to find references to pregnant women as "the maternal environment." Fetal surgeons now have at their disposal a repertoire of sophisticated technology that can save the lives of dangerously ill fetuses; in light of the excitement of such heroic successes, it is perhaps understandable that women have disappeared from their view. These specialists see the fetuses as their patients, not the women who nurture the fetuses. As the "active" agents in saving fetal lives (unlike the pregnant women, whose role is seen as purely passive), doctors perceive themselves as developing independent relationships with the fetuses they treat. Barbara Katz Rothman observes: "The medical model of pregnancy, as an essentially parasitic and vaguely pathological relationship, encourages the physician to view the fetus and mother as two separate patients, and to see pregnancy as inherently a conflict of interests between the two" (Rothman 1986, 25).

Perhaps even more distressing than the tendency to ignore the woman's agency altogether and view her as a passive participant in the medically controlled events of pregnancy and childbirth is the growing practice of viewing women as genuine threats to the well-being of the fetus. Increasingly, women are described as irresponsible or hostile toward their fetuses, and the relationship between them is characterized as adversarial. Concern for the well-being of the fetus is taken as license for doctors to intervene to ensure that women comply with medical "advice." Courts are called upon to enforce the doctors' orders when moral pressure alone proves inadequate, and women are being coerced into undergoing unwanted cesarean deliveries and technologically monitored hospital births (Annas 1982; Rodgers 1989; Nelson and Milliken 1990). Some states have begun to imprison women for endangering their fetuses through drug abuse and other socially unacceptable behaviors (Annas 1986). Mary Anne Warren reports that a bill was recently introduced in an Australian state that makes women liable to criminal prosecution "if they are found to have smoked during pregnancy, eaten unhealthful foods, or taken any other action which can be shown to have adversely affected the development of the fetus" (Warren 1989, 60).

In other words, some physicians have joined antiabortion campaigners in fostering a cultural acceptance of the view that fetuses are distinct individuals who are physically, ontologically, and socially separate from the women whose bodies they inhabit and that they have their own distinct interests. In this picture, pregnant women are either ignored altogether or are viewed as deficient in some crucial respect, and hence they can be subject to coercion for the sake of their fetuses. In the former case, the interests of the women concerned are assumed to be identical with those of the fetus; in the latter, the women's interests are irrelevant, because they are perceived as immoral, unimportant, or unnatural.

Focus on the fetus as an independent entity has led to presumptions that deny pregnant women their roles as active, independent, moral agents with a primary interest in what becomes of the fetuses they carry. The moral question of the fetus's status is quickly translated into a license to interfere with women's reproductive freedom.

A Feminist View of the Fetus

Because the public debate has been set up as a competition between the rights of women and those of fetuses, feminists have often felt pushed to reject claims of fetal value, in order to protect women's needs. As Kathryn Addelson (1987) has argued, however, viewing abortion in this way "rips it out of the context of women's lives." Other accounts of fetal value are more plausible and less oppressive to women.

On a feminist account fetal development is examined in the context in which it occurs, within women's bodies, rather than in the isolation of imagined abstraction. Fetuses develop in specific pregnancies that occur in the lives of particular women. They are not individuals housed in generic female wombs or full persons at risk only because they are small and subject to the whims of women. Their very existence is relationally defined, reflecting their development within particular women's bodies; that relationship gives those women reason to be concerned about them. Many feminists argue against a perspective that regards the fetus as an independent being and suggest that a more accurate and valuable understanding of pregnancy would involve regarding the pregnant woman "as a biological and social unit" (Rothman 1986, 25).

On this view, fetuses are morally significant, but their status is relational rather than absolute. Unlike other human beings, fetuses do not have any independent existence; their existence is uniquely tied to the support of a specific other. Most nonfeminist accounts have ignored the relational dimension of fetal development and have presumed that the moral status of fetuses could be resolved solely in terms of abstract, metaphysical criteria of personhood as applied to the fetus alone (Tooley 1972; Warren 1973). Throughout much of the nonfeminist literature, commentators argue that some set of properties (such as genetic heritage, moral agency, self-consciousness, language use, or self-determination) will entitle all who possess it to be granted the moral status of persons. They seek some feature by which we can neatly divide the world into moral persons (who are to be valued and protected) and others (who are not entitled to the same group privileges).

This vision, however, misinterprets what is involved in personhood and what is especially valued about persons. Personhood is a social category, not an isolated state. Persons are members of a community, and they should be valued in their concrete, discrete, and different states as specific individuals, not merely as conceptually undifferentiated entities. To be a morally significant category, personhood must involve personality as well as biological integrity.[20] It is not sufficient to consider persons simply as Kantian atoms of rationality, because persons are embodied, conscious beings with particular social histories. Annette Baier has developed a concept of persons as "second persons," which helps explain the sort of social dimension that seems fundamental to any moral notion of personhood:

A person, perhaps, is best seen as one who was long enough dependent upon other persons to acquire the essential arts of personhood. Persons essentially are *second* persons, who grow up with other persons. . . . The fact that a person has a life *history*, and that a people collectively have a history depends upon the humbler fact that each person has a childhood in which a cultural heritage is transmitted, ready for adolescent rejection and adult discriminating selection and contribution. Persons come after and before other persons (Baier 1985: 84–5).

Persons, in other words, are members of a social community that shapes and values them, and personhood is a relational concept that must be defined in terms of interactions and relationships with others.[21]

Because humans are fundamentally relational beings, it is important to remember that fetuses are characteristically limited in the "relationships" in which they can "participate"; within those relationships, they can make only the most restricted "contributions."[22] After birth human beings are capable of a much wider range of roles in relationships with a broad variety of partners; that very diversity of possibility and experience leads us to focus on the abstraction of the individual as a constant through all these different relationships. Until birth, however, no such variety is possible, so the fetus must be understood as part of a complex entity that includes the woman who currently sustains the fetus and who will, most likely, be principally responsible for it for many years to come.

A fetus is a unique sort of human entity, then, for it cannot form relationships freely with others, and others cannot readily form relationships with it. A fetus has a primary and particularly intimate sort of "relationship" with the woman in whose womb it develops; connections with any other persons are necessarily indirect and must be mediated through the pregnant woman. The relationship that exists between a woman and her fetus is clearly asymmetrical, because she is the only party to it who is capable of even considering whether the interaction should continue; further, the fetus is wholly dependent on the woman who sustains it, whereas she is quite capable of surviving without it.

Most feminist views of what is valuable about persons reflect the social nature of individual existence. No human, especially no fetus, can exist apart from relationships; efforts to speak of the fetus itself, as if it were not inseparable from the woman in whom it develops, are distorting and dishonest. Fetuses have a unique physical status — within and dependent on particular women. That gives them also a unique social status. However much some might prefer it to be otherwise, no one other than the pregnant woman in question can do anything to support or harm a fetus without doing something to the woman who nurtures it. Because of this inexorable biological reality, the responsibility and privilege of determining a fetus's specific social status and value must rest with the woman carrying it.

Many pregnancies occur to women who place a very high value on the lives of the particular fetuses they carry and choose to see their pregnancies through to term, despite the possible risks and costs involved; it would be wrong of anyone to force such a woman to terminate her pregnancy. Other women, or some of these same women at other times, value other things more highly (for example, their freedom, their health, or previous responsibilities that conflict with those generated by the pregnancies), and so they choose not to continue their pregnancies. The value that women ascribe to individual fetuses varies dramatically from case to case and may well change over the course of any particular pregnancy. The fact that fetal lives can neither be sustained nor destroyed without affecting the women who support them implies that whatever value others may attach to fetuses generally or to specific fetuses individually should not be allowed to outweigh the ranking that is assigned to them by the pregnant women themselves.

No absolute value attaches to fetuses apart from their relational status, which is determined in the context of their particular development. This is not the same, however, as saying that they have no value at all or that they have merely instrumental value, as some liberals suggest. The value that women place on their own fetuses is the sort of value that attaches to an emerging human relationship.

Nevertheless, fetuses are not persons, because they have not developed sufficiently in their capacity for social relationships to be persons in any morally significant sense (that is, they are not yet second persons). In this way they differ from newborns, who immediately begin to develop into persons by virtue of their place as subjects in human relationships; newborns are capable of some forms of communication and response. The moral status of fetuses is determined by the nature of their primary relationship and the value that is created there. Therefore, feminist accounts of abortion emphasize the importance of protecting women's rights to continue or to terminate pregnancies as each sees fit.

The Politics of Abortion

Feminist accounts explore the connections between particular social policies and the general patterns of power relationships in our society. With respect to abortion in this framework, Mary Daly observes that "one hundred percent of the bishops who oppose the repeal of antiabortion laws are men and one hundred percent of the people who have abortions are women. . . . To be comprehended accurately, they [arguments against abortion] must be seen within the context of sexually hierarchical society" (Daly 1973, 106).

Antiabortion activists appeal to arguments about the unconditional value of life. When we examine their rhetoric more closely, however, we find other ways of interpreting their agenda. In addition to their campaign to criminalize abortion, most abortion opponents condemn all forms of sexual relations outside of heterosexual marriage, and they tend to support patriarchal patterns of dominance within such marriages. Many are distressed that liberal abortion policies support permissive sexuality by allowing women to "get away with" sex outside of marriage. They perceive that ready access to abortion supports women's independence from men.[23]

Although nonfeminist participants in the abortion debates often discount the significance of its broader political dimensions, both feminists and antifeminists consider them crucial. The intensity of the antiabortion movement correlates closely with the increasing strength of feminism in achieving greater equality for women. The original American campaign against abortion can be traced to the middle of the nineteenth century, that is, to the time of the first significant feminist movement in the United States (Luker 1984). Today abortion is widely perceived as supportive of increased freedom and power for women. The campaign against abortion intensified in the 1970s, which was a period of renewed interest in feminism. As Rosalind Petchesky observes, the campaign rested on some powerful symbols: "To feminists and antifeminists alike, it came to represent the image of the 'emancipated woman' in her contemporary identity, focused on her education and work more than on marriage or childbearing; sexually active outside marriage and outside the disciplinary boundaries of the parental family; independently supporting herself and her children; and consciously espousing feminist ideas" (Petchesky 1984, 241). Clearly, much more than the lives of fetuses is at stake in the power struggle over abortion.

When we place abortion in the larger political context, we see that most of the groups active in the struggle to prohibit abortion also support other conservative measures to maintain the forms of dominance that characterize patriarchy (and often class and racial oppression as well). The movement against abortion is led by the Catholic church and other conservative religious institutions, which explicitly endorse not only fetal rights but also male dominance in the home and the church. Most opponents of abortion also oppose virtually all forms of birth control and all forms of sexuality other than monogamous, reproductive sex; usually, they also resist having women assume positions of authority in the dominant public institutions (Luker 1984). Typically, antiabortion activists support conservative economic measures that protect the interests of the privileged classes of society and ignore the needs of the oppressed and disadvantaged (Petchesky 1985). Although they stress their commitment to preserving life, many systematically work to dismantle key social programs that provide life necessities to the underclass. Moreover, some current campaigns against abortion retain elements of the racism that dominated the North American abortion literature in the early years of the twentieth century, wherein abortion was opposed on the grounds that it amounted to racial suicide on the part of whites.[24]

In the eyes of its principal opponents, then, abortion is not an isolated practice; their opposition to abortion is central to a set of social values that runs counter to feminism's objectives. Hence antiabortion activists generally do not offer alternatives to abortion that support feminist interests in overturning the patterns of oppression that confront women. Most deny that there are any legitimate grounds for abortion, short of the need to save a woman's life — and some are not even persuaded by this criterion (Nicholson 1977). They believe that any pregnancy can and should be endured. If the mother is unable or unwilling to care for the child after birth, then they assume that adoption can be easily arranged.

It is doubtful, however, that adoptions are possible for every child whose mother cannot care for it. The world abounds with homeless orphans; even in the industrialized West, where there is a waiting list for adoption of healthy (white) babies, suitable homes cannot always be found for troubled adolescents; inner-city, AIDS babies, or many of the multiply handicapped children whose parents may have tried to care for them but whose marriages broke under the strain.

Furthermore, even if an infant were born healthy and could be readily adopted, we must recognize that surrendering one's child for adoption is an extremely difficult act for most women. The bond that commonly forms between women and their fetuses over the full term of pregnancy is intimate and often intense; many women find that it is not easily broken after birth. Psychologically, for many women adoption is a far more difficult response to unwanted pregnancies than abortion. Therefore, it is misleading to describe pregnancy as merely a nine-month commitment; for most women, seeing a pregnancy through to term involves a lifetime of responsibility and involvement with the resulting child and, in the overwhelming majority of cases, disproportionate burden on the woman through the child-rearing years. An ethics that cares about women would recognize that abortion is often the only acceptable recourse for them.

Expanding the Agenda

The injunction of feminist ethics to consider abortion in the context of other issues of power and oppression means that we need to look beyond the standard questions of its moral and legal acceptability. This implies, for instance, that we need to explore the moral imperatives of ensuring that abortion services are actually available to all women who seek them. Although medically approved abortions are technically recognized as legal (at least for the moment) in both Canada and the United States, many women who need abortions cannot obtain them; accessibility is still associated with wealth and privilege in many regions.[25] In

Canada vast geographical areas offer no abortion services at all, so unless the women of those regions can afford to travel to urban clinics, they have no meaningful right to abortion. In the United States, where there is no universal health insurance, federal legislation (under the Hyde amendment) explicitly denies the use of public money for abortions. Full ethical discussion of abortion reveals the necessity of removing the economic, age, and racial barriers that currently restrict access to medically acceptable abortion services.[26]

The moral issues extend yet further. Feminism demands respect for women's choices; even if the legal and financial barriers could be surpassed, this condition may remain unmet. The focus of many political campaigns for abortion rights has been to make abortion a matter of medical, not personal, choice, suggesting that doctors (but not necessarily women) can be trusted to choose responsibly. Feminists must insist on respect for women's moral agency. Therefore feminism requires that abortion services be provided in an atmosphere that is supportive of the choices that women make. This could be achieved by offering abortions in centers that deal with all matters of reproductive health in an open, patient-centered manner, where respectful counseling on all aspects of reproductive health is available.[27]

Furthermore, the moral issues surrounding abortion include questions of how women are treated when they seek abortions. All too frequently hospital-based abortions are provided by practitioners who are uneasy about their role and treat the women involved with hostility and resentment.[28] Health care workers involved in providing abortions must recognize that abortion is a legitimate option that should be carried out with respect and concern for the physical, psychological, and emotional well-being of the patient. In addition, we need to turn our moral attention to the effects of antiabortion protests on women. Increasingly, many antiabortion activists have personalized their attacks and focused their energies on harassing the women who enter and leave abortion clinics, thereby requiring them to pass a gauntlet of hostile protesters to obtain abortions. Such arrangements are not conducive to positive health care, so these protests, too, must be subject to moral criticism within the ethics of health care.

Feminist ethics promotes the value of reproductive freedom, which is defined as the condition under which women are able to make truly voluntary choices about their reproductive lives. Women must have control over their reproduction if patriarchal dominance over women is to be brought to an end. In addition to reliable and caring abortion services, then, women also need access to safe and effective birth control, which would provide them with other means of avoiding pregnancy.[29]

Moreover, we must raise questions about the politics of sexual domination in this context. Many men support women's right to abortion because they perceive that if women believe that they can engage in intercourse without having to accept an unwanted pregnancy, they will become more sexually available. Some of the women who oppose abortion resist it for this very reason; they do not want to support a practice that increases women's sexual vulnerability. Feminists need to develop an analysis of reproductive freedom that includes sexual freedom as it is defined by women, not men. Such an analysis would, for example, include women's right to refuse sex. Because this right can only be assured if women have power equal to men's and are not subject to domination because of their sex, women's freedom from oppression is itself an element of reproductive freedom.

Finally, it is important to stress that feminist accounts do not deny that fetuses have value. They ask that fetuses be recognized as existing within women's pregnancies and not as separate, isolated entities. Feminists positively value fetuses that are wanted by the women who carry them; they vigorously oppose practices that force women to have abortions they do not want. No women should be subjected to coerced abortion or sterilization. Women must be assured of adequate financial and support services for the care of their children, so that they are not forced to abort fetuses that they would otherwise choose to carry. Further, voluntarily pregnant women should have access to suitable pre- and postnatal care and nutrition, lest wanted fetuses be unnecessarily harmed or lost.

Feminists perceive that far more could be done to protect and care for fetuses if the state directed its resources toward supporting women who choose to continue their pregnancies, rather than draining those resources to police the women who try to terminate undesired pregnancies. Unlike their conservative counterparts, feminists recognize that caring for the women who maintain the lives of fetuses is not only a more legitimate policy than is regulating them but also probably more effective at ensuring the health and well-being of more fetuses and, ultimately, of more infants.

In sum, then, feminist ethics demands that moral discussions of abortion reflect a broader agenda than is usually found in the arguments put forth by bioethicists. Only by reflecting on the meaning of ethical pronouncements on actual women's lives and the connections that exist between judgments on abortion and the conditions of domination and subordination can we come to an adequate understanding of the moral status of abortion in a particular society.

NOTES

1. Much of the philosophic literature on abortion characterizes the possible moral positions on the issue as falling within three slots along a continuum: conservative (no abortions are morally acceptable, except, perhaps, when the woman's life is at stake), moderate (abortions are permissible under certain circumstances), or liberal (abortion should be available "on demand"). See, e.g., Wertheimer (1971) or Sumner (1981).

2. Technically, the term "fetus" does not cover the entire period of development. Medical practitioners prefer to distinguish between differing stages of development with such terms as "conceptus," "embryo" (and, recently, "pre-embryo"), and "fetus." Because these distinctions are not relevant to the discussion here, I follow the course common to discussions in bioethics and feminism and use the term "fetus" to cover the entire period of development from conception to the end of pregnancy through either birth or abortion.

3. Bearing a child can keep a woman within a man's sphere of influence against her will. The Canadian news media were dominated in the summer of 1989 by the story of Chantel Daigle, a Quebec woman who faced injunctions granted to her former boyfriend by two lower courts against her choice of abortion before she was finally given permission for abortion by the Supreme Court of Canada. Daigle's explanation to the media of her determination to abort stressed her recognition that if she was forced to bear this child, she would never be free from the violent father's involvement in her life.

4. Feminists believe that it is wrong of society to make childbearing a significant cause of poverty in women, but the reality of our social and economic structures in North America is that it does. In addition to their campaigns for greater reproductive freedom for women, feminists also struggle to ensure that women receive greater support in child-rearing; in efforts to provide financial stability and support services to those who provide care for children, feminists would welcome the support of those in the antiabortion movement who sincerely want to reduce the numbers of abortions.

5. Among the exceptions here, see Overall (1987), who seems willing to specify some conditions under which abortion is immoral (78–79).

6. Critics continue to base the debate on the possibility that women might make frivolous abortion decisions; hence they want feminists to agree to setting boundaries on acceptable grounds for choosing abortion. Feminists, however, should resist this injunction. There is no practical way of

drawing a line fairly in the abstract; cases that may appear "frivolous" at a distance often turn out to be substantive when the details are revealed. There is no evidence to suggest that women actually make the sorts of choices worried critics hypothesize about: for example, the decision of a woman eight-months pregnant to abort because she wants to take a trip or gets in "a tiff" with her partner. These sorts of fantasies, on which demands to distinguish between legitimate and illegitimate personal reasons for choosing abortion rest, reflect an offensive conception of women as irresponsible. They ought not to be perpetuated. Women seeking moral guidance in their own deliberations about choosing abortion do not find such hypothetical discussions of much use.

7. In her monumental historical analysis of the early roots of Western patriarchy, Lerner (1986) determined that patriarchy began in the period from 3100 to 600 b.c., when men appropriated women's sexual and reproductive capacity; the earliest states entrenched patriarchy by institution-alizing the sexual and procreative subordination of women to men.

8. Some women claim to be feminist yet oppose abortion; some even claim to offer a feminist argument against abortion (see Callahan 1987). For reasons that I develop in this chapter, I do not believe a thorough feminist analysis can sustain a restrictive abortion policy, although I do acknowledge that feminists need to be wary of some of the arguments proposed in support of liberal policies on abortion.

9. The state could do a lot to ameliorate this condition. If it provided women with adequate financial support, removed the inequities in the labor market, and provided affordable and reliable child care, pregnancy need not so often lead to a woman's dependence on a particular man. That it does not do so is evidence of the state's complicity in maintaining women's subordinate position with respect to men.

10. The IUD has proven so hazardous and prone to lawsuits, it has been largely removed from the market in the United States (Pappert 1986). It is also disappearing from other Western countries but is still being purchased by population-control agencies for use in the developing world (LaCheen 1986).

11. For a more detailed discussion of the limitations of current contraceptive options, see Colodny (1989); for the problems of cost, see esp. 34–35.

12. See Petchesky (1985), esp. chap. 5, where she documents the risks and discomforts associated with pill use and IUDs and the increasing rate at which women are choosing the option of diaphragm or condom, with the option of early, legal abortions as backup.

13. Eisenstein (1988) has developed an interesting account of sexual politics, which identifies the pregnant body as the central element in the cultural subordination of women. She argues that pregnancy (either actual or potential) is considered the defining characteristic of all women, and because it is not experienced by men, it is classified as deviance and considered grounds for different treatment.

14. Thomson (1971) is a notable exception to this trend.

15. Because she was obviously involved in sexual activity, it is often concluded that the noncoerced woman is not innocent but guilty. As such, she is judged far less worthy than the innocent being she carries within her. Some who oppose abortion believe that an unwanted pregnancy is a suitable punishment for "irresponsible" sex.

16. This seems reminiscent of Aristotle's view of women as flowerpots where men implant the seed with all the important genetic information and the movement necessary for development and the woman's job is that of passive gestation, like the flowerpot. See Whitbeck (1973) and Lange (1983).

17. Some are so preoccupied with the problem of fetuses being "stuck" in women's bodies that they seek to avoid this geographical complication altogether, completely severing the ties between woman and fetus. For example, Bernard Nathanson, an antiabortion activist with the zeal of a new convert, eagerly anticipates the prospect of artificial wombs as alternative means for preserving the lives of fetuses and "dismisses the traditional reverence for birth as mere 'mythol-ogy' and the act of birth itself as an 'insignificant event'" (cited in McDonnell 1984, 113).

18. Cf. Warren (1989) and Tooley (1972).

19. The definition of pregnancy as a purely passive activity reaches its ghoulish conclusion in the increasing acceptability of sustaining brain-dead women on life-support systems to continue their functions as incubators until the fetus can be safely delivered. For a discussion of this trend, see Murphy (1989).

20. This apt phrasing is taken from Petchesky (1985), 342.

21. E.g., Held (1987b) argues that personhood is a social status, created by the work of mothering persons.
22. Fetuses are almost wholly individuated by the women who bear them. The fetal "contributions" to the relationship are defined by the projections and interpretations of the pregnant woman in the latter stages of pregnancy, if she chooses to perceive fetal movements in purposeful ways (e.g., "it likes classical music, spicy food, exercise").
23. See Luker (1984), esp. chaps. 6 and 7, and Petchesky (1985), esp. chaps. 7 and 8, for documentation of these associations in the U.S. antiabortion movement and Collins (1985), esp. chap. 4, and McLaren and McLaren (1986) for evidence of similar trends in the Canadian struggle.
24. See McLaren and McLaren (1986) and Petchesky (1985).
25. When abortion was illegal, many women nonetheless managed to obtain abortions, but only the relatively privileged women with money were able to arrange safe, hygienic abortions; poor women were often constrained to rely on dangerous, unacceptable services. In the United States court rulings have ensured that rich and middle-class women have, for the moment, relatively easy access to well-run clinics and hospitals, but because public hospitals are mostly unwilling to offer abortion services and federal law prohibits the use of Medicaid funding for abortion, many poor women still find legal, safe abortions out of reach (Petchesky 1985). In Canada, too, abortion services are most readily available to middle-class, urban, mature women. This suggests that financial circumstances may be a more significant factor in determining women's access to abortion than abortion's legal status.
26. Some feminists suggest we seek recognition of the legitimacy of nonmedical abortion services. This would reduce costs and increase access dramatically, with no apparent increase in risk as long as services were provided by trained, responsible practitioners who were concerned with the well-being of their clients. It would also allow the possibility of increasing women's control over abortion. See, e.g., McDonnell (1984).
27. For a useful model of such a center, see Van Wagner and Lee (1989).
28. A poignant collection of some women's unfortunate experiences with hospital abortions is offered in *Telling Our Secrets*, produced by CARAL (1990).
29. Therefore, the Soviet model, in which abortions have been relatively accessible, is also unacceptable, because there the unavailability of birth control forces women to rely on multiple abortions to control their fertility.

QUESTIONS

1. Susan Sherwin takes the position that women facing an unwanted pregnancy should be free to make their decision to have an abortion in light of their own values. What are the key steps in her reasoning that lead her to that conclusion?
2. What is it to be a second person? Is this a helpful idea for understanding the morality of abortion? Can this idea answer some of the questions raised by Celia Wolf-Devine's account of a feminist defence of abortion?
3. Sherwin distinguishes between feminist and non-feminist approaches to abortion. Based on her way of making the distinction, would you classify the approaches to abortion of Jane English, Judith Jarvis Thomson, and Celia Wolf-Devine as feminist or non-feminist? Why?
4. Does Sherwin offer convincing reasons for thinking that the development of fetal medicine should not play a decisive role in determining the rights of the unborn? Compare her views on this issue with those of the Grants and Judith Jarvis Thomson.
5. Do you agree that if the abortion debate is broadened in the way Sherwin suggests in her closing paragraph, the case for limiting access to abortion is seriously undermined? In your view, should the debate be broadened in this way? If the debate is broadened, does this address some of Wolf-Devine's concerns about a feminist approach?
6. In what ways can Sherwin's feminist approach shed light on the moral dilemmas presented by New Reproductive Technologies?

SUGGESTIONS FOR FURTHER READING

An Important Supreme Court of Canada Judgement

- *Chantal Daigle v. Jean-Guy Tremblay* This judgement resulted from a request made by Jean-Guy Tremblay for an injunction by the court to prevent Chantal Daigle, with whom he had conceived a child, from having an abortion. The injunction was granted by a Quebec Court and confirmed by the Quebec Court of Appeal. The Supreme Court unanimously overruled the decision taken by the lower courts.

Canadian Government Report

- Canada. Royal Commission on New Reproductive Technologies. *Proceed with Care: Final Report of the Royal Commission on New Reproductive Technologies* (Ottawa: Supply and Services Canada, 1993). In addition to the final two-volume report, this Royal Commission chaired by Patricia Baird produced fifteen volumes of Research Studies and separately authored reports and bibliographies. One of these reports, volume 1 of the Research Studies called *New Reproductive Technologies: Ethical Aspects*, was designed to set the ethical framework for examining the issues.

Other Readings

- Ian Gentles (ed.), *A Time to Choose Life: Women, Abortion and Human Rights* (Toronto: Stoddart, 1990). This book is a collection of articles that reflect on the implications for the development of social policy in Canada of the Supreme Court judgement striking down the abortion law. The various authors argue that in spite of the Supreme Court judgement, and perhaps even because of it, Canadians should be concerned with the protection of prenatal human life.
- Edward W. Keyserlingk, "The Unborn Child's Right to Prenatal Care," *Health Law in Canada* (Fall 1982). This article points to the apparent inconsistency of legal systems that allow abortion without legal impediment while extending the protection of the law to unborn children in other respects.
- John T. Noonan Jr., "An Almost Absolute Value in Human History," in *The Morality of Abortion: Legal and Historical Perspectives* (Cambridge, Mass.: Harvard University Press, 1970). This is a widely quoted study of the history of abortion and its legal treatment. The book contains a number of other articles by prominent commentators and is one of the early collections of philosophical essays to address what has become a topic of wide philosophical debate.
- Donald B. Marquis, "Why Abortion is Immoral," *Journal of Philosophy*, v. 86 (1989). By examining the deficiencies in the arguments concerning the status of the fetus on both sides of the debate, Marquis argues that "abortion is, except possibly in rare cases, seriously immoral, that it is in the same moral category as killing an innocent human being."
- Maureen Muldoon (ed.), *The Abortion Debate in the United States and Canada: A Source Book* (New York: Garland, 1991). This book is a compendium of sources of material relevant to the abortion debate. Its chapter headings are: "Demographics, Sociological Research, and Opinions"; "Philosophical Perspectives on Abortion"; "The Positions of Religious Denominations"; "The Advocates and Advocate Groups"; and "Law and Politics." This last chapter identifies the significant court decision and legislative initiatives over the past two decades in both the United States and Canada.

- Christine Overall, *Ethics and Human Reproduction: A Feminist Analysis* (Boston: Unwin Hyman, 1987). In this book, the author reviews the development of new reproductive technologies and their implications for women. The purpose of the book is to explore the value context appropriate for the decisions and policy development that the new reproductive technologies are making unavoidable. One chapter of the book addresses the topic of abortion directly.
- Christine overall (ed.), *The Future of Human Reproduction* (Toronto: Women's Press, 1989). This anthology gathers together a number of important essays by feminist scholars on the topic of human reproduction.
- L.W. Sumner, *Abortion and Moral Theory* (Princeton, N.J.: Princeton University Press, 1981). This book, referred to by Justice Wilson in the *Morgentaler* decision, defends a view similar to that of Jane English. Sumner argues for a developmental view of the point at which a human fetus becomes a human being with a right to life.
- Michael Tooley, "In Defense of Abortion and Infanticide," *Philosophy & Public Affairs*, v. 2, no. 2 (Fall 1972). Tooley argues that neither abortion nor infanticide are matters of moral concern because neither fetuses nor very young infants have the right to life.

Chapter 3

Capital Punishment

Introduction
Background Considerations

Capital punishment is thought of today as a punishment inflicted on persons who have been found guilty of murder. But the idea that capital punishment should be reserved only for murderers has gained wide acceptance only in this century. At one time in English history, for example, the penalty of death might be imposed for the theft of anything worth more than 12 pence. Blackstone, an influential eighteenth-century commentator on the law, discovered 166 crimes punishable by death in English law. By 1810, there were 300 offences, including forgery, for which the death penalty could be imposed in England.

The view that capital punishment should be reserved for murder is the product of more than one hundred years of law reform, the result of which has been increasing moderation in the use of capital punishment in many countries in the Western world.

Execution by hanging for murder has been a feature of Canadian law throughout our history. Until the 1950s murder was rather broadly defined as the unlawful killing of a human being by someone who intended to bring about his victim's death or who intended to inflict bodily harm on his victim, and where the harm inflicted resulted in his victim's death. For such a crime the mandatory sentence was death by hanging. A judge had no discretion in the matter and only the Governor General, acting on the advice of the Canadian government, could intervene to prevent the execution from taking place. Such interventions were relatively rare.

Toward the end of the 1950s support for moderation in the use of capital punishment began to grow. It resulted first in a decision that no one under the age of 18 was to be executed. A second step was taken in 1960: the law was altered to differentiate between murder and capital murder. Capital murder, for which capital punishment was the mandatory sentence, comprised those murders which were planned and deliberate. The change was not intended to be a step in the direction of the abolition of capital punishment. Nevertheless, from 1957 to 1963, the Conservative government commuted 80 percent of all death sentences. And from 1963 to 1967, the Liberal government commuted one hundred percent of all death sentences. Thus, by 1967 abolition of capital punishment had in fact come about, though in law capital punishment continued to exist.

By 1967, substantial pressure for the formal abolition of capital punishment was being felt by the government. The result was a bill restricting capital murder to situations where the victim was a police officer or a prison guard. All other acts of murder were to result in a sentence of life imprisonment. The bill was to remain in force for an experimental period of five years. After a stormy debate, the bill was adopted in a vote in which members were free of party discipline and could vote according to what they believed to be right. In 1973, the same bill was renewed for a further five-year period by a vote of 119 in favour, 106 opposed. At the same time, public-opinion polls suggested that a majority of Canadians wished to return to a wider definition of capital murder.

Between 1967 and 1977 all death sentences were commuted to life imprisonment by the Governor General on the advice of the government.

The final step toward the abolition of capital punishment was taken in 1978 when capital punishment was eliminated. Murder is now classified as first-degree murder or second-degree murder. If a murder is planned or deliberate, carried out for pay, or committed in the course of an actual or attempted hijacking of an aircraft, kidnapping, sexual assault with or without a weapon, or aggravated sexual assault, or if the victim is a police officer or prison employee or the murderer has been convicted of murder before, it is first-degree murder. Most other acts of murder are second-degree. Both are punishable by a mandatory sentence of life imprisonment. However, persons convicted of first-degree murder must serve a minimum sentence of 25 years before they are eligible for parole. A conviction for second-degree murder now results in a minimum of ten years in jail before becoming eligible for parole.

The Current Situation

In Canada, although capital punishment has been abolished, there is considerable pressure for its reinstatement. At the time of the abolition debate, public-opinion polls indicated that two-thirds of Canadians wished capital punishment retained. More recent polls indicate that a majority of Canadians continue to favour a return to capital punishment, a position which police associations across the country advocate strongly.

In England, abolition was brought about in 1965 by a free vote in spite of the fact that a public-opinion poll taken at the time showed that 79 percent of the British people were opposed. In 1969, abolition was reaffirmed, a situation which has continued to the present. The current situation in the United States is somewhat different. There, criminal law is established by each state; hence the situation varies from one part of the country to another. In those states which have retained capital punishment, executions are increasingly common.

The Moral Dimension

Any form of punishment inflicts suffering on the offender being punished. For that reason, punishment needs to be justified. The death penalty is a particularly severe form of punishment because it inflicts suffering on an offender by taking his life. How then can a society that claims to be committed to the view that human life is sacred tolerate capital punishment?

Those who endorse the death penalty tend to justify their position by appealing to one of two views. The first view is that, because the protection of human life is a fundamental obligation which the community has toward its members, it must do everything it legitimately can do to deter those who might otherwise commit murder. Capital punishment is the most effective deterrent available and so is justified. In short, capital punishment is a means to securing respect for the principle that both individually and collectively we have an obligation to preserve and respect human life.

Evaluating the merits of the view that capital punishment is justified as a deterrent requires that we address two questions. First, does the threat of capital punishment deter people from committing murder? Some have argued that it does not. They point to a host of studies undertaken in several countries over the past several decades which have failed to provide any evidence for the view that capital punishment is a deterrent to murder. Others have argued that the studies which have been done are inconclusive; further, the suggestion that capital punishment is not a deterrent conflicts with practical experience and common sense. Assessing the merits of these conflicting points of view is a theme which runs through several of the readings.

There is a second question to be considered. Let us assume for the moment that the death penalty is a deterrent. Does it follow that capital punishment is justified? Many people are prepared to accept that it does. But for others, harming some individuals as a way of securing benefits for others is not acceptable, particularly where taking human life is involved.

Let us turn now to a second view — namely, that justice requires that those who break the law should be punished. On this view justice requires that offenders receive the punishment they deserve for the crime which they have committed. That is, the punishment should fit the crime. The punishment which those who commit murder deserve, that is the punishment which fits the crime of murder, is death.

Assessing the merits of this view requires, once again, that we address two questions. First, does justice require that those who break the law be punished? A complex variety of arguments have been advanced by those who reject a "just deserts" view of punishment. Some have suggested that those who commit serious crimes like murder are not autonomous moral agents responsible for their actions; rather they are mentally ill; or they are victims of their upbringing or their environment. The findings of the social sciences are frequently cited in support of these arguments. Others argue that we are never justified in imposing suffering in the form of punishment unless we can establish that punishment will serve to reform or rehabilitate the offender, or that it will result in benefits to the community. Obviously, reform or rehabilitation of the offender is not the point of capital punishment. And empirical research has failed to establish that capital punishment reduces the volume of crime in general or murder in particular. Hence, they conclude that capital punishment is immoral.

Those who advocate capital punishment on the grounds that execution is the fitting punishment for those who commit murder must address a second question. Let us assume that justice requires that those who break the law be punished. Does it follow that execution is a just punishment for those who commit murder? This question requires serious consideration. Murder is frequently committed in a moment of uncontrollable anger or while the offender is heavily intoxicated. Frequently the victim is closely related to the murderer, a husband or wife, a parent, or a son or daughter. Of course, not all cases of murder fall into this category. But here, too, there are objections. For example, courts have been known to make mistakes. Innocent people have been found guilty in the past. This has led some to argue that the death penalty is simply too final a punishment to be inflicted by fallible human institutions. Those who commit very serious crimes like murder should be given very long prison sentences, to leave open the possibility for errors to be corrected.

The Readings

Because capital punishment is no longer practised in Canada, our courts have not had to examine it from a legal and constitutional perspective. In this respect, Canadian jurisprudence is quite different from that of the United States, where the constitutionality of capital punishment has been extensively tested in the courts and has been the subject of important American Supreme Court judgements. However, the Canadian Supreme Court has not escaped debating this issue entirely. In recent years, two persons accused of murder in the United States escaped to Canada, where they were subsequently arrested by Canadian authorities. In both cases, the United States requested that they be extradited to stand trial in an American court. In both cases, the individuals appealed against extradition on the grounds that if returned to the United States they faced the death penalty on conviction. That appeal eventually made its way to the Supreme Court.

Our first reading sets out the majority and the dissenting judgements in the case. The majority ruled that given the history of the sanction in Canada, the lack of consensus in parliament on those occasions where the issue was addressed and voted on, and the continuing public debate about its reinstatement, capital punishment is not seen by Canadians to be morally abhorrent or absolutely unacceptable. Therefore extraditing an accused to the United States where he might face execution is not unconstitutional. The dissenting opinion argues in contrast that capital punishment is regarded with abhorrence by Canadians and is a cruel and unusual punishment of the sort prohibited by the Charter of Rights and Freedoms. Extradition of an accused to a jurisdiction in which he might be executed was therefore unconstitutional.

The Supreme Court judgement is followed by a speech in defence of capital punishment by John Stuart Mill made in the British Parliament in 1868. Many of Mill's points are still being argued today. For example, Mill emphasizes the role of executions in deterring violent crime. Our third reading, by Ezzat Fattah, examines this argument and concludes, on empirical grounds, that execution is no more effective in deterring people from committing murder than imprisonment. A statistical analysis of violent crime and murder rates since 1975 in the United States and Canada by the John Howard Society of Ontario follows. The study indicates that there has been no increase in the murder rate since the abolition of capital punishment in Canada. Neither has either Canada or the United States seen a sharp increase in violent crime over that same period.

Alan Brudner's article then shifts the focus of discussion. Justifying punishment by reference to its consequences, he argues, is a mistake. Retributivism with its emphasis on just desserts offers a more convincing alternative. But does it follow that capital punishment is therefore justified? Brudner offers a cautious no to this question.

The final reading in the chapter examines the practice of capital punishment in the United States. Anthony Amsterdam argues that American courts have not found a way to apply capital punishment in a non-discriminatory way and that therefore it should be abolished.

RE KINDLER AND MINISTER OF JUSTICE; AMNESTY INTERNATIONAL, INTERVENER

[Indexed as: Kindler v. Canada (Minister of Justice), 1991]

Supreme Court of Canada, Lamer C.J.C., La Forest, L'Heureux-Dubé, Sopinka, Gonthier, Cory and McLachlin JJ.   September 26, 1991.

Madame Justice B. McLachlin

This appeal, and the companion case, *Reference re: Ng Extradition (Can.)* [*post*, p 498], raise the issue of whether the Minister of Justice can order the extradition of fugitives to the United States without obtaining an assurance from that country's authorities that the death penalty will not be imposed. Canadian law does not impose the death penalty, except for certain military offences. The question is whether our government is obliged, in all cases, to obtain assurances from the state requesting extradition that the death penalty will not be carried out by them. In my view the two cases raise the same issues. I have, therefore, chosen to deal with the cases together in the reasons for this appeal.

The Minister's orders of extradition are attacked on two grounds: (1) that the section of the *Extradition Act*, R.S.C. 1985, c. E-23, under which they are made is unconstitutional, and (2) that the Minister's exercise of his discretion under the order was unconstitutional.

For the reasons that follow, I conclude that it is not contrary to the *Canadian Charter of Rights and Freedoms* to give the Minister discretion on the question of whether to seek assurances from the requesting state that the death penalty will not be carried out. I further conclude that the Minister did not err in the way he exercised his discretion in the cases of Ng and Kindler.

Facts

Kindler stands convicted of first degree murder, conspiracy to commit murder, and kidnapping in the State of Pennsylvania. The jury which convicted him, after hearing further evidence, recommended the imposition of the death penalty. Before he was sentenced, however, Kindler escaped from prison and fled to Canada, where he was subsequently arrested and, after a hearing before Pinard J., committed for surrender, [1985] C.S. 1117.

Ng is charged in the State of California with 19 charges arising from multiple and brutal killings. On 12 of those charges, Ng, if found guilty, could receive the death penalty. He was arrested in Calgary following a bungled shoplifting attempt during which he shot and wounded a store security guard. At the end of a six-week hearing, Trussler J. committed Ng for extradition: 93 A.R. 204, 6 W.C.B. (2d) 214.

Section 25 of the *Extradition Act* leaves the final decision to surrender with the Minister of Justice. Article 6 of the Extradition Treaty Between Canada and the United States of America, Can. T.S. 1976, No. 3, provides that the country from which extradition of a fugitive has been requested may seek assurances from the arresting country that the death penalty will not be imposed where the offences involved carry the possibility of capital punishment. In the case of both Kindler and Ng, the Minister ordered final extradition without asking for such assurances. . . .

Issues

The essence of these cases is not whether the death penalty offends the Charter. It is rather whether the Canadian extradition procedure, as expressed in the *Extradition Act* and in the Minister's decision, violates the Charter. In addition to the submissions advanced by the fugitives, this court stated two constitutional questions directed at whether s. 25 of the *Extradition Act* violates s. 7 or 12 of the Charter, and if so, whether such violation is justified under s. 1.

Treaties and legislation

Canadian Charter of Rights and Freedoms

> 7. Everyone has the right to life, liberty and security of the person and the right not to be deprived thereof except in accordance with the principles of fundamental justice.

• • • • •

> 12. Everyone has the right not to be subjected to any cruel and unusual treatment or punishment.

Extradition Treaty Between Canada and the United States of America, Can. T.S. 1976, No. 3, in force March 22, 1976.

ARTICLE 6

> When the offense for which extradition is requested is punishable by death under the laws of the requesting State and the laws of the requested State do not permit such punishment for that offense, extradition may be refused unless the requesting State provides such assurances as the requested State considers sufficient that the death penalty shall not be imposed, or, if imposed, shall not be executed.

Extradition Act, R.S.C., 1985, c. E-23

> 25. Subject to this Part, the Minister of Justice, on the requisition of the foreign state, may, under his hand and seal, order a fugitive who has been committed for surrender to be surrendered to the person or persons who are, in the Minister's opinion, duly authorized to receive the fugitive in the name and on behalf of the foreign state, and the fugitive shall be so surrendered accordingly. . . .

II. Which sections of the Charter apply?

The Charter clearly applies to extradition matters, including the executive decision of the Minister that affects the fugitive's surrender: *Schmidt, supra; Argentina (Republic) v. Mellino* (1987), 33 C.C.C. (3d) 334, 40 D.L.R. (4th) 74, [1987] 1 S.C.R. 536; and *United States of America v. Allard* (1987), 33 C.C.C. (3d) 501, 40 D.L.R. (4th) 102 [1987] 1 S.C.R. 564.

The narrower question is what provisions of the Charter apply to extradition proceedings — s. 12, s. 7, or both?

In my view, the guarantee against cruel and unusual punishment found in s. 12 of the Charter does not apply to s. 25 of the *Extradition Act* or to ministerial acts done pursuant to s. 25. The Charter's reach is confined to the legislative and executive acts of Canadian governments. The question then is whether the decision to surrender a fugitive under s. 25

can constitute the imposition of cruel and unusual punishment by a Canadian government. In my view, it cannot. Neither s. 25 nor orders made under it impose or authorize punishment. The purpose and effect of the provision is to permit the fugitive to be extradited to face the consequences of the judicial process elsewhere. Any punishment which is imposed will be the result of laws and actions in that jurisdiction.

The fact that the Minister may seek assurances that the death penalty will not be demanded or enforced in the foreign jurisdiction does not change this situation. The punishment, if any, to which the fugitive is ultimately subject will be punishment imposed not by the Government of Canada, but by the foreign state. To put it another way, the effect of any Canadian law or government act is too remote from the possible imposition of the penalty complained of to attract the attention of s. 12. To apply s. 12 directly to the act of surrender to a foreign country where a particular penalty may be imposed, is to overshoot the purpose of the guarantee and to cast the net of the Charter broadly in extraterritorial waters. Effective relations between different states require that we respect the differences of our neighbours and that we refrain from imposing our constitutional guarantees on other states under the guise of refusing to assist them (and extradition is a form of assistance) unless they conform to our Charter. . . .

The practice of extradition, as has been noted, has deep roots in this country, and the practice *per se* has never been controversial. This reflects a strong belief that crime must not go unpunished. Fairness requires that alleged criminals be brought to justice and extradition is the normal means by which this is achieved when the offence was committed in a foreign jurisdiction.

When an accused person is to be tried in Canada, there will be no conflict between our desire to see an accused face justice, and our desire that the justice he or she faces conforms to the most exacting standards which have emerged from our judicial system. However, when a fugitive must face trial in a foreign jurisdiction if he or she is to face trial at all, the two desires may come into conflict. In some cases the social consensus may clearly favour one of these values above the other, and the resolution of the conflict will be straightforward. This would be the case if, for instance, the fugitive faced torture on return to his or her home country. In many cases, though, neither value will be able to claim absolute priority; rather, one will serve to temper the other. There may be less unfairness in requiring an accused to face a judicial process which may be less than perfect according to our standards, than in having him or her escape the judicial process entirely.

For this reason, in considering the attitude of Canadians toward the death penalty we must consider not only whether Canadians consider it unacceptable, but whether they consider it to be so absolutely unacceptable that it is better that a fugitive not face justice at all rather than face the death penalty.

With this in mind I turn to consider Canadian attitudes to the death penalty. Much has been said and written in this country on the death penalty. While it is difficult to generalize about a subject so controverted, this much can be ventured. There is no clear consensus in this country that capital punishment is morally abhorrent and absolutely unacceptable.

Capital punishment was a component of Canadian criminal law from this country's colonial beginnings until it was abolished by Parliament in 1976. For most of that period the penalty was accepted with little question, although executions became increasingly rare in the latter years of its existence in Canada. The last execution in Canada was in 1962. Yet, while the death penalty has been formally abolished in this country, its possible return continues to be debated. In 1987, in response to persistent calls to bring back the death penalty, Members of Parliament conducted a free vote on a resolution to reinstate capital punishment. The result was a defeat of the motion, but the vote — 148 to 127 — fell far short of reflecting a broad consensus even among Parliamentarians.

To this day, capital punishment continues to apply to certain military offences. At the same time, public opinion polls continue to show considerable support among Canadians for the return of the death penalty for certain offences. Can it be said, in light of such indications as these, that the possibility that a fugitive might face the death penalty in California or Pennsylvania "shocks" the Canadian conscience or leads Canadians to conclude that the situation the fugitive faces is "simply unacceptable"? The case is far from plain.

When other considerations are brought into the picture, the matter becomes even less clear. In some cases, the unconditional surrender of a fugitive to face the death penalty may "sufficiently shock" the national conscience as to render it mandatory that the Minister seek an assurance that the penalty will not be imposed. But in other cases, this may not be so. These instances provide an example. Both fugitives are sought for crimes involving brutal, and in the case of Ng, multiple, murders. In both Pennsylvania and California the legal system is the product of democratic government, and includes the substantial protections of a constitutional rights document which dates back over two centuries. The variance between cases supports legislation which accords to the Minister a measure of discretion on the question of whether an assurance that the death penalty will not be imposed should be demanded.

The importance of maintaining effective extradition arrangements with other countries in a world where law enforcement is increasingly international in scope, likewise supports the ministerial discretion found in s. 25. As discussed above, an effective extradition process is founded on respect for sovereignty and differences in the judicial systems among various nations. Canada displays confidence in the fairness of the justice systems of other nations by entering into treaties with them. If Canada is to be assured of co-operation when it seeks extradition from states whose laws may not conform exactly to ours, it must be prepared to reciprocate.

Another relevant consideration in determining whether surrender without assurances regarding the death penalty would be a breach of fundamental justice is the danger that if such assurances were mandatory, Canada might become a safe haven for criminals in the United States seeking to avoid the death penalty. This is not a new concern. The facility with which American offenders can flee to Canada has been recognized since the 19th century: *Cotroni, supra*, at p. 219.

It was argued that there was little statistical evidence that criminals routinely cross the border into Canada. On the other hand, there must be few cases indeed where a person facing the death penalty in the United States is able to escape and make his or her way to the border. What is certain is that this is precisely what happened in the two cases before the court, and that the result endangered Canadians; Ng, arrested in the course of committing a crime here, shot and wounded a security guard. Given our long undefended common border with the United States, it is not unreasonable for the Minister, in deciding whether to seek the assurance that the death penalty will not be imposed, to consider the danger of encouraging other fugitives to do what Ng and Kindler did.

The fugitives, in suggesting that s. 25 should be struck down, in effect urge that the only constitutional law is one which absolutely forbids extradition in the absence of assurances that the death penalty will not be imposed. The foregoing discussion suggests that such a law might well prove too inflexible to permit the Government of Canada to deal with particular situations in a way which maintains the required comity with other nations, while at the same time going beyond what is required to conform to our fundamental sense of fairness. What is required is a law which permits the Minister, in the particular case before her, to act in a way which preserves the effectiveness of the extradition process, while conforming to the Canadian sense of what is fundamentally just. Section 25 does this; the less flexible alternative proposed by the fugitives would not.

I conclude that the fugitives have not established that the law which permits their extradition without assurances that the death penalty will not be applied in the requesting states offends the fundamental principles of justice enshrined in s. 7 of the Charter.

CORY J. (dissenting) —

The House of Commons votes to abolish the death penalty

In free votes in both 1976 and 1987, a majority of the members of the House of Commons supported the abolition of the death penalty. These votes, held after extensive and thorough debate, demonstrate that the elected representatives of the Canadian people found the death penalty for civil crimes to be an affront to human dignity which cannot be tolerated in Canadian society. These votes are a clear indication that capital punishment is considered to be contrary to basic Canadian values.

The rejection of the death penalty by the majority of the members of the House of Commons on two occasions can be taken as reflecting a basic abhorrence of the infliction of capital punishment either directly, within Canada, or through Canadian complicity in the actions of a foreign state.

The position under the Charter

What then is the constitutional status of the death penalty under s. 12 of the Charter?

The American experience provides no guidance. Cases dealing with the constitutional validity of the death penalty were decided on very narrow bases unique to the wording of the American Constitution and rooted in early holdings of the United States Supreme Court. Canadian courts should articulate a distinct Canadian approach with respect to cruel and unusual punishment based on Canadian traditions and values.

The approach to be taken by this court in determining whether capital punishment contravenes s. 12 of the Charter should, in my view, be guided by two central considerations. First is the principle of human dignity which lies at the heart of s. 12. It is the dignity and importance of the individual which is the essence and the cornerstone of democratic government. Second is the decision of this court in *Smith, supra.*

1. *Human dignity under the Charter*

The fundamental importance of human dignity in Canadian society has been recognized in numerous cases. In *R. v. Oakes,* (1986), 24 C.C.C. (3d) 321 at p. 346, 26 D.L.R. (4th) 200, [1986] 1 S.C.R. 103, Dickson C.J.C. referred to the basic principles and values which are enshrined in the Charter. He wrote:

The court must be guided by the values and principles essential to a free and democratic society which I believe embody, to name but a few, respect for the inherent

dignity of the human person, commitment to social justice and equality, accommodation of a wide variety of beliefs, respect for cultural and group identity, and faith in
social and political institutions which enhance the participation of individuals and
groups in society. The underlying values and principles of a free and democratic
society are the genesis of the rights and freedoms guaranteed by the Charter and the
ultimate standard against which a limit on a right or freedom must be shown, despite
its effect, to be reasonable and demonstrably justified.

In her reasons in *R. v. Morgentaler* (1988), 37 C.C.C. (3d) 449 at p. 550, 44. D.L.R. (4th)
385, [1988] 1 S.C.R. 30, Wilson J. stressed the importance of human dignity in understanding the protections afforded by the Charter. She wrote:

> The idea of human dignity finds expression in almost every right and freedom
> guaranteed in the Charter. Individuals are afforded the right to choose their own
> religion and their own philosophy of life, the right to choose with whom they will
> associate and how they will express themselves, the right to choose where they will
> live and what occupation they will pursue.

Again in *Andrews v. Law Society of British Columbia* (1989), 56 D.L.R. (4th) 1, [1989] 1
S.C.R. 143, 25 C.C.E.L. 255, this court emphasized the importance of human dignity.
McIntyre J. wrote at p. 15:

> It is clear that the purpose of s. 15 is to ensure equality in the formulation and
> application of the law. The promotion of equality entails the promotion of a society in
> which all are secure in the knowledge that they are recognized at law as human
> beings equally deserving of concern, respect and consideration.

In *Reference re: s. 94(2) of Motor Vehicle Act, supra*, the court once again noted the
fundamental importance of human dignity to the provisions of the Charter. Lamer J., as he
then was, stated at p. 309:

> Sections 8 to 14 address specific deprivations of the "right" to life, liberty and
> security of the person in breach of the principles of fundamental justice, and as such,
> violations of s. 7. They are therefore illustrative of the meaning, in criminal or penal
> law, of "principles of fundamental justice"; they represent principles which have been
> recognized by the common law, the international conventions and by the very fact of
> entrenchment in the Charter as essential elements of a system for the administration
> of justice which is founded upon the belief in the dignity and worth of the human
> person and the rule of law.

Let us now turn to consider the second guiding consideration, the decision of this court in
Smith.

2. Section 12 and the Smith case

In *Smith, supra*, this court considered a challenge to the minimum sentencing provision
of the *Narcotic Control Act*, R.S.C. 1970, c. N-1. The penalty prescribed by the *Narcotic*

Control Act for importing a narcotic into Canada was imprisonment for a minimum of seven years up to life. The minimum term was challenged on the ground that it constituted cruel and unusual punishment contrary to s. 12 of the Charter. It was argued that the punishment was unduly severe and disproportionate to the offence committed. The decision focused upon the element of proportionality.

Lamer J., as he then was, carefully considered the nature of the protection afforded by s. 12 of the Charter. In giving a broad interpretation to the s. 12 right, Lamer J., at p. 139, held that punishments "must not be grossly disproportionate to what would have been appropriate". He later held, at p. 140, that certain punishments will by their very nature always be grossly disproportionate:

> Finally, I should add that some punishments or treatments will always be grossly disproportionate and will always outrage our standards of decency: for example, the infliction of corporal punishment, such as the lash, irrespective of the number of lashes imposed, or, to give examples of treatment, the lobotomisation of certain dangerous offenders or the castration of sexual offenders.

From this decision two principles emerge. First punishments must never be grossly disproportionate to that which would have been appropriate to punish, rehabilitate, or deter the particular offender or to protect the public from that offender. Secondly, and more importantly for the purposes of this case, punishments must not in themselves be unacceptable no matter what the crime, no matter what the offender. Although any form of punishment may be a blow to human dignity, some form of punishment is essential for the orderly functioning of society. However, when a punishment becomes so demeaning that all human dignity is lost, then the punishment must be considered cruel and unusual. At a minimum, the infliction of corporal punishment, lobotomisation of dangerous offenders and the castration of sexual offenders will not be tolerated.

3. *Does the death penalty violate s. 12 of the Charter?*

In light of both the decisions stressing the importance of human dignity under the Charter and the principles espoused in the *Smith* case, it remains to be determined whether the death penalty violates s. 12 of the Charter. In my view, there can be no doubt that it does.

A consideration of the effect of the imposition of the death penalty on human dignity is enlightening. Descriptions of executions demonstrate that it is state-imposed death which is so repugnant to any belief in the importance of human dignity. The methods utilized to carry out the execution serve only to compound the indignities inflicted upon the individual.

In his book *Condemned to Die: Life Under Sentence of Death* (1981), at pp. 86–7, Johnson makes this reference to executions in the electric chair:

> Electrocution has been described by one medical doctor as "a form of torture [that] rivals burning at the stake". Electrocutions have been known to drag on interminably, literally cooking the prisoners. In one instance a man's brain was found to be 'baked hard', the blood on his head had turned to charcoal, and his entire back was burnt black. One man somehow survived electrocution and was returned months later, with the approval of the Supreme Court, for a second (and unsuccessful) encounter with

the chair. More recently, John Spenkelink's electrocution lasted over six minutes and required three massive surges of electricity before he finally died. Although we have no accounts of the damage to Spenkelink's body caused by his execution, allegations that Florida prison officials stuffed his anus with cotton and taped his mouth shut suggest that they may have anticipated the forbidding spectacle typically provided by electrocution, and made every effort to make the sanction cosmetically acceptable.

This description of the imposition of the death penalty clearly indicates that persons executed by the state are deprived of all semblance of human dignity. The stuffing of the anus with cotton wool and the taping shut of the mouth suggest that even the authorities carrying out the execution were not only insensitive to human dignity but fully expected a horrible reaction to a dreadful punishment. Even so, these indignities are simply adjuncts to the ultimate attack on human dignity, the destruction of life by the state.

The following description by the Reverend Myer Tobey of the execution by lethal gas of Eddie Daniels is to similar effect:

In the chamber now, he was strapped to the chair. The cyanide had been prepared, and was placed beneath his chair, over a pan of acid that would later react with the cyanide to form the deadly gas. Electrocardiographic wires were attached to Daniels' forearms and legs, and connected to a monitor in the observation area. This lets the doctor know when the heart stops beating.

This done, the prison guards left the room, shutting the thick door, and sealing it to prevent the gas from leaking. I took my place at one of the windows, and looked at Eddie, and he looked at me. We said the prayer together, over and over.

At a motion of the warden, a prison guard then pulled a lever releasing the cyanide crystals beneath the chair. Eddie heard the chemical pellets drop, and he braced himself. We did not take our eyes off each other.

In an instant, puffs of light white smoke began to rise. Daniels saw the smoke, and moved his head to try to avoid breathing it in. As the gas continued to rise he moved his head this way and that way, thrashing as much as his straps would allow still in an attempt to avoid breathing. He was like an animal in a trap, with no escape, all the time being watched by his fellow humans in the windows that lined the chamber. He could steal only glimpses of me in his panic, but I continued to repeat "My Jesus I Love You", and he too would try to mouth it.

Then the convulsions began. His body strained as much as the strips would allow. He had inhaled the deadly gas, and it seemed as if every muscle in his body was straining in reaction. His eyes looked as if they were bulging, much as a choking man with a rope cutting off his windpipe. But he could get no air in the chamber.

Then his head dropped forward. The doctor in the observation room said that that was it for Daniels. This was within the first few minutes after the pellets had dropped. His head was down for several seconds. Then, as we had thought it was over, he again lifted his head in another convulsion. His eyes were open, he strained and he looked at me. I said one more time, automatically, "My Jesus I Love You". And he went with me, mouthing the prayer. He was still alive after those several minutes, and I was horrified. He was in great agony. Then he strained and began the words with me again. I knew he was conscious, this was not an automatic response of an unconscious man. But he did not finish. His head fell forward again.

There were several more convulsions after this, but his eyes were closed. I could not tell if he were conscious or not at that point. Then he stopped moving, approximately ten minutes after the gas began to rise, and was officially pronounced dead.

The death penalty not only deprives the prisoner of all vestiges of human dignity, it is the ultimate desecration of the individual as a human being. It is the annihilation of the very essence of human dignity.

Let us now consider the principles set out in *Smith* to determine whether the death penalty is of the same nature as corporal punishment, lobotomy or castration which were designated as cruel and unusual punishment.

What is acceptable as punishment to a society will vary with the nature of that society, its degree of stability and its level of maturity. The punishments of lashing with the cat-o'-nine tails and keel-hauling were accepted forms of punishment in the 19th century in the British navy. Both of those punishments could, and not infrequently, did result in death to the recipient. By the end of the 19th century, however, it was unthinkable that such penalties would be inflicted. A more sensitive society had made such penalties abhorrent.

Similarly, corporal punishment is now considered cruel and unusual, yet it was an accepted form of punishment in Canada until it was abolished in 1973. The explanation, it seems to me, is that a maturing society has recognized that the imposition of the lash would now be a cruel and intolerable punishment.

If corporal punishment, lobotomy and castration are no longer acceptable and contravene s. 12 then the death penalty cannot be considered to be anything other than cruel and unusual punishment. It is the supreme indignity to the individual, the ultimate corporal punishment, the final and complete lobotomy and the absolute and irrevocable castration.

As the ultimate desecration of human dignity, the imposition of the death penalty in Canada is a clear violation of the protection afforded by s. 12 of the Charter. Capital punishment is *per se* cruel and unusual.

If Kindler had committed the murder in Canada, then not simply the abolition of the death penalty in this country but, more importantly, the provisions of s. 12 of the Charter would prevent his execution. The next question is whether the fact that American, not Canadian, authorities would carry out the execution is fatal to Kindler's s. 12 claim. That is, does the Minister's decision to surrender Kindler to American authorities who may impose the death penalty "subject" him, within the meaning of s. 12, to cruel and unusual punishment?

VIII. The Relevance of the Fact That the Death Penalty Would Be Inflicted by the United States and Not Canada

The respondent contends that even if it is assumed that the death penalty constitutes cruel punishment, the Charter protections should not apply to a fugitive. In support of this position it was said that the surrender of Kindler did not mean that the government of Canada would be subjecting the fugitive to cruel and unusual punishment, since the punishment would be inflicted by the requesting state. It was argued that so long as the trial procedure the fugitive had undergone or would undergo in the requesting state was fair, the punishment that followed a finding of guilt was not something which could be subject to the provisions of the Charter. Based on the Charter jurisprudence of this court, this argument must be rejected.

The approach that should be taken in applying the Charter

Although the Charter has no extraterritorial application, persons in Canada who are subject to extradition proceedings must be accorded all the rights which flow from the Charter. The approach to be taken is indicated by this court in *Singh v. Canada (Minister of Employment and Immigration)* (1985), 17 D.L.R. (4th) 422, [1985] 1 S.C.R. 177, 14 C.R.R. 13. In that case, the refugee claimants contended that Canada's decision not to extend convention refugee status to them placed them at risk that they would be prosecuted in their home country for their political beliefs. Wilson J., for the plurality, found that this decision deprived the claimants of their s. 7 right to security of the person and that this was sufficient to trigger the protection of the Charter. Specifically, Wilson J. stressed that the Charter affords freedom not only from actual punishment but also from the threat of punishment.

The *Singh* principle was applied in the extradition context in *Schmidt, supra*, where La Forest J. held that the manner in which the foreign state will deal with the fugitive upon surrender may, in some situations, violate the Charter. When such a likelihood arises, Canada, as the extraditing state, must accept responsibility for the ultimate consequence of the extradition. This, I believe, is the conclusion to be drawn from the reasons of La Forest J., at p. 214:

> I have no doubt either that in some circumstances the manner in which the foreign State will deal with the fugitive on surrender, whether that course of conduct is justifiable or not under the law of that country, may be such that it would violate the principles of fundamental justice to surrender an accused under those circumstances. To make the point, I need only refer to a case that arose before the European Commission on Human Rights. *Altun v. Germany* (1983), 5 E.H.R.R. 611, where it was established that prosecution in the requesting country might involve the infliction of torture. *Situations falling far short of this may well arise where the nature of the criminal procedures or penalties in a foreign country sufficiently shocks the conscience as to make a decision to surrender a fugitive for trial there one that breaches the principles of fundamental justice enshrined in s. 7.*

(Emphasis added.)

• • • • •

The responsibility of the extraditing state

Given all of the above, the respondent's contention that the Charter would not apply to cruel and unusual punishments inflicted by the requesting state must be rejected. In my view, since the death penalty is a cruel punishment, that argument is an indefensible abdication of moral responsibility. Historically such a position has always been condemned. The ceremonial washing of his hands by Pontius Pilate did not relieve him of responsibility for the death sentence imposed by others and has found little favour over the succeeding centuries.

Notwithstanding the fact that it is the United States and not Canada which would impose the death penalty, Canada has the obligation not to extradite a person to face a cruel and unusual treatment or punishment. To surrender a fugitive who may be subject to the death penalty violates s. 12 of the Charter just as surely as would the execution of the fugitive in Canada. Therefore, the Minister's decision to extradite Kindler without obtaining art. 6. assurances violates Kindler's s. 12 rights. The only remaining question is whether this violation can be justified under s. 1 of the Charter.

IX. Section 1 of the Charter

The death penalty for civil crimes cannot be justified under s. 1 of the Charter. Indeed, it is difficult to imagine how it could ever be justified. However, let us assume that there could be a s. 1 justification for a punishment which would be, *per se*, a violation of s. 12. Even then, capital punishment could not meet the proportionality test except, perhaps, in very rare circumstances such as conviction for a very serious military offence committed during time of war or emergency.

The safe haven argument

The primary s. 1 justification put forth by the respondent was the so-called "safe haven" argument. The respondent argued that if the death penalty was found to be cruel and unusual punishment *per se*, then to require the Minister to insist upon an art. 6 assurance in every case where the death penalty might be imposed would result in Canada becoming a safe haven for murderers. It was said that to retain such a ministerial discretion constitutes a reasonable limit on the Charter proscription against punishment which would be, *per se*, a breach of s. 12.

I cannot accept this contention. This submission is an *in terrorem* argument put forward without any evidentiary basis.

It is not an unreasonable supposition that people facing criminal charges may flee. But in Europe the decision not to extradite without death penalty assurances has not led to any known exodus of violent criminals from one state to another. The respondent would exclude any comparison to Europe because of the stricter enforcement of national boundaries and its language differences which make it more difficult for a fugitive to flee. However, even if the relatively open border and the similarity in language invites flight from the United States to Canada, the reasons for flight are not necessarily dependent on a presumption that Canada will seek an art. 7 assurance before surrendering a fugitive. Flight may often be undertaken to avoid detection or trial. These are reasons enough to flee without an art. 6 assurance. It should be remembered that any fugitive must first escape from the authorities in the United States and then successfully enter Canada. With that accomplished the fugitive still has to avoid detection in this country.

The respondent alleges that Canada is seeking to prevent an influx of murderers in the future. An allegation that there will be a future danger can best be substantiated by past history. In this case the past history gives little indication of a flood of future problems. Article 6 has been in existence since 1976, yet only two instances are known of American murderers or alleged murderers fleeing to Canada: Kindler and Ng. In the case of Ng it was not surprising that he would attempt to flee to Calgary where his sister resided [see *Reference re: Ng Extradition (Can.)*, p. 498, *post*]. There is simply no evidence that the existence of art. 6 has led to a flood of American murderers into Canada. Nor is there any reason to believe that this would occur if Ministers of Justice uniformly sought art. 6 assurances. . . .

→ ←

SPEECH IN FAVOUR OF CAPITAL PUNISHMENT (1868)

John Stuart Mill

. . . It would be a great satisfaction to me if I were able to support this Motion. It is always a matter of regret to me to find myself, on a public question, opposed to those who are called — sometimes in the way of honour, and sometimes in what is intended for ridicule — the philanthropists. Of all persons who take part in public affairs, they are those for whom, on the whole, I feel the greatest amount of respect; for their characteristic is, that they devote their time, their labour, and much of their money to objects purely public, with a less admixture of either personal or class selfishness, than any other class of politicians what-ever. On almost all the great questions, scarcely any politicians are so steadily and almost uniformly to be found on the side of right; and they seldom err, but by an exaggerated application of some just and highly important principle. On the very subject that is now occupying us we all know what signal service they have rendered. It is through their efforts that our criminal laws — which within my memory hanged people for stealing in a dwell-ing house to the value of 40s. — laws by virtue of which rows of human beings might be seen suspended in front of Newgate by those who ascended or descended Ludgate Hill — have so greatly relaxed their most revolting and most impolitic ferocity, that aggravated murder is now practically the only crime which is punished with death by any of our lawful tribunals; and we are even now deliberating whether the extreme penalty should be retained in that solitary case. This vast gain, not only to humanity, but to the ends of penal justice, we owe to the philanthropists; and if they are mistaken, as I cannot but think they are, in the present instance, it is only in not perceiving the right time and place for stopping in a career hitherto so eminently beneficial. Sir, there is a point at which, I conceive, that career ought to stop. When there has been brought home to any one, by conclusive evidence, the greatest crime known to the law; and when the attendant circumstances suggest no palliation of the guilt, no hope that the culprit may even yet not be unworthy to live among mankind, nothing to make it probable that the crime was an exception to his general character rather than a consequence of it, then I confess it appears to me that to deprive the criminal of the life of which he has proved himself to be unworthy — solemnly to blot him out from the fellowship of mankind and from the catalogue of the living — is the most appropriate, as it is certainly the most impressive, mode in which society can attach to so great a crime the penal consequences which for the security of life it is indispensable to annex to it. I defend this penalty, when confined to atrocious cases, on the very ground on which it is commonly attacked — on that of humanity to the criminal; as beyond comparison the least cruel mode in which it is possible adequately to deter from the crime. If, in our horror of inflicting death, we endeavour to devise some punishment for the living criminal which shall act on the human mind with a deterrent force at all comparable to that of death, we are driven to inflections less severe indeed in appearance, and therefore less efficacious, but far more cruel in reality. Few, I think, would venture to propose, as a punishment for aggravated murder, less than imprisonment with hard labour for life; that is the fate to which a mur-derer would be consigned by the mercy which shrinks from putting him to death. But has it been sufficiently considered what sort of a mercy this is, and what kind of life it leaves to him? If, indeed, the punishment is not really inflicted — if it becomes the sham which a

Reprinted from Hansard's Parliamentary Debates, *3rd Series, 21 April 1868 (London, 1868).*

few years ago such punishments were rapidly becoming — then, indeed, its adoption would be almost tantamount to giving up the attempt to repress murder altogether. But if it really is what it professes to be, and if it is realized in all its rigour by the popular imagination, as it very probably would not be, but as it must be if it is to be efficacious, it will be so shocking that when the memory of the crime is no longer fresh, there will be almost insuperable difficulty in executing it. What comparison can there really be, in point of severity, between consigning a man to the short pang of a rapid death, and immuring him in a living tomb, there to linger out what may be a long life in the hardest and most monotonous toil, without any of its alleviations or rewards — debarred from all pleasant sights and sounds, and cut off from all earthly hope, except a slight mitigation of bodily restraint, or a small improvement of diet? Yet even such a lot as this, because there is no one moment at which the suffering is of terrifying intensity, and, above all, because it does not contain the element, so imposing to the imagination, of the unknown, is universally reputed a milder punishment than death — stands in all codes as a mitigation of the capital penalty, and is thankfully accepted as such. For it is characteristic of all punishments which depend on duration for their efficacy — all, therefore, which are not corporal or pecuniary — that they are more rigorous than they seem; while it is, on the contrary, one of the strongest recommendations a punishment can have, that it should seem more rigorous than it is; for its practical power depends far less on what it is than on what it seems. There is not, I should think, any human infliction which makes an impression on the imagination so entirely out of proportion to its real severity as the punishment of death. The punishment must be mild indeed which does not add more to the sum of human misery than is necessarily or directly added by the execution of a criminal. As my hon. Friend the Member for Northampton (Mr Gilpin) has himself remarked, the most that human laws can do to anyone in the matter of death is to hasten it; the man would have died at any rate; not so very much later, and on the average, I fear, with a considerably greater amount of bodily suffering. Society is asked, then, to denude itself of an instrument of punishment which, in the grave cases to which alone it is suitable, effects its purposes at a less cost of human suffering than any other; which, while it inspires more terror, is less cruel in actual fact than any punishment that we should think of substituting for it. My hon. Friend says that it does not inspire terror, and that experience proves it to be a failure. But the influence of a punishment is not to be estimated by its effect on hardened criminals. Those whose habitual way of life keeps them, so to speak, at all times within sight of the gallows, do grow to care less about it; as, to compare good things with bad, an old soldier is not much affected by the chance of dying in battle. I can afford to admit all that is often said about the indifference of professional criminals to the gallows. Though of that indifference one-third is probably bravado and another third confidence that they shall have the luck to escape, it is quite probable that the remaining third is real. But the efficacy of a punishment which acts principally through the imagination, is chiefly to be measured by the impression it makes on those who are still innocent; by the horror with which it surrounds the first promptings of guilt; the restraining influence it exercises over the beginning of the thought which, if indulged, would become a temptation; the check which it exerts over the graded declension towards the state — never suddenly attained — in which crime no longer revolts, and punishment no longer terrifies. As for what is called the failure of death punishment, who is able to judge of that? We partly know who those are whom it has not deterred; but who is there who knows whom it has deterred, or how many human beings it has saved who would have lived to be murderers if that awful association had not been thrown round the idea of murder from their earliest infancy? Let us not forget that the most imposing fact loses its power over the imagination if it is made too cheap. When a punishment fit only for the most atrocious crimes is lavished on small offences until human feeling recoils from it, then, indeed, it ceases to intimidate, because it ceases to be believed in. The failure of capital punishment in cases of theft is easily accounted for; the thief did not believe that it would be inflicted. He had learnt by experience that jurors would perjure themselves rather than find him guilty; that Judges would seize any excuse for not sentencing him to death, or for recommending him to mercy; and that if neither jurors nor Judges were merciful, there were still hopes from an authority above both. When things had come to this pass it was high time to give up the vain attempt. When it is impossible to inflict a punishment, or when its infliction becomes a public scandal, the idle threat cannot too soon disappear from the statute book. And in the case of the host of offences which were formerly capital, I heartily rejoice that it did become impracticable to execute the law. If the same state of public feeling comes to exist in the case of murder; if the time comes when jurors refuse to find a murderer guilty; when Judges will not sentence him to death, or will recommend him to mercy; or when, if juries and Judges do not flinch from their duty, Home Secretaries, under pressure of deputations and memorials, shrink from theirs, and the threat becomes, as it became in the other cases, a mere *brutum fulmen*; then, indeed, it may become necessary to do in this case what has been done in those — to abrogate the penalty. That time may come — my hon. Friend thinks that it has nearly come. I hardly know whether he lamented it or boasted of it; but he and his Friends are entitled to the boast; for if it comes it will be their doing, and they will have gained what I cannot but call a fatal victory, for they will have achieved it by bringing about, if they will forgive me for saying so, an enervation, an effeminancy, in the general mind of the country. For what else than effeminancy is it to be so much more shocked by taking a man's life than by depriving him of all that makes life desirable or valuable? Is death, then, the greatest of all earthly ills? *Usque adeone mori miserum est?* Is it, indeed, so dreadful a thing to die? Has it not been from of old one chief part of a manly education to make us despise death — teaching us to account it, if an evil at all, by no means high in the list of evils; at all events, as an inevitable one, and to hold, as it were, our lives in our hands, ready to be given or risked at any moment, for a sufficiently worthy object? I am sure that my hon. Friends know all this as well, and have as much of all these feelings as any of the rest of us; possibly more. But I cannot think that this is likely to be the effect of their teaching on the general mind. I cannot think that the cultivating of a peculiar sensitiveness of conscience on this one point, over and above what results from the general cultivation of the moral sentiments, is permanently consistent with assigning in our own minds to the fact of death no more than the degree of relative importance which belongs to it among the other incidents of our humanity. The men of old cared too little about death, and gave their own lives or took those of others with equal recklessness. Our danger is of the opposite kind, lest we should be so much shocked by death, in general and in the abstract, as to care too much about it in individual cases, both those of other people and our own, which call for its being risked. And I am not putting things at the worst, for it is proved by the experience of other countries that horror of the executioner by no means necessarily implies horror of the assassin. The stronghold, as we all know, of hired assassination in the 18th century was Italy; yet it is said that in some of the Italian populations the infliction of death by sentence of law was in the highest degree offensive and revolting to popular feeling. Much has been said of the sanctity of human life, and the absurdity of supposing that we can teach respect for life by ourselves destroying it. But I am surprised at the employment of this argument, for it is one which might be brought against any punishment whatever. It is not human life only, not human life as such, that ought to be sacred to us, but human feelings. The human capacity of suffering is what we should cause to be respected, not the mere capacity of existing. And we may imagine somebody asking how we can teach people not to inflict suffering by ourselves inflicting it? But to this I should answer — all of us would answer — that to deter by suffering from inflicting suffering is not only possible, but the very purpose of penal justice. Does fining a criminal show want of respect for property, or imprisoning him, for personal freedom? Just as unreasonable is it to think that to take the life of a man who has taken that of another is to show want of regard for human life. We show, on the contrary, most emphatically our regard for it, by the adoption of a rule that he who violates that right in another forfeits it for himself, and that while no other crime that he can commit deprives him of his right to live, this shall. There is one argument against capital punishment, even in extreme cases, which I cannot deny to have weight — on which my hon. Friend justly laid great stress, and which never can be entirely got rid of. It is this — that if by an error of justice an innocent person is put to death, the mistake can never be corrected; all compensation, all reparation for the wrong is impossible. This would be indeed a serious objection if these miserable mistakes — among the most tragical occurrences in the whole round of human affairs — could not be made extremely rare. The argument is invincible where the mode of criminal procedure is dangerous to the innocent, or where the Courts of Justice are not trusted. And this probably is the reason why the objection to an irreparable punishment began (as I believe it did) earlier, and is more intense and more widely diffused, in some parts of the Continent of Europe than it is here. There are on the Continent great and enlightened countries, in which the criminal procedure is not so favourable to innocence, does not afford the same security against erroneous conviction, as it does among us; countries where the Courts of Justice seem to think they fail in their duty unless they find somebody guilty; and in their really laudable desire to hunt guilt from its hiding places, expose themselves to a serious danger of condemning the innocent. If our own procedure and Courts of Justice afforded ground for similar apprehension, I should be the first to join in withdrawing the power of inflicting irreparable punishment from such tribunals. But we all know that the defects of our procedure are the very opposite. Our rules of evidence are even too favourable to the prisoner; and juries and Judges carry out the maxim, 'It is better that ten guilty should escape than that one innocent person should suffer', not only to the letter, but beyond the letter. Judges are most anxious to point out, and juries to allow for, the barest possibility of the prisoner's innocence. No human judgement is infallible; such sad cases as my hon. Friend cited will sometimes occur; but in so grave a case as that of murder, the accused, in our system, has always the benefit of the merest shadow of a doubt. And this suggests another consideration very germane to the question. The very fact that death punishment is more shocking than any other to the imagination, necessarily renders the Courts of Justice more scrupulous in requiring the fullest evidence of guilt. Even that which is the greatest objection to capital punishment, the impossibility of correcting an error once committed, must make, and does make, juries and Judges more careful in forming their opinion, and more jealous in their scrutiny of the evidence. If the substitution of penal servitude for death in cases of murder should cause any declaration in this conscientious scrupulosity, there would be a great evil to set against the real, but I hope rare, advantage of being able to make reparation to a condemned person who was afterwards discovered to be innocent. In order that the possibility of correction may be kept open wherever the chance of this sad contingency is more than infinitesimal, it is quite right that the Judge should recommend to the Crown a commutation of the sentence, not solely when the proof of guilt is open to the smallest suspicion, but whenever there remains anything unexplained and mysterious in the case, raising a desire for more light, or making it likely that further information may at some future time be obtained. I would also suggest that whenever the sentence is commuted the grounds of the commutation should, in some authentic form, be made known to the public. Thus much I willingly concede to my hon. Friend; but on the question of total abolition I am inclined to hope that the feeling of the country is not with him, and that the limitation of death punishment to the cases referred to in the Bill of last year will be generally considered sufficient. The mania which existed a short time ago for paring down all our punishments seems to have reached its limits, and not before it was time. We were in danger of being left without any effectual punishment, except for small offences. What was formerly our chief secondary punishment — transportation — before it was abolished, had become almost a reward. Penal servitude, the substitute for it, was becoming, to the classes who were principally subject to it, almost nominal, so comfortable did we make our prisons, and so easy had it become to get quickly out of them. Flogging — a most objectionable punishment in ordinary cases, but a particularly appropriate ones for crimes of brutality, especially crimes against women — we would not hear of, except, to be sure, in the case of garrotters, for whose peculiar benefit we re-established it in a hurry, immediately after a Member of Parliament had been garrotted. With this exception, offences, even of an atrocious kind, against the person, as my hon. and learned Friend the Member for Oxford (Mr Neate) well remarked, not only were, but still are, visited with penalties so ludicrously inadequate, as to be almost an encouragement to the crime. I think, Sir, that in the case of most offences, except those against property, there is more need of strengthening our punishments than of weakening them; and that severer sentences, with an apportionment of them to the different kinds of offences which shall approve itself better than at present to the moral sentiments of the community, are the kind of reform of which our penal system now stands in need. I shall therefore vote against the Amendment.

QUESTIONS

1. Mill argues that capital punishment is "the least cruel mode in which it is possible adequately to deter from the crime" of murder. What support does he offer for this view? What would he say to the author of the dissenting opinion in *Kindler v. Canada*?
2. Does it matter to Mill that capital punishment may not be a unique deterrent? How does his position differ from that of Fattah in this regard?
3. How does Mill respond to the argument that capital punishment should be abolished since it is a punishment that cannot be corrected once administered should a court reach an incorrect verdict of guilt?
4. Mill voices a view which is commonly heard today; namely, that the penalties in place for dealing with crime, particularly violent crime, are too lenient. Is John Howard of the Ontario *Report on Violent Crime* relevant here?

IS CAPITAL PUNISHMENT A UNIQUE DETERRENT?

Ezzat A. Fattah

The Deterrence Argument: Why Is It Popular?

Retributive, religious and philosophical arguments in support of the death penalty have lost favour with many of its advocates. The radical change in penal philosophy that took place in the second half of the twentieth century was bound to bring about a change in retentionists' rhetoric and strategy. At a time when correctional philosophy was dominated by the rehabilitative ideal and when correctional efforts were geared towards treatment and change, it was no longer fashionable to advocate the principles of Talion Law and to claim a life for a life, an eye for an eye and a tooth for a tooth. Advocates of the death penalty chose to focus instead on its presumed preventive effects and protective functions. Gradually, the deterrent effect of capital punishment became the focal point in arguments to support its retention or its reintroduction and continues to be presented by its supporters as the indisputable justification for the State's deliberate taking of human life. This change in focus that characterized death penalty debates of recent years is understandable. The deterrence argument is, in many respects, an attractive one:

Firstly, deterrence makes sense. It is common knowledge that people are afraid of death and will do everything they can to avoid it. The threat of execution is, therefore, likely to deter them from committing the criminal offences carrying the death penalty. In fact, the logic of the deterrence argument is impeccable. After all, what can be more obvious than the assumption that people cherish life above everything else and will not willingly and deliberately put it in peril? Common sensical views, however, are not always correct. And if we are to justify the retention of the death penalty solely, or mainly, on grounds of its preventive effects, its supporters will have to come up with a more solid and convincing proof than mere conventional wisdom.

Secondly, the deterrence argument is more civilized than arguments based on revenge and retribution. Retaliation and expiation are no longer acceptable as the ultimate goals of criminal sanctions. Changes in philosophy are not always accompanied by changes in people's sentiments. Since vindictive, retributive feelings continue to exist it is only appropriate to cloak them in rational arguments such as deterrence and protection of society. The deterrence argument thus serves to disguise the primitive desire to see the murderer pay for his crime with his life. As Hanz Zeisel puts it:

> It is the belief in retributive justice that makes the death penalty attractive, especially when clothed in a functional rationalization.[52]

Thirdly, the deterrence argument provides a utilitarian rationale for the shedding of blood since this is supposedly indispensable for saving innocent lives.

The superiority of the deterrence argument to others advanced in support of the death penalty was reaffirmed by the Subcommittee on Moral Arguments For and Against the Death Penalty. The Subcommittee stated that:

From the Canadian Journal of Criminology, *vol. 23, no. 3 (July 1981). Reprinted by permission of the Canadian Criminal Justice Association.*

The only moral ground on which the State could conceivably possess the right to destroy human life would be if this were indispensable for the protection or preservation of other lives. This places the burden of proof on those who believe that capital punishment exercises a deterrent effect on the potential criminal. Unless they can establish that the death penalty does, in fact, protect other lives, at the expense of one, there is no moral justification for the State to take life.[48]

Not only did the Subcommittee proclaim deterrence as the only legitimate justification for the death penalty, but it also squarely placed the burden of proof on the shoulders of the retentionists.

Is Capital Punishment a Unique Deterrent?

Discussions around the deterrent effect of capital punishment usually center on a wrong question. The question to be asked is not whether the death penalty deters would-be murderers, but whether it deters them more than the prospect of life imprisonment. The question is not whether the death penalty has a deterrent effect but whether it provides a unique and supreme deterrent, whether it is the most powerful and most effective of all deterrents. It seems obvious that the death penalty cannot be justified on grounds of its deterring function alone unless and until it has been proved beyond a reasonable doubt that it supplies an additional increment of deterrence above and beyond the alternative which, in most jurisdictions, is life imprisonment. Has such a unique deterrent effect been unequivocally proven? The answer to this question is no.

Early deterrence research failed to show any relationship between the abolition or reinstatement of the death penalty and homicide rates. Despite the fact that several different studies reached the same conclusion, namely that the death penalty has no noticeable effect on the rates of homicide, these studies were dismissed by retentionists as "extremely primitive statistically" and as having been done by "not very good statisticians." Retentionists, on the other hand, were quick to hail the one study that reached an opposite conclusion, namely the now famous Ehrlich study.[14] They either failed to detect the flaws in Ehrlich's data and methodology or simply decided to ignore whatever defects the study suffered from.

Empirical Tests of the Deterrence Hypothesis

Scholars who tried to assess the preventive functions of the death penalty used various methods to test the deterrence hypothesis. And proponents and opponents of the death penalty used various types of evidence to support or to challenge its unique deterrent effect. This evidence may be divided into two main categories: anecdotal stories and statistical findings.

Anecdotal Stories

Proponents of the death penalty usually argue that almost every prisoner under sentence of death seeks a reprieve and welcomes it when it comes. This is seen as evidence that men fear death more than anything else and far more than life imprisonment. It seems fallacious to assume from the terror of death experienced and manifested by an individual on death row that the same fear was operative in his mind at the time of the crime. This argument overlooks one indisputable fact: the difference between a potential and remote danger and one that is imminent and seemingly inevitable. In Sellin's words:

> Surely a murderer for whom a possible death penalty had proved to be no deterrent, would be considered abnormal were he not to make every effort to escape death after being discovered and sentenced to die.[41]

Another fact this argument overlooks is that the murderer on death row who is showing extreme fear and terror in face of execution has not been deterred by the threat of death in the first place. It seems illogical to use the words or the psychological state of those who were not deterred by the death penalty to prove this penalty's unique deterrent effect!

Proponents of the death penalty also cite real-life stories of criminals who have told the police that they refrained from killing the victim or from shooting at the pursuing police officer to avoid being put to death. For example, the Los Angeles Police Department reported to a California Senate Committee considering the abolition of the death penalty[47] that during the course of one year, 13 robbery suspects had told the police that they used unloaded or simulated guns "rather than take a chance on killing someone and getting the gas chamber." The unreliability of such anecdotal evidence is too obvious and for every story alleging that the fear of the death penalty has acted as a deterrent there are ten others alleging that it has not. Clinton Duffy, former warden of San Quentin prison, asked thousands of prisoners convicted of homicide or armed robbery whether they had thought of the death penalty before their act. Not one had!

Among the most frequently quoted stories to deny the deterrent effect of capital punishment are those of the English pickpockets who actively plied their trade in the shadow of the gallows from which their fellow knaves were strung. Another often cited story is the one of an Ohio convict named Charlie Justice who devised the clamps that held the condemned man in the electric chair. After his release, he was convicted of murder and electrocuted. A similar fate befell Alfred Wells, who helped install San Quentin's gas chamber in 1938. It was his conversational cachet around the prison yard, usually with the moral: "That's the closest I ever want to come. . . ." Four years later, back at San Quentin for a triple killing, he was sealed in the chamber to die.

Needless to say that arguments and claims based on this kind of anecdotal evidence tend to neutralize each other and are of little help in settling the basic factual question whether or not the death penalty is a unique deterrent.

Statistical Evidence

Earlier studies on the preventive functions of the death penalty tried to ascertain its deterrent effect in five different ways:

a. examining the effect of a declining rate of executions on criminal homicide rates;
b. comparing homicide rates within countries and/or states before and after they abolished or restored the death penalty;
c. comparing homicide rates between adjacent and apparently congruent states with and without the death penalty;
d. ascertaining whether law-enforcement officers and prison guards were safer from murderous attacks in states with the death penalty than in those without it; and

e. examining homicide trends in cities where executions were carried out and were presumed to have been widely publicized.

The Effect of a Declining Rate of Executions on Homicide Rates. If capital punishment is as its supporters claim, a unique deterrent to murder, then a declining use of it reflected in a decreasing rate of executions (which necessarily means an improved chance of escaping it) should be accompanied or followed by an increase in the murder rate. Yet statistics available from many countries, and particularly from the United States, tend to show that this is not the case. These statistics indicate, in fact, that murder rates have either remained constant or declined despite trends away from the use of capital punishment.

Chambliss[12] compared the number of prisoners executed under civil authority and murder rate from 1951 to 1966 in the United States and found that the substantial decline in executions has not been accompanied by any significant change in the murder rate.

Another study carried out in Ohio[49] tested the relationship between execution rates and homicide rates. Both rates for the entire state for a half-century (1909–1959) were computed. The statistical correlation did not indicate that homicides have increased as executions have decreased, or the reverse. Any correlation between the two rates seemed to be direct rather than inverse, indicating only that homicide rates and execution rates have risen and fallen together. The researchers concluded that the statistical analysis of Ohio execution and homicide rates over the fifty-year period revealed no evidence that executions have any discernible effect on homicide rates.

A third study conducted in Australia by Barber and Wilson[5] similarly revealed that the relationship between execution and murder rates tends to be a positive rather than a negative one. It was found that the State of Queensland has had a higher execution rate than the other Australian states over a longer period of time (1860–1915) and that the murder rate in that state during the pre-abeyance period (1901–1914) was also considerably greater than in New South Wales and South Australia. Barber and Wilson concluded that:

> The apparently disproportionately high frequency of executions in Queensland during this period would not, then, seem to have had a very great deterrent effect on potential murderers in Queensland. Indeed the evidence is more supportive of Sir Samuel Romilly's contention that brutal punishments accustom people to brutality, and tend to create attitudes conducive to the commission of violent crimes.

The Effect of Repeal and Reintroduction of Capital Punishment on Homicide Rates. The experience of those European countries which abolished the death penalty in the nineteenth or early twentieth century and for whom statistics are available shows that the abolition was followed by a decrease rather than an increase in homicide rates. But it is the experience of those countries which more recently repealed capital punishment statutes that is really worth mentioning.

Morris and Blom-Cooper evaluated the British experience and reported their findings in an article published by the *Observer*, in 1979. The authors analyzed murder statistics in England and Wales since 1957 when hanging was partially abolished and concluded that the abolition has had no visible effect on the murder rate in Britain:

> One aspect stands out starkly. The penalty of the crime of murder has no discernible influence on the rate at which murder is committed.[26]

Following the suspension of the death penalty in Canada in 1967 for a trial period of five years I conducted a study[15] in which I attempted to assess the impact this suspension has had on homicide rates. The study clearly showed that the statistical increase in criminal homicide in Canada could in no way be attributed to the suspension of the death penalty. The large differences in homicide rates among the Canadian provinces suggested that the rates are conditioned by factors other than the death penalty. They confirmed what criminologists have held for a long time namely that the causes of criminal homicide are not related to any single factor but to a total social situation in which a special law or a particular punishment can have little or no effect.

The effect of reinstating capital punishment on criminal homicide rates has been thoroughly researched by Professor Sellin. He examined and analyzed statistics for eleven American states that experimented with abolition for periods of time varying in duration. Here is the conclusion he reached:

> If any conclusion can be drawn from all the above data, it is that there is no evidence that the abolition of the death penalty generally causes an increase in criminal homicides or that its reintroduction is followed by a decline. The explanation of changes in homicide rates must be sought elsewhere.[37]

Professor Sellin's conclusion is almost identical to the one reached by the British Royal Commission on Capital Punishment (1949–1953):

> The general conclusion which we have reached is that there is no clear evidence in any of the figures we have examined that the abolition of capital punishment had led to an increase in the homicide rate or that its reintroduction has led to a fall.[46]

Comparisons of Homicide Rates in States With and Without Death Penalty. Professor Sellin[35,40] compared homicide rates for states with similar outlook in the United States. He selected five sets of three states each and compared their crude homicide death rates. The comparisons covered a 43-year span for each set of states, extending from 1920 to 1963. In each set, at least one of the three states did not provide the death penalty for all or a part of the period while the others did provide it. Each of the three states in each set borders one or both of the other two. The figures showed clearly that homicide death rates in all the states have followed the same trends, whether or not the death penalty was provided. In all of the 15 states covered by the comparisons, homicide death rates reached peaks in the 1920s and early 1930s, then followed a general downward trend, leveled out in the 1940s and continued through 1960 at about that level. Comparison of trends and rates revealed no differences among adjacent states with and without the death penalty which can be ascribed to either its presence or absence. Professor Sellin found that:

1. the level of rates is not the same in all regions;
2. within each group of contiguous states it would be impossible to identify the abolitionist state, were it not designated as such; and
3. the trends of the rates of the states compared are similar.

The inevitable conclusion, therefore, is that the presence of the death penalty, either in law or practice, does not influence homicide death rates. As Professor Sellin puts it:

The important thing to be noticed is that, whether the death penalty is used or not, or whether executions are frequent or not, both death penalty States and abolition States show rates which suggest that these rates are conditioned by other factors than the death penalty.

Comparisons of Risks to Law Enforcement Officers in States With and Without the Death Penalty. Proponents of the death penalty claim that it provides superior protection to law-enforcement officers and prison guards whose job, it is argued, would become more difficult and more hazardous if it were abolished. Since the 1950s the truth of this assumption has been subjected to several tests.

In 1956 Father Donald Campion published a study of 24 American police forces, 18 of which represented death-penalty states and six of which represented abolition states. The study covered a fifty-year period from 1905 to 1954 and took many factors into account, such as the varying size of the police forces and the populations they served. Father Campion concluded that the data

> do not lend empirical support to the claim that the existence of the death penalty in the statutes of a State provides a greater protection to the police than exists in States where the penalty has been abolished."[10]

Professor Sellin[36,38] did an extensive study of police homicide rates over a 25-year period. He examined the rates for 183 cities in eleven capital-punishment states and for eighty-two cities in six abolition states. The general results of the study demonstrated that between the years 1919 and 1954 the cities in death-penalty states had a police homicide rate of 1.3 per 100,000 population, while the cities in abolition states had a police homicide rate of only 1.2 per 100,000 population. Commenting on his findings Professor Sellin writes:

> It is obvious from an inspection of the data that it is impossible to conclude that the States which had no death penalty had thereby made the policeman's lot more hazardous. It is also obvious that the same differences observable in the general homicide rates of the various States were reflected in the rates of police killings.

Sellin concluded further that:

> The claim that if data could be secured they would show that more police are killed in abolition States than in capital punishment States is unfounded. On the whole, the abolition States, as is apparent from the findings of this particular investigation, seem to have fewer police killings but the differences are small. If this, then, is the argument upon which the police are willing to rest their opposition to the abolition of capital punishment, it must be concluded that it lacks any factual basis.

Some years later, Professor Sellin[38], using statistics of policemen killed in the U.S.A. by offenders or suspects during 1961–1963 (140 policemen) and using as a base the number of police in the 15 states where the killing occurred according to the 1960 census, found that the annual average risk for the three years was 1.312 per 10,000 police in abolition states and 1.328 in the bordering states. There was, then, no significant difference.

Cardarelli[11], analyzing the same data (police killed by criminal action from 1961–1963) came to the conclusion that data "lend no weight to the argument that the death penalty states afford more protection."

Robin[30, 31] found that in any given year the policemen in the U.S.A. are approximately six times more likely to kill than to be killed in the course of their duty; at the same time the probability of either event occurring is very small.

More recently, Professor Sellin[41] did yet another study of police killings in abolitionist and retentionist states based on data published in 1975 in the FBI annual report. His conclusion did not differ from his earlier ones:

> Not only did the police in retentionist States run a greater risk of being feloniously killed, but so did the slayers and suspects involved in these homicides. . . .
>
> The data presented in these pages permit only one conclusion, namely that the belief of the police that in order to be safer in their occupation they need laws that threaten potential murders with death has no factual basis. Indeed, it is evident that the police are more efficient executioners than the public hangman and should inspire more fear than any capital law could do if deterrence were operative.

Studies by Morris,[25] Sellin[29], Akman[4] and Buffum[8] clearly show that the hazards involved in prison life are not increased by the abolition of the death penalty. Neither does such abolition result in an increase in homicidal or assaultive behaviour in those penal institutions where convicted murderers are detained. Moreover, it is obvious that those who present the greatest danger are insane murderers. Yet, these murderers are by definition excluded from the possible infliction of the death penalty and nobody is calling for their execution as a way of protecting the staff or the patients in the psychiatric institutions in which they are usually held.

Examining Homicide Trends Following Widely Publicized Executions. In 1935 Dann[13] conducted a study to assess the impact of publicity of executions on deterrence. He hypothesized that if the death penalty is a deterrent, its greatest effect should be shown through executions which are well publicized. Furthermore, the effect should be more noticeable in the community where the offence occurred, where the trial aroused wide publicity and the offender lived and had relatives, friends and acquaintances. To test the hypothesis, Dann compiled the dates of executions of Philadelphia residents for a period of several years and was able to find five cases that met the study's specifications. Three of the five cases were of great notoriety. The study found no significant difference in homicide rates for equal periods before and after the execution. There was a total of 105 days free from homicides during the 60-day periods before the executions and 74 in the periods after the executions. There were a total of 91 homicides in the "before the execution" periods and 113 in the "after" periods. Of the 204 homicides included in the study 19 resulted in sentences for murder in the first degree. Nine of them had occurred during the 60-day periods preceding and ten in the corresponding periods following the executions. During the ten days just before the executions there were two, and during the ten days immediately following there were three such first-degree murders in Philadelphia.

Another study was undertaken, also in Philadelphia, by Savitz.[32] After examining homicide trends before and after four widely publicized trials during the 1940s, Savitz concluded that no pattern emerges that would indicate deterrence and that the assumption that the deterrent effect of the imposition of the death penalty might be felt shortly after the date of sentencing is not borne out by the data. He further concluded that on the basis of the data "there was no significant decrease or increase in the murder rate following the imposition of the death penalty on four separate occasions."

Recently, Phillips[19] examined weekly murder statistics for the city of London, England for the period 1858–1921 and came to the conclusion that the homicide rate drops during the week of a highly publicized execution and during the following week then it begins rising again.

> Within five or six weeks of a publicized execution, the drop in homicides is cancelled by an equally large rise in homicides.

Phillips' results were in contrast to those of Bowers and Pierce[7] who used monthly rather than weekly murder rates. They found an increase of two murders during the month following a highly publicized execution.

Isaac Ehrlich's Study and Its Replications

Until 1975, researchers analyzing murder or criminal homicide statistics were unanimous in their conclusion: they found no empirical evidence to support the presumed unique deterrent effect of the death penalty and could discern no visible effect this penalty has on the rates of homicide. But in 1975 a study reporting an opposite conclusion was published.[14] The study was done by I. Ehrlich, an economist at the University of Chicago. Ehrlich used a set of assumptions to construct an econometric model, employed aggregate data and claimed to have found evidence that a capital execution would indeed deter some potential killers and perhaps save as many as eight lives:

> Empirical analysis suggests that on average the trade-off between the execution of an offender and the lives of potential victims it might have saved was of the order of magnitude of one for eight for the period 1933–1967 in the U.S.A.

Not only was Ehrlich's claim at odds with the findings of all studies done in the U.S. and elsewhere but it was the first time ever a researcher has claimed to have been able to estimate the number of murders prevented by each execution. Ehrlich's findings received a great deal of publicity and were circulated widely by many police forces in the U.S.A. and Canada. More important still was their presentation as evidence in support of the death penalty before U.S. courts. Until then the deterrence debate was largely an academic one and was rarely used in the courtroom. But in 1976 statistical evidence in support of the deterrence hypothesis was submitted to the U.S. Supreme Court in Fowler vs. North Carolina (428 U.S. 904, 1976). It was in this case that the Solicitor-General submitted to the court an *amicus curiae* brief citing Ehrlich's conclusion that capital punishment deters murder. And in another case, Gregg vs. Georgia (428 U.S. 153, 169, 1976), the Supreme Court ruled that "the punishment of death does not invariably violate the constitution" and added that for many murderers "the death penalty undoubtedly is a significant deterrent." One would have expected the Court to substantiate such claim with empirical evidence but the Court did not although such evidence was not totally ignored. The Court stated that although some of the studies suggest that the death penalty may not function as a significantly greater deterrent than less penalties, there is no convincing empirical evidence either supporting or refuting this view.[17] Zeisel[52] took issue with the Court's statement arguing that the evidence about the deterrent effect is, indeed, "quite sufficient" and that the request for more proof is but "the expression of an unwillingness to abandon an ancient prejudice."

Because of the nature of Ehrlich's claim and the publicity they received there were several replications of his study. The replications revealed fundamental weaknesses in his assumptions, his model and his analysis. His detractors claimed that his evidence of deterrence depends upon a restrictive assumption about the mathematical relationship between homicides and executions,[6,18,28] the inclusion of a particular set of observations, the use of a limited set of control variables and a peculiar construction of the execution rate, the key variable.

One important criticism of Ehrlich's study is his use of time-series data for 1933–1969 in which homicides and executions were aggregated for the entire U.S. The Panel of the National Academy of Science[50] pointed out that Ehrlich's findings were particularly sensitive to the time period included. This sensitivity was largely due to the fact that during 1962–1969, executions in the U.S. ceased while homicides increased though not more than did other crimes. When Bowers and Pierce[6] reproduced Ehrlich's analysis using data from slightly different periods, all beginning in 1935 but each ending in a different year in the 1960s, their findings were entirely different from those of Ehrlich. They concluded that:

> It becomes evident that the so-called deterrent effect of execution risk altogether disappears when the effective time period is foreshortened by dropping recent data points.

Another researcher, Passell,[27] used cross-sectional data in various states in the U.S. from the period 1950 and 1960. He also concluded that there was no reasonable way of interpreting the cross-sectional data that would lend support to the deterrence hypothesis.

A third researcher, Forst,[17] replicated Ehrlich's analysis while avoiding some of the major flaws that were identified in Ehrlich's research. For instance, he focused on a unique decade during which the homicide rate increased by over 50% and the use of the death penalty ceased. He examined, as well, changes in homicides and executions over time and across states. His findings did not support Ehrlich's claim that capital punishment deters homicides. His final conclusion:

> The results of this analysis suggest . . . that it is erroneous to view capital punishment as a means of reducing the homicide rate.

Probably the most detailed critique of Ehrlich's research was published in Canada.[21] Hahn is very conscious of the serious policy implications defective studies might have and is particularly perturbed by the great publicity Ehrlich's study received. His final comments contain both a warning and an advice:

> The techniques introduced by the economists may represent significant advances over those used in the past. These techniques and the behavioural models used by economists are, however, useless unless they are combined with sufficient, accurate and relevant data. Unfortunately, it will be many years before data of sufficient quality and quantity is available for undertaking research which is adequate for supporting deterrence policy.

Until that time, uncritical publicity of the earlier economic findings, publicity that has in the past bordered on the irresponsible, should cease. Economists like Ehrlich should also exercise more professional responsibility in undertaking and reporting what amounts to circumstantial results.

How Effective Is the Death Penalty as a Means of Prevention and Societal Protection?

The nature of the death penalty, its irrevocability, together with the safeguards necessary to avoid errors in its application are such that it can never become an effective means of crime prevention or of societal protection. This point will be illustrated through a discussion of three aspects related to the application of the death penalty.

Capital Punishment Is the Least Certain of All Punishments

More than two hundred years ago Beccaria noted that severity and certainty of punishment are hard to reconcile. In this he was referring to the inverse relationship that often exists between the two variables: the more severe the punishment, the less certain it is. The same point was well stated in what is known as the "Rejected Preamble" of Sir Samuel Romilly's Bill of 1808:

> Whereas the extreme severity of penal laws has not been found effectual for the prevention of crimes; but, on the contrary, by increasing the difficulty of convicting offenders, in some cases affords them immunity and in most cases renders their punishment extremely uncertain.

This rule applies to capital punishment more than to any other. In my study of the deterrent effect of capital punishment[15] I compiled data on charges and sentences for murder, manslaughter and for other violent offences in Canada during the period 1881–1967. The average yearly conviction rate for murder proved to be the lowest among all crimes of violence.

Capital Punishment Endangers Society by Preventing Convictions

Capital punishment is known to exercise an inhibitory effect on juries and judges in capital cases. Those who are familiar with the administration of justice know that retaining the death penalty, especially if it is made mandatory, reduces the likelihood that indicted offenders will be convicted. In this way, the menace of the death penalty tends more to protect the accused through intimidation of the jury than to protect society through the conviction of the murderer. In a democratic, fair system of justice it is doubtful that the death penalty can ever reach the certainty level necessary for it to operate effectively as a deterrent. This difficulty was outlined in the introduction to the British criminal statistics furnished by the Home Office.

> In consequence of the strong proof of guilt necessary for conviction of crimes punishable by death, the proportion of acquittals for murder is higher than for most other crimes, and an acquittal in such a case does not necessarily imply failure to detect the perpetrator of the crime.[44]

One of the paradoxes of the death penalty is that if it is made mandatory it results in a high acquittal rate and leads to many murderers being let free. If, on the other hand, it is made discretionary then its application becomes arbitrary, discriminatory and erratic.

The Paradoxical Nature of the Death Penalty

If capital punishment is really a unique deterrent then a scarce and sporadic use of it would undoubtedly weaken its deterrent value by reducing the possibility and the threat of execution. It is in this fact that the real paradox of capital punishment lies. If it is used lavishly it loses its horror, people become accustomed to it and are no longer affected or deterred by it; if it is rarely applied, then the probability of incurring it sinks to insignificance in the minds of potential offenders.[33] This led him to declare that "the death penalty probably can never be a deterrent. Its very life seems to depend on its rarity and therefore on its ineffectiveness as a deterrent."

Another paradox of the death penalty relates to the nature of the crimes for which it is provided. Where it is wanted and used, that is for crimes of violence and sex, it is not likely to be effective. Where it might be effective (such as for rational economic crimes) it is not wanted.

Why Capital Punishment Fails as a Deterrent

The belief, shared by many, in the effectiveness of the death penalty as a deterrent and in its uniqueness as a means of dissuasion can usually be traced to a lack of knowledge as to the penalty's applications, to an inadequate understanding of the nature of criminal homicide, to psychology of the killer and to a failure to realize that deterrence has its limits.

The Odds Against Incurring the Death Penalty

In his study of the death penalty in Canada, Topping made the following statement:

> It seems clear that there is an inverse relationship between severity of punishment and certainty of punishment, and that Canadians are suffering under a delusion when they assert that they know how to hang. The net result of the administration of justice in Canada as it relates to capital offences is that murder has become the least risky of any or all the offences which a citizen might choose to commit.[43]

In an attempt to assess the level of certainty of the death penalty in Canada and the odds against incurring it, I compiled statistics for the 80-year period from 1881 to 1960.[16] The 80 years were then divided into periods of five years each. The highest percentage of death sentences to charges (45.9%) was recorded in the period from 1931 to 1935 when a person charged with murder had approximately an even chance of being sentenced to death. The last period, 1956 to 1960, revealed a low percentage of death sentences (33%), the highest percentage of commutations (73%) and the lowest percentage of executions (23.8%). In other words, during that period, although capital punishment was still the mandatory penalty for murder, a person charged with murder had only one chance in three of being sentenced to death. Once sentenced to death, he had more than three chances out of four of escaping the death penalty. The chances of being executed during that period for a person accused with the capital offence of murder was eight in a hundred, a very low probability indeed. If the period is examined as a whole, we find that out of a total of 3,249 persons charged with murder, only 634 were actually executed. The percentage of executions to charges was 19.5 meaning that only one charge in five led to an execution, again a very weak probability.

Those who feel that the death penalty, despite the very low probability of incurring it, still provides an effective means of societal protection simply forget that the other risks the potential killer takes are far greater than the risk of legal execution. Comparisons between the rates of legal executions and the rates of offenders killed by the police, the intended victim or by some bystander during or after the crime, show that this latter risk is much higher than the former. If the potential killer is not deterred by the greater threat of being killed on the spot while committing his crime or while escaping could it be claimed that he would be deterred by the minor and remote threat of being legally executed? The fact is, the potential killer rarely contemplates the consequences of his acts, calculates the risk involved or makes a rational consideration of gain or loss.

To illustrate the differential risks to which the potential killer is exposed, Sellin[34,35] made the following calculations:

> During the period 1934–1954, in Chicago, for instance, policemen killed 69 and private citizens 261 criminals or suspects involved in homicide, or a total of 330. During the same period there were 45 persons executed for murder in the Cook County jail. In other words, there were nearly 8 times as many homicidal offenders killed unofficially, so to speak, as were those electrocuted. There were 5,132 murders and non-negligent manslaughters known to the police during those years. In connection with 6.45% of these homicides, a criminal or suspect met his death at the hands of police or citizens, while 0.88% were put to death in the electric chair.

The Impulsive and Pathological Character of Many Homicides

Paradoxically the crime for which the death penalty is most often provided and applied, namely murder, is one of the offences least likely to be deterred. It is universally recognized that homicide is most frequently an emotional and impulsive crime, rarely subject to control by reason of fear of consequences. In the majority of cases the crime is the result of a sudden impulse or a violent over-mastering passion. The high emotions and strong motivations involved are likely to preclude a careful consideration of consequences or to outweigh the threat of any punishment be it life imprisonment or even death. Quite often the victim is closely associated with the offender.

A large number of homicides are committed under the influence of alcohol, drugs, sexual stimulation or provocation with the thought of punishment hardly crossing the mind of the killer. Only a small percentage of all criminal homicides are truly thought out and premeditated. This small percentage is usually perpetrated by persons [so] convinced of their ability to escape detection as to rule out all thought of consequences. As Calvert[9] pointed out, one of the most common characteristics exhibited by the murderer who commits an apparently cold-blooded crime is an exaggerated sense of confidence in his ability to escape detection.

The Undeterrability of Many Potential Killers

The act of killing is quite commonly committed by mentally deranged or psychologically abnormal individuals under the spell of an obsession, an irresistible impulse or under the pressure of some unusual circumstances. Abnormal offenders, offenders suffering from mental illness, those reacting to provocation and those acting under the influence of alcohol or drugs commit their crimes while in a state of mind that does not enable them to foresee or to consider the consequences of their actions. The more savage, heinous and atrocious the crime is, the greater is the likelihood that the criminal will be declared not guilty by reason of insanity. Many of the cases cited in support of the death penalty or to justify its retention are cases to which the death penalty does not apply because of the insanity of the offender.

Another category of murderers comprises individuals who are actually attracted by the prospect of death. And still another type is attracted by the notoriety the principal actor in a murder trial gets. In such cases the death penalty is likely to act as an incentive rather than a deterrent. It might even exercise a morbid fascination.

Professional killers, or "hired guns" as they are sometimes called, often mentioned in discussions advocating the death penalty, consider punishment, be it death or otherwise, a professional risk in the same way a physician considers the risk of contamination or a race-driver the risk of a car crash. The great majority of these killers are adventurers who are not afraid of death; they are rather attracted by it in the same way mercenaries are attracted to the dangers of war.

As to terrorists and other political criminals, often singled out as a group to whom the death penalty should be applied, their fanaticism and dedication to their cause counteract and neutralize whatever legal threat is meant to deter them. Moreover, many of them do seek through their actions their own self-destruction, destruction which they view as the easiest and quickest way to the state of martyrdom [to which] they aspire.

Murderers' Indifference to Death

The death penalty cannot be an effective deterrent to those who are indifferent to death, are not afraid of it or those who have a conscious or unconscious desire to die. The large percentage of murderers who commit or attempt suicide fall into this category. Figures from some European countries show that one quarter to one half of murder cases are followed by the suspects' suicide.

According to West[51] something like half of the murders in England are followed by the suicide or attempted suicide of the aggressor.

Home Office researchers Gibson and Klein[19,20] report in their study of murder in England and Wales in the years 1952–1960 that about one third of all suspects in cases finally recorded as murder committed suicide. In over half of the murders known to have been committed by females, suicide followed the crime.

A Danish study by Siciliano[42] covering all homicides in Denmark over a period of 28 years reported that 42.2% of the Danish killers subsequently killed themselves and a further 9.6% made a serious suicidal attempt. The incidence of suicide was particularly high among female offenders with 63.9% killing themselves and 16.1% making serious suicidal attempts. Obviously none of these murders would have been prevented had the death penalty been in effect in Denmark during that period.

Another category of potential killers unlikely to be deterred by the prospect and threat of the death penalty are those who see the ultimate sentence as a way of achieving a death wish. In such cases capital punishment acts as a direct incentive to murder.

Abrahamsen[2,3] and Hurwitz[23] cite the epidemic of indirect suicides that took place in Norway and Denmark in the seventeenth and eighteenth centuries when depressed people committed murder in order to be put to death since they would not commit suicide for religious reasons. These cases were so frequent that a special law had to be passed excluding such individuals from the death penalty to stop this particular type of homicide. Several recent cases reported in the literature confirm that this form of indirect suicide by means of the death penalty still exists.

Man's Inability to Conceive of His Own Death

Two important factors that weaken to a considerable extent whatever deterrent effect the death penalty may have are the time dimension and man's inability to conceive of his own death. This latter phenomenon has been discussed and documented by many psychiatrists.

Modern life is full of hazards. But the dangers in every-day life do not stop people from going about their daily activities oblivious to the risks involved. This is made possible by this peculiar aspect of human psychology: the inability of man to conceive of his own death. It is this inability that explains why the risk of accidental death does not prevent people from driving or flying, auto-racers or bullfighters from competing, etc. It explains why the risk of death from lung cancer or from liver cirrhosis does not prevent people from smoking or drinking.

The British Select Committee on Capital Punishment noted that

> The mass of mankind put death in the far distance and push it into the doubtful future. Men peril it for trifling aims. Some are reckless of others, reckless of life itself. Be its consequences what they may, they will take them. Some dodge death and think they can evade all its penalties; and flatter themselves that, whatever the penalty, they will never be found out.[45]

The Remoteness of the Threat

For punishment to elicit the desired behavioural response from the potential killer it has to pose an immediate threat of unavoidable dire consequences. The threat the death penalty poses is both remote and improbable. It is well known that the threat of the most dire consequences can have little effect if the prospect is uncertain and distant in time. The threat of hell and damnation has not been effective in deterring people from sin and it would be too naive and too optimistic to expect the death penalty to deter them from crime. In both cases the effectiveness of the threat is greatly weakened by its remoteness and uncertainty. Even if potential killers were rational and careful calculators of gain and loss, as some assume they are, the remoteness of the threat would always tip the scale against the death penalty. As Honderich puts it

> . . . it is a truism that people do not choose between possible courses of action in a prudential way if the possible consequences of one course are distant in time and the consequences of the other immediate. A penalty is a distant possibility, the gain from an offence is usually immediate.[22]

Summary

1. If the death penalty is a unique deterrent to murder, then a declining use of it should be followed by an increase in murder rates. Yet statistics from many countries and

particularly from the United States show that murder rates have remained constant or declined despite trends away from the use of the death penalty.

2. The experience of European countries that abolished the death penalty in the nineteenth or early twentieth century shows that abolition was followed by a decrease rather than an increase in criminal homicides. Moreover, countries that recently abolished the death penalty (U.K., Canada) report that abolition has had no discernible influence on the rate at which murder is committed.

3. The reintroduction of the death penalty after it has been abolished for some or many years does not lead to a decline in homicide rates.

4. Comparisons of homicide rates in adjacent, congruent states with or without the death penalty clearly show that the presence or absence of capital punishment has no visible influence on homicide rates.

5. Comparisons of homicide rates in Canadian provinces suggest that such rates are not related to the penalty provided by law but to a total social situation in which a particular punishment can have little or no effect.

6. Comparisons of police killing in abolitionist and retentionist states in the U.S.A. do not lend empirical support to the assumption that law-enforcement officers are better protected when the death penalty is retained or that their occupational risks are increased by its abolition.

7. The abolition of the death penalty does not increase the hazards involved in prison life and does not result in an increase in homicidal or assaultive behaviour in those penal institutions where convicted murderers are detained.

8. Capital punishment tends to defeat its own purpose, that is protection of society, by increasing the number of acquittals in capital cases. Its presence especially when it is made mandatory, reduces the likelihood that indicted offenders will be convicted.

9. Comparisons of execution rates and rates of offenders killed by the police, the intended victim or others, during or immediately after the crime, reveal that this latter risk is much greater than the former. If death is a deterrent, potential killers should be more deterred by the risk of being killed than by the threat of legal execution.

10. In a system of a fair and democratic justice, the application of the death penalty can probably never attain the certainty and expediency levels necessary for it to operate as a deterrent.

11. If the death penalty is used lavishly it loses its horror, people become accustomed to it and are no longer affected or deterred by it. Conversely, if it is rarely applied, then the probability of incurring it sinks to insignificance in the minds of potential offenders.

12. The alleged deterrent effect of the death penalty is based on the assumption of free and rational choice. Yet the crime for which the death penalty is most frequently prescribed, that is criminal homicide, is mostly committed in circumstances that preclude the existence of free will or a rational consideration of the consequences.

13. The death penalty is not likely to be an effective deterrent for those who are unafraid of death, those seeking martyrdom, or those who have a conscious or unconscious wish to die.

14. For certain categories of potential offenders the death penalty may act as an incentive to murder and for certain personalities it has a morbid fascination and a pathological attraction.

15. The deterrent effect of the death penalty is considerably weakened by the remoteness and uncertainty of the threat it presents and by man's inability to conceive of his own death.

NOTES

1. Revised version of a paper presented at the VI UN Congress on the Prevention of Crime and the Treatment of Offenders — Session on Capital Punishment Organized by Amnesty International, Tuesday, August 26, 1980.
2. Abrahamsen, D. *Crime and the Human Mind.* New York: Columbia University Press, 1944.
3. Abrahamsen, D. "The Dynamic Connection between Personality and Crime, and the Detection of the Potential Criminal, Illustrated by Different Types of Murder." *Journal of Criminal Psychology.* 5:481–488. 1944.
4. Akman, D.P. "Homicides and Assaults in Canadian Penitentiaries." *Canadian J. of Corrections.* Pp. 284–299. 1966.
5. Barber, R.N. and Wilson, P.R. "Deterrent Aspect of Capital Punishment and Its Effect on Conviction Rates: The Queensland Experience." *Australian and New Zealand Journal of Criminology.* 1:2, 100–108. 1968.
6. Bowers, W. and Pierce, G. "The Illusion of Deterrence in Isaac Ehrlich's Research on Capital Punishment." *Yale Law Journal,* 85, pp. 187–208, 1975.
7. Bowers, W. and Pierce, G. Research on Publicity of Executions and Homicide Rates. Reported by Associated Press, Monday, October 6, 1980.
8. Buffum, P.C., "Prison Killings and Death Penalty Legislation." *Prison Journal.* Pp. 49–57. 1976.
9. Calvert, R. *Capital Punishment in the Twentieth Century.* London and New York: G.P. Putnam's Sons. 1927.
10. Campion, D. "The State Police and the Death Penalty." *Congressional Record.* March 6, 1956, A2076–2080. Also in Appendix F of *Minutes of the Proceedings and Evidence.* No. 22. Joint Committee of the Senate and the House of Commons on Capital Punishment. Ottawa: Queen's Printer.
11. Cardarelli, A.P. "An Analysis of Police Killed by Criminal Action: 1961–1963." *Journal of Criminal Law, Criminology and Police Science.* 59:3, pp. 447–453. 1968.
12. Chambliss, W.J. "The Deterrent Influence of Punishment." *Crime and Delinquency.* 12:1, 70–75. 1966.
13. Dann. R.H. "The Deterrent Effect of Capital Punishment." *Friend's Social Service Series Bulletin.* 29, March. 1935.
14. Ehrlich, I. "The Deterrent Effect of Capital Punishment: A Question of Life and Death." *American Economic Review.* 65, pp. 397–417. 1975.
15. Fattah. E.A. *A Study of the Deterrent Effect of Capital Punishment with Particular Reference to the Canadian Situation.* Ottawa: Information Canada. 1972.
16. Fattah, E.A. "Sentencing to Death: The Inherent Problem." In B. Grosman (ed.). *New Directions in Sentencing.* Pp. 157–193. Toronto: Butterworths. 1980.
17. Forst, B.E. "The Deterrent Effect of Capital Punishment: A Cross-state Analysis of the 1960's." *Minnesota Law Review.* 61, p. 764. 1977.
18. Forst, B., Filatov, V. and Klein, L.R. "The Deterrent Effect of Capital Punishment: An Assessment of the Estimates." In A. Blumstein, J. Cohen and D. Nagin (eds.). *Deterrence and Incapacitation: Estimating the Effects of Criminal Sanctions on Crime Rates.* Pp. 336–360. Washington, D.C.: National Academy of Sciences. 1978.
19. Gibson, E. and Klein, S. *Murder: A Home Office Research Unit Report.* London: H.M.S.O. 1961.
20. Gibson, E. and Klein, S. *Murder 1957 to 1968: A Home Office Statistical Division Report on Murder in England and Wales.* London: H.M.S.O. 1969.
21. Hahn, R.G. *Deterrence and the Death Penalty: A critical Review of the Research of Isaac Ehrlich.* Ottawa: Ministry of Supply and Services. 1977.
22. Honderich, T. *Punishment: The Supposed Justification.* London: Pelican Books. 1971.
23. Hurwitz, S. *Criminology.* London: George Allen and Unwin Ltd. 1952.
24. Mattick, H.W. *Unexamined Death: An Analysis of Capital Punishment.* Centre for Studies in

Criminal Justice. University of Chicago Law School. Chicago: John Howard Association. 46 pp. 1966.

25. Morris, A. *Homicide: An Approach to the Problem of Crime*. Boston: Boston University Press. 1955.

26. Morris, T. and Blom-Cooper, L. "Research on the Effect of Abolition of the Death Penalty on Homicide Rates in England and Wales." Reported in the *Observer* of London. 1979.

27. Passell, P. "The Deterrent Effect of the Death Penalty: A Statistical Test." *Standford Law Review*. 28. Pp. 61–80. 1975.

28. Passell, P. and Taylor, J.B. "The Deterrence Controversy: A Reconsideration of the Time Series Evidence." In H.A. Bedau and G. Pierce (eds.). *Capital Punishment*. New York: AMS Press. Pp. 359–371. 1976.

29. Phillips, David P. "The Deterrent Effect of Capital Punishment: New Evidence on an Old Controversy." *American J. of Sociology*. 86: 1 (July), 139–148. 1980.

30. Robin, G.D. "Justifiable Homicide by Police Officers," *J. of Criminal Law, Criminology and Police Science*. 54:2, 225–231. 1963.

31. Robin, G.D. "Justifiable Homicide by Police Officers." In M.E. Wolfgang (ed.). *Studies in Homicide*. New York: Harper and Row, 88–100. 1967.

32. Savitz, L.D. "Study in Capital Punishment." *Journal of Criminal Law, Criminology and Police Science*. 49:338–341. 1958.

33. Sellin, Th. "Common Sense and the Death Penalty." *Prison Journal*. 12:4 (Oct. 1932).

34. Sellin, Th. *The Death Penalty: A Report for the Model Penal Code Project of the American Law Institute*. Philadelphia Executive Office of the American Law Institute. 1959.

35. Sellin, Th. "Capital Punishment." *Federal Probation*. 25:3, 3–11. 1961.

36. Sellin, Th. "The Death Penalty Relative to Deterrence and Police Safety." In N. Johnson et al. (eds.). *The Sociology of Punishment and Corrections*. New York: John Wiley and Sons. 1962.

37. Sellin, Th. "Effect of Repeal and Reintroduction of the Death Penalty on Homicide Rates." In H.A. Bedau (ed.). *The Death Penalty in America*. Chicago: Aldine. Pp. 339–343. 1966.

38. Selling, Th. *Capital Punishment*. New York: Harper and Row. 1967.

39. Selling, Th. "Prison Homicides." In Sellin, T. (ed.). *Capital Punishment*. New York: Harper and Row. 1967.

40. Sellin, Th. "Homicides in Retentionist and Abolitionist States." In Sellin, T. (ed.). *Capital Punishment*. New York: Harper and Row. 1967.

41. Sellin, Th. *The Penalty of Death*. California: Sage Publications. 1980.

42. Siciliano, S. "Risultati Preliminari di Un'indagine sull Homicidio in Danimarca." *La Scuola Positiva*. 3: 4, 718–729. 1965.

43. Topping, C.W. "The Death Penalty in Canada." *The Annals of the American Academy of Political and Social Science*. 284 (Nov.): 147–157. 1952.

44. U.K. Home Office. *British Criminal Statistics*. London: HMSO. 1924.

45. U.K. *British Select Committee on Capital Punishment — Report*. London: HMSO. 1930.

46. U.K. *Royal Commission on Capital Punishment 1949–1953 — Report*. London: HMSO. 1953.

47. U.S.A. California, *Senate Committee's Report on the Death Penalty*. California. Pp. 16–17. Quoted in H.A. Bedau (1976). *The Death Penalty in America*. New York: Anchor Books. 1960.

48. U.S.A. Massachusetts, *Report*, Sub-committee on Moral Arguments For and Against the Death Penalty. 1958.

49. U.S.A. Ohio, Ohio Legislative Commission. *Capital Punishment: Report*. Columbus, Ohio. 1961.

50. U.S.A. The Panel of the National Academy of Sciences. *Deterrence and Incapacitation: Estimating the Effects of Criminal Sanctions on Crime Rates*, by A. Blumstein, J. Cohen and D. Nagin. Washington, D.C.: National Academy of Sciences. 1978.

51. West, D.J. *Murder Followed by Suicide*. London: Heneman. 1965.

52. Zeisel, H. "The Deterrent Effect of the Death Penalty: Facts v. Faith." In P.B. Kurland (ed.). *The Supreme Court Review*, 1976. Chicago: University of Chicago Press. 1976.

QUESTIONS

1. Is the deterrence argument more civilized than arguments based on revenge and retribution, as Fattah implies?

2. Should the burden of proving that capital punishment is a deterrent be placed on the retentionists?
3. Is Fattah right in saying: "The question is not whether the death penalty has a deterrent effect but whether it provides a unique and supreme deterrent"?
4. Is capital punishment a unique deterrent? If not, does it follow that capital punishment should be abolished?

FACT SHEET #2: CHANGES IN REPORTING MASK VIOLENT CRIME TRENDS

John Howard Society of Ontario

What Is Really Happening with Violent Crime Rates?

Violent crime represents a relatively small percentage of all Criminal Code offences, but because of the serious nature of the offences, it is violent crime that we fear the most.

Believing that rates of violent crime are increasing dramatically makes us feel more vulnerable and at risk. Increasing public fear of crime results in demands for more incarceration and for longer sentences. The fact is, however, that official statistics and media reports can be very misleading. No amount of violent crime is acceptable, but being panicked into costly and ineffective responses to crime by incomplete information is not acceptable either. In this Fact Sheet we will explore violent crime statistics and victimization studies in order to show why we have been saying, *"Now is not the time to panic"*.

The evidence suggests that while the *rate* of violent crime in Canada has not been increasing dramatically the *reporting* of violent crime has increased. This is particularly the case with the reporting of assault offences not involving serious injury or a weapon (assault level 1 and non-sexual assault level 1).

It is important to understand that even a small increase in the rate at which the public reports crime to the police can result in a large increase in police reported crime rates.

According to the 1987 Canadian victimization survey, an estimated 1,104,000 violent offences were *not* reported to the police. If an additional 1% of these victimizations were reported, 11,040 offences would have been added to the reported number of violent crimes for that year (i.e., 219,381 + 11,040 = 230,421), representing an increase in violent crime of 5%.

The entire increase in the violent crime rate over the 1987–1991 period (28.4%) might be accounted for by an increase in victimization reporting of slightly more than 1% each year.

The issues relating to violent crime generate strong feelings of anger and fear — that is to be expected — but, if we are to take the best course of action to reduce violent crime, we must also use our intellect and examine the facts carefully. Exaggerated claims, misunderstood statistics, and panic responses are not helpful or likely to result in effective social policy.

Reprinted by permission of the John Howard Society of Ontario.

CRIMINAL CODE OFFENSES — CANADA 1991

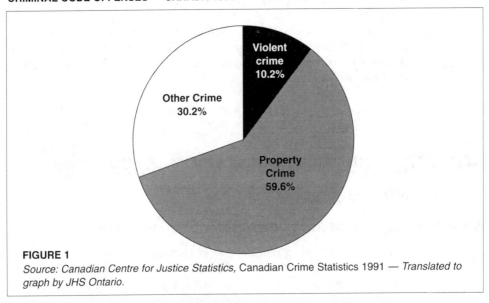

FIGURE 1
Source: Canadian Centre for Justice Statistics, Canadian Crime Statistics 1991 *— Translated to graph by JHS Ontario.*

Critical Analysis of Statistics Essential

The primary source of Canadian crime statistics is the Uniform Crime Reporting system (UCR) developed by Statistics Canada in 1962. This survey is completed by the federal, provincial and municipal police and contains only information on crimes which are reported by police.

Researchers and statisticians always caution the reader that increases in violent crime as defined by UCR data may be partly due to changes in reporting practices of citizens and the police.

But, how much of the increase in crime is really attributable to changes in reporting practices?

Comparing trends in reported crime with estimates of actual crime based on victimization studies helps to illustrate the effect of changing reporting practices.

Canadian victimization data are available for 1982 and 1987 but, because the groups surveyed and the methodology used differ, the data cannot be compared and trends cannot be identified. In the United States, however, national victimization studies have been conducted annually since 1973.

What Does the U.S. Information on Crime Tell Us?

American data show that changes in reporting practices can generate quickly escalating violent crime statistics when, in fact, violent crime is actually stable *or even declining.*

An analysis of trends in the rates of specific violent offences in the United States shows the convergence between reported crime and victimization estimates. Figures 3, 4 and 5 show this converging pattern with the three key indicators of violent crime in the United States.

It is worth noting that the Canadian equivalent of assault level 1 (not involving serious injury or use of a weapon) is not classified as a violent crime in the United States. As the

VIOLENT CRIME AND VICTIMIZATION RATES UNITED STATES 1975–1990

(per 100,000 population)

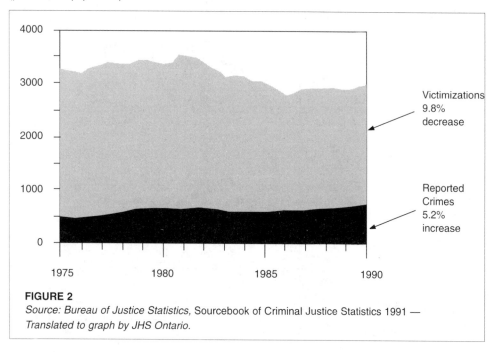

FIGURE 2

Source: Bureau of Justice Statistics, Sourcebook of Criminal Justice Statistics 1991 —
Translated to graph by JHS Ontario.

AGGRAVATED ASSAULT RATES — U.S.

(per 100,000 population)

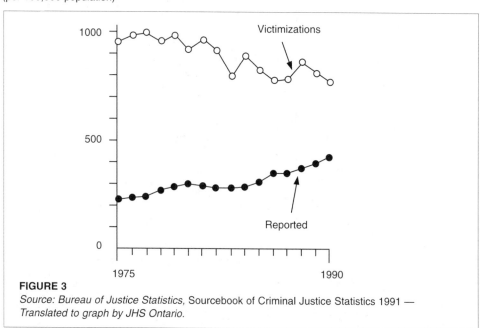

FIGURE 3

Source: Bureau of Justice Statistics, Sourcebook of Criminal Justice Statistics 1991 —
Translated to graph by JHS Ontario.

ROBBERY RATES — U.S.

(per 100,000 population)

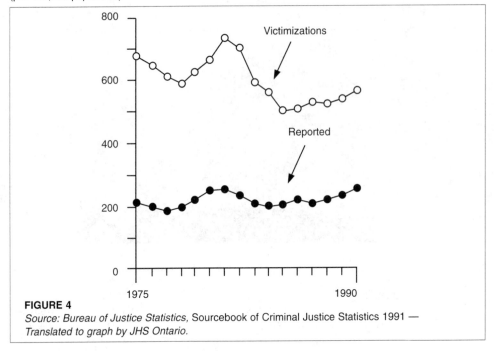

FIGURE 4

Source: Bureau of Justice Statistics, Sourcebook of Criminal Justice Statistics 1991 —
Translated to graph by JHS Ontario.

RAPE RATES — U.S.

(per 100,000 population)

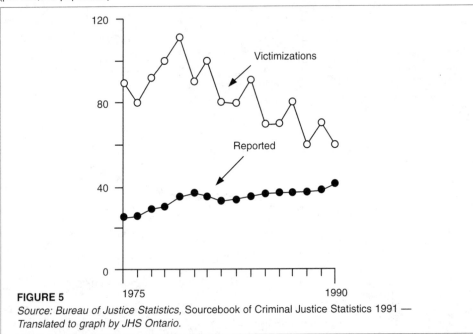

FIGURE 5

Source: Bureau of Justice Statistics, Sourcebook of Criminal Justice Statistics 1991 —
Translated to graph by JHS Ontario.

Canadian data which follow will show, most of the increase in the rate of violent crime in Canada is attributable to this *lowest* level of violent crime.

Most Violent Crime in Canada Stable

In Canada, the least serious offences account for *virtually all* of the growth in official violent crime between 1984 (after the laws for assault and sexual assault changed) and 1991. As Figure 6 shows, when the lowest levels of violent crime are excluded, there has been very little change in the rate of violent crime.

Trends in assault level 1 and sexual assault level 1 are more likely to be reflective of changes in reporting practices rather than changes in the rate of actual assaults. When sexual assault level 1 and assault level 1 are excluded from the violent crime rate (Fig. 6), the pattern is similar to that of property crime rates over the same period (Fig. 7).

It is likely that the patterns of crime reflected in property and "other" violent crime (Fig. 6 & 7), are a more accurate reflection of actual trends.

Violence Less Tolerated

Assaultive behaviour — particularly sexual assaults, domestic assault, and child abuse — has been the target of legislative action, public education and media attention within the past decade. Citizens and police have been encouraged, and in some cases required, to report and record offences.

As we turn our attention and criminal justice resources to combat violent crimes that were "tolerated" in the past, we should *expect* to see a disproportionate increase in the rate at which these offences are reported.

For example, fights between youths appear to be tolerated much less now than was the case in past years. The police are more likely to be called and, therefore, more charges are laid.

Sexual assaults on children are now being reported more frequently — often many years after the offence took place. More charges are being laid in cases of domestic assault as police are now required or expected to lay charges for offences which, in the past, would have been dealt with informally and not recorded.

Because the worst cases of violent crime have always had a high rate of reporting, we should expect to see changes with the least serious offences (Fig. 6).

Assault cannot be tolerated, dismissed, or ignored. But neither should increased reporting of these incidents lead Canadians to the conclusion that our society is becoming *more* violent and that Canadians are more at risk than they were in the past.

Attempts to address previously hidden or tolerated violence will result in more reporting of those offences and, in turn, an increase in the rates of those offences should be expected. The irony here is that our success in addressing issues of violence may result in us believing that we are more at risk.

Legislative Changes Can Affect Reporting Practices

New legal definitions of criminal behaviour affect how police charge offenders. For instance, the rate of sexual offences began to increase dramatically in 1983 — the year of the criminal code changes for sexual assault.

VIOLENT CRIME RATE — CANADA

(per 100,000 population)

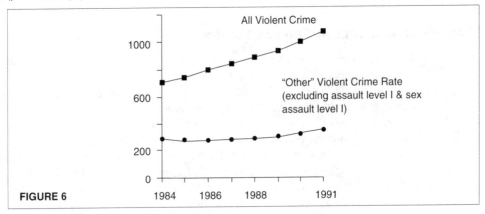

FIGURE 6

PROPERTY CRIME RATE — CANADA

(per 100,000 population)

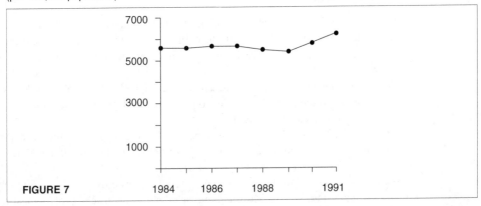

FIGURE 7

ASSAULT AND SEXUAL ASSAULT RATES — LEVEL I — CANADA

(per 100,000 population)

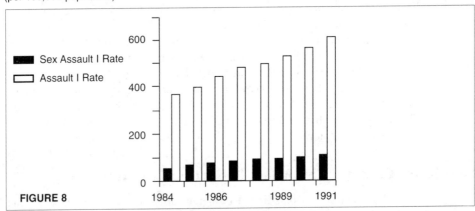

FIGURE 8

Source: Canadian Centre for Justice Statistics, Canadian Crime Statistics *(1984–1991) — Translated to graph by JHS Ontario (Figures 6, 7, and 8).*

As Figure 8 shows, the rates for sexual assault as compared to those for general assault are relatively low. At the same time, the increase in the number of general assaults has been much greater than is the case with sexual assaults, even though the rate of increase has been greater with sexual assault. *Even a small shift in charging practices from assault to sexual assault would generate a large increase in the officially recorded rate of sexual assaults.*

Robberies Linked to Tough Times

As Figure 9 shows, other violent offences not affected by legislative changes show very different trends. The homicide rate was relatively stable between 1976 and 1991. The pattern of robbery rates have traditionally mirrored the economic conditions of Canada with the peaks occurring during periods of recession and high unemployment.

Most Violent Crimes Not Reported to Police

Victimization studies in Canada show that only about 30% of violent crimes are reported to police. Victims frequently report that "the offence was too minor" or that "there was nothing the police could do" as the reasons for not reporting. In other cases, such as domestic and sexual assault, victims may be reluctant to report due to fears about reprisals or the impact on the family of a public prosecution.

Considering that about 70% of violent crime goes unreported, there is obviously room for enormous growth in the official violent crime rates whether or not there is any change in actual rates of violent crime.

SELECTED VIOLENT CRIME RATES — CANADA — 1976 TO 1991

(per 100,000 population)

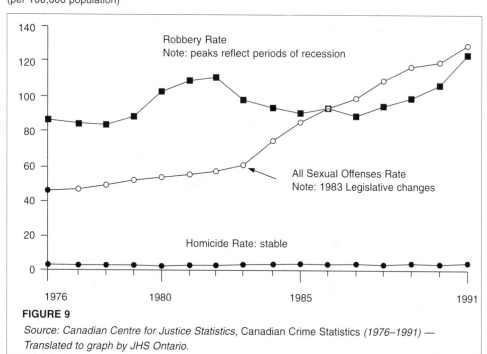

FIGURE 9

Source: Canadian Centre for Justice Statistics, Canadian Crime Statistics *(1976–1991) — Translated to graph by JHS Ontario.*

HOMICIDE RATES
(per 100,000 population)
CANADA 1970 TO 1994

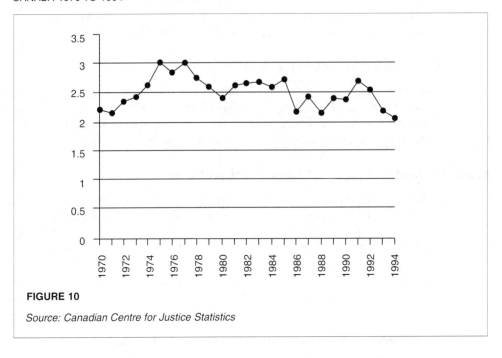

FIGURE 10

Source: Canadian Centre for Justice Statistics

**TOTAL REPORTED HOMICIDES AND YOUTHS AGED 12 TO 17 CHARGED WITH HOMICIDES
CANADA 1975–1994**

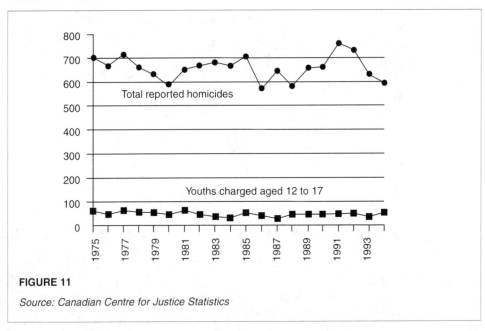

FIGURE 11

Source: Canadian Centre for Justice Statistics

Public Policy Choices Shaped by Public Perception of Violent Crime

It seems likely that some violent crime is increasing while other violent crimes are remaining level or even decreasing. What is certain, however, is that the changes in the rate of violent crime are much more gradual than official crime statistics suggest.

A critical analysis of violent crime is essential to the development of good public policy in criminal justice. Much more Canadian research is necessary if we are to determine whether violent crime is actually increasing, the nature of the increase, who is being victimized, the causes of the increase, and how it can be prevented.

We cannot afford to be either paralysed by sensational reports of increasing violent crime or pressured to adopt short-sighted solutions. With a better understanding of what is really happening with violent crime rates, an environment can exist which allows for careful and thoughtful analysis and proposals.

FACT SHEET #2 SUPPLEMENT: HOMICIDE TRENDS

John Howard Society of Ontario

Homicides remain stable over 25 years

Unlike most other crimes, the reporting rate for homicide is considered to be a reliable indicator of actual rates of homicide. This reliability is a function of the fact that because homicide is so serious reporting rates are always very high and are not influenced by changes in public attitude or legislative changes.

Overall homicide rates and incidence show no discernable trends for either adults or youth over the last 25 years in Canada. As shown in Figure 10, Canadian homicide rates have ranged between 2 and 3 per 100,000. In 1994, the homicide rate was the lowest in 25 years but that could change dramatically in subsequent years and still fall within the normal range. For instance, if the homicide rate increases from 2 to 3 per 100,00 that would be reported as a 50% increase yet still be lower than the rate in 1974.

Figure 11 shows the overall *number* of homicides in Canada as well as the number of youths aged 12 to 17 who were *charged* with homicide. It should be noted that the homicides committed by youth are also included in the total. Comparing total number of crimes to youth charged is normally problematic but in this case, because homicide has a very high clearance rate the comparison is still instructive.

The chart shows that youth are responsible for a relatively small proportion of all homicides. The chart also shows no discernable trend with either category. It should be noted that neither the abolition of the death penalty in 1976 nor the introduction of the Young Offenders Act in 1984 has had any observable impact on homicides committed by either adults or youth.

QUESTIONS

1. Do the statistics on the incidence of murder and violent crime in Canada since 1975 prove that capital punishment is not a uniquely effective deterrent against murder? Does it matter whether it is or is not?

RETRIBUTIVISM AND THE DEATH PENALTY

Alan Brudner

A reasoned approach to the death penalty presupposes a comprehensive theory of punishment. A comprehensive theory of punishment is an account of punishment which distinguishes it from arbitrary and unjust violence and which, in doing so, provides a criterion for the legitimate deprivation of rights. Whether or not the death penalty is just, whether it should or should not be retained or restored can be decided only with reference to the criterion of justice generated by a true account of punishment.

Since Beccaria, the argument for the abolition of the death penalty has customarily been advanced from within the framework of a utilitarian theory of punishment. According to this theory, punishment is an expression of the impulse for self-defence moralized by the feeling of sympathy.[1] Whereas the former is rooted in the self-regarding desire for pleasure and aversion to pain, the latter allows us to transcend the narrow bounds of self and identify our own with collective pleasures and pains. Thus punishment is collective self-defence. Since the aim of collective defence is what constitutes punishment as a moral phenomenon in contradistinction to private revenge, it alone can provide grounds for the legitimate pursuit of the aim. For punishment is an evil that can be justified only as a means of avoiding greater evil; that is, only if its social benefits exceed its social costs.[2] That punishment is an evil follows from the hedonistic psychology and ethics of utilitarian thought. For Bentham the good at which all human beings aim is happiness, understood as the excess of pleasure over pain. Therefore the good at which all just policy must aim is the maximization of pleasure in the social aggregate. Now punishment inflicts suffering and so belongs in the debit column of the social utility ledger. It is acceptable, therefore, only if it yields a return of pleasure greater than its cost in pain. The benefits to be derived from punishment are: deterrence of potential offenders, the protection of society against actual offenders, and the rehabilitation of the criminal. Accordingly, the decision as to whether a particular instance of punishment is moral or immoral is basically an accounting decision. If the punishment works more harm than good, or if the same benefits can be obtained at less cost in suffering, then the punishment is unjust in the only sense intelligible to a utilitarian. It is especially the latter criterion that has provided the major focus for policy research on the death penalty and that has structured whatever rational debate one can find on the subject. Once the utilitarian premises are granted, it remains to determine by means of empirical studies whether, as compared with long-term imprisonment, the death penalty is either a uniquely effective deterrent to murder or a uniquely effective protection against those convicted of murder. Of its rehabilitative effects nothing need be said.

From a utilitarian standpoint the death penalty is difficult to justify. The statistical evidence fails to confirm (though neither does it decisively refute) the common intuition that capital punishment deters potential murderers and protects society from actual ones more effectively than incarceration for life.[3] It is true that no study of the deterrent effect of capital punishment can be conclusive, since it is impossible to compare the effects of retention and abolition within the same jurisdiction over the same time period. But since the burden of justification rests with those who would take a life, inconclusive data ought

From the University of Toronto Law Journal, Vol. XXX, No. 4, 1980. Reprinted by permission of University of Toronto Press.

properly to weigh in favor of abolition. Ernest van den Haag has, to be sure, formulated a retentionist case that takes into account the lack of firm proof for the marginal deterrent value of the death penalty.[4] He argues that, given our uncertainty about deterrence, capital punishment should be retained in order to minimize the costs of our being wrong. The risk of causing unnecessary suffering to the criminal is preferable to that of exposing innocent people to murderers who might have been deterred. Though ingenious, this argument can, I think, be countered on utilitarian grounds. One could point out that, in retaining capital punishment, we choose the alternative that carries a risk of injustice over the one which carries none. For if we abolish the death penalty and people murder who would have been deterred, we have committed no injustice because we could not have known they would be deterred. But if we retain it and execute someone in vain, then we have done wrong in killing someone without sufficient reason. A more plausible justification of capital punishment from a utilitarian perspective is that of John Stuart Mill, who simply challenged the commonplace assumption that life imprisonment inflicts less suffering on the criminal than death.[5] Yet even this point argues less in favor of capital punishment than for granting the convict the right to choose, and so merely shifts the moral dilemma from capital punishment to suicide or euthanasia.

Were the utilitarian account of punishment the true one, therefore, we should have no doubt but that the movement toward abolition in the western world is securely grounded in reason, and that opposition to this movement, however broadly based, can be justly disregarded. However, a number of legal philosophers have insistently called attention to shocking inadequacies in the theory, and the result of their efforts is that the classic or pure utilitarian position outlined above now stands discredited even among philosophers whom one could still class as utilitarians.[6] As yet little has been done to assess the implications of this development for the moral status of the death penalty.[7] Such an assessment is, however, an urgent necessity, because the downfall of utilitarianism directs our attention once again to retributivism, a theory of punishment that has traditionally furnished arguments in favor of the death penalty.[8] Accordingly, the next section of this paper recapitulates the main objections to the utilitarian position and argues that recent efforts to rescue it by retreating to a qualified utilitarianism are in vain. The succeeding sections attempt both to vindicate retributivism as the only morally defensible account of punishment and to explore its implications for the death penalty. I intend to show that, far from specifically enjoining capital punishment for first-degree murder, retributivism provides grounds for favouring abolition as an ideal, though also for opposing it in circumstances which make the realization of the ideal imprudent.

The test of an adequate theory of punishment is whether it can save, provide an explicit ground for, and so confirm the prephilosophic distinction between punishment and arbitrary violence. Sense-perception alone cannot distinguish between murder and judicial killing, or between abduction and judicial detention. Our common-sense conviction that a difference nonetheless exists must therefore remain a prejudice vulnerable to skeptical questioning unless a philosophy of punishment can disclose the real basis of the distinction and so confirm it to rational insight. Now there are two levels at which thought can seek to clarify punishment. At one level it attempts merely to analyse the concept of punishment, to isolate the various elements implicit in its definition that distinguish it from wrongful injury. Although this approach yields important results, it can never produce a "justification" of punishment, for it deals only with a conventional object, with what we mean by punishment, without ever showing that what we mean has a foundation in reality. Thus analysis merely describes — it cannot confirm — the content of moral opinion.

The second level is that of theory. Here thought aims at a scientific account of the phenomenon of punishment. Rather than analysing an abstract concept, it seeks to disclose the real nature of the thing. The effect of such a theory may well be to debunk the common opinion regarding the essential distinction between judicial and criminal force, or it may be to confirm that opinion — that is, to provide a justification of punishment. But although only theory can justify punishment, the analytic approach is a necessary preliminary, because it alone can provide standards for the verification of theory. By specifying the conceptual elements of the distinction between punishment and violence, analysis furnishes the criteria by which we can assess the validity of justificatory theories of punishment.

There are at least three factors which distinguish punishment from violence for common sense. One of these is purpose. Punishment differs from unjust violence in that it is directed towards a good that is genuinely common — that is, common both to those who punish and to him that is punished — while unjust violence aims at some particular or exclusive interest. It is this factor of aim that distinguishes punishment not only from criminal aggression but also from that form of violence with which it is in all other essential respects identical, namely, revenge. Second, punishment differs from unjust violence in that it is intrinsically related to desert. Punishment, we may say, is the deserved infringement of a right. That it is connected with desert further implies that punishment can only be (a) a reaction to wrongdoing, and (b) a measured reaction — measured, that is, to the gravity of the wrong. The question as to the meaning and criterion of an appropriate measure is of course the crucial one in a discussion of the death penalty, and I shall return to it presently. For now let us simply say that implicit in the notion of punishment (as connected with desert) is a relation of fitness between punishment and crime. This means that penalties must be measured not only to the seriousness of the objective but also to the degree of subjective responsibility, since it is responsibility alone that constitutes wrongdoing. Thus civilized criminal codes recognize various degrees of culpable homicide ranging from manslaughter to first-degree murder, the degrees of guilt or desert corresponding to degrees of intent (or what is called *mens rea*), and they prescribe penalties which vary in severity according to the degree of intent. The converse of this principle of proportionality is that of strict liability, according to which the intention of the individual is irrelevant to the determination either of guilt or of the appropriate statutory penalty. Accordingly, a morally sound theory of punishment must (a) justify punishment with reference to a good that is genuinely universal, (b) save the connection between punishment and wrongdoing, and (c) save the rule of proportionality as between punishment and crime.

As has been frequently argued, the utilitarian theory fails on all three counts. In the first place, it views punishment as an evil inflicted on one individual for the benefit of others. The criminal is sacrificed, or used as a means, to the welfare of the majority, so that punishment becomes indistinguishable from the criminal use of force. Secondly, the utilitarian theory can countenance "punishment" of the innocent. This is because it defines just punishment in terms of aims that are only contingently related to desert. If punishment is justified by its deterrent effect, then in circumstances which made the risks of disclosure worth bearing, the state could legitimately fabricate evidence against an innocent man in order to make an example of him. Moreover, collective or vicarious punishment could, in extreme cases, also be socially expedient, and where expedient, just. And if punishment is justified by the protection it affords society, then justified in certain cases are preventive detention and the indeterminate sentence — that is, punishment related not to actual wrong-doing but to expected wrongdoing. From the standpoint of self defence, waiting for a known psychopath to strike is absurd.

What of the requirement that punishment be proportioned to the offence? At first sight the utilitarian theory seems to preserve this relation, at least with respect to the nature of the objective act. Deterrence requires that the punishment be severe enough to make the crime a bad risk to the potential offender; utilitarian justice demands that it be no more severe than what is needed to deter the crime, and no more socially injurious than the crime unpun-ished. Furthermore, penalties must be so graded that anyone embarking on a criminal course will be encouraged to commit the less rather than the most harmful offence. How-ever, we must recall that deterrence is only one of three aims contemplated by utilitarian punishment, and that of these three only deterrence looks to the crime. The goals of self-protection and reform have regard not to the offence but to the offender. They consider the criminal in terms of psychological rather than legal categories: not as the responsible author of a particular offence but as a dangerous or deviant personality, the subject of unique characterological attributes and propensities of which the crime is but a particular manifes-tation. Accordingly, since a penal practice which aimed exclusively at minimum deterrence would accomplish these other goals only accidentally, utilitarianism must fix penalties which leave sufficient room for judicial discretion in imposing individualized sentences. In doing so, however, it defines the moral degree of punishment by reference to something other than the offence, hence in a way that subverts the rule of natural justice requiring that punishments be proportioned to crimes. On utilitarian principles the pathological petty offender may warrant more severe punishment than the "normal" armed robber.

It is questionable, moreover, whether utilitarianism preserves the rule of proportionality respecting punishment and responsibility. Bentham, to be sure, claimed that it did. He argued that the circumstances recognized in the common law as excusing or extenuating wrongdoing — namely, accident, insanity, coercion, and provocation — are all confirmed by utilitarian theory as factors which render punishment "inefficacious."[9] Punishment of the insane, for example, would serve no useful deterrent purpose; and punishing a provoked crime with the same severity as a premeditated one would mean paying more than is necessary for the deterrence purchased, since a man provoked is not the rational maximizer of utilities envisaged by Benthamite psychology. Bentham, however, was wrong on two counts. He was wrong, first of all, in supposing that because the threat of punishment in cases where intent is absent is useless for deterrence, it is also useless for other utilitarian goals. From the standpoint of self-protection, for example, doing away with excusing con-ditions might conceivably be socially beneficial, for it would eliminate the opportunities that criminals now have for deceiving juries. He was wrong, secondly, in supposing that because the threat of punishment in such cases is useless for particular deterrence, it is also useless for general deterrence. As H.L.A. Hart has pointed out, punishing the insane will not deter them from striking again, but it may effectively deter others, especially if they know that a defence of insanity will do them no good.[10] From the standpoint of deterrence, in other words, excusing conditions are just so many loopholes in the law which the unscrupulous may be encouraged to exploit. Furthermore, persons engaged in an activity governed by a statute of strict liability are likely to exercise added caution, knowing that a plea of accident or of reasonable mistake will not excuse them; indeed they may be discour-aged from undertaking the activity altogether. For all these reasons it can be said that any conduct which society wants to prevent is more effectively prevented by a statute of strict liability than by one which recognizes excusing or extenuating conditions. Hence the requirement of natural justice that responsibility be a condition of criminal liability finds in utilitarianism only contingent support. No doubt the question of responsibility would still be relevant for a utilitarian at the sentencing stage, where it would serve to indicate the kind of reformative or protective measures that need to be taken.[11] But adapting measures of social hygiene to the mental condition of the offender is a far different thing from proportioning punishments to legal responsibility. And it would be a sheer accident if their results were congruent. A crime of passion deserves less punishment than a calculated one; but the offender may require a more prolonged period of "treatment."

There have been several recent attempts to rescue the utilitarian position from the moral anomalies to which it leads. The weakest consist in definitionally limiting punishment to mean infliction of pain on the deserving, as if by calling "punishment" of the innocent by some other name utilitarians could stop worrying about sanctioning it.[12] Others have held that punishing innocents is condemned by a utilitarianism rightly interpreted, one that judges the morality of acts by their utility not in isolated circumstances but when generalized as a rule.[13] If sacrificing innocent persons for the sake of deterrence were standard policy, it is argued, the costs in terms of public anxiety would far outweigh the benefits of a reduced crime rate. Yet surely it is quite consistent with "rule-utilitarianism" for governments to empower themselves to use all expedient means (including collective punishment) for coping with emergencies, provided that the type of emergency is specified in law and is sufficiently grave to warrant such extraordinary powers. Because, in other words, it is possible to formulate rules not only for the general case but also for exceptional circumstances of a given type, rule-utilitarianism cannot, any more than act-utilitarianism, absolutely exclude punishing innocents under the colour of right. A third defence is in the nature of a strategic retreat. Professor Hart has acknowledged the pitfalls of a thoroughly consistent utilitarianism yet sees no need to discard it once it is suitably qualified. Deterrence and self-protection continue to justify punishment in general but cannot alone guide us in determining whom and how much to punish. For these questions principles (e.g., that punishment be only for an offence) must be applied that limit the extent to which the individual can be sacrificed for social ends — principles that guarantee a calculable world in which choices have a bearing on one's fate.[14] This solution is similar to that of John Rawls, in that it consists in splitting up the phenomenon of punishment into the general institution and the particular applications and in applying different moral criteria to each — a salutary eclecticism.[15] Whereas social utility justifies the former, principles associated with (but, according to Hart, not exclusive to) retributive punishment must guide us in the latter.

A number of rejoinders can be made to this argument. First, the splitting up of punishment in this way denies the organic link between the universal and its particularization. Just as a law is properly a law only if it is regularly enforced, so a set of penalties affixed to rules is a system of punishment only insofar as the penalties are imposed for violations of the rules. Conversely, a specific imposition of a sanction is an instance of punishment only insofar as it is carried out under the system of rules and procedures defining the legal use of force. While distinct, therefore, the institution of punishment and its particular applications are united in essence; neither is apart from the other. Consequently, one cannot coherently adopt one set of principles to govern the institution of punishment and another set to govern its concrete applications. Taking a utilitarian position on the universal commits one to taking it on the particular as well, because the latter is the realization of the former. Of course one may wish to limit the application of deterrence and security considerations by other values, but either these values are likewise grounded in social utility or they are not. If they are not, then we must abandon utilitarianism as a general justifying theory. If they are, then they lie at the mercy of the utilitarian calculus and so cannot serve as an unconditional stop to the encroachments of society. Secondly, the mixed theory of punishment is designed to extricate utilitarianism only from the charge that it justifies punishment of the innocent. It is no answer to the objection that utilitarianism fails to provide a morally acceptable justification for punishing the guilty. On the mixed theory, law-breakers are still harmed to satisfy the particular interests of others. Finally, the solution of Hart and Rawls involves a refusal to submit to rigorous standards of theoretical adequacy. The test of a theory of a natural phenomenon is the empirical one of whether it is confirmed by the observed facts. The test of a theory of a moral phenomenon is the dialectical one employed by Socrates. If an account of the phenomenon (e.g., courage, justice, punishment) logically entails, or is consistent with, consequences that involve the collapsing of the phenomenon into its opposite (e.g., punishment into arbitrary violence), then the account must be abandoned as a resting point, because it has failed to grasp the thing's specific essence. Certainly one cannot think to have rescued it by holding it aloof from its contradictions. Had Cephalus replied to Socrates in *Republic I*, "While I grant that in certain circumstances paying one's debts may work injustice, and that in those cases difference principles would have to guide us, nevertheless I maintain that justice in general is paying one's debts," he would have responded in the manner of Hart and Rawls. It might be objected, however, that the utilitarian theory of punishment offers not an account of punishment in this explanatory sense but only as a set of justifying conditions, and so is not rigorously committed to all its logical implications. But this is not the case. The utilitarian position is ultimately an answer to the question, What is punishment? It offers criteria and conditions for distinguishing authentic punishment from arbitrary violence. Explanation and justification are thus inextricably meshed: what justifies punishment is also what constitutes its essence and vice-versa. The utilitarian position is thus a full-fledged "account" of punishment, which, to be tenable, must offer non-collapsible criteria for distinguishing it from criminal force.

Given the very serious deficiencies of the utilitarian account of punishment, the impressive array of statistics adduced to question the superior deterrent force of the death penalty suddenly becomes irrelevant. Whether or not capital punishment is a uniquely effective deterrent to murder or the only sure-fire means of self protection is beside the point if these criteria are not the ones we should be using to determine the justice of capital punishment. But not only are these questions theoretically irrelevant. Inasmuch as they orient research that determines our policy, they implicate us in immorality, because they suppose the criteria of an immoral view of punishment.

Let us then consider the chief rival to the utilitarian account of punishment and inquire as to the implications it bears for the death penalty. I refer to the retributivist account, the classic formulations of which are by Immanuel Kant and G.W.F. Hegel.[16] In contrast to utilitarianism, the retributive theory views punishment as a moral good rather than as an evil requiring justification in terms of extrinsic advantages. Whether or not punishment yields these advantages is irrelevant to its justification, because the principal end of punishment is neither to deter, nor to protect, nor to reform, but to annul wrong and thereby vindicate right. This is not to say that the retributivist is indifferent to these other goals or regards them as improper objects of policy. The criteria of reform, deterrence, and protection do have their place, but it is a very subordinate one. Specifically, they are relevant only to the secondary question of how we shall punish and not to the primary question of whether we have the right to punish. Furthermore, even within the limits of the secondary question (with which we are here concerned) they have relevance only *after* the moral issue has been settled and what remains is merely the choice, judicial or administrative, between various morally acceptable types and measures of punishment. For the retributivist the sole criterion of just punishment as well as of a just measure of punishment is whether it annuls the wrong.

But precisely how, we may ask, does punishment annul wrong? "Can the shrieks of a wretch recall from time, which never reverses its course, deeds already accomplished?" thundered Beccaria. Obviously punishment cannot undo the deed, for the past is irrevocable. And yet by "annulment" of the wrong retributivists must mean something more than mere restitution, for restitution is not punishment. According to Hegel, punishment annuls wrong by demonstrating the non-being of the criminal principle, which might otherwise have seemed to possess validity.[17] The principle of crime is the claim to a right of the arbitrary and unrestrained freedom of the will. Seen in this way, crime is more than, as Plato thought, a sickness in the individual soul; it is a challenge to the natural moral order underpinning civilized society. This is because it denies the validity of natural law and gives this denial itself a show of validity. Punishment, then, is the denial of the denial and so the vindication or reaffirmation of natural law. It is, in other words, the objective demonstration that the criminal claim is without natural support or sanction, without reality.

Because it looks backward to a crime over and done with rather than forward to its social effects, retributive punishment has always seemed to utilitarians a relic of more barbarous times, a mere rationalization of the lust for revenge. In part this judgment reflects the utilitarian's rationalist suspicion of popular sentiment, in which he is wont to see only vulgar prejudice and blind emotionalism. Beccaria saw in the penal law of his time only "the accumulated errors of centuries," and this attitude finds its modern counterpart in the demand to keep separate the questions, Why do men punish? and What justifies punishment?[18] On the other hand, because of his commitment to natural law, the retributivist is more inclined to see in public opinion a dim perception of moral truth. And he is thus also inclined to see his task as one of providing a rational account of action already in itself moral rather than one of excogitating a criterion of morality to which society may be indifferent. To his utilitarian critic, therefore, the retributivists would reply that his punishment is not a form of revenge, but that revenge and punishment are both forms of natural retribution, punishment being alone the adequate form because emancipated from subjective interest. He would, moreover, counter with the charge that whereas utilitarianism plays havoc with our common-sense notions of penal justice, retributivism confirms them.

First of all, retributivism justifies punishment by reference to a good that is genuinely common. Punishment vindicates human rights. It thus affirms and makes objective the real rights of the criminal himself, who, in asserting a right to unlimited freedom, had undermined right as such, his own no less than others'. In receiving punishment, therefore, the criminal is subjected not to someone else's good, but to his own true good, hence to his own rational will. His autonomy and dignity are thus respected.

Secondly, retributivism accounts for the connection between punishment and desert. If punishment is the vindication of right against wrong or the denial of a denial, then it logically presupposes wrongdoing. Thus retributivism condemns punishment of the innocent. Furthermore, if what requires annulment is not the criminal deed itself but rather its claim to validity, then clearly intent or *mens rea* is saved as a determinant of wrongdoing and hence of criminal desert. Retributivism thus condemns strict liability.

Thirdly, retributivism saves the rule of proportionality respecting the relation between punishment and crime. The punishment must annul the wrong. This it does by demonstrating the self-contradictoriness — that is, the inherent nullity — of the criminal act. If I steal, I deny the existence of property even for me. My act recoils upon itself and so destroys itself. Now punishment simply brings home this contradiction, or is this contradiction objectively manifest? I assert a right to unbridled freedom; I thereby deny the existence of right, which denial punishment brings home to me by depriving me of mine. I am the author of my punishment, inasmuch as the latter is simply the inner consequence of my deed. "The Eumenides sleep," says Hegel, "but crime awakens them, and hence it is the very act of crime itself which vindicates itself."[19] Now this account of punishment explains the demand that the punishment fit the crime. Punishment must be related to the gravity of the wrong because it must signify nothing but the recoiling of the criminal's own act against itself. Only as such is punishment natural retribution and not another act of violence. It is in this sense that Hegel speaks of the criminal's "right" to punishment — that is, to be subjected only to the consequences immanent in his act and never to the alien exigencies of society.[20] To punish the offender in accordance with the principle laid down by his deeds is to honour his human subjectivity, his essential self-determination, while to fix penalties according to the requirements of deterrence or correction is to degrade him to an object and a tool. Moreover, only if the measure of punishment is derived from the deed itself does the punishment logically annul the wrong. Were a fine the penalty for murder, we would feel that murder had not been sufficiently repaid, hence not decisively invalidated. The Biblical *lex talionis* as well as the common opinion that the criminal incurs a debt that can be discharged only by suffering the appropriate punishment are prephilosophic apprehensions of punishment as nemesis.

Before considering the implications of retributivism for the death penalty, I should briefly mention a third view of punishment often linked with retributivism but in reality quite distinct from it. Variously referred to as the denunciatory, the reprobative, or the expressive view of punishment, this theory holds that punishment is the emphatic denunciation of crime by society, an authoritative expression of disapproval that both vents popular indignation towards the criminal and reaffirms the positive morality of a people. The most frequently quoted exponent of this view is Sir James Fitzjames Stephen, a Victorian judge and the author of *Liberty, Equality, Fraternity*, a contemporary attack on Mill's *On Liberty*. "It is highly desirable," wrote Stephen in 1883, "that criminals should be hated, that punishments inflicted upon them should be so contrived as to give expression to that hatred, and to justify it so far as the public provision of means for expressing and gratifying a healthy natural sentiment can justify and encourage it."[21] A somewhat more temperate version of this position was expressed by Lord Justice Denning in hearings before the Royal Commission on Capital Punishment. "The punishment inflicted for grave crimes," said Denning, "should adequately reflect the revulsion felt by the great majority of citizens for them. It is a mistake to consider the objects of punishment as being deterrent or reformative or preventive and nothing else. . . . The ultimate justification of any punishment is not that it is a deterrent, but that it is the emphatic denunciation by the community of a crime."[22] Denning thus opposed the denunciatory view of punishment to the deterrence school and saw it as implying a retentionist position on the death penalty. The vilest of crimes demanded the most emphatic of all denunciations. Nevertheless, the two positions are not as incompatible as they may seem, nor does the denunciatory theory necessarily entail retention of capital punishment. If the public condemnation of crime is held to be desirable as a salutary outlet for moral indignation and as a vindication of social norms, then the denunciatory theory is a species of utilitarianism, and the rivalry between it and the deterrence school is a rivalry between siblings. It has thus been quite a simple matter in practice for utilitarian policy-makers to assimilate the criterion of reprobative power to their own theoretical framework and to formulate alternatives to the death penalty which take into account this desideratum.

On the other hand, if the apparent opposition between the denunciatory and the deterrence schools conceals a fundamental agreement, the affinity between the former and the retributivists masks a real opposition. There is, to be sure, an element of denunciation in retributive punishment, but the author of this condemnation is nature rather than society. Punishment expresses the objective nemesis of crime, not the revulsion of men. Of course feelings of revenge, revulsion, and moral indignation enter into punishment, but they have nothing to do with its essence or justification. In retributive punishment, furthermore, denunciation is linked to a principle of fitness in the light of which one can distinguish between natural retribution and human violence. By itself the denunciatory theory contains no such principle; it sets a minimum limit to punishment but not a maximum. In short, the question as to whether a particular punishment is sufficient to denounce a crime is indeed relevant to the issue of a just measure, but it has to be developed out of a morally acceptable theory of punishment in general. The denunciatory theory is not such a one. Either it justifies punishment by reference to the social benefits of denouncing crime, in which case it is a disguised utilitarianism; or it justifies punishment as an expression, good in itself, of moral indignation, without bothering to explain why this feeling should lend moral weight to violence. We do not allow anger as an excuse, let alone a moral justification, for assault or homicide; why then should we admit it just because it is also self-righteous?

What guidance does the classic retributivist theory offer in the matter of capital punishment? It is usually assumed that retributivism logically entails retention of the death penalty for first-degree murder because of its apparent confirmation of the *lex talionis*. Certainly this connection was maintained by Kant, for whom fitness meant, quite simply, equality. The murderer must die, insists Kant, because "there is no sameness of kind between death and remaining alive even under the most miserable conditions, and consequently there is also no equality between the crime and the retribution unless the criminal is judicially condemned and put to death."[23] Theorists of punishment have had little difficulty in demolishing this conception of justice, thinking in having done so to have dealt a death-blow to retributivism. If by equality is meant equality in kind, then we must repay theft with theft, adultery with adultery, forgery with forgery, and so on. If equal value is meant, then we must punish mass murderers on a scale repugnant to our moral sense. Moreover, even if it were possible to compare qualitatively different injuries in terms of their painfulness according to an average preference scale, the commensurability of crimes and punishment would be destroyed as soon as we added considerations of *mens rea* to the balance. For although suffering can be compared with suffering, how can suffering be compared with wickedness?[24] All these and other arguments are useful and valid against the *lex talionis*, but against retributivism itself they are quite harmless. For the demand that, as the criminal has done, so shall it be done to him is merely a sensuous representation or image of the inner identity of crime and its nemesis. The conceptual likeness is represented by the popular imagination as a qualitative (or quantitative) one, and, as in the allegory of the cave, the representation is taken for the thing represented. That retributive justice has nothing to do with crude conceptions of equality was emphasized by Hegel. While agreeing that equivalence is the criterion of justice in the distribution of punishment, he pointed out that "in crime, as that which is characterized at bottom by the infinite aspect of the deed, the purely external, specific character vanishes."[25] In other words, the injury to be annulled by punishment is not the determinate injury done to the victim but the noumenal injury done to the moral order. Hence the measure of punishment is properly derived not from the qualitative or quantitative aspects of the crime (as in revenge) but from its moral significance. The seriousness of the criminal's infringement of Right must be matched by an infringement of his right of "equal" weight. Since, however, the first of these variables eludes measurement in quantitative terms, "equal weight" cannot mean more than "proportionate severity." That is to say, the principle of equivalence properly understood translates into the rather vague demand for a graded proportionality, whereby more serious crimes are punished with severer penalties. Thus retributivism does not specifically enjoin the death penalty for first-degree murder, but neither of course does it absolutely condemn it. This result is not as unenlightening as it may seem, for that capital punishment is neither a moral imperative nor a moral wrong is no trivial conclusion.

Can we, however, go further? Can retributivism offer any guide as to how to go about matching punishments to crimes? Let us immediately grant the argument that, given the impossibility of assigning values to degrees of "seriousness" or "wickedness," we cannot fit penalties to offences according to the principle of proportionality literally construed. We may regard murder as a more serious crime than robbery, but as we have no way of assigning a numerical ratio to this comparison, we cannot achieve proportional equality between the relative severity of punishments and the relative seriousness of crimes. But although there is no principle of fitness by which we could establish natural correspondences between specific penalties and specific crimes, we can at least seek considerations relevant to determining the overall severity of the punishment scale taken by itself. And I want now to suggest that such considerations may be supplied by the retributivist understanding of mercy.

The charge is often heard that retributivism leaves no room for mercy, that it establishes not only the right to punish but also the positive duty to do so, so that any waiving of the right appears, on this theory, to be itself an injustice.[26] I shall argue, however, that it is not retributivism as such which leads to this conclusion so much as Kant's metaphysical assumptions, and that Hegel offers a metaphysical context for retributivism significantly different from Kant's, one that saves mercy. Furthermore, the difference between the two accounts of mercy will suggest a criterion for determining whether and for what crimes death is an appropriate punishment.

Let us first notice what Kant says about the right to pardon. In *The Metaphysical Elements of Justice* he writes:

> The right to pardon a criminal . . . is certainly the most slippery of all the rights of the sovereign. By exercising it he can demonstrate the splendor of his majesty and yet thereby wreak injustice to a high degree. With respect to crime of one subject against another, he absolutely cannot exercise this right, for in such cases exemption from punishment constitutes the greatest injustice toward his subjects. Consequently he can

make use of this right to pardon only in connection with an injury committed against himself.[27]

Kant is clearly uneasy about the right to pardon; indeed, he is totally at a loss to account for it and would restrict its application to the crime of treason. This is precisely what one would expect from a philosopher who regards punishment as a categorical imperative, an unconditional duty to be performed for its own sake and irrespective of its consequences. Kant would have the whole human race perish rather than exempt a criminal from punishment, for "if legal justice perishes, then it is no longer worthwhile for men to remain alive on this earth."[28]

Now consider what Hegel says about the right to pardon.

> The right to pardon criminals arises from the sovereignty of the monarch since it is this alone which is empowered to actualize Spirit's power of making undone what has been done and wiping out a crime by forgiving and forgetting it.
>
> Pardon is the remission of punishment, but it does not annul the law. On the contrary, the law stands and the pardoned man remains a criminal as before. This annulment of punishment may take place through religion, since something done may by Spirit be made undone in Spirit. But the power to accomplish this on earth resides in the king's majesty alone and must belong solely to his self-determined decision.[29]

Here there is no uneasiness. The right of pardon exhibits the majesty, the supreme self-confidence of Spirit in its cosmic authority, and Hegel places no limitations on its exercise. How can we account for this difference within retributivism between the Kantian and Hegelian attitudes towards mercy?

The answer lies, I believe, in their different understandings of the basis of human dignity. For Kant, the individual's dignity, and thus his title to rights, rests on his sharing the common personality of the human species. This common personality — Kant's pure ego — is a human essence abstracted from the empirical personality, which is ruled by self-love and which remains as a fixed reality opposed to the rational self. Now the fixed reality or naturalness of the self-seeking person poses an ever-present challenge to the objective reality of human dignity. For Kant this dignity is inherently insecure, because it is nothing more than a subjective claim asserted over against a hostile nature, a claim that must therefore be continually vindicated through the external conquest of its antithesis. From this perspective, therefore, to grant mercy to a criminal would be to leave standing the claim of selfishness to validity and thus to leave justice unsatisfied.

For Hegel, by contrast, the basis of human dignity is not solely a human essence of personality. It is a transcendent or divine Personality of which human selfhood is a subordinate though essential element. And this divine Person is no mere abstraction which leaves evil as a fixed reality outside it. Rather it is a Spirit which itself submits to negation by evil in order that, by the annulment of evil's claim to positive reality, its sovereignty might be objectively manifest. Stated otherwise, the natural (self-centred) will is for Hegel not primary and absolute, but is rather posited within the divine ground as an appearance of something independent, in order that, by the demonstration of its independence as appearance, the divine ground of being might be vindicated as such.[30] This means that the naturalness of egoism is inherently a show, a passing phase in the self-reintegration of Spirit. Punishment is just the practical demonstration that the right of egoism is a mere show, and this constitutes its justification. But now mercy is a more perfect demonstration of this truth. For Kant, mercy was opposed to justice because it meant leaving unrefuted the claim of egoism to reality. For Hegel, mercy is a form of justice because it is itself the refutation of that claim. The passage quoted above suggests a distinction as well as a relation between divine and human forgiveness. Divine forgiveness flows from the divine nature as that which incorporates as a constituent element of itself the individual's alienation from, and return to, the divine ground. From the divine standpoint, therefore, mercy is reconciled with justice because, far from leaving the natural will in its otherness, it is the very process of positing and conquering it. Human forgiveness flows from the recognition that divine mercy robs evil of its power of being and so establishes man's dignity beyond threat of subversion.[31] Thus, not even from the human standpoint is mercy opposed to justice, for it too attests to the nullity of evil. Like punishment, mercy presupposes wrongdoing; but it affirms that the wrong is insignificant, that its claim to validity is a mock claim, that it is powerless to prevail against right. This, then, is how mercy can have a place within a retributive theory of punishment. Mercy, no less than punishment, "wipes out" the wrong, not by repaying it but by forgetting it.

Now the relevance of all this to the death penalty is simply this. If the purpose of punishment is to vindicate human rights against the pretended validity of the criminal act, it seems consequent to suppose that the severity of punishment in any epoch will depend on the perceived magnitude of the threat that crime poses to the reality of human dignity. A claim of human worth resting on the supposed sovereignty of individual personhood finds its sole objective confirmation in outward possessions. It will therefore see in any offence against property an infinite challenge to itself and punish it accordingly. Since, moreover, the absolutization of the isolated person brings the state of nature into political society, the penal system will take upon itself the enforcement of the law of private revenge, centralizing without reconstituting it. Retribution will thus take the form of the qualitative and quantitative redress of personal injury, and torture, the giving back of pain for pain, will be the paradigmatic form of punishment.[32] On the other hand, a claim of dignity resting, like Kant's, on the assumed sovereignty of a common humanity (and hence of law) will view this dignity as established independently of external things, though still challenged by a natural will now regarded as evil. Since the state of nature is here abrogated as a normative principle, the law of retaliation will be reinterpreted as the impersonal vengeance of the general will, and minutely differentiated corporal punishments will give way to the uniform abstraction of imprisonment, corresponding to the abstraction of crime as an offence against right in general. Moreover, since it is now the principle of the criminal will and not the criminal act itself that challenges the objective reality of human worth, punishments will be adjusted more subtly to the evil quality of the will, and, in particular, the death penalty will be reserved for the only crime which, by destroying the body, also destroys the person. Finally, a people confident that human dignity is no mere subjective claim pitted against an indifferent nature but an objective fact rooted in a divinely governed cosmos; a people confident, in short, that the human personality cannot be destroyed will be inclined to temper punishment with mercy. We may imagine, therefore, that there exists an ideal penal code corresponding to the highest strength of the human spirit and in which the death penalty perhaps plays no part. But like representative government, this simply best penal code is not suited to all peoples at all stages of their moral development. At any stage, the strength of the basis of self-definition will determine the scale of punishments needed to preserve and reinforce the positive morality (understood as a particular perception of natural morality) on which the social order is founded. And any attempt to impose a higher, less severe code on a people unprepared for it risks undermining the belief in a natural moral order on which depends the conviction of personal worth as well as the habit of self-restraint.

Somewhat surprisingly, therefore, retributivism issues in a counsel of pragmatism with respect to the use of the death penalty. It leads to the Montesquieuian conclusion that that penal code is best which suits the "spirit" of a people, by which is here understood the system of life-organizing beliefs regarding the foundation of human value. Not to be confused with this result is the conclusion of Beccaria, who thought that the scale of punishments ought to be relative to the level of civility of a people, the more savage requiring stronger deterrents. The question legislators must ask is not how much punishment is needed to deter potential criminals in the present state of society, but how much is needed to reassure decent men in the present state of their self-knowledge. Obviously these questions lead to different oracles. The first directs us to data on differential crime rates, the second to public opinion.

NOTES

1. Mill, "Utilitarianism," in Lerner (ed.), *Essential Works of John Stuart Mill* (1961), 236.
2. Bentham, *The Principles of Morals and Legislation* (Darien, Hafner 1970), 170.
3. Sellin, "Death and Imprisonment as Deterrents to Murder," in Bedau (ed.), *The Death Penalty in America* (1964) 274–284; Sellin, "Does the Death Penalty Protect Municipal Police?" in Bedau, 284–301; Sellin, "Effect of Repeal and Reintroduction of the Death Penalty on Homicide Rates," in Bedau, 339–343. Stronger, though still not conclusive, evidence for the uniquely effective deterrent force of the death penalty is offered by Ehrlich, "The Deterrent Effect of Capital Punishment," 65 *American Economic Review* (1975), 397–417.
4. Van Den Haag, "On Deterrence and the Death Penalty," 78 *Ethics* (1968), 280–287. See also Goldberg, "On Capital Punishment," 85 *Ethics* (1974) 67–74.
5. Mill, "Speech in Favor of Capital Punishment," 1868 in Ezorsky (ed.), *Philosophical Perspectives on Punishment* (1972), 271–278.
6. See, e.g., Mabbott, "Punishment," 48 Mind (1939); McCloskey, "A Non-utilitarian Approach to Punishment," 8 *Inquiry* (1965); Armstrong, "The Retributivist Hits Back," 70 *Mind* (1961).
7. See, however, Hart, "Murder and the Principles of Punishment," in Hart, *Punishment and Responsibility* (1968), 54–89. My disagreements with Hart will be spelled out below.
8. For a recent retributivist argument in favor of retention see Berns, *For Capital Punishment* (1979).
9. Bentham, supra note 2, 172–175.
10. Hart, *Punishment and Responsibility*, supra note 7, 77 and passim.
11. See Wootton, *Social Science and Social Pathology* (1959), ch. 8, and Crime and the Criminal Law (1963) 47–57.
12. Quinton, "On Punishment," in Acton (ed.), *The Philosophy of Punishment* (1969), 55–64.
13. Rawls, "Two Concepts of Rules," in Acton, supra note 12, 105–114.
14. Hart, *Punishment and Responsibility*, supra note 2, 22–24, 44–49, 80–81, 181–183.
15. Rawls, supra note 13.
16. Kant, *The Metaphysical Elements of Justice* (trans. Ladd, 1965), 99–108; Hegel, *Hegel's Philosophy of Right* (trans. Knox, 1952), paras. 90–103.
17. *Philosophy of Right*, supra note 16, paras. 97, 99.
18. Beccaria, *On Crimes and Punishments* (trans. Paolucci, 1963), 9; Hart, *Punishment and Responsibility*, supra note 2, 74.
19. *Philosophy of Right*, supra note 16, addition to para. 101.
20. Ibid. para. 100.
21. Stephen, *A History of the Criminal Law of England* (1883), Volume 2, 81.
22. Quoted in Ezorsky, supra note 5, 250.
23. Kant, supra note 16, 102.

24. The problems in matching punishments to crimes are discussed in two recent articles. See Wertheimer, "Should the Punishment Fit the Crime?" 3 *Social Theory and Practice* (1975), 403–423; Goldman, "The Paradox of Punishment," 9 *Philosophy and Public Affairs* (1979), 42–58.
25. Hegel, supra note 16, para. 101.
26. This accusation has been repeated by Honderich, *Punishment: The Supposed Justifications* (1969), 12–13. Here we may note that it is really utilitarianism that abolishes mercy. The latter presupposes the right to punish; it is a forgoing of the right. Now if the circumstances of utility give us the right to punish, then we must do so, since to forgo the right is to satisfy the criminal's interest at the expense of the general welfare, which is to commit an injustice. On the other hand, if considerations of utility lead us to forgo punishment, this is not to show mercy, for we had no right to punish.
27. Kant, supra note 16, 107–108.
28. Ibid., 100.
29. Hegel, supra note 16, para. 282 and addition.
30. Hegel, *The Phenomenology of Mind* (trans. Baillie, 1931), 93–94, 96–99, 789–790, 806–807.
31. Hegel, *Early Theological Writings* (trans. Knox, 1971), 224–244; *Phenomenology of Mind*, supra note 30, 6680–679.
32. See Foucault, *Discipline and Punish* (trans. Sheridan, 1977), 32–69.

QUESTIONS

1. Based on the materials in this chapter, can you construct a utilitarian or what is sometimes called a forward-looking justification of punishment? What are the central strengths and weaknesses to this approach?
2. What are Alan Brudner's objections to utilitarian justifications of punishment?
3. Brudner argues that retributivism offers the only morally defensible account of punishment. Why? Do you find his arguments persuasive?

RACE AND THE DEATH PENALTY

Anthony G. Amsterdam

There are times when even truths we hold self-evident require affirmation. For those who have invested our careers and our hopes in the criminal justice system, this is one of those times. Insofar as the basic principles that give value to our lives are in the keeping of the law and can be vindicated or betrayed by the decisions of any court, they have been sold down the river by a decision of the Supreme Court of the United States less than a year old.

I do not choose by accident a metaphor of slavery. For the decision I am referring to is the criminal justice system's *Dred Scott* case. It is the case of Warren McCleskey, a black man sentenced to die for the murder of a white man in Georgia. The Supreme Court held that McCleskey can be constitutionally put to death despite overwhelming unrebutted and unexplained statistical evidence that the death penalty is being imposed by Georgia juries in a pattern which reflects the race of convicted murderers and their victims and cannot be accounted for by any factor other than race.

From Criminal Justice Ethics, *v. 7, no. 2 (Summer/Fall 1988), pp. 2, 84–86. Reprinted by permission of The Institute for Criminal Justice Ethics, 899 Tenth Ave., New York, NY 10019, and Anthony Amsterdam.*

This is not just a case about capital punishment. The Supreme Court's decision, which amounts to an open license to discriminate against people of color in capital sentencing, was placed upon grounds that implicate the entire criminal justice system. Worse still, the Court's reasoning makes us all accomplices in its toleration of a racially discriminatory administration of criminal justice.

Let us look at the *McCleskey* case. His crime was an ugly one. He robbed a furniture store at gunpoint, and he or one of his accomplices killed a police officer who responded to the scene. McCleskey may have been the trigger-man. Whether or not he was, he was guilty of murder under Georgia law.

But his case in the Supreme Court was not concerned with guilt. It was concerned with why McCleskey had been sentenced to death instead of life imprisonment for his crime. It was concerned with why, out of seventeen defendants charged with the killings of police officers in Fulton County, Georgia, between 1973 and 1980, only Warren McCleskey — a black defendant charged with killing a white officer — had been chosen for a death sentence. In the only other one of these seventeen cases in which the predominantly white prosecutor's office in Atlanta had pushed for the death penalty, a black defendant convicted of killing a black police officer had been sentenced to life instead.

It was facts of that sort that led the NAACP Legal Defense Fund to become involved in McCleskey's case. They were not unfamiliar facts to any of the lawyers who, like myself, had worked for the Legal Defense Fund for many years, defending blacks charged with serious crimes throughout the South. We knew that in the United States black defendants convicted of murder or rape in cases involving white victims have always been sentenced to death and executed far out of proportion to their numbers, and under factual circumstances that would have produced a sentence of imprisonment — often a relatively light sentence of imprisonment — in identical cases with black victims or white defendants or both.

Back in the mid-sixties the Legal Defense Fund had presented to courts evidence of extensive statistical studies conducted by Dr. Marvin Wolfgang, one of the deans of American criminology, showing that the grossly disproportionate number of death sentences which were then being handed out to black defendants convicted of the rape of white victims could not be explained by any factor other than race. Prosecutors took the position then that these studies were insufficiently detailed to rule out the influence of every possible non-racial factor, and it was largely for that reason that the courts rejected our claims that our black death-sentenced clients had been denied the Equal Protection of the Laws. Fortunately, in 1972 we had won a Supreme Court decision that saved the lives of all those clients and outlawed virtually every death penalty statute in the United States on procedural grounds; and when the States enacted new death-penalty laws between 1973 and 1976, only three of them reinstated capital punishment for rape. Now that it no longer mattered much, the prosecutors could afford to take another tack. When we argued against the new capital murder statutes on the ground that the Wolfgang studies had shown the susceptibility of capital sentencing laws to racially discriminatory application, the Government of the United States came into the Supreme Court against us saying, Oh, yes, Wolfgang was "a careful and comprehensive study, and we do not question its conclusion that during the twenty years between [1945 and 1965] . . ., in southern states, there was discrimination in rape cases." However, said the Government, this "research does not provide support for a conclusion that racial discrimination continues, . . . or that it applies to murder cases."

So we were well prepared for this sort of selective agnosticism when we went to court in the *McCleskey* case. The evidence that we presented in support of McCleskey's claim of racial discrimination left nothing out. Our centerpiece was a pair of studies conducted by Professor David Baldus, of the University of Iowa, and his colleagues, which examined 2,484 cases of murder and non-negligent manslaughter that occurred in Georgia between 1973, the date when its present capital murder statute was enacted, and 1979, the year after McCleskey's own death sentence was imposed. The Baldus team got its data on these cases principally from official state records, supplied by the Georgia Supreme Court and the Georgia Board of Pardons and Paroles.

Through a highly refined protocol, the team collected information regarding more than five hundred factors in each case — information relating to the demographic and individual characteristics of the defendant and the victim, the circumstances of the crime and the strength of the evidence of guilt, and the aggravating and mitigating features of each case: both the features specified by Georgia law to be considered in capital sentencing and every factor recognized in the legal and criminological literature as theoretically or actually likely to affect the choice of life or death. Using the most reliable and advanced techniques of social-science research, Baldus processed the data through a wide array of sophisticated statistical procedures, including multiple-regression analyses based upon alternative models that considered and controlled for as few as 10 or as many as 230 sentencing factors in each analysis. When our evidentiary case was presented in court, Baldus reanalyzed the data several more times to take account of every additional factor, combination of factors, or model for analysis of factors suggested by the State of Georgia's expert witnesses, its lawyers, and the federal trial judge. The Baldus study has since been uniformly praised by social scientists as the best study of any aspect of criminal sentencing ever conducted.

What did it show? That death sentences were being imposed in Georgia murder cases in a clear, consistent pattern that reflected the race of the victim and the race of the defendant and could not be explained by any non-racial factor. For example:

(1) Although less than 40 percent of Georgia homicide cases involve white victims, in 87 percent of the cases in which a death sentence is imposed, the victim is white. White-victim cases are almost eleven times more likely to produce a death sentence than are black-victim cases.

(2) When the race of the defendant is considered too, the following figures emerge: 22 percent of black defendants who kill white victims are sentenced to death; 8 percent of white defendants who kill white victims are sentenced to death; 1 percent of black defendants who kill black victims are sentenced to death; 3 percent of white defendants who kill black victims are sentenced to death. It should be noted that out of the roughly 2,500 Georgia homicide cases found, only 64 involved killings of black victims by white defendants, so the 3 percent death-sentencing rate in this category represents a total of two death sentences over a six-year period. Plainly, the reason why racial discrimination against black defendants does not appear even more glaringly evident is that most black murderers kill black victims; almost no identified white murderers kill black victims; and virtually nobody is sentenced to death for killing a mere black victim.

(3) No non-racial factor explains these racial patterns. Under multiple regression analysis, the model with the maximum explanatory power shows that after controlling for legitimate non-racial factors, murderers of white victims are still being sentenced to death 4.3 times more often than murderers of black victims. Multiple regression analysis also shows that the race of the victim is as good a basis for predicting whether or not a murderer will be sentenced to death as are the aggravating circumstances which the Georgia statute explicitly says should be considered in favor of a death sentence, such as whether the

defendant has a prior murder conviction, or whether he is the primary actor in the present murder.

(4) Across the whole universe of cases, approximately 5 percent of Georgia killings result in a death sentence. Yet when more than 230 non-racial variables are controlled for, the death sentencing rate is 6 percentage points higher in white-victim cases than in black-victim cases. What this means is that in predicting whether any particular person will get the death penalty in Georgia, it is less important to know whether or not he committed a homicide in the first place than to know whether, if he did, he killed a white victim or a black one.

(5) However, the effects of race are not uniform across the entire range of homicide cases. As might be expected, in the least aggravated sorts of cases, almost no one gets a death sentence; in the really gruesome cases, a high percentage of both black and white murderers get death sentences; so it is in the mid-range of cases — cases like McCleskey's — that race has its greatest impact. The Baldus study found that in these mid-range cases the death-sentencing rate for killers of white victims is 34 percent as compared to 14 percent for killers of black victims. In other words, out of every thirty-four murderers sentenced to death for killing a white victim, twenty of them would not have gotten death sentences if their victims had been black.

The bottom line is this: Georgia has executed eleven murderers since it passed its present statute in 1973. Nine of the eleven were black. Ten of the eleven had white victims. Can there be the slightest doubt that this revolting record is the product of some sort of racial bias rather than a pure fluke?

A narrow majority of the Supreme Court pretended to have such doubts and rejected McCleskey's Equal-Protection challenge to his death sentence. It did not question the quality or the validity of the Baldus study, or any of the findings that have been described here. It admitted that the manifest racial discrepancies in death sentencing were unexplained by any non-racial variable, and that Baldus's data pointed to a "likelihood" or a "risk" that race was at work in the capital sentencing process. It essentially conceded that if a similar statistical showing of racial bias had been made in an employment-discrimination case or in a jury-selection case, the courts would have been required to find a violation of the Equal Protection Clause of the Fourteenth Amendment. But, the Court said, racial discrimination in capital sentencing cannot be proved by a pattern of sentencing results: a death-sentenced defendant like McCleskey must present proof that the particular jury or the individual prosecutor, or some other decision-maker in his own case, was personally motivated by racial considerations to bring about his death. Since such proof is never possible to obtain, racial discrimination in capital sentencing is never possible to prove.

The Court gave four basic reasons for this result. First, since capital sentencing decisions are made by a host of different juries and prosecutors, and are supposed to be based upon "innumerable factors that vary according to the characteristics of the individual defendant and the facts of the particular capital offense," even sentencing patterns that are explicable by race and inexplicable except by race do not necessarily show that any single decision-maker in the system is acting out of a subjective purpose to discriminate. Second, capital punishment laws are important for the protection of society; the "[i]mplementation of these laws necessarily requires discretionary judgments"; and, "[b]ecause discretion is essential to the criminal justice process, we [sh]ould demand exceptionally clear proof before we . . . infer that the discretion has been abused." Third, this same respect for discretionary judgments makes it imprudent to require juries and prosecutors to explain their decisions, so it is better to ignore the inference of racial discrimination that flows logically from their behavior than to call upon them to justify such behavior upon non-racial grounds.

Fourth, more is involved than capital punishment. "McCleskey's claim . . . throws into serious question the principles that underlie our entire criminal justice system." This is so because "the Baldus study indicates a discrepancy that appears to correlate with race," and "[a]pparent disparities in sentencing are an inevitable part of our criminal justice system." "Thus," says the Court, "if we accepted McCleskey's claim that racial bias has impermissibly tainted the capital sentencing decision, we could soon be faced with similar claims as to other types of penalty. Moreover, the claim that . . . sentence rests on the irrelevant factor of race easily could be extended to apply to claims based on unexplained discrepancies that correlate to membership in other minority groups, and even to gender" — and even to claims based upon "the defendant's facial characteristics, or the physical attractiveness of the . . . victim." In other words, if we forbid racial discrimination in meting out sentences of life or death, we may have to face claims of discrimination against blacks, or against women, or perhaps against ugly people, wherever the facts warrant such claims, in the length of prison sentences, in the length of jail sentences, in the giving of suspended sentences, in the making of pretrial release decisions, in the invocation of recidivist sentencing enhancements, in the prosecutor's decisions whether to file charges, and how heavily to load up the charges, against black defendants as compared with white defendants or against ugly defendants as compared with ravishingly beautiful defendants; and of course the whole criminal justice system will then fall down flat and leave us in a state of anarchy. In thirty years of reading purportedly serious judicial opinions, I have never seen one that came so close to Thomas De Quincy's famous justification for punishing the crime of murder: "If once a man indulges himself in murder, very soon he comes to think little of robbing; and from robbing he next comes to drinking and Sabbath-breaking, and from that to incivility and procrastination."

Notice that the Court's version of this slippery-slope argument merely makes explicit what is implied throughout its opinion in the *McCleskey* case. Its decision is not limited to capital sentencing but purports to rest on principles which apply to the whole criminal justice system. Every part of that system from arrest to sentencing and parole, in relation to every crime from murder to Sabbath-breaking, involves a multitude of separate decision-makers making individualized decisions based upon "innumerable (case-specific) factors." All of these decisions are important for the protection of society from crime. All are conceived as "necessarily requir[ing] discretionary judgments." In making these discretionary judgments, prosecutors and judges as well as jurors have traditionally been immunized from inquiry into their motives. If this kind of discretion implies the power to treat black people differently from white people and to escape the responsibility for explaining why one is making life-and-death decisions in an apparently discriminatory manner, it implies a tolerance for racial discrimination throughout the length and breadth of the administration of criminal justice. What the Supreme Court has held, plainly, is that the very nature of the criminal justice system requires that its workings be excluded from the ordinary rules of law and even logic that guarantee equal protection to racial minorities in our society.

And it is here, I suggest, that any self-respecting criminal justice professional is obliged to speak out against this Supreme Court's conception of the criminal justice system. We must reaffirm that there can be no justice in a system which treats people of color differently from white people, or treats crimes against people of color differently from crimes against white people.

We must reaffirm that racism is itself a crime, and that the toleration of racism cannot be justified by the supposed interest of society in fighting crime. We must pledge that when anyone — even a majority of the Supreme Court — tells us that a power to discriminate on grounds of race is necessary to protect society from crime, we will recognize that we are probably being sold another shipment of propaganda to justify repression. Let us therefore never fail to ask the question whether righteous rhetoric about protecting society from crime really refers to protecting only white people. And when the answer, as in the McCleskey case, is that protecting only white people is being described as "protecting society from crime," let us say that we are not so stupid as to buy this version of the Big Lie, nor so uncaring as to let it go unchallenged.

Let us reaffirm that neither the toleration of racism by the Supreme Court nor the pervasiveness of racism in the criminal justice system can make it right, and that these things only make it worse. Let us reaffirm that racism exists, and is against the fundamental law of this Nation, whenever people of different races are treated differently by any public agency or institution as a consequence of their race and with no legitimate non-racial reason for the different treatment. Let us dedicate ourselves to eradicating racism, and declaring it unlawful, not simply in the superficial, short-lived situation where we can point to one or another specific decision-maker and show that his decisions were the product of conscious bigotry, but also in the far more basic, more intractable, and more destructive situation where hundreds upon hundreds of different public decision-makers, acting like Georgia's prosecutors and judges and juries — without collusion and in many cases without con- sciousness of their own racial biases — combine to produce a pattern that bespeaks the profound prejudice of an entire population.

Also, let us vow that we will never claim — or stand by unprotestingly while others claim for us — that, because our work is righteous and important, it should be above the law. Of course, controlling crime is vital work; that is why we give the agencies of criminal justice drastic and unique coercive powers, including the powers of imprisonment and death. And of course discretion in the execution of such powers is essential. But it is precisely because the powers that the system regulates are so awesome, and because the discretion of its actors is so broad, that it cannot be relieved of accountability for the exercise of that discretion. Nor can it be exempted from the scrutiny that courts of law are bound to give to documented charges of discrimination on the ground of race by any agency of government. Let us declare flatly that we neither seek nor will accept any such exemp- tion, and that we find it demeaning to be told by the Supreme Court that the system of justice to which we have devoted our professional lives cannot do its job without a special dispensation from the safeguards that assure to people of every race the equal protection of the law.

This is a stigma criminal justice practitioners do not deserve. Service in the criminal justice system should be a cause not for shame but for pride. Nowhere is it possible to dedicate one's labors to the welfare of one's fellow human beings with a greater sense that one is needed and that the quality of what one does can make a difference. But to feel this pride, and to deserve it, we must consecrate ourselves to the protection of all people, not a privileged few. We must be servants of humanity, not of caste. Whether or not the Supreme Court demands this of us, we must demand it of ourselves and of our coworkers in the system. For this is the faith to which we are sworn by our common calling: that doing justice is never simply someone else's job; correcting injustice is never simply someone else's responsibility.

QUESTIONS

1. Evaluate the U.S. Supreme Court concern that if arguments pointing to discrimination against black Americans facing capital charges were acknowledged by the court, the entire criminal justice sentencing process would be threatened.
2. Discretion is an important element in sentencing for capital crimes. Does the fact that discretion must enter into such sentencing decisions explain, excuse, or justify the kinds of patterns that Amsterdam is pointing to?
3. Is the fact of discrimination against black Americans in assigning the penalty of death for capital crimes a persuasive reason for abolishing capital punishment?

SUGGESTIONS FOR FURTHER READING

Books

- Hugo Adam Bedau, *Matters of Life and Death*, ed. Tom Regan (New York: Random House, 1980). In the fifth chapter, "Capital Punishment," Bedau explores the various justifications for capital punishment. (Regan's book is a useful resource for exploring the issues of abortion and euthanasia as well as capital punishment.)
- Walter Berns, *For Capital Punishment* (New York: Basic Books Inc., 1979). The various arguments against capital punishment are set out and systematically examined and rejected. The author then constructs a defence of capital punishment in a manner similar to that set out in the article included in this chapter.
- David Chandler, *Capital Punishment in Canada* (Toronto: McClelland and Stewart, 1976). The author describes his book as a study in the sociology of law. It provides a background study of the history of capital punishment in Canada. Key debates in Parliament are set out; the positions of political parties and individuals are described and analyzed and conclusions with respect to the capital punishment debate are suggested.
- *Crime and Delinquency* is a journal published by the American National Council on Crime and Delinquency. Their October 1980 issue, which is devoted to the topic of capital punishment, includes the article by Walter Berns in this chapter.

The other articles are, for the most part, opposed to the use of capital punishment. The emphasis is on research designed to establish the effect of capital punishment on the occurrence of murder. One particularly interesting article argues that there is no evidence that capital punishment deters people from committing murder; and that there is empirical evidence suggesting that capital punishment has a brutalizing effect — that is to say, that capital punishment is actually a stimulant to murder.

Government Reports

These reports should be available in the public-documents section of your university library.

- *Capital Punishment: New Material 1965–1972*. This was prepared for the Solicitor-General of Canada in 1972 as a resource document for the public and for Parliament in the 1972 abolition debate. It is an update of a similar study done in 1965. The report, though somewhat out of date, provides an interesting summation of the arguments for and against capital punishment.

- *A Study of the Deterrent Effect of Capital Punishment with Special Reference to the Canadian Situation*. This research report was prepared by E.A. Fattah for the department of the Solicitor-General as a resource document to be used in the debate of 1972. The report is a somewhat dated but highly regarded study. Much of the information it contains is still of value.

Articles

- E.A. Fattah, "Perceptions of Violence, Concern about Crime, Fear of Victimization and Attitudes to the Death Penalty," *Canadian Journal of Criminology*, Vol. 21, No. 1 (January 1979). This is an empirical survey of available information and studies of attitudes in Canada and the United States with a view to discovering relationships among the factors indicated. The findings suggest that the attitude toward the death penalty is stable, resistant to change, and not "greatly influenced by the level of general concern about crime, or by the degree of personal fear of victimization."
- J. Feinberg, "The Expressive Function of Punishment," *The Monist*. La Salle, Illinois, Vol. 49 (1965), No. 3.

   Over the past two or three decades there has developed in legal and government circles the view that denunciation of crime is a central purpose of punishment. Among punishments, capital punishment is the strongest tool of denunciation available; therefore, capital punishment is appropriate where the most emphatic form of denunciation is required — namely, murder. This view is set out and defended by Feinberg in this article, which is reprinted in *Punishment*, referred to below. For a critical assessment of Feinberg's argument see "Crime, Punishment and Emphatic Denunciation," an article by me printed in the special issue, Vol. 11, No. 1 (November 1981), of *The Laurentian University Review* devoted to the topic "Law and Justice." It is argued here that the justification of punishment as denunciation is at root simply a variation on the deterrence justification. For such a view to support the use of capital punishment it would have to be shown that capital punishment is a unique deterrent. Adopting a view similar to that developed by Fattah in this chapter, the argument is that it is not. The article is available from me on request.

On Punishment in General

Discussion of the merits of capital punishment inevitably leads to discussions on the justification of punishment. A good deal of worthwhile material is available on this issue. For example, the Law Reform Commission of Canada has prepared a number of reports and commissioned a number of studies. Of these the following are certainly of interest:

- *The Meaning of Guilt* (Working Paper 2). In this paper the Commission argues that punishment is justified in name of fairness to those who obey the law and in the name of self-defence.
- *Imprisonment and Release* (Working Paper 11). As the title suggests, this study examines the justification of punishment and what that justification implies for sentencing and imprisonment.
- *Studies on Sentencing* (Working Paper 3). This paper includes two studies of interest. The first, by John Hogarth (then chairman of the B.C. Police Commission), examines alternatives to our adversary system of justice with their implications for the imposition

of punishment. The second (by Paul Weiler, professor of law at Osgoode Law School), "The Reform of Punishment," examines a variety of theories of punishment. A deterrence justification is rejected and a retribution model advanced.

- *Fear of Punishment.* This study was published in 1976. It contains two essays. The first, by E.A. Fattah, is "Deterrence: A Review of the Literature." The second, "Deterrent Effects of Punishment for Breaking and Entering and Theft," is an empirical analysis.
- Finally, a good source of articles written from a philosophical perspective on the subject of punishment is *Punishment,* edited by Gertrude Ezorsky and published by the State University of New York Press (1972).

Audiovisual Resources

- As is the case for the topics of Abortion and Euthanasia, the Ontario Education Authority has produced two half-hour videotapes on capital punishment. The first tape is called "The Last Hangings in Canada." It is built around an account of the last days of the last two people to be executed in Canada and includes discussions with a number of academics, American prison personnel who supervised executions, and a number of men on death row in American prisons at the time of filming. The second, "Capital Punishment," is a round-table discussion. Participants include Hugo Bedau and Walter Berns, both of whose work is included in this chapter.
- Finally, a 1996 American film called *Dead Man Walking* explores a relationship between a man on death row in the United States and a Roman Catholic nun. The story takes the viewer through a series of appeals, through the final hours of the prisoner's life and into the death chamber, where the prisoner is executed by lethal injection.

Chapter 4

Pornography

Introduction

The concept of moral autonomy explored in the first two chapters on euthanasia and abortion also plays a central role in discussions of the morality of censorship, particularly the censorship of pornographic materials. How do we assess the limits beyond which the exercise of freedom on the part of some becomes an unacceptable threat to the freedom or well-being of others? This question provides a focus for the discussions of this chapter.

Background Considerations

The Criminal Code of Canada has contained provisions restricting the circulation of obscene material from its earliest formulations. The 1892 Code prohibited the sale or display of anything that tended to "corrupt public morals" or was "disgusting" or "immoral." It also banned the use of postal services for the transmission of anything that was "immoral," "obscene," or "indecent." The law did provide, however, that serving the public good was an adequate defence to an obscenity charge.

The code was expanded in 1927 to include the sale, public display, circulation, distribution, and possession of "obscene" materials or "materials tending to corrupt public morals." No further major change was made until shortly after the Second World War, when the code was expanded once more to include crime comics — material that through the use of pictures depicted the commission of real or fictitious crimes. The code was also revised to remove any reference to "the tendency to corrupt public morals."

The 1950s were a period of social change. Increasing wealth and sophisticated printing and distribution techniques led to dramatic increases in the circulation of pornographic materials. Concern with this trend resulted in the creation of a Senate Committee on Salacious and Indecent Literature. The committee hearings provided a public forum for debate, and individuals and groups used the occasion to set out their views. Those who advocated stricter control argued that the Criminal Code should be strengthened. There was clear concern about the involvement of children.

Those who opposed further regulation did so on two grounds. Some argued that current provisions provided adequate control. Others argued that any control limited freedom of speech, interfered with the right of adults to read what they wished, and was objectionable except where needed to protect people from direct harm.

In 1958, a series of changes were proposed to Parliament by the Minister of Justice, Davie Fulton, who presented his amendments with two objectives in mind. To begin with, there was no statutory definition of obscenity. Prior to 1958, material was judged obscene by the courts if it had a "tendency to deprave and corrupt those whose minds were open to such immoral influences and into whose hands a publication of the sort in question might fall." This test, laid down by a British judge, Chief Justice Cockburn, in the case of *R. v. Hicklin* in 1868, was known as the Hicklin test. And it had come under severe criticism as being subjective and open to uneven application. Davie Fulton proposed in his amendments to supplement this test with a more objective standard. The courts were to regard as obscene "any publication a dominant characteristic of which was the undue exploitation of sex or of sex and crime, horror, cruelty, and violence." Fulton was also concerned to stem the circulation of what he described in the House of Commons as "the kind of muck on the newsstands against which our main efforts in this definition are directed." The aim, therefore, was to strengthen control of pornographic materials.

The proposed amendments were adopted in 1959 under s. 159 of the *Criminal Code* (now s. 163 and included in the first reading). This legislation regarding obscenity remains to this day.

It is perhaps ironic that legislation designed to reduce the amount of objectionable material in circulation had the opposite effect. The key to this development was the case of *Queen v. Brodie*, which was finally decided in the Supreme Court and in which the court was asked to determine whether the unexpurgated text of *Lady Chatterley's Lover* was an obscene publication under the 1959 provisions of the Criminal Code. The Court decided, five votes to four, that it was not. Although the Supreme Court was divided on a number of issues, its decision had a decisive impact on Canadian law and its treatment of obscene materials. To begin with, the Hicklin test ceased to be used. This in itself had a liberalizing impact. Secondly, a book could be judged obscene only if undue exploitation of sex was a dominant theme of the whole publication. Judgement could no longer be based on passages taken out of context. Further, artistic merit could now be considered, with the result that today it is unlikely that works of serious literary merit could be judged obscene under the code no matter how explicit their treatment of subjects defined by the law as obscene. Finally, the notion of "community standards" was introduced. A publication could be judged obscene only if it exceeded community standards of tolerance.

The 1970s saw a strong renewal of public concern with pornography in response to a flood of increasingly explicit, widely circulated pornographic publications. Relaxation of legal controls was widely criticized. By 1977 a number of private members' bills dealing with pornography had been proposed. The government of the day felt itself under increasing pressure to tighten legislative controls. The result was a decision to examine all the proposed amendments to the Criminal Code through public hearings to be conducted by the Justice and Legal Affairs Committee of the House of Commons.

The pattern followed in the hearings was similar, in many respects, to that of the Senate inquiry that had taken place two decades previously. Those who advocated stricter controls called for an objective test of obscenity. There was a sharply focused desire to eliminate child pornography. And the theme of violence played a significant role in the discussions. Those opposed to increased control argued that current provisions were adequate if properly applied and pointed to the undesirable aspects of censorship in any form.

The committee reported in 1978 and indicated that it was concerned with the depiction and advocacy "in clear and explicit terms" of such activities as "sodomy, cunnilingus, fellatio, incest, masturbation, bestiality, necrophilia, sadism, and masochism." It argued that "the effect of this type of material is to reinforce male-female stereotypes to the detriment of both sexes," and went on to say that "such literature attempts to make degradation, humiliation, victimization and violence in human relationships appear normal and acceptable." The committee concluded that Canadians were justified in controlling the circulation of this kind of material and proposed a series of amendments. However, the report was not acted upon.

Another government report, *Pornography and Prostitution in Canada: Report of the Special Committee on Pornography and Prostitution*, chaired by Paul Fraser and produced in 1985, concluded that "with respect to pornography, its availability and its control, it is overwhelmingly apparent that the current legal proscriptions are unsatisfactory to everyone." Once again, changes were proposed in 1987 in response to that report and growing public concern. However, as in the past, the proposed amendments generated serious controversy, and the proposed legislation died on the order paper.

The most recent development with respect to censoring pornography is a landmark Supreme Court decision in 1992. In *R. v. Butler*, a unanimous 9-0 decision by the justices held that pornography depicting child sex and violent, degrading, or dehumanizing sex is illegal in Canada. The first set of readings in this chapter are excerpts from that case.

Concern with pornography has not been an exclusively Canadian phenomenon. Over the past two decades, studies have been commissioned in both the United States and Great Britain. The resulting reports (mentioned in the bibliography at the end of the chapter) have concluded that, in spite of obvious public concern, research has not established conclusively that exposure to pornography stimulates an increase in sexual crimes such as rape or indecent exposure. On the basis of these findings, these committees have recommended that, because controls limit freedom of choice and expression, and because no direct harm in the form of criminal activity can be proven to result from exposure to such materials, legislative control of pornographic material should be reduced or eliminated.

The Current Situation

Pornography today is big business. Moreover, if the report of the Justice and Legal Affairs Committee is to be believed, a substantial portion of the business is controlled by organized crime in the United States. Of course, not all pornography is illegal, as a visit to the magazine shelf of the corner store would quickly reveal. Of the ten best-selling magazines in Canada today, six are explicitly sexual in content. Two examples are *Playboy* and *Penthouse*.

The public attitude toward pornography is not easy to gauge. Over the past ten years the courts have accepted a wider and wider range of materials as not exceeding community standards of tolerance. At the same time, Parliament has been under constant political pressure since the mid-1970s to strengthen the law. Some of this pressure has come from feminists who argue that because pornography depicts women in ways that endorse messages about their unequal and subordinate status, restricting its circulation is one strategy for achieving the goal of equality. Discussions of and challenges to this feminist analysis of pornography are evident in the reasoning of the Supreme Court Justices in the *Butler* case and in the readings by Lorenne Clark and Wendy McElroy.

Pornography continues to be controversial as rapid technological developments have made it possible for people to freely access information on the World Wide Web. Pornography is now readily available in virtually every home by computer. These developments raise new and difficult problems with respect to censorship. In summary, the nature and availability of pornography continue to pose vexing questions for Canadians both as individuals and as a community.

The Moral Dimension

Some people believe that pornography is beneficial, in part because it provides an outlet for sexual fantasies that might otherwise find expression in violent or coercive behaviour. None of the readings in this chapter adopts this stance, though some of the readings examine it. Others have argued that pornography is a form of sexual expression that is simply a matter of personal preference, and, as such, morally neutral if participation is voluntary and those participating are adults capable of deciding their own lifestyle. This view, too, is examined in the readings. Much more common is the view that pornography is objectionable either because of the way it depicts human sexuality and because of the sexual morality it appears to advocate, or because of specific and common ingredients such as violence or the way it represents women or children.

However, the debate does not end here, for two reasons. First, those who feel quite strongly that pornography is seriously objectionable face further questions. Should pornography be censored in general or only in certain cases? If in certain cases, how do we define pornography so as to target only that material which is objectionable? For those who do not feel strongly on the subject, a slightly different question is raised. When is a majority entitled to override the moral autonomy of individuals and impose, by law, a standard of conduct?

We have already examined possible answers to this last question. In the first three chapters, we have seen it argued that communities are justified in creating legal constraints on individual autonomy in order to protect human life. People should be allowed to pursue their own lifestyle and determine their own behaviour up to the point at which the behaviour begins to harm themselves or others. The question around which the pornography debate usually revolves is whether the voluntary use of pornography by some is harmful to non-users or the community at large.

The suggestion that the basic issue in assessing the justifiability of censorship is its harmfulness for non-users carries with it a deceptive air of simplicity and masks several difficulties with respect to determining the harm of pornography. In its most basic form, harm is associated with direct physical harm resulting in death or injury. But there are more complex dimensions to the concept. We can cause *psychological* harm through insults or misrepresentations or bad faith. Furthermore, at a social level each of us is dependent on others in a wide variety of ways. That dependence results in cooperation. But cooperation is possible only if there are shared rules and patterns of behaviour. If confidence in those rules and patterns of behaviour is undermined, the consequences can be damaging. For example, yelling "Fire!" in a crowded theatre may well cause panic. Panic is a state of mind in which confidence in normal rules or patterns of behaviour has collapsed. The results of these psychological and social aspects are invariably harmful, but its effects can be described as indirect.

Even if we could reach agreement about the kinds of harm relevant to an assessment of pornography, there is an additional difficulty in determining the level of harm. Are all types of harm to be given equal weight? Or do some kinds of harm have a higher priority than others? If so, how are the priorities to be determined? That is, by reference to what system of values are decisions to be made?

A third type of difficulty complicates the debate about the harm of pornography. Even if we agree on what we are looking for, how do we trace in a definitive way the impact of pornography on its users and on the community generally? The answer might be thought to be relatively straightforward. We can set up research studies designed to provide us with the facts. The simplicity of the suggestion hides the complexity of the situation. The tools available to social scientists in analyzing and explaining human conduct are not precision instruments. In addition, there are serious moral limitations on the kinds of studies that are allowed.

The task of measuring harm for purposes of restricting pornography is complicated in a fourth way. Where does the onus of proof lie? Should we take the view that obscenity legislation is justified only if substantial harm can be demonstrated to flow from free and uncontrolled circulation of pornography? Or should we take the view that until pornography is shown to be harmless, legislative control is justified? Furthermore, should we resolve this issue in the case of pornography differently than we would in the case of pollution or safety standards? The question is important, at least in part because available research about the effect of pornography on users and on the community is inconclusive.

Thus far, we have four difficulties that lie in the way of ready agreement on the consequences of exposure to pornography. Yet another difficulty arises when we consider the possibility that the relevant harm of pornography is not direct harm to individuals, but indirect harm to members of particular groups. It may be that the most important characteristic of pornography is its impact on how people think about others and the world in which they live. Some people are opposed to anti-Semitic literature not because research shows it leads directly to harm to Jews. In fact, it is unlikely that any direct cause/effect relationship could be demonstrated. Rather, the concern is with the way in which such literature affects how its users and members of society generally think about or see themselves and others. The harmful impact of pornography may as a consequence be at the level of ideas or concepts. Some argue that pornography perpetuates beliefs about the inferiority of women, beliefs that result in discrimination and unequal treatment. The idea that groups can be harmed in ways that justify restrictions to individual freedom is central to the discussion of discrimination in the next chapter and will be a recurring theme in the remaining chapters.

The Readings

In the previous section, we identified several types of difficulty that lie in the way of agreement on the nature and impact of pornography. Each is encountered in the readings that follow.

The first reading is drawn from the 1992 Supreme Court decision in *Butler.* Speaking for the majority, Justice Sopinka ruled that the standard of "undue exploitation" as defined in s. 163 of the Criminal Code is appropriate. Because it can be reasonably concluded that pornography causes harm both directly and indirectly, the restriction on freedom of expression is justified.

A second group of readings by Raymond Gastil, Leo Groarke, and Lorenne Clark all defend censorship, but each presents a different analysis of the kind of harm that justifies restricting pornography. Each author begins the assessment of pornography and the moral problems it generates by evaluating the traditional liberal defence of an individual's right to produce and consume material that causes no direct harm to others. Raymond Gastil defends the view that the majority has the moral right to place limits on what is permissible in society. He supports a case for saying that the majority can claim that pornography is harmful because it reinforces and popularizes a diminished view of humanity and sexuality. The reading by Groarke makes use of the traditional liberal distinction articulated by John Stuart Mill between private and public morality. The distinction justifies state interference with individual freedom only when failure to intervene will result in direct harm to others. Using this standard, Groarke targets violent pornography and argues that placing limits on its production and circulation is in keeping with traditional liberal justifications for restricting individual freedom. His approach differs from Gastil's in that he defends the view that "pornography is unacceptable because it promotes harm to others and not because the views expressed contravene the views of the community."

Lorenne Clark agrees with the conclusions reached by Gastil and Groarke regarding censorship. However, she rejects the liberal distinction between private and public morality. She argues that the kind of liberty this distinction has traditionally supported has resulted in inequalities for women in both the public and private spheres. Because pornography endorses messages about women's inferior status, it causes harm to women as a group. Censorship of pornography can then be justified as one of a number of strategies for promoting women's equality.

In the final reading, Wendy McElroy rejects the analyses presented thus far regarding the harms of pornography and the justifications for censorship. She presents a series of challenges to the kind of radical feminist analysis provided by Lorenne Clark. She defends a libertarian approach, which she refers to as "individualist feminism," in which she sees pornography as serving the important function of enhancing human sexual diversity and women's right to choose, "regardless of the content of their choices."

DONALD VICTOR BUTLER V. HER MAJESTY THE QUEEN, 1992

[Supreme Court of Canada, 1992]

Mr. Justice J. Sopinka

1. Facts and Proceedings

In August 1987, the appellant, Donald Victor Butler, opened the Avenue Video Boutique located in Winnipeg, Manitoba. The shop sells and rents "hard core" videotapes and magazines as well as sexual paraphernalia. Outside the store is a sign which reads:

Avenue Video Boutique; a private members only adult video/visual club. Notice: if sex oriented material offends you, please do not enter. No admittance to persons under 18 years.

On August 21, 1987, the City of Winnipeg Police entered the appellant's store with a search warrant and seized all the inventory. The appellant was charged with 173 counts in the first indictment: three counts of selling obscene material contrary to s. 159(2)(*a*) of the *Criminal Code*, R.S.C. 1970, c. C-34 (now 163(2)(*a*)), 41 counts of possessing obscene material for the purpose of distribution contrary to s. 159(1)(*a*) (now 163(1)(*a*)) of the *Criminal Code*, 128 counts of possessing obscene material for the purpose of sale contrary to s. 159(2)(*a*) of the *Criminal Code* and one count of exposing obscene material to public view contrary to s. 159(2)(*a*) of the *Criminal Code*. . . .

2. <u>Relevant Legislation</u>

Criminal Code, R.S.C., 1985, c. C-46.

163. (1) Everyone commits an offence who,

(*a*) makes, prints, publishes, distributes, circulates, or has in his possession for the purpose of publication, distribution or circulation any obscene written matter, picture, model, phonograph record or other thing whatever; or

(*b*) makes, prints, publishes, distributes, sells or has in his possession for the purpose of publication, distribution or circulation a crime comic.

(2) Every one commits an offence who knowingly, without lawful justification or excuse,

(*a*) sells, exposes to public view or has in his possession for such a purpose any obscene written matter, picture, model, phonograph record or other thing whatever;

(*b*) publicly exhibits a disgusting object or an indecent show;

(*c*) offers to sell, advertises or publishes an advertisement of, or has for sale or disposal, any means, instructions, medicine, drug or article intended or represented as a method of causing abortion or miscarriage; or

(*d*) advertises or publishes an advertisement of any means, instructions, medicine, drug or article intended or represented as a method for restoring sexual virility or curing venereal diseases or diseases of the generative organs.

(3) No person shall be convicted of an offence under this section if he establishes that the public good was served by the acts that are alleged to constitute the offence and that the acts alleged did not extend beyond what served the public good.

(4) For the purposes of this section, it is a question of law whether an act served the public good and whether there is evidence that the act alleged went beyond what served the public good, but it is a question of fact whether the acts did or did not extend beyond what served the public good.

(5) For the purposes of this section, the motives of an accused are irrelevant.

(6) Where an accused is charged with an offence under subsection (1), the fact that the accused was ignorant of the nature or presence of the matter, picture, model, phonograph record, crime comic or other thing by means of or in relation to which the offence was committed is not a defence to the charge.

(7) In this section, "crime comic" means a magazine, periodical or book that exclusively or substantially comprises matter depicting pictorially

(*a*) the commission of crimes, real or fictitious; or

(*b*) events connected with the commission of crimes, real or fictitious, whether occurring before or after the commission of the crime.

(8) For the purposes of this Act, any publication a dominant characteristic of which is the undue exploitation of sex, or of sex and any one or more of the following subjects, namely, crime, horror, cruelty and violence, shall be deemed to be obscene.

3. Issues

The following constitutional questions are raised by this appeal:

1. Does s. 163 of the *Criminal Code* of Canada, R.S.C, 1985, c. C-46, violate s. 2(*b*) of the *Canadian Charter of Rights and Freedoms*?

2. If s. 163 of the *Criminal Code* of Canada, R.S.C., 1985, c. C-46, violates s. 2(b) of the *Canadian Charter of Rights and Freedoms*, can s. 163 of the *Criminal Code* of Canada be demonstrably justified under s. 1 of the *Canadian Charter of Rights and Freedoms* as a reasonable limit prescribed by law?

4. Analysis

The constitutional questions, as stated, bring under scrutiny the entirety of s. 163. However, both lower courts as well as the parties have focused almost exclusively on the definition of obscenity found in s. 163(8). Other portions of the impugned provision, such as the reverse onus provision envisaged in s. 163(3) as well as the absolute liability offence created by s. 163(6), raise substantial *Charter* issues which should be left to be dealt with in proceedings specifically directed to these issues. In my view, in the circumstances, this appeal should be confined to the examination of the constitutional validity of s. 163(8) only. . . .

Pornography can be usefully divided into three categories: (1) explicit sex with violence, (2) explicit sex without violence but which subjects people to treatment that is degrading or dehumanizing, and (3) explicit sex without violence that is neither degrading nor dehumanizing. Violence in this context includes both actual physical violence and threats of physical violence. Relating these three categories to the terms of s. 163(8) of the *Code*, the first, explicit sex coupled with violence, is expressly mentioned. Sex coupled with crime, horror or cruelty will sometimes involve violence. Cruelty, for instance, will usually do so. But, even in the absence of violence, sex coupled with crime, horror or cruelty may fall within the second category. As for category (3), subject to the exception referred to below, it is not covered.

Some segments of society would consider that all three categories of pornography cause harm to society because they tend to undermine its moral fibre. Others would contend that none of the categories cause harm. Furthermore there is a range of opinion as to what is degrading or dehumanizing. See *Pornography and Prostitution in Canada: Report of the Special Committee on Pornography and Prostitution* (1985) (the Fraser Report), Vol. 1, at p. 51. Because this is not a matter that is susceptible of proof in the traditional way and because we do not wish to leave it to the individual tastes of judges, we must have a norm that will serve as an arbiter in determining what amounts to an undue exploitation of sex. That arbiter is the community as a whole.

The courts must determine as best they can what the community would tolerate others being exposed to on the basis of the degree of harm that may flow from such exposure. Harm in this context means that it predisposes persons to act in an anti-social manner as, for example, the physical or mental mistreatment of women by men, or, what is perhaps debatable, the reverse. Anti-social conduct for this purpose is conduct which society formally recognizes as incompatible with its proper functioning. The stronger the inference of a risk of harm the lesser the likelihood of tolerance. The inference may be drawn from the material itself or from the material and other evidence. Similarly evidence as to the community standards is desirable but not essential.

In making this determination with respect to the three categories of pornography referred to above, the portrayal of sex coupled with violence will almost always constitute the undue exploitation of sex. Explicit sex which is degrading or dehumanizing may be undue if the risk of harm is substantial. Finally, explicit sex that is not violent and neither degrading nor dehumanizing is generally tolerated in our society and will not qualify as the undue exploitation of sex unless it employs children in its production.

If material is not obscene under this framework, it does not become so by reason of the person to whom it is or may be shown or exposed nor by reason of the place or manner in which it is shown. The availability of sexually explicit materials in theatres and other public places is subject to regulation by competent provincial legislation. Typically such legislation imposes restrictions on the material available to children. See *Nova Scotia Board of Censors v. McNeil*, [1978] 2 S.C.R. 662. . . .

Does the prevention of the harm associated with the dissemination of certain obscene materials constitute a sufficiently pressing and substantial concern to warrant a restriction on the freedom of expression? In this regard, it should be recalled that in *Keegstra, supra*, this Court unanimously accepted that the prevention of the influence of hate propaganda on society at large was a legitimate objective. Dickson C.J. wrote with respect to the changes in attitudes which exposure to hate propaganda can bring about:

> . . . the alteration of views held by the recipients of hate propaganda may occur subtly, and is not always attendant upon conscious acceptance of the communicated ideas. Even if the message of hate propaganda is outwardly rejected, there is evidence that its premise of racial or religious inferiority may persist in a recipient's mind as an idea that holds some truth, an incipient effect not to be entirely discounted. . . .
>
> The threat to the self-dignity of target group members is thus matched by the possibility that prejudiced messages will gain some credence, with the attendant result of discrimination, and perhaps even violence, against minority groups in Canadian society. [At pp. 747–48.]

This Court has thus recognized that the harm caused by the proliferation of materials which seriously offend the values fundamental to our society is a substantial concern which justifies restricting the otherwise full exercise of the freedom of expression. In my view, the harm sought to be avoided in the case of the dissemination of obscene materials is similar. In the words of Nemetz C.J.B.C. in *R. v. Red Hot Video Ltd.* (1985), 45 C.R. (3d) 36 (B.C.C.A.), there is a growing concern that the exploitation of women and children, depicted in publications and films can, in certain circumstances, lead to "abject and servile victimization" (at pp. 43–44). As Anderson J.A. also noted in that same case, if true equality between male and female persons is to be achieved, we cannot ignore the threat to equality resulting from exposure to audiences of certain types of violent and degrading material. Materials portraying women as a class as objects for sexual exploitation and abuse have a negative impact on "the individual's sense of self-worth and acceptance".

In reaching the conclusion that legislation proscribing obscenity is a valid objective which justifies some encroachment of the right to freedom of expression, I am persuaded in part that such legislation may be found in most free and democratic societies. As Nemetz C.J.B.C. aptly pointed out in *R v. Red Hot Video, supra*, for centuries democratic societies have set certain limits to freedom of expression. He cited (at p. 40) the following passage of Dickson J.A. (as he then was) in *R. v. Great West News Ltd.*, [1970] 4 C.C.C. 307 (Man. C.A.):

> . . . all organized societies have sought in one manner or another to suppress obscenity. The right of the state to legislate to protect its moral fibre and well-being has long been recognized, with roots deep in history. It is within this frame that the Courts and Judges must work. [At p. 309.]

The advent of the *Charter* did not have the effect of dramatically depriving Parliament of a power which it has historically enjoyed. It is also noteworthy that the criminalization of obscenity was considered to be compatible with the *Canadian Bill of Rights*. As Dickson J.A. stated in *R. v. Prairie Schooner News Ltd.* (1970), 1 C.C.C. (2d) 251:

> Freedom of speech is not unfettered either in law or civil law. The *Canadian Bill of Rights* was intended to protect, and does protect, basic freedoms of vital importance to all Canadians. It does not serve as a shield behind which obscene matter may be disseminated without concern for criminal consequences. The interdiction of the publications which are the subject of the present charges in no way trenches upon the freedom of expression which the *Canadian Bill of Rights* assures. [At p. 271.]

The enactment of the impugned provision is also consistent with Canada's international obligations. (*Agreement for the Suppression of the Circulation of Obscene Publications* and the *Convention for the Suppression of the Circulation of and Traffic in Obscene Publications*).

Finally, it should be noted that the burgeoning pornography industry renders the concern even more pressing and substantial than when the impugned provisions were first enacted. I would therefore conclude that the objective of avoiding the harm associated with the dissemination of pornography in this case is sufficiently pressing and substantial to warrant some restriction on full exercise of the right to freedom of expression. The analysis of whether the measure is proportional to the objective must, in my view, be undertaken in light of the conclusion that the objective of the impugned section is valid only insofar as it relates to the harm to society associated with obscene materials. Indeed, the section as interpreted in previous decisions and in these reasons is fully consistent with that objective. The objective of maintaining conventional standards of propriety, independently of any harm to society, is no longer justified in light of the values of individual liberty which underlie the Charter. . . .

Finally, I wish to address the arguments of the interveners, Canadian Civil liberties Association and Manitoba Association for Rights and Liberties, that the objectives of this kind of legislation may be met by alternative, less intrusive measures. First, it is submitted that reasonable time, manner and place restrictions would be preferable to outright prohibition. I am of the view that this argument should be rejected. Once it has been established that the objective is the avoidance of harm caused by the degradation which many women feel as "victims" of the message of obscenity, and of the negative impact exposure to such material has on perceptions and attitudes towards women, it is untenable to argue that these harms could be avoided by placing restrictions on access to such material. Making the materials more difficult to obtain by increasing their cost and reducing their availability does not achieve the same objective. Once Parliament has reasonably concluded that certain acts are harmful to certain groups in society and to society in general, it would be inconsistent, if not hypocritical, to argue that such acts could be committed in more restrictive conditions. The harm sought to be avoided would remain the same in either case.

It is also submitted that there are more effective techniques to promote the objectives of Parliament. For example, if pornography is seen as encouraging violence against women, there are certain activities which discourage it — counselling rape victims to charge their assailants, provision of shelter and assistance for battered women, campaigns for laws against discrimination on the grounds of sex, education to increase the sensitivity of law enforcement agencies and other governmental authorities. In addition, it is submitted that education is an under-used response.

It is noteworthy that many of the above suggested alternatives are in the form of *responses* to the harm engendered by negative attitudes against women. The role of the impugned provision is to control the dissemination of the very images that contribute to such attitudes. Moreover, it is true that there are additional measures which could alleviate the problem of violence against women. However, given the gravity of the harm, and the threat to the values at stake, I do not believe that the measure chosen by Parliament is equalled by the alternatives which have been suggested. Education, too, may offer a means of combating negative attitudes to women, just as it is currently used as a means of addressing other problems dealt with in the *Code*. However, there is no reason to rely on education alone. It should be emphasized that this is in no way intended to deny the value of other educational and counselling measures to deal with the roots and effects of negative attitudes. Rather, it is only to stress the arbitrariness and unacceptability of the claim that such measures represent the sole legitimate means of addressing the phenomenon. Serious social problems such as violence against women require multi-pronged approaches by government. Education and legislation are not alternatives but complements in addressing such problems. There is nothing in the *Charter* which requires Parliament to choose between such complementary measures.

Balance Between Effects of Limiting Measures and Legislative Objective

The final question to be answered in the proportionality test is whether the effects of the law so severely trench on a protected right that the legislative objective is outweighed by the infringement. The infringement on freedom of expression is confined to a measure designed to prohibit the distribution of sexually explicit materials accompanied by violence, and those without violence that are degrading or dehumanizing. As I have already concluded, this kind of expression lies far from the core of the guarantee of freedom of expression. It appeals only to the most base aspect of individual fulfilment, and it is primarily economically motivated.

The objective of the legislation, on the other hand, is of fundamental importance in a free and democratic society. It is aimed at avoiding harm, which Parliament has reasonably concluded will be caused directly or indirectly, to individuals, groups such as women and children, and consequently to society as a whole, by the distribution of these materials. It thus seeks to enhance respect for all members of society, and non-violence and equality in their relations with each other.

I therefore conclude that the restriction on freedom of expression does outweigh the importance of the legislative objective.

THE MORAL RIGHT OF THE MAJORITY TO RESTRICT OBSCENITY AND PORNOGRAPHY THROUGH LAW

Raymond D. Gastil

Obscenity and pornography may be defined as the use of language or images relating to the body, violence, or sex that exceed the bounds of propriety that a significant part of the public finds appropriate for the context and requirements of the situation in which they are used. Efforts to limit obscenity and pornography either legally or informally are frustrated by the lack of an acceptable intellectual basis in liberal societies for such limitations. Appeals to community standards or lack of redeeming social value are weakened by a widespread feeling, especially in academic circles and the media, that the majority has no right to impose its standards on individuals or to decide on social values unless clear physical harm is involved. Moreover, attempts to regulate obscenity are frequently criticized on the ground that the regulators are enforcing standards that neither they nor the majority observe in their own lives.

The recent controversy that has focused on the works of H.L.A. Hart and Lord Devlin on the one hand, and the reports of government commissions to look into the regulation of obscenity on the other, has summarized but not greatly advanced the argument.[1] In his defense of controls, Lord Devlin fails to accept the intellectual weakness and thus ultimate unsatisfactoriness of controls defended largely by populism and conservatism, nor is he sufficiently aware of the dangers of an open-ended appeal to the popular will. On the other hand, in the Mill tradition, Hart fails to stake out the rights of the majority as firmly as he does those of the minority. He promotes a form of libertarian elitism that should be rejected because it represents an undue infringement on the freedom of potential majorities that they will not freely accept. Devlin's intuition that law and morality should reinforce one another cannot simply be ignored. Since inadequacies in the Hart position lead to a purely instrumental view of freedom, both may lay the groundwork for a new "escape from freedom."[2]

In order to avoid this danger, I suggest that we build a case for the control of obscenity by establishing the following: (1) a distinction of private from public rights to expression, (2) a distinction of political from non-political rights to expression, and (3) a plausible case that the majority can claim harm from public obscenity.

From Ethics, *vol. 86, no. 3 (April 1976), pp. 231–240. Reprinted by permission of The University of Chicago Press and Raymond D. Gastil.*

The Private/Public Distinction

In a free society, the majority is responsible for establishing the laws of the community, while at the same time this responsibility is limited by certain absolute privileges granted to minorities and individuals because of attachment to a concept of basic rights or freedoms. Aside from those rational political and civil freedoms that are necessary to guarantee a democratic structure, these include rights to that degree of freedom that is consonant with the freedom of others. Yet what are the rules for this consonance? For example, surely one freedom of those in the majority is to have the kind of social and aesthetic environment that they desire in the moral mode. It is with this in mind that nudists are asked to disrobe only in private or in camps segregated for that purpose. If the clash between the majority and minority over nudism meant that nudists could appear anywhere in public, then in this case majority rights would be nugatory while the minority rights would be guaranteed. To expect majorities to long accede to such situations is to imagine that people will give up being interested in determining many aspects of their social environment that have formerly been considered of importance.

The problem for the liberal, therefore, is to define basic civil rights in such a way that they preserve a meaningful area of freedom both to individuals who can form majorities capable of determining a way of life for themselves and to individuals who have not or cannot form a majority. The right to try to form new majorities is the basic right given to individuals in both the majority and the minority that makes meaningful the right of either. Adding to this an absolute right to a private sphere of life guarantees the development of that degree of individuality that would seem consonant with human dignity in the liberal view. Once he has staked out a private realm for minority rights beyond the public political sphere, the liberal may go on to make the utilitarian case that the majority will also benefit from eschewing regulation of most social behaviour. But this is an area appropriate for continual readjustment of interests and not for basic guarantees.

David Conway has recently argued in regard to pornography that there is little sense to the private/public distinction that H.L.A. Hart and the *Wolfenden Report* have affirmed as a basis for distinguishing between what may or may not be prohibited.[3] He suggests that it is not the public nature of acts that prohibitionists wish to control but the acts themselves. He believes that public and private acts lie along a continuum that cannot be arbitrarily demarcated without a clear moral boundary. Finally, Conway suggests that since many personal actions, such as marriage, are necessarily public, the public/private distinction does not adequately preserve an arena of personal freedom.

Conway's last point is an unavoidable weakness of the distinction, but the first two objections are unconvincing. First, the public or private value of an action may be an integral part of its "rightness" or "wrongness," for, physically, and biologically, actions are generally neutral and their morality or immorality is in most cases judged with reference to the context of their occurrence. Opposition to sexual obscenity might be founded upon a desire to control the tone of sexual behaviour by reinforcing one set of meanings associated with it rather than another. If so, the place and the participants in expression determine its relative desirability. Second, there are many continuums upon which we wish to start and do not desire to finish but where nevertheless the exact stopping point must be arbitrary and conventional. For example, everyone should have equal political and civil rights, but how we define "everyone" is necessarily conventional. It would be foolish to give one-year-olds voting rights, but whether the age at which one receives this right should be twelve, eighteen, twenty-one, or twenty-five can be discussed as a matter of reasoned argument. Therefore, as a basis of compromise between majority and minority rights, the private/public distinction remains the most salient available — a view supported by its acceptance in both of the reports cited above.

The Political/Nonpolitical Distinction

In the United States, the argument against controls on obscenity is frequently made in the context of the right of free speech under the First Amendment to the Constitution. Yet as Alexander Meiklejohn has pointed out: ". . . the principle of freedom of speech is derived . . . from the necessities of self-government by universal suffrage. . . . The guarantee by the First Amendment is . . . assured only to speech which bears, directly or indirectly, upon issues with which voters have to deal — only, therefore, to a consideration of matters of public interest. Private speech, or private interest in speech — has no claim whatever to the protection of the First Amendment."[4] Therefore, it is wrong for the authors of the *Report of the Commission on Obscenity and Pornography* to assert that controls should not be imposed because of the American tradition of free speech.[5] American history has not been remarkable for libertarianism, except in regard to politically related speech and behaviour. This is even more true of a democracy such as Switzerland.

There are borderline cases. Profanity and nudity are sometimes regarded as political expression, or random violence may carry a political message. However, if the courts were not confused by the claim that the First Amendment gave an unlimited right to all expression, they might plausibly determine what is an authentic political message.

But they have been so confused.[6] Although in the Roth case (1957) the Supreme Court exempted obscenity from coverage by the First Amendment, the stipulation that any redeeming social value would lift a work of art or literature into legality was based more on J.S. Mill than the writers of the Constitution. A more recent (1973) Supreme Court decision that work must have serious literary, artistic, political, or scientific value to escape potential condemnation as obscene gives more recognition to the fact that the majority has a right to intervene when it feels there is more social disvalue than value in a particular unit of expression. Yet the court signally fails to distinguish politically and nonpolitically relevant rights and by adding "scientific" appears to rest its justification on utilitarian arguments for freedom that may unfortunately wilt when calculations change. In a majoritarian state, freedom of speech must, instead, be protected by a more absolute but less all-inclusive principle that refers to rational political discourse as an ineluctable requirement of political democracy.

A Plausible Case That the Majority Can Claim Harm From Public Obscenity

Since regulation of obscenity and pornography limits freedom, and since they bring pleasure to many, their legal restriction in a liberal society cannot be advocated unless a plausible case can be made that lack of restriction does substantial harm to potential majority interests.

Both Mill and Hart assert that only harm to individuals can be a basis of regulation, and primarily harm to individuals other than the actors. But this is hardly a confining limit if the concept of harm may be extended through psychic to social and spiritual harm to individuals or to the society of which they are a part. Three broad extensions of the principle of harm have been proposed.[7] The first is the conservative hypothesis that since received moral and legal codes are the tested results of trial and error, they are likely to meet social needs better than untested alternatives. The second is the disintegration hypothesis that lack of regulation of conduct offensive to the majority will result in the loss of a unified moral consensus in the community and thus undercut its whole moral structure, washing away finally even the limitations that the libertarian would hate to lose. In Lord Devlin's hands, the disintegration hypothesis is often defended by an additional consequentialist appeal to what would happen if we were to lose present restraints.[8] It is, then, both a claim that any code is better than none and a claim that the code on which we have built our civilization is apt to be more supportive of social goods common even to libertarians than would be a truly libertarian world. By easy stages, this brings us to the third or majoritarian hypothesis[9] that the people of any community have a right to legislate their way of life. If wearing clothes, for example, is a part of their way of life, they have a right to enforce this custom irrespective of lack of proof as to the harm of individual nudity to others.

These arguments are supportive of control, yet they are not enough for a plausible case. As to the majoritarian hypothesis, in a democracy, of course, a majority can force its will eventually, but this fact does not help us decide whether majorities or their leaders should be taught that they have a right to exert force in a particular sphere of life. Majorities are often wrong and frivolous, and this is one reason for constitutions and basic civil rights. The disintegration hypothesis may be correct — dashing views do lead to instability — but this is a weak case for enforcing old standards. It is true that attitudes about decency in the arts and on the streets have been changing rapidly, and the wide dissemination of pornography is speeding up the change. One result of any social change is instability, and instability has losses. Yet it might be possible in the future to achieve consensus that "anything goes" in obscene expression, and in these terms stability could be restructured. Conservatively, I would argue that those who launch confusion have the heavier burden of proof. Yet this does not alter the fact that the defender of the old assumptions of a society has the responsibility to give a rational case for those assumptions or to suggest revisions in those assumptions that accord with a rational case. A living conservative tradition must be a changing tradition, or else it will fail to preserve social integration, community identity, and cherished values.

In a recent review of the relevant theoretical and empirical evidence for potential harm that has been developed by the social sciences, James Q. Wilson compared two attempts to summarize such evidence for policy purposes in the United States.[10] He found that in both cases the supporting evidence for the conclusions was weak and often only tangentially related to real-world concerns. Nevertheless, the National Commission on the Causes and Prevention of Violence recommended that violence in the media should be controlled, or further investigated with an eye to control, because of the probability that fictional violence may make individuals behave violently. On the other hand, the Commission on Obscenity and Pornography recommended widespread decontrol of sexually explicit materials because no negative results of their general dissemination could be demonstrated. Wilson reasonably surmises that the reason for the disparity between the treatment of the relation between evidence and conclusion in the two reports is due to the bias of their authors against violence and in favor in sex.

Wilson, however, goes on to point out that almost all recent major American studies testing the hypothesis that major long-term behavior changes result from particular social policy or educational inputs have provided inconclusive or negative findings. Thus, studies have in recent years shown that the type of school or educational method makes no difference (Coleman report), that Head Start accomplishes little, that prison correction systems produce little gain, and that psychiatry does little for the patient. He suggests, and it is probably true, that in real-life situations there is too much going on, too many cycles of reinforcement stretched over too many years, for particular interventions to get up out of the noise. Still this does not mean that there is not a great deal of change over time[11] and that the arts, the schools, and the media do not participate in positive or negative feedback relationships that eventuate in these changes. Because Head Start did not work very well does not mean early education is not important. As the violence commission report suggests, since advertisers feel that exposure to certain symbols and fictional experiences will influence buying behavior, it is reasonable to suppose that an increasing flow of violent pornography will influence other social behavior. The "no harmful effects" of sexual pornography reported by the pornography commission included an observation that exposure led to a more open attitude toward sex and, after initial increase in sexual interest, a general adaptation to pornography.[12]

But what is behavior? One of the curious aspects of the claim that obscenity and pornography are not significant influences on behavior is that both their production and consumption (direct and indirect) are forms of behavior. In this sense, there are then two significant but not unrelated results of uncontrolled pornography and obscenity. First, we are granted only so much time in our lives, and our minds have only so much capacity for attention at any one time. Therefore, if there is more of X there will be less of Y in our attention. And so if there is more obscenity there is less of something else. Our lives are changed (of course, some not at all, many to a degree, and few greatly changed). Second, the parts of our lives are unlikely to be either watertight compartments or tightly interconnected. The verbal and artistic forms and images we use are just that, and yet at the same time they carry meanings that habituate us to different attitudes and eventually to different qualities of behavior. With the generalization of violent and sexual pornography, our bodies become depersonalized emotive machines with many buttons to push. As Walter Berns writes:

> Consider the case of the parent who wants to convince his children of the impropriety of the use of the four-letter verb meaning to copulate. At the present time the task confronting him is only slightly less formidable than that faced by the parent who would teach his children that the world is flat. Until recently propriety required the use of the verb "to make love," and this delicacy was not without purpose. It was meant to remind us — to teach us, or at least to allow us to be taught — that whereas human copulation can be physically indistinguishable from animal copulation generally, it ought to be marked by the presence of a passion of which other animals are incapable. Now, to a quickly increasing extent, the four-letter verb — more "honest" in the opinion of its devotees — is being used openly and therefore without impropriety. The parent will fail in his effort to educate because he will be on his own, trying to teach a lesson his society no longer wants taught — by the law, by the language, or by the schools.[13]

As an analogy, let us imagine an attractive but small square in a large city surrounded by medium-sized apartments. Among those who used the square, 25 percent were inclined to be disorderly and kept trash lying around their apartments for days, while 75 percent were neat. However, the square was always neat, for few people dropped trash in the square and a weekly cleaning by the city was quite enough for even its neatest users.

One year, however, 5 percent of the users began to drop their trash in the square. Those disturbed by the change in its appearance asked for the enforcement of antilittering laws, but the courts held that no one was being injured, for there was no danger to health because of the weekly municipal cleanup. Yet, toward the end of each week trash grew so thick that users who had not previously dropped their trash began to become less careful, and so the percentage of litterers grew to at least equal the percentage who were also disorderly inside their own apartments. By now many of those who had formerly enjoyed the square partially because of its appearance stayed away, so that finally more than 50 percent of the users were also litterers, and in the end dropping trash casually about became the social custom. For health reasons cleanup was now three times a week, but with the heavy population it was a rather trashy park most of the time. By now, many of those who formerly had kept clean apartments but had become litterers in public also kept littered apartments.

This is the course of events which those disturbed with pornography and obscenity believe they are witnessing today. I do not know if any court has ruled against littering laws in the way they have against blue laws. But if the question of the extra cost of cleanup were kept out of the legal calculation, I see no reason why in the name of individual freedom the courts should not equally do away with such laws. Why is the filling of the public arena with pornography and obscenity to be regarded as different from the delict of littering? When the movie marquee, newsstands, and popular songs all blare out *Deep Throat* and its equivalents, the city becomes a different place to walk in just as it does when everyone carelessly drops his lunch sack, candy wrapper, or pop bottle. Since everyone's likes and dislikes cannot be accommodated in the same square, the obvious basis of decision as to regulation becomes the desire of the majority of its users.

Let me, then, somewhat formalize the case for restriction of obscenity in perfectionist terms such as those of Rashdall, Moore, or de Jouvenal.

First, I define the moral-action mode as one in which a person assumes that one of his interests will be to act in ways that accord with his highest image of how a man should act. He knows he will have other interests at other times and from other vantage points, but in the moral mode he wants to act in terms of this image, and he wants to advocate that others act in these terms. If we view all actions as basically self-interested, we will assume that the actor believes that his moral actions will improve the esteem in which he is held and thus his status, and that this gain is better than other possible gains. If we assume that an actor can internalize desires to achieve the good of others or of society, then he may act morally or support such action when projected gain to self-esteem outbalances other possible gains by other means.

Since the moral code is only one of several, there is no obvious hypocrisy in a society prohibiting obscenity or pornography that most of its members in fact enjoy. One may believe that it would be better for him to eat less ice cream; he will avoid ice-cream shops, but when faced with an ice-cream counter he will always order two scoops.

Let us, then, define morality as action that is guided in the moral-action mode by a reasoned balancing of the claims to consideration of a variety of ultimate goods for man or society, limited by a set of basic moral rules placed outside immediate consideration. A moral society is one that forms its customs and laws in terms of trade-offs within limits among the ultimate goods accepted by its members. The ultimate goods are many, and no two people will have the same list. But moral persons will, in fact, develop lists that have a great deal of overlap.

For the purposes of this discussion I will classify ultimate goods under three headings. First are the goods of pleasure in all of the manifold forms in which they occur. Second are the good of creativity, the making and doing of something beyond the self. Creativity may be intellectual, technical, organizational, or artistic. Third are the goods of significance. Most people are concerned with their place in time, with their dignity as men and women, with their specialness. It is true of course that heroic generalization would allow us to reduce all goods to those of pleasure. Yet ancient Athens was not as remarkable for the pleasures of its inhabitants as for Athenian creativity and the significance that Athenian high culture gave to man as separate from nature. For many, satisfaction with life does not come from a quantum of fun but from the significance that they find in it. The rights and dignities afforded by policies that guarantee individual freedom offer one basis of individual significance, but not the only one.

In the moral society, limits are placed on the balancing of ultimate goods both because of a mistrust of rationalization and because of the hierarchical relation of ultimate goods. For example, if an analyst hypothesizes basic social rights such as those to food, respect, and life and basic civil rights such as those to freedoms that do not infringe on the freedom of others, he in effect sets limits that he will not recommend infringing except in such extreme circumstances as a danger of imminent destruction of the human race. On the other hand, less basic ultimate goods may in ordinary circumstances be traded off against other personal and social interests in deciding upon moral action.

In order to go beyond conservative, disintegration, and majoritarian hypotheses to build a case for limiting pornography and obscenity, it is necessary to show that it is not irrational for men to value the ultimate goods of creativity and significance equally with those of pleasure. For those who evaluate in these terms, actions that move society away from a balanced mix of the ultimate goods do moral harm to individuals both separately and collectively.

As I have pointed out, moral harm may come in a variety of forms. The *Brave New World* could offer most people manifold pleasures yet fall short in offering what the reader might consider sufficient significance to the average human life. Therefore, the controls of this society would harm its members. Similarly, lack of sufficient discipline may result in a person who is so unable to put off immediate gratification that he falls short of what others consider true humanity. Lack of discipline has harmed this person as surely as dropping a rock on his foot.

In perfectionist terms, the case against obscenity is either that it diminishes man or reduces his creativity. Since the second case depends on an analysis of extensive empirical evidence that I do not have, I shall limit the argument largely to the first. Historically, one way to achieve human significance has been to emphasize the specialness of man either as an individual or as a human group. This may be because many feel that there can be no meaning to a life except to itself if it is a replaceable part in a process that could do without it. And to have meaning only to oneself is ultimately to seem to have no meaning at all.

An obvious way to establish meaning is to sharply distinguish human from animal life. No civilization has placed human and prehuman life on a plane, even when, as in Hinduism and Buddhism, animal life is highly respected. Only in recent years has man come, by means of science, to concentrate on the similarities among existences — to flatten all differences, including those between animate and inanimate matter. This is one reason why the naive reaction to Darwin was so strong. If man is only part of a process and probably not a final stage, then his consciousness, ideals, and creativity are only epiphenomena. Since what is really important is his biology, beyond eugenics the reformer's goal can only be to make the progress of individuals through the stages of life as painless as possible for all. For a person to believe that he should really live up to a set of symbolic standards or should not try to get away with whatever he can seems to be to allow oneself to be brainwashed by a social machine justified as oiling the succession of the generations. Self-fulfillment becomes letting everything happen to oneself that can, enjoying all the possibilities before it is too late. From this perspective, even self-actualization is a mocking game.

Maintaining a system of symbolic restraints on language and the arts has historically been a means of underscoring the difference between man and the process from which he emerged. Let me pose as a critical difference between man and animal the development of symbolic systems that allow us to disvalue public viewing of biological processes such as defecation, urination, or sexual intercourse. Why? There is nothing "wrong" with these actions. I suggest that what is wrong, just as what is "wrong" with the naked body, is that they remind us of our biology, of our presymbolic connections. This is why Duncan Williams attacks modern literature as the depiction of the "trousered ape,"[14] and this is why he sees pornography as both violent and sexual — the realm of the forbidden and animal in the popular mythology.

The spread of obscenity through the popular arts and up and down the streets can be interpreted as a reflection of the victory of science over religious belief. The Marquis de Sade reasoned that since man was determined and essentially a machine, anything that he might do that he found pleasurable he should do. As Francis Shaeffer has pointed out, as this view of man has come to be popularly accepted, it has been accompanied by an overriding mood of despair in the arts.[15] But literary and artistic critics have gone further to note the resulting shattering of a sense of purpose and order and standards in the arts, with dependence on sex and violence as the most universal and easiest to understand common denominator.[16] It may be plausibly argued, then, that once casual sex and violence fill our viewing and creating lives, this feeds back to further reinforce and popularize a diminished view of man.

The case, then, is that the presentation or acting out of sex or violence in public, or advertising such activities in public, will tend to popularize and familiarize a view of man and an attitude toward the self that will diminish the view that people have of the significance through specialness of human life and also divert creative artists from creative activity through the diversion of the time and money of the public toward an art world whose standards have been undermined, both directly (through taking up the space and time of the audience) and indirectly (through its feedback support of nihilism) by pornography. In the account of some people, the losses in significance and creativity are not made up for by gains in creativity and significance (freedom) released by the decontrol of pornography, or by the gains in sensual pleasure. These judgments are contingent upon a time and place in which nihilism is already far advanced and in which culture as "adversary culture" is the accepted stance.[17] The relative gains and losses in a Victorian age such as that which Freud encountered might well be different.

Concluding Note

In making these arguments, it is well to note that I have not tried to prove the contentions of those who would regulate obscenity but only to establish the extent of their moral right. The majority has a moral right to legislate, outside of the political realm, their not unreasonable conclusions as to what should be permitted in public in a moral society. In the case of pornography and obscenity, their representatives can make a plausible case for regulation. Beyond this, for any particular legislation or mode of enforcement, advocates must establish more detailed consequentialist arguments for particular definitions of public and private, political and nonpolitical, and obscenity and pornography before a framework for effective control can be preserved or constructed.

NOTES

1. See Patrick Devlin, *The Enforcement of Morals* (London: Oxford University Press, 1965); H.L.A. Hart, *Law, Liberty and Morality* (Stanford, Calif.: Stanford University Press, 1963); Basil Mitchell, *Law, Morality and Religion in a Secular Society* (London: Oxford University Press, 1967); the *Wolfenden Report: Report of the Committee on Homosexual Offenses and Prostitution* (New York: Stein & Day, 1963); and *Report of the Commission on Obscenity and Pornography* (Washington, D.C., 1970), esp. p. 53.
2. On the undermining of freedom by liberalism see Thomas Molnar, "Zur Gesellschaft der Zukunft," *Schweizer Monatshefte* 54, no. 2 (1974): 97–104.
3. David Conway, "Law, Liberty and Indecency," *Philosophy* 49, no. 188 (1974): 135–148.
4. Alexander Meiklejohn, *Free Speech and Its Relation to Self-Government* (New York: Harper & Row, 1948), pp. 93–94.
5. *Report of the Commission on Obscenity and Pornography*, pp. 53–54.
6. See ibid., pp. 295–370.
7. *New York Times* (January 24, 1973).
8. In addition to Hart and Devlin, see C.L. Ten, "Enforcing a Shared Morality," *Ethics* 82, no. 4 (1972): 321–329; and Basil Mitchell, pp. 45–47.
9. Mislabeled "conservative" by Ten, ibid.
10. James Q. Wilson, "Violence, Pornography, and Social Science," *Public Interest* 22 (Winter 1971): 45–61. Even a strong defender of the report of the pornography commission agrees with this analysis. See Weldon Johnson, "The Pornography Report," *Duquesne Law Review* 10 (Winter 1971): 190–219 (note, p. 219).
11. For example, a Gallup poll shows a 20 percent drop in the percent opposing premarital sexual relations over the four years 1969–1973 (*New York Times* [August 12, 1973]).
12. *Report of the Commission on Obscenity and Pornography*, pp. 139–264.
13. Walter Berns, "Pornography vs. Democracy: The Case for Censorship," *Public Interest* 22 (Winter 1971): 19–20.
14. Duncan Williams, *Trousered Apes: A Study in the Influence of Literature on Modern Society* (London: Churchill Press, 1971).
15. Francis A. Schaeffer, *Escape from Reason* (Downer's Grove, Ill.: Intervarsity Press, 1968).
16. In addition to Williams, see Paul Horgan, "The Abdication of the Artist," *Proceedings of the American Philosophical Society* 109, no. 5 (1965): 267–271; Katherine Ann Porter, "A Country and Some People I Love," *Harper's Magazine* 231 (September 1965): 58–68.
17. See Daniel Bell and Irving Kristol, *Capitalism Today* (New York: Basic Books, 1971), p. 22; and Irving Howe, *Decline of the New* (New York: Harcourt, Brace & World, 1963).

QUESTIONS

1. Raymond Gastil argues that lack of restriction in the circulation of pornography does substantial harm to "potential majority interests." Does he provide good reasons for his argument?
2. Gastil argues that pornography affects creative activity and diminishes humanity. Do you agree? If so, do you think this justifies censorship?
3. In deciding the question of censorship, where should the burden of proof lie?

PORNOGRAPHY, CENSORSHIP, AND OBSCENITY LAW IN CANADA[1]

Leo Groarke

Recent discussions of pornography and censorship focus on the question whether violence in pornography legitimates new restrictions on freedom of expression. In 1987, the Canadian government proposed new laws that would prohibit such material.[2] Though I take issue with some aspects of their proposals, I defend restrictions on violent pornography, arguing that it is a mistake to think they violate traditional limits on freedom of expression. I conclude that the censorship of pornography can be made compatible with free speech, and that commentators who have defended and attacked censorship — among them, Feinberg, Cohen, Clark, Lederer,[3] and North American civil libertarians — have mistakenly assumed that this is not the case.

Examples of the images and themes that have fuelled debates about pornography and censorship are enumerated by Laura Lederer in her introduction to the anthology *Take Back the Night: Women on Pornography*. She describes the investigations undertaken by the California group Women Against Violence in Pornography and the Media. In one three-month period, they viewed twenty-six pornographic films to gain some understanding of their content. Twenty-one of the films featured rape, sixteen celebrated bondage and torture, two were films of child molestation, and two condoned the killing of women for sexual satisfaction. In their investigation of pornographic magazines, members of the group found stories, articles, and photographs that glorified pain, violence against women, kidnapping, and assault and torture for sexual stimulation. As Thelma McCormack remarks in her discussion of similar material,

> A new hard-edged sado-masochistic pornography has appeared in which women are mutilated and abused with chains, whips and fists. The women in this pornography are presented as seeking and enjoying their own punishment, while violence heightens the erotic excitement of both partners.[4]

Many commentators respond to such trends by calling for censorship, but McCormack and others still reject it. The basis of their views is an appeal to freedom of expression and it is in this sense the heart of the debate on censorship.

The classic defence of freedom of expression is John Stuart Mill's *On Liberty*. It is difficult to exaggerate its influence, and it is enough for us to note that its account of freedom of expression has become a rarely questioned part of liberal theory that is routinely invoked by contemporary theorists, both in discussions of pornography and in the more general accounts of justice proposed by influential thinkers like John Rawls, Jan Narveson,[5] and Michael Walzer.

The crux of Mill's account is his claim that freedom is a general good that must be maximized, and his consequent conclusion that "the only purpose for which power can be rightfully exercised over any member of a civilized community, against his will, is to prevent harm to others."[6] Given this principle, freedom of expression is a fundamental right,

---

From Windsor Review of Legal and Social Issues, *vol. 2 (May 1990). Reprinted by permission of Leo Groarke.*

for the expression of thoughts and opinions does not itself harm others. The freedom this implies must, says Mill, include the freedom to live as one chooses, so long as one does not transgress the rights of others. As Mill himself puts it:[7]

> This, then, is the appropriate region of human liberty. It comprises, first, the inward domain of consciousness, demanding liberty of thought and feeling, absolute freedom of opinion and sentiment on all subjects. . . . The liberty of expressing and publishing opinions . . . [is] almost of as much importance as the liberty of thought itself and resting in great part on the same reasons, is practically inseparable from it. Secondly, the . . . liberty of tastes and pursuits, of framing the plan of our life to suit our own character, of doing as we like, subject to such consequences as may follow, without impediment from our fellow creatures, so long as what we do does not harm them, even though they should think our conduct foolish, perverse, or wrong.

Elsewhere, Mill contends that we must not infringe on freedom of expression even when it becomes "intemperate" and is "pushed to an extreme."[8] It is natural to conclude that he would oppose the censorship of pornography, for viewing it does not itself cause harm to others. *On Liberty* does allow the prohibition of public actions that "are a violation of good manners,"[9] and this may justify a ban on the public display of pornographic matter, but has no implications for its use in private.[10]

In response to this interpretation of Mill, Kathleen Okruhlik has argued that Mill would accept the censorship of pornography, for current psychological research links the viewing of pornography to subsequent harm and violence against women. This is, she concludes, a case where the state can legitimately prohibit a particular action (the publication of pornography) because it causes harm to others. The research she cites[11] is important, and we shall see that her conclusion contains an important element of truth, but it is based on an account of harm that is broader than the one that Mill allows. At most, the publication and viewing of pornography harms others indirectly — in the sense that they may lead to other acts (rape, assault, for instance), which cause actual harm. Mill does not, however, allow the state to interfere with acts that are only indirectly harmful. On the contrary, he explicitly declares that we must permit all acts that do not harm others "directly and in the first instance."[12] According to his account, all such acts are "self-regarding" and should not be prohibited.

Mill's unwillingness to allow the state to interfere with indirectly harmful acts is clear when he discusses drunkenness and other "extravagances" that may lead to other acts that are directly harmful. Rather than argue for a ban on such activities, he holds that individuals have the responsibility to ensure that their extravagances do not lead to harmful acts and that society may intervene only when they abrogate this responsibility.

> I fully admit that the mischief which a person does to himself may seriously affect, both through their sympathies and their interests, those nearly connected with him and, in a major degree, society at large. When [and only when], by conduct of this sort, a person is led to violate a distinct and assignable obligation to any other person or persons, the case is taken out of the self-regarding class. . . . If a man, through intemperance or extravagance becomes unable to pay his debts, or having undertaken the moral responsibility of a family, becomes from the same cause incapable of

supporting or educating them, he is deservedly reprobated and might be justly punished; but it is for the breach of duty to his family or creditor, not for the extravagance. . . .

. . . [T]he merely contingent . . . injury which a person causes society by conduct which neither violates any specific duty to the public, nor occasions perceptible hurt to any assignable individual except himself . . . is one which society can afford to bear, for the sake of the greater good of human freedom.[13]

It is, on this account, the harmful effects that may be produced by one's self regarding habits, not the habits and attitudes themselves that must be the focus of reproach and legal sanction. If the habitual viewing of violent pornography leads someone to commit a rape, for example, it would seem to follow that they can be justly punished, but it is for the rape rather than the habits that precipitated it.

In answer to such considerations, it might be said that the distinction between directly and indirectly harmful acts may sometimes be ignored. When someone yells "Fire!" in a crowded theatre, the effects are so immediate and so obvious that we might, for example, count this as an attempt at direct harm. Such cases have little consequence for the questions we are discussing here, however, for such a situation is not analogous to the viewing of pornography, which is not so obvious and immediate an attempt to provoke harm. Rather, the viewing of pornography can better be compared to the situation Mill discusses when he argues that "an opinion that corn dealers are starvers of the poor, or that private property is robbery, ought to be unmolested when . . . circulated through the press."[14] Such claims obviously promote a view of corn dealers and the owners of private property that might inflame someone who reads them, thus precipitating violence. Mill is not, however, willing to suppress such remarks on this account though he does claim that context can make them unacceptable — as when they are yelled to an angry mob gathered outside the residence of a corn dealer.[15] In the latter, *but not the former*, case the difference between directly and indirectly harmful acts is, on Mill's account, insignificant. Yet it is the former case that is analogous to the publication of pornography, and it seems to follow that the link between it and harm is not direct enough to provide sufficient grounds for censorship.

One might still defend the censorship of pornography by arguing that we should extend Mill's ban on harmful acts so that it applies to indirectly harmful acts, but such a move is difficult to justify. It must be granted that some indirectly harmful acts lead to actual harm, but this is the price of liberty and the prohibition of such acts is compatible with the most extreme paternalism. Gambling in the stock market, consuming alcohol, betting on horse races, watching crime on television, frequenting pool halls, and attending soccer games and rock and roll concerts may lead to harmful acts, but it is difficult to justify the suggestion that we should ban them on these grounds. Analogous restrictions on freedom of expression are still more difficult to justify, for the publication of anything that fuels emotions — stories that offend religious convictions (e.g., Salman Rushdie's *The Satanic Verses*), government exposés, and harsh criticisms of any individual or groups — may be indirectly harmful, for they may lead, in one way or another, to anger and ultimately violence. The censorship of material that may be indirectly harmful, therefore, implies an enormous infringement on the freedom of expression, which is difficult to make compatible with free political discussion.

It may seem to follow that Mill's defence of freedom of expression is incompatible with the censorship of pornography, but it would be a mistake to draw this conclusion. For although Mill does not accept the prohibition of all indirectly harmful acts, he does allow the state to interfere in specific cases, and a careful look at *On Liberty* shows that he would hold that the state can justifiably suppress freedom of expression in cases where individuals promote harm to others. This is not a principle he explicitly propounds, but it can be deduced from his discussion of the promotion of self-regarding acts of which society disapproves. There is, he says in this regard, "considerable force" in the arguments for interfering with anyone who "makes it his occupation, for subsistence of pecuniary gain, to promote" self-regarding acts that "society and the State consider to be an evil."[16] Taking fornication and gambling as examples, he claims that they must be accepted, but that the question whether one should be allowed to be a pimp or the keeper of a gambling house "is one of those which lie on the exact boundary line . . ." between what is and what is not acceptable.[17] This is enough to show that Mill would not tolerate the attempt to benefit by promoting directly harmful acts, for they are more objectionable than the self-regarding acts in question, and the attempt to promote them must, therefore, cross the boundary line between what should and should not be tolerated. Mill himself does not discuss such cases, but this is not because he thinks they are acceptable, but because he cannot envision such a possibility.

At first glance, it may seem that this account of Mill implies a new restriction on freedom of expression, but the principle that individuals may not promote harm to others is not a radically new suggestion. On the contrary, it is the implicit basis of laws against inciting an offence, aiding and abetting, conspiracy, intimidation, threatening, and counselling an offence. In all these cases, actions are prohibited because they promote harm to others, even though they themselves are only indirectly harmful and lead at most to other acts that are the immediate cause of harm. The extent to which the promotion of harm to others is rejected in standard legal principles is seen in the law of torts, which defines "defamation" as any visible or audible matter or act that tends "to diminish the esteem, respect, goodwill or confidence in which the plaintiff is held, or to excite adverse, derogatory or unpleasant feelings against him."[18] Defamation is not, it should be emphasized, confined to communication that actually harms another's reputation, but applies to any communication that has *a general tendency* to this effect.

Given limits on freedom of expression that rule out the promotion of harm to others, the censorship of a great deal of contemporary pornography can be justified, for it suggests that kidnapping, rape, assault, and torture are a legitimate means of achieving sexual satisfaction. It is the explicit promotion of harm that this implies that distinguishes it from other indirectly harmful acts (e.g., drinking and gambling) that cannot be legitimately prohibited. Within the arena of free speech, publications that may indirectly lead to harm by stirring up emotions are, in contrast, permissible as long as they do not suggest that violence and the infringement of other people's rights are appropriate. Much violent pornography does not literally state that rape, assault, torture, etc., is acceptable, but this is still its obvious message, as is clear from its heroes (men and sometimes women who perpetrate assault, torture, and violence), its lack of compassion for their victims, and its complete disregard and insensitivity to the unacceptability of the acts that it depicts. To imagine something similar in a more explicitly political realm, we would have to imagine political pamphlets that glorified or made light of the vivid torture of political opponents. In both cases, the promotion of violence that this implies is a clear case where freedom of expression is used to condone the harm to others that Mill and traditional legal sanctions both reject.

Though she does not discuss the links between her views and traditional accounts of freedom of expression, Rosemarie Tong[19] recognizes this aspect of contemporary pornography in an analysis she has proposed. Arguing that violent pornography defames women as a class, she proposes "group libel" as a means of preventing the dissemination of "degrading thanatica" (from the Greek thanatos for "death"). Appropriate plaintiffs and damages can, she suggests, be determined by standard libel law principles, while injunctions against the future publication of similar materials may be adopted as a remedy.[20]

Such moves are in keeping with a rejection of the promotion of harm to others, but there are many practical problems with such a strategy. Thus the courts have not been receptive to the notion of group libel on the grounds that it is difficult to define defamed groups,[21] injunctions are possible only in very restricted circumstances,[22] and the cost of civil actions would impede them. As Tong herself suggests, group libel is an "undeveloped" legal concept. Changes to obscenity law therefore seem a better answer to contemporary pornography, although they could have an effect similar to the one that she defends.

We can better understand the proposed defense of the censorship of violent pornography if we compare it to censorship as it presently operates in North America. Originally, both Canadian and United States courts employed the common law test of obscenity — the "Hicklin test" enunciated by Lord Cockburn, chief justice of the Court of Queen's Bench in 1868. It asks ". . . whether the tendency of the matter charged as obscenity is to deprave and corrupt those whose minds are open to such immoral influences, and into whose hands a publication of this sort may fall."[23]

In American courts, the Hicklin test was first rejected when Judge Augustus Hand ruled that James Joyce's *Ulysses* was not obscene.[24] In lieu of Hicklin, he proposed a new standard that emphasized the dominant theme of a work as viewed by the average reader. In 1957, the United States Supreme Court confirmed this rejection of Hicklin in *Roth v. U.S.* Roth further held that obscenity was "utterly without redeeming social importance" and not protected by the First Amendment. In 1973, in *Miller v. California*, the Supreme Court established as the present test of obscenity the questions:

(a) whether the "average person, applying contemporary community standards" would find that the work, taken as a whole appeals to the prurient interest . . .
(b) whether the work depicts or describes, in a patently offensive way, sexual conduct specifically defined by the applicable state law, and
(c) whether the work, taken as a whole, lacks serious literary, artistic, political, or scientific value.

According to Miller, local communities must be appealed to in determining standards of tolerance, though it is unclear whether these communities are states or smaller units.

In Canada, the Hicklin test was modified by the introduction of the Criminal Code[25] definition of obscenity in 1959. Subsection 159 (8) of the code states that

any publication a dominant characteristic of which is the undue exploitation of sex, or of sex and any one or more of the following subjects, namely crime, horror, and violence, shall be deemed to be obscene.[26]

Originally intended as a mechanism that would support the Hicklin test, case law soon adopted the Criminal Code definition as an exhaustive test. Initially introduced as a remedy to the "vague subjective" common law criteria,[27] it soon proved to be inadequate, and case law turned to "the community standards test,"[28] employing community standards to establish what constitutes the "undue exploitation" central to the statutory definition of obscenity.

In 1985, the Supreme Court of Canada made possible a broader understanding of obscenity, suggesting that community standards were merely one of a number of ways to measure undue exploitation. Any legal definition of undueness must, it declared, also encompass publications that might pass the community standards test but are harmful to members of society and, therefore, society as a whole.[29] In *R v. Wagner*, the Alberta Court of Appeal subsequently concluded that video tapes could be judged obscene if they could result in probable harm to the public.[30] Sociological studies, research, and experiments of the kind we have already noted were accepted as evidence that could establish the probability of such harm.

Unlike courts in the United States, Canadian courts interpret their appeal to community standards as an appeal on a national rather than a local level.[31] Despite this difference, obscenity law has, for the most part, been applied similarly in both jurisdictions.[32] For our purposes, the important point is that obscenity law is founded, in both cases, on an appeal to community attitudes and opinions. The legal constitutionality of such appeals under the Canadian Charter of Rights and Freedoms[33] has yet to be decided by the Supreme Court,[34] but there is, from a moral point of view, no way to escape the conclusion that present day obscenity law represents an arbitrary infringement on freedom of expression. Indeed, it would be difficult to find a clearer example of the "tyranny of the majority," which prompted Mill's defence of freedom of expression. As he says repeatedly, the imposition of the majority's view on other individuals is the most serious threat to liberty in a democratic state, and freedom of expression must protect us from such interference. Instead, obscenity law as it is now exercised has the opposite effect, enforcing the majority's view of what is unacceptable and obscene.

I have already argued that there are instances where the censorship of pornography can be justified, but this censorship should not be confused with censorship as it now operates in North America. In the cases in question, pornography is unacceptable because it promotes harm to others and *not* because the views expressed contravene the views of the community. The conflict between the rationale behind present-day obscenity law and censorship, which is compatible with traditional accounts of freedom of expression, is very clearly seen in the decision, by the British Columbia Court of Appeal, that sexually explicit material can be deemed to be obscene even when no violence is involved and women are not subjugated to degrading and dehumanizing roles.[35] Though I know of no such case, it is also easy to imagine how the standard appeal to community standards of tolerance might be used to justify restrictions that allow society to act against material it finds politically offensive — e.g., the defence of gay and lesbian rights. Any such action is, however, an arbitrary infringement on freedom of expression, which endorses the principle that society can interfere with individual expression it finds disagreeable even if it has no clear connection to direct harm to others.

American and Canadian appeals to obscenity law are, it should be noted, also problematic from a practical point of view, for they are vague and indeterminate. "The determination of 'community standards' by the experts appearing in obscenity trials is . . . left largely to their hunches, impressions and subjective judgments."[36] The uncertain and inconsistent standard this implies makes it difficult to apply obscenity law and asks defendants to abide by standards that are not clearly demarcated in the first place. Within such a context, those involved in obscenity trials have good reason to criticize the unavailability of advance notice that specific materials are obscene. It is in view of the vague, subjective, and indeterminate nature of Canadian obscenity law that it has been called "the most muddled law in Canada." In a 1948 decision in the United States, Judge Struble of Ohio captured the frustration that surrounds obscenity law in both the United States and Canada when he remarked that "'obscenity' is not a legal term. It cannot be defined so that it will mean the same thing to all people, all the time, everywhere. Obscenity is very much a figment of the imagination." This may overstate the case, but it is hard to deny that the vagueness and inconsistency of present-day standards of obscenity supports Lawrence Tribe's suggestion that "the American Supreme Court's bare majority in 1973 for yet another definition of the obscene and yet another set of rationales for its suppression has produced a formula as likely to be as unstable as it is unintelligible."

Instead of resolving these practical problems, many of those who have attacked pornography have proposed analyses that are likely to exacerbate them. Helen Longino has, for example, argued that the degradation of women and their portrayal "as mere sexual objects to be exploited and manipulated" is what is unacceptable in present-day pornography.[37] The Canadian Parliament's Standing Committee on Justice and Legal Affairs endorsed a similar account of obscenity in 1978, suggesting that we define it in terms of degradation and humiliation. In *R v. Towne Cinema Theatres Ltd.*[38] Madam Justice Wilson concurred with the majority decision, but further defined the undue exploitation of sex prohibited by the present law to include degrading and dehumanizing treatments of sex. What is exploitative, degrading, and dehumanizing is very much a matter of individual taste, however, and changes to obscenity law along these lines would allow for arbitrary infringements on freedom of expression rather than a clear account of what should and should not be censored. It is a similar lack of clear criteria that created the present appeal to community standards in the first place, and it is likely that courts would be forced to use some such standards in interpreting such notions. The end result is likely to be yet another version of the practical problems that presently exist.

One finds a more promising attempt to deal with the problems with present-day obscenity law in the changes to the Canadian Criminal Code proposed in 1987 — changes that are founded on detailed definitions of "pornography" and "erotica."[39] Pornography is defined to include written and visual matter that shows (or incites, promotes, encourages, or advocates) "a person causing, attempting to cause or appearing to cause, in a sexual context, permanent or extended impairment of the body or bodily functions of that person or any other person," or "sexually violent conduct, including sexual assault and any conduct in which physical pain is inflicted or apparently inflicted on a person by that person or any other person in a sexual context."[40] A person is guilty of "dealing in pornography" if he or she "imports, makes, prints, publishes, distributes," and so forth, pornography as it is defined.

Such legislation is in keeping with the account of the limits of freedom of expression I have defended, but goes too far when it prohibits material that depicts consenting sexual acts that do not involve harm to others, e.g., consenting intercourse or masturbation.[41] The proposed prohibitions on the public display of erotica are especially heavy-handed, prohibiting erotica that may be in keeping with public taste and the rejection of the promotion of harm that I have already elaborated.[42] As many commentators have pointed out, there seems no way to justify such infringements on freedom of expression. Judging by the account I have proposed, the emphasis on sex, which continues to be the cornerstone of obscenity law, is very much misguided, for it is the promotion of harm that can justifiably be prohibited and it follows that objectionable material may contain no sex at all.

A further problem with the proposed changes to Canadian law is their failure to make clear enough the distinction between material that depicts and promotes harm to others. It must in this regard be emphasized that some specific film, book, video, sign, etc., must be judged by considering its attitude to the content it includes. A film that contains a rape scene is not ipso facto unacceptable, and the crucial factor is whether it condones the rape. A magazine, like *Brutal Trio*, which glorifies rape as a means of sexual stimulation should be prohibited, while an anti-rape film like *Scream From Silence* (which graphically portrays a rape) cannot legitimately be censored. Rather, its attempt to dispel myths that make rape acceptable is a laudable attempt to reinforce the principle that harm to others is unacceptable — the very principle attacked by objectionable pornography. It is in view of this principle that unacceptable pornography should be defined as material that *incites, advocates, promotes or, encourages* (and not merely as material that "depicts") harm to others. The context in which a particular publication is presented may, therefore, be important to a determination of its status as pornography. The publication of Marquis de Sade's *One Hundred and Twenty Days of Sodom* may, for example, be permissible as a basis for the study of history or sexual deviance though it should be published in a way that reflects the attitude this implies. It is one thing to make it available for serious study, it is another to publish and promote it as illustrated popular bedtime reading. Dworkin and MacKinnon have suggested one way to allow such contexts in their proposal to amend the Minneapolis Code of Ordinance on Civil Rights in a way that would ban "trafficking in pornography," for their amendment would exempt public libraries from this ban.

Accepting the limit on censorship implied by a consideration of the attitude that is displayed by pornographic material, it should by now be clear that the censorship of violent pornography proposed by the Canadian government can be made compatible with liberal notions of freedom of expression. The key to such censorship is the principle that the promotion of harm to others should not be tolerated, a principle that can be used to justify the changes to obscenity law that prohibit such material, though not the changes that allow a broader censorship.

In closing, it should perhaps be noted one should not expect the proposed censorship to eliminate every problematic case, even though it will eradicate much of the vagueness inherent in the present appeal to community standards. A definition of obscenity that focuses on the promotion of harm will substantially clarify obscenity law, but questions of intent and meaning are inherently difficult and complex. Indeed, the problems they produce are not unique to censorship and inevitably permeate any legal system. It is impossible to anticipate every possible problem here, and it must instead be said that such censorship must be refined by a discussion of a multitude of examples, and that this is best accomplished by case law and the evolution this implies. Granting the need for such discussion, the fundamental principle behind the account of obscenity I have proposed is (unlike the principles behind present-day obscenity law) relatively straightforward and easily applied.[43] More importantly perhaps, it provides a basis for obscenity that is very much in keeping with traditional accounts of freedom of expression.

NOTES

1. For detailed references, see the version of the present paper published in the *Windsor Review of Legal and Social Issues*, Vol. II, May 1990.

2. The legislation died on the order paper when Parliament was dissolved for the federal election in 1988.
3. Laura Lederer, ed., *Take Back the Night: Women on Pornography* (New York: William Morrow & Company, 1980); ". . . the liberal approach . . . presents pornography as just one more aspect of our ever expanding sexuality" (19).
4. Thelma McCormack, "Passionate Protests: Feminists and Censorship," *Canadian Forum* (March, 1980).
5. Jan Narveson, *The Libertarian Idea* (Philadelphia: Temple University Press, 1988). Narveson discusses the issues raised in the present paper on pp. 284–95, but his account is inconclusive and does not address the distinctions I make here.
6. John Stuart Mill, *On Liberty* (Markham: Penguin Books, 1974), 68.
7. Ibid., 71.
8. Ibid., 116–17, 81.
9. Ibid., 148.
10. In very extreme cases where the making of ("snuff") pornography depends on actual rape and murder, the state must intervene, but this leaves the bulk of pornography untouched.
11. For relevant material, see supra, note 1.
12. Supra, note 6 at 71. It is important to separate: (1) the distinction between directly and indirectly harmful acts, and (2) the distinction between acts which are always or only sometimes directly harmful. Mill allows society to take action against the latter when he suggests that acts may be forbidden if they promote "a definite risk of damage" or "probability of damage," ibid., pp. 149 and 163, though he fails to give a precise account of how much risk warrants prohibition. The important point is that the acts that might thus be prohibited (drunken driving, for example) cause direct harm when they cause harm, and that this aspect of Mill's discussion is not, therefore, applicable to the viewing of pornography, which is at most indirectly harmful.
13. Ibid., 148–49.
14. Ibid., 119.
15. Ibid., 119.
16. Ibid., 168–69.
17. Ibid., 170.
18. *Black's Law Dictionary*, 5th ed. (St. Paul: West Publishing Co., 1983), 217. See also P. Lewis, ed., *Gatley on Libel and Slander*, 8th ed. (London: Sweet and Maxwell, 1981).
19. Rosemarie Tong, "Feminism, Pornography and Censorship," *Social Theory and Practice* 8 (1982).
20. Ibid., 12. A similar approach is discussed in Susan G. Cole, *Pornography and the Sex Crisis* (Toronto: Amanita Enterprises, 1989), 95–106. For a detailed discussion of group libel, see David Reisman, "Democracy and Defamation: Control of Group Libel," *Columbia Law Review* (1942) 42:727.
21. Especially as different individuals (including different individuals from the groups that have allegedly been defamed) disagree over the question whether pornography is objectionable.
22. *Natural Resources Ltd. v. Saturday Night Ltd.* (1910), 2 O.W.N. 9. See *Robinson v. Adams* (1924), 56 O.L.R. 217 (C.A.) for the principles outlining the limited cases where an injunction should be granted.
23. *R v. Hicklin* (1868), 3 L.R.Q.B. 360.
24. *United States v. One Book Called "Ulysses"*: 5 F. Supp. 182 (S.D.N.Y., 1983) affirmed 72 F. 2d 705 (2d Cir. 1934). See L. Tribe, *American Constitutional Law* (Mineola: The Foundation Press Inc. 1978), 659.
25. *Canadian Criminal Code*, S.C. 1953–54 c. 51.
26. Ibid., a. 159(8), as am. S.C. 1959, c. 41, s. 11.
27. Canada, House of Commons Debates 1959, Vol. V, p. 5517, Standing Committee on Justice and Legal Affairs, "Report on Pornography" by the Hon. E. Davie Fulton in *House of Commons Journal*, Vol. 123, No. 86, 1978.
28. *R v. Brodie; R v. Times Square Cinemas Ltd.* (1971), 3 O.R. 688, 4 C.C.C. (2d) 229 (C.A.).
29. *R v. Towne Cinema Theatres Ltd.* [1985] 1 S.C.R. 494, 18 D.L.R. (4th) 1.
30. *R v. Wagner* (1986), 26 C.C.C. (3d) 242, 43 Alta. L.R. (2d).

31. *R v. Times Square Cinemas Ltd.,* supra; *R v. Adriadne Dev. Ltd.* (1974), 19 C.C.C. (2d) 49, 8 N.S.R. (2dd) 560.

32. "The definitions of obscenity in these two countries, although developing from different sources, have been interpreted and applied similarly." R.E. Dean, *Obscenity Standards in Canada and the United States: A Comparative Study in Constitutional Law* (Ph.D. Dissertation, University of Tennessee, 1974), 11.

33. *Canadian Charter of Rights and Freedoms,* 1 of the *Constitution Act,* 1982, being Schedule B of the *Canada Act* 1982 (U.K.) 1982, c. 11.

34. Lower court rulings on the issue are found in the decisions of the British Columbia Court of Appeal in *R v. Red Hot Video* (1985), 15 C.R.R. 206, 18 C.C.C. (3d) 1, and the Ontario Court of Appeal in *Re Ontario Film and Video Appreciation Society and the Ontario Board of Censors* (1984), 7 C.R.R. 129, 5 D.L.R. (4th) 766. In *R v. Butler* (1989), 50 C.C.C. (3d) 97, 60 M.R. (2d) 82, the Manitoba Court of Queen's Bench ruled in favour of prohibitions on obscene material if their purpose is to protect people from, among other things, material that effectively reduces the human, equality, or other Charter rights of individuals (but not if their purpose is to control the morals of society).

35. *R v. Pereira-Vasquez* (1988),43 C.C.C. (3d) 82, 26 B.C.L.R. (2d) 273.

36. Supra, note 49, 532.

37. Supra, note 7.

38. *R v. Towne Cinema Theatres Ltd.,* [1985] 1 S.C.R. (S.C.C.), 494.

39. Bill C-54, *An Act to Amend the Criminal Code and other Acts in Consequence Thereof,* 2d Sess., 33d Parl., 1986–87, s. 1.

40. Ibid. at 1 a(ii) & 1 a(iii).

41. Ibid. at 1 a(vi).

42. Though "erotica" is defined very broadly to include almost any vaguely sexual representation, section 159.7 would make it an offence to publicly display it.

43. It should be emphasized that such censorship implies a very specific restriction on freedom of expression and cannot be rejected on the grounds that other kinds of censorship have often been abused (Leach and other critics of censorship seem oblivious to the differences that distinguish different kinds of censorship).

QUESTIONS

1. Is Mill right in thinking that freedom is a general good that must be maximized? Why or why not?

2. Is Mill's view that "the only purpose for which power can be rightfully exercised over any member of a civilized community against his will is to prevent harm to others" sound? How would you test its validity?

3. Leo Groarke argues that censoring some kinds of pornography is compatible with Mill's principle. What reasons does he give for this view? How do these reasons differ from Gastil's? Are Groarke's reasons convincing? Why or why not?

4. The fact that censoring some kinds of pornography is compatible with Mill's principle does not show that violent pornography should be censored. Does Leo Groarke provide convincing arguments to show that the kind of pornography that he thinks should be censored is sufficiently harmful to warrant this kind of legal intervention?

SEXUAL EQUALITY AND THE PROBLEM OF AN ADEQUATE MORAL THEORY: THE POVERTY OF LIBERALISM

Lorenne Clark

One of the fundamental principles endorsed by a liberal ethic is that there must be some areas of one's life in which one has the freedom to do what one wants, free from interference by others. It has been argued that there simply are some areas of life which are none of the law's business. For those familiar with the Wolfenden Report on Homosexuality in England, and the subsequent debate that this started both within and outside academic circles, this phrase, "none of the law's business," will have an all too familiar ring. Philosophically, this is reflected in debates about which areas of one's life should be essentially characterized by negative freedom, the ability to act free of restraints and scrutiny of others. Legally, it is reflected in debates about privacy, about the areas of one's life into which others should be legally prohibited from interfering.[1] There is virtually no one who would want to say that we should have no negative liberty or no privacy, but the debate still rages as to which areas of one's life should be guaranteed as areas of negative liberty through the creation of a legal right to privacy.

The difficulty is that no one has found a satisfactory method of drawing the boundaries between the private and other areas of life. In the past, the boundary was thought to be a *natural* one, based on the traditional distinction between the public and the private. The private just *was* "the private," and, as such should be guaranteed as an area of negative liberty and fully protected by means of a legally enforceable right to privacy. This was the basis of the argument in the Wolfenden Report. Here it was alleged that sexual relations between consenting adults simply are none of the law's business and the underlying rationale was that such behaviour should justifiably be left to the absolute discretion of individuals because it has effects on no one other than the participants. This was the rationale provided by John Stuart Mill in "On Liberty," and which was reiterated and defended by Herbert Hart in *Law, Liberty, and Morality*.[2] The best defence of this liberal tenet is the view developed by Mill that the law is justified in prohibiting actions if and only if doing them results in the inability of others to exercise rights of a similar kind. The underlying view is that rights should be distributed equally, which entails that no one can have rights the exercise of which would prevent others from exercising similar rights. The difficulty with the position is that it is virtually impossible to say with certainty of any action or pattern of behaviour that it has in principle no potential effects on others, either in terms of causing harm, or in terms of limiting the effective exercise of rights. Thus it is impossible *in principle* to draw a defensible boundary between the public and the private.

And certainly it has been indefensible to draw the legal boundary on the basis of the historical division between public and private. As is now abundantly clear, privacy functioned historically to protect those who were privileged to begin with. Privacy was a consequence of the ownership of private property, and, hence, was a commodity purchased with property. It has been a privilege accorded those of wealth and high social status. But more importantly from a feminist perspective, it protected not only the dominant class in

This is a shortened version of a paper originally published in In Search of the Feminist Perspective: The Changing Potency of Women, *Mary Kathryn Shirley and Rachel Emma Vigier, eds. Toronto: Resources for Feminist Research, Special Publication no. 5 (Spring 1979). Reprinted by permission of Lorenne Clark.*

the Marxist sense, but the dominant sex-class as well. The traditionally "private" was the sphere of the personal, home and hearth. And that area was the area within which women and children were forms of private property under the exclusive ownership and control of males. As the person in whom the absolute personality of the family rested, male heads of households had virtually absolute rights over their wives and children. The family, clearly, was not and is not a partnership of equals. There is no mutuality in the marital relations and the rights and duties are decidedly one-sided.

Of course it is not the concept of privacy which is responsible for this state of affairs. But in drawing a boundary between the historically private and public, for the purpose of entrenching a legal right to privacy in the area of the traditionally private, it certainly functioned to condone and encourage the abusive and unjustified practices which were possible within this unequal relation. As is now clear, the family has been characterized by a great deal of physical violence. The legitimate basis of authority in the family is physical coercion, and it is and has been regularly relied on to secure to the male head of the house the attitudes and behaviours he wants. Women, much less children, had no right to protest such behaviour but were expected to suffer it, willingly, or otherwise. Thus, the last place feminists want to see a right to privacy is in the family. What possible sense can be made of the notion of being a consenting adult when one is in a relation in which one has no right to say no? Clearly, if we want privacy at all, where we do not want it is in the home.

The area of life most in need of regulation and control in the interest of creating more liberty and equality for women is the area of the traditionally private and personal. But greater liberty and equality for women can be purchased only at the cost of less liberty, and loss of status, for men. To the extent that women are given more rights within marriage, men are less able to do as they please; what was before permissible would now be either mandatory, as, for example, in making it a duty for men to share the housework and childcare, or prohibited, as for example in allowing a charge of rape between spouses. Within terms of the basic principle, such changes are justified. The past operation of the law has permitted many forms of behaviour which in fact caused physical and other direct and tangible harms to others, and which certainly prevented the effective exercise of like rights on the part of others. On the principle of like liberties for all, marriage must be turned into a relation of mutuality, and the relationships within it must be subject to regulation and control.

Why, then, has the demand for privacy centred so exclusively on preserving the traditional domain of male privilege? And why do the staunchest defenders of that view fail to see that in invoking these principles within a domain characterized by fundamental sexual inequality they are in fact both reinforcing that inequality and sanctioning its worst abuses? Thus, at the very least, adherents of the liberal ethic must acknowledge that there is no *natural* basis for deciding on what is private and what is public for the purpose of entrenching a legal right to privacy, and that the traditional area of the private is the area most in need of loss of privacy, in the name of promoting greater positive liberty and greater equality. How this fares on a purely utilitarian principle is of course problematic, for since men and women each make up roughly half the population, we cannot be sure that the benefits to women will in fact outweigh the losses to men.

In my view, the whole debate about privacy has been totally miscast because it has relied on the historical division between public and private. Thus, its liberal adherents continue to stress the need for privacy in just the areas where it is least defensible. Where we need the most protection, the legally enforceable right to prevent others from gaining access to information about us, and from disseminating that information to others without either our knowledge or our consent, is in the public world, the world of computers and charge-cards, credit ratings, and security forces. But this will mean much more regulation and control of the people and institutions which determine the structure and organization of the economic and social order. It will mean confronting the dominant class and the dominant sex in the public as well as the private sphere, and we should hardly be surprised to find that we are forced to part company with radical adherents of the liberal ethic. Equality cannot flourish without limiting the privileges some already have in both the private and the public spheres because the inequalities of the present system were a product of the unequal attribution of rights in the first instance; thus greater equality and liberty for those least advantaged under the present system necessitates placing restrictions on the privileged rights of those who are presently most advantaged. And since this must be done by creating obligations either to do or to forbear actions previously permitted, it can be accomplished only at the expense of negative liberty.

While the principles of the liberal ethic itself do not require the historical division between public and private, it has certainly been presupposed in liberal thinking about these issues. Recognition of the extent to which this has played a role must lead to a reappraisal of what it is that people should be at liberty to do, and it must find a basis for this which does not rest on traditional views of the different spheres of life, and the different roles of the sexes.

What is needed, at base, is a reappraisal of what is *harmful*. That, too, has historically been defined in terms of what the dominant sex and the dominant economic class find "harmful." An analysis of rape law demonstrates that point as well as anything could. Physically coerced sexual intercourse has been regarded as constituting a redressable harm if and only if the female victim was a dependent female living under either parental or matrimonial control, and in possession of those qualities which made her desirable as a piece of sexual and reproductive property available for the exclusive use of a present or future husband.[3] I dare say that when we start pressing for legal reform which will prohibit sexual harassment on the job we will find few adherents of liberalism rallying to our cause. It remains to be seen whether or not liberalism can survive and transcend the limitations of its own historical perspective, but in so far as it must renounce much of its accepted thinking about what sorts of actions individuals ought to be free to do, and must recognize that negative liberty must at least temporarily take a back seat to the promotion of equality, I cannot say I am hopeful about the outcome. But the ethics of liberalism will not do as the moral framework for the achievement of sexual equality unless it can meet this challenge.

But it is clear from a consideration of the issue of pornography that so far at least the ethics of liberalism has been unable to rethink its concept of harm in a way which is consistent with sexual equality. Feminists and civil libertarians are now at complete loggerheads over the issue. The trend among feminists is clear. More and more of them are coming to see that pornography is a species of hate literature.[4] To achieve its impact, it relies on depicting women in humiliating, degrading, and violently abusive situations. To make matters worse, it frequently depicts them willingly, even avidly, suffering and inviting such treatment. As is obvious to even the naivest of eyes, such recreations of heterosexual behaviour and rela-tionships feed traditional male fantasies about both themselves and women.

Pornography is a method of socialization; it is the tangible, palpable embodiment of the imposition of the dominant sexual system which is a part of the dominant sex-class system.

It is a vivid depiction of how to deploy male sexuality in just the way that will achieve maximum effect in maintaining the *status quo*. Pornography would be neither desired nor tolerated within any system other than one which sprang from the differential attribution of rights of ownership in which women and children are forms of sexual property, and in which they must either like it or quite literally lump it. It is the obverse of a morality which stresses female passivity and submissiveness, and it encourages the actualization of such states through active aggression and violence. Pornography has very little to do with sex, certainly with any conception of egalitarian sexual relations between the sexes, but it has everything to do with showing how to use sexuality as an instrument of active oppression, and that is why it is wrong. Some allege that it also feeds female fantasies about themselves and men, but that is certainly being questioned, at least in so far as it can be said that there is any hard empirical data to support it.[5]

That there should be no laws prohibiting the manufacture, sale, and distribution of pornography has traditionally and increasingly been defended as a freedom of speech, and freedom of press, issue. It is alleged that the reading or viewing of such material does not cause harm, or that if it does, it is harm only to those who willingly consent to it. The premise that it doesn't cause harm is defended by arguing that it relates only to the fantasy level and does not translate itself into interpersonal behaviour. And it goes further than this to argue that, indeed, it provides a healthy outlet, a cathartic effect, for those who might otherwise be tempted to act out their fantasies. Those who oppose pornography, particularly those who advocate its prohibition, are treated as Victorian prudes with sexual hang-ups. Women who object to it are seen as uptight, unliberated, and just not "with it" sexually speaking.

The general principle underlying the liberal view is of course that expressed by Mill in "On Liberty," who argued against any form of censorship on the ground that it was only through the free flow of information that the true and false could be separated. Prohibitions against the dissemination of any form of information functions to preserve the *status quo* and to prevent the development of a critically reflective morality which is itself necessary to pave the way for needed social change. The principle has much to be said for it. But that cannot change the fact that when it is uncritically made to apply within a domain character-ized by inequality and by frankly abusive behaviour, a domain which is fundamentally shaped by a framework of social relations and institutions which makes all sexual relation-ships between men and women fundamentally coercive in nature,[6] it is bound to produce results which will be unacceptable because harmful to those who are in the pre-existing inferior position and who stand to be most affected by the attitudes and beliefs, as well as the practices, of those who use it.

The liberal argument has been that such material isn't harmful at all, and certainly cannot be seen as harmful to anyone other than the user, if harmful even to him. It isn't harmful because it functions merely to inflame male sexual desire. What is the harm if all it does is give a guy a bit of a rush? And it is right here that we must begin our critique. Surely we must acknowledge at least two things. First, it is not "normal" to get one's rushes from just anything. Secondly, if one gets desirable reactions from things which create a clear and substantial risk to others, then one can justifiably be prohibited from getting them that way. Persons who get their sexual stimulation from watching the atrocities perpetrated against the Jews during the Holocaust are not regarded as "normal," and rightly so. Furthermore, we do not feel that we are infringing any legitimate rights of others in preventing them access to material designed to provide sexual stimulation by this means. And the reasons for that are at least two-fold. First, as history has made all too clear, actions of this particular species do not remain at the level of mere fantasy. They have been acted out on the grand scale, so grand as to make any rational and reflective person aware that the possibility of a correlation between thought and action is at least strong enough to justify the imposition of prohibitions against material of this sort. Second, it stems from recognizing that even if the actual actions themselves are not acted out, the attitudes and beliefs of the persons enjoying them reflect attitudes toward the objects of the actions which are in themselves intrinsically bad and which are bound to produce practical effects in real life, if only to be expressed in bigoted and racist attitudes. All of the same arguments apply to material which depicts black people in degrading, humiliating, and abusive circumstances. Such material is, in itself, an affront to the dignity of the objects depicted, not least because they *are* being depicted purely as objects, dehumanized and depersonalized instruments for the satisfaction of someone else's perverted tastes.

The same case can be made with respect to heterosexual pornography.[7] As Camille Le Grand puts it, "pornography teaches society to view women as less than human. It is this view which keeps women as victims."[8] The typical way in which women are depicted in pornography certainly reflects a view of them as inferior to men, as inherently masochistic, and as primarily of value as instrument for the satisfaction of male lust. That is, in itself, intrinsically offensive to women, and is a straightforward objective affront to their dignity as equal persons. So on that ground alone, pornography ought to be prohibited just as we prohibit material depicting other social groups in such a fashion.

Of course, we could hardly argue within the parameters of our present culture that it is abnormal for males to react as they do to pornography. It is, unfortunately, all too normal, at least where we have any notion of statistical normality in mind. But neither is it unusual for rape victims to feel shamed, humiliated, and degraded by being raped; this is "normal" in the culture, but from any more rational perspective, it certainly is not "normal" in any normative sense. Much of recent efforts around the issue of rape have been designed specifically to change the perspective which rape victims have on that experience. Rape victims can come to see the assaultive behaviour perpetrated against them as legitimizing the anger which is appropriate to the nature of the attack. In short, it is possible both to identify the specific effects of socialization within a male supremacist and sexually coercive society, and to offset those effects with appropriate reconceptualization of the event. Women can come to identify the masochism and victimization into which they have been socialized, and can then act both to counteract it, and to be sublimely angry at a culture which socialized them into that mode. So, too, it should be possible for men to identify the sadism and attitudes of sexual aggressivity into which they are socialized and so act both to counteract them, and to be angry at a social system that produced that response. In short, *it is not a mark of personal depravity or immorality to be aroused by such material.* Given the cultural pattern of which it is a manifestation that is not at all surprising. Indeed, it is just what we would expect. But what must be recognized is that it is a socialized response, and that it is a response about which men should be both concerned and angry. And certainly, once its cultural roots are exposed, it is a response which should not be seen as needing or justifying the sale and distribution of the material which elicited it. Women must object to pornography because it both reflects and reinforces the patterns of socialization appropriate to a system based on the unequal status of the sexes, in which women are consistently regarded and treated as the inferiors, and the sexual property, of men. The socialization it brings about is *in itself* a limitation of the autonomy of women. Men ought to object to it for the same reason, and they ought to recognize that the socialization it brings about in terms of their self-images and internalized standards of conduct is also intrinsically undesirable given any commitment to the notion of sexual equality. To the extent that men are able to internalize the conviction that women and men are equal persons, they must recognize that the pleasurable responses they get from pornography are inappropriate to that conviction and are destructive to their ability to form self-images consistent with it. But that does not entail that they are in any sense to blame for those responses: they had as little choice about that as they did about their names. But we have, then, given strong arguments in support of the view that the eliciting of a pleasurable response is not in itself any reason to condone the sale and distribution of pornography, and that a proper understanding of the nature and causes of that response gives men as well as women solid grounds for objecting to the material which occasioned it. I believe that many more men would be able to understand and accept the feminist perspective on pornography if they could come to realize that they are not responsible for their sexual responses to it given the patterns of socialization which exist to mould us all into a set of social relations which institutionalizes male aggression and female passivity.

Thus, pornography is intrinsically harmful, both to women and to men. However, that does not end the argument with defenders of liberalism because their argument then moves on to the assertion that the harm to women is not direct enough to justify the legal prohibition of pornography. Frankly, I think that the argument that pornography is intrinsically offensive to the dignity of women ought to carry the day, but in the interests of completeness I want to go on to consider the other arguments that are brought to pornography's defence. Apart from this notion of an intrinsic harm and infringement of the rights of women, it will be argued that even if pornography is harmful to the user, it does not lead to direct harm to women, because the fantasies it supports remain fantasies, and it in fact prevents direct harm to women through its cathartic effect. I may say at the outset that I'm not at all impressed with either of these arguments. So far as the first is concerned, there is plenty of hard evidence available which supports the contention that modeling has a powerful effect on human behaviour. Studies of wife and child abuse consistently attest to the fact that there is a strong correlation between those who are abusers and those who come from family situations which were themselves abusive. The battered child becomes the battering parent; the son who witnessed his father battering his mother, and who was himself battered, becomes a battering husband.[9] Also, the evidence about the effect of violence depicted on television on the behaviour of children also points strongly in this direction.[10] People tend to act out and operationalize the behaviour that they see typically acted out around them. And surely that is hardly surprising. It is what has kept civilization going. If we weren't able to perpetuate the patterns of behaviour developed through cultural organization we wouldn't have come very far. So far as I know, however, there is no hard data to support the catharsis theory. It is a theory espoused by those who are looking for a rationale, though doubtless it has its roots in their awareness that they read pornography but don't rape and brutalize women. But raping and brutalizing women isn't the only harm that can be perpetrated against women. But so far there is little empirical support offered for the view that pornography feeds only the fantasy. Most psychiatric literature dealing with the "perversions" asserts that some people remain content with the fantasy while others do not.[11] But no one knows what differentiates the one who does actualize it from the one who doesn't. If this argument is going to be effective, it must be empirically demonstrated that this is so, and surely we cannot predict until the data are in that those who don't so outnumber those who do that we should, in the interests of an open society, tolerate the risk that some will. And since we are all imprisoned by the cultural stereotypes and the patterns of socialization appropriate to a society based on sexual coercion, how can those who do read it assert with certainty that they do not cause harm to women? They are hardly the best judges! As rape makes clear again, there is nowhere greater difference in perception than there is in the confusion surrounding rape and seduction. The men believe they are merely seducing, but the women perceive it as rape! And who is to judge? Certainly it is intrinsically unfair to permit only those who are the perpetrators of such behaviour to have a say in its interpretation.

While the liberal principle behind opposition to censorship is based on a recognition that desirable social change requires public access to information which challenges the beliefs and practices of the *status quo*, what it does not acknowledge is that information which supports the *status quo* through providing role models which advocate the use or threat of coercion as a technique of social control directed at a clearly identifiable group depicted as inferior, subordinate, and subhuman works against the interest both of desirable social change and of the members of the subgroup so identified. This has been clearly acknowledged in the case of violently anti-Semitic and other forms of racist literature. The same principles apply with respect to violently anti-female literature, and the same conclusion should follow. But this cannot come about until it is recognized and acknowledged that the dissemination of such material is itself a harm to the members of the group involved. It remains to be seen whether liberalism can accomplish this, but until it does, we cannot hope for its support on this issue.

In refusing to count as "harms" actions and practices which serve the interest of the dominant sex by reinforcing the patterns and effects of modes of socialization which support the sexist system, it renders itself incapable of changing that system and of promoting greater equality and positive liberty for women. Liberalism serves the interest of the dominant sex and the dominant class, though it contains within itself the potential for promoting greater equality and greater positive liberty for all. It can realize this potential, however, only by reconceptualizing harm in a way consistent with sex and class equality, and by recognizing that negative liberty must take second place to the promotion of equality at least until we have achieved a framework of enforceable rules which guarantees equality within both the public and the private spheres. When no one is allowed to do what is harmful to others, and/or what prevents them from effectively exercising liberty rights to autonomy and equality consistent with the equal attribution and effective exercise of like rights on the part of others, then we will have achieved a state in which liberty is concrete, and not a chimera which upholds the liberty of some at the expense of inequality to the rest. As women we are members of the disadvantaged sex. We are thus acting contrary to the interests of our sex in accepting any position which does not place the achievement of legally enforceable sexual equality at the forefront of its program.

That entails that we have to challenge traditional concepts of harm, and of liberty as the absence of restraint. We have been successful in removing most of the legal restraints which made both equality and liberty impossible, and that was the stage at which the ethics of liberalism served our purpose. But it has now outlived its usefulness to us. The achievement of *real*, rather than merely *possible*, equality and liberty now depends on placing effective, enforceable restraints on others; we can expect little support from liberalism as we move into this stage of our liberation.

NOTES

1. A more detailed account of the relationship between the philosophical and legal debates, as well as a discussion of the complexity of the legal issue of privacy itself, is found in Clark, Lorenne M.G., "Privacy, Property, Freedom, and the Family," *Philosophical Law*, (Ed.) R. Bronaugh, Greenwood Press, Conn., 1978.

2. Hart, H.L.A., *Law, Liberty, and Morality*, O.U.P. London, 1963. This was Hart's answer to the objections raised by Lord Devlin to the recommendations and theory expressed in the Wolfenden Report. Devlin's position on this and other related matters is found in Devlin, Lord Patrick, *The Enforcement of Morals*, O.U.P., London, 1965.

3. For a discussion of the way in which the historical evolution and conception of rape law functioned to maintain the sexual *status quo*, and indeed continues to produce just the results we should expect to find with respect to the treatment and handling of rape cases within the criminal justice system, see Clark, Lorenne M.G., and Lewis, Debra J., *Rape: The Price of Coercive Sexuality*, The Women's Press, Toronto, 1977.

4. Among the articles that spring readily to mind are Morgan, Robin, "Theory and Practice: Pornography and Rape," *Going Too Far*, Random House, N.Y., 1977, Ch. IV, pp. 163–169; Russell, Diana, "Pornography: A Feminist Perspective," unpublished paper; Brownmiller, Susan, *Against Our Will*, Simon & Schuster, N.Y., 1975, pp. 394–396; and Shear, Marie, "Free Meat Talks Back," *J. of Communication*, Vol. 26, No. 1, Winter, 1976, pp. 38–39.

5. For an excellent discussion of the way in which the empirical research that has been done on obscenity reflects a decidedly male bias, see McCormack, Thelma, "Machismo in Media Research: A Critical Review of Research on Violence and Pornography," *Social Problems*, Vol. 25, No. 5, 1978, pp. 544–555.

6. Clark and Lewis, *Rape: The Price of Coercive Sexuality*, Chs. 7 and 8 in particular.

7. Indeed, it is true of male homosexual pornography as well. But in the interest of not legislating in the interest of others, I am not advocating that we should prohibit this species of pornography. If men object to it, as in my view they should, whether homo- or heterosexual, it is up to them to express their opposition. Certainly I do not wish to infringe the rights homosexuals have to look at what they like, even though I cannot say with certainty that I am not adversely affected by it.

8. Quoted in Russell, Diana, "Pornography: A Feminist Perspective," op. cit., p. 7, no reference given.

9. See, for example, Martin, Del, *Battered Wives*, Glide Publications, San Francisco, 1976, pp. 22–23; Pizzey, Erin, *Scream Quietly or the Neighbours Will Hear*, Penguin Books, England, 1974, Ch. 4; Van Stolk, Mary, *The Battered Child in Canada*, McClelland & Stewart, Toronto, 1972, pp. 23–27.

10. Bandura, A., Ross, D., and Ross, S.A., "Transmission of Aggression through Imitation of Aggressive Models," *J. Abnormal and Social Psychology*, 63, No. 3, 575–582.

11. Kraft-Ebbing, Richard von, *Psychopathia Sexualis*, 11th ed. rev. and enlarged, Stuttgard, 1901, pp. 94–95; Freud, S., *Introductory Lectures on Psycho-Analysis*, Standard Edition, 16:306.

QUESTIONS

1. Is Lorenne Clark right in thinking that the separation of law and morality as it relates to human sexuality and reproduction is not sound?

2. In what respects does Clark's critique of the public-private distinction differ from the critique offered by Raymond Gastil?

3. Is the idea of harm used by those opposing the censorship of pornography adequate, or is it in need of revision, as Clark suggests?

4. To what extent does the idea of harm suggested by Clark differ from that suggested by the authors of the other selections?

5. Is pornography a species of hate literature?

6. Does pornography reinforce a sexist view of women? If so, does this fact provide adequate grounds for censorship?

LIBERAL FEMINISM: THE GLIMMER OF HOPE

Wendy McElroy

In the maelstrom of anti-pornography hysteria, liberal feminism often provides the few voices of sanity heard above the storm. Liberal organizations like Feminists for Free Expression (FFE) have consistently and courageously stood up against measures like the Victims of Pornography Compensation Act, and for sexual expression. Some liberal feminists like Nadine Strossen have been staunch and tireless in their defense of freedom of speech. It is difficult to imagine better companions in the fight for sexual choice.

Other liberals seem to have forgotten their roots and are now willing to sacrifice free speech for the greater good of protecting women from pornography.

There is a growing schism within liberal feminism, which threatens to disrupt such key liberal organizations as the National Organization for Women (NOW) and the American Civil Liberties Union (ACLU).

What are the arguments that are causing such turmoil in liberal ranks?

Liberal Feminist Arguments Against Censorship

In general, liberal feminists offer three types of arguments against censoring pornography: Freedom of speech is a necessary condition for human freedom; the suppression of pornography will hurt women (in the several ways presented below); and, pornography offers certain benefits to women.

Let us examine the first two arguments. The third will be discussed in the following chapter.

Freedom of speech is a necessary condition for human freedom.

This argument says little about women's relationship to pornography, except in the most general sense. Even feminists who believe porn degrades and humiliates women sometimes argue against censorship as the greater threat. These are the feminists who say: As a woman I am appalled by *Playboy* . . . but as a writer I understand the need for free speech.

Such feminists are not pro-pornography. They are anti-censorship. They argue on several grounds: Great works of art and literature would be banned; the First Amendment would be breached; political expression would be suppressed; and a creative culture requires freedom of speech.

The suppression of pornography will hurt women.

This argument specifically addresses the relationship of women to pornography. But, again, it is not so much a defense of pornography as it is an attack on censorship. Liberal feminists point to the real problems involved in implementing the anti-pornography program. Among the insightful questions they ask are:

Who Will Act as Censor?

Whoever acts as censor will wield tremendous power, because words such as *degrading* are so subjective they will be interpreted to mean whatever the censor wants them to. In the August 1993 *Virginia Law Review*, Nadine Strossen worries that the anti-pornography definitions are so vague that they could be used against homosexual and lesbian material:

"It is not clear whether Andrea Dworkin or Catharine MacKinnon would classify homoerotic photographs or films as 'pornography.' Although their model law defines 'pornography' as the 'sexually explicit subordination of *women* through pictures, and/or words,' it expressly stipulates that even images of men could be interpreted as portraying the subordination of women."[1]

The state that banned Margaret Sanger because she used the words *syphilis* and *gonorrhea* is no different, in principle, than the one that interprets obscenity today.

There will be nothing — not even the paper shield of the First Amendment — to stand between the state and feminist literature. There will be no protection even for the feminist classics such as *Our Bodies, Ourselves*, which provided a generation of women with an explicit glimpse of their own sexuality.

Inevitably, censorship will be used against the least popular views, against the weakest members of society — including feminists and lesbians. When the Canadian Supreme Court decided (1992) to protect women by restricting the importation of pornography, one of the first targets was a lesbian/gay bookstore named Glad Day Bookstore, which had been on a police "hit list." Canadian officials also targeted University and radical bookstores. Among the books seized by Canadian customs were two books by Andrea Dworkin: *Pornography: Men Possessing Women* and *Women Hating*.

Even narrowing the definition of pornography to include only the depiction of explicit violence would not protect feminist works. It would not, for example, protect Susan Brownmiller's pivotal *Against Our Will*, which offers a "history" of rape, complete with graphic detail. Nor would it exempt Kate Millett's *The Basement*, a novel-chronicle of sexual torture.

Doesn't the Anti-Pornography Crusade Perpetuate the Myth of Women as Victims?

Refusing to acknowledge the contracts of women in pornography places them in the same legal category as children or mental incompetents. In Indianapolis, the anti-pornography ordinance argued that women, like children, needed special protection under the law:

"Children are incapable of consenting to engage in pornographic conduct. . . . By the same token, the physical and psychological well-being of women ought to be afforded comparable protection, for the coercive environment . . . vitiates any notion that they consent or 'choose' to perform in pornography."[2]

This attitude of "I'm a helpless victim" could easily backfire on women who may be required to prove they are able to manage their own finances, or to handle custody of their own children. Moreover, the idea of men "emotionally or verbally coercing" women reenforces the concept of men as intellectually and psychologically stronger than women. It is the old "Man of Steel/Woman of Kleenex" myth.

Who Will Protect Women from the Anti-Feminist Conservatives, with Whom Radical Feminists Are Aligning?

By joining hands with conservatives, anti-pornography feminists have strengthened the political power of the Religious Right, who attack abortion and other fundamental rights of women. Radical feminists are being used. For example, in 1992, the promotional material of the conservative National Coalition Against Pornography featured quotes from Andrea Dworkin; in other contexts, these same people crucify her as a lesbian.

This alliance may be a tragic mistake for women's rights. With tragic results. Feminists are lending credibility and power to organizations which will turn on a dime against them.

Aren't Radical Feminists Diverting Attention from the Real Issues That Confront Women?

Feminists used to address the complex network of cultural, political, and biological factors that contributed to the real issues confronting women. Now the beginning and ending of all discussion seems to be the specter of patriarchy — of white male culture in league with capitalism. Pornography is merely one aspect of this single-minded assault. Radical feminist analysis is imposed on all forms of women's sexuality, including childbirth.

Consider the furor that is brewing around the New Reproductive Technologies (NRTs), which have been called "the pornography of pregnancy." These technologies — which include *in vitro* fertilization, surrogate motherhood, and embryo transfer — are behind the recent news stories announcing that sixty-year-old women are giving birth. Men have always been able to become parents at sixty; that door has just opened for women.

The NRTs raise many questions of medical and genetic ethics, including: how to redefine the family, what of population control; and what of world hunger. For radical feminists, however, there is but one issue. Medical science and technology are the products of white male culture, which oppresses women; therefore, the NRTs are medicalized terror conducted against women.

(Interestingly enough, the women who clamor for such medical procedures are dismissed in the same manner as women in pornography: namely, they are said to be brainwashed and no longer capable of true consent.)

Patriarchy seems to be blamed for everything from sexual harassment to stretch marks. It is a common saying: When all you have is a hammer, everything looks like a nail. When your ideology sounds only one note, all songs are in the same key.

Increasingly, violence against women seems to be linked — almost attributed — to one source: pornography. This is not an opening up of feminist theory and consciousness; it is a closing down.

Doesn't Blaming Pornography Exonerate Rapists?

To blame words or images for the actions of people is simplistic. It retards any real examination into what motivates violent crimes, such as rape. Radical feminists are handing a "pornography made me do it" excuse to rapists. Nothing should be allowed to mitigate the personal responsibility of every man who physically abuses a woman.

Radical feminists are allowing men to introduce "extenuating circumstances" into their defense. For example, in appealing *Schiro v. Clark*,[3] the defendant — a rapist — argued that in sentencing, the judge had failed to take into account his consumption of "rape" pornography. Fortunately, his argument fell deservedly flat.

How Can Women Chronicle Their Oppression if They Do Not Have Access to Its History?

Censorship removes the evidence of women's oppression and limits their ability to learn from it. For example, if it had been up to Comstock and his nineteenth-century censorship drive, no evidence of the fledgling birth control movement would have survived. The record of this struggle survives only because individuals preserved periodicals and pamphlets, which were archived decades later by universities and historical societies.

How much lesbian history will be available if censorship prevails?

The Flaw in Liberal Feminist Arguments

Those liberals who defend pornography do not generally address the ideological underpinnings of the onslaught against it. They continue to view anti-porn feminists as fellow travelers, instead of seeing them as dangerous companions.

One reason for this is that liberal feminists share many of the ideological assumptions underlying the radical feminist attack. For example, both liberal and radical feminists condemn the free market for making a profit by using women as "body parts." Both believe that the commercialization of sex demeans women. In an essay meant to defend the rights of pornographers, Lisa Steel comments: "Sexist representation of women . . . is all part of the same system that, in the service of profits, reduces society to 'consumer groups.' And marketing is every bit as conservative as the military . . . we pay dearly for the 'rights' of a few to make profits from the rest of us."[4]

Is this a defense or an attack?

Liberal feminists also tend to use the radical feminist definition of pornography — a definition tremendously slanted in favor of censorship. Once women accept the anti-pornography definition, it is difficult to arrive at any position other than censorship. The Canadian sociologist Jill Ridington argues for free speech. Nevertheless, she defines pornography as: ". . . a presentation . . . of sexual behavior in which one or more participants are coerced, overtly or *implicitly*, into participation; or are injured or abused physically or *psychologically*; or in which an *imbalance of power* is obvious, or *implied* . . . and in which such behavior can be taken to be advocated or endorsed." (Emphasis added.)[5]

By this definition, what isn't pornography? What can't be interpreted as an imbalance of power? Since almost every sexual presentation is capable of causing psychological harm to someone, almost every presentation can be considered pornographic.

Pornography needs stauncher advocates.

Fortunately, it has them. . . .

NOTES

1. *Virginia Law Review,* August 1993, p. 1118.
2. Indianapolis-Mercer Country; Indiana, General Ordinances Nos. 24 and 25 (1984), amendments to code of Indianapolis and Marion Country.
3. *Schiro v. Clark,* 63 F.2d. 962, 972 (7th Cir. 1992).
4. Lisa Steel, "A Capital Idea," *Women Against Censorship,* ed. Varda Burstyn (Vancouver, Can.: Douglas & McIntyre, 1985), p. 63.
5. Jill Ridington, as quoted in *Women Against Censorship,* p. 34.

INDIVIDUALIST FEMINISM: A TRUE DEFENSE OF PORNOGRAPHY

Wendy McElroy

Individualist feminism provides the best defense of pornography because its ideology is the mirror image of radical feminism, from which the most effective attack on porn is coming. Individual feminism insists on the principle of self-ownership: a woman's body, a woman's right. It insists that women be free to choose, regardless of the content of their choices.

The key concept here is *choice*, which is present whenever a woman acts without physical coercion. Certainly, it is present whenever the woman herself says the actions are voluntary, because she is the only person truly capable of judging that claim. The peaceful choices of every woman must be respected; the voice of every woman should be heard.

This is a profoundly individualistic approach, which leaves little room for class analysis as presented by anti-porn feminists. Such feminists view individual rights and personal preferences as irritating bumps on the road to the greater good of class interest. To them, "the personal is political."

To individualist feminists, the personal is personal. There is a political door that closes to separate and protect individuals from society. People call this protection by different names: the Bill of Rights, self-ownership, individual rights, or natural law. In the shadow of this protection, individual women make decisions about matters that concern them and them alone. For example, they decide about sex.

This is not to say that one woman's sexual choices cannot have implications for another woman, or an impact upon her. Every action you take and every word you utter can impact upon another human being. Exhaling can have an impact, especially if you have a cold or some other contagious disease. The question is: At what point does another woman have a right to restrict your actions on the grounds of self-protection?

Individualist feminism answers: When, and only when, those actions involve physical force, threat of force, or fraud. In the absence of force, women should be free to make any and every sexual choice they wish.

I may not personally approve of their choices. I may find their choices distasteful. Nevertheless, every choice a woman makes enriches me, because it expands my range of alternatives — even if it is an alternative I can't imagine ever pursuing myself.

The nineteenth-century individualist feminist Lillian Harman made a similar point:

> I consider uniformity in mode of sexual relations as undesirable and impractical as enforced uniformity in anything else. For myself, I want to profit by my mistakes . . . and why should I be unwilling for others to enjoy the same liberty? If I should be able to bring the entire world to live exactly as I live at present, what would that avail me in ten years, when as I hope, I shall have a broader knowledge of life, and my life therefore probably changed.[1]

To repeat: the key is choice. With regard to pornography, this means: Let individual women decide for themselves. Let them weigh the evidence and come to their own conclusions.

From XXX: A Woman's Right to Pornography. New York: St. Martin's Press, 1995. (Extracts.) © *1995 Wendy McElroy. Reprinted by permission of St. Martin's Incorporated.*

But what of the women who are upset by the mere fact that pornography exists? Aren't they "forced" to live in a pornographic world? In a word, yes. Women who like pornography force others to live in a pornographic world in the same manner that women who lack taste in clothes force others to live with their fashion sense. *Every* peaceful act can affect someone else. Again, the question is: Do the effects deny to anyone what they have the right to demand?

The answer is no. My decision to consume pornography in no way infringes on another woman's ability to walk right past it. She can express her disapproval — through speaking out, picketing, and boycott. What she must not do is introduce the force of law.

The mere fact that some women are upset by the presence of pornography tells us very little. It tells us nothing about whether porn is right or wrong, valuable or useless. After all, feminism distresses a great many people. Yet feminists would argue that the movement should not only be tolerated, it should be nurtured. They consider women's rights to have a positive, rather than a negative effect on society — even if it causes distress. Perhaps the same is true of the graphic depiction of sex.

This is the position I maintain. I argue that the benefits pornography provides to women far outweigh any of its disadvantages. But, at its root, the argument for pornography is not utilitarian.

Pornography should be defended out of respect for women's choices and for human sexual diversity.

NOTES

1. Lillian Harman as quoted in Hal D. Sears, *The Sex Radicals,* p. 258.

QUESTIONS

1. In your view, does Wendy McElroy provide a fair assessment of the kind of feminist analysis offered by Lorenne Clark?
2. McElroy is critical of both radical and liberal feminist analyses of pornography. What sorts of objections does she raise against liberal feminism's defence of pornography?
3. McElroy claims that in practice censorship laws have tended to target material such as homosexual pornography and even radical feminist pro-censorship literature. Do you think this sort of evidence of what happens in practice should influence policies regarding censorship?
4. What is individualist feminism? Why does McElroy say that it is the best defence of pornography? Do you agree with McElroy that "women should be free to make any and every sexual choice they want"?

SUGGESTIONS FOR FURTHER READING

Canadian Government Reports

- *Limits of Criminal Law — Obscenity: A Test Case* (Working Paper 10) prepared by the Law Reform Commission of Canada. This report sets the discussion within the context of an analysis of the function of the criminal law with respect to censoring pornographic materials.

- *Pornography and Prostitution in Canada* is the report of a committee commissioned by the Canadian government and chaired by Paul Fraser. It submitted its findings in 1985.
- *Note*: Both of these reports should be available in public document sections of university libraries.

Other Reports

- *The Report on the Commission on Obscenity and Pornography* (New York: Bantam Books, 1970). One of the first government reports commissioned by the U.S. government to study the effects of pornography on users.
- *Report of the Attorney General's Commission on Pornography* (Washington, D.C.: United States Government Printing office, 1986). This report, prepared by the Meese Commission, suggests that, contrary to the findings of the 1970 U.S. Commission, exposure to some types of pornography has harmful consequences.
- *Obscenity and Film Censorship*, the report of a committee commissioned by the British government and chaired by Bernard Williams, a prominent British philosopher. The report was published under the same title by Cambridge University Press in 1979.

Recent Books

- Alison Assiter, *Pornography, Feminism and the Individual* (London: Pluto Press, 1989). The author takes issue with radical feminists who seek the total elimination of pornography as well as liberals who see censorship as an unjustified violation of individual liberty. The book argues that "the consumption of pornography is an individualist pursuit that violates the autonomy of those who model for pornographic films and magazines but that it is a symptom rather than a cause of the power relations that exist within our society."
- F.M. Christensen, *Pornography: The Other Side* (New York: Praeger, 1990). This book explores the "other side" of the censorship debate, arguing that anti-pornography campaigns are themselves morally evil and rest on irrational attitudes toward human sexuality.
- David Copp and Susan Wendell (eds.), *Pornography and Censorship: Scientific, Philosophical and Legal Studies* (Buffalo: Prometheus Books, 1983). This anthology reviews a wide range of arguments both for and against censorship of pornography. It includes an extensive evaluation of the results of research into the harmfulness of pornography. It also includes the Williams report referred to above.
- Laura Lederer (ed.), *Take Back the Night: Women on Pornography* (New York: Morrow, 1980). This collection is representative of the early feminist analysis of pornography. It includes essays that are critical of studies used in the Copp collection, referred to above, as evidence that pornography does not have harmful social consequences.
- *Pornography and Sexual Violence: Evidence of the Links* (London: Everywoman, 1988). This is the published transcript of the 1983 hearings in Minneapolis, Minnesota, of the MacKinnon/Dworkin Ordinance referred to in some of the readings. The book includes the text of the ordinance as well as the testimony of women who came before the hearings to give personal accounts of how they had been harmed by pornography.
- Susan Dwyer (ed.), *The Problem of Pornography* (Belmont: Wadsworth, 1995). A collection of papers covering various topics in the pornography debate including definitions, pornography and equality, pornography and sexuality, and pornography and speech acts. The collection includes an interesting philosophical exchange between Ronald

Dworkin and Rae Langton about the tension between liberty and the principle of equality as it relates to the issue of pornography.

- Carole S. Vance (ed.), *Pleasure and Danger: Exploring Female Sexuality* (Boston: Routledge, 1984). A collection of papers originating at a conference held at Barnard College in New York in 1982 called "Towards a Politics of Sexuality." Many of the papers challenge a feminist analysis that emphasizes the dangers of pornography at the expense of making it difficult for women to explore sexuality and express desire.

Films

- *Not a Love Story* is a film about pornography that has been widely distributed in Canada. It is available from the National Film Board.
- *Killing Us Softly* is the first of two films, the second being *Still Killing Us Softly*, put out by the Media Education Foundation. These films examine the role of the advertising industry in perpetuating myths and stereotypes about women and sexuality.

[Editor's note: A bibliography of Canadian material on pornography, which resulted from research leading to the publication of the first edition of this book has now been updated by Christine Koggel, who did background research for the writing of this chapter. That revised bibliography is available from the editor or from Christine Koggel.]

Chapter 5

Discrimination

Introduction

In the introduction to the discussion of euthanasia, three principles that have a central role in the discussion of contemporary moral issues — the protection-of-life principle, the avoidance-of-suffering principle, and the moral-autonomy principle — were introduced. There is a fourth principle, what we shall call the *principle of equal worth*, that has an equally important role to play in discussions of contemporary moral issues. One of the central tasks of this chapter is to bring the significance of that principle into focus. We will then see that this principle plays a role in all of the remaining chapters.

Although in modern democratic societies of the sort in which we live we often forget the fact, discrimination on grounds of race, colour, sex, ethnic origin, and so on has a long and deeply entrenched history; a history in which some people have been explicitly judged as having unequal worth and deserving of unequal treatment. It is easy to forget that slavery was an institution in our society until less than two centuries ago, that visible minorities often have difficulty finding jobs and adequate housing because of skin colour, and that women have been and in the view of many still are actively discouraged from following career paths open to men because of their sex.

These examples of kinds of discrimination bring into sharp relief an idea introduced in the last chapter that will be central to a discussion of discrimination; the idea that it is not only individuals who can be harmed by the actions and attitudes of others, but groups as well. Discriminatory actions, of the kind in the examples above, result from judgements that certain individuals are unequal or inferior merely because they are members of particular groups. Discrimination is widely thought to be morally unacceptable because it prevents people who are discriminated against from participating fully in the life of their society for irrelevant or immoral reasons.

Indeed, the elimination of discrimination is thought to be so central to creating a just society that the principle of equal worth is found in all modern charters, bills, and declarations of human rights. The United Nations Universal Declaration of Human Rights, adopted in 1948, is a good example. It proclaims that "all human beings are born free and equal in dignity and rights" and that "everyone is entitled to all the rights and freedoms set forth in this Declaration, without distinction of any kind, such as race, colour, sex, language, religion, political or other opinion, national or social origin, property, birth or other status."

The UN declaration is one example of numerous articulations of our current commitment to equality. However, propounding a commitment to the principle of equal worth is but one step on the road to actually achieving equality. Our emergence from a long history in which discrimination against members of particular groups was overt and explicitly defended in legislation and theory continues to make the topic of discrimination current and important for several reasons. Identifying at least two of these now will serve to highlight the complexity of issues of discrimination.

First, different groups experience discrimination in various ways and at multiple levels and this variation creates different sorts of inequalities and disadvantages for particular groups. This complexity with respect to discrimination provides a second reason for identifying discrimination as an important topic of investigation. Even though we have reached agreement that the principle of equal worth ought to be foundational to any society, this does not yet tell us what is needed to satisfy the principle in various social contexts and particular cases. We will see, in fact, that even within liberal societies there is a great deal of disagreement about what counts as the fair application of the principle of equal worth. This chapter will introduce some of the main concepts and begin the exploration of issues central to a discussion of discrimination. These issues will then be examined in more detail in each of the remaining chapters.

Background Considerations

Canada is a signatory country to the Universal Declaration of Human Rights and many other international human rights agreements. In Canada, enshrining human rights into law is a fairly recent phenomenon. One of the first pieces of anti-discrimination legislation, "An Act to prevent the Further Introduction of Slaves and to limit the term of Enforced Servitude within this Province," was passed in the province of Upper Canada in 1793. One of its objectives was to free the children of slaves once they reached the age of twenty-five. This legislation remained in force until 1833, when Britain abolished slavery throughout the British Empire. However, up until 1944 the message given in court decisions dealing with cases of racial discrimination was that discrimination was neither immoral nor illegal.

In 1940, the Supreme Court ruled in *Christie v. York Corporation* that no wrong was done to Christie, a black man who was refused entry in a tavern in the Montreal Forum. Christie's claim for damages sought for humiliation was dismissed because, in the words of Rinfret J.: "The general principle of the law of Quebec is that of complete freedom of commerce. Any merchant is free to deal as he may choose with an individual member of the public." In 1944, Ontario passed the Ontario Racial Discrimination Act, which was to change this view that human rights were subordinate to the rights of property and commerce. The act prohibited public endorsements of discrimination on the basis of "race or creed" and specifically targeted the public display of "whites only" signs. This act allowed the Ontario High Court in 1945 to prevent the prohibition of the sale of land to Jews.

Parallelling the advances made against discrimination on the basis of "race or creed" was the fight for women's rights. In 1916, women were granted voting rights for the first time in Manitoba, Saskatchewan, and Alberta. They won the vote federally in 1918. In 1916, Emily Murphy became one of the first woman magistrates in the British Empire. Soon after, her judgements were challenged, based on the argument that she did not qualify as a person under the British North America Act. In 1927, Murphy and four other women from Alberta requested a constitutional interpretation to determine the eligibility of women for appointment to the Senate. In what has become known as "the Persons Case," the Supreme Court ruled that only men were eligible under the "qualified persons" provision in Section 24 of the BNA Act. Murphy appealed to the British Privy Council, the final interpreter of the

BNA Act at that time, and won the case in 1929, when it ruled that the word persons "may include members of both sexes." The following year, Cairine Wilson became the first woman senator.

Women's participation in politics and the labour force was practically negligible in the decades that followed. During the Second World War, an exemption was made when women were recruited into jobs left vacant by men who had joined the armed forces. However, when the war was over, women were laid off and their jobs made available to returning armed forces personnel. Policies providing incentives to stay home and raise children were also instituted. In 1967 Florence Bird was the first woman to head a royal commission, the Royal Commission on the Status of Women. In many of the first attempts to enact human rights into provincial codes, sex was absent from the lists that enumerated the grounds for discrimination.

The first Bill of Rights in Canada was enacted by the province of Saskatchewan in 1947. It prohibited discrimination on the basis of race, creed, religion, colour, ethnic, or national origin. In 1951, Ontario enacted the first Fair Employment Practices Act. This legislation was important because it expanded procedures for investigating complaints, launching inquiries, and seeking redress, and made non-compliance with the Act an offense. After the Canadian Bill of Rights was enacted in 1960, various individual provinces introduced human rights codes. Notable among these was the 1962 Ontario consolidation of various anti-discrimination provisions into a comprehensive human rights code.

The Current Situation

In 1982, the Canadian Charter of Rights and Freedoms was enacted. Section 15, the equality rights section of the Charter, came into force three years later on April 17, 1985. The delay in implementation of Section 15 was intended to allow time for federal and provincial governments to amend any legislation that did not conform with the section. If anything, this was an acknowledgement of the possibly far-reaching effects of the equality provisions. The Charter has been viewed as a powerful tool for righting the imbalance of decades of discrimination and unequal access.

The government and various concerned groups responded to the equality rights provisions in Section 15 by providing an abundance of research into its potential effects. An example was the Royal Commission on Equality in Employment headed by Judge Rosalie Abella. Its report, Equality in Employment, provides factual information on four groups about which the government was particularly concerned; namely, women, the disabled, native people, and visible minorities. The Commission also made recommendations for alleviating the discrimination and disadvantages suffered by these groups.

One of the results of the report was the passage of Bill C-62, which outlined the measures that the government would take to improve the participation of women, native people, disabled persons, and visible minorities in both the public service and companies with more than 100 employees. These measures, commonly referred to as affirmative action, and the justifications for them are the topics of the text chapter.

Cases invoking Section 15 of the Charter are only now finding their way into the courts. Some take the 1989 Supreme Court decision in *Andrews v. Law Society of B.C.* to be an important contribution to the project of articulating Canada's own vision of what constitutes equality. Excerpts from that decision, which includes the text and interpretation of the equality provisions in Section 15 of the Charter, are included in the readings. The readings also include recent federal legislation adding sexual orientation as a prohibited ground of discrimination under the *Canadian Human Rights Act*. Some take these developments to be a charting of new and exciting territory, one that departs from the direction taken by our neighbours to the south. Others view the interpretations of equality and the new legislation as either unnecessary or unjustifiable applications of the principle of equal worth.

The Moral Dimension

Making wise choices requires the capacity to discriminate between and among things and people in ways designed to help us accomplish our objectives. We applaud the ability to identify things that are well made from things that are not. And normally, it is a compliment to describe someone as a person of discriminating taste. Seen from this perspective, discrimination is an unavoidable feature of human life. Discrimination is normally considered to be unjustified, however, when it interferes arbitrarily with the application of such moral principles as moral autonomy by unfairly limiting the capacity of some individuals to participate fully in the life of their community, or to enjoy the rights, privileges, and benefits to which they are entitled.

The principle of equal worth is an important one for several reasons. Articulating some of them here will give us an idea of the various complex dimensions of discrimination. First, our emergence from a long history in which discrimination against certain groups was defended and entrenched in laws and behaviour should undermine confidence that we have succeeded in eliminating discrimination and achieving equality. While legal barriers that once prohibited some people from participating as full members of a community have been removed, informal barriers in the form of discriminatory beliefs, judgements, and actions continue to have an impact on the freedom and opportunities of individuals who are members of traditionally disadvantaged groups.

Second, an examination of the nature of discrimination and of its various manifestations raises questions about the connections between the principle of equal worth and the principles of moral autonomy and avoidance of suffering. What sort of barriers to the full exercise of autonomy stand in the way of those who are disadvantaged because their membership in a group continues to determine in advance their life prospects and goals? Do members of these kinds of groups suffer particular inequalities in a society that prizes an individual's freedom from the interference of law and policy? Does an emphasis on individual freedom in abstraction from social and political contexts of discrimination prevent us from seeing certain limitations of freedom and autonomy experienced by those who are members of traditionally disadvantaged groups?

This set of questions about individual freedom and group disadvantage raises another set of questions that suggest a third important dimension in a discussion of the principle of equal worth. Does discrimination have an impact on how individuals who are members of disadvantaged groups see themselves and the world? If there are differences in perspectives on societies and social relations, does it follow that only those individuals who are members of a particular group can understand or interpret the experiences of that group? Is what members of disadvantaged groups say about their experiences important to understanding discrimination for the purpose of eliminating conditions of disadvantage?

Taken together, all of the questions posed thus far demonstrate the complexity of the moral issues surrounding discrimination. The questions also point to a fourth and final reason for acknowledging the importance of the principle of equal worth, one that is introduced in this chapter and developed more fully in the next. The principle of equal worth is grounded on the assumption that all people are equal. But how do we apply this principle when we are confronted with particular cases of inequality? In the tradition of Western political thought, theorists have developed two different approaches to applying the principle of equal worth.

On the one side are those theorists who believe that equality is achieved when legal barriers to obtaining certain goods are removed: everyone then has the same opportunity to participate in society and acquire their share of social, educational, and economic goods. This approach to satisfying the principle of equal worth has been referred to as "formal equality," an approach that advocates that everyone be treated the same or equally no matter what their differences. Under formal equality, the emphasis is on individual and negative freedom, the freedom from artificial barriers and state interference in the lives of citizens.

Other theorists have pointed out that removing legal barriers and providing equal treatment has not resulted in vast improvements to the condition or prospects of disadvantaged groups. These theorists conclude that the damage and injustice that has been inflicted on groups that have suffered from discrimination can only be overcome if they are given special, favourable consideration, the purpose of which is to bring the members of those groups to a position where they are treated equally as a matter of course. This second approach to the principle of equal worth is generally referred to as "substantive equality." The suggestion is that achieving meaningful or substantive equality sometimes requires respecting difference and providing special treatment. Special educational opportunities, job training, and affirmative action programs are examples of positive measures endorsed by substantive equality theorists. While these measures limit the freedom of some individuals, they have the effect of increasing the freedom of members of traditionally disadvantaged groups by broadening their range of opportunities and improving their life prospects.

Each of these approaches is explored in the contributions to this chapter. A central issue in the next chapter's discussion of affirmative action is whether the second approach of providing special or positive measures violates the principle of equal worth or can be morally justified. We will see that moral justifications for special treatment or positive measures are central to the discussions in the remaining chapters on poverty and the right to welfare, aboriginal rights, and environmental ethics.

The Readings

The first group of readings set out the legal background to current discussions of discrimination in Canada. The first includes excerpts from the 1989 landmark Supreme Court decision in *Andrews v. Law Society of B.C.* The case presents the first attempt by the Supreme Court to interpret the equality provisions in Section 15 of the Charter. Because it provides analyses of the concepts of discrimination and equality, it has become the benchmark for subsequent cases to which the equality provisions apply. The second reading is recent federal legislation that has added sexual orientation to the list of morally irrelevant grounds for discrimination specified in the *Canadian Human Rights Act.* This legislation is widely viewed as having potentially radical social and economic implications for benefits to same sex couples.

The readings in the second group discuss the moral dimensions of various manifestations of discrimination: whether and what sorts of restrictions to individual freedom are experienced by members of different disadvantaged groups; whether differences do exist and can form the basis for justifying different or unequal treatment; and whether and what sorts of positive measures designed to address inequalities by providing special treatment can be morally justified.

In the first reading of this second group, Karen Selick takes issue with recent demands for special consideration by disadvantaged groups in general and people with disabilities in particular. In her view, human rights legislation of the sort specified in the Charter is not only unnecessary, but has been used to condone morally unjustifiable policies. She argues that ordinary business people who are required by law to build ramps for the disabled, for example, are the ones who have their rights violated because their freedom to run their business as they wish is restricted.

The second reading by Alex Wellington focuses specifically on discrimination on the basis of sexual orientation. Wellington questions the idea that sexual orientation is a difference that justifies unequal treatment. She argues that a purely formal equality approach can form the moral justification for same sex marriage. By rejecting the accounts of harm that some argue would result from state-sanctioned same-sex marriage, Wellington concludes that formal equality demands that same-sex couples be treated in the same way and be given the same benefits as heterosexual couples.

In the context of an examination of issues of gender, Marilyn Frye provides numerous descriptions and examples that would appear to support the idea that there are relevant differences between the sexes that justify assigning different roles to women. Frye argues, however, that these differences are constructed in and through social practices and political contexts that have assumed women's inferiority and unequal status. The results are manifested in the various aspects of sexism that, Frye argues, need our moral attention.

Questions about differences, whether biologically based or socially constructed, raise issues about whether it is possible or morally appropriate for one group or culture to represent or speak for the experiences of another group. The two readings by James O. Young and Cornell West discuss "voice appropriation" in the context of issues of race. They each use the example of cultural communities, but present two different perspectives and reach different conclusions. Young uses the context of art to argue against programs and policies, for example, that base decisions about allocating funds or restricting public displays of works by particular artists on considerations of cultural or group representation. White men, Young argues, can and should play the blues. Cornell West argues that because the history and experiences of African Americans, for example, have been suppressed or ignored, it is morally incumbent on societies to give such groups a forum for representing and expressing those experiences and challenging existing stereotypes. Art is one forum that serves this purpose.

The final reading by J.E. Bickenbach provides a perspective on issues of disability that can be read as challenging ideas in the piece by Karen Selick. By carefully outlining the complexities involved in describing and understanding disability, Bickenbach argues that the inequalities associated with disabilities result from public perceptions and beliefs about the capacities of people with disabilities. Bickenbach evaluates a "civil rights" approach to disability, one that dominates the treatment of discrimination and focuses on addressing discriminatory actions. He argues that while this approach has resulted in changes to both the physical environment to accommodate people with disabilities and to attitudes and stereotypes about disability, it has not succeeded in broadening the range of choices available to people with disabilities. A better approach, he argues, is one that views disability as a condition each of us does or will experience in a lifetime. Issues of disability can then be seen as issues of the fair distribution of social goods, including positive liberty.

LAW SOCIETY OF BRITISH COLUMBIA ET AL. V. ANDREWS ET AL., 1989

[Indexed as: Andrews v. Law Soc. of B.C.]

[The 1989 Judgement of the Supreme Court of Canada]

Mr. Justice Wm. R. McIntyre

This appeal raises only one question. Does the citizenship requirement for entry into the legal profession contained in s. 42 of the Barristers and Solicitors Act, R.S.B.C. 1979, c. 26 (the "Act"), contravene s. 15(1) of the Canadian Charter of Rights and Freedoms? Section 42 provides:

> 42. The benchers may call to the Bar of the Province and admit as solicitor of the Supreme Court
>
> (*a*) a Canadian citizen with respect to whom they are satisfied that he . . .

and s. 15 of the Charter states:

> 15. (1) Every individual is equal before and under the law and has the right to the equal protection and equal benefit of the law without discrimination and, in particular, without discrimination based on race, national or ethnic origin, colour, religion, sex, age or mental or physical disability.
>
> (2) Subsection (1) does not preclude any law, program or activity that has as its object the amelioration of conditions of disadvantaged individuals or groups including those that are disadvantaged because of race, national or ethnic origin, colour, religion, sex, age or mental or physical disability. . . .

The concept of equality

Section 15(1) of the Charter provides for every individual a guarantee of equality before and under the law, as well as the equal protection and equal benefit of the law without discrimination. This is not a general guarantee of equality; it does not provide for equality between individuals or groups within society in a general or abstract sense, nor does it impose on individuals or groups an obligation to accord equal treatment to others. It is concerned with the application of the law. No problem regarding the scope of the word "law", as employed in s. 15(1), can arise in this case because it is an Act of the legislature which is under attack. Whether other governmental or quasi-governmental regulations, rules or requirements may be termed laws under s. 15(1) should be left for cases in which the issue arises.

The concept of equality has long been a feature of Western thought. As embodied in s. 15(1) of the Charter, it is an elusive concept and, more than any of the other rights and freedoms guaranteed in the Charter, it lacks precise definition. As has been stated by John H. Schaar, "Equality of Opportunity and Beyond", in Nomos IX: Equality (1967), J. Roland Pennock and John W. Chapman eds., at p. 228:

> Equality is a protean word. It is one of those political symbols — liberty and frater-nity are others — into which men have poured the deepest urgings of their heart.

Every strongly held theory or conception of equality is at once a psychology, an ethic, a theory of social relations, and a vision of the good society.

It is a comparative concept, the condition of which may only be attained or discerned by comparison with the condition of others in the social and political setting in which the question arises. It must be recognized at once, however, that every difference in treatment between individuals under the law will not necessarily result in inequality and, as well, that identical treatment may frequently produce serious inequality. This proposition has found frequent expression in the literature on the subject but, as I have noted on a previous occasion, nowhere more aptly than in the well-known words of Frankfurter J. in *Dennis v. U.S.*, 339 U.S. 162 at 184, 94 L. Ed. 736 (1950):

It was a wise man who said that there is no greater inequality than the equal treatment of unequals. . . .

In simple terms, then, it may be said that a law which treats all identically and which provides equality of treatment between "A" and "B" might well cause inequality for "C", depending on differences in personal characteristics and situations. To approach the ideal of full equality before and under the law — and in human affairs an approach is all that can be expected — the main consideration must be the impact of the law on the individual or the group concerned. Recognizing that there will always be an infinite variety of personal characteristics, capacities, entitlements and merits among those subject to a law, there must be accorded, as nearly as may be possible, an equality of benefit and protection and no more of the restrictions, penalties or burdens imposed upon one than another. In other words, the admittedly unattainable ideal should be that a law expressed to bind all should not because of irrelevant personal differences have a more burdensome or less beneficial impact on one than another. . . .

It is not every distinction or differentiation in treatment at law which will transgress the equality guarantees of s. 15 of the Charter. It is, of course, obvious that legislatures may — and to govern effectively — must treat different individuals and groups in different ways. Indeed, such distinctions are one of the main preoccupations of legislatures. The classifying of individuals and groups, the making of different provisions respecting such groups, the application of different rules, regulations, requirements and qualifications to different persons is necessary for the governance of modern society. As noted above, for the accommodation of differences, which is the essence of true equality, it will frequently be necessary to make distinctions. What kinds of distinctions will be acceptable under s. 15(1) and what kinds will violate its provisions?

In seeking an answer to these questions, the provisions of the Charter must have their full effect. In *R. v. Big M Drug Mart Ltd.*, this court emphasized this point at p. 344, where Dickson C.J.C. stated:

This Court has already, in some measure, set out the basic approach to be taken in interpreting the *Charter.* In *Hunter v. Southam Inc.*, [1984] 2 S.C.R. 145, this Court expressed the view that the proper approach to the definition of the rights and freedoms guaranteed by the *Charter* was a purposive one. The meaning of a right or freedom guaranteed by the *Charter* was to be ascertained by an analysis of the *purpose* of such a guarantee; it was to be understood, in other words, in the light of the interests it was meant to protect.

In my view this analysis is to be undertaken, and the purpose of the right or freedom in question is to be sought by reference to the character and the larger objects of the *Charter* itself, to the language chosen to articulate the specific right or freedom, to the historical origins of the concepts enshrined, and where applicable, to the meaning and purpose of the other specific rights and freedoms with which it is associated within the text of the *Charter*. The interpretation should be, as the judgment in *Southam* emphasizes, a generous rather than a legalistic one, aimed at fulfilling the purpose of the guarantee and securing for individuals the full benefit of the *Charter's* protection. At the same time it is important not to overshoot the actual purpose of the right or freedom in question, but to recall that the *Charter* was not enacted in a vacuum, and must therefore, as this Court's decision in *Law Society of Upper Canada v. Skapinker*, [1984] 1 S.C.R. 357, illustrates, be placed in its proper linguistic, philosophic and historical contexts [emphasis in original]. . . .

The principle of equality before the law has long been recognized as a feature of our constitutional tradition and it found statutory recognition in the Canadian Bill of Rights. However, unlike the Canadian Bill of Rights, which spoke only of equality before the law, s. 15(1) of the Charter provides a much broader protection. Section 15 spells out four basic rights: (1) the right to equality before the law; (2) the right to equality under the law; (3) the right to equal protection of the law; and (4) the right to equal benefit of the law. The inclusion of these last three additional rights in s. 15 of the Charter was an attempt to remedy some of the shortcomings of the right to equality in the Canadian Bill of Rights. It also reflected the expanded concept of discrimination being developed under the various Human Rights Codes since the enactment of the Canadian Bill of Rights. The shortcomings of the Canadian Bill of Rights as far as the right to equality is concerned are well known. In *A.G. Can. v. Lavell; Isaac v. Bedard*, [1974] S.C.R. 1 1349, 23 C.R.N.S. 197, 11 R.F.L. 333, 38 D.L.R. (3d) 481 [Fed.], for example, this court upheld s. 12(1)(*b*) of the Indian Act which deprived women, but not men, of their membership in Indian bands if they married non-Indians. The provision was held not to violate equality *before* the law although it might, the court said, violate equality *under* the law if such were protected. In *Bliss*, supra, this court held that the denial of unemployment insurance benefits to women because they were pregnant did not violate the guarantee of equality before the law because any inequality in the protection and benefit of the law was "not created by legislation but by nature" (p. 190). The case was distinguished from the court's earlier decision in *Drybones*, supra, as not involving (pp. 191–92) the imposition of a penalty on a racial group to which other citizens are not subjected, but as involving rather "a definition of the qualifications required for entitlement to benefits". It is readily apparent that the language of s. 15 was deliberately chosen in order to remedy some of the perceived defects under the Canadian Bill of Rights. The antecedent statute is part of the "linguistic, philosophic and historical context" of s. 15 of the Charter.

It is clear that the purpose of s. 15 is to ensure equality in the formulation and application of the law. The promotion of equality entails the promotion of a society in which all are secure in the knowledge that they are recognized at law as human beings equally deserving of concern, respect and consideration. It has a large remedial component. Chief Justice

Howland (with Robins J.A. dissenting in the result but not with respect to this comment) in *Ref. re An Act to Amend the Education Act* (1986), 53 O.R. (2d) 513, 25 D.L.R. (4th) 1, 23 C.R.R. 193, 13 O.A.C. 241 (C.A.), attempts to articulate the broad range of values embraced by s. 15. He states at p. 554:

> In our view, s. 15(1) read as a whole constitutes a compendious expression of a positive right to equality in both the substance and the administration of the law. It is an all-encompassing right governing all legislative action. Like the ideals of "equal justice" and "equal access to the law", the right to equal protection and equal benefit of the law now enshrined in the Charter rests on the moral and ethical principle fundamental to a truly free and democratic society that all persons should be treated by the law on a footing of equality with equal concern and equal respect.

It must be recognized, however, as well that the promotion of equality under s. 15 has a much more specific goal than the mere elimination of distinctions. If the Charter was intended to eliminate all distinctions, then there would be no place for sections such as s. 27 (multicultural heritage); s. 2(a) (freedom of conscience and religion); s. 25 (aboriginal rights and freedoms); and other such provisions designed to safeguard certain distinctions. Moreover, the fact that identical treatment may frequently produce serious inequality is recognized in s. 15(2), which states that the equality rights in s. 15(1) do "not preclude any law, program or activity that has as its object the amelioration of conditions of disadvantaged individuals or groups . . . ."

Discrimination

The right to equality before and under the law, and the rights to the equal protection and benefit of the law contained in s. 15, are granted with the direction contained in s. 15 itself that they be without discrimination. Discrimination is unacceptable in a democratic society because it epitomizes the worst effects of the denial of equality, and discrimination reinforced by law is particularly repugnant. The worst oppression will result from discriminatory measures having the force of law. It is against this evil that s. 15 provides a guarantee.

Discrimination as referred to in s. 15 of the Charter must be understood in the context of pre-Charter history. Prior to the enactment of s. 15(1), the legislatures of the various provinces and the federal Parliament had passed during the previous 50 years what may be generally referred to as Human Rights Acts. With the steady increase in population from the earliest days of European emigration into Canada and with the consequential growth of industry, agriculture and commerce and the vast increase in national wealth which followed, many social problems developed. The contact of the European immigrant with the indigenous population, the steady increase in immigration bringing those of neither French nor British background, and in more recent years the greatly expanded role of women in all forms of industrial, commercial and professional activity led to much inequality and many forms of discrimination. In great part these developments, in the absence of any significant legislative protection for the victims of discrimination, called into being the Human Rights Acts. In 1944 the Racial Discrimination Act, 1944, S.O. 1944, c. 51, was passed, to be followed in 1947 by the Saskatchewan Bill of Rights Act, 1947, S.S. 1947, c. 35, and in 1960 by the Canadian Bill of Rights. Since then every jurisdiction in Canada has enacted broad-ranging Human Rights Acts which have attacked most of the more common forms of discrimination found in society. This development has been recorded and discussed by Walter Tarnopolsky, now Mr. Justice Tarnopolsky, in Discrimination and the Law, revised ed. (1985).

What does discrimination mean? The question has arisen most commonly in a consideration of the Human Rights Acts and the general concept of discrimination under those enactments has been fairly well settled. There is little difficulty, drawing upon the cases in this court, in isolating an acceptable definition. In *Ont. Human Rights Comm. v. Simpsons-Sears Ltd.*, [1985] 2 S.C.R. 536 at 551, 17 Admin. L.R. 89, 9 C.C.E.L. 185, 86 C.L.L.C. 17,002, 23 D.L.R. (4th) 321, 7 C.H.R.R. D/3102, 12 O.A.C. 241, 64 N.R. 161, discrimination (in that case, adverse effect discrimination) was described in these terms:

> It arises where an employer . . . adopts a rule or standard . . . which has a discriminatory effect upon a prohibited ground on one employee or group of employees in that it imposes, because of some special characteristic of the employee or group, obligations, penalties, or restrictive conditions not imposed on other members of the work force.

It was held in that case, as well, that no intent was required as an element of discrimination, for it is in essence the impact of the discriminatory act or provision upon the person affected which is decisive in considering any complaint. At p. 547, this proposition was expressed in these terms:

> The Code aims at the removal of discrimination. This is to state the obvious. Its main approach, however, is not to punish the discriminator, but rather to provide relief for the victims of discrimination. It is the result or the effect of the action complained of which is significant. If it does, in fact, cause discrimination; if its effect is to impose on one person or group of persons obligations, penalties, or restrictive conditions not imposed on other members of the community, it is discriminatory.

In *C.N.R. v. Can. (Can. Human Rights Comm.)*, [1987] 1 S.C.R. 1114, 27 Admin. L.R. 172, 87 C.L.L.C. 17,022, 40 D.L.R. (4th) 193, 8 C.H.R.R. D/4210, 76 N.R. 161 (sub nom. *Action Travail des Femmes v. C.N.R.*) [Fed.], better known as the *Action Travail des Femmes* case, where it was alleged that the Canadian National Railway was guilty of discriminatory hiring and promotion practices contrary to s. 10 of the Canadian Human Rights Code, S.C. 1976-77, c. 33, in denying employment to women in certain unskilled positions, Dickson C.J.C., in giving the judgment of the court, said at pp. 1138-39:

> A thorough study of "systemic discrimination" in Canada is to be found in the Abella Report on equality in employment. The terms of reference of the Royal Commission instructed it "to inquire into the most efficient, effective and equitable means of promoting employment opportunities, eliminating systemic discrimination and assisting individuals to compete for employment opportunities on an equal basis" (Order in Council P.C. 1983-1924 of 24 June 1983). Although Judge Abella chose not to offer a precise definition of systemic discrimination, the essentials may be gleaned from the following comments, found at p. 2 of the Abella Report.
>
> "Discrimination . . . means practices or attitudes that have, whether by design or impact, the effect of limiting an individual's or a group's right to the opportunities generally available because of attributed rather than actual characteristics . . .

"It is not a question of whether this discrimination is motivated by an intentional desire to obstruct someone's potential, or whether it is the accidental by-product of innocently motivated practices or systems. If the barrier is affecting certain groups in a disproportionately negative way, it is a signal that the practices that lead to this adverse impact may be discriminatory."

There are many other statements which have aimed at a short definition of the term "discrimination". In general, they are in accord with the statements referred to above. I would say then that discrimination may be described as a distinction, whether intentional or not but based on grounds relating to personal characteristics of the individual or group, which has the effect of imposing burdens, obligations or disadvantages on such individual or group not imposed upon others, or which withholds or limits access to opportunities, benefits and advantages available to other members of society. Distinctions based on personal characteristics attributed to an individual solely on the basis of association with a group will rarely escape the charge of discrimination, while those based on an individual's merits and capacities will rarely be so classed.

The court in the case at bar must address the issue of discrimination as the term is used in s. 15(1) of the Charter. In general, it may be said that the principles which have been applied under the Human Rights Acts are equally applicable in considering questions of discrimination under s. 15(1). Certain differences arising from the difference between the Charter and the Human Rights Acts must, however, be considered. To begin with, discrimination in s. 15(1) is limited to discrimination caused by the application or operation of law, whereas the Human Rights Acts apply also to private activities. Furthermore, and this is a distinction of more importance, all the Human Rights Acts passed in Canada specifically designate a certain limited number of grounds upon which discrimination is forbidden. Section 15(1) of the Charter is not so limited. The enumerated grounds in s. 15(1) are not exclusive and the limits, if any, on grounds for discrimination which may be established in future cases await definition. The enumerated grounds do, however, reflect the most common and probably the most socially destructive and historically practised bases of discrimination and must, in the words of s. 15(1), receive particular attention. Both the enumerated grounds themselves and other possible grounds of discrimination recognized under s. 15(1) must be interpreted in a broad and generous manner, reflecting the fact that they are constitutional provisions not easily repealed or amended but intended to provide a "continuing framework for the legitimate exercise of governmental power" and, at the same time, for "the unremitting protection" of equality rights. . . .

BILL C-33, 1996

["Act to amend the Canadian Human Rights Act"]

2nd Session, 35th Parliament
45 Elizabeth II, 1996

THE HOUSE OF COMMONS OF CANADA

Preamble   Whereas the Government of Canada affirms the dignity and worth of all individuals and recognizes that they have the right to be free from discrimination in employment and the provision of goods and services, and that that right is based on respect for the rule of law and lawful conduct by all;

And whereas the Government recognizes and affirms the importance of family as the foundation of Canadian society and that nothing in this Act alters its fundamental role in society;

Now, therefore, Her Majesty, by and with the advice and consent of the Senate and House of Commons of Canada, enacts as follows:

1. Section 2 of the *Canadian Human Rights Act* is replaced by the following:

Purpose   **2.** The purpose of this Act is to extend the laws in Canada to give effect, within the purview of matters coming within the legislative authority of Parliament, to the principle that all individuals should have an equal opportunity to make for themselves the lives that they are able and wish to have, consistent with their duties and obligations as members of society, without being hindered in or prevented from doing so by discriminatory practices based on race, national or ethnic origin, colour, religion, age, sex, sexual orientation, marital status, family status, disability or conviction for an offence for which a pardon has been granted.

2. Subsection 3(1) of the Act is replaced by the following:

Prohibited grounds of discrimination   **3.** (1) For all purposes of this Act, the prohibited grounds of discrimination are race, national or ethnic origin, colour, religion, age, sex, sexual orientation, marital status, family status, disability and conviction for which a pardon has been granted.

Summary   These amendments add sexual orientation as a prohibited ground of discrimination under the *Canadian Human Rights Act.*

THE RAMP TO HELL

Karen Selick

Perhaps the people who first dreamed up Ontario's Human Rights Code had good intentions but as the old saying goes, that's what the road to hell is paved with. A recent decision of a Board of Inquiry shows just how far we've travelled down that road.

The case involved a disabled woman who uses a wheelchair. She made an appointment with a chiropractor whose office was not accessible by wheelchair. He offered her three alternatives: two doctors would carry her up the stairs, or he would treat her at her home, or he would borrow accessible premises from another chiropractor and treat her there.

Not good enough, said the lady, and lodged a complaint with the Human Rights Commission. Almost seven years later, the decision has come down: the chiropractor is guilty of discrimination. He has to pay the lady $500 in damages and install a ramp in his building at a cost of almost $20,000.

Reading this decision reminds me of the Emperor's new clothes: everyone seems either too embarrassed, too fearful or too politically correct to say what was so pathetically obvious.

For example, one recurrent theme is that the disabled are "seen both by themselves and by society as not the same as everyone else." Okay, I'll be the kid in the crowd who blurts out what everyone already knows: installing wheelchair ramps won't change this. People in wheelchairs will still be unmistakably different — they'll be the ones rolling up the ramps while other people will be walking. To make their differences genuinely unobservable, we'd have to pass a law compelling everyone to use wheelchairs.

A second theme in the judgment is that the disabled don't want charity or pity; they don't want to be dependent upon others. That's understandable — who does? But to pretend that this decision — or indeed, any application of the Human Rights Code — makes the disabled any less the recipients of charity or any more independent requires a prodigious feat of self-delusion. They may not be dependent on someone else to carry them up the stairs, but they are still dependent on someone else to build them a ramp.

If the complainant had wanted to demonstrate true independence, she would have gone to the other chiropractor's office where someone had already installed wheelchair access voluntarily, instead of burdening a stranger with a $20,000 expense. Or she could have offered to pay for the ramp herself, rather than forcing an unwilling victim to provide it for her. The route she chose, of using the coercive power of a state agency to appropriate someone else's assets for her benefit, underscores the very dependency she is attempting to deny.

A third theme of the decision is dignity. We're told that the alternatives offered by the chiropractor offended the woman's dignity. One wonders what she and the Board of Inquiry expected him to do when initially confronted with the situation. Was he supposed to say, "Okay, just wait a few weeks while I get a zoning variance from the city, arrange a new mortgage, and spend $20,000 installing a ramp so we can see whether you really want me as your chiropractor?"

Most people who need chiropractic services need them now, not a few weeks from now. It made far more sense for the doctor to offer quick expedients than to offer to install a ramp. Even if he had proposed a ramp, the woman might well have sought treatment elsewhere in the meantime, and might either have had her problem completely remedied, or

From Fraser Forum, December 1995. First appeared in Canadian Lawyer. *Copyright 1995, Karen Selick. Reprinted by permission of The Fraser Institute and Karen Selick.*

might have been so satisfied with the second chiropractor that she would never have come back to the first one.

In my view, the complainant's own behaviour robbed her of dignity. A dignified response would have been for her to realize that the doctor was trying to accommodate her and to have met him half-way. Instead, she insisted that everything be done entirely *her* way. That's not dignified — that's bullying.

The Human Rights Code says its purpose is to enhance the dignity of "every person," not just disabled people, but the decision — indeed, the whole proceeding — overlooks any consideration of the chiropractor's dignity. The judgment reveals details of his assets, his debts, and his earnings over several years. There it all is, in black and white, for his colleagues, his patients, his neighbours, or any other nosy stranger to read. I'm sure he finds that very dignified.

Even worse, his judgment as a businessman regarding the appropriate financial conduct of his business has been completely overridden. No doubt he would willingly have installed a ramp, in order to expand his potential client base, if he had perceived a reasonable prospect that the extra traffic would justify the expense. His opinion was that it wouldn't. The Board of Inquiry couldn't care less. He is the child, it is the parent, and he has to do what it says, regardless of how foolish its decision may be from a business point of view. I'm sure he finds that very dignified too.

One witness, quoted approvingly by the Board, described the proceedings this way: "It really is . . . about persons with disabilities taking control of their own lives." Not at all. It's really about the Human Rights Commission, in the name of a few legally privileged groups, taking control of *other people's* lives. . . .

CALLING A SLAVE A SLAVE

Karen Selick

The business and professional community in London — and indeed, all of Ontario — must be shaking in their boots. Every doctor, dentist, accountant, lawyer, restaurateur, or merchant whose business premises are inaccessible to wheelchairs has to pray that this woman never decides to patronize his establishment, lest it cost him $20,000 for the favour.

Ontario's Human Rights Code divides the population into two classes who are given completely different treatment. The first group can be broadly described as consumers. They can't be discriminated against on the grounds of race, sex, handicap, etc., by anyone providing services, goods, facilities, or accommodation. If they think they have been discriminated against, they can complain to the Human Rights Commission.

The second group can be broadly described as business people. They are the ones who provide the services, goods, facilities, and accommodations, in exchange for money. The first group can freely discriminate against the second on every imaginable ground, because there is nothing in the Code that forbids discrimination in the spending of money.

So if a person in a wheelchair chooses to eat at an English-style pub rather than at the French, Jewish, or Chinese restaurants (all ramped) in the same block, the snubbed restaura-

From Fraser Forum, January 1996. First appeared in Canadian Lawyer. *Copyright 1995, Karen Selick. Reprinted by permission of The Fraser Institute and Karen Selick.*

teurs can't go bleating to the Human Rights Commission about her cruel ethnic discrimination. Nor can any of the ethnic restaurateurs claim "systemic discrimination" if his restaurant fails while those of his neighbours succeed. The Human Rights Commission won't force the locals in the neighbourhood to eat their "fair share" of Chinese food. Business people simply have to live with the fact that in a market economy, consumers are free to deal with whomever they choose.

Here's another example. Clients occasionally tell me they picked my name out of the yellow pages because they wanted a female lawyer. Presumably, there are other people who choose *not* to hire me for the same reason. Ontario's benchers endorsed this discriminatory practice last year by allowing the Lawyer Referral Service to fill gender-specific requests. A Law Society Committee was even asked to consider permitting clients to request a referral by race or ethnicity. But the Rules of Professional Conduct make it clear that lawyers cannot screen out clients on the basis of sex, race, or ethnicity.

Why should there be any such dichotomy? Every commercial transaction consists of two parties making an exchange: goods, services, facilities, or accommodation flow in one direction, and money flows in the other. Both parties to the transaction must feel that what they are getting is more valuable to them than what they are giving up; otherwise, they wouldn't agree to the deal. So why should one group be free to select the identity of the person they wish to profit from, while the other isn't?

Don't get me wrong — I am certainly not advocating that the Human Rights Code should apply in both directions. On the contrary, I am suggesting that it should be scrapped, so that freedom of contract can prevail for all.

The only way to make sense of the dichotomy is to realize that the Code is not about protecting minorities against racism, sexism or other -isms at all. No, what it's really about is subjugating those classes of people who are presumed to be powerful to those who are presumed to be powerless. Business people and landlords of all races, sexes, and abilities are the targets; consumers and tenants are the beneficiaries.

Of course, the presumptions about power are not particularly accurate. There are many consumers and tenants who are wealthier and more influential than business people and landlords. But little facts like this never bother those who want to dismantle the free-market system.

The chiropractor decision contains the unspoken declaration that the doctor has some sort of obligation to provide services to the disabled woman, even though she is under no corresponding obligation to purchase his services. Interestingly, he has no general obligation to provide chiropractic services to the world. He can retire from practice and take his services off the market entirely if he chooses. But if he has no obligation to provide his services to anyone at all, then how can he have an obligation to provide services to the disabled woman in particular?

What the Human Rights Code actually does is to impose a form of involuntary servitude on certain members of society — the goods and service providers. It transforms others — consumers who belong to one of the privileged minority groups — into overlords. The latter have the right to force the former to perform services for them against their will. There was a time when this was called "slavery," but it's unfashionable to call a slave a slave these days.

According to the preamble of the Ontario Human Rights Code, its purpose is to create "a climate of understanding and mutual respect." What it is bound to create instead is a climate of privilege and resentment.

QUESTIONS

1. Do you think the chiropractor in Karen Selick's example is guilty of discrimination? If so, is requesting that he build a ramp into his building a fair decision on the part of the Human Rights Commission?
2. Do you think that either of the two options that Selick suggests, having the woman in the wheelchair go to another chiropractor or having her pay for the ramp herself, are acceptable?
3. Do you agree with Selick that anti-discrimination legislation divides the population into classes of consumers and business people and that it is business people who are unfairly discriminated against?

WHY LIBERALS SHOULD SUPPORT SAME SEX MARRIAGE

Adrian Alex Wellington

This paper is about the state sponsorship of same sex unions, or about "family values, queer-style," as one commentator has put it.[1] The simple claim of this paper is that gays, lesbians, and bisexuals should have the right to legally marry if they so choose.[2] This simple claim can be characterized as a claim about formal equality — the same sex marriage bar is a denial of the formal equality rights of lesbians, gays,[3] and bisexuals. However, the simple claim does not adequately capture the complexity of the issue, either for those who argue against same sex marriage or for those who argue for it.

In this paper I will present a more complex version of the above argument in the context of contemporary secular liberalism. The argument can be broken down into the following components:

1. In a liberal society, sexual relations between consenting adults is beyond the purview of the state — "the state has no business in the bedrooms of the nation."[4]
2. It is not possible to justify anything other than a functional account of marriage in contemporary secular liberal society.
3. If some relationships — namely opposite sex ones — are to be given state sponsorship, there must be rational reasons consistent with liberal principles to deny that sponsorship to analogous relationships.
4. On a functional account of marriage same sex relationships are analogous to opposite sex relationships.
5. As a matter of formal equality, same sex unions should be entitled to state sponsorship.
6. Any other arguments against the provision of state sponsorship to same sex unions could only make claim to liberal principles by reference to some formulation of the harm principle.
7. There is no valid argument against same sex marriage based on the grounds of harm consistent with the harm principle.

From the Journal of Social Philosophy, *v. 26, no. 3 (Winter 1995), pp. 5–32. Reprinted by permission of the* Journal of Social Philosophy.

All of these claims taken together provide a compound argument for the claim that gays, lesbians, and bisexuals should have the right to participate in state sponsored same sex unions if they so choose. The policy claim that corresponds to my argument is that legislative reform would be required in order to ensure the provision of that right.

The main claim of this paper is that as a matter of social justice liberalism requires the provision of the opportunity for state sponsorship and state recognition of same sex couples. The paper is concerned with an issue of political philosophy — whether a commitment to liberalism entails a commitment to support the rights of lesbians, gays, and bisexuals to marry persons of the same sex, should they so desire. Whether gays, lesbians, and bisexuals should choose to exercise the option, if available, of marrying persons of the same sex is a separate issue. The position that liberalism must, as a matter of political philosophy, recognize the validity of same sex marriage as an option for gays, lesbians, and bisexuals as well as for heterosexuals (should any heterosexuals choose to marry persons of the same sex) is distinct from the position that state sponsorship of same sex marriages should be pursued as a strategy for achieving gay rights or gay liberation. One can acknowledge that liberalism entails the commitment to support state sponsorship of same sex marriage without insisting that lesbians, gays, and bisexuals should participate in, or even advocate the provision of the opportunity to participate in same sex marriages.

I

This paper begins with certain crucial assumptions about the basic claims of liberalism and the fluidity of human sexuality and emotional attachment. The first basic claim of liberalism as a broadly defined concept is the claim that each person in a liberal society should be able to determine for her/himself just what constitutes the "good life." Corollary to that claim is another basic claim that the state should be neutral between conceptions of the "good life." The third basic claim is that liberal society not only need not, but actually should not, be based on any specific picture of "human nature." A liberal society is one in which there are many diverse conceptions of "human nature," as with conceptions of the "good life," and that none should be accorded primacy or specific state endorsement. The fourth basic claim is that legal intervention in the lives of the members of a liberal society should be constrained as far as possible by the notion of liberty contained in the formulation of the harm principle.[5]

The claims concerning human sexuality and emotional attachment are simpler, but probably no less contentious. These claims are that human beings as a species have a remarkably diverse range of potential sexual practices and emotional affiliations. Even given tremendous levels of socialization aimed at producing compulsory heterosexuality, many people resist this socialization and choose to reject, partly or completely, heterosexuality. One can assume that many more people would adopt homosexuality or bisexuality in practice or identify with either by inclination if those socialization pressures were ameliorated. The picture of a traditional marriage is that of heterosexual adults taking on a pair bonding union sanctioned by religion and/or the state involving fidelity and reproduction. Yet, many, many people who enter into the state of marriage, who partake of the status of the social practice of marriage, actually do not adhere to that traditional picture. Many marriages do not rest upon fidelity, and many marriages do not result in procreation. Further, many marriages are between parties, or involve parties, who do not primarily perceive themselves as heterosexual.

It seems clear that a liberal conception of sexuality must be one that recognizes the contingency of heterosexuality. There may be many subcultures or segments of a liberal society — religious fundamentalists, certain kinds of anti-homosexual moralists — which do not accept the assertion of heterosexuality as contingent. These groups may wish to entrench heterosexuality socially, morally, and legally, yet the very fact that they seek to entrench it and to force compliance with the norm of heterosexuality itself attests to the very contingency of the norm. It is because some people are unwilling to live in compliance with the norm, and are able to resist the supposed necessity of the norm, that these groups wish to adopt harsh measures of policing and enforcement of the norm. These groups who categorically oppose the assertion of contingent heterosexuality, nevertheless, are only part of liberal society. Liberal society also includes those who wish to partake in homosexual or bisexual pair bonding unions as well as those who wish to, or at least are willing to, tolerate such unions.

A liberal society is one that rests upon the provision of choice for individuals to determine what sorts of people they want to be, as well as what sorts of lives they want to lead. Part of the choices that one undertakes during the process of self construction and life construction is whether, and to what extent, to participate in pair bonding unions. In a society which is premised upon the separation of religion and democratic governance, indicated by the institution of civil marriage, these unions must be interpreted in the context of liberal and not religious norms. Despite the holdover of religious notions in the wording of the marriage ceremony itself, it is clear that people can engage in the practice of marriage without any specific commitment to religious conceptions of marriage. Marriage thus becomes a state sanctioned pair bonding union, an affirmation of state endorsement of the pair bonding itself. There is no requirement that one engage in heterosexual practices with one's marriage partner, and no requirement that one attempt to produce children. The only conditions one need meet in order to undertake civil marriage are that the partners are of opposite sex, of sufficient age, legally sane, and not too closely related (consanguinity conditions).[6] Of course, the partners must also be able to pay the required fee for the ceremony.

It is interesting to note that once the religious basis for marriage is removed or at least elided that there is no longer any rational reason — rational in the sense of related to the purpose of the practice — to insist that parties to a civil marriage be of the opposite sex. A civil marriage is a self-defining ceremony, intended to accord a certain social status. The state cannot require that marriage partners endorse and live up to the ideal of fidelity, or endorse and live by the norm of heterosexuality, or endorse and live in accordance with the intention to reproduce. The marriage union in a secular liberal society is one that is interpreted by the parties in the context of the purported absence of teleological conceptions of human nature and of state sanctioned conceptions of the good life. The parties themselves determine what marriage means to them, and shape the practice to their needs and wants. How then can the state insist upon the condition that parties must be of opposite sexes in order to participate in that kind of practice?

Marriages are intended to be unions, unions which apparently automatically create "couples" and then "families." There are of course couples outside of marriage and marriage partners who do not perceive themselves to be couples. There are of course families outside of marriage and marriages which do not actually function like families. The point is that civil marriages produce a certain kind of coupling — state sanctioned coupling. Other than the requirement that the parties be adults and be of opposite sex, the civil marriage ceremony can be tailored by the parties to incorporate their values and beliefs and preferences.

The parties can undertake civil marriage in order to attain the social status of marriage but intend to be "unfaithful" to one another sexually with persons of the opposite or same sex. The parties can intend to be celibate, to avoid procreation or to engage in procreation, to have sex only with each other, or to never have sex with each other. In other words, marriage does not depend upon any particular set of sexual or emotional practices. Why then does it depend upon an arbitrary condition of membership in the opposite sex to one's intended partner?

If a homosexual person can marry another homosexual person of the opposite sex or a heterosexual person of the opposite sex, or a bisexual person marry a homosexual or heterosexual person of the opposite sex, why should lesbians, gays, and bisexuals be excluded from marrying a homosexual or bisexual or heterosexual person of the same sex? Heterosexuals are also prevented from marrying a heterosexual or homosexual person of the same sex as well. If one looks at marriage in the context of a liberal conception of the practice, divorced from the religious interpretation of the practice and the historical background of the practice, these restrictions make no sense. Apart from social prejudice and discrimination, there is no reason to insist that individuals of the same sex cannot form couples in the same way that parties to marriage form couples. Civil marriage is a self-defining, self-obligating union. The parties will determine what the union provides for them, and what need they have for the state sanction — from expression of commitment to tax breaks. Same sex couples are no less capable of determining this than opposite sex couples.

One does not have to able to recognize the capacity in oneself to respond sexually to persons of either sex or of the same sex in order to recognize that the capacity exists in many others. One does not have to be able to recognize the capacity in oneself to form emotional affiliations with persons of either sex or of the same sex in order to recognize that the capacity exists in many others. There is no biological, or psychological reason that human beings must have sex or emotional affiliations only with persons of the opposite sex. There are only political or social reasons that motivate people to insist that heterosexuality is natural, or normal. Liberals are predisposed to resist arguments of the form that it is only "natural" or "normal" for humans to be X or to do Y. On my reading of liberalism the central driving force behind the adoption of liberal political philosophy and policy historically was to counteract precisely those kind of arguments in favor of the divine right of monarchs or in favor of religious morality. Divorce is one of the clearest examples of the movement towards a secularization of social practices that were initially the exclusive preserve of religion.

It seems clear that secular liberal societies can no longer rely upon outdated and archaic religious notions about the purposes of coupling and specifically of marriage. The attempts of courts to deal with common law opposite sex coupling point to several interesting things about contemporary civil marriage. The courts in some cases have attempted to develop functional characterizations of "spouses" and thus functional definitions of "couples."[7] These definitions include factors like the following: Did the parties share a bank account? Did the parties own property in common? Did the parties visit each other's relatives? Did the parties purchase shared items? Did the parties entertain guests together? Did the parties divide up household chores between them? Did the parties share meals? Did the parties provide nurturance and caring for each other when ill?

It is obvious that all these factors apply equally to same sex couples as to opposite sex couples. Same sex couples share bank accounts, own property in common, visit each other's relatives, purchase shared items, entertain guests together, divide up household chores, share meals, and provide nurturance and care for each other when ill. And of course, same sex couples, like opposite sex couples, have sex with each other. Any functional characterization of a couple — which I would argue is the only kind that could be endorsed by a full-fledged liberalism — is going to apply equally to same sex couples as to opposite sex couples.

If functional definitions are appropriate to determine whether unmarried couples were or are effectively married, and thus fall under "common law" marriage provisions of family law, then would functional definitions not be appropriate to determine whether same sex couples are suitable candidates for characterizations of "spouses" and thus suitable candidates to be deemed effectively married as well? Same sex couples look indistinguishable from opposite couples on the basis of functional definitions — that is, the differences among particular opposite and same sex couples would be as great as differences between opposite and same sex couples. The only reason that same sex couples do not fall under "common law" marriage provisions of family law is that same sex couples cannot marry, and thus they cannot be "effectively married." I should point out that "common law" marriage designation has to do with both the division of property and family assets, and the custody of, and access to, children. Both of these factors can be relevant to same sex couples who may own property together, have been in a relationship of economic dependence and support, and have children together (not the children of both of them together, but the children of each of them who they parent together or the children they have adopted together or singly previously).

None of the criteria in a functional definition of "spouse" — a person with whom one may share a bank account, own property, visit relatives, purchase shared items, entertain guests, divide up household chores, share meals, and have sex, and for whom one may provide nurturance and care — are gender specific. All are functional and relational. The significant issue in the determination of "spouse" is whether the two people relate to each other, and think of each other, in the manner of a "couple." What is a couple then, on this account, is a provisional definition that is something along the lines of a "voluntary relation premised on intimacy and connection." This phrase is my choice of wording; similar ideas based on functional definitions are suggested by the wording found in domestic partnership provisions and in certain court decisions.[8] My functional definition of marriage explicitly excludes the requirement of procreation, or even intended procreation. It is inconsistent, I argue, with a liberal account of marriage to include such a requirement. Thus, there is no basis to the attempt to privilege procreative or potentially procreative heterosexual marriage to encourage reproduction. Such an attempt could not be justified on my account.

Of course, the phrase "voluntary relation premised on intimacy and connection" could apply to affairs, and special friendships, so what needs to be added is the clause intended to produce the union of coupling. Thus, it is self-defining. What is distinctive about "couples" is that two people self-identify as a couple, and then other people identify those two people as a couple. There is no reason, once the notion of "couple" is characterized as functional and self-defining, to restrict the notion to opposite sex couples. And then if marriage is simply the legitimation by state sanction of self-defined, functional couples, there is no reason to restrict civil marriage to opposite sex couples.

The argument might be made that a significant feature of marriage is that the status of marriage represents a certain expression of social approval for the union. Thus, the state provides for couples to marry to express social approval for opposite sex coupling. It is of course arguments like this that make advocates of gay rights argue that gays, lesbians, and bisexuals need to have the opportunity to marry in order to be accorded the expression of social approval for their unions. The idea is that marriage is a legitimating social practice — that the status of marriage legitimates the coupling. Therefore, some lesbians, gays, and bisexuals wish to have their same sex coupling legitimated. The counter argument then is that "society," whatever that is, does not wish to bestow social approval on same sex coupling. Therefore, same sex couples should not be provided with the option of legitimating state sanctioned marriage.

This counter argument does not work, for several reasons. One reason is that people who marry engage in myriad forms of coupling which are not socially approved by large segments of the population — for example, childless marriages (by choice), open marriages, adulterous marriages, opportunistic marriages or marriages of convenience (for immigration purposes, for example), tabloid marriages ("grandmother- or grandfather-aged person marries teen" type of thing). It simply is not the case that whatever unions result from opposite sex marriages would be subject to social approval. It is not simply by virtue of the fact that parties are of opposite sexes that civil marriage expresses social approval. Another reason is that many, many people do support the idea of state sanctioned social approval for same sex unions. Obviously, most if not all gays, lesbians, and bisexuals support the idea of state sanctioned social approval for same sex unions.[9] Whether or not all gays, lesbians, and bisexuals would actually want to participate in the practice of same sex marriages, they would nevertheless not want to endorse a continuation of a source of discrimination against gays, lesbians, and bisexuals. There may be some homosexuals who object to the campaign for gay marriage, but the basis of their denial of support may be something other than a wish to see discrimination against gays, lesbians, and bisexuals continued.

It is also the case that some heterosexuals who would not wish to have the option to undertake same sex marriages for themselves would still support the provision of state sanctioned same sex marriages to those who do want them. Liberals are notorious for arguing for the rights of people to do things that liberals themselves may not want to do, and that other people (non liberals) do not support for anyone. Why should same sex marriage be any different? A liberal society is one in which the fullest possible range of options for human flourishing is to be encouraged, consistent with the need for respect of the civil rights and liberties of individuals. One important civil liberty is the freedom to engage in a state sanctioned union. The only possible reason that a liberal could have for rejecting same sex marriage is that the practice would in some way violate the harm principle.

It is important to clarify why the harm principle is even relevant in this context. The harm principle purports to stipulate the conditions under which the state could legitimately interfere with the liberty of its citizens; it sets out the bounds of individual liberty which must be respected by liberal government. The harm principle is clearly germane to the issue of whether (homosexual) sodomy should be subject to criminal prohibition.[10] It makes sense therefore to apply the harm principle to that issue, but it is less clear why the harm principle should be applied to the issue of same sex marriage. There are several reasons why the application may be problematic.

Criminal prohibitions against sexual activity between consenting adults obviously violate the liberty of those subject to them. Thus, these prohibitions could only be justified if there was sufficient reason to do so, reasons which satisfy the requirements of the harm principle. If it could be shown that some harm — harm of the sort envisaged by Mill —

results from the activity, then the prohibition could be justified. It cannot be shown that any harm of the sort envisaged by Mill results from the activity, and thus the criminal prohibition of homosexual activity cannot be justified. Any justifications of such criminal prohibitions could only be based on illiberal principles and prejudices.

The question of permitting homosexual marriage does not involve any clear violation of liberty. It could be argued that marriage law is an instance of power-conferring and entitlement-allocating legislation. Marriage law determines which couples are entitled to state sanction for their unions, and which couples are not. Marriage constitutes "an affirmation by the state, a larger-than-life acknowledgment of one's relationship, a seal of approval."[11] The question of whether the state can legitimately deny same sex couples the right to marry seems thus to be a question of equality. Are same sex couples equal to opposite sex couples, such that they should be entitled to the same state sponsorship of their unions? I argue that on a functional account of marriage formal equality would dictate that same sex couples are entitled to the same state sponsorship as opposite sex couples. I also argue that a functional account of marriage is the only type of account consistent with contemporary secular liberal society.

It should be sufficient, then, to say that the same sex marriage bar violates the formal equality of gays, lesbians, and bisexuals. Yet, it is not sufficient because the literature addressing the issue of same sex marriage does not facilitate a straightforward treatment in terms of formal equality. To respond to the objections that have been raised by critics of homosexual marriage, it is necessary to depart from a neat and simple analysis of equality.

The critics of homosexual marriage (both straight and gay) are not satisfied with the characterization of the issue as one of formal equality. Those critics who object to homosexual marriage because they object to homosexuality will not accept the claim of equality between same sex couples and opposite sex couples. That claim is contentious for them, and their response to that claim is typically to point out some kind of harm that is imputed to homosexual marriage. Those critics who object to homosexual marriage, or at least raise concerns about the pursuit of state sponsorship, but who do not object to homosexuality *per se* are concerned with issues of substantive equality. To address same sex marriage in the context of substantive equality is to talk about benefit and disbenefit, it is to talk about harm to interests.

Some readers might wonder whether the kind of harm that is being discussed in this section of the paper is really the kind of harm that Mill would have had in mind when he proposed the Harm Principle. I have two responses to that potential interjection. Firstly, what Mill would have had in mind is not determinative of the articulation of harm to be covered by the Principle for contemporary society. The debates over hate literature, pornography, and the limits of free speech are not really foreshadowed in Mill's formulation, yet these issues have become an integral part of how the Harm Principle is understood in contemporary liberal society. Secondly, the kinds of harms that are covered by the term stigmatization include the loss of jobs, physical assaults ("gay bashing"), and other violations of the civil rights of gays, lesbians, and bisexuals. These are certainly the kinds of things Mill's own formulation would have been intended to cover.

On the usual reading of Mill's harm principle, preventing harm to others is the only justified rationale for state interference with the liberty of individuals.[12] I propose to apply a variant of the harm principle which can accommodate the concerns about putative harm raised by both sets of critics of same sex marriage, but still does justice to liberal principles. That variant is the following: the only justification for the denial by the state of a benefit required by formal equality is that the provision of that benefit would harm others in the society. Thus, as a matter of public policy, the state must sponsor power-conferring or entitlement-allocating legislation required by formal equality unless it can be shown that significant harm (of the kind covered by the harm principle) would result from that sponsorship. It could be argued that my formulation has departed so far from Mill's principle that it could not be included under the same label. Nevertheless, I think that the term harm is irreplaceable in this context — since it is harm that justifies the denial of state benefits. My version could be called the State Benefits Version of the Harm Principle.

The objections to same sex marriage which need to be countered involve conceptions of harm. I contend that in order to make sense of the objections, and in order to make a valid case for state sponsorship, it is necessary to respond to the assertions about putative harm. I have found that the most efficacious way to do so is examine the application of my proposed formulation of the harm principle in the context of the legitimation of homosexual marriage.

II

There are effectively two distinct sets of criticisms of same-sex marriage on the grounds of imputed harm resulting from state sanction. One set of criticisms includes several variations on the idea that allowing same-sex marriages will bring about a threat to the nuclear family, marriage in general, or even to society. This set of criticisms is based on a claim that I will call the Harm to Heterosexuality claim. The other set of criticisms includes several variations on the idea that advocating and pursuing state sponsorship of same sex marriage will bring about a threat to the goals and objectives of gay liberation. This set of criticisms is based on a claim that I will call the Harm to Homosexuality claim. The objection to same sex marriage can make use of conceptions of harm that are either symbolic or empirical, or both. In other words, the kind of harm that is imputed can be harm that can be determined and measured empirically or it can be symbolic harm that is simply perceived.

The Harm to Heterosexuality is supposed to consist in the threat that same sex marriages pose to opposite sex marriages, harm in the form of decline in the sanctity of the institution of marriage, inconsistency with traditional definitions of family, or even in the most extreme articulations of the position, harm in the form of a contribution to an overall breakdown in social order. People who make these kinds of criticisms are motivated by the rejection of gay rights and liberation, and often even a "fear and loathing" of homosexuality.

Many versions of the Harm to Heterosexuality position are premised upon religious conceptions of sex, family, and society. As such, the harm that is claimed tends to be more symbolic than empirical. Insofar as the Harm to Heterosexuality position is based upon religious conceptions of sex, family, and society, it is easily dispensed with in the context of a discussion of liberalism. Given that liberalism requires the separation of church and state, it cannot be argued that the state should outlaw same sex marriages because such marriages are inconsistent with religious morality. Insofar as the Harm to Heterosexuality position is based upon some empirical sounding claim about actual harm to the institutions of marriage and family, or to "society" itself, it is obvious that this would have to be based on some kind of evidence. What kind of evidence could one possibly produce to argue that same sex marriages would erode the institutions of marriage and family?

Someone who wants to claim that same sex marriages will produce some kind of distinct social harm has to be able to show what harm is caused by the state sponsorship of marriage that is distinct from the harm that is imputed to same sex relationships themselves. Same sex coupling will continue with or without state sponsorship, and even with or without criminalization of some of the acts that are targeted as part of an attempt to outlaw homosexuality. People who object to same sex marriage may also object to homosexuality, but the point is that to make any kind of a case for why a liberal society should not provide legal sanction for relationships that are already occurring, an argument specifically against state sponsorship of marriage is needed. If liberalism is based, as I want to argue, on the notions of privacy, autonomy, and individual liberty, no argument against homosexuality based on mere moral or social disapproval is acceptable. There has to be evidence of actual harm that will be experienced by members of the society that amounts to more than mere offense at the actions or choices of others. Therefore, the critics of same sex marriage cannot argue that they object to state sponsorship because they object to homosexuality and state sponsorship legitimates homosexuality.

What quickly becomes clear once one looks at the various articulations of the Harm to Heterosexuality position is that it is difficult to separate the objection to same sex marriage from the objection to homosexuality. It is of course important to be able to separate these objections, because the only basis a liberal could accept for outlawing, or denying legitimacy to, same sex relationships, is that those relationships will actually cause harm to others. If we recognize that the harm that can be considered is not harm that consists of mere offense, then the symbolic element of the objection is disallowed. That leaves the empirical element of the objection.

One candidate for the requisite kind of harm that is proposed is the potential for gay marriage to undermine the legitimacy of straight marriage. This claim can be understood in two ways: one in which the delegitimation consists of symbolic harm to the institution and the other in which the delegitimation consists of actual harm to the institution in the form of decreased participation. The notion of symbolic harm to the sanctity of heterosexual marriage rests upon illiberal commitments and concerns, and thus does not raise issues germane to the consideration of what liberals should support.

The notion of the latter form of harm, one of decreased participation, underlies the claim that the opportunity for gay marriage will weaken the institution of heterosexual marriage. Yet, as others have pointed out, this argument rests upon (at least one) fallacy. As one commentator puts it, "[g]ay marriage could only delegitimize straight marriage if it were a real alternative to it."[13] That is, it could only delegitimize it if those who would otherwise participate in straight marriage chose to participate instead in gay marriage. Obviously, heterosexuals will continue to marry other heterosexuals. The people who will no longer participate in straight marriages if offered the opportunity to participate in gay marriages will be gays, lesbians, and bisexuals. Assuming that some gays who marry straights do so in order to be married and to have families, and not simply to avoid social stigma, then they would continue to do so. Those gays who marry straights in order to stay closeted and to avoid social stigma would continue to do so as long as the social stigmatization continues. Of course, the legalization of gay marriage would contribute to the erosion of the social stigma surrounding homosexuality, which would in turn encourage lesbians, gays, and bisexuals to participate in gay marriage. None of this suggests that there would be any real threat of significantly decreased participation in heterosexual marriage.

It thus seems as if the objection to same sex marriage characterized in terms of harm rests solely upon the objection to homosexuality itself. There is no argument against marriage of same sex persons that is not an argument against homosexuality. I want to assert that there is no valid empirical evidence that same sex relationships, in and of themselves, cause actual harm to any other persons. The claim that these relationships are harmful to the participants — even assuming there could be shown to be a factual basis to this dubious supposition — is of course an irrelevant claim, given liberalism's *prima facie* commitment to non-paternalism. It is particularly illegitimate when the paternalism is based on contentious moral, religious, or social conceptions of the "good" of the intended beneficiaries of the paternalism.[14]

The Harm to Homosexuality is supposed to consist in the threat that state sponsorship poses to the achievement of gay liberation and to the project of reconceiving heterosexuality, homosexuality, and relations between the sexes. People who make these kinds of claims are motivated by a commitment to gay liberation, and to some articulations of gay rights — ones that do not amount to presumption of the notion of "sameness" between gays and straights but rather assume the notion of "difference" between gays and straights. The position of those in gay, lesbian, and bisexual communities[15] who reject the pursuit of state sponsorship for same sex relationships, is not of course that there is anything wrong with same sex relationships. Their position is that there is something wrong with state sponsorship, and something wrong with marriage.

It should be pointed out that those in lesbian, gay, and bisexual communities who raise objections to the prospect of gay marriage do so largely on grounds of strategy and tactics. The debate over gay marriage within gay, lesbian, and bisexual communities is mainly a debate over the priority of different venues or policies for the allocation of resources and the expenditure of efforts. The discussion in much of the literature thus addresses the advisability of pursuing gay marriage as a strategy for gay activists, and raises concerns about the diversion of efforts and resources from other significant issues. These debates — whether putting too much effort into this one option will divert efforts from other options that may be more central to sexual liberation, whether the pursuit of domestic partnership legislation should take priority over removal of the same sex marriage bar,[16] whether the potential backlash from the pursuit of this particular option will have repercussions, or whether the gay, lesbian, and bisexual community is too divided over the option to make it a priority — could all be seen to involve questions about goals and strategies for queer activism.[17] For instance, some "regard domestic partnership agreement registration as a distraction from the need to gain full rights to marry with full access to benefits and protections," while others perceive that registration is better because it "recognizes alternative family structures."[18] These questions about which is the better target begin with the assumption that gays, lesbians, and bisexuals are entitled to equality and then move to the attempt to articulate and clarify the appropriate way to characterize and pursue that equality.

The point is that gays, lesbians, and bisexuals who call into question the desirability of gay marriage generally do not dispute the position that the opposite sex requirement of marriage laws is "socially discriminatory and offensive to the basic liberal principles that underlie human rights legislation."[19] Even those who raise objections to same sex marriage do not deny that the same sex marriage bar is illiberal. Yet, it is still possible to construct an objection to state sponsorship to same sex marriage that imputes some type of potential harm that would result from the policy. This objection could take several different forms:

1. one based on an objection to perceived conformity to "straight standards;[20]
2. one based on an objection to the oppressive patriarchal nature of the institution of marriage; and

3. one based on an objection to the involvement of the state in the regulation of lesbian, gay, and bisexual intimate relationships. These objections tend to overlap and are difficult to disentangle.

The first form of the objection, based on rejection of the perceived conformity to "straight standards" inherent in same sex marriage, implies that the pursuit of conformity on the part of some gays, lesbians, and bisexuals — namely those who would want to get married — could indirectly harm the interests of those who would not want to get married, and thus who do not conform. The harm would consist of the further stigmatization of those lesbians, gays, and bisexuals who choose not to get married once the option becomes available.[21]

It is possible to construct the imputed argument along the following lines. Homosexual sex is stigmatized and a cause for oppression of gays, lesbians, and bisexuals. If homosexuals could marry, those who would already tend to benefit from certain social privileges (class, race, ethnicity, and so forth) will likely be the ones to exercise the option. Those homosexuals who do not marry will be further stigmatized and oppressed, relative to the otherwise more privileged homosexuals who will marry.[22]

It is difficult to determine in what sense there would be more stigmatization or oppression of the lesbians, gays, and bisexuals who choose not to marry — absolutely or in terms of perception of relative privilege. It is at least partly an empirical question. What is relevant to the issue in question is whether the provision of state sponsorship for same sex marriage would result in more harm overall, harm of the sort that is germane to liberalism.

The significant issue for the question of whether liberalism should support same sex marriage is whether the resulting "extra" stigmatization would result from the provision of same sex marriage itself, or would be an unintended byproduct of pre-existing homophobia.[23] It is unclear whether the stigmatization of non-married or single gays, lesbians, and bisexuals would be more after the option of state sponsored same sex marriage is available or whether it would be the same amount of stigmatization, but would seem more in relation to the other married gays, lesbians, and bisexuals. That is, it is unclear whether it would be extra stigmatization or simply continuing stigmatization. Either way, the "extra" stigmatization should be the focus of additional efforts to reduce and eventually overcome homophobic societal attitudes. Unless one could show that denying same sex couples the right to marry would, in and of itself, decrease the stigmatization, it is necessary to address the resulting harm by other measures than continuing the same sex marriage bar.

The first objection to same sex marriage can be presented still more abstractly, in terms of the "politics of validating difference,"[24] and a general critique of "rights discourse" and "rights claims." The presumption is that there is something one could identify as lesbian and gay identity and culture that resists assimilation. There is no denial, however, that some gays and lesbians as individuals do not resist, and even welcome, assimilation. The concern is that whenever society extends rights to some previously disenfranchised group of persons — in this case the lesbians, gays, and bisexuals who do want to get married — then other members of the group who "forswear or forego such rights risk being even more marginalized than before."[25] The objection seems to highlight the tension between individual rights which would be asserted by the group of same sex couples who want to marry, and collective interests which would be represented by the interests of the remainder of the group, the non-marrying gays and lesbians.[26]

The second form of the Harm to Homosexuality objection is the claim that marriage is an oppressive institution which lesbians and gay men should condemn, rather than lobby to join.[27] There are two different aspects of characterizing the harm of marriage in this objection. One aspect concerns the patriarchal nature of marriage as a social institution.[28] The other aspect emphasizes the balance of benefits and burdens that marriage may provide for particular same sex couples. The latter aspect is related to the former in that the reason some couples would not realize the potential benefits of marriage would have to do with the underlying oppressive features, and structural constraints of society. What Nitya Duclos calls the "hierarchy of privilege" ensures that some couples — whether opposite sex or same sex couples — will benefit more from the bundle of benefits that constitute marriage.[29] The provision of state-sponsored marriage for same sex couples will also have effects on cohabiting same sex couples that may or may not be welcomed by those cohabiting couples.

Both aspects of the second objection — the particular and the general — have in common the focus on marriage. It is marriage as a social institution that is an oppressive patriarchal institution. It is marriage as a particular legislative scheme that has better or worse effects for particular couples. The important point for the purposes of this paper is that the putative harm does not result from the provision of same sex marriage, but rather from marriage itself. For the liberal, the question is whether it is justifiable for the state to continue to deny to same sex couples the option that is available to opposite sex couples — to participate in the potentially undesirable, arguably harmful institution of marriage. The liberal rejection of paternalism entails that individuals should be allowed to choose for themselves whether or not to participate in activities that may be harmful to themselves. The issue is not the desirability of marriage, but the desirability of the right.[30]

Several feminists have argued for the position that while marriage may be oppressive in its present form, it need not always be that way. Marriage, the argument goes, is a creature of law dependent upon the power of the state; as such, it is an historically and culturally contingent institution.[31] The further claim is made that same sex marriage could have the potential to "disrupt both the gendered definition of marriage and the assumption the marriage is a form of socially, if not legally, prescribed hierarchy".[32] At the very least, same sex marriages would require the rethinking of the content of the marriage vows and the exercise of linguistic creativity to replace the "husband" and "wife" terminology. These improvements would have symbolic value, and would contribute to the larger project of reforming marriage as a social institution. Same sex marriage, then, would produce no distinctive harm and might even ameliorate the current harm produced by marriage.

What makes the issue complicated is that it is possible to characterize the benefits that would accrue to lesbians, gays, and bisexuals upon provision of the right to state sponsorship of same sex marriage in two ways. One way is to emphasize the benefits that would be realized by individual members of same sex couples who could participate in marriage. The other way is to emphasize the benefits that would be realized by all queers consisting of increased tolerance of homosexuality and increased legitimacy for same sex unions. Some advocates of state sponsorship of same sex marriage argue that it is actually the "issue most likely to lead ultimately to a world free of discrimination against lesbians and gay men."[33] The characterization of benefits — the determination of which benefits will result and who specifically will benefit — is addressed in the literature in the context of the identification of attendant harms — the determination of which harms will result and who specifically will be harmed.

It is important to distinguish between the claim that same sex couples should be entitled to equal treatment with opposite sex couples — whether through domestic partnership arrangements or civil marriage — and the claim that these legal measures should be the focus of advocacy and struggle for gay rights. It is also important to distinguish between the claim that the right to choose X — for example, the right to choose to marry — will benefit those for whom X is a likely option and the claim that the right to choose X is a benefit to only those who do choose X. There is a difference between the concern that gay activists should not direct their energies to the pursuit of marriage and domestic partnership arrangements because only some gays and lesbians would want to participate in these institutions and the claim that only those who (will) participate in those institutions will be benefited by the existence of the choice.

The objection to same sex marriage based on the rejection of conformity should properly locate the harm in homophobia. The objection to same sex marriage based on the suspicion of marriage should properly locate the harm in marriage itself. The objection to same sex marriage based on the perniciousness of state regulation of sexuality should properly locate the harm in the combination of homophobia and marriage itself. It is obvious why queers would be suspicious of any manifestation of state regulation of sexuality.[34] The question, however, is whether gays, lesbians, and bisexuals would be worse off with the provision of state sponsorship for same sex coupling. It is hard to see how they would be. The problem rests with state initiatives that amount to the entrenchment of intolerance of homosexuality.

According to the third form of the Harm to Homosexuality objection, marriage simply presents yet another vehicle of state regulation of sexuality. Marriage, however, does present some potential for protection from state regulation and other benefits. Nitya Duclos lists four objectives of the advocates of gay and lesbian marriage:

1. "to revolutionize marriage and force society to rethink its collective views of sex and sexuality;"
2. to provide validation and legitimation of same sex relationships;
3. to enable lesbian and gay families to partake in the range of socioeconomic benefits of marriage;
4. to legitimate gay and lesbian relationships in the eyes of courts to help lesbians and gays keep their children.[35]

It is clear that merely removing the obstacles to same sex marriage is not going to be sufficient for the realization of these objectives.

State sponsorship of same sex coupling will entail toleration of homosexuality, but it alone will not provide for respect and full equality without other social, political, legal, and economic changes.[36] For example, changes in judicial attitudes and child custody legislation will be necessary for the achievement of the fourth objective.[37] The effect of marriage breakdown will cause same sex couples to come under the purview of courts under divorce legislation. Same sex couples who separate and divorce will be subject to provisions concerning division of property, support, and custody of children. For some people, that will be a benefit and for others that will be a burden. The point is that it is not same sex marriage that increases the points of contact but the legislative regime governing marriage and divorce. The fear of state regulation should not amount to a fear of same sex marriage, but rather a fear of homophobia and a fear of the potential effects of the legislative regime governing marriage and divorce. Thus, harm would result from homophobia and the effects of marriage and divorce, but not from same sex marriage itself.

The consideration of the Harm to Homosexuality objections points to the need to distinguish between formal and substantive equality. The conceptions of harm contained in the various forms of the objection indicate concerns of substantive equality. The question of whether same sex couples should be denied the state sponsorship available to opposite sex couples is really a question of formal equality. The position of this paper is that the same sex marriage bar is a clear denial of formal equality for gay, lesbians and bisexuals. It is important to make clear, then, the relation between formal equality and substantive equality on this issue, if there is any relation.

The opponents to same sex marriage who are motivated by some version of the Harm to Homosexuality objection could be making one of three different claims about the effects of same sex marriage on substantive equality. These three claims are:

1. same sex marriage would increase substantive equality;
2. same sex marriage would decrease substantive equality; or
3. same sex marriage would neither decrease nor increase substantive equality.

On the basis of the above discussion it seems that the three forms of the Harm to Homosexuality objection — the rejection of conformity, the suspicion of marriage, and the fear of state regulation — all attempt to implicate same sex marriage in the charge of jeopardizing substantive equality.

I have tried to argue, however, that what actually jeopardizes substantive equality is not the possibility of same sex marriage, in and of itself, but the effects of pre-existing inequalities resulting from homophobia, the legal regime governing marriage and divorce, and other social inequalities. I would contend then, that same sex marriage at the least could be said to neither decrease nor increase substantive equality. It may even increase substantive equality if the claims concerning the potential liberatory effects of same sex marriage upon the institution of marriage are viable. The provision of state sponsored same sex marriage would certainly further the pursuit of formal equality for homosexuals, and for that reason it is incumbent upon liberals to support it.

NOTES

1. Chris Bull, "Till Death Do Us Part", *The Advocate*, Issue 643, November 30, 1993, 40 at 41. As Bull and others point out gays and lesbians are "openly marrying, raising children, and demanding official recognition of their partners as spouses." Bull says that same sex marriage is the "new hot issue in the nation's [the U.S.] gay and lesbian community." See Michelangelo Signorile's article "Bridal Wave" for an account of how the issue is developing in Hawaii, which may end up being the first U.S. state to legally recognize homosexual marriages.
2. Gays and lesbians have been participating in commitment ceremonies (also called bonding or union ceremonies) for some time, but these, of course, do not have the "stamp of approval" nor the legal consequences of state-sponsored marriage. In Canada, several challenges to the exclusion of same sex couples from legal provisions concerning "spouses" are working their way through the courts. These challenges are typically based on equality claims involving section 15 of the Canadian Charter of Rights and Freedoms. See Bruce Ryder's "Equality Rights and Sexual Orientation: Confronting Heterosexual Family Privilege", *Canadian Journal of Family Law*, Volume 9, 1990, 39 for more on the specifics of the Canadian context.
3. As per common usage, I will assume that gay refers to gay men and lesbian refers to gay women. Some people take the term "queer" to refer to gay men, lesbian women, bisexual women, bisexual men, transsexuals, and transvestites collectively.
4. This is the gist of what then Prime Minister Pierre Elliot Trudeau said when recommending the decriminalization of any sexual activity between consenting adults in private. This claim is a prior assumption to my version of a functional definition of marriage.
5. Clearly, I am developing my formulation of liberalism and its basic assumptions and commitments in reliance upon certain exponents of the liberal tradition — namely John Stuart Mill in

On Liberty, Ronald Dworkin in "Liberalism," from Hampshire, ed., *Public and Private Morality*, and Joel Feinberg in *Harmless Wrongdoing*. There is a vast literature on liberalism, but interestingly very little of that literature that I am aware of actually addresses the question of a liberal position on the state sponsorship of same sex marriages.

6. These are the usual conditions for marriage – there will likely be some variation among jurisdictions. Nitya Duclos, in "Some Complicating Thoughts on Same Sex Marriage," says the common bars to marriage include: "minimum age limits, insanity, absence of consent (mistake, duress, and fraud), prohibited degrees of affinity and consanguinity, and a prior existing marriage." Nitya Duclos, "Some Complicating Thoughts on Same Sex marriage", *Law and Sexuality: A Review of Lesbian and Gay Legal Issues*, Volume 1, Summer 1991, 31 at 44, fn. 48.

7. Nan Hunter, in "Marriage, Law and Gender: A Feminist Inquiry", points out that the functionalist approach — which posits the identification of objective criteria to determine which relationships are the functional equivalents to marriage — underlay the recognition of common law marriage. See Nan Hunter, "Marriage, Law and Gender", *Law and Sexuality: A Review of Lesbian and Gay Issues*, Volume 1, Summer 1991, 9 at 21 ff.

8. The San Francisco Domestic Partnership law states "[d]omestic partners are two adults who have chosen to share one another's lives in an intimate and committed relationship of mutual caring, who live together, and who have agreed to be jointly responsible for basic living expenses incurred during the Domestic Partnership". See Appendix A: San Francisco Domestic Partnership Ordinance (1990) in David Chambers's article "Tales of Two Cities: AIDS and the Legal Recognition of Domestic Partnerships in San Francisco and New York", *Law and Sexuality: A Review of Lesbian and Gay Legal Issues*, Volume 2, Summer 1992, 181 at 204. The New York Court of Appeals found in *Braschi v. Stahl Associates* that a gay couple must be treated as a family in relation to New York's rent control law. The Court found that the couple satisfied the following criteria: "the exclusivity and longevity of the relationship, the level of emotional and financial commitment, the manner in which the parties have conducted their everyday lives and held themselves out to society, and the reliance placed upon one another for daily family services". Chambers provides an extended discussion of that case from p. 192 ff. See Hunter, supra, p. 23.

9. I should point out that the support is often a qualified support, for a series of complicated reasons. I will touch briefly on some of those reasons in the section concerning the Harm to Homosexuality objection to same sex marriages below, but it will not be possible for me to do justice in this paper to the fascinating complexity of the debates over same sex marriage in the lesbian, gay and bisexual community. For some sense of what the issues are see the papers by Nitya Duclos, Mary Dunlap and Nan Hunter in the Symposium on Lesbian and Gay Marriage in *Law and Sexuality: A Review of Lesbian and Gay Legal Issues*, Volume 1, Summer 1991 and see the papers by Thomas Stoddard and Paula Ettelbrick in *Lesbian and Gay Marriage*, edited by Suzanne Sherman. See also Chris Bull, "Till Death Do Us Part", supra, and Michelangelo Signorile, "Bridal Wave", *Out*, December/January 1994, 69.

10. Laws in several states in the United States which criminalize sodomy do not distinguish between heterosexual and homosexual sodomy. Yet, in *Bowers vs. Hardwick* the Georgia law was challenged by a homosexual man and the court dealt with the issue as if the law were intended to outlaw homosexual sodomy. In Canada, the federal criminal code was amended in May 1969 to remove the criminalization of any sexual acts between consenting adults.

11. Harlon Dalton, "Reflections on the Lesbian and Gay Marriage Debate", *Law and Sexuality: A Review of Lesbian and Gay Legal Issues*, Volume 1, Summer 1991, 1 at 7.

12. This general conception covers both narrower and broader conceptions of the Harm Principle. See Lyons, "Liberty and Harm to Others", for a discussion of the debate over how narrowly or broadly Mill's principle — which he calls the Principle of Liberty — should be construed. Brown argues that the principle should cover only harm producing conduct and Lyons argues that it should be expanded to include harm preventing conduct, which may not itself be harm producing — for example, good samaritan behaviour and joint cooperation behaviour. My conception differs from that of both of these versions in that I focus on the justification of the denial of state benefits rather than the justification of the interference with liberty.

13. Andrew Sullivan, in "Here Comes the Groom: A (Conservative) Case for Gay Marriage", *The New Republic*, August 28, 1989, 20. Catherine MacKinnon points out that "persons secure in their heterosexuality would not be threatened by the availability of this option", ie. gay marriage.

MacKinnon, *Feminism Unmodified: Discourses on Life and Law*, Harvard University Press, 1987, at 27.

14. Michael Levin, in "Why Homosexuality is Abnormal," for example, attempts to provide a teleological account of the harm that homosexuality presents. If his argument were persuasive, then paternalism would seem to follow. Michael Ruse's discussion of the claim that homosexuality is unnatural in "Is Homosexuality Bad Sexuality?" tends to undercut Levin's claims. Both papers can be found in *Moral Controversies: Race, Class, and Gender in Applied Ethics*, edited by Steven Jay Gold, Wadsworth, 1993.

15. It would be inaccurate and inappropriate to speak of "the" gay, lesbian, and bisexual community; but it would be equally inaccurate and inappropriate to speak of "the" gay, "the" lesbian, or "the" bisexual community. There are communities, and communities within communities. It might be possible to speak of a community of communities, but even that might be misleading. One can get a sense of the remarkable range of conceptions of equality for gays, lesbians and bisexuals and of the range of recommended strategies from reading Paul Berman's essay "Democracy and Homosexuality", in *The New Republic,* and from the following books (two of which Berman reviews): Bruce Bawer, *A Place at the Table: The Gay Individual in American Society*; Mark Blasuis, *A Politics of Sexuality: The Emergence of a Lesbian and Gay Ethos*; Diana Fuss, *Essentially Speaking: Feminism, Nature and Difference*; Marshall Kirk and Hunter Madsen, *After the Ball: How America Will Conquer Its Fear and Hatred of Gays in the 1990s*; Shane Phelan, *Identity Politics: Lesbian Feminism and the Limits of Community*; Michelangelo Signorile's *Queer in America: Sex, the Media and the Closets of Power*. There are many more references that could be given, but this list is sufficient to cover the range from separatist liberation perspectives to conservative assimilationist perspectives. Chris Bull's article in the *Advocate*, "Till Death Do Us Part" and Michelangelo Signorile's article in *Out*, "Bridal Wave" gave some indication of the range of positions on same sex marriage among gays and lesbians.

16. See David Chambers, "Tales of Two Cities: AIDS and the Legal Recognition of Domestic Partnerships in San Francisco and New York". Domestic Partnership ordinances have been enacted by municipalities in various U.S. cities. The domestic partnership arrangements usually contain a requirement that same sex couples register as partners — "two people who have chosen to share one another's lives in an intimate and committed relationship of mutual caring". Chambers, supra, at 185. The other feature of the arrangements is the provision by public and private employers that those couples who have registered will be entitled to the benefits provided to "spouses". Domestic Partnership regimes in the U.S. have usually been open to both homosexual and heterosexual unmarried couples. See Dunlap, at 94 and Posner, at 313–314 on the arrangements in Denmark and Sweden. Richard Posner's discussion is part of a larger work, *Sex and Reason*, Harvard University Press, 1992.

17. Many of the discussions of the issue by gay and lesbian activists focus on this aspect. For example, Michael Lowenthal in "Wedding Bells and Whistles" says that "[w]inning domestic-partnership privileges won't lead to acceptance for all lesbians and gay men, only for those in domestic partnerships". He then goes on to say: "[r]ather than lobbying for policies that will benefit only those who choose to register domestic partnerships, we should be fighting for the fundamental civil rights that will guarantee equal treatment for us all". See Lowenthal, *The Advocate*, December 4, 1993, 5.

18. Suzanne Sherman points to the divided opinion on the topic among the interviewees for her book, *Lesbian and Gay Marriage: Private Commitments, Public Ceremonies*, Temple University Press, 1992. See p. 8.

19. Nitya Duclos, "Some Complicating Thoughts on Same Sex Marriage", supra at 31. Paula Ettelbrick, one of those most strongly opposed to same sex marriages admits that: "[w]hen analyzed from a standpoint of civil rights, certainly lesbians and gay men should have a right to marry". Ettelbrick, "Since When Is Marriage a Path to Liberation?", in Sherman, ed., *Lesbian and Gay Marriage*, at 21.

20. Michael Lowenthal says in "Wedding Bells and Whistles" that he was part of efforts to obtain legal recognition of domestic partnerships but came to realize that the administration of the college where he worked "would accept us only to the degree that we conformed to straight standards". Lowenthal, p. 5.

21. The objection is framed this way by Mary Dunlap in "The Lesbian and Gay Marriage Debate: A Microcosm of Our Hopes and Troubles in the Nineties", *Law and Sexuality: A Review of Lesbian*

and Gay Legal Issues, Volume 1, Summer 1991, 63 at 78 and Nan Hunter in "Marriage, Law and Gender . . .", supra, at 12. Dunlap asks "If Outlaws Can Have In-Laws Then Won't Those Without In-Laws Become Outer Outlaws?" Nitya Duclos discusses the issue several times in "Some Complicating Thoughts on Same Sex Marriage". Paula Ettelbrick says, "gay marriage, instead of liberating gay sex and sexuality, would further outlaw all gay and lesbian sex that is not performed in a marital context". See Ettelbrick, "Since When Is Marriage a Path to Liberation?", supra, at 23.

22. This is a reconstruction of the various positions presented in the papers by Hunter, Duclos, and Ettelbrick.

23. Homophobia has become a common term for the unjust denial of civil rights to homosexuals, as well as to the irrational fear and hatred of homosexuals and homosexuality. The term was initially used in psychiatric literature to refer to the 'phobia' that one might be a homosexual oneself. The term has taken on a broader meaning, one which functions in many respects analogously to sexism, racism, ableism, and classism. The term heterosexism is often used in the same contexts as homophobia.

24. Nan Hunter, supra, at 11.

25. Harlon Dalton, "Reflections on the Lesbian and Gay Marriage Debate", supra, at 5. As Dalton points out, "legal rights would never be extended if the bare fact that a subset of the class might thereby be disadvantaged were deemed to constitute a sufficient ground for inaction". He goes on to say that it is still problematic to pursue policies which will have the unintended effects of favouring some class members over others.

26. While this conflict is most readily treated as a conflict between individual and collective interests, it can also be conceived as a conflict between different collective interests and thus competing versions of collective rights – the interests of assimilationists and the interests of anti-assimilationists respectively. C.f. Leslie Green, "Two Views of Collective Rights". *Canadian Journal of Law and Jurisprudence*, Volume 4(2), 1991, 315 at 325.

27. Hunter, supra, at 11. Hunter identifies two arguments that opponents to same sex marriage within lesbian, gay, and bisexual communities have relied on: the one about assimilation and stigmatization and the other one about the oppressiveness of marriage. Duclos and Dunlap also provide extensive discussion of the claim concerning marriage.

28. See Duclos, Dunlap, and Hunter for extensive discussions of marriage as a patriarchal institution. Duclos points out that the provision of same sex marriage may serve to legitimate marriage, which would have bad consequences for heterosexually identified women. It is of course the legitimation of marriage that would have the bad consequences.

29. Dunlap, supra at 86 reproduces the following list of rights enjoyed by persons who marry: the right to obtain health insurance, bereavement leave, and make decisions when the partner is incapacitated; the right to visit the partner in hospitals, jails, mental institutions and other places restricted to family members; the right to claim dependency deductions and statuses; the right to claim estate and gift tax benefits; the right to file joint tax returns; the right of inheritance (particularly in case of intestacy); the right to sue for infliction of emotional distress by injury to the partner, for loss of consortium, wrongful death and other personal injuries; the right to claim marital communication privilege; the right to live in housing for married persons; and more. See Duclos, pp. 52–53 for a more extensive list. Duclos also sets out a list of burdens the marriage brings, which includes the following: "spouse in the house" rules for state welfare assistance; "spouse's" credit history taken into account in credit rating; disentitlement from government student loans on the basis of "spouse's" income; anti-nepotism rules in employment, and more. See Duclos, supra, at 53–54 for the complete list.

30. Thomas Stoddard makes this point in "Why Gay People Should Seek the Right to Marry", in Sherman, ed., *Lesbian and Gay Marriage*, at 18.

31. Nan Hunter, supra, at 13. See also Dunlap and Duclos for similar arguments.

32. Hunter, supra, at 16. As Catherine MacKinnon puts it in "Not By Law Alone" from *Feminism Unmodified: Discourses on Life and Law*: "I do think it might do something amazing to the entire institution of marriage to recognize the unity of "two" persons between whom no superiority or inferiority could be presumed on the basis of gender". MacKinnon, supra, at 27.

33. Thomas Stoddard, "Why Gay People Should Seek the Right to Marry", supra at 17.

34. See Dunlap for an extensive discussion of the harmful effects of the *Bowers v. Hardwick* decision and other homophobic state measures.

35. Duclos, supra, at 42.
36. Nan Hunter suggests that more encompassing changes be based on "gender dissent", which she says does not connote identity based on sexual orientation but rather conveys an active intent to disconnect power from gender and conveys an adversary relationship to dominance. Hunter, supra, at 29–30. She argues that the pursuit of domestic partnership laws should complement the pursuit of legalizing lesbian and gay marriage, and that "neither strategy is complete without the other". Hunter, supra, at 26. For more, on domestic partnership agreements, see David Chambers, "Tales of Two Cities . . .", supra.
37. It is interesting, and disconcerting, to note that the Danish government which provided the right to marry for same sex couples by an act of Parliament still restricted the right of lesbian and gay couples to adopt children. There would be no rationale for the continuing restriction on a liberal treatment of the issue such as I have been developing. See Dunlap, supra, at 94.

QUESTIONS

1. According to Alex Wellington, what are the basic tenets of liberalism?
2. What aspects of the functional definition of heterosexual couples does Wellington see as analogous to the case for same-sex couples?
3. Why is the harm principle relevant to an analysis of the issue of same-sex marriage? Wellington identifies two distinct sets of criticisms of same-sex marriage that have relied on an account of harm. What are they? What reasons does Wellington give for rejecting these accounts of harm?
4. Does Wellington provide a convincing case for seeing same-sex couples as the same as heterosexual couples and, thus, deserving of equal treatment under the law?

SEXISM

Marilyn Frye

The first philosophical project I undertook as a feminist was that of trying to say carefully and persuasively what sexism is, and what it is for someone, some institution or some act to be sexist. This project was pressed on me with considerable urgency because, like most women coming to a feminist perception of themselves and the world, I was seeing sexism everywhere and trying to make it perceptible to others. I would point out, complain and criticize, but most frequently my friends and colleagues would not see that what I declared to be sexist was sexist, or at all objectionable.

As the critic and as the initiator of the topic, I was the one on whom the burden of proof fell — it was I who had to explain and convince. Teaching philosophy had already taught me that people cannot be persuaded of things they are not ready to be persuaded of; there are certain complexes of will and prior experience which will inevitably block persuasion, no matter the merits of the case presented. I knew that even if I could explain fully and clearly what I was saying when I called something sexist, I would not necessarily be able to convince various others of the correctness of this claim. But what troubled me enormously

From The Politics of Reality: Essays in Feminist Theory *by Marilyn Frye. Crossing Press, 1983. Reprinted by permission of Crossing Press.*

was that I could not explain it in any way which satisfied me. It is this sort of moral and intellectual frustration which, in my case at least, always generates philosophy.

The following was the product of my first attempt to state clearly and explicitly what sexism is:

> The term 'sexist' in its core and perhaps most fundamental meaning is a term which characterizes anything whatever which creates, constitutes, promotes or exploits any irrelevant or impertinent marking of the distinction between the sexes.[1]

When I composed this statement, I was thinking of the myriads of instances in which persons of the two sexes are treated differently, or behave differently, but where nothing in the real differences between females and males justifies or explains the difference of treatment or behavior. I was thinking, for instance, of the tracking of boys into Shop and girls into Home Ec, where one can see nothing about boys or girls considered in themselves which seems to connect essentially with the distinction between wrenches and eggbeaters. I was thinking also of sex discrimination in employment — cases where someone otherwise apparently qualified for a job is not hired because she is a woman. But when I tried to put this definition of 'sexist' to use, it did not stand the test.

Consider this case: If a company is hiring a supervisor who will supervise a group of male workers who have always worked for male supervisors, it can scarcely be denied that the sex of a candidate for the job is relevant to the candidate's prospects of moving smoothly and successfully into an effective working relationship with the supervisees (though the point is usually exaggerated by those looking for excuses not to hire women). Relevance is an intrasystematic thing. The patterns of behavior, attitude and custom within which a process goes on determine what is relevant to what in matters of describing, predicting or evaluating. In the case at hand, the workers' attitudes and the surrounding customs of the culture make a difference to how they interact with their supervisor and, in particular, *make* the sex of the supervisor a relevant factor in predicting how things will work out. So then, if the company hires a man, in preference to a more experienced and knowledgeable woman, can we explain our objection to the decision by saying it involved distinguishing on the basis of sex when sex is irrelevant to the ability to do the job? No: sex is relevant here.

So, what did I mean to say about 'sexist'? I was thinking that in a case of a candidate for a supervisory job, the reproductive capacity of the candidate has nothing to do with that person's knowing what needs to be done and being able to give properly timed, clear and correct directions. What I was picturing was a situation purified of all sexist perception and reaction. But, of course. *If* the whole context were not sexist, sex would not be an issue in such a job situation; indeed, it might go entirely unnoticed. It is precisely the fact that the sex of the candidate is relevant that is the salient symptom of the sexism of the situation.

I had failed, in that first essay, fully to grasp or understand that the locus of sexism is primarily in the system or framework, not in the particular act. It is not accurate to say that what is going on in cases of sexism is that distinctions are made on the basis of sex when sex is irrelevant; what is wrong in cases of sexism is, in the first place, that sex *is* relevant; and then that the making of distinctions on the basis of sex reinforces the patterns which make it relevant.

In sexist cultural/economic systems, sex is always relevant. To understand what sexism is, then, we have to step back and take a larger view.

Sex-identification intrudes into every moment of our lives and discourse, no matter what the supposedly primary focus or topic of the moment is. Elaborate, systematic, ubiquitous and redundant marking of a distinction between two sexes of humans and most animals is customary and obligatory. One *never* can ignore it.

Examples of sex-marking behavior patterns abound. A couple enters a restaurant; the headwaiter or hostess addresses the man and does not address the woman. The physician addresses the man by surname and honorific (Mr. Baxter, Rev. Jones) and addresses the woman by given name (Nancy, Gloria). You congratulate your friend — a hug, a slap on the back, shaking hands, kissing; one of the things which determines which of these you do is your friend's sex. In everything one does one has two complete repertoires of behavior, one for interactions with women and one for interactions with men. Greeting, storytelling, order-giving and order-receiving, negotiating, gesturing deference or dominance, encouraging, challenging, asking for information: one does all of these things differently depending upon whether the relevant others are male or female.

That this is so has been confirmed in sociological and socio-linguistic research,[2] but it is just as easily confirmed in one's own experience. To discover the differences in how you greet a woman and how you greet a man, for instance, just observe yourself, paying attention to the following sorts of things: frequency and duration of eye contact, frequency and type of touch, tone and pitch of voice, physical distance maintained between bodies, how and whether you smile, use of slang or swear words, whether your body dips into a shadow curtsy or bow. That I have two repertoires for handling introductions to people was vividly confirmed for me when a student introduced me to his friend, Pat, and I really could not tell what sex Pat was. For a moment I was stopped cold, completely incapable of action. I felt myself helplessly caught between two paths — the one I would take if Pat were female and the one I would take if Pat were male. Of course the paralysis does not last. One is rescued by one's ingenuity and good will; one can invent a way to behave as one says "How do you do?" to a human being. But the habitual ways are not for humans: they are one way for women and another for men.

Interlaced through all our behavior is our speaking — our linguistic behavior. Third person singular pronouns mark the sex of their referents. The same is true for a huge range of the nouns we use to refer to people ('guy', 'boy', 'lady', 'salesman', etc., and all the terms which covertly indicate the sex of the referent, like 'pilot', 'nurse', etc.), and the majority of given proper names ('Bob', 'Gwen', etc.).* In speaking, one constantly marks the sexes of those one speaks about.

The frequency with which our behavior marks the sexes of those we interact with cannot be exaggerated. The phenomenon is absolutely pervasive and deeply entrenched in all the patterns of behavior which are habitual, customary, acceptable, tolerable and intelligible. One can invent ways of behaving in one situation or another which are not sex-marking,

---

* Languages differ in their degree of "gender-loading" and there is evidence that these differences correlate with differences in the ages at which children "attain gender identity." In "Native Language and Cognitive Structures — A Cross-cultural Inquiry," Alexander Z. Guiora and Arthur Herold detail this evidence. They characterize English as having "minimal" gender-loading, Hebrew as having "maximum gender-loading" and Finnish as having "zero." If English, whose gender-marking seems so very prevalent to me, is an example of "minimal gender-loading," it seems safe to assume that gender-marking in human languages is indeed a significant factor in human experience generally. (The Guiora and Herold article may be requested from Dr. Guiora at Box No. 011, University Hospital, The University of Michigan, Ann Arbor, Michigan 48109.) I am indebted to Barbara Abbott for bringing this article to my attention.

which do not vary with the sexes of the persons involved, but if one were to succeed in removing sex-marking from one's behavior altogether, one's behavior would be so odd as to precipitate immediate crises of intelligibility and strenuous moral, religious or aesthetic objections from others. Everything one did would seem strange. And this is a matter of no small moment. We are a gregarious species. Our lives depend on our abilities to interact with others in relations of work, of exchange and of sympathy. What one cannot do without seeming excessively odd or unintelligible, one cannot do without severe disturbance to patterns of interaction upon which one's life depends. Sex-marking behavior is not optional; it is as obligatory as it is pervasive.

Closely connected with habitual and obligatory sex-marking is a constant and urgent need to know or be able to guess the sex of every single person with whom one has the slightest or most remote contact or interaction. If we are going to mark people's sexes in every situation, then we have to know their sexes. I needed to know whether "Pat" was endowed with a clitoris or a penis prior to making the first step in getting acquainted. If I am writing a book review, the use of personal pronouns to refer to the author creates the need to know whether that person's reproductive cells are the sort which produce ova or the sort which produce sperm. I cannot ask the time of day without first knowing or presuming I know my informant's potential role in reproduction. We are socially and communicatively helpless if we do not know the sex of everybody we have anything to do with, and for members of such a species as ours, such helplessness can be life-threatening. Our habitual behavior patterns make knowledge of each person's sex both pervasively pertinent and of the *first* importance. Furthermore, the importance and urgency of having such knowledge is intensified by another sort of factor which I think most people rarely notice because they *do* usually know the sexes of others.

In a culture in which one is deemed sinful, sick or disgusting (at least) if one is not heterosexual, it is very important to keep track of one's sexual feelings and the sexes of those who inspire them. If one is permitted sexual expression or gratification, or even mere feeling, with persons of one sex but not of the other, one has to know what sex each person is before one can allow one's heart to beat or one's blood to flow in erotic enjoyment of that person. Much of our ordinary and apparently nonsexual interaction and communication involves elements of sexual or erotic message, and these are *rigidly* regulated by sex taboos, including the taboo on homosexuality. The adjustment or maladjustment of these messages to the sex of the person in question can have wonderful or disastrous consequences. The thought that one might misapprehend the sex of another conjures nothing less than the holy dread of unwitting violation of powerful taboo. Thus all the tension connected with sexual taboo and repression intensifies the urgency of being acceptable and intelligible, and our need to know everyone's sex carries much of the weight of an acute and emotionally fraught survival need.

The pressure on each of us to guess or determine the sex of everybody else both generates and is exhibited in a great pressure on each of us to *inform* everybody all the time of our sex. For, if you strip humans of most of their cultural trappings, it is not always that easy to tell without close inspection which are female, which are male. The tangible and visible physical differences between the sexes are not particularly sharp or numerous. Individual variation along the physical dimensions we think of as associated with maleness and femaleness are great, and the differences between the sexes could easily be obscured by bodily decoration, hair removal and the like. One of the shocks, when one does mistake someone's sex, is the discovery of how easily one can be misled. We could not ensure that we could identify people by their sex virtually any time and anywhere under any conditions if they did not announce themselves, did not *tell* us in one way or another.

We do not, in fact, announce our sexes "in one way or another." We announce them in a thousand ways. We deck ourselves from head to toe with garments and decorations which serve like badges and buttons to announce our sexes. For every type of occasion there are distinct clothes, gear and accessories, hairdos, cosmetics and scents, labeled as "ladies'" or "men's" and labeling us as females or males, and most of the time most of us choose, use, wear or bear the paraphernalia associated with our sex. It goes below the skin as well. There are different styles of gait, gesture, posture, speech, humor, taste and even of perception, interest and attention that we learn as we grow up to be women or to be men and that label and announce us as women or as men. It begins early in life: even infants in arms are color coded.

That we wear and bear signs of our sexes, and that this is compulsory, is made clearest in the relatively rare cases when we do not do so, or not enough. Responses ranging from critical to indignant to hostile meet mothers whose small children are not immediately sex-identifiable, and hippies used to be accosted on the streets (by otherwise reserved and polite people) with criticisms and accusations when their clothing and style gave off mixed and contradictory sex-announcements. Anyone in any kind of job placement service and any Success Manual will tell you that you cannot expect to get or keep a job if your clothing or personal style is ambiguous in its announcement of your sex. You don't go to a job interview wearing the other sex's shoes and socks.

The buzz on this last example indicates another source of pressure to inform each other of our sexes, namely, once again, the requirement that one be and appear heterosexual. Queerly enough, one appears heterosexual by informing people of one's sex *very* emphatically and *very* unambiguously, and one does this by heaping into one's behavior and upon one's body ever more and more conclusive sex-indicators. For homosexuals and lesbians who wish to pass as heterosexual, it is these indicators that provide most of the camouflage; for those who wish to avoid being presumed heterosexual, the trick is to deliberately cultivate ambiguous sex-indicators in clothes, behavior and style. In a culture in which homosexuality and lesbianism are violently and almost universally forbidden, and heterosexuality is announced by announcing one's sex, it always behooves one to announce one's sex.

The information as to what sex one is is always wanted, and supplying it is always appropriate to one's own and others' most constant and pervasive interests — interests in being and remaining viable in the available human community.

The intense demand for marking and for asserting what sex each person is adds up to a strenuous requirement that there *be* two distinct and sharply dimorphic sexes. But, in reality, there are not. There are people who fit on a biological spectrum between two not-so-sharply defined poles. In about 5 percent of live births, possibly more, the babies are in some degree and way not perfect exemplars of male and female. There are individuals with chromosome patterns other than XX or XY and individuals whose external genitalia at birth exhibit some degree of ambiguity. There are people who are chromosomally "normal" who are at the far ends of the normal spectra of secondary sex characteristics — height, musculature, hairiness, body density, distribution of fat, breast size, etc. — whose overall appearance fits the norm of people whose chromosomal sex is the opposite of theirs.[3]

These variations not withstanding, persons (mainly men, of course) with the power to do so actually *construct* a world in which men are men and women are women and there is nothing in between and nothing ambiguous; they do it by chemically and/or surgically altering people whose bodies are indeterminate or ambiguous with respect to sex. Newborns with "imperfectly formed" genitals are immediately "corrected" by chemical or surgical means, children and adolescents are given hormone "therapies" if their bodies seem not to be developing according to what physicians and others declare to be the norm for what has been declared to be that individual's sex. Persons with authority recommend and supply cosmetics and cosmetic regimens, diets, exercises and all manner of clothing to revise or disguise the too-hairy lip, the too-large breast, the too-slender shoulders, the too-large feet, the too-great or too-slight stature. Individuals whose bodies do not fit the picture of exactly two sharply dimorphic sexes are often enough quite willing to be altered or veiled for the obvious reason that the world punishes them severely for their failure to be the "facts" which would verify the doctrine of two sexes. The demand that the world be a world in which there are exactly two sexes is inexorable, and we are all compelled to answer to it emphatically, unconditionally, repetitiously and unambiguously.

Even being physically "normal" for one's assigned sex is not enough. One must *be* female or male, actively. Again, the costumes and performances. Pressed to acting feminine or masculine, one colludes (co-lude: play along) with the doctors and counselors in the creation of a world in which the apparent dimorphism of the sexes is so extreme that one can only think there is a great gulf between female and male, that the two are, essentially and fundamentally and naturally, utterly different. One helps to create a world in which it seems to us that we *could* never mistake a woman for a man or a man for a woman. We never need worry.

Along with all the making, marking and announcing of sex-distinction goes a strong and visceral feeling or attitude to the effect that sex-distinction is the most important thing in the world: that it would be the end of the world if it were not maintained, clear and sharp and rigid; that a sex-dualism which is rooted in the nature of the beast is absolutely crucial and fundamental to all aspects of human life, human society and human economy. Where feminism is perceived as a project of blurring this distinction, antifeminist rhetoric is vivid with the dread that the world will end if the feminists have their way.[4] Some feminists' insistence that the feminist goal is not a "unisex" society is defensive in a way that suggests they too believe that culture or civilization would not survive blurring the distinction. I think that one of the sources of the prevalence and profundity of this conviction and dread is our immersion in the very behavior patterns I have been discussing.

It is a general and obvious principle of information theory that when it is very, very important that certain information be conveyed, the suitable strategy is redundancy. If a message *must* get through, one sends it repeatedly and by as many means or media as one has at one's command. On the other end, as a receiver of information, if one receives the same information over and over, conveyed by every medium one knows, another message comes through as well, and implicitly: the message that this information is very, very important. The enormous frequency with which information about people's sexes is conveyed conveys implicitly the message that this topic is enormously important. I suspect that this is the single topic on which we most frequently receive information from others throughout our entire lives. If I am right, it would go part way to explaining why we end up with an almost irresistible impression, unarticulated, that the matter of people's sexes is the most important and most fundamental topic in the world.

We exchange sex-identification information, along with the implicit message that it is very important, in a variety of circumstances in which there really is no concrete or experientially obvious point in having the information. There are reasons, as this discussion has shown, why you should want to know whether the person filling your water glass or your tooth is male or female and why that person wants to know what you are, but those reasons are woven invisibly into the fabric of social structure and they do not have to do with the bare mechanics of things being filled. Furthermore, the same culture which drives us to this constant information exchange also simultaneously enforces a strong blanket rule requiring that the simplest and most nearly definitive physical manifestations of sex difference be hidden from view in all but the most private and intimate circumstances. The double message of sex-distinction and its pre-eminent importance is conveyed, in fact, in part *by* devices which systematically and deliberately cover up and hide from view the few physical things which do (to a fair extent) distinguish two sexes of humans. The messages are overwhelmingly dissociated from the concrete facts they supposedly pertain to, and from matrices of concrete and sensible reasons and consequences.

Small children's minds must be hopelessly boggled by all this. We know our own sexes, and learn to think it a matter of first importance that one is a girl or a boy so early that we do not remember not knowing — long before physical differences in our young bodies could make more than the most trivial practical differences. A friend of mine whose appearance and style have a little bit about them that is gender-ambiguous walked past a mother and child, and heard the child ask the mother, "Is she a man or a woman?" The struggle to divine some connection between social behavior and physical sex, and the high priority of it all, seem painfully obvious here.

If one is made to feel that a thing is of prime importance, but common sensory experience does not connect it with things of obvious concrete and practical importance, then there is mystery, and with that a strong tendency to the construction of mystical or metaphysical conceptions of its importance. If it is important, but not of mundane importance, it must be of transcendent importance. All the more so if it is *very* important.*

This matter of our sexes must be very profound indeed if it must, on pain of shame and ostracism, be covered up and must, on pain of shame and ostracism, be boldly advertised by every means and medium one can devise.

There is one more point about redundancy that is worth making here. If there is one thing more effective in making one believe a thing than receiving the message repetitively, it is rehearsing it repetitively. Advertisers, preachers, teachers, all of us in the brainwashing professions, make use of this apparently physical fact of human psychology routinely. The redundancy of sex-marking and sex-announcing serves not only to make the topic seem transcendently important, but to make the sex-duality it advertises seem transcendently and unquestionably *true*.

It is quite a spectacle, really, once one sees it, these humans so devoted to dressing up and acting out and "fixing" one another so everyone lives up to and lives out the theory that

---

* For some readers it will be useful to note a connection here with H.P. Grice's doctrine of conversational implicatures. There is a conversational "rule" to the effect that a speaker should "be relevant." As audiences we assume information given us is relevant, and if we cannot see its relevance we generally assume the relevance is to something hidden or that we are somehow missing something others see; or we invent a relevance by reconstruing the information as about something other than it initially appeared to be about. (Grice, "Logic and Conversation," *The Logic of Grammar*, edited by Donald Davidson and Gilbert Harman [Dickenson Publishing Company, Inc., Encino, California and Belmont, California, 1975], pp. 64-75.)

there are two sharply distinct sexes and never the twain shall overlap or be confused or conflated; these hominids constantly and with remarkable lack of embarrassment marking a distinction between two sexes as though their lives depended on it. It is wonderful that homosexuals and lesbians are mocked and judged for "playing butch-femme roles" and for dressing in "butch-femme drag," for nobody goes about in full public view as thoroughly decked out in butch and femme drag as respectable heterosexuals when they are dressed up to go out in the evening, or to go to church, or to go to the office. Heterosexual critics of queers' "role-playing" ought to look at themselves in the mirror on their way out for a night on the town to see who's in drag. The answer is, everybody is. Perhaps the main difference between heterosexuals and queers is that when queers go forth in drag, they know they are engaged in theater — they are playing and they know they are playing. Heterosexuals usually are taking it all perfectly seriously, thinking they are in the real world, thinking they *are* the real world.

Of course, in a way, they are the real world. All this bizarre behavior has a function in the construction of the real world.

Sex-marking and sex-announcing are equally compulsory for males and females; but that is as far as equality goes in this matter. The meaning and import of this behavior is profoundly different for women and for men.

Imagine. . .

A colony of humans established a civilization hundreds of years ago on a distant planet. It has evolved, as civilizations will. Its language is a descendant of English.

The language has personal pronouns marking the child/adult distinction, and its adult personal pronouns mark the distinction between straight and curly pubic hair. At puberty each person assumes distinguishing clothing styles and manners so others can tell what type she or he is without the closer scrutiny which would generally be considered indecent. People with straight pubic hair adopt a style which is modest and self-effacing and clothes which are fragile and confining; people with curly pubic hair adopt a style which is expensive and prepossessing and clothes which are sturdy and comfortable. People whose pubic hair is neither clearly straight nor clearly curly alter their hair chemically in order to be clearly one or the other. Since those with curly pubic hair have higher status and economic advantages, those with ambiguous pubic hair are told to make it straight, for life will be easier for a low-status person whose category might be doubted than for a high-status person whose category might be doubted.

It is taboo to eat or drink in the same room with any person of the same pubic hair type as oneself. Compulsory heterogourmandism, it is called by social critics, though most people think it is just natural human desire to eat with one's pubic-hair opposite. A logical consequence of this habit, or taboo, is the limitation to dining only singly or in pairs — a taboo against banquetism, or, as the slang expression goes, against the group gulp.

Whatever features an individual male person has which tend to his social and economic disadvantage (his age, race, class, height, etc.), one feature which never tends to his disadvantage in the society at large is his maleness. The case for females is the mirror image of this. Whatever features an individual female person has which tend to her social and economic advantage (her age, race, etc.), one feature which always tends to her disadvantage is her femaleness. Therefore, when a male's sex-category is the thing about him that gets first and most repeated notice, the thing about him that is being framed and emphasized and given primacy is a feature which in general is an asset to him. When a female's sex-category is the thing about her that gets first and most repeated notice, the thing about her that is being framed and emphasized and given primacy is a feature which in general is a liability to her. Manifestations of this divergence in the meaning and consequences of sex-announcement can be very concrete.

Walking down the street in the evening in a town or city exposes one to some risk of assault. For males the risk is less; for females the risk is greater. If one announces oneself male, one is presumed by potential assailants to be more rather than less likely to defend oneself or be able to evade the assault and, if the male-announcement is strong and unambiguous, to be a noncandidate for sexual assault. If one announces oneself female, one is presumed by potential assailants to be less rather than more likely to defend oneself or to evade the assault and, if the female-announcement is strong and unambiguous, to be a prime candidate for sexual assault. Both the man and the woman "announce" their sex through style of gait, clothing, hair style, etc., but they are not equally or identically affected by announcing their sex. The male's announcement tends toward his protection or safety, and the female's announcement tends toward her victimization. It could not be more immediate or concrete; the meaning of the sex-identification could not be more different.

The sex-marking behavioral repertoires are such that in the behavior of almost all people of both sexes addressing or responding to males (especially within their own culture/race) generally is done in a manner which suggests basic respect, while addressing or responding to females is done in a manner that suggests the females' inferiority (condescending tones, presumptions of ignorance, overfamiliarity, sexual aggression, etc.). So, when one approaches an ordinary well-socialized person in such cultures, if one is male, one's own behavioral announcement of maleness tends to evoke supportive and beneficial response and if one is female, one's own behavioral announcement of femaleness tends to evoke degrading and detrimental response.

The details of the sex-announcing behaviors also contribute to the reduction of women and the elevation of men. The case is most obvious in the matter of clothing. As feminists have been saying for two hundred years or so, ladies' clothing is generally restrictive, binding, burdening and frail; it threatens to fall apart and/or to uncover something that is supposed to be covered if you bend, reach, kick, punch or run. It typically does not protect effectively against hazards in the environment, nor permit the wearer to protect herself against the hazards of the human environment. Men's clothing is generally the opposite of all this — sturdy, suitably protective, permitting movement and locomotion. The details of feminine manners and postures also serve to bind and restrict. To be feminine is to take up little space, to defer to others, to be silent or affirming of others, etc. It is not necessary here to survey all this, for it has been done many times and in illuminating detail in feminist writings. My point here is that though both men and women must behave in sex-announcing ways, the behavior which announces femaleness is in itself both physically and socially binding and limiting as the behavior which announces maleness is not.

The sex-correlated variations in our behavior tend systematically to the benefit of males and the detriment of females. The male, announcing his sex in sex-identifying behavior and dress, is both announcing and acting on his membership in a dominant caste — dominant within his subculture and to a fair extent across subcultures as well. The female, announcing her sex, is both announcing and acting on her membership in the subordinated caste. She is obliged to inform others constantly and in every sort of situation that she is to be treated as inferior, without authority, assaultable. She cannot move or speak within the usual cultural norms without engaging in self-deprecation. The male cannot move or speak without engaging in self-aggrandizement. Constant sex-identification both defines and maintains the caste boundary without which there could not be a dominance-subordination structure.

The forces which make us mark and announce sexes are among the forces which constitute the oppression of women, and they are central and essential to the maintenance of that system.

Oppression is a system of interrelated barriers and forces which reduce, immobilize and mold people who belong to a certain group, and effect their subordination to another group (individually to individuals of the other group, and as a group, to that group). Such a system could not exist were not the groups, the categories of persons, well defined. Logically, it presupposes that there are two distinct categories. Practically, they must be not only distinct but relatively easily identifiable; the barriers and forces could not be suitably located and applied if there were often much doubt as to which individuals were to be contained and reduced, which were to dominate.[5]

It is extremely costly to subordinate a large group of people simply by applications of material force, as is indicated by the costs of maximum security prisons and of military suppression of nationalist movements. For subordination to be permanent and cost effective, it is necessary to create conditions such that the subordinated group acquiesces to some extent in the subordination. Probably one of the most efficient ways to secure acquiescence is to convince the people that their subordination is inevitable. The mechanisms by which the subordinate and dominant categories are defined can contribute greatly to popular belief in the inevitability of the dominance/subordination structure.

For efficient subordination, what's wanted is that the structure not appear to be a cultural artifact kept in place by human decision or custom, but that it appear *natural* — that it appear to be a quite direct consequence of facts about the beast which are beyond the scope of human manipulation or revision. It must seem natural that individuals of the one category are dominated by individuals of the other and that as groups, the one dominates the other.[6] To make this seem natural, it will help if it seems to all concerned that members of the two groups are *very* different from each other, and this appearance is enhanced if it can be made to appear that within each group, the members are very like one another. In other words, the appearance of the naturalness of the dominance of men and the subordination of women is supported by anything which supports the appearance that men are very like other men and very unlike women, and that women are very like other women and very unlike men. All behavior which encourages the appearance that humans are biologically sharply sex-dimorphic encourages the acquiescence of women (and, to the extent it needs encouragement, of men) in women's subordination.

That we are trained to behave so differently as women and as men, and to behave so differently toward women and toward men, itself contributes mightily to the appearance of extreme natural dimorphism, but also, the *ways* we act as women and as men, and the *ways* we act toward women and toward men, mold our bodies and our minds to the shapes of subordination and dominance. We do become what we practice being.

Throughout this essay I have seemed to beg the question at hand. Should I not be trying to prove that there are few and insignificant differences between females and males, if that is what I believe, rather than assuming it? What I have been doing is offering observations which suggest that if one thinks there are biologically deep differences between women and men which cause and justify divisions of labor and responsibility such as we see in the modern patriarchal family and male-dominated workplace, one may *not* have arrived at this belief because of direct experience of unmolested physical evidence, but because our customs serve to construct that appearance; and I suggest that these customs are artifacts of culture which exist to support a morally and scientifically insupportable system of dominance and subordination.[7]

But also, in the end, I do not want to claim simply that there are not socially significant biologically-grounded differences between human females and males. Things are much more complex than that.

Enculturation and socialization are, I think, misunderstood if one pictures them as processes which apply layers of cultural gloss over a biological substratum. It is with that picture in mind that one asks whether this or that aspect of behavior is due to "nature" or "nurture." One means, does it emanate from the biological substratum or does it come from some layer of the shellac? A variant on this wrong picture is the picture according to which enculturation or socialization is something mental or psychological, as opposed to something physical or biological. Then one can think of attitudes and habits of perception, for instance, as "learned" versus "biologically determined." And again, one can ask such things as whether men's aggressiveness is learned or biologically determined, and if the former is asserted, one can think in terms of changing them while if the latter is asserted, one must give up all thought of reform.

My observations and experience suggest another way of looking at this. I see enormous social pressure on us all to act feminine or act masculine (and not both), so I am inclined to think that if we were to break the habits of culture which generate that pressure, people would not act particularly masculine or feminine. The fact that there are such penalties threatened for deviations from these patterns strongly suggests that the patterns would not be there but for the threats. This leads, I think, to a skeptical conclusion: we do not know whether human behavior patterns would be dimorphic along lines of chromosomal sex if we were not threatened and bullied; nor do we know, if we assume that they would be dimorphous, *what* they would be, that is, *what* constellations of traits and tendencies would fall out along that genetic line. And these questions are odd anyway, for there is no question of humans growing up *without* culture, so we don't know what other cultural variables we might imagine to be at work in a culture in which the familiar training to masculinity and femininity were not going on.

On the other hand, as one goes about in the world, and in particular as one tries out strategies meant to alter the behaviors which constitute and support male dominance, one often has extremely convincing experiences of the *inflexibility* of people in this respect, of a resistance to change which seems to run much, much deeper than willingness or willfulness in the face of arguments and evidence. As feminist activists, many of us have felt this most particularly in the case of men, and it has sometimes seemed that the relative flexibility and adaptability of women and the relative rigidity of men are so widespread within each group respectively, and so often and convincingly encountered, that they must be biologically given. And one watches men and women on the streets, and their bodies seem so different — one hardly can avoid thinking there are vast and profound differences between women and men without giving up the hard won confidence in one's powers of perception.

The first remedy here is to lift one's eyes from a single culture, class and race. If the bodies of Asian women set them apart so sharply from Asian men, see how different they are also from Black women; if white men all look alike and very different from white women, it helps to note that Black men don't look so like white men.

The second remedy is to think about the subjective experience we have of our *habits*. If one habitually twists a lock of one's hair whenever one is reading and has tried to break this habit, one knows how "bodily" it is; but that does not convince one it is genetically determined. People who drive to work every day often take the same route every day, and if they mean to take another route one day in order to do an errand on the way, they may find themselves at work, conveyed along the habitual route, without having revised the decision to do the errand. The habit of taking that course is mapped into one's body; it is not a matter of a decision — a mental event — that is repeated each day upon a daily re-judgment of the reasonableness of the course. It is also not genetic. We are animals. Learning is physical, bodily. There is not a separate, nonmaterial "control room" where socialization, enculturation and habit formation take place and where, since it is nonmaterial, change is independent of bodies and easier than in bodies.

Socialization molds our bodies; enculturation forms our skeletons, our musculature, our central nervous systems. By the time we are gendered adults, masculinity and femininity *are* "biological." They are structural and material features of how our bodies are. My experience suggests that they are changeable just as one would expect bodies to be — slowly, through constant practice and deliberate regimens designed to remap and rebuild nerve and tissue. This is how many of us *have* changed when we chose to change from "women" as culturally defined to "women" as we define ourselves. Both the sources of the changes and the resistances to them are bodily — are among the possibilities of our animal natures, whatever those may be.

But now "biological" does not mean "genetically determined" or "inevitable." It just means "of the animal."

It is no accident that feminism has often focused on our bodies. Rape, battering, reproductive self-determination, health, nutrition, self-defense, athletics, financial independence (control of the means of feeding and sheltering ourselves). And it is no accident that with varying degrees of conscious intention, feminists have tried to create separate spaces where women could exist somewhat sheltered from the prevailing winds of patriarchal culture and try to stand up straight for once. One needs space to *practice* an erect posture; one cannot just will it to happen. To retrain one's body one needs physical freedom from what are, in the last analysis, physical forces misshaping it to the contours of the subordinate.

The cultural and economic structures which create and enforce elaborate and rigid patterns of sex-marking and sex-announcing behavior, that is, create gender as we know it, mold us as dominators and subordinates (I do not say "mold our minds" or "mold our personalities"). They construct two classes of animals, the masculine and the feminine, where another constellation of forces might have constructed three or five categories, and not necessarily hierarchically related. Or such a spectrum of sorts that we would not experience them as "sorts" at all.

The term 'sexist' characterizes cultural and economic structures which create and enforce the elaborate and rigid patterns of sex-marking and sex-announcing which divide the species, along lines of sex, into dominators and subordinates. Individual acts and practices are sexist which reinforce and support those structures, either as culture or as shapes taken on by the enculturated animals. Resistance to sexism is that which undermines those structures by social and political action and by projects of reconstruction and revision of ourselves.

NOTES

1. "Male Chauvinism — A Conceptual Analysis," *Philosophy and Sex*, edited by Robert Baker and Frederick Elliston (Prometheus Books, Buffalo, New York, 1975), p. 66. The inadequacies of such an account of sexism are reflected in the inadequacies of a standard legal interpretation of what sex discrimination is as it is analyzed by Catharine A. MacKinnon in *Sexual Harassment of Working Women* (Yale University Press, New Haven and London, 1979), cf. Chapters 5 and 6. See also my review of this book, "Courting Gender Justice," *New Women's Times Feminist Review*, No. 17, September-October 1981, pp. 10–11.
2. See, for example, such works as *Body Politics: Power, Sex and Nonverbal Communication*, by Nancy Henley (Prentice-Hall, Englewood Cliffs, New Jersey, 1977); *Language and Sex: Difference and Dominance*, edited by Barrie Thorne and Nancy Henley (Newbury House Publishers, Rowley, Massachusetts, 1975); and *Gender and Nonverbal Behavior*, edited by Clara Mayo and Nancy M. Henley (Springer-Verlag, New York, 1981).
3. I rely here on lectures by Eileen Van Tassell in which she interpreted the generally available data on sex-characteristics, sex-differences and sex-similarities. One can refer, in particular, to *Man and Woman, Boy and Girl*, by John Money and Anke A. Ehrhardt (The Johns Hopkins University Press, 1972) and *Intersexuality*, edited by Claus Overzier (Academic Press, New York and London, 1963). See also, for instance: "Development of Sexual Characteristics," by A.D. Jost in *Science Journal*, Volume 6, No. 6 (especially the chart on page 71) which indicates the variety of "sex characteristics" which occurs in normal females and males; and "Growth and Endocrinology of the Adolescent," by J. M. Tanner in *Endocrine and Genetic Diseases of Childhood*, edited by L. Gardner (Saunders, Philadelphia & London, 1969), which tries to give clinical standards for evaluating the hormonal status of adolescent youth, and in which the author characterizes individuals which are well within the normal curve for males as "feminized males," thus, by implication, as "abnormal" males; and similarly, *mutatis mutandis*, for females.
4. See, for example, *Sexual Suicide*, by George F. Gilder (Quadrangle, New York, 1979). For an eloquent example of the Victorian version of this anxiety and the world view which underlies it, see "The Emancipation of Women," by Frederic Harrison in *Fortnightly Review*, CCXCVII, October 1, 1891, as quoted in a talk given by Sandra Siegel at the Berkshire Conference on Women's History, April 1981, entitled "Historiography, 'Decadence,' and the Legend of 'Separate Spheres' in Late Victorian England," which connects Victorian conceptions of civilization and the separateness and differentness of women and men.
5. See "Oppression," in this collection.
6. See "Feminist Leaders Can't Walk On Water," by Lorraine Masterson, *Quest: A Feminist Quarterly* (Volume II, Number 4, Spring, 1976), especially pp. 35–36 where the author refers to Paulo Freire's *Pedagogy of the Oppressed* and speaks to the special case of women's belief that our subordination is inevitable because rooted in biology.
7. Cf., the early and powerful article by Naomi Weisstein, "Psychology Constructs the Female," in *Woman in Sexist Society: Studies in Power and Powerlessness*, edited by Vivian Gornick and Barbara K. Moran (Basic Books, Inc., New York, 1971). Weisstein documents clearly that neither laypersons nor psychologists are the least bit dependable as observers of sex-correlated traits of people, and that theories of sex-difference based on "clinical experience" and based on primate studies are scientifically worthless.

QUESTIONS

1. Why does Frye revise her initial definition of sexism as that which promotes or exploits any irrelevant distinction between the sexes?
2. According to Frye, why do we need to examine the system or framework and not the particular discriminatory act in order to explore the moral dimensions of sexism?
3. Do you think the examples Frye provides of the marking of the distinction between the sexes succeed in revealing aspects of the immorality of sexism?
4. What does Frye mean when she says that "whatever features an individual male person has which tend to his social and economic disadvantage (his age, race, class, height, etc.), one feature which never tends to his disadvantage in the society at large is his maleness"? Do you agree with this claim?
5. Frye suggests that her analysis of sexism can also be applied to an analysis of discrimination on the basis of sexual orientation. How would this analysis differ from Wellington's?

SHOULD WHITE MEN PLAY THE BLUES?

James O. Young

1.

For the past few years the Canadian arts community has been racked by a debate about voice, or cultural, appropriation. Voice appropriation is supposed to occur when an artist from one cultural group (usually the member of a majority culture) makes the lives or experiences of members of another group (usually from a minority culture) the subject of an artwork. Appropriation of voice is also supposed to take place when members of one culture incorporate into their work images, stories, or other artistic elements which have been produced by another culture. A number of reasons have been advanced for thinking that voice appropriation is morally and aesthetically objectionable. While the debate has focused on the Canadian context, the issue of voice appropriation can arise in the context of any multicultural society. The issue is pressing in countries such as Australia, New Zealand, and the United States, which have a disadvantaged indigenous population, and nations, such as Britain and France, which have substantial immigrant communities from distinct cultures. Voice appropriation has been widely debated in the popular press and in the publications of the artistic community, but it has not yet received any rigorous and sustained philosophical attention. Once the matter receives such attention, we will see that nothing is inherently morally or aesthetically objectionable about artists borrowing from other cultures or making them the subject of their works.

The debate about voice appropriation has practical implications. If something is objectionable about voice appropriation, the question of what is to be done arises. Already one exhibition (at Montreal's Concordia University) has refused to display a picture of a black

From Journal of Value Inquiry, *v. 28 (1984), pp. 415–425. Reprinted by permission of Kluwer Academic Publishers and James O. Young.*

woman on the grounds that it was painted by a white woman and perpetuated racial stereotypes. One women's press has considered not publishing stories by white women about black women. The Canada Council, the country's primary granting agency for the arts, has asked its juries to be sensitive to the matter of cultural appropriation when adjudicating applications for funding.[1] What is to be done about the artistic treatment of other cultures is another question which cries out for careful philosophical scrutiny. Since I believe nothing is wrong with such treatments, the answer to the practical question is easily given: nothing need be done. Besides the normal criteria for judging works of art, no aesthetic or moral grounds exist for passing negative judgment on works of art which involve treatment of cultures other than the artist's. Any granting agency errs which uses voice appropriation as a criterion in apportioning funds.

At least three distinct lines of argument have been advanced in favor of the view that voice appropriation is morally and aesthetically suspect.[2] The first argument begins with the claim that members of one cultural group (call them "outsiders") will misrepresent the lives of members of another cultural group (call them "insiders"). By misrepresenting other cultures, outsiders harm the members of these cultures. Some opponents of voice appropriation have taken an even harder line and held, for example, that men should not write about women, heterosexuals should not write about homosexuals, and so on. I will limit the discussion to cultural appropriation. For example, the representation in Hollywood Westerns of native Americans as dim-witted and mendacious perpetuates harmful racial stereotypes. Harm could take more subtle forms. By presenting a distorted picture of another culture an outsider may hinder the ability of insiders to understand themselves. This is especially a danger when a minority culture is represented by outsiders from a majority culture. In this case, a danger may be that the voices of insiders will be overwhelmed by the voices of outsiders. Since it is wrong to harm people in these ways, opponents of voice appropriation conclude, artists should not treat cultures other than their own.

The second argument against cultural appropriation holds that when outsiders from a majority culture treat a minority culture, they limit the opportunity for insiders to find audiences for their treatments of their own cultures. The suggestion is that, in appropriating culture, outsiders also appropriate audiences. Audiences will read or view only a limited number of works about insider culture. Every time they view a work by an outsider, the probability decreases that they will view one by an insider. Moreover, if an outsider gets a grant to write, or make a film, about insider life, this entails less opportunity for insiders to get a grant. For economic and other reasons, when outsiders appropriate an audience, they also take away the insiders' ability to pursue their artistic activities. After all, artists need an audience to survive. This appropriation is particularly problematic when the outsiders are members of a majority, while insiders are of a minority. Minority cultures are likely to be more fragile and more in need of nurturing.

According to the third argument, some forms of voice appropriation are a kind of theft. Stories and visual imagery have been created by cultures. The aboriginal peoples of North America and Australasia have their legends and styles of pictorial representation. The legends or carved images of some societies frequently have religious or cultural significance. Arguably, insiders own the stories and images created by their culture. If so, outsiders who, without permission, make use of the products of another culture are guilty of theft. This argument, as well as the second, does not suggest that works which involve cultural appropriation are aesthetically objectionable. Advocates of this objection will likely believe, however, that such works are aesthetically problematic as well. Taken together, the objections to voice appropriation put a new spin on the old question of whether white men can play the blues.

2.

The first argument against voice appropriation is the strongest of the three, but four reasons show that it fails. The first argument has both an aesthetic and a moral element, and the moral case depends on an aesthetic premise. This premise states that all artworks which involve voice appropriation present distortions of insider culture. Consequently, the first grounds for rejecting the first argument are found in the many counter-examples to the thesis that works by outsiders always distort the culture of insiders. Secondly, the case that any such distortion leads to an amount of harm which always outweighs any good is difficult to make. The third rejoinder to the first argument grants that some works by outsiders distort and harm other cultures. The problem with such works, however, is not that they involve cultural appropriation but that they are poor works of art. The fourth counter-argument charges that the first argument is based on a mistaken conception of the relationship between works of art and cultures.

Those who hold that voice appropriation is harmful have a hard row to hoe when they claim that *all* treatments of alien cultures involve harmful distortion. The universal claim is the one they must make, however, or else they are compelled to admit that nothing is inherently wrong with treating other cultures. No one will deny that some objectionable cultural appropriation occurs or that something is wrong with harmful distortions. Room does exist for skepticism about the necessity of harmful distortions. Two claims are being made by opponents of voice appropriation. The first is that *all* such treatments involve distortion. The second is that *all* works by outsiders cause more harm than good. Both claims are highly dubious.

Begin by considering the first. The charge is that no amount of imagination and empathetic understanding on the part of outside artists could avoid distortion. The advocates of this argument are committed to saying that the works of Gauguin and Conrad, to mention two notable outsiders, misrepresent the cultures which they treat. Within the context of the treatment of native North Americans, the film *Black Robe* (1991), widely praised for its sensitivity to Indian culture, would involve distortion. If artists are unable to represent accurately cultures other than their own, we have no reason to suppose that anyone else can do so. So opponents of voice appropriation are committed to the claim that any treatment of other cultures, artistic or otherwise, involves distortion. Any histories of alien cultures or any social scientific studies will similarly involve distortion. Many histories and social scientific studies have involved distortion as outsiders impose their standards and values, but the thesis entails that *all* do.

Even if all works by outsiders involve distortion, that all such works are objectionable does not follow. The distortion could take a harmless form or even be beneficial. The insiders' culture, for example, could be represented in an unduly favorable manner which leads to increased interest in the culture, greater job opportunities for members of the culture, and so on. We need only think of the film *Dances with Wolves* (1990) to see that this is possible. Yet, grant for the sake of argument that all distortion of a culture by outside artists is harmful. The conclusion that all treatments of alien cultures are objectionable still would not follow. This conclusion would follow only given the premise that the amount of harm caused by such treatments outweighed the amount of good they cause. We have little reason to suppose this premise is true. Consider, for example, *The Merchant of Venice* and *Othello*. We can have little doubt but that both involve treatments and distortions of minority cultures by a member of a majority culture. Nevertheless, that Shakespeare penned them is a good thing on balance. Few Jews or blacks have been disadvantaged as a result of these plays. (Almost no one reads about Shylock and then smashes the windows of the local synagogue.) Nowhere near enough people have been harmed so badly as to outweigh the enjoyment and understanding which the Bard's plays have made possible. Many of those who have enjoyed and gained from the plays have been Jewish or black.

Nevertheless, some works by outsiders harmfully distort other cultures. The example of Hollywood Westerns has been provided but many more could be given. Stories about North American Indians by W.P. Kinsella (best known for his baseball stories) have been singled out (rightly or wrongly) as perpetuating harmful stereotypes. This concession is not enough, however, to establish the conclusion that voice appropriation is objectionable. Such works are not objectionable because they purport to be accurate representations of an alien culture but fail to provide such a representation. They attempt, in a rudimentary fashion, to increase an audience's understanding of historical events (the "heroic" settlement of the West) but are unsuccessful. Such works are morally objectionable because they fail aesthetically in this manner, and this failure leads to social harm. They are not objectionable because they are created by outsiders. Anyone who has any doubt about this should reflect that the works would be just as objectionable if they were created (through incompetence or self-loathing) by insiders.

The most basic rejoinder to the argument that cultural appropriation involves harmful distortion suggests that the argument completely misconstrues the relationship between an artwork and a culture. Artists who treat any culture do not simply copy it. All art involves interpretation and imaginative creation. In a sense, any artwork could be said to distort its object. This distortion is not grounds for saying that a work is aesthetically objectionable. The claim that it is grounds for negative aesthetic judgment would make *Hamlet* an aesthetic failure because people in Denmark do not speak English or see ghosts. Similarly, to object to *Heart of Darkness* on the grounds that it misrepresents the people of central Africa is to miss the point of the work.

The second and third arguments against voice appropriation are less serious. The second argument is an economic argument which cuts both ways. Every time an insider benefits from an audience, some outsider does not. There are no moral grounds for saying that an insider should receive an audience in preference to an outsider. No artist has a right to an audience. Artists may deserve an audience, but not because they are insiders or outsiders. They deserve an audience if they create worthwhile works. That good works of art are created is important. Who creates them is not important. If some reason exists for supposing that only insiders are able to create worthwhile artworks which treat their culture, we would have some reason to object to voice appropriation. But this claim has been seen to be highly dubious. Even if this claim were not dubious, the grounds for objecting to the works by outsiders would be ordinary aesthetic grounds: the works would not be aesthetically successful. Moreover, the claim that outsiders take economic advantages away from insiders is extremely questionable. Artists are not playing a zero-sum game. Consider, for example, in the realm of pop art, Paul Simon's appropriation of the music of South Africa's townships. The result of this appropriation has been an increased interest in the music of South Africa and more opportunities for South African musicians.

The consideration that art, not the artist, matters also tells against the view that insiders have some sort of inviolable right to their cultural creations. I can only endorse the views of

R.G. Collingwood on this matter. He wrote, "this fooling about personal [or cultural] property must cease. Let painters and writers and musicians steal with both hands whatever they can use, wherever they can find it."[3] Like Collingwood, I am not inclined to think that property rights count for much when it comes to artistic ideas. Even if we grant that members of a culture have property rights in the products of their culture, the opponents of voice appropriation would have to demonstrate that such rights could *never* be overridden. We should ask ourselves whether more good results from giving some artists a monopoly on certain artistic ideas or whether more good will come from allowing all artists to seek ideas wherever they are to be found. We have good reason to suppose that property rights could be overridden by our desire to maximize freedom of artistic expression and the production of valuable art.

The fact is that cultural appropriation does lead to good art. Consequently, I am inclined to say that Picasso did nothing wrong when he incorporated elements of non-Western art into his painting. No more did Stravinsky when he appropriated the rhythms and harmonies of other cultures. More recently, the American minimalist, Steve Reich, has learned from a master drummer of Ghana's Ewe tribe and, like so many other Western composers of this century, studied Balinese Gamelan music. Such influences have considerably enriched Western culture, and no reason has been presented for supposing that this appropriation has harmed anyone. In calculating the importance of property rights, we would do well to remember that truly new ideas are hard to come by in the arts. The incorporation into our culture of ideas developed in others is a valuable source of artistic inspiration. Ideas from different cultures can be combined to form new ideas. Arguably, in the hope that they will come up with new ideas, artists ought to be obliged to appropriate elements of other cultures into their works, not forbidden to do so.

One important context exists in which artists should, at least, hesitate before appropriating artistic forms of another culture. As has already been noted, many cultures endow certain images, stories, and compositions with religious or cultural significance. The use of these artistic elements in the art of outsiders might be regarded as sacrilege by insiders. The treatment of certain religious or cultural phenomena can be similarly controversial. In such cases, insiders are not being denied economic or artistic opportunity by voice appropriation. The suggestion is, rather, that the insiders are being done (what may be called) *moral harm*. The insiders feel, that is, that something essential to their cultural being is offended in some way. Salman Rushdie may be said to have done Moslems moral harm in writing *The Satanic Verses*, when he treated certain elements of Islamic culture. Since he was raised a Moslem, this is not obviously a case of voice appropriation. A clearer example is provided by the British television program *Spitting Image*, which ceased using a Jesus puppet at the request of some Moslems, who regard Jesus as a prophet and were offended by the program.

The possibility that insiders may be done moral harm should lead artists to be careful when appropriating artistic elements from other cultures (or treating sensitive aspects of other cultures: the same considerations apply). This possibility does not entail, however, that all instances of voice appropriation are objectionable. At least two reasons can be found for rejecting such an inference. For a start, not every artistic element of every community is fraught with religious or cultural significance. Consequently, artists need not refrain from appropriating some elements even if they ought not to commandeer others. Consequentialist reflections provide a second reason for thinking that the possibility of moral harm is not a decisive consideration. Suppose that an outsider incorporates the melody of a sacred hymn into a (secular) symphony and that members of culture which produced this hymn are offended by the use to which it is put. Suppose, however, that the resulting symphony is a great work of art and the insiders in question are only mildly annoyed. The aesthetic enjoyment that the symphony produces in many could easily outweigh the mild vexation felt by some insiders. The opponents of voice appropriation are, again, hobbled by the difficulty of proving that all instances are objectionable.

The consequentialist observation just offered perhaps understates the case against those who object to voice appropriation. Even if some instances of cultural appropriation could give rise to considerable moral harm, however, there is good reason to suppose that artists should not be denied access to any subjects or artistic forms. The value of artistic freedom is so great that artists should not be constrained in any way. Even if some artists who appropriate voice are insensitive, no effort ought to be made to prevent their work.

3.

The question of what is to be done about voice appropriation is much less pressing now that we see that it is not inherently objectionable. Still, investigating this question is worthwhile, since one national granting agency has already made a practice of taking cultural appropriation into account. Few opponents of voice appropriation have advocated a censorship which would ban works by outsiders about insiders. More have suggested that the members of majority cultures should regulate themselves and voluntarily refrain from treating minority cultures. The most controversial proposals have suggested that granting agencies should take steps to discourage voice appropriation. An agency could refrain from funding those who engage in voice appropriation and encourage artists from minority groups to treat their own cultures. An agency could also ensure that members of minority cultures play a role in adjudicating applications. If the goal of an agency is to support the best art, all of these steps are unnecessary, and some of them conflict with the goal.

The key practical question is concerned with what a granting agency should do when faced with applications from two artists, one an outsider and one an insider, who treat the same minority culture. The outsider has engaged in voice appropriation, while the insider has not. Several writers have suggested that, in choosing which artist to support, the agency can and should take into account that one artist has engaged in cultural appropriation while the other has not. The previous section established that nothing is inherently aesthetically or morally wrong with the artistic treatment of other cultures. That one work of art is by an insider and another is by an outsider is completely irrelevant in the aesthetic assessment of the works. Perhaps insiders, when writing about or otherwise treating their culture, will create more successful works. If so, then their works are to be preferred on purely aesthetic grounds, and the insiders should be funded because their works are better, not because they do not involve voice appropriation. Special criteria are not necessary. On the other hand, outsiders who attempt to portray an aspect of an alien culture but only create a clumsy and harmful distortion should not be funded because their works are aesthetically unsuccessful. Again, it does not matter who creates a work of art. All that matters is that good works are created.

When faced with instances of voice appropriation where the members of some community will be offended by the treatment of their culture or the use of certain of their artistic products, a granting agency may be tempted to take cultural appropriation into account when adjudicating applications. In practice, little danger exists that an agency will be in a position to fund artists whose works cause uncompensated moral harm. Artists engaged in voice appropriation which causes moral harm, without more than countervailing aesthetic benefits, are poor candidates for funding. After all, an agency should only fund artists who are likely to produce works with substantial aesthetic value. Artists whose works cannot counterbalance some moral harm will probably be denied support on purely aesthetic grounds. Quite apart from any consequentialist considerations, however, a granting agency should not lose sight of its primary goal: supporting artists of the highest quality. To a large measure, an agency should leave out of account any offense felt by members of any culture. An agency should not leave off funding overtly homosexual art, even if many people are seriously offended by this art. Similarly, an agency should not be unduly worried by the fact that members of some culture are aggrieved by appropriation of their voice.

Even if no grounds exist on which to discriminate against artists who depict other cultures, perhaps agencies should include minority members on juries to ensure that artists from minorities are not discriminated against. The Canada Council's Advisory Committee for Racial Equality in the Arts recommends that at least two members of each jury with five or more members be from minority groups and that the Council employ special assessors when considering non-Western art.[4] The suggestion is that only members of some culture will be able to appreciate fully the artistic methods and media of that culture. This is an extremely implausible claim. Many Western artists have admired the art of non-Western cultures. Critics have been equally receptive to the art of other cultures. We need look no further than Clive Bell, one of the most influential critics of this century, to see that this is the case. Bell was the great champion of what used to be called "primitive" art.[5] Even Kenneth Clark, whose name is almost synonymous with the study of Western civilization, was a connoisseur of many non-Western arts. If, however, we grant that critics can only appreciate the works of their cultures, the very idea of a national funding agency is undermined. We will have to settle for an aesthetic apartheid. Members of each culture will have to judge and appreciate the works of their culture and no other.

Those worried about voice appropriation have one last ditch to defend. They could point out that many members of minority groups are denied the training and education which would allow them to give artistic expression to their cultures. This fact is scarcely deniable when many aboriginal peoples live on unspeakable reserves and other minority groups are largely confined to decaying inner cities. While the plight of minority cultures is undeniable, it is scarcely relevant to the matter at hand. Their plight is not the result of voice appropriation. Any decent society will take immediate and energetic steps to improve the condition and the education of minority groups, but this is hardly a job for an agency whose role is to support accomplished and promising artists.

We are now in a position to answer the question which forms the title of this essay. White musicians should feel free to play the blues, even though the blues were developed by members of a minority culture. White musicians may even compose songs about black culture. Common decency dictates that, in doing so, they should be sensitive to the integrity of black culture. More generally, artists from one cultural group should feel free to appropriate elements from the art of other cultures and take other cultures as the subjects of their art. If these artists produce aesthetically successful works, they are deserving of support from granting agencies.[6]

NOTES

1. Canada Council, *Recommendations of the Advisory Committee to the Canada Council for Racial Equality in the Arts and the Response of the Canada Council* (Ottawa, 1992), p. 6.
2. For this taxonomy of the arguments against voice appropriation see, Thomas Hurka, "Should Whites Write about Minorities?" *Globe and Mail* (19 December 1989), p. 8. I am grateful to Professor Hurka for providing me with a copy of this article and for drawing my attention to several other pieces on the subject of cultural appropriation.
3. R.G. Collingwood, *The Principles of Art* (Oxford: Oxford University Press, 1958), p. 320.
4. Canada Council, *Recommendations*, pp. 4–5. The Council did not agree that a quota should be accepted for minority members on its juries, although it does express commitment to the inclusion of more members of minority groups on its juries.
5. Clive Bell, *Art* (London: Chatto and Windus, 1914).
6. In the course of writing this essay I profited from the comments of C.B. Daniels, Lana Simpson, Mark Tatchell, and Sheldon Wein. A version of this essay was read at a session of the Northwest Conference on Philosophy, Boise, Idaho, 7 November 1992. I am grateful to the audience at this session and particularly to John Rowell, the commentator, and Paul Tate, the chair.

QUESTIONS

1. James Young identifies three distinct lines of argument that have been used to defend the view that voice appropriation is morally suspect. What are they?
2. How does Young answer the charge that representations of cultures by outsiders to that culture are harmful?
3. Compare and contrast Young's account of the relevance of differences to Frye's account.
4. Do you agree with Young that voice appropriation is not morally objectionable?

THE NEW CULTURAL POLITICS OF DIFFERENCE

Cornel West

In the last few years of the twentieth century, there is emerging a significant shift in the sensibilities and outlooks of critics and artists. In fact, I would go so far as to claim that a new kind of cultural worker is in the making, associated with a new politics of difference. These new forms of intellectual consciousness advance new conceptions of the vocation of critic and artist, attempting to undermine the prevailing disciplinary divisions of labor in the academy, museum, mass media, and gallery networks while preserving modes of critique within the ubiquitous commodification of culture in the global village. Distinctive features of the new cultural politics of difference are to trash the monolithic and homogeneous in the name of diversity, multiplicity, and heterogeneity; to reject the abstract, general, and universal in light of the concrete, specific, and particular; and to historicize, contextualize, and pluralize by highlighting the contingent, provisional, variable, tentative, shifting, and changing. Needless to say, these gestures are not new in the history of criticism or art, yet what makes them novel — along with the cultural politics they produce — is what constitutes difference and how it is constituted, the weight and gravity it is given in representation, and

From October, *53 (Summer 1990), pp. 93–109. Copyright ©1990 by permission of October Magazine, Ltd. and the Massachusetts Institute of Technology.*

the way in which highlighting issues like exterminism, empire, class, race, gender, sexual orientation, age, nation, nature, and region at this historical moment acknowledges some discontinuity and disruption from previous forms of cultural critique. To put it bluntly, the new cultural politics of difference consists of creative responses to the precise circumstances of our present moment — especially those of marginalized first world agents who shun degraded self-representations, articulating instead their sense of the flow of history in light of the contemporary terrors, anxieties, and fears of highly commercialized North Atlantic capitalist cultures (with their escalating xenophobias against people of color, Jews, women, gays, lesbians, and the elderly). The nationalist revolts against the legacy of hegemonic party henchmen in second world excommunist cultures, and the diverse cultures of the majority of inhabitants on the globe smothered by international communication cartels and repressive postcolonial elites (sometimes in the name of communism, as in Ethiopia) or starved by austere World Bank and IMF policies that subordinate them to the North (as in free-market capitalism in Chile), also locate vital areas of analysis in this new cultural terrain.

The new cultural politics of difference are neither simply oppositional in contesting the mainstream (or *male*stream) for inclusion nor transgressive in the avant-gardist sense of shocking conventional bourgeois audiences. Rather they are distinct articulations of talented (and usually privileged) contributors to culture who desire to align themselves with demoralized, demobilized, depoliticized, and disorganized people in order to empower and enable social action and, if possible, to enlist collective insurgency for the expansion of freedom, democracy, and individuality. This perspective impels these cultural critics and artists to reveal, as an integral component of their production, the very operations of power within their immediate work contexts (i.e., academy, museum, gallery, mass media). This strategy, however, also puts them in an inescapable double bind — while linking their activities to the fundamental, structural overhaul of these institutions, they often remain financially dependent on them. (So much for "independent" creation.) For these critics of culture, theirs is a gesture that is simultaneously progressive and co-opted. Yet without social movement or political pressure from outside these institutions (extraparliamentary and extracurricular actions like the social movements of the recent past), transformation degenerates into mere accommodation or sheer stagnation, and the role of the "co-opted progressive" — no matter how fervent one's subversive rhetoric — is rendered more difficult. In this sense there can be no artistic breakthrough or social progress without some form of crisis in civilization — a crisis usually generated by organizations or collectivities that convince ordinary people to put their bodies and lives on the line. There is, of course, no guarantee that such pressure will yield the result one wants, but there is a guarantee that the status quo will remain or regress if no pressure is applied at all.

The new cultural politics of difference faces three basic challenges — intellectual, existential, and political. The intellectual challenge — usually cast as a methodological debate in these days in which academicist forms of expression have a monopoly on intellectual life — is how to think about representational practices in terms of history, culture, and society. How does one understand, analyze, and enact such practices today? An adequate answer to this question can be attempted only after one comes to terms with the insights and blindnesses of earlier attempts to grapple with the question in light of the evolving crisis in different histories, cultures, and societies. I shall sketch a brief genealogy — a history that highlights the contingent origins and often ignoble outcomes — of exemplary critical responses to the question. . . .

By 1914 European maritime empires had dominion over more than half of the land and a third of the peoples in the world — almost seventy-two million square kilometers of territory and more than 560 million people around colonial rule. Needless to say, this European control included brutal enslavement, institutional terrorism, and cultural degradation of black diaspora people. The death of roughly seventy-five million Africans during the centuries-long, transatlantic slave trade is but one reminder, among others, of the assault on black humanity. The black diaspora condition of New World servitude — in which people of African descent were viewed as mere commodities with production value, who had no proper legal status, social standing, or public worth — can be characterized, following Orlando Patterson, as natal alienation. This state of perpetual and inheritable domination that diaspora Africans had at birth produced the *modern black diaspora problematic of invisibility and namelessness.* White supremacist practices — enacted under the auspices of the prestigious cultural authorities of the churches, print media, and scientific academics — promoted black inferiority and constituted the European background against which African diaspora struggles for identity, dignity (self-confidence, self-respect, self-esteem), and material resources took place.

An inescapable aspect of this struggle was that the black diaspora peoples' quest for validation and recognition occurred on the ideological, social, and cultural terrains of non-black peoples. White supremacist assaults on black intelligence, ability, beauty, and character required persistent black efforts to hold self-doubt, self-contempt, and even self-hatred at bay. Selective appropriation, incorporation, and rearticulation of European ideologies, cultures, and institutions alongside an African heritage — a heritage more or less confined to linguistic innovation in rhetorical practices, stylizations of the body as forms of occupying an alien social space (e.g., hairstyles, ways of walking, standing, and talking, and hand expressions), means of constituting and sustaining camaraderie and community (e.g., antiphonal, call-and-response styles, rhythmic repetition, risk-ridden syncopation in spectacular modes in musical and rhetorical expressions) — were some of the strategies employed.

The modern black diaspora problematic of invisibility and namelessness can be understood as the condition of *relative lack of power for blacks to present themselves to themselves and others as complex human beings, and thereby to contest the bombardment of negative, degrading stereotypes put forward by white supremacist ideologies.* The initial black response to being caught in this whirlwind of Europeanization was to resist the misrepresentation and caricature of the terms set by uncontested non-black norms and models and to fight for self-recognition. Every modern black person, especially the cultural disseminator, encounters this problematic of invisibility and namelessness. The initial African diaspora response was a mode of resistance that was *moralistic in content and communal in character.* That is, the fight for representation and recognition highlighted moral judgements regarding black "positive" images over and against white supremacist stereotypes. These images "re-presented" monolithic and homogeneous black communities in a way that could displace past misrepresentations of these communities. Stuart Hall has discussed these responses as attempts to change the "relations of representation."

These courageous yet limited black efforts to combat racist cultural practices uncritically accepted non-black conventions and standards in two ways. First, they proceeded in an *assimilationist manner* that set out to show that black people were really like white people — thereby eliding differences (in history and culture) between whites and blacks. Black specificity and particularity were thus banished in order to gain white acceptance and approval. Second, these black responses rested upon a *homogenizing impulse* that assumed that all black people were really alike — hence obliterating differences (class, gender, region, sexual orientation) between black peoples. I submit that there are elements of truth in both claims, yet the conclusions are unwarranted owing to the basic fact that non-black paradigms set the terms of the replies.

The insight in the first claim is that blacks and whites are in some important sense alike — i.e., positively, in their capacities for human sympathy, moral sacrifice, service to others, intelligence, and beauty; or negatively, in their capacity for cruelty. Yet the common humanity they share is jettisoned when the claim is cast in an assimilationist manner that subordinates black particularity to a false universalism, i.e., non-black rubrics and prototypes. Similarly, the insight in the second claim is that all blacks are in some significant sense "in the same boat"—that is, subject to white supremacist abuse. Yet this common condition is stretched too far when viewed in a *homogenizing* way that overlooks how racist treatment vastly differs owing to class, gender, sexual orientation, nation, region, hue, and age.

The moralistic and communal aspects of the initial black diaspora responses to social and psychic erasure were not simply cast into binary oppositions of positive/negative, good/ bad images that privileged the first term in light of a white norm, so that black efforts remained inscribed within the very logic that dehumanized them. They were further complicated by the fact that these responses were advanced principally by anxiety-ridden, middle-class black intellectuals (predominantly male and heterosexual) grappling with their sense of double-consciousness — namely their own crisis of identity, agency, audience — caught between a quest for white approval and acceptance and an endeavor to overcome the internalized association of blackness with inferiority. And I suggest that these complex anxieties of modern black diaspora intellectuals partly motivate the two major arguments that ground the assimilationist moralism and homogeneous communalism just outlined.

Kobena Mercer has talked about these two arguments as the *reflectionist* and the *social engineering* arguments. The reflectionist argument holds that the fight for black representation and recognition — against white racist stereotypes — must reflect or mirror the real black community, not simply the negative and depressing representations of it. The social engineering argument claims that since any form of representation is constructed — i.e., selective in light of broader aims — black representation (especially given the difficulty for blacks to gain access to positions of power to produce any black imagery) should offer positive images, thereby countering racist stereotypes. The hidden assumption of both arguments is that we have unmediated access to what the "real black community" is and what "positive images" are. In short, these arguments presuppose the very phenomenon to be interrogated and thereby foreclose the very issues that should serve as the subject matter to be investigated.

Any notions of "the real black community" and "positive images" are value laden, socially loaded, and ideologically charged. To pursue this discussion is to call into question the possibility of such an uncontested consensus regarding them. Hall has rightly called this encounter "the end of innocence or the end of the innocent notions of the essential Black subject . . . the recognition that 'black' is essentially a politically and culturally constructed category" (Hall, 1988, p. 28). This recognition — more and more pervasive among the postmodern African diaspora intelligentsia — is facilitated in part by the slow but sure dissolution of the European Age's maritime empires and the unleashing of new political possibilities and cultural articulations among ex-colonized peoples across the globe.

One crucial lesson of this decolonization process remains the manner in which most third world authoritarian bureaucratic elites deploy essentialist rhetorics about "homogeneous national communities" and "positive images" in order to repress and regiment their diverse and heterogeneous populations. Yet in the diaspora, especially among first world countries, this critique has emerged not so much from the black male component of the left as from the black women's movement. The decisive push of postmodern black intellectuals toward a new cultural politics of difference has been made by the powerful critiques and constructive explorations of black diaspora women (e.g., Toni Morrison). The coffin used to bury the innocent notion of the essential black subject was nailed shut with the termination of the black male monopoly on the construction of the black subject. In this regard, the black diaspora womanist critique has had a greater impact than have the critiques that highlight exclusively class, empire, age, sexual orientation, or nature.

This decisive push toward the end of black innocence — though prefigured in various degrees in the best moments of W.E.B. DuBois, James Baldwin, Amiri Baraka, Anna Cooper, Frantz Fanon, C.L.R. James, Claudia Jones, the later Malcolm X, and others — forces black diaspora cultural workers to encounter what Hall has called "the politics of representation." The main aim now is not simply access to representation in order to produce positive images of homogeneous communities — though broader access remains a practical and political problem. Nor is the primary goal here that of contesting stereotypes — though contestation remains a significant albeit limited venture. Following the model of the African diaspora traditions of music, athletics, and rhetoric, black cultural workers must constitute and sustain discursive and institutional networks that deconstruct earlier modern black strategies for identity formation, demystify power relations that incorporate class, patriarchal, and homophobic biases, and construct more multivalent and multidimensional responses that articulate the complexity and diversity of black practices in the modern and postmodern world.

Furthermore, black cultural workers must investigate and interrogate the other of blackness/whiteness. One cannot deconstruct the binary oppositional logic of images of blackness without extending it to the contrary condition of blackness/whiteness itself. However, a mere dismantling will not do — for the very notion of a deconstructive social theory is oxymoronic. Yet social theory is what is needed to examine and *explain* the historically specific ways in which "whiteness" is a politically constructed category parasitic on "blackness," and thereby to conceive of the profoundly hybrid character of what we mean by "race," "ethnicity," and "nationality." Needless to say, these inquiries must traverse those of "male/female," "colonizer/colonized," "heterosexual/homosexual," et al., as well.

Demystification is the most illuminating mode of theoretical inquiry for those who promote the new cultural politics of difference. Social structural analyses of empire, exterminism, class, race, gender, nature, age, sexual orientation, nation, and region are the springboards — though not the landing grounds — for the most desirable forms of critical practice that take history (and herstory) seriously. Demystification tries to keep track of the complex dynamics of institutional and other related power structures in order to disclose options and alternatives for transformational praxis; it also attempts to grasp the way in which representational strategies are creative responses to novel circumstances and conditions. In this way the central role of human agency (always enacted under circumstances not of one's choosing) — be it in the critic, artist, or constituency, and audience — is accented.

I call demystificatory criticism "prophetic criticism" — the approach appropriate for the new cultural politics of difference — because while it begins with social structural analyses it also makes explicit its moral and political aims. It is partisan, partial, engaged, and crisis centered, yet it always keeps open a skeptical eye to avoid dogmatic traps, premature closures, formulaic formulations, or rigid conclusions. In addition to social-structural analyses, moral and political judgements, and sheer critical consciousness, there indeed is evaluation. Yet the aim of this evaluation is neither to pit art objects against one another like racehorses nor to create eternal canons that dull, discourage, or even dwarf contemporary achievements. We listen to Laurie Anderson, Kathleen Battle, Ludwig van Beethoven, Charlie Parker, Luciano Pavarotti, Sarah Vaughan, or Stevie Wonder; read Anton Chekhov, Ralph Ellison, Gabriel Garcia Márquez, Doris Lessing, Toni Morrison, Thomas Pynchon, William Shakespeare; or see the works of Ingmar Bergman, Le Corbusier, Frank Gehry, Barbara Kruger, Spike Lee, Martin Puryear, Pablo Picasso, or Howardena Pindell — not in order to undergird bureaucratic assents or enliven cocktail party conversations, but rather to be summoned by the styles they deploy for their profound insights, pleasures, and challenges. Yet all evaluation — including a delight in Eliot's poetry despite his reactionary politics, or a love of Zora Neale Hurston's novels despite her Republican Party affiliations — is inseparable from, though not identical or reducible to, social structural analyses, moral and political judgements, and the workings of a curious critical consciousness.

The deadly traps of demystification — and any form of prophetic criticism — are those of reductionism, be it of the sociological, psychological, or historical sort. By reductionism I mean either one-factor analyses (crude Marxisms, feminisms, racialisms, etc.) that yield a one-dimensional functionalism or hypersubtle analytical perspectives that lose touch with the specificity of an artwork's form and the context of its reception. Few cultural workers of whatever stripe can walk the tightrope between the Scylla of reductionism and the Charybdis of aestheticism — yet demystificatory (or prophetic) critics must. Of course, since so many art practices these days also purport to be criticism, this also holds true for artists.

The Existential Challenge

The existential challenge to the new cultural politics of difference can be stated simply: How does one acquire the resources to survive and the cultural capital to thrive as a critic or artist? By cultural capital (Pierre Bourdieu's term), I mean not only the high-quality skills required to engage in cultural practices but more importantly, the self-confidence, discipline, and perseverance necessary for success without an undue reliance on the mainstream for approval and acceptance. This challenge holds for all prophetic critics, yet it is especially difficult for those of color. The widespread modern European denial of the intelligence, ability, beauty, and character of people of color puts a tremendous burden on critics and artists of color to "prove" themselves in light of norms and models set by white elites whose own heritage devalued and dehumanized them. In short, in the court of criticism and art — or any matters regarding the life of the mind — people of color are guilty (i.e., not expected to meet standards of intellectual achievement) until "proven" innocent (i.e., acceptable to "us").

This is more a structural dilemma than a matter of personal attitudes. The profoundly racist and sexist heritage of the European Age has bequeathed to us a set of deeply ingrained perceptions about people of color, including, of course, the self-perceptions that people of color bring. It is not surprising that most intellectuals of color in the past exerted much of their energies and efforts to gain acceptance and approval by "white normative gazes." The new cultural politics of difference advises critics and artists of color to put aside this mode of mental bondage, thereby freeing themselves both to interrogate the ways in which they are bound by certain conventions and to learn from and build on these very norms and models. One hallmark of wisdom in the context of any struggle is to avoid knee-jerk rejection and uncritical acceptance.

Self-confidence, discipline, and perseverance are not ends in themselves. Rather they are the necessary stuff of which enabling criticism and self-criticism are made. Notwithstanding inescapable jealousies, insecurities, and anxieties, one telling characteristic of critics and artists of color linked to the new prophetic criticism should be their capacity for and promotion of relentless criticism and self-criticism — be it the normative paradigms of their white colleagues that tend to leave out considerations of empire, race, gender, and sexual orientation, or the damaging dogmas about the homogeneous character of communities of color.

There are four basic options for people of color interested in representation — if they are to survive and thrive as serious practitioners of their craft. First, there is the Booker T. Temptation, namely the individual preoccupation with the mainstream and its legitimizing power. Most critics and artists of color try to bite this bait. It is nearly unavoidable, yet few succeed in a substantive manner. It is no accident that the most creative and profound among them — especially those who have staying power beyond being mere flashes in the pan to satisfy faddish tokenism — are usually marginal to the mainstream. Even the pervasive professionalization of cultural practitioners of color in the past few decades has not produced towering figures who reside within the established white patronage system, which bestows the rewards and prestige for chosen contributions to American society.

It certainly helps to have some trustworthy allies within this system, yet most of those who enter and remain tend to lose much of their creativity, diffuse their prophetic energy, and dilute their critiques. Still, it is unrealistic for creative people of color to think they can sidestep the white patronage system. And though there are indeed some white allies conscious of the tremendous need to rethink identity politics, it is naive to think that being comfortably nested within this very same system — even if one can be a patron to others — does not affect one's work, one's outlook, and most important, one's soul.

The second option is the Talented Tenth Seduction, namely, a move toward arrogant group insularity. This alternative has a limited function — to preserve one's sanity and sense of self as one copes with the mainstream. Yet it is, at best, a transitional and transient activity. If it becomes a permanent option it is self-defeating in that it usually reinforces the very inferiority complexes promoted by the subtly racist mainstream. Hence it tends to revel in parochialism and encourage a narrow racialist and chauvinistic outlook.

The third strategy is the Go-It-Alone Option. This is an extreme rejectionist perspective that shuns the mainstream and group insularity. Almost every critic and artist of color contemplates or enacts this option at some time in his or her pilgrimage. It is healthy in that it reflects the presence of independent, critical, and skeptical sensibilities toward perceived constraints on one's creativity. Yet it is, in the end, difficult if not impossible to sustain if one is to grow, develop, and mature intellectually, as some semblance of dialogue with a community is necessary for almost any creative practice.

The most desirable option for people of color who promote the new cultural politics of difference is to be a Critical Organic Catalyst. By this I mean a person who stays attuned to the best of what the mainstream has to offer — its paradigms, viewpoints, and methods — yet maintains a grounding in affirming and enabling subcultures of criticism. Prophetic critics and artists of color should be exemplars of what it means to be intellectual freedom fighters, that is, cultural workers who simultaneously position themselves within (or alongside) the mainstream while clearly being aligned with groups who vow to keep alive potent traditions of critique and resistance. In this regard one can take clues from the great musicians or preachers of color who are open to the best of what other traditions offer, yet are rooted in nourishing subcultures that build on the grand achievements of a vital heritage. Openness to others — including the mainstream — does not entail wholesale co-optation, and group autonomy is not group insularity. Louis Armstrong, Ella Baker, W.E.B. DuBois, Martin Luther King, Jr., Jose Carlos Mariatequi, Wynton Marsalis, M.M. Thomas, and Ronald Takaki have understood this well.

The new cultural politics of difference can thrive only if there are communities, groups, organizations, institutions, subcultures, and networks of people of color who cultivate critical sensibilities and personal accountability — without inhibiting individual expressions, curiosities, and idiosyncrasies. This is especially needed given the escalating racial hostility, violence, and polarization in the United States. Yet this critical coming together must not be a narrow closing of ranks. Rather it is a strengthening and nurturing endeavor that can forge more solid alliances and coalitions. In this way prophetic criticism — with its stress on historical specificity and artistic complexity — directly addresses the intellectual challenge. The cultural capital of people of color — with its emphasis on self-confidence, discipline, perseverance, and subcultures of criticism — also tries to meet the existential requirement. Both are mutually reinforcing. Both are motivated by a deep commitment to individuality and democracy — the moral and political ideals that guide the creative responses to the political challenge.

The Political Challenge

Adequate rejoinders to intellectual and existential challenges equip the practitioners of the new cultural politics of difference to meet the political ones. This challenge principally consists of forging solid and reliable alliances to people of color and white progressives guided by a moral and political vision of greater democracy and individual freedom in communities, states, and transnational enterprises — i.e., corporations and information and communications conglomerates. Jesse Jackson's Rainbow Coalition is a gallant yet flawed effort in this regard: gallant due to the tremendous energy, vision, and courage of its leader and followers; flawed because of its failure to take seriously critical and democratic sensibilities within its own operations.

The time has come for critics and artists of the new cultural politics of difference to cast their nets widely, flex their muscles broadly, and thereby refuse to limit their visions, analyses, and praxis to their particular terrains. The aim is to dare to recast, redefine, and revise the very notions of "modernity," "mainstream," "margins," "difference," "otherness." We have now reached a new stage in the perennial struggle for freedom and dignity. And while much of the first world intelligentsia adopts retrospective and conservative outlooks that defend the crisis-ridden present, we promote a prospective and prophetic vision with a sense of possibility and potential, especially for those who bear the social costs of the present. We look to the past for strength, not solace; we look at the present and see people perishing, not profits mounting; we look toward the future and vow to make it different and better.

To put it boldly, the new kind of critic and artist associated with the new cultural politics of difference consists of an energetic breed of new world *bricoleurs* with improvisational and flexible sensibilities that sidestep mere opportunism and mindless eclecticism; persons of all countries, cultures, genders, sexual orientations, ages, and regions, with protean identities, who avoid ethnic chauvinism and faceless universalism; intellectual and political freedom fighters with partisan passion, international perspectives, and, thank God, a sense of humor to combat the ever-present absurdity that forever threatens our democratic and libertarian projects and dampens the fire that fuels our will to struggle. We will struggle and stay, as those brothers and sisters on the block say, "out there" — with intellectual rigor, existential dignity, moral vision, political courage, and soulful style.

REFERENCES

Arnold, M. ([1869] 1925). *Culture and Anarchy: An essay in political criticism*. New York: MacMillan.

—. ([1855] 1969). Stanzas from the Grand Chartreuse. In C. B. Tinker & H. F. Lowry (eds.), *Poetical Works* (299–306). London: Oxford.

Eliot, T. S. ([1919] 1950). Tradition and the individual talent. In *Selected Essays* (pp. 3–11). New York: Harcourt.

—. ([1923] 1948). Ulysses, order, and myth. In S. Givens (ed.), *James Joyce: Two decades of criticism* (198–202). New York: Vanguard.

Fanon, F. (1963). *The Wretched of the Earth*. New York: Grove.

Hall, S. (1988). *New Ethnicities*. In K. Mercer (ed.), *Black Film, British Cinema*. ICA documents, 7 (27–31). London: ICA.

Joyce, J. ([1922] 1934). *Ulysses*. New York: Random.

Trilling, L. ([1961] 1965). On the teaching of modern literature. In *Beyond Culture: Essays on literature and learning* (3–30). New York: Viking.

Valéry, P. ([1919] 1962). The crisis of the mind. In D. Folliot & J. Mathews (eds.), *The Collected Works of Paul Valéry* (Vol. 10, 23–36). New York: Bollingen.

QUESTIONS

1. What does Cornel West mean by the term "the new cultural politics of difference"?
2. According to West, why is an account of African American history relevant to an analysis of cultural representations and voice appropriation?
3. Do you think that West is right to suggest that critics and artists have an important role to play in challenging stereotypes of group members and changing conditions of disadvantage?

DISABILITY AND EQUALITY

Jerome E. Bickenbach

When census-takers first tried to count the number of their citizens with mental or physical disabilities it proved to be surprisingly difficult. They found that two people with precisely the same medical condition — a visual impairment, spinal injury, cerebral palsy, neurosis or depression — often experience the condition in very different ways. Some will be limited in what they can do, others will not. They also discovered something sociologists had known for years: disability is not merely a medical condition, it is a negative social status that people may, justifiably, be reluctant to apply to themselves. Disability, it turns out, is a complex notion, both logically and sociologically. But a careful analysis of it has shed light on the wider issue of human diversity and the political ideal of equality.

Although philosophers have only very recently thought much about disability, it has been scrutinized by other disciplines for decades. The profession of physical therapy, for example, broke away from medicine in part because of the practical need to distinguish the medical domain of pathologies and impairments — which affect cells, tissues, organs and other parts of people — from the disfunctionings and inabilities that limit the range of activities people perform in the world as they find it. Social psychologists have emphasized the role of stereotyping and stigmatization in the construction of the public perception of disability. Economists, for their part, have analyzed disability as a limitation on the repertoire of functional capacities of people. And political theorists have identified disability as an administrative category used to set people apart for special treatment, sometimes to their advantage, but usually not.

In 1980, the World Health Organization published a remarkable document that brought together many of these isolated strains of thought about disability. It was called the *International Classification of Impairments, Disabilities, and Handicaps* (or ICIDH), and, though designed primarily as a classification tool, it embodied a sophisticated three-part analysis of disability in terms of Impairments, Disabilities* and Handicaps:

An Impairment is any loss or abnormality of physiological, psychological or anatomical structure or function, described and explained by biomedical scientists. Sometimes, an Impairment forms the physical basis of a Disability, defined as a restriction or lack of an ability to perform an activity in the manner or range considered normal. This transition is not inevitable, not only because some Impairments are so trivial they normally would not limit significant abilities (for example, being born with a thumb that is a millimetre shorter than normal), but also because people with a potentially disabling Impairment are not disabled because, for them in their circumstances, lacking that ability has no affect on their lives (for example, being unable to tolerate very hot weather if one lives out one's life in the arctic). Having a Disability, in short, is in part a function of the physical and social circumstances in which one lives.

Lastly, the complex phenomenon of disability includes the aspect of Handicap, defined as those disadvantages that are created by the social reception of perceived Impairments or Disabilities. If I am ridiculed for my limp, or prohibited from being a school teacher

---

Reprinted by permission of Jerome E. Bickenbach.

* *From now on, to avoid confusion, the specially defined WHO notion will be capitalized (Disability) while the ordinary, inclusive and ambiguous notion will be left in lower case.*

because of my blindness, or denied a place in the movie theatre because I am in a wheelchair, then I am disadvantaged (I am denied benefits and opportunities available to others) because of the reception of my perceived Impairment or Disability. Handicaps, in a word, are denials of equality based on perceived Disability or Impairment.

But why 'perceived' Disability or Impairment? Because, interestingly, since Handicaps are the products of stigma, stereotype, ill-will, pity, misperception, ignorance, or benign neglect, it is the perception, not the reality, that is important. Suppose I am denied an apartment because the landlord thinks that I have AIDS (when in fact I do not). Were I HIV serio-positive I would have an Impairment, and would eventually have a collection of Disabilities as well; and if I were denied the apartment for these reasons, then I would have a Handicap. But if I am falsely believed to have AIDS, and denied an apartment on that ground, I still have a Handicap, since I am still disadvantaged because of someone's perception of my physical state.

The WHO model helpfully explains why the purely medical understanding of disability is incomplete. There is no direct, causal link between Impairments, Disabilities and Handicaps: each aspect of disability interacts with the background social and physical context in which the person lives, and it is the interaction, not just the physical or mental condition, that yields Disabilities and Handicaps. This model of disability is sometimes called the ecological model because of the essential role played by environment factors (social, attitudinal, physical) in the creation of the various dimensions of disability.

Understanding disability ecologically, or interactively, helps also to clarify basic confusions about what it means to have a disability. First of all, many Disabilities involve chronic Impairments that do not get better. So, if one is blind, or an amputee, or post-polio, the 'problems' one faces are not really medical, but rehabilitative: getting around, finding employment, acquiring and using prosthetic devices. To insist that Disability is a medical problem, moreover, can be stigmatizing. People with medical problems we believe have a responsibility to see a physician, follow her advice, and get better. But if Disability is medicalized, people with Disabilities will be viewed either as irresponsible, or as medical 'failures'.

Secondly, Disabilities often, and Handicaps always, are created by social circumstances wholly separate from the Impairment a person may have, and this has obvious, and profound, social and political consequences. Suppose I am in a wheelchair and I wheel up to the front door of a building that has no ramp. I might describe my situation by saying, either that I am unable to enter the building, because of my Impairment, or else that I am unable to enter because of the absence of a ramp. The word 'able' and its cognants (including 'ability') are ambiguous in this respect. But notice that in the first case the problem is functional, while in the second, it is architectural. In the first case, if medicine and rehabilitative therapy can do nothing, then I cannot enter the building because of my inability; but in the second case, I cannot enter the building because it is inaccessible.

How does our interactive notion of Disability help us here? It does by insuring that we describe the situation accurately: my Disability (being unable to get into the building) is the result of what happens when my Impairment interacts with a particular architectural environment. This means that my Disability can be 'fixed' by altering the environment: first of all, and for many purposes, by giving me a wheelchair; but, secondly, as in this instance, by providing a ramp or elevator.

The ecological model, in another words, makes it clear that there are two distinct social responses to Impairments and Disabilities: On the one hand, we can direct social and individual resources to try to *correct* the Impairment or Disability. In the standard case, this would mean either looking for a medical therapy or cure, where possible and appropriate, or else a rehabilitative response. Performing surgery to alter the configuration of muscles in my legs, or training me to walk by means of exercises and physical therapy are thus modes of correction.

But on the other hand, we can direct social and individual resources to altering the physical or social environment in order to *accommodate* a person's functional limitations. Wheelchairs and ramps are accommodations; so too are alterations in job descriptions that make it possible for me to work on one floor rather than having to go up and down stairs, or changes in employers' attitudes to hiring people in wheelchairs, or passing legislation that requires governments to put ramps in public buildings and to share the cost of doing so in private employment sites, and on and on. An accommodation alters that part of the social and physical environment that Disables people who have Impairments.

Significantly, though, the line between correction and accommodation is drawn politically, not medically. Take the case of finding employment for people with disabilities. As a society we are faced with a choice: should we correct the person by providing her or him with new or augmented skills in order to overcome the physical obstacles in the workplace; or should we make the workplace accessible to the person with a Disability by means of accommodations. (For years physiotherapists trained people in wheelchairs to 'jump' curbs so that they could get around; now we put in curb cuts.) Although medical and other expertise is obviously relevant to our decision, ultimately our choice is grounded in our political and moral understanding of what society owes to people with disabilities. We need to ask ourselves, what does equality demand?

Hence the third philosophically important consequence of the ecological model is that it identifies the social-political dimension of disability. In nearly every nation, some provision is made for people with disabilities; in the wealthier, Western countries social policy for and on behalf of people with disabilities constitutes a substantial portion of what is usually called the 'welfare state': disability pensions, worker's compensation, medical insurance, drug and assistive device programmes, mental health care, vocational rehabilitation, and so on. Increasingly too, anti-discrimination laws have extended protection to those who are Handicapped by discrimination on the basis of disability. The three-part WHO model makes it clear that this complex social policy addresses different aspects of disability: Impairment issues (medical care, medications, chronic care); Disability issues (rehabilitation, assistive devices, architectural and other accommodations); and Handicap Issues (anti-discrimination protections; accommodation requirements; access to services).

In recent years, with the ecological approach to disability in hand, advocates for people with disabilities have made the link, both as a matter of political theory and practice, between the nature of Disability and Handicap and the political ideal and promise of equality. These efforts have been primarily in the political arena, where, for example in the United States, we have witnessed an increased politicalization of people with disabilities which has resulted in legislation such as the *Americans with Disabilities Act*. At the theoretical level, though, there remains much turmoil, and considerable need for philosophical investigation that goes to the very heart of the theory of political and social equality.

It is clear that whatever our social policy arrangements happen to be, wherever we choose to draw the line between correction and accommodation, and whether we have legal protections against discrimination or not, at bottom the politics of disability rests on the political value of equality. Bluntly put, the issue comes to this: What does a social and political commitment to equality require in the case of people with disabilities?

So far — but the day is still young in theorizing about disability — two major strategies have been tried to answer this question. One approach, and to date by far the most popular, is to characterize all forms and manifestations of Handicaps as discriminatory denials of equality of opportunity. Treatment is discriminatory, on this account, if it is either insulting, demeaning, trivializing or marginalizing, or else if it indirectly disadvantages people with disabilities by failing to provide them with the resources required to meet the needs created by their Impairments and Disabilities. This means that people with disabilities consti-tute a kind of minority group who have historically faced systemic discrimination. The solution is political action to ensure protection against discrimination, through explicit anti-discrimination legislation and system-wide changes to remedy the marginalized status of people with disabilities, as a group.

As a political strategy, the civil rights approach (as this first strategy may be called) is a proven success. Born out of the consumer and civil rights movements of the 1960s, the disability rights movement can be credited with nearly every change in attitude and treat-ment of people with disabilities in the last two decades — from curb cuts and accessible bathrooms, to programs to integrate developmentally disabled children into the public schools to protections of the rights of people in mental institutions. As it has matured, the civil rights approach has adopted some of the theoretical developments introduced by feminists and black theorists, notably identity politics and separatist cultures (as evidenced by the Deaf Culture).

Another strategy, still in its infancy, might be called the universalistic, or distributive justice, approach. It is founded on the principle that disability is not the characteristic of some discrete and insular minority of people, it is rather a human phenomenon experienced by everyone, to one degree or another, and at one time or another. On this account, a failure to make public transportation accessible, or to integrate people with different cognitive abilities into schools, are not acts of discrimination but rather instances of distributive injustice. By catering to people whose range of abilities falls within an artificially narrow range we call 'normal', our society and its economic institutions, public and private, are unfairly and irrationally privileging one group of people over another. Equality is best served by distributive justice, and justice requires that the range of variation in human abilities and capabilities should not be artificially narrowed to advantage some at the ex-pense of others.

The universalistic approach has the advantage of providing a theoretical answer to why disability is an issue of political equality. Since Disabilities and Handicaps are limitations on an individual positive liberty — the freedom to do or become what a person chooses — to the extent that these limitations are socially-constructed, they are instances of unjust distribution of positive liberty across members of society. People who are currently not disabled (the disability rights community jokingly calls these people TABs — the 'tempo-rarily able bodied') enjoy a disproportionate share of the benefits from social arrangements because the existing social environment has been arbitrarily designed to cater to their range of abilities. Moreover, they enjoy these benefits, not because they deserve them, but simply because of good luck: in the 'natural lottery' they happened to be born without potentially Disabling conditions, or they happen not to have Disabling accidents. On the other hand, people who came out differently in the natural lottery and as a result cannot perform within the socially-constructed and artificially narrow range of abilities enjoy fewer social benefits, and must confront more socially-created burdens that limit their positive freedom.

From the point of view of distributive justice, the appropriate response to this situation is to remove the unfairness by redistributing positive liberty more equitably across the population. That may be accomplished either by correcting, or by accommodating or both. Those who are reaping the unearned benefits of the natural lottery (the TABs) can in fairness be required to return this unearned benefit (or, alternatively, to take on their fair share of social burdens) through the standard social redistributive mechanisms of taxation and regulation. This is not a matter, it should be noted, of punishing the TABs for their discriminatory behaviour; it is rather a matter of securing a more equitable distribution of the positive liberty that it is society's obligation to secure for all its citizens.

The universalistic approach, in other words, focuses our social energies on the task of finding the right balance of correction and accommodation that can secure full equality of social participation for everyone, regardless of their functional capacities. The civil rights approach, by contrast, is diverted from this important, and extremely difficult task, by two preliminary tasks: first, that of determining whether a particular person with a Disability has been disadvantaged because of an act of discrimination; and secondly, assigning responsibility for the discrimination in order determine who must repair the damage caused by it. The first task determines the eligibility of the complainant, the second, the identity of the culprit. In practice, both of these tasks require an adjudicator (such as a judge or tribunal) and, in fairness, the opportunity for the putative culprit to defend herself. All of these take up time, and social resources, both of which could be more fruitfully expended on the task of securing equality through redistribution.

Another contrast between the two strategies is illuminating. To employ the notion of discrimination in order to remedy a Handicap the person with the disability can not themselves have contributed to the creation of the Handicap, since it would be unfair to hold one person responsible for a disadvantage that the victim has helped to create. That means that it matters how the Impairment or Disability came about, and in particular, it matters whether the person with the disability is in part, or entirely, to blame for it (by leading a risky or unhealthy life, for example). So, on the civil rights approach, if someone is denied employment because they are in a wheelchair, it will make a difference to the social response to the discrimination whether the individual acquired the Disability innocently or brought it on themselves through careless living.

The universalistic approach does not see it this way. Here we do not care how the Disability was acquired, or who was to blame for it, but merely whether the individual has access to a fair share of positive liberty, in order to participate equally in all areas of social life. Knowing about a person's risky or careless life habits is important, for these habits are themselves Disabilities that may need to be corrected or accommodated. But, on the universalistic approach, being denied employment because you are in a wheelchair is unjust, irrespective on why you are in the wheelchair or whose fault it is that you are.

Now, although historically the civil rights approach has proven its usefulness, the universalistic or distributive justice approach may in the long run prove to have a stronger theoretical foundation. In part this is because many of the basic assumptions of the civil rights approach are dubious. For example, it is doubtful whether people with disabilities constitute a distinct minority group, or that all of the systemic Handicaps that they face are the product of discrimination (unless that term is given an uncomfortably wide, and loose, characterization). Intuitively, it makes more sense to say that, unlike race, ethnicity, gender, and religion, disability is a universal feature of the human condition, shared by all to one degree or another. Indeed, the ultimate Handicap may just be that of assuming that disability is confined to one group of people.

To prove its theoretical superiority, however, the universalistic approach to disability must secure the link between disability, understood on the ecological model, and the political and moral value of equality. That in turn requires what so far has not been successfully achieved, namely, a theory of distributive justice that takes disability seriously. So far, most theories of distributive justice treat disability as a 'special case' that can be added on to a theory of justice designed primarily for 'normal people'. Increasingly, political and moral philosophers are turning to the ecological understanding of disability as a cure for their unaccommodating accounts of equality and justice.

FURTHER READING

Amundson, Ron "Disability, Handicap, and the Environment" (1992) 9 *Journal of Social Philosophy*

Bickenbach, Jerome *Physical Disability and Social Policy* (Toronto, University of Toronto Press, 1993)

Goffman, Erving *Stigma: Notes on the Maintenance of Spoiled Identity* (Englewood Cliffs, NJ, Prentice Hall, 1963)

Hahn, Harlan "The Politics of Physical Differences: Disability and Discrimination" (1988) 44 *Journal of Social Issues* 39

McCluskey, Martha "Rethinking Equality and Difference: Disability Discrimination in Public Transportation" (1988) 97 *Yale Law Journal* 863

Minow, Martha *Making All the Difference: Inclusion, Exclusion, and American Law* (Ithaca, NY, Cornell University Press, 1990)

Oliver, Michael *Understanding Disability: From Theory to Practice* (London, MacMillan, 1996)

Zola, Irving K. "Toward the Necessary Universalizing of a Disability Policy" (1989) 67 *The Milbank Quarterly* 401

QUESTIONS

1. What are the definitions of "Impairment," "Disabilities," and "Handicaps" given by the World Health Organization?
2. What does Bickenbach mean by an ecological model? Do you think this idea helps us to understand the nature of disability? In what ways can an ecological model be used to raise objections against Selick's account of our obligations to people with disabilities?
3. What are the differences between a civil rights approach and a distributive justice approach to issues of disability? What reasons does Bickenbach give for saying that the civil rights approach has limitations?
4. Bickenbach claims that "it makes more sense to say that, unlike race, ethnicity, gender, and religion, disability is a universal feature of the human condition, shared by all to one degree or another." How does Bickenbach use this claim to defend a distributive justice approach? Do you think this claim has implications for other issues of discrimination examined in this chapter?

SUGGESTIONS FOR FURTHER READING

Government Reports

- Canada. Parliament. House of Commons. Special Committee on Participation of Visible Minorities in Canadian Society. *Equality Now!: Report of the Special Committee on Visible Minorities in Canadian Society*. Ottawa: Supply and Services, 1984.
- Canada. Parliament. House of Commons. Standing Committee on Justice and Legal Affairs. Sub-Committee on Equality Rights. *Equality For All: Report of the Parliamentary Committee on Equality Rights*. Ottawa: Supply and Services, 1985.
- Canadian Advisory Council on the Status of Women. *Canadian Charter Equality Rights for Women: One Step Forward or Two Steps Back?* Ottawa: Canadian Advisory Council on the Status of Women, 1989.
- Canada. House of Commons Standing Committee on Human Rights and the Status of Disabled Persons. *A Consensus for Action: The Economic Integration of Disabled Persons*. Ottawa: Supply and Services, 1990.

Recent Collections

- Anne Bayefsky and Mary Eberts, eds., *Equality Rights and the Canadian Charter of Rights and Freedoms* (Toronto: Carswell, 1985). This collection of essays explores the ways in which interpretations of the charter may affect various disadvantaged groups. It includes chapters that discuss aspects of discrimination on the grounds of ethnicity, religion, sex, age, mental and physical disability, marital status, and sexual orientation.
- Carl E. James, ed., *Perspectives an Racism and the Human Services Sector: A Case for Change* (Toronto: University of Toronto Press, 1996). A collection of essays by Canadian academics, lawyers, public servants, and policy workers that "examines race and racism in Canada from historical and contemporary perspectives and explores the extent to which these factors operate within social services systems related to immigration, settlement, the justice system, health, and education."
- Will Kymlicka, ed., *The Rights of Minority Cultures* (Oxford: Oxford University Press, 1995). A collection of essays on the rights of minority cultures by prominent political theorists such as Joseph Raz, Jeremy Waldron, Michael Walzer, Iris Marion Young, and Allen Buchanan.
- D. Kelly Weisberg, ed. *Feminist Legal Theory: Foundations* (Philadelphia: Temple University Press, 1993). This book is a comprehensive collection of essays that examines the treatment of difference in law and social policy. While the focus is on issues of gender, the book contains a broader and more general discussion of discrimination and equality theory. Some of the chapter headings are: "The Equality Debate: Equal Treatment versus Special Treatment"; "New Approaches to Equality and Difference"; "The Debate over Essentialism: Gender and Race"; "Theories of Law"; and "Feminist Legal Methods."

Books and Articles

The sources cited in the bibliographies by the individual authors to this chapter will be helpful for identifying material on different issues of discrimination. This list supplements those sources and provides perspectives on the issues different from those in the chapter.

- Evelyn Kallen, *Ethnicity and Human Rights in Canada* (2nd ed). (Toronto: Oxford University Press, 1995). This book examines key issues central to the concerns of Canada's three major ethnic constituencies: aboriginal peoples, racial and ethnic immigrant groups, and Franco-Québécois.
- J.R. Lucas, "Because You Are a Woman," Philosophy 48 (1973), pp. 161–171. Lucas argues that sex is a relevant difference that justifies different treatment.
- Laurence Thomas, "Sexism and Racism: Some Conceptual Differences," *Ethics*, v. 90 (January 1980). As the title suggests, Thomas compares the issues of racism and sexism and argues that unlike racism, sexism is tied to the positive self-concept of men in a way that racism is not tied to the positive self-concept of whites. This difference, he argues, suggests that sexism is more difficult to erase than racism.
- Kwame Anthony Appiah, "Racisms," in *Anatomy of Racism* edited by David Theo Goldberg. University of Minnesota Press, 1990. Appiah distinguishes aspects of racism. Appiah argues that racialism, the view that people divide up into distinct races and possess traits and tendencies that are not shared with members of other races, is false. He then examines the theoretical and moral difficulties of two other theories of race that he refers to as intrinsic and extrinsic racism.
- David Theo Goldberg, "Racist Exclusions," *Philosophical Forum* 26 (1) (Fall 1994). Goldberg argues that the standard view of racism as an "irrational prejudice predicated upon the arbitrary and so morally irrelevant category of 'race'" fails to capture critical features of racism and what is wrong with it.
- Jeffrey Jordon, "Is it Wrong to Discriminate on the Basis of Homosexuality?", *Journal of Social Philosophy*, v. 26, no. 1 (Spring 1995). This article discusses the issue of same-sex marriages and argues that it is morally permissible to discriminate against homosexuals because public sentiments favour the "neutral" approach of not giving public recognition to same-sex marriages.
- Christine Overall, "Heterosexuality and Feminist Theory," *Canadian Journal of Philosophy*, v. 20, no. 1 (March 1990), pp. 1–17. Overall argues that because our institutions enforce heterosexuality in a myriad of ways, it is problematic to view homosexuality as "abnormal." As an institution, heterosexuality contributes to women's unequal status in relationships and reduces their choices for sexual expression.

A fairly comprehensive bibliography on discrimination and equality that covers material dealing with court decisions, government reports, legal discussions of the charter, specific issues of discrimination, general theoretical works on equality, and feminist critiques of equality theory is available upon request from Christine M. Koggel.

Chapter 6

Affirmative Action

Introduction

In the last chapter, we introduced the principle of equal worth and explored its relevance to various moral dimensions of discrimination. One of these dimensions will be the focus of this chapter: the moral implications of and justifications for policies that advocate special or favourable treatment for disadvantaged groups as a way of achieving the goal of equality. These policies have come to be known as affirmative action and are nowhere more controversial than in the context of hiring and promoting people in the workplace.

The last chapter's reading from the Supreme Court decision in *Andrews* contained an interpretation of the equality provisions in Section 15 of the *Canadian Charter of Rights and Freedoms*. Having the text of Section 15 before us now for our current topic will be useful for revealing an apparent tension that cuts to the heart of the controversy about affirmative action. Section 15(1) reads: "Every individual is equal before and under the law and has the right to the equal protection and equal benefit of the law without discrimination and, in particular, without discrimination based on race, national or ethnic origin, colour, religion, sex, age or mental or physical disability." More importantly for purposes of this chapter, Section 15(2) explicitly accepts the legitimacy of affirmative action programs: "Subsection (I) does not preclude any law, program or activity that has as its object the amelioration of conditions of disadvantaged individuals or groups including those that are disadvantaged because of race, national or ethnic origin, colour, religion, sex, age or mental or physical disability." The margin notes to Section 15(2) identify the programs as affirmative action.

Section 15(1) seems to be a strict defence of what we referred to in the last chapter as formal equality, an equal treatment application of the principle of equal worth. Section 15(2), however, defends an understanding of the principle of equal worth as requiring positive measures, an approach we referred to as substantive equality. In Section 15(2), affirmative action programs are identified as policies that do not fall under the class of discriminatory actions listed in Section 15(1). Implicit in the Charter is a distinction between two kinds of discrimination: the discrimination in affirmative action programs, which has as its object or goal the amelioration of conditions of disadvantage, and the discrimination specified in Subsection (1), which perpetuates conditions of disadvantage.

When taken together, the two sections of the Charter appear to be in tension and to generate a paradox. Affirmative action programs have many of the characteristics that count as violating the principle of equal worth and constitute unjustified discrimination; that is, differential treatment based on religion, race, sex, and so forth. Affirmative action discriminates, only in reverse. Some argue that this feature alone makes affirmative action morally unjust. In response, others argue the difference in the case of affirmative action is that the goal of these policies is to enhance the operation of the principle of equal worth. Whether this kind of policy is morally justifiable has now become a significant issue in our society. It is this issue which we propose to explore in this chapter.

Background Considerations

As a stated policy, affirmative action has had a longer history in the United States than in Canada. From 1941 on, American presidents began to require that companies doing construction work financed by the federal government stipulate their intention not to discriminate in employment. The stipulation was replaced by an affirmative action requirement by President Kennedy and strengthened further by President Johnson in 1965 when he passed an executive order that set goals of certain percentages of minority group employees in the contractors' work force. Thus began the well-known and controversial system of quota hiring. In the now famous analogy to a race, Johnson compared opportunities for African Americans to those of competitors in a race who are shackled. Like runners shackled in competition, he argued, blacks deserve a head start.

In the decades that followed, such policies as quota hiring were voluntarily adopted throughout the States by private employers and educational institutions. Affirmative action has continued to be controversial. In fact, as a result of changing tides and growing opposition in the last few years, some states have recently removed affirmative action legislation.

In its broadest interpretation, affirmative action covers any kind of measure or policy designed to improve the life prospects of members of disadvantaged groups. Understood in this way, many policies implemented in Canada from earliest times can be described as affirmative action even though the label was not attached to these kinds of policies until fairly recently. For example, the *British North American Act,* 1867 specified special status for minority Roman Catholic schools and for French language rights. Other examples that can be characterized as early affirmative action measures are the scheme of equality in regional representation for appointment to the Senate (accommodating the interests of the less populous geographic regions in Canada) and the veteran's preference program that gave veterans special access to educational and employment opportunities following World War II.

The first steps toward developing affirmative action programs occurred in the late '60s and early '70s, when the federal and Quebec governments implemented programs designed to increase francophone participation in the public service. In another development, concerns in the 1970s about the "Americanization" of Canadian universities resulted in regulations that made universities advertise for and evaluate Canadian candidates before seeking foreign academics.

Yet, the legal foundation for affirmative action was not put in place at the federal level until the passage of the *Canadian Human Rights Act (Bill C-25)* in 1977. As in Section 15(2) of the Charter, the *Human Rights Act* specified that programs designed to alleviate conditions of inequality for disadvantaged groups do not count as discriminatory. Today, in addition to the *Canadian Human Rights Act* and the Charter, virtually all Canadian jurisdictions assert that affirmative action programs are not a form of discrimination prohibited by law.

The *Canadian Human Rights Act* also established the Canadian Human Rights Commission (CHRC) with powers to investigate complaints of discrimination by employees of federal departments, crown corporations, and businesses under federal jurisdiction. Amendments to the Act allowed the CHRC to broaden its mandate and deal with allegations of less overt or what is called "systemic" forms of discrimination and to do so even in the absence of complaints by particular individuals. This provision allowed the CHRC's recent investigation into discrimination on the basis of sexual orientation, an investigation that led to Bill C-33, the text of which is included in the readings of the last chapter. The Canadian Employment and Immigration Commission (CEIC) is another federal body that since 1976 has had major responsibilities for affirmative action initiatives. Part of their function is to provide advice, workplace audits, and assistance regarding affirmative action measures to private sector employees.

Current Situation

The 1984 Royal Commission called *Report of the Commission on Equality in Employment* headed by Judge Rosalie Abella called for legislation to require all federally regulated employers in both the public and private sector to implement mandatory affirmative action programs. In that report, Judge Abella also called for the use of a new term, "employment equity," to remove the negative connotations associated with "affirmative action" and to distinguish the Canadian from the American debate on affirmative action. Bill C-62, The Employment Equity Act, was the federal response to the Abella report. The Act does not mandate affirmative action hiring, but instead requires that federally regulated employers with more than 100 employees develop affirmative action programs and file annual reports about the results of those programs.

The 1987 Supreme Court decision *Action Travail des Femmes v. Canadian National Railway Company Co. et al.* was the first and most explicit decision rendered by the highest court on the legitimacy of affirmative action. Because it examines a specific context of workplace discrimination as the basis for justifying empowering federal courts to mandate affirmative action measures, it is an interesting case for introducing some of the main issues in the current debate.

Action Travail des Femmes, a private organization promoting the participation of women in occupations traditionally dominated by men, brought a complaint before the Federal Human Rights Tribunal charging that CN discriminated against women. The evidence showed that women were significantly under-represented at CN (0.7 percent, well below the national average of 13 percent for women's participation in blue-collar jobs across the country). Evidence also showed widespread discrimination in recruitment, hiring, and promotion policies that prevented or discouraged women from applying for or remaining in jobs at CN (CN restricted its career information promotions to trade schools, encouraged women applicants in interviews to consider traditional secretarial work as a more suitable alternative, and created an environment for women in which hostility and open insults were rampant). Finally, skills unrelated to the job (experience in welding, for example) were specified as job requirements for any position at CN and this had the effect of excluding women in large numbers.

The Human Rights Tribunal agreed that the evidence showed that discrimination formed a whole pattern of reactions and behaviour towards women that had entrenched and systemic effects on the workplace environment at CN and on all women. They thereby ruled that affirmative action was necessary in this context and mandated a program of quota hiring. Canadian National Railway appealed the Tribunal decision to the Federal Court of

Appeal in 1985, arguing that it was not within the powers of the Tribunal to enforce mandatory affirmative action measures on CN. The Federal Court agreed and quashed the mandated affirmative action hiring of women as beyond the powers of the Human Rights Tribunal. The Federal Court of Appeal decision was taken to the Supreme Court, and in a unanimous decision in 1987, the Supreme Court restored the mandatory affirmative action order by the Human Rights Tribunal.

In its decision, the Supreme Court acknowledged the full impact that systemic, entrenched discrimination has on opportunities for the disadvantaged as members of groups. The judges emphasized that the specific references to affirmative action programs in Sections 15(1) and 41(2)(a) of the Canadian Human Rights Code were intended to save affirmative action programs from attack on the ground of "reverse discrimination." Whereas discrimination against members of disadvantaged groups prevents or restricts achievement of equal opportunity for those individuals, discrimination in favour of members of disadvantaged groups is designed to promote equality for those same individuals. On a formal interpretation of equality under the law, women had an equal opportunity. The Supreme Court rendered a substantive interpretation of equality and determined that women at CN were not treated equally in the substantive sense.

The Moral Dimension

As we saw in the last chapter, it is widely accepted that unjustified discrimination is a feature of modern social life that should be eliminated. Because employment is so central to people's lives and welfare, discrimination in this domain has far-reaching effects on an individual's life prospects and goals. Obviously, an employer is justifiably interested in finding employees who have the skills needed for the work he or she proposes to do. Unjust discrimination occurs when hiring decisions are based not on objective assessments of a person's skills, but on judgements about what that person "is" or "must be" like because he or she is a member of a particular group. Various studies show that members of some groups in our society often have obstacles to overcome in finding or being selected for employment that people who are not members of those groups do not have to face. These obstacles are often traceable to patterns of discrimination in hiring and promotion practices that may be deliberate, but are also sometimes unconscious.

We examined the two distinct and apparently incompatible remedies to these unjustified inequalities, formal and substantive equality, in the last chapter. The favoured approach until recently has been formal equality, an approach of equal treatment that calls for the elimination of legal and formal barriers. The development of Canadian law provides a good example of this process in its entrenchment of what have come to be called equality rights in the Constitution and various human rights codes. The goal aimed at by this approach is to ensure that everyone has an equal opportunity to share in what our society has to offer, including an equal opportunity to compete for jobs and to be promoted.

In recent years, partly in response to unhappiness with the results produced by the formal equality approach, some have argued that real, substantive, or concrete equality cannot be achieved unless we do more than simply ensure formal legal equality. This theory, which we referred to as "substantive equality," argues that positive or affirmative action is sometimes required. The growing influence of this approach in Canada is reflected in part by the fact that the equality rights section of our Charter gives to governments the right to institute programs designed to help people disadvantaged because of unjust discrimination.

Substantive equality theorists argue that features such as race, sex, and disability normally regarded as morally irrelevant for purposes of discriminating amongst people can justifiably be used to identify people deserving of special or favourable treatment. Approaching the problem of discrimination in this way is controversial because it seems to require the acceptance of what would otherwise be regarded as unjustified discrimination in the achievement of its goals.

Most people have come to associate affirmative action with preferential hiring practices and with such controversial policies as setting quotas, practices that have been variously described as reverse discrimination, employment equity, justified discrimination, positive sexism, and responsive hiring. *Preferential* hiring raises issues of fairness because it suggests that, at least in some instances, jobs are given to people not because they are the most deserving or qualified candidates, but merely because they are members of disadvantaged groups. Is it morally acceptable to treat members of disadvantaged groups preferentially as a way of overcoming patterns of conscious and unconscious or systemic discrimination? If so, what sorts of justifications can be offered for employing these means as a way of achieving the goal of equality?

The Readings

The first reading is an example of affirmative action legislation enacted by the New Democratic Party in Ontario in 1993, *An Act to provide for Employment Equity for Aboriginal People, People with Disabilities, Members of Racial Minorities and Women*. Bill 79, as it is called, is currently slated for dismantling by Ontario's new government.

In the second reading, Michael Walker of the Fraser Institute argues that affirmative action measures violate the principle of equal treatment, unjustly punish current generations for wrongs that were committed by others in the past, and have not generated the kind of benefits they were intended to achieve. Walker believes that Canada should reverse its current trend of strengthening affirmative action measures and instead follow the lead of Americans, who he sees as rightly abandoning affirmative action.

The third reading by Thomas Hurka provides a general description of the directions that affirmative action hiring practices have taken and compares Canada's situation with that of the United States. After reviewing many of the arguments that have been used both for and against affirmative action programs, Hurka concludes that at least in some of its forms affirmative action is justified.

In the fourth reading, Jan Narveson argues that because the goal of business is to make profit, business people have a natural incentive to select candidates on the basis of criteria relevant to performing the job that needs doing and, therefore, to choose the most qualified candidates. He then argues that discrimination is not a problem because it does not pay for businesses to engage in discriminatory hiring. Narveson concludes not only that anti-discrimination laws are redundant, but that affirmative action measures are positively harmful to businesses and the workplace.

The last two readings provide two quite distinct and what appear to be conflicting approaches to the justification of affirmative action. Wayne Sumner defends the view that hiring policies that discriminate in favour of women are justified if there is good reason to believe that they will help to correct historical patterns of discrimination against women. He concludes that affirmative action is discrimination, but that it is justified by the goal of achieving greater equality.

In the final article, Christine Koggel develops an argument rejected by Sumner as a justification for affirmative action. Role modelling arguments escape the charge of reverse discrimination by holding that factors such as sex or race can be seen as qualifications for particular jobs because, at least in part, they serve the important function of increasing the participation of disadvantaged groups. Koggel moves the focus from seeing role models as the means for achieving a goal of greater representation for disadvantaged groups to the contexts and relationships within which the traditionally disadvantaged can interact with those in positions of power and influence when affirmative action measures are in place. Koggel expands the role of role modelling by showing how affirmative action allows those who were formerly excluded and are currently under-represented to challenge beliefs about their inferiority and unequal status.

BILL 79, 1993

[Act to Provide for Employment Equity for Aboriginal People, People with Disabilities, Members of Racial Minorities and Women]

Preamble

The people of Ontario recognize that Aboriginal people, people with dis-abilities, members of racial minorities and women experience higher rates of unemployment than other people in Ontario. The people of Ontario also recognize that people in these groups experience more discrimination than other people in finding employment, in retaining employment and in being promoted. As a result, they are underrepresented in most areas of employment, especially in senior and management positions, and they are overrepresented in those areas of employment that provide low pay and little chance for advancement. The burden imposed on the people in these groups and on the communities in which they live is unacceptable.

The people of Ontario recognize that this lack of employment equity exists in both the public and private sectors of Ontario. It is caused in part by systemic and intentional discrimination in employment. People of merit are too often overlooked or denied opportunities because of this discrimi-nation. The people of Ontario recognize that when objective standards govern employment opportunities, Ontario will have a workforce that is truly representative of its society.

The people of Ontario have recognized in the *Human Rights Code* the inherent dignity and equal and inalienable rights of all members of the human family and have recognized those rights in respect of employment in such statutes as the *Employment Standards Act* and the *Pay Equity Act*. This Act extends the principles of those Acts and has as its object the amelioration of conditions in employment for Aboriginal people, people with disabilities, members of racial minorities and women in all workplaces in Ontario and the provision of the opportunity for people in these groups to fulfil their potential in employment.

The people of Ontario recognize that eliminating discrimination in employment and increasing the opportunity of individuals to contribute in the workplace will benefit all people in Ontario.

Therefore, Her Majesty, by and with the advice and consent of the Legislative Assembly of the Province of Ontario, enacts as follows:

Part I
Employment Equity

Entitlement

1.—(1) All people are entitled to equal treatment in employment in accordance with the *Human Rights Code*.

Aboriginal people

(2) Aboriginal people are entitled to be considered for employment, hired, retained, treated and promoted in accordance with employment equity principles.

People with disabilities, racial minorities and women

(3) People with disabilities, members of racial minorities and women are entitled to be considered for employment, hired, retained, treated and promoted in accordance with employment equity principles.

Employment equity principles

2. The following principles of employment equity apply throughout Ontario:

1. Every Aboriginal person, every person with a disability, every member of a racial minority and every woman is entitled to be considered for employment, hired, retained, treated and promoted free of barriers, including systemic and deliberate practices and policies, that discriminate against them as an Aboriginal person, as a person with a disability, as a member of a racial minority or as a woman.

2. Every employer's workforce, in all occupational categories and at all levels of employment, shall reflect the representation of Aboriginal people, people with disabilities, members of racial minorities and women in the community.

3. Every employer shall ensure that its employment policies and practices, including its policies and practices with respect to recruitment, hiring, retention, treatment and promotion, are free of barriers, both systemic and deliberate, that discriminate against Aboriginal people, people with disabilities, members of racial minorities and women.

4. Every employer shall implement positive measures with respect to the recruitment, hiring, retention, treatment and promotion of Aboriginal people, people with disabilities, members of racial minorities and women.

5. Every employer shall implement supportive measures with respect to the recruitment, hiring, retention, treatment and promotion of Aboriginal people, people with disabilities, members of racial minorities and women which also benefit the employer's workforce as a whole. . . .

Part III
Obligations

Obligations

Implementation and maintenance of employment equity

9.—(1) Every employer shall implement and maintain employment equity by recruiting, hiring, retaining, treating and promoting employees according to employment equity principles and in accordance with the employment equity plan that applies in respect of those employees.

Role of supervisors, etc.

(2) Every employer shall ensure that the employer's staff who have responsibility for recruiting, hiring, supervising, evaluating or promoting employees are aware of, and observe, the requirements of this Act, the regulations and the employment equity plan that applies in respect of those employees.

Same

(3) Every member of staff who has responsibility for recruiting, hiring, supervising, evaluating or promoting employees shall work in accordance with this Act, the regulations and the employment equity plan that applies in respect of those employees.

Collection of workforce information

10.—(1) Every employer shall, in accordance with the regulations, conduct employment equity workforce surveys and collect other information to determine the extent to which members of the designated groups are employed in the employer's workforce.

Voluntary giving of information

(2) An employee has the right to decide whether to answer questions asked by an employer under subsection (1).

Review of employment policies

11.—(1) Every employer shall review the employer's employment policies and practices in accordance with the regulations.

Purpose of review

(2) The purpose of the review is to identify and enable the employer to remove barriers to the recruitment, hiring, retention, treatment and promotion of members of the designated groups, including terms and conditions of employment that adversely affect members of the designated groups.

Seniority rights

(3) For the purpose of this Act, employee seniority rights with respect to a layoff or recall to employment after a layoff that are acquired through a collective agreement or an established practice of an employer are deemed not to be barriers to the recruitment, hiring, retention, treatment or promotion of members of the designated groups.

Same

(4) For the purpose of this Act, employee seniority rights, other than those referred to in subsection (3), that are acquired through a collective agreement or an established practice of an employer are deemed not to be barriers to the recruitment, hiring, retention, treatment or promotion of members of the designated groups unless a board of inquiry under the *Human Rights Code* finds that the seniority rights discriminate against members of a designated group in a manner that is contrary to the *Human Rights Code*.

Employment equity plan

12.—(1) Every employer shall prepare an employment equity plan in accordance with the regulations. It must provide for,

(a) the elimination of barriers identified under section 11;

(b) the implementation of positive measures with respect to the recruitment, hiring, retention, treatment and promotion of members of the designated groups;

(c) the implementation of supportive measures with respect to the recruitment, hiring, retention, treatment and promotion of members of the designated groups which also benefit the employer's workforce as a whole;

(d) the implementation of measures to accommodate members of the designated groups in the employer's workforce;

(e) specific goals and timetables for the matters referred to in clauses (a) to (d);

(f) specific goals and timetables with respect to the composition of the employer's workforce; and

(g) such other matters as may be prescribed by the regulations.

More than one plan

(2) An employer may prepare more than one plan, in accordance with the regulations, for the purpose of meeting the employer's obligations under subsection (1), so long as each plan meets the requirements set out in subsection (1), and so long as, together, the plans cover all of the employer's employees and all of the employer's workplaces.

Plan certificates

(3) After preparing a plan, the employer shall prepare a certificate respecting the plan in accordance with the regulations.

Additional requirements (4) The certificate of every employer other than an employer in the broader public sector that has fewer than fifty employees and a private sector employer that has fewer than 100 employees shall, in accordance with the regulations, include information with respect to the provisions of the plan for the elimination of barriers and for the implementation of positive measures, supportive measures and measures to accommodate members of the designated groups.

Filing of certificate (5) The employer shall file the certificate with the Employment Equity Commission in a form approved by the Commission and in accordance with the regulations.

Copy of plan (6) The Commission may require the employer to file a copy of the plan.

Filing of copy of plan (7) Despite subsection (6), after preparing a plan, the Crown in right of Ontario shall file a copy of the plan with the Commission.

Standard re contents of plan **13.** Every employer shall ensure that the matters referred to in subsection 12 (1) that are contained in an employment equity plan would, if implemented, constitute reasonable progress toward achieving compliance with the principles of employment equity that are set out in section 2.

Implementation of plan **14.** Every employer shall make all reasonable efforts to implement each of the employer's employment equity plans and to achieve the goals set out in each plan in accordance with the timetables set out in the plan.

Review and revision of plan **15.**—(1) Every employer shall review and revise each of the employer's employment equity plans in accordance with the regulations.

Plan certificate (2) After revising a plan, the employer shall prepare a certificate respecting the revised plan in accordance with the regulations.

Additional requirements (3) The certificate of every employer other than an employer in the broader public sector that has fewer than fifty employees and a private sector employer that has fewer than 100 employees shall, in accordance with the regulations, include,

(a) information with respect to the efforts made to implement the previous plan and the results achieved; and

(b) information with respect to the provisions of the revised plan for the elimination of barriers and for the implementation of positive measures, supportive measures and measures to accommodate members of the designated groups.

Filing of certificate

(4) The employer shall file the certificate with the Employment Equity Commission in a form approved by the Commission and in accordance with the regulations.

Copy of plan

(5) The Commission may require the employer to file a copy of the revised plan.

Filing of copy of plan

(6) Despite subsection (5), after revising a plan, the Crown in right of Ontario shall file a copy of the revised plan with the Commission.

Joint responsibilities, employer and bargaining agent

16.—(1) This section applies if any of an employer's employees are represented by a bargaining agent.

Same

(2) The employer and the bargaining agent shall jointly carry out the responsibilities described in sections 10, 11, 12, 13 and 15 in respect of the part of the employer's workforce in which employees are represented by the bargaining agent.

More than one bargaining agent

(3) If the employees of the employer are represented by more than one bargaining agent, the employer and the bargaining agents shall establish a committee to co-ordinate the carrying out of their joint responsibilities.

Composition of committee

(4) The committee shall be composed of representatives of the bargaining agents and up to an equal number of representatives of the employer, in accordance with the regulations.

Good faith, etc.

(5) The joint responsibilities shall be carried out in good faith, separately from the normal collective bargaining process and in the manner prescribed by the regulations.

Right to information

(6) The employer shall provide the bargaining agent with all information in the employer's possession or control in respect of the part of the employer's workforce in which employees are represented by the bargaining agent that is necessary for the bargaining agent to participate effectively in carrying out their joint responsibilities, including the information prescribed by the regulations.

Exception

(7) Subsection (6) does not require the employer to provide the bargaining agent with information of a scientific, technical, commercial, financial, personal or other nature if,

(a) the disclosure of the information could reasonably be expected to prejudice the employer's competitive position; or

(b) the disclosure of the information meets the criteria prescribed by the regulations.

Consultation with
unrepresented
employees

17. Every employer shall, in accordance with the regulations, consult with the employer's employees who are not represented by a bargaining agent concerning the conduct of the employer's employment equity workforce survey, the review of the employer's employment policies and practices, and the development, implementation, review and revision of the employment equity plan that applies in respect of those employees.

Duty to post
information

18.—(1) Every employer shall post in each of the employer's workplaces,

    (a) a copy of each certificate that the employer has filed with the Employment Equity Commission in respect of each employment equity plan that applies in respect of the employees in the workplace; and

    (b) such other information in respect of this Act and employment equity as may be prescribed by the regulations.

Same

(2) The information described in clauses (1) (a) and (b) shall be posted in prominent places in the workplace that are accessible to all employees to whom the information applies.

Duty to make
information available

(3) Every employer shall provide or make available to the employer's employees information in respect of this Act and employment equity, in accordance with the regulations.

Duty to make copy of
plan available

(4) Every employer shall make available in each of the employer's workplaces a copy of each plan that applies in respect of the employees in the workplace.

Same

(5) A plan shall be made available in the workplace in such a manner that it is accessible to all employees to whom it applies.

Employment equity
records

19.—(1) Every employer shall establish and maintain employment equity records in respect of the employer's workforce.

Self-identification

(2) The employer shall keep in the employer's records concerning employees' membership in designated groups only the information, if any, that is provided by each employee about himself or herself.

Reports to the
Commission

20. Every employer shall submit reports and other information to the Employment Equity Commission in accordance with the regulations concerning the composition of the employer's workforce and the development, implementation, review and revision of the employer's employment equity plans.

Access to information

21. Any person may apply to the Employment Equity Commission for access to a copy of any information provided to the Commission under this Act and in the possession of the Commission.

EXEMPTIONS

Regulations re
Aboriginal workplaces

22.—(1) The Lieutenant Governor in Council may, by regulation, vary the application of any of the provisions of this Part and the regulations as they apply to Aboriginal workplaces. The regulation may define what constitutes an Aboriginal workplace.

Broader public sector employers

(2) The Lieutenant Governor in Council may, by regulation,

(a) exempt employers in the broader public sector that have fewer than fifty employees from any provision of this Part and the regulations;

(b) vary the application of any provision of this Part and the regulations to impose less stringent requirements on those employers.

Regulation ceases to apply

(3) A regulation made under subsection (2) ceases to apply to an employer who employs fifty or more employees at any time after the effective date.

Private sector employers

(4) The Lieutenant Governor in Council may, by regulation,

(a) exempt private sector employers that have fewer than 100 employees from any provision of this Part and the regulations;

(b) vary the application of any provision of this Part and the regulations to impose less stringent requirements on those employers.

Regulation ceases to apply

(5) A regulation made under subsection (4) ceases to apply to an employer who employs 100 or more employees at any time after the effective date. . . .

PART V
ADMINISTRATION

EMPLOYMENT EQUITY COMMISSION

Commission established

45.—(1) A commission is established to be known in English as the Employment Equity Commission and in French as Commission de l'équité en matière d'emploi.

Composition   (2) The Commission is composed of one or more members to be appointed by the Lieutenant Governor in Council.

Employment Equity Commissioner   (3) One member shall be designated by the Lieutenant Governor in Council as the Employment Equity Commissioner.

Employees   (4) Such employees as are necessary for the proper conduct of the Commission's work may be appointed under the *Public Service Act.*

Delegation   (5) The Commission may delegate any powers or duties to its employees.

Functions of the Commission   **46.**—(1) The Employment Equity Commission has the following functions:

1. To further the principles of employment equity.

2. To monitor the implementation of employment equity and the effectiveness of this Act.

3. To conduct research and develop policy in relation to employment equity.

4. To assist employers, employees and bargaining agents in complying with Part III.

5. To educate the public about employment equity.

6. To carry out any function assigned to the Commission under this or any other Act.

Public consultations   (2) The Commission may engage in public consultations which may include public hearings.

Policy directives   **47.**—(1) The Commission may issue policy directives on matters related to employment equity.

When effective   (2) A policy directive takes effect on the day it is published in *The Ontario Gazette.*

Effect of directive   (3) The Employment Equity Tribunal shall consider the Commission's policy directives in making decisions.

Commission rules   **48.** The Commission may make rules for the conduct and management of its affairs and for the practice and procedure to be observed in relation to matters it deals with.

Annual report	**49.**—(1) Each year the Employment Equity Commissioner shall make an annual report to the Minister of Citizenship on the activities and affairs of the Commission.
Same	(2) The report shall include data and information in respect of the progress made toward achieving employment equity in Ontario.
Tabling of report	(3) The Minister shall table the report before the Assembly if it is in session or, if not, at the next session.
When due	(4) Each annual report is due on or before the 31st day of March.
First annual report	(5) The first annual report is not due until the second anniversary of the 31st day of March following the coming into force of this section.
Advisory councils	**50.**—(1) The Minister of Citizenship may appoint one or more advisory councils to advise the Commission.
Provincial or regional	(2) An advisory council may be appointed for the province as a whole or for a region of the province.
Minimum representation	(3) An advisory council must include a representative of employers, a representative of labour and a representative of the designated groups.

BLOWING THE WHISTLE ON DISCRIMINATION

Michael Walker

Nothing quite offends the sensibilities of normal folk like discrimination. It starts in the family. Siblings rile at being treated differently. "It's not fair that XYZ got something that I did not. You are not treating us as equals."

It was not surprising, therefore, that when the issue of discrimination broke on the public policy scene it quickly became a driving force for the overhaul of legislation. First was the treatment of the races, principally in the United States. Then the treatment of genders. Then the differently-abled. From the right to vote, to sit at the front of the bus, and to use public washrooms, we progressed to the requirement that to operate within the law, a business must have a certain mix of visible minorities or of particular genders on its staff.

Along the road from Selma, Alabama, to Toronto and Victoria's pay and employment equity laws, the original notions of fair play have been left in the ditch. What began as a movement to ensure that every citizen would be treated equally before the law in every respect has become a device whereby special interests have sought to settle scores for real or imagined wrongs or, more practically, to pursue incomes which could not be achieved on

---

From Fraser Forum, *September 1995. Reprinted by permission of The Fraser Institute.*

merit alone. So-called affirmative action programs have become reverse discrimination mechanisms punishing current generations for past outcomes.

Canada has generally lagged the process in the United States, but we have in most particulars followed in their footsteps, usually five or ten years later.

But the worm has turned. In a recent decision, based on the careful research of the San Francisco-based Pacific Research Institute, the Board of Governors of the University of California threw out its "affirmative action" admissions policy. They did so because it so obviously discriminated against groups who were not the specific targets of the policy. Bright Koreans and other visible minorities, as well as whites, were getting the shaft in order to accommodate the named minorities.

More generally, the new Republican-dominated Congress in the United States is determined to overhaul many of the laws which attempt to accomplish nationally the ends sought by the University of California rules. And with the characteristic lag, these sentiments will eventually come to Canada. Indeed, the new government of Ontario has already announced that it will abolish the so-called employment equity legislation brought in by its predecessors.

The reason for this shift in attitude is not that Republicans or the Conservatives in Ontario or the Board of the University of California have become "unfair" in their outlook, or decided to indulge a taste for discrimination. The change in policy is coming because of the evidence of the unanticipated consequences of these well-intentioned but flawed policies, and because genuine minority groups themselves are recognizing that the laws often do not serve their interests.

There is nothing surprising about this outcome. In the early 1980s I co-authored two books which tried to warn Canadians about the problems with such policies. In *Discrimination, Affirmative Action and Equal Opportunity*, my co-author, Walter Block, and I pointed out that the prospective impact of these polices was such that Canada should avoid following in the footsteps of the United States. Wage differentials, we noted, are caused primarily by productivity differences, not discrimination. For example, equally trained, equally experienced single men and single women have been and are paid almost identically. In fact, women, at some ages, actually receive higher average wages than men of the same age.

Perhaps the most pernicious notion of all to come out of the attempt to legislatively pursue perceived discrimination has been the attempt to legislate equal pay for work of equal value. While seemingly fair, such policies ignore all of the important insights of modern economics, such as how value is determined. Markets and not wage bureaucrats determine value, and, as has been impressively demonstrated in experiments in China, the Soviet Union, and even here in Canada, markets have a way of making themselves felt even in the face of the most energetic effort to suppress them.

The practical side of all of this is that those groups and businesses who have been benefiting from reverse discrimination policies would do well to reconsider their options. While the protection of equal opportunity is likely to continue, affirmative action legislation which is exposed to the effect of markets is highly unlikely to survive the decade. Regrettably, it will take somewhat longer to expunge the sort of affirmative action programs which the University of California has just abandoned, but which some Canadian schools, like the University of Alberta, have just adopted.

→ ←

GIVING WOMEN AN EVEN BREAK AT WORK

Thomas Hurka

In the United States, important social policies are mandated by the courts and become the subjects of intense political controversy. In Canada, they get introduced by bureaucrats against only mild murmurs of protest.

So it has been when affirmative action (a.k.a. reverse discrimination) crossed the border and took up Canadian residence under the name "employment equity."

Affirmative action means giving preference in hiring, promotion or university admission to the members of disadvantaged groups. In Canada, the selected groups are women, natives, visible minorities and the employable handicapped.

Administratively, affirmative action can take three forms.

The mildest is a tie-breaking scheme. If two candidates are judged to be equally well qualified you prefer, say, the woman to the man.

Next is an extra-points scheme. A candidate gets extra credit, over and above her normal qualifications, for being a woman. This means she can be hired ahead of a man who would otherwise be judged more qualified.

Finally, there are quotas. Certain places are set aside for women, and men cannot compete for them.

Opponents of affirmative action often say they don't mind tie-breaking; supporters loudly deny they favor quotas. But in fact these administrative differences are morally trivial. The important question is: what morally justifies any affirmative action?

Here the move across the border has made a difference.

U.S. discussions assume that affirmative action means hiring someone who is in a traditional sense less qualified — that is, who will do less well in the job on a day-to-day basis. But the official Canadian line is that affirmative action is needed to ensure that the most qualified person is hired, that "systemic" barriers don't prevent talented women from advancing as they should.

Isn't this contradictory? How can telling managers *not* to hire the most qualified person help them hire the most qualified?

The objection assumes that the candidate managers *think* is most qualified is *in fact* most qualified. This is often not so.

Affirmative action began in the federal civil service when it was found that, although women held 40 per cent of civil service jobs, they had only 5 per cent of the top jobs. Faced with this statistic, no one could pretend that civil service promotions were based on actual merit. Civil service managers were preferring less qualified men to more qualified women.

One reason for this could be conscious sexism, the conscious belief that women are inferior or should not have important jobs. Although once common, this is less so now.

More persistent is subconscious sexism, or the subconscious use of sexist stereotypes. Someone who believes himself free of prejudice may have a subconscious picture of women as inferior that he applies to women candidates and that makes him find them less qualified.

Or the cause may be more innocent. Even if men and women can do some jobs equally well, they may do them differently, using different talents and personal strengths. But if only men have had the job before, managers may think the male way of doing it is the only

Reprinted from The Globe and Mail *with permission of Thomas Hurka, University of Calgary.*

way. They may, honestly and understandably, not count as qualifications female traits that haven't been able to show they're qualifications.

These factors are pervasive and enduring. When they exist — and the statistics show they often exist — there is a morally uncontestable case for affirmative action.

Given the factors, if managers think a woman is equally or nearly equally qualified with a man, she is probably more qualified. This justifies tie-breaking and extra points.

If a candidate is rated among the best women she is probably among the best, period. This can justify quotas.

Deciding exactly how many extra points to give or what quotas to use requires estimating the percentage of women who would be hired if actual merit were decisive. This is a controversial matter, about which honest people can differ. But if we allow that managers can misrate candidates, we can justify some affirmative action without giving up the traditional idea that hiring should be by merit.

We can't however, justify all the affirmative action proposed in Canada.

Imagine there's a job you think should be filled 50 per cent by women, but that now has only 20 per cent women. If you use the official Canadian argument you can now start hiring 50 per cent women. But then the percentage of women in the job as a whole will only reach 50 per cent after a generation, when the last male hired before your scheme started retires.

Most Canadian supporters of affirmative action don't want their targets reached this slowly.

As recently reported, the Ontario College of Art will hire 100 per cent women for the next 10 years. A proposal at a university department I know is for two-thirds women over the next 15 years.

These schemes can't be justified on the grounds of removing barriers or ensuring that the best candidates are hired. They clearly involve selecting people who are not, in the traditional sense, most qualified. An honest defence of them must recognize this, and show why, despite it, they're still justified.

AFFIRMATIVE ACTION: HOW FAR SHOULD WE GO?

Thomas Hurka

One argument points to the consequences of affirmative action. It admits affirmative action has short-term costs in lost job efficiency, but claims these are outweighed by long-term benefits.

For some the benefit is just achieving, as quickly as possible, a representative work force, one where the proportion of women in top jobs equals that in the population. This is morally dubious. Any morally significant benefits must go to individuals, not groups.

But there are such benefits, operating through changes in people's attitudes.

If the belief that women are inferior persists in Canada, either consciously or subconsciously, it's partly because women aren't sufficiently prominent in Canadian life. Moving them quickly into important jobs can help dispel that belief and the many harms it does.

Reprinted from The Globe and Mail *with permission of Thomas Hurka, University of Calgary.*

Equally important are the changes in women's attitudes. What you aspire to in life depends on what you think you can do, which depends on what people like you have done before. Women in prominent jobs can be role models, encouraging young women to work for similar success. If the young women achieve success this will benefit both them and society, which now wastes much of their potential.

If affirmative action has these benefits, is it therefore justified? Some say no: any policy is wrong that discriminates by race or gender. Affirmative action's end is good, but it doesn't justify these means.

But the issue is tricky. Imagine there's a job for which intelligence is a qualification, so the more intelligent are hired ahead of the less intelligent. Can the less intelligent complain of discrimination? We want, obviously, to say no. But on what basis?

There seems only one argument. Hiring by intelligence isn't wrong, we can say, because intelligent candidates will do the job better. And that's important because society benefits when the job is done better.

This argument implies a more general one. Discrimination on any basis is wrong if its social consequences are bad, but not otherwise.

By this test, race and sex discrimination are usually wrong. They hire less able candidates and, when the group discriminated against is disadvantaged, perpetuate harmful attitudes against it.

But there's an exception for discrimination in favor of the disadvantaged, as in affirmative action. It can have over-all good consequences, and so be justified.

This thinking appears in the Charter of Rights and Freedoms, whose equality clauses explicitly exempt programs aimed at "the amelioration of conditions of disadvantaged individuals or groups."

We've looked at a second justification of affirmative action: that, even when it doesn't hire the most qualified person, it has good long-term consequences. A third argument says that affirmative action is required as compensation for past injustice. If women and natives have been treated unjustly, they should be compensated by preferential hiring.

Although common in U.S. discussions, this argument is heard much less frequently in Canada. Despite this, the objections to it are often, irrelevantly, introduced into Canadian debate.

One is that affirmative action benefits only the least disadvantaged members of the selected groups, those doing well enough to apply for high-profile jobs. Another is that it places the entire burden of compensation on a few white males who are no more guilty of the injustice than anyone.

Even if successful, these objections concern only one justification of affirmative action. They don't touch the arguments that affirmative action hires the best person or has good consequences.

The objections may also be answerable. If the effects of injustice are pervasive they may affect all members of the group, including those doing comparatively well. And the white males, although not specially guilty of the injustice, may be its prime beneficiaries, competing successfully against women and natives who would beat them given an equal chance.

In the United States it would be vital to evaluate these answers. But in Canada the compensation argument merely supplements two other justifications of affirmative action. Honest people can disagree how much affirmative action these justifications support, but, as our charter recognizes, they do support some.

QUESTIONS

1. Thomas Hurka identifies three different forms that affirmative action programs can take. What are they? Do you agree that from a moral point of view they are not significantly different?
2. Does Hurka give any reasons for not heeding Michael Walker's call that Canadians follow the American lead and dismantle affirmative action programs?
3. Hurka identifies two of the main arguments used to justify hiring less qualified people. What are they? Are they convincing?

FAIR HIRING AND AFFIRMATIVE ACTION

Jan Narveson

1. The Subject of This Essay

In recent times, policies that have now become generally known as "Affirmative Action" have been prominent on the agendas of governments at all levels. These policies have two notable features. First, in marked contrast and apparent opposition to previous practice, they call for positive preference to be given to certain groups of people in particular. And second, they do so on the ground that those groups have previously been, or perhaps are still, the subjects of discrimination on the part of hirers, or of society at large. The assumption is that the second feature *justifies* the first one: that an appropriate way to correct the injustices to which such groups have been subjected is to impose mandatory preferential hiring on potential employers. This practice raises major and basic questions of justice and fairness. In this short treatment, I will query the soundness of the argument. Many have raised the question whether this is the correct response to injustices of this kind. I agree with those queries and will pose them in this essay. In addition, though, I will raise the more basic question, of just how and indeed whether "discrimination in hiring" is unjust in the first place. Getting these things right will, I believe, greatly improve our practice in this vexed area. There is no doubt that affirmative action has been and will continue to be a highly divisive kind of policy. We urgently need to set matters right.

2. Is Discrimination in Hiring Unjust?

Few beliefs among contemporary writers, at least, are more solidly entrenched than the view that discriminating against people is morally wrong, unjust. It is a belief with an air of self-evidence about it. And like many other such beliefs held by many people in the past, that air is seen to consist largely of fog when subjected to more careful analysis. It may seem obvious that to hire someone because he is a "he" rather than a "she", or white rather than, say, black, is somehow unfair. And if it is, of course, then by parity of reason it ought

Jan Narveson, 1996. Reprinted by permission of Jan Narveson.

to seem equally obvious that it is unfair to hire a "she" rather than a "he", or a black person rather than a white person. This last inference is extremely important. For if it did not follow, then the first claim would itself be extremely implausible; but if it does, then it is hard to see how "affirmative action" policies could be just. To get a start on this, we had better look with some care at the subjects of discrimination and fairness.

2.1 Definitions

What do we mean by 'discrimination', anyway? The basics are not so hard to come by. To begin with, we should appreciate that this word, like so many, has more than one familiar meaning. It can even refer to what is generally regarded as a good thing: to be "discriminating" in matters of taste, for example, is to be able to make fine and subtle distinctions which perhaps escape the eye of the less perceptive. That Jonathan is a "discriminating judge of wines", for instance, is a compliment rather than a slam. But in moral and political matters, discrimination is regarded as a bad thing. Why?

First, to discriminate among persons, in contexts such as hiring, is always to discriminate *against* someone. The person discriminated against is passed over in favor of some other person, such as the rival candidate. (Which brings up a point: hiring is by no means the only area in which we can discriminate. We will concentrate on hiring, especially because it is the area on which most current political "action" is concerned. But one can discriminate in many contexts of choice: whom to designate as the class valedictorian, or any of an immense variety of honors or rewards.)

Second, in all these cases, there is a common element: namely, that the persons favored have been favored because of the possession of an *irrelevant* characteristic or set of characteristics. This idea of "relevance" is absolutely essential to the whole subject. If there is no way in which people should be treated, no basis for supposing that these are the features on the basis of which choices *should* be made, then it makes no sense at all to say that someone has been selected on the basis of the *wrong* ones.

Combining these two, we get the general definition of 'discrimination': a person has been discriminated against if he or she has been passed over in favor of someone else, but on the basis of characteristics having no relevance to the choices made by the persons with the power to make them.

In all discrimination, we may say, there are three basic positions involved: (1) the person who makes the selection — the hirer, who, in the cases we are concerned with, is the "discriminator"; (2) the person discriminated *against*, the person passed over — the "discriminatee"; and finally, (3) the beneficiary of this action, the person who gets the choice made in his or her favor. A fourth term should also be noted: the characteristics on the basis of which the supposedly wrongful choice is made — the "discriminandum", as we might call it.

The plot now thickens quite rapidly. If we are to claim that someone was wrongfully passed over for some situation, we must be claiming that there are certain characteristics such that the chooser — in the cases we are especially concerned with, the hirer — has a duty to choose on the basis of those rather than anything else. What those who think that "discrimination" is fundamentally wrong must think, then, is that we, or at least hirers, have a duty to choose on the basis of relevant characteristics. That raises the questions, (1) what is "relevance" here?; and (2) why would we — or, indeed, do we, really — have a duty to hire only on the basis of relevant features?

2.2 What Constitutes "Relevance"?

Suppose you are the operator of a business: you own and operate a hardware store, for instance. The business expands enough that you think it would benefit from an extra employee. On the basis of what will you hire such a person? Knowledge of the hardware business, surely; good work habits, such as punctuality — showing up at the store on time so that the business can open for the public when it advertises it will be open; and so on. In other walks of life, very different characteristics might be important. If you are in need of a creative writer, the factor of showing up for work on time may be beside the point, though getting the story in by the deadline may well be important. Knowledge of the writer's subject will be crucial, but politeness to customers will not. And so on.

What do all these cases have in common? There is a fairly straightforward answer to this. Every organization that is in a position to hire anybody has a purpose or purposes for which it exists. It will, then, hire the people who can *best promote those purposes.* If the organization, by hiring applicant A at the level of remuneration it can get A for, as compared with applicant B at B's pay level, is likely, on the whole, to achieve more of what the organization is trying to achieve, then A should get the nod. That seems, on reflection, entirely obvious.

In some of these cases, the organization will be a private business which, in whatever specific way it is trying to do so, is endeavoring to make money, that is, profit. Private businesses sell something to certain people, and they incur various costs in the process. Among their costs is their wage bill, the amount they pay their employees. (This may be complex: there may be not only a monetary wage or salary for each hour, week or month worked, or perhaps each unit of product produced, but benefits such as pensions and insurance schemes, and perhaps also various "perks". For brevity, we will lump these all into one, which we'll call the "wage"; and we'll refer to the organization as the "firm".) A firm makes money by selling enough of its product at prices such that overall, their income exceeds their expenses. Moreover, since it wants to make as much money as possible, it will want to make the excess of income over costs as great as possible. It wants to "maximize" its profits.

In other cases, profit isn't what the firm is "into". It may, for instance, be a charitable organization, or a church, or school. Even so, it will be concerned with costs. And though it does not pursue monetary profit, it pursues some objectives that can be, very broadly, "quantified". If it is a church, it will be concerned to "save more souls" rather than less; if it is a University, it will want to educate people more rather than less, and contribute more rather than less to the sum of human knowledge.

In all cases, then, our hirer hires for a discernible, more or less clearly formulated general purpose, which it pursues by utilizing a set of resources, such that it makes sense to think those resources can be used more or less effectively in relation to its goals. This general characterization is enough to generate the set of relevant features on the basis of which it will be able to make rational hiring decisions. The applicant who is such that the firm will do better by its purposes if it hired that one rather than any other is the one to hire.

2.3 Is Relevance Always Possible? Is "Irrelevance" Sometimes Rational?

What if more than one applicant appears likely to be equal in ability to accomplish the firm's purposes? The firm now has a problem, which must be solved, since *somebody* must be hired. Here are three familiar ways of dealing with such problems.

1. It can *randomize* over the applicants — flip a coin, say.
2. It can take the *first* applicant that applied.
3. It can hire the one who seems more appealing in respect of some *irrelevant* feature, so far as the firm is concerned. For example, the first cousin of the "boss", or the woman who looks nicer, or the applicant who is likely to be more popular with fellow employees.

Or, of course, a combination of the above. For example, there will be a cut-off date, and only applicants who got there in time will be considered; but among them, the winner is decided by lottery.

Notice another thing: there is a decidedly *not irrelevant* way of shortening any potential list of equally capable applicants: the firm can *bargain* with them, choosing the applicant who will do the job for the lowest pay. Indeed, given the purpose of the firm, it *should* do this. Since this is, obviously, relevant rather than irrelevant, we have implicitly assumed that this has already been done: the list of equal-best applicants can't be got for anything less than a certain wage — the one offered. One of the sources of contemporary problems in this area is a feeling that this last method, bargaining, is somehow itself "unfair". If the reader is inclined to think that, he had better think again. To have a purpose is to devote a limited set of resources toward a certain end that is achievable to greater or less degree; and to want to achieve more of it, rather than less, with the available resources. That means minimizing costs and maximizing efforts toward the goal. Wages are *costs* to any firm; obviously it has an interest in minimizing them. To say that it is "unfair" to do so is to fail to appreciate the basics of the subject. Some romantic writers have apparently felt that we should never engage in organized, rational activity toward definite ends, relative to which we can assess costs which we therefore want to minimize. That view makes it impossible to talk sensibly of "fairness" in any case.

2.4 Freedom

Well, which of the three listed ways, then, is required? That brings up another question, really: Why are we in this business in the first place? At this point, a fundamental feature of our society comes into view. For the answer to that question is — *whatever!* People go into business, or a particular business, for any number of reasons: because they simply want to make a living, because they happen to like the particular kind of activity that that firm specialized in (this is very likely in the case of academic employment); and so on. And, what is most important here, *any* of these reasons is perfectly okay. What we believe, surely, is that people have a free choice about what if any business they will go into.

Free choice is lack of specific obligation. If you are free to do whatever you want in a certain area, then that is to say that you have no obligation to do one thing rather than another in it. Nobody can force you to make one choice rather than another. There may be good reasons for your making one choice rather than another, to be sure; but still, what you choose and why is *your* business.

Because this is so obviously true, however, a fundamental problem arises concerning the most primary of the questions we are investigating here. For if nobody has any duty to go into any particular business, or any business at all, then that is as much as to say that nobody has any fundamental *duty* to hire *anybody* for *any* reason. And if they don't have any such duty, it is at least not obvious how they could nevertheless have the duty to hire A rather than B, for *no matter what reason* the hirer does so. This last may seem surprising to some people. Let us look a bit more closely.

Suppose I want my lawn mowed. I can do it myself, or induce somebody else to. To do the latter, I might use money or any number of other inducements. But suppose I hire my friend Tom — not because he's an expert lawnmower, but because I simply like him and, he being perhaps in need of a bit of money, offering him the job is doing him a favor. Is this wrong? Am I unfairly discriminating against all the expert mowers out there who might have done a better job or at lower cost? Indeed I am not. It's my lawn, it's up to me not only how it will be mown but whether it will be, and in general, there simply are no duties in this area. I am perfectly free to accept a poorer job for a higher price, if I want to. And in any case, it may not be worth my while trying to locate these more efficient workers.

2.5 The Purposes of Firms

We noted above that what constitutes a relevant criterion for such things as hiring is a function of the purpose for which the hiring is done. Jobs differ, very greatly, and they do so because the purposes of the organizations doing the hiring differ. What sets these purposes? That is obviously a crucial question, for whether a criterion of selection is relevant, as we have seen, is determined by that purpose.

And it is a further implication of the point made above that the purpose of the firm is, basically, the purpose of the people whose firm it is. If it's a one-person firm, that person's purposes in setting up the firm are the purposes of the firm. If it's a company, they must jointly work out those purposes — though it's usually likely that its purpose will be to make money, whatever else; and even when that isn't so, cost-effectiveness will always be an important consideration.

Firms could of course, have evil purposes: the Mafia is a "firm" we can do without. But short of that, any purpose that isn't downright malevolent is perfectly acceptable in a free society. And those who worry about discrimination are worried about it in acceptable, normal firms and organizations, not criminal ones.

So let's think about what a firm's purposes might be like. One of my favorite imaginary examples is the "Irish-Canadian Distillery Corporation", which makes Irish whiskey, but whose purpose is only partly to make money; the other purpose is to employ fellow Irish-men, those wonderful people! Ethnic clubs and churches are further examples. When the ICD employs an Irishman rather than someone equally or even somewhat more competent at the job, it is fulfilling its somewhat complex purpose — it's not "discriminating". Examples like this make life very difficult for those who think it is easy to identify cases of wrongful discrimination.

Among the popular discriminanda nowadays are sex and race. It is thought to be wrong to discriminate on the basis of either. Yet if your ladies' dress shop hires only women, you can very reasonably claim that being a woman is quite relevant to the job; or if you want to write for Ebony magazine, you don't have much of a complaint if they don't take you because you're white or oriental. It is easy for these popular examples of supposedly irrelevant characteristics to become quite relevant.

2.6 Discrimination Is Irrational

We can now draw a general conclusion about what is normally referred to as "discrimination". Since hiring on the basis of irrelevant characteristics means hiring on the basis of characteristics that don't promote the purposes of the firm, it must follow that attending to such characteristics is, so far as it goes, contrary to the purpose of the firm. If Firm F's purpose is to make money, and plain Ms. X is a much more efficient secretary than beautiful Ms. Y, then if X is available for about the same wage as Y, Firm F will hire Ms. X, if it knows what it's doing. If it doesn't, there are two possibilities. Either it doesn't know what it's doing, and hiring Ms. Y is irrational; or else F has a more complicated purpose than making money: e.g., it also wants to create attractive environments for its managerial-level employees who have secretaries.

Is there something wrong with that? If there is, then how about the man who marries a beautiful woman, in part because she is beautiful? After all, plain women might be just as good at all the other things a man might want a wife for, and some of the available candidates might well have been a good deal better! And indeed, it might be irrational for John to marry pretty Mary instead of plain Matilda. But then again it might not. You're going to be looking at your mate a great deal in the next fifty years, after all: isn't it worth sacrificing some other variables to have the sight you are greeted with each time a pleasant one? And if it's pleasant in a wife, mightn't it also be so in a secretary?

If we are entitled to run businesses and undertake endeavours for our *own purposes*, whatever they are, so long as their pursuit does not harm others, how can there be any basic objection? Ms. X can complain, in the above case — and she can also try lowering her price. But why should her complaint get more than a polite hearing and a rejection? How can the outside world have any business, any right, preventing this firm from doing what it likes?

Of course, if hiring Ms. Y is irrational, the company is going to pay for it. Its costs of production of the goods it makes its money by selling will be higher. And, on the other hand, the firm down the road, G, which doesn't have this particular expensive habit about secretaries will, on the contrary, have a better-running office that gets more done for the same money, thus making it more competitive.

In short, then, the situation is that market forces tend to extinguish discrimination in employment, just as they would any other inefficient business practice. So long as we are using the proper criteria for hiring, this has to be our result. There is, to be sure, a tendency for discussants of this subject to suppose that businesses ought to hire on the basis of various criteria whose relevance to those businesses is marginal, indirect, or nonexistent. The fact that A would "work just as hard" as B, for example, is uninteresting if the sort of "work" that A does is simply not the sort that will promote the company's purposes, whereas B's is. Nor is the fact that A is an overall excellent worker, if meanwhile B, who is merely quite good, will do the job for half the price, or can be relied on to stay around a lot longer, and so on. Pinning down the complex of factors that make one person on the whole a better buy than another from an employer's point of view is not a simple matter.

Many readers will scoff at the above, citing what they claim to be relevant statistical facts concerning salaries and employment of, say, blacks versus whites. We will discuss some of the pitfalls of uncareful use of statistics below. (An example: a widely-cited figure has it that women earn on average about 70% or so of what men do, the implication being than women are "discriminated against". It is not noted that this statistic is a gross figure covering both part-time and full-time employment. Since about half of all employed women are in part-time employment, it is hardly surprising that when you add up all the wages paid to women and all the wages paid to men, the average for women is much lower. Correcting for that one mistake alone closes the gap to within less than 10%. More careful work on obviously relevant factors closes it up altogether.[1])

2.7 Discrimination Does Not Harm People

People tend to talk about discrimination as if it were "harmful". Those who do so, however, have probably fallen afoul of a very important, but quite plain, distinction. For it certainly is possible to harm people from discriminatory motives. When Negroes were lynched in the American South, for example, the motive was probably racist, indeed. However, what's wrong with being lynched *isn't* that one was discriminated against thereby! It is that lynching tends to be fatal, which certainly *is* an injury, and about as serious a one as we could readily find. Obviously it is wrong to kill innocent people, or to assault them, or hit them, or steal from them, and in general, to harm them.

You harm someone when you intervene in his or her life in such a way that the situation, the life, of the victim is worsened by what you do. If I hit you, then after the hit you are damaged and in pain, whereas before you were in a better condition: hitting worsens your situation. But *not hiring* someone doesn't do this. The applicant would like the job, to be sure. But he doesn't now have it. After rejection, he is in the same situation as before, *not a worse* one — still no job.

Remember, you have no general *duty* to give people jobs, just as (and for the same reason that) you have no duty to go into business at all. No one is *entitled* to a job, although frequently people *deserve* them.

2.8 Anti-Discrimination Laws Nonsensical

Since it is not in a company's interest to discriminate, properly understood, laws forbidding discrimination in hiring are, in that regard, redundant. Laws are needed when people have an interest in doing what the law forbids. Theft, for instance, hurts the victim but benefits the thief, so long as he gets away with it. But the person who is "hurt" by discrimination is, primarily, the employer — which implies an important point, that will be brought out in the next section.

Meanwhile, we have to point out that the greater society surrounding a business has no business, so to speak, passing laws that command these companies to be "efficient". Such laws are certain to be at least as counterproductive as the practices they forbid. Laws forcing people to do what is in those people's interest anyway are called "paternalistic" laws; such laws are widely condemned by thinkers on these matters, and for good reason. Moreover, the public has no basic interest in a firm's efficiency — not of anything like the kind it has in its own safety, for instance. If there are inefficient people out there, that had better *not* be a subject for the law to go to work on — who among us can claim to be totally efficient?

2.9 Within-Firm Duties vs. General Duties

However, we must not conclude too hastily that the whole concern about discrimination is a mistake, and that one cannot have a duty to hire fairly. Who would have such duties and why would they have them? Here the answer is straightforward. Since discrimination is counterproductive, those who are working for the firm, and have duties to it, are indeed under an obligation to hire, among other things, "fairly". A sizable organization will appoint certain people to do the hiring, or certain bits of the hirings. These people have duties that go with, indeed define, their positions. All such people may be presumed to have a general duty to the organization to do their jobs well, and in the case of hiring, that means, among other things, to refrain from discrimination, should the officer in question be inclined to do so. If you are a racist manager, you will be inclined to turn away what might have been productive employees, and to hire ones that are less productive. Clearly this is contrary to what your firm has hired you to do.

However, these are *within-firm* duties, duties laid upon particular people by the terms of their jobs, and owed to the company who hires them. Indirectly, of course, they will then be owed to applicants for jobs. If the company wants a good tool-and-die maker, the staff person whose job is to find such people must avoid looking at skin-color or religious belief, and so on, instead. But the society in which this company is embedded does not, in its turn, have the right to enforce those requirements: that's the business of the company, which can discipline or dismiss any employee for failing to do his job properly. Society is not in the tool-and-die-making business, nor any other particular business. Its business is to enable people to live the sort of lives they want to live, on terms that are mutually agreeable. If you'd prefer that a factory had different work procedures and practices, and you can't persuade its management to alter them, then you can go somewhere else, or try to set up your own factory.

3. Affirmative Action

"Affirmative action" policies are supposedly designed to undo the effects of injustice, the injustice being discrimination. We have seen that what is ordinarily called discrimination is not obviously unjust. Since affirmative action presupposes this, if our previous reflections are correct, affirmative action programs lack the rationale for which they were originally designed. Nevertheless, we will discuss the subject — not just because we may, conceivably, be wrong in our previous reflections, but because items of independent interest are raised thereby. Moreover, I shall argue that this would be the wrong cure for the disease even if it were a disease.

A further general observation is in order before we proceed. In view of my previous arguments, discrimination isn't morally wrong in the first place. But doesn't it follow, then, that affirmative action, which is "discrimination in reverse", must be okay? No. For 'affirmative action' isn't just preferential hiring. If that's all it were, it would, of course, be all right. If your firm wants to hire nothing but left-handed people, and to do so because in your view left-handed people haven't been getting a fair shake, you are welcome to do that. But we are discussing government-imposed *policies* of reverse discrimination. Anti-discrimination regulations would *prohibit* people from hiring on the basis of job-unrelated features such as race and sex: it doesn't allow people to do these dumb things, even if they wanted to. Similarly, affirmative action programs *force* the employer to hire persons on the basis of color or sex, or whatever, whether they want to or not, and whether it's in their interest or not. Affirmative action programs are, in principle, much worse in their effects on the free conduct of business and other activities, because at least discrimination, properly speaking, is against the interests of business anyway, and so if those programs were properly run, they would not be hampering businesses from operating as they would anyway. Indeed, it follows from the foregoing analysis that genuine anti-discrimination regulations are essentially superfluous. But that is not true of "affirmative action" programs. A new and seriously insidious idea has crept into the design of those programs. It is no longer enough to forbid the employer from intentionally taking the supposedly irrelevant variables, such as race and sex, into account: these programs also forbid having a work-force whose proportions of members of the groups in question are deemed to be "wrong", e.g. by being different from what they are in society at large. This new idea requires careful discussion in its own right.

3.1 Definitions

When is a program an "affirmative action" program? A program is an "affirmative action" program when it requires employers to give more than ordinary weight to the applications of members of those groups which the authorities fostering the program deem to have been the subjects of wrongful discrimination.

This time we have explicitly confined the concept to the context of employment, even though it is similarly true that any number of other contexts could possibly be the subject of such programs. For example, the author recently saw a photograph of the San Francisco Bay Area Youth Orchestra. Its members are not employed, since their positions are not jobs that somebody is paying for — but they are, after all, selected, and on the basis of the overwhelmingly relevant criterion of ability to play their instruments well. Strikingly, over half of the 90 or so young players were oriental, and all but one of the remainder were white, leaving only one black player and no Hispanics.[2] Had this been a professional orchestra, it could have been accused of massive "discrimination". Had it been any of a great range of other professions, it surely would have been. The reader should think about this point. After all, what's wrong with awarding jobs on the basis of race or whatever is that to do so is "discriminatory", then so is awarding positions on the pee wee league baseball team, prizes in the local gardening competition, and so on, for all of the cases in which we single some people out for reward or benefit. But we will say no more about those contexts here.

3.2 What Constitutes Unfair Employment?

In one sense, we know the answer to this: it's using criteria other than those relevant to the purposes of the employer — job competence, broadly speaking. But this raises the question of when one has done that. Affirmative action programs get off the ground when this question is answered in a particular way: namely, by *inferring* that "discrimination" has taken place from employment statistics concerning the distribution of persons from the allegedly oppressed groups in the ranks of jobholders of the kind in question.

How is this to be done? In my example of the Bay Area Youth Orchestra, the fact was that not quite half the players were white, and only about 1% were black. What made that "striking" was the fact that perhaps 80% of the population in that area are white, some 10% black and 10% Asian. The proportion of Asians and blacks in the orchestra was strikingly different from the percentages of those groups in the area's populace. A defender of affirmative action might conclude that there must have been a great deal of discrimination in the assembling of that orchestra.

He might. But why couldn't we draw a very different conclusion: namely, that a surprisingly high percentage of oriental people are highly talented at the playing of classical music, and a much lower percentage of black people are so. Had there been, for instance, a "Bay Area Youth Jazz Band", the story would surely have been very different: probably there would be as many black players as there were Asians in the classical orchestra, and perhaps no Asians at all, or only one or so. It was black people who invented jazz, after all, and a not implausible hypothesis that it is a kind of music that speaks to something in the "souls", or the genes, or certainly the broad cultures, of blacks. And so on.

The point is that it is certainly not true that those who selected the players in the Youth Orchestra explicitly chose Asians over others regardless of their ability. The fact is that the most able youths, within the limits of reliability of the selection procedures, turned out to be Asian.

Disparities in many, many walks of life are common, and strike most of us as quite unsurprising. American professional basketball teams, for instance, are dominated by tall black males. If you have any interest and rudimentary knowledge of the game of basketball, it cannot fail to strike you that the players on those teams are extremely good at what they do. The managements of those teams, it is easy to believe, didn't do anything remotely like looking at the ranks of applicants and saying "OK, all you white or Asian folks, forget it! We only take blacks. . ." Nor do they say, "Sorry, our quota of whiteys is full . . . !" We have every reason to suppose that they hire what they judge to be the best players they can afford — for the very good reason that winning teams make more money than losing ones, and these teams are trying to make money. As we saw in the previous section, we can expect "market forces" to induce professional sports teams' owners to hire strictly on the basis of ability, modified by budget limitations. If it nevertheless turns out that most of the players are black, as in basketball, or white, as in hockey, or Asian, as in table tennis, we conclude that whatever it is that makes for skill at those respective sports is found in quite different proportions in those respective races. It is, in short, on the face of it, a *strictly empirical question* how ability at job X correlates with membership in Group Y.

Or, of course, ability plus inclination. Which brings up another question. We all know what it's like, I'm sure, to find that we are reasonably good at something which, nevertheless, we simply aren't *interested* in doing. It seems not to be universally true by any means that people love to do what they are good at. It seems quite possible that a large group of people might be averse to doing something that they would be very good at IF they felt like doing it — but, alas, they don't. I mention this as just one more factor in the puzzle about the relating of statistical data about who does what to underlying variations in basic ability and such.

We should, though, say one thing about this. Very few writers really think that the equality they posit holds at the individual level. It is simply beyond the bounds of scientific credulity to suppose that Mozart or Euler were just another of the kids on the block, who happened to develop their amazing abilities only because of the right kind of socialization. And we also know that the human genome, which has enormous influence on every imaginable facet of development and which affords the potential for an unbelievable amount of variations, should nevertheless be resolutely identical for every single human being when it comes to abilities of the kind that are relevant to such things as earning incomes in particular ways. The hypothesis of "basic human equality" in these matters is not scientifically credible, let alone plausible. And in all sorts of respects on the physical front, it is also, in a word, exploded.

There is, then, no rational *basis* in relation to today's science for any substantial hypothesis about "human equality". And there is also no rational basis for supposing that the human genetic system has taken any steps whatever to reassure us that none of the variation correlates well with race, sex, or whatever. Very much to the contrary, in fact.

A hypothesis to the effect that ability *must* be distributed equally, at root, between the Xs and the Ys has no scientific standing, and no real credibility. In all kinds of specific cases, we know perfectly well that it is not. Thus statistical arguments intended to convict employers of racism or sexism simply aren't valid. And legislation based on such assumptions is unfounded.

3.3 Affirmative Action as Overkill

Let us suppose that some person has been done an injustice by another. The inflicter then has a duty to compensate the victim: she has done him a wrong and, if possible, can make it up to him by a transfer from herself to him. Determining what the right amount is will not be easy, and then securing her cooperation in making good her injury of him will, very likely, not be so easy either. But in the most favorable cases, this will all happen and justice, given the initial injustice, will have been fully done.

But the case is very different when one *group* claims to have been badly treated by another group. For in whatever way this is true, it is virtually certain that many and perhaps most members of the alleged oppressor group have never engaged in any of the specific actions in which the alleged injustice consists. And it is likewise essentially certain that most members of the oppressed group will not have been individually mistreated in the claimed ways. In recent times, few persons will have been refused a job, for example, on the ground that they were female or black.

But consider the character and effect of explicitly "affirmative action" legislation. *All* members of the victim group are to be given preference in hiring contexts; *all* hirers in the supposed oppressor group are required to give that preference. What will be the result? The hirers will wish, of course, to hire the most nearly competent among the victim group. Those in the victim-group who would have been hired anyway will be snapped up — perhaps for positions more demanding than those for which they are suited. Those among the hirers — probably close to 100% — who would never refuse to hire on the ground of race, sex, or whatever, will now have to hire people who are reliably believed to be less competent than their new colleagues when hired. And those who are well below any reasonable threshold of competence, if hired, will be a menace to the firm that hires them; or if they are not hired, on the other hand, they will have the dissatisfaction of knowing that they have not been able to meet even the lowered standards that the law imposes on hirers.

What group-imposed requirements entail, in short, is that the innocent among the alleged oppressor group are treated as if they were guilty, while the non-victims among the alleged victim group are treated as if they were victims. A double injustice is thus committed.

What should be done instead? The answer to this is simple enough. If discrimination is the problem, then discrimination should be *eliminated* — not reapplied in reverse. If individual persons can be shown to have been discriminated against, then those individual persons should be compensated, and by the very persons who supposedly discriminated against them.

At this point, though, we really must remember that the whole story is wrong to start with. The really correct solution, as opposed to the "politically correct" solution currently in vogue, is to eliminate *both* the laws against discrimination *and* the "affirmative action" programs supposedly designed to correct the problems supposed to have been caused by the former.

3.4 The "Victim" Industry

A program of affirmative action, like every other program that transfers taxpayers' money or work from some people to others who are claimed to be "victims" or oppressed, etc., has the inevitable consequence that it now pays to be a victim. People who cannot plausibly be thought, in any serious way, to have been discriminated against will now so regard themselves, because there's money or other advancement awaiting if one succeeds.

Nor is that all. Because affirmative actions programs are anti-efficient, they must be administered, imposed, by officials, people with authority to impose them. The victim industry spawns its own kind of employment. Normally, awarding a job is a matter of mutual advantage: the employer wants this candidate, and the candidate wants this job at this wage. Being a matter of mutual advantage, officials and laws are not fundamentally required to make the thing work. If one party doesn't like it, he leaves the relation: the employee quits if he doesn't like the job; the employer fires him, within the limits that their employment contract allows, if he isn't happy with the employee's performance. In a rare case, one party might steal from, or lie to, or cheat the other, and in such cases, perhaps, outside intervention might be needed to enforce the rules. But such cases are the exception. On the other hand, though, when the employer is *forced* to hire the employee, he must have someone standing over him with punitive measures ready to hand if he doesn't conform to the law, and further, monitoring things later on to be sure that the employer doesn't revert to performing in the rational way that is the standard way in economic matters between individuals. These necessary administrative positions, however, create an interest that is also contrary to general economic efficiency. It is in the administrator's interest to find people guilty, to crack the whip: that way, his job is seen to be necessary. The more he does, the more secretaries he gets to hire — and, of course, the more authority he exercises over other people's lives. (I say 'he', though nowadays it's more likely to be 'she'. During its heyday, the Office of Employment Equity under the New Democratic Government of Ontario (1990–1995) employed approximately 100 persons; of these, precisely none were white males, and only about 9 were males of any race. "Affirmative action" — if not exactly what one might think of as "equity" — was alive and well in the Office of Employment Equity!)

3.5 The Divisiveness of Affirmative Action and "Equity" Programs

Programs of the "equity" type, which establish preferential treatment for some parts of the populace at the expense of the rest, are bound to be political boondoggles. They are also certain to operate in a highly charged atmosphere of controversy. When rules and procedures are established to ensure that a "spoil" is divided among several contending parties, none of which has any natural claim to what is being divided, we have a sure recipe for trouble. We will see splinter groups within the victim groups clamoring that their particular set of victims has been inadequately served. And we will see litigation, verbal and sometimes even nonverbal battles breaking out. At the extreme, terrible conditions such as that prevailing in what used to be Yugoslavia, or in Sri Lanka[3], will result. In those countries people are murdered by politically-engendered armies for the "crime" of being members of the "wrong" ethnic group. Neighbors who were good friends all their lives are suddenly set against each other, by the drawing of lines that have no bearing on the real life interests of the people concerned. Those lines *impose* a "bearing" where there was none before. "Affirmative action" indeed. And in the end, hundreds of thousands of lives are lost or, in the case of Nazi Germany with its fanatical selection of Jews as the cause of all its troubles, millions. In all of this, there is no gain for the public, nor for most of the people concerned.

The public does not gain when people are hired for political reasons rather than for reasons of efficiency. It does not gain when businesses are forced to operate in worse ways rather than better. And one must wonder whether the immediate beneficiaries — those who get jobs that they would not have gotten had they been competing solely on the basis of ability — really benefit. The nagging sense that one was not hired on the basis of one's real abilities, but rather of political considerations, is not one that many people would want to live with. And worse, that same sense is hard to avoid even among those who would have been hired on the basis of their abilities.

4. Conclusion

Affirmative action is the wrong solution to the wrong problem. Everyone is entitled to be treated with respect. No person may be subordinated to any other by force, nor are people to be treated on the basis of deception or fraud. There is no reason why the context of hiring should be an exception to these fundamental and obvious moral requirements.

Organizations have goals, and bend their efforts as effectively as they can toward achieving them. Whether their essential goal is to make profits, or, instead, some cultural or social end is being pursued, an organization taking on employees does so with a view to best helping to promote its ends. It naturally and reasonably hires on that basis. What is normally called discrimination in employment consists in employing people on the basis of other considerations, irrelevant ones. That is a counterproductive practice, and therefore it is unreasonable, indeed irrational for organizations to engage in it. Moreover, in the case where it is a private business operating in a competitive environment, it is a habit that will tend toward extinction. But while non-discrimination is a duty of officials and managers in firms, it is not obvious that it is a suitable subject for legal intervention. We should not use force to get people to do what they should, in their own interests, be doing anyway.

Meanwhile, programs of preferential treatment for the erstwhile "victims" of discrimination are not justifiable on the basis of compensation. Such programs do not, are not intended to, and could not possibly compensate all and only all the actual "victims" of discrimination; instead, they bestow advantages on all members of the group, whether or not they are relevantly sufferers from past discrimination. And they inflict serious disadvantages on all employers — again, whether or not those employers are "guilty". In the process, what ought to have been straightforward procedures of trying to hire the best people for the job are instead *politicized*. Undisciplined use of statistics regarding past hiring patterns with respect to the politically favored grounds of discrimination — race and sex are the most popular such at present — will be invoked to "prove" that discrimination has taken place, and quotas or the equivalent imposed on the unwilling potential employers. All of this makes for substantial and in some cases massive inefficiency, and of course substantial injustice to individuals hoping to be considered on their job-related merits rather than their color or sex.

And it makes for divisiveness among the populations thus treated. Taxpayers and consumers — in short, the public — suffer the further consequences, just as employers and potential employees suffer the immediate effects of mandatory imposition of irrelevant standards on employment by persons knowing nothing about the businesses they take a major hand in administering. This is a formula for social disaster if pressed seriously; in the meanwhile, it is a formula for reduced prosperity, much resentment and confrontation, and massive injustice.

Do we need all that?

NOTES

1. See the careful discussion in the Fraser Institute's *Focus: On Employment Equity* (Vancouver, 1985). This is a critique of an extremely influential Royal Commission report — a report whose statistical insensitivity to known relevant variables should have been regarded as shocking. Most important was its failure to assess the influence of marital status. It is interesting, for instance, that in 1971, the average pay of never-married, University-degree possessing women as compared with never-married University educated males was 9% *greater*. (p. 52).
2. This is purely a recollection; it may have been difficult to discern Hispanics, and in any case my figures may well be wrong by a few percent either way.
3. See Thomas Sowell, *Preferential Policies* (New York: William Morrow, 1990) for a careful account of preferential policies in Malaysia, India, Nigeria, and Sri Lanka that led to extensive violence.

QUESTIONS

1. Jan Narveson provides this definition of discrimination: "a person has been discriminated against if he or she has been passed over in favour of someone else, but on the basis of characteristics having no relevance to the choices made by the persons with the power to make them." Is this understanding of discrimination different from that provided by the authors in the previous chapter?
2. According to Narveson, it is not morally wrong for a business person to select a secretary, for example, who is the best-looking candidate. Does he take the case of discriminating on the basis of sex or race as different? Do you?
3. Do you agree with Narveson when he says that "since it is not in a company's interest to discriminate, properly understood, laws forbidding discrimination in hiring are, in that regard, redundant"? How would the other contributors to this chapter respond?
4. Why does Narveson think that statistical evidence of the under-representation of members of particular groups does not establish the case for discrimination?
5. What reasons does Narveson give for saying that affirmative action measures are not justifiable on the basis of compensation? Do you think that affirmative action programs create the kinds of social divisiveness that Narveson describes?

POSITIVE SEXISM

L. W. Sumner

No one who cares about equal opportunity can derive much comfort from the present occupational distribution of working women. In the various industrial societies of the West, women comprise between one-quarter and one-half of the national labor force. However,

From Social Philosophy & Policy, *vol. 5, no. 1, pp. 204–22. Reprinted by permission of Blackwell Publishers and L.W. Sumner.*

An earlier version of this paper was presented to the Moral, Political, and Legal Philosophy Discussion Group at All Souls College, Oxford. I am grateful for the valuable suggestions I received from the members of the audience on that occasion, especially from Ronald Dworkin and Janet Radcliffe Richards. I have also benefited from comments by G.A. Cohen, Marilyn Friedman, Nathan Isgur, Larry May, Kathryn Morgan, Ronald de Sousa, Mark Thornton, Heather Wright, and the editors of Social Philosophy & Policy.

they tend to be clustered in employment sectors — especially clerical, sales, and service occupations — which rank relatively low in remuneration, status, autonomy, and other perquisites. Meanwhile, the more prestigious and rewarding managerial and professional positions, as well as the major categories of blue-collar labor, remain largely a male preserve. In the same societies the average income earned by full-time female workers is one-half to two-thirds that of their male counterparts. Although this disparity owes much to other factors, including lower pay for work similar or even identical to that standardly done by men, much of it can be explained only by the concentration of working women in traditional female job ghettos.

A pattern as widespread and persistent as this one has many roots. Women may be underrepresented in some positions because they possess a lesser share of the necessary native skills (such as physical strength), or because they are (authentically) less attracted to them, or (more commonly) because while lacking neither ability nor motivation they find it harder to free themselves from domestic responsibilities, or (more commonly still) because they have been indoctrinated to believe that these occupations are unsuitable for them. However, even after due allowance has been made for all of these sources, much of the pattern remains unexplained and can be attributed only to discriminatory practices on the part of employers. These practices — whether at the initial stage of hiring or at subsequent stages of progress through the ranks — are often less overt than they were before the level of social consciousness about sexism was raised. But they continue to exist, and they continue to retard the occupational advancement of even highly qualified and highly motivated women.

Over the past two decades many countries have initiated programs of affirmative action or employment equity which aim to counteract these traditional forms of discrimination. During that period women have made palpable progress in some economic sectors in most of these countries — especially in those sectors and those countries where the programs have been most vigorously pursued. Nowhere, however, has discrimination, whether overt or covert, ceased to be a major factor in explaining the occupational maldistribution of women. Affirmative action is an umbrella category embracing a wide variety of programs designed to improve the employment opportunities of women and other disadvantaged groups. Some of these programs, though by no means all, aim to counteract discrimination against women by authorizing or even mandating discrimination against men. When these policies of positive or reverse discrimination were first proposed, a spirited philosophical and political debate ensued concerning their legitimacy. Given the stubborn survival of sexist employment practices, the time is ripe for reopening that debate.

My focus in this discussion will be deliberately narrow. Women are not the only victims of systematic or institutionalized discrimination, and employment is not the only social domain in which such discrimination is practiced. I shall pay no heed either to other victims (racial or ethnic groups, homosexuals, the physically or mentally handicapped, immigrants, etc.) or to other domains (education, housing, law, the family, social services, etc.). My inquiry will therefore be doubly incomplete, both because it ignores all of these cognate practices and also because the one case on which it focuses — discrimination against women in the workplace — can be neither fully understood nor effectively combated in isolation from the rest. My conclusions will therefore be provisional; they may well need to be amended in the light of wider investigation. Furthermore, they cannot safely be extrapolated to other cases. Both the efficacy and the justice of positive discrimination programs depend on a number of social contingencies. Even if, as I shall argue, a policy of positive sexism could well be both efficacious and just in many jurisdictions, the same need not hold for other formally similar measures. The situation of other groups, or in other social sectors, or in other jurisdictions may be importantly different.

1. Preliminaries

We need a working account of what it is for an employment policy to be discriminatory. For ease of exposition I focus on one particular phase of the employment process, namely, initial appointment. If we can isolate what counts as discrimination in hiring, we should be able to generalize the result to subsequent stages of advancement. Imagine, then, that a number of candidates have applied for a single position in some workplace. In one legitimate sense, of course, any means of selecting the successful candidate must discriminate among them, for it must distinguish them on some ground or other. The very weakness of this notion of discrimination, however, will prevent us from uncovering what is peculiar to those employment practices which we ordinarily classify as discriminatory. Let us therefore try to determine which grounds for selecting the successful applicant would justify the losers in thinking that they had been discriminated against.

Because the possible forms of discrimination are legion, it will be easier to begin by trying to identify the grounds which would count as nondiscriminatory. Let us assume, therefore, that the position in question consists of specific tasks or duties for which different grades or levels of performance can be at least roughly distinguished. Let us further assume that among the many attributes displayed by the candidates, some are *performance-related*, where this means that they are fairly reliable predictors of a successful applicant's subsequent level of performance. To assess candidates by means of performance-related criteria is to assess them in terms of their qualifications for the position or, as we are wont to say, on the basis of merit. It is then tempting to say that a selection process is nondiscriminatory just in case it is purely merit-based, and thus that it is discriminatory when any candidate is either preferred or not at least partly on the basis of some attribute which is not performance-related.

This account of discrimination certainly seems to be in the right neighborhood, since it goes a long way toward capturing our intuitive sense that a female job applicant has been discriminated against if she has been rejected, on account of her gender, in favor of some less qualified male. The discrimination here seems to consist in allowing gender to override the ranking of the candidates on the basis of their qualifications. Furthermore, she has been discriminated against even if gender is itself a qualification for the job in question, since whatever weight it deserves on that score will already have been taken into account in the merit ranking. In order to be nondiscriminatory, therefore, a hiring procedure need not be gender-blind. Gender is a performance-related attribute for some jobs, such as sperm donors and wet nurses.

However, allowing that gender may itself affect job performance requires us to complicate our initial account of discrimination. The problem is that some connections between gender and performance depend on attitudes or practices which are themselves discriminatory. To illustrate how these mechanisms can work, I relate a story told to me recently by an academic acquaintance. His university department, which is entirely male, advertised a tenure-track position for which it received a large number of applications. Believing that no further candidates would present themselves, the hiring committee met sometime before the advertised deadline in order to draw up a short list. The candidates were assessed on the basis of qualifications previously agreed upon, and each committee member compiled a separate ranking of them. When these rankings were combined by means of a previously established procedure, the candidate at the top of the list was a woman and all of the others were men. Subsequently, a few additional applications came in. Some members of the committee insisted that the ranking procedure be repeated on the ground that one of these late applicants appeared to have a chance of supplanting someone on the short list. When the procedure was repeated the latecomer was a distant last on the revised list, but one of the male applicants now finished first. Furthermore, the reason given by those who had downgraded the female contender in this second round was that they would have found it difficult to work with someone as outspoken and forthright as she was.

This woman was passed over because, it was claimed by her prospective male colleagues, she would not fit in well "as a member of the team". However, it was clear (at least to my informant) that they would not have found it equally difficult to work with a male colleague of the same disposition. To the extent that harmony among its members was necessary in order for "the team" to function efficiently, her gender was in this case a performance-related attribute: because she was a woman she was, to that extent, less qualified to work with a group of men. But her gender counted as a (dis)qualification only because of the sexist attitudes of those men. This kind of "secondary sexism" is depressingly common; it is one of the main mechanisms whereby employment practices continue to discriminate against women.[1] However, it would not count as discriminatory on our initial account, since the final ranking was (we may suppose) based exclusively on performance-related attributes and was not then overridden on grounds of gender. Clearly, we need to revise the account so as to filter out attributes whose correlation with subsequent performance itself depends on prior sexist attitudes or practices (whether on the part of co-workers, superiors, customers, or anyone else). This amendment introduces an awkwardly recursive element into our account, but it will not be viciously circular as long as we can identify some cases of primary or direct discrimination (which should not be difficult). It also raises some difficult practical questions, since we must now decide when impaired performance is due to latent or covert sexism. I shall not address these problems here, except to say that some solution to them appears to be essential to any adequate account of sex discrimination.

We can now say that a hiring procedure is sexist whenever it either overtly or covertly assigns more weight to gender than it deserves as a legitimate performance-related attribute. Traditional sexism has favored men at the expense of women. Programs of affirmative action or employment equity have been designed to counteract this competitive advantage. Such programs have generally included some or all of the following policies.

1. *Special recruitment:* ensuring that women are informed of job openings and encouraged to apply for them.
2. *Tiebreaking:* preferring female applicants to equally qualified male applicants.
3. *Handicapping:* preferring female applicants to more qualified male applicants.
4. *Lexical assessment:* ignoring male applicants altogether unless there is no suitably qualified female applicant.
5. *Numerical goals or quotas:* achieving or maintaining some stipulated minimum female complement in particular occupational categories in particular workplaces.

The first of these policies is plainly nondiscriminatory. The purpose of special measures to recruit women is to offset the informational and motivational advantages traditionally enjoyed by men; if they are effective, they will therefore expand the pool of female applicants without contracting the pool of males. Tiebreaking, on the other hand, does employ gender as a basis for hiring independently of its weight (if any) as a qualification for the position in question. However, because it does not authorize choosing a less qualified woman on grounds of her sex, it is a rather anodyne form of discrimination.

Both handicapping and lexical assessment, by contrast, do authorize hiring a less qualified woman. The former does so directly by giving gender a weight which is not performance related, while the latter invites women to a prior competition from which men are entirely excluded. Because they are discriminatory, both have been widely criticized as unfair to any male candidates who are better qualified than the successful woman. (The less qualified male contenders presumably have no ground for complaint, since they would have lost anyway in a purely merit-based competition.) However, the distinction between these controversial measures and their more benign predecessors is considerably clearer in theory than in practice. Since qualifications for a position can seldom be measured precisely, rankings of candidates on their merits are often inherently uncertain. In many situations it will therefore be difficult to distinguish between a set of candidates judged to be equally qualified and a merit ranking in which the differences among the candidates are agreed to be relatively slight. In any such case it will be equally difficult to distinguish between tiebreaking and handicapping.

Merit rankings are also often corrupted by sexist biases. (Readers who are unconvinced might recall the story I told earlier.) If gender can be appealed to only to break ties, then employers who are determined not to hire even qualified women need only ensure that their ranking of applicants contains no ties. If, on the other hand, it is necessary for them to argue that the best qualified woman is so inferior to the best qualified man that the independent weight to be accorded to her gender is incapable of making up the difference, or to argue that none of the female applicants is suitably qualified at all, then their task is made considerably more difficult. Not impossible, as experience sadly shows, just more difficult. Because even an ostensibly merit-based ranking can be infected by secondary sexism, affirmative action measures which are discriminatory *de jure* may not be so in their actual effects. Both handicapping and lexical assessment may be seen as ways of introducing into the hiring process a bias favoring women to cancel out the existing bias favoring men, in which case the vector sum of these opposing forces may tend toward genuinely merit-based selection on a case-by-case basis. In this way, either policy might be less discriminatory in its actual outcome than the milder measures which contain no effective counterweight against covert forms of sexism.

Finally, no components of affirmative action programs have been as controversial as the establishment of numerical goals or quotas.[2] Because quotas can be both calculated and applied in many different ways, I will simplify the discussion by focusing on a policy with the following ingredients. Different quotas will be established for different occupational categories, the quota for any given category reflecting the percentage of women in the national pool of qualified candidates for the position in question. Quotas will therefore be readjusted from time to time to reflect fluctuations in their base lines. Whatever the quota for a particular category, employers will be required to achieve at least that complement of female workers in that echelon of their work force by some stipulated deadline. The task of setting and enforcing quotas will fall to a public regulatory agency which will also be empowered to take account of any special circumstances — size of work force, rate of turnover, regional disparities in the labor pool, and so forth — which may render compliance by particular employers unusually difficult.

It is curious that quota systems have attracted such a hostile reaction since, unlike handicapping and lexical assessment, they are not intrinsically discriminatory. A quota provides an employer with a goal to be achieved but does not stipulate the means to be used in achieving it. If the target can be hit by means of scrupulously nondiscriminatory procedures such as special recruitment, or mildly discriminatory procedures such as tiebreaking, then no one will have any serious ground for complaint. Of course, a quota system will compel employers to discriminate as a matter of practical necessity if these weaker measures will not suffice. However, it might well result in less discrimination overall than would a straightforward policy of either handicapping or lexical assessment.

This brief review of affirmative action policies has carefully bracketed the question of their legitimacy. That is the question to which we must now turn. In order to keep the issues at stake as sharp as possible, I shall henceforth assume that the policy whose legitimacy is in question is a quota system of the sort outlined above, the implementation of which would lead to some actual discrimination against men. In the next two sections I shall raise what I consider to be the two central moral questions about such a policy: (1) Might it be the best means of combating traditional discrimination in hiring, at least in some jurisdictions? (2) Where this is the case, would the implementation of such a policy be just? I shall defend affirmative answers to both questions. I shall also contend that the issues raised by the two questions are more closely connected than they are commonly thought to be.

2. The Justification of Positive Sexism

Defenses of positive discrimination tend to divide into two sorts. Some appeal to norms of corrective justice, arguing that women who have been the victims of traditional discrimination deserve preferential treatment by way of compensation for their past injuries.[3] This retrospective strategy has been widely criticized, largely on the ground that such schemes are unlikely either to deliver their compensatory benefits to those very women who have been penalized by past discrimination or to impose their correlative burdens on those very men who have profited from such discrimination.[4] Although some considerable headway can be made against this objection by urging that because both the harms and the benefits are group-based they have been diffused throughout the two groups,[5] positive sexism will always be deeply flawed as a social program of corrective justice. Even if we agree that to some extent or other every woman is disadvantaged (and every man advantaged) whenever any woman is discriminated against, nonetheless both the costs and the benefits of past discrimination have been very unequally distributed. A compensatory program of reverse discrimination will also distribute its costs and benefits unequally, and will be quite unable either to impose its heaviest burdens or to confer its greatest rewards on those who most deserve them. Thus, it is inevitable that some women will gain, and some men lose, either much more or much less than corrective justice would require. If the aim of corrective justice is to impose rectificatory transfers in accordance with desert, then positive sexism will require some other form of justification.

By contrast, a prospective or consequentialist defense may appeal to norms of distributive, as opposed to corrective, justice. Here the central claim is that the injustice represented by traditional discrimination can best be combated by a policy of counterbalancing reverse discrimination. This argument adds a diachronic dimension to the balance-of-forces analysis in the preceding action. There the suggestion was that introducing an element of positive discrimination into employment procedures might make merit-based outcomes more likely in particular cases. While the present argument need not eschew these immediate payoffs, it also does not depend on them. It is therefore prepared to concede that the measures it supports may be genuinely discriminatory in particular cases. But it urges that as women are enabled to make their presence felt in the traditional bastions of male privilege, the sexist attitudes which now prejudice their chances in a purely merit-based competition will gradually loosen their grip. If this process reaches a stage at which women will no longer be threatened by (primary or secondary) sexism in hiring practices, and if a quota system is not needed to counteract competitive disadvantages resulting from sexism in other domains, then the policy will eventually become redundant and can then be dismantled.

It is this consequentialist case in favor of positive sexism that I wish to support. I shall not try to show that a quota system would be the best means of combating sexist hiring practices in any particular society. To demonstrate this would require marshaling far more empirical evidence than is possible in this essay. Instead, I shall argue that it might well be such a means, under the conditions which now obtain in the industrialized countries of the West. I shall thus offer a *prima facie* justification of positive sexism which will point to the way in which it could be made conclusive for some chosen jurisdiction.

Although the argument to follow is consequentialist, it is not (necessarily) utilitarian. Whereas utilitarians acknowledge only one basic good — welfare — I shall presuppose a plurality of goods without raising the question of their underlying unity. Furthermore, whereas utilitarians aggregate welfare I shall assume that the distribution of goods also matters, without raising the question of whether it is valuable merely as a means to some deeper and purely aggregative goal. My main assumption will be the very weak one that traditional discrimination against women is a bad thing, and thus that its eradication would be a good thing.[6] But I am also happy to recognize any other goods or evils commonly agreed to be such, since even if positive sexism turns out to be the best means of eliminating traditional sexism, it might have other consequences sufficiently pernicious to condemn it on balance.

The centerpiece of the consequentialist argument is the claim that introducing a measure of discrimination against men will be the most effective means of eliminating discrimination against women, and thus of minimizing discrimination in the long run.[7] It is no objection against this claim merely to point out that it fights discrimination with its own weapons. The argument has the same logic as the justification sometimes offered for imposing temporary restrictions on basic liberties in order to safeguard or expand such liberties in the more distant future. Liberals should, of course, always be suspicious of such authoritarian measures, for the reality is usually that repression is accelerated in the short run in order that it may be further increased in the long run. But this merely reminds us that consequentialist arguments in favor of repression are usually sophistical or hypocritical. It has no bearing on any case in which the temporary or partial restriction of some social good is truly necessary for its ultimate expansion.

But is positive discrimination necessary in order to eradicate traditional discrimination? Might we not combat it just as effectively by nondiscriminatory measures? Certainly the level of social consciousness concerning discrimination against women has been raised both by the public debate and by the affirmative action remedies of the past two decades. Nowadays, with the conspicuous exception of the hierarchy of some of our larger religious institutions, men are less likely to argue openly that women are unqualified for traditionally male occupations simply by virtue of their gender. But all too often these overt manifestations of sexism have merely been supplanted by more devious tactics: "I agree that she has excellent qualifications on paper but will she fit in, or isn't she a bit strident and aggressive, or how do we know she won't leave in a few years to raise a family, or doesn't her male competitor really need the job more, or. . . ."[8]

Although milder affirmative action policies have the virtue of wide acceptance, they are powerless to remove these stubborn stains of secondary sexism. None of the special pains which employers take to recruit qualified female candidates ensures that they will then assess them fairly on their merits. They can satisfy affirmative action guidelines by interviewing lots of women and then proceed to hire a man, secure in the buoyant conviction that they have, after all, done all that could be expected. Likewise, allowing gender to break ties between male and female applicants who are judged to be equally qualified does nothing to neutralize the sexist assumptions at work in ranking the applicants in the first place. Women can benefit from this limited form of preferential treatment only if they can somehow get to the top of the short list, but therein lies the problem. The basic and ineradicable defect of these relatively uncontroversial measures is that because they can be easily subverted, they are unenforceable. One need not believe in a patriarchal conspiracy in order to harbor the suspicion that the measures are so popular in part because they are so ineffectual.

However, other nondiscriminatory policies are also available. We could, for instance, either establish or improve grievance procedures, in order to provide an avenue of appeal for women who are convinced that they have been the victims of discrimination. For decisions concerning progress through the ranks, grievance procedures within a particular workplace may prove quite effective. But they are far less effective for rejected job candidates, whose only recourse is to an outside body. Given the difficulty of proving that the more covert sexist biases have influenced hiring in a particular case, and given also the length of time needed to conduct a proper investigation, it seems clear that this avenue will do little to guarantee women fair consideration at the crucial point of initial entry.

It is time to accentuate the positive by pointing to the benefits which seem likely to flow from a quota system. The great advantage which such a system enjoys over all other affirmative action policies is that because its requirements are objective and verifiable, they are also enforceable. As such, a quota system would enable us to combat traditional discrimination in two important ways. In the first place, it would go some distance toward neutralizing the pervasive influence of secondary sexism. An employer who needs to hire women in order to meet a stipulated quota will be less likely to worry whether this particular woman is too pushy, or will not be a good team player, or is likely to get pregnant, or whatever. Although numerical quotas will come as an acute shock to many employers, I know of no other way to concentrate their minds as wonderfully on the genuine qualifications of female job candidates. Second, the widespread achievement of the mandated goals is likely to have a significant effect on women who contemplate seeking entry into traditional male preserves. Women often drop out of the competition for these positions long before hiring decisions are made: they are discouraged either by propaganda suggesting that these jobs are not really suitable for them or by the expectation that even if they are successful, they will merely join a tiny and embattled minority in an overwhelmingly male world. Only the toughest and the most able are likely to persist as matters now stand; but if women become increasingly numerous and visible in these domains, then their sisters and daughters (and mothers) may receive additional encouragement to stay in (or enter) the chase. Furthermore, since the quotas will be set so as to reflect the percentage of women in the pool of qualified applicants, as this complement grows the quota will rise correspondingly, in a self-reinforcing upward spiral.

A quota system is not a panacea for the many ills which presently afflict working women in capitalist societies. Because it attacks only one of the ways in which their employment opportunities are limited, it will need to work in tandem with a variety of complementary measures: the elimination of sexist stereotypes in education, the funding of day-care facilities, the expansion of part-time employment and the introduction of more flexible working hours, equal remuneration for work of equal value, more efficient grievance procedures, improved protection against sexual harassment in the workplace, and so on. Furthermore, to the extent that all of these measures address problems which afflict women in only one sector of their lives, they must all be seen as components of a much broader assault on sexist social structures. We should therefore not expect revolutionary results to flow from a policy of positive sexism alone. However, discriminatory hiring practices remain an important barrier in the path of working women, and thus an important factor in the oppression of all women. If a quota system promises to remove this particular barrier more effectively than any other remedial measure, then this provides a strong case for its implementation.

We must also, however, consider its probable costs. Since a quota system will (we are assuming) be discriminatory in its effects, it will penalize those male job applicants who would have been hired but for its operation. We should bear in mind that the victims of such a policy will not be easy to identify. No rejected candidate can safely conclude that he has been victimized solely on the ground that a woman has been hired in his stead. After all, she might have been hired even if the firm were not trying to fill its quota, or in a genuinely merit-based competition untinged by all forms of covert sexism. (Likewise, just as unsuccessful male candidates should not automatically blame a quota system for their rejection, successful female candidates should not assume that the scheme is responsible for their selection.) However, though we may not be sure who they are, there will be victims, each of whom will have suffered a loss. The extent of this loss in a particular case will obviously depend on the other avenues open to the unlucky loser. However this may be, the costs imposed on men by positive discrimination will be real, just as the costs imposed on women by traditional discrimination have been real.

Since the alternative to a quota system appears to be the indefinite survival of traditional discrimination, there is, at least in the short run, no way to avoid imposing costs on some victims. However, since the aim of such a system is the eventual achievement of equal employment opportunity, it promises to minimize such costs over the long run.[9] There is, moreover, an important difference between the impact of the two forms of discrimination. When women are discriminated against the message they receive, whether overtly or covertly, is that they are inferior to men. A program of positive sexism, by contrast, is premised not on a myth of male inferiority, but on the necessity of giving women a competitive advantage so that they can achieve real equality. Its victims need not, therefore, suffer any loss of self-esteem. The men who fail to get jobs which they would otherwise have won (or would have won in a purely merit-based competition) will suffer real losses, but they will not thereby be either stereotyped or stigmatized.

This concern for the victims of a quota system might take a more structural shape. Positive sexism is a remedial measure which will have outlived its usefulness when women come to enjoy equal employment opportunities. However, supposedly transitional programs have a nasty habit of prolonging their own lives once they have achieved institutional status. Why should we suppose that positive sexism would be any easier to dismantle than those dictatorships whose ostensible purpose is to pave the way to democracy or to the withering away of the state? And what is to prevent this officially sanctioned discrimination against men from spreading into other social domains? There is, however, an obvious answer to these questions. Local and remedial measures become pervasive and entrenched when they are supported by other forms of social power, such as capital, or the church, or a dominant ideology. A program of positive sexism, however, runs against the grain of virtually all other influential social institutions. Because it denies employers a free hand in the labor market it is unlikely to be popular in business circles. More importantly, its aim is to eliminate some of the privileges which have long been enjoyed by men. The tenacity of traditional sexism in the workplace is due in large part to its power base in wider forms of male domination. Were anyone to propose a transitional program of discrimination in favor of men, there would be a genuine danger of its permanent entrenchment. But whereas women need special protection against male oppression, men are well positioned to take care of themselves. We need not fear the advent of a new epoch of female domination.

Finally, some may worry that a quota system will lead to inefficiency in the workplace, because less qualified women will at least sometimes be preferred to more qualified men. How costly this will be to the firm in question, and to its clients, will depend on the degree to which the successful woman is inferior to the best qualified male candidate. If quotas are set so as to reflect the percentage of women among qualified applicants, then this gap should not in general be sizable, and where special problems of labor supply do obtain, then either quotas or deadlines can be adjusted so as to take them into account. Furthermore, when debating the inefficiency of positive sexism we must also keep in mind the inefficiency of traditional sexism, which favors less qualified men over more qualified women. Like the other values which it promotes, positive sexism also promises to maximize efficiency over the long run.

The foregoing considerations do not constitute a decisive consequentialist case in favor of positive discrimination. To make such a case for any particular jurisdiction would require an empirical inquiry which is quite beyond the means of this discussion. My aim has been to show not that a quota system would be the best way to combat discriminatory hiring practices in this society or that, but only that it could well be such in many of the industrial societies of the West. There is a strong policy argument in its favor, whose conclusiveness for a particular jurisdiction could be demonstrated only by examining more closely the special circumstances of that jurisdiction.

3. The Justice of Positive Sexism

Even if the consequentialist case in favor of a quota system were quite solid, there would remain an important issue to consider. Opponents of such a scheme need not doubt its effectiveness, even though they often do. Instead, they may object to it on the ground that the discrimination which it authorizes is unjust. However desirable the goal of eradicating traditional discrimination, these critics will say, it is impermissible to employ unjust means in order to achieve it.

The large question here is whether a policy of positive sexism treats men unjustly. But suppose such a policy were unjust: would that be sufficient by itself to condemn it? Those who concede the injustice of positive discrimination but still wish to support it clearly have some room for maneuver. After all, the payoff to be expected from the policy is not merely any old good, but justice itself. Positive sexism discriminates against men in order to combat precisely the same sort of discrimination against women; injustice is therefore being done for the sake of eradicating injustice. We might take the view that whereas justice is too important to be sacrificed in favor of other social goods, nonetheless we should always prefer more of it to less. If so, then we will be prepared to tolerate unjust discrimination against men if this is necessary in order to minimize discrimination overall.

Although this line of defense seems initially promising, the issues which it raises are very complex.[10] In any case, they need to be confronted only if we concede that a quota system is unjust. Whether this should be conceded is the question which will occupy the remainder of my discussion. I shall assume, for the purpose of the argument, a close connection between justice and rights, so that positive sexism is unjust if, and only if, it violates some right on the part of those men who are its victims. Which right might this be? The most obvious contender is the right not to be discriminated against on the basis of gender. After all, this is the right, on the part of women, which is violated by traditional discrimination and which seems to explain why we think that practice is unjust.

If this is the right in question, then there are two ways to avoid the conclusion that a quota system is unjust: we can either deny that men have such a right, or we can deny that such a system is discriminatory. Libertarians offer one way of taking up the first option. They argue that since employers are not obliged to offer jobs to anyone in the first place, they are free to assess applicants on any basis they please. Thus, if employers voluntarily adopt a policy of reverse discrimination, they do not thereby violate the rights of men. However, the problems raised by this argument for defenders of positive sexism are obvious. In the first place, the argument will exonerate only voluntary programs; their mandatory imposition would violate freedom of contract. Second, and more important, it will equally exonerate a voluntary program of traditional discrimination. The libertarian offers us no means of distinguishing the justice of traditional and positive sexism.

Meanwhile, the second option is precluded by the account of discriminatory hiring practices which I offered in Section 1. Since that account ties job qualifications to performance-related attributes and defines a hiring procedure as discriminatory if it assigns more weight to gender than it deserves as a genuine qualification, then it yields the result that in practice a quota system will discriminate against men. Pursuing the second option would therefore require some alternative concept of discrimination. One such alternative has recently been proposed by Janet Radcliffe Richards.[11] She argues that because assigning gender some independent weight in hiring decisions is necessary in order to equalize employment opportunities between men and women, gender is after all a relevant attribute of job applicants, in which case favoring female applicants on this basis does not discriminate against men. Her proposal therefore severs the connection between job qualifications and (narrowly defined) performance-related attributes. Its upshot is that since the traditional favoring of men over women widens the opportunity gap, it is genuinely discriminatory, while the remedial favoring of women over men, which promises to narrow that gap, is not.

Unlike the libertarian argument, this line of defense would enable us to affirm the justice of favoritism toward women without also affirming the justice of favoritism toward men. However, it would do so at the cost of erasing the distinction between discriminatory and nondiscriminatory affirmative action policies, since this distinction depends on tying qualifications to specific job descriptions. Now this might be a price worth paying, since the same substantive boundaries could doubtless be drawn in some other terms. But it is an advantage of the conceptual framework outlined in Section 1 that it explains why such measures as handicapping and quota systems have been so controversial in public debate. For better or worse, these measures are now labeled as positive or reverse discrimination by their proponents and their opponents alike. We therefore appear to be well past the point at which their justice can be defined by merely revising our concept of discrimination.

The prospects of defending the justice of positive sexism appear to be dim. On the one hand, we seem compelled to admit that it is genuine discrimination. But the only way we have found of denying that it violates the rights of men also commits us to denying that traditional sexism violates the rights of women. In order to escape this unpleasant dilemma we need some means of distinguishing between just and unjust discrimination. Furthermore, if what makes traditional hiring practices unjust is the fact that they violate the right of women not to be subjected to discrimination on grounds of gender, then we will need to show that men have no such right. But how could we show this? How, indeed, do we know in general which rights people have and when they are being violated?

I have a proposal concerning the way in which we should set about answering such questions, one which I have developed at length elsewhere[12] and can only briefly summarize here. The proposal begins by underlining the difference between moral rights — the sorts of rights presently in question — and conventional rights. The latter are established by conventional rule systems. While legal systems are the most developed and visible sources of such rights, they may also be conferred by the rules of nonlegal institutions (corporations, churches, clubs, etc.), as well as less formal associations (families, peer groups, communes, etc.). Whatever the conventional rule system in question, whether or not it confers a particular right on some particular individuals is determined by the decisions of those authorized to create and/or apply the rules of the system. The existence of conventional rights is therefore entirely a matter of authoritative decision. This is obviously not the case for moral rights; here an individual may have such a right even though it has been recognized in no conventional rule system. This gap between the existence conditions for conventional and moral rights raises the question of how the existence of the latter could ever be either confirmed or disconfirmed.

My answer to this question is that whether we have some particular moral right is determined not by whether the right is actually recognized in some conventional rule system, but by whether its recognition is (or would be) morally justified. The effect of this proposal is to shift our attention away from the abstract existence of moral rights to the ways in which policies of creating and protecting conventional rights might be given a moral justification. It follows immediately, of course, that this justification cannot consist ultimately in an appeal to moral rights. The existence of a moral right cannot be a final or ultimate reason for according it conventional recognition; instead, this reason — whatever shape it might take — will entail the existence of the moral right by virtue of justifying the policy of recognizing it in some conventional rule system. Arguments will therefore run not from the existence of moral rights to the justification of social policies, but in the opposite direction.

This much of the proposal is merely conceptual or analytic: it tells us what it is for someone to have some particular moral right. It is therefore compatible with a wide variety of different moral frameworks, any one of which might provide the needed justification for our social policies of creating and protecting conventional rights. My further substantive thesis is that the best account of this justification is consequentialist. Thus, substantively, moral rights are those rights whose conventional recognition will advance some set of favored consequentialist goals. In order to show how rights might, in principle, be incorporated within and supported by a consequentialist moral framework, we need not decide which particular goals should be favored. For present purposes, the goal which has been central to this discussion — equal employment opportunity — will do quite nicely.

Now I do not expect anyone to be persuaded of the wisdom of this proposal on the basis of a mere outline. But I do want to illustrate its *modus operandi* by applying it to the question currently in dispute, namely, whether positive sexism violates the rights of men. The problem, recall, is that it is difficult to see how we could give a negative answer to that question without giving the same answer to the question of whether traditional sexism violates the rights of women. However, a consequentialist theory of rights provides the resources for securing just this result by making the considerations which are decisive concerning the justification of positive sexism also decisive concerning its justice. Suppose that we are convinced that the establishment of a quota system is, all things considered, the best policy for some jurisdiction on the ground that it will eliminate the evil of traditional discrimination at a reasonable cost. The adoption of that policy in that jurisdiction is then morally justified, in which case the conventional rights which it confers are also moral rights. Clearly the policy confers on women both a negative right not to be discriminated against and a positive right to those forms of preferential treatment which are necessary in order to meet the stipulated quotas. Both of these rights are therefore moral rights.

However, it does not follow immediately that the policy denies men the conventional right not to be subjected to sexist hiring practices, and thus that they have no such moral right. It is true, of course, that the policy permits discrimination against them. But a conventional rule system may confer rights whose infringement it then permits under stipulated circumstances. Thus, for all we yet know, the policy in question might confer on men a general right not to be discriminated against on grounds of gender, which it then allows to be overridden in particular cases by the necessity of meeting a quota. In that case, the quota system would infringe a moral right held by men, but only in order to safeguard a competing moral right held by women. That is to say, it would employ unjust means to achieve a just end.

We must therefore look more closely at the way in which a quota system might operate. There are two possibilities: either it simply denies men the right not to be subjected to sexist hiring practices, or it gives them this right while permitting it to be overridden when necessary to achieve a quota. The difference between these two options turns on such matters as whether or not male applicants are given any avenue of redress when employers elect to discriminate in favor of women. A legal right must be capable of being exercised, and its exercise must include access to some procedure for seeking compensation in the event of its infringement. The question then becomes whether there are good consequentialist reasons for building any such procedure into a program of positive sexism.

Should a quota system, for instance, allow disappointed male applicants to grieve before some public tribunal? Alternatively, should being rejected in favor of a less qualified woman count as a ground of action for a legal remedy? Or should employers be required to compensate those male candidates who might have been hired were the quota system not in force?[13] If a quota system is to achieve its intended result, then it is likely that the answers to all these questions must be negative. As we saw earlier, those men who fail to gain jobs because of the operation of such a system suffer real losses. However, if every case of perceived discrimination could be brought either to a tribunal or to the courts, then the resulting flood of arbitration or litigation would in all probability render the policy utterly ineffective. On the other hand, any requirement that employers offer compensation to every male applicant victimized by the operation of a quota would stumble over the problem that the victims can be identified only counterfactually. In order to minimize costs, employers would have a strong incentive to conceal or distort their decision mechanisms, while in order to maximize gains men would have an equally strong incentive to get themselves short-listed for as many positions as possible. Considerations of efficiency therefore seem to dictate that a quota system will have to deny men any form of redress for their losses. In closing these avenues, however, this policy denies men a conventional right — in this case a legal right — not to be discriminated against on the basis of their gender. The recognition of any such right would be unjustified, since it would disserve the goals which the policy is meant to achieve. But then it follows that men have no moral right not to be subjected to discriminatory hiring practices. And if they have no such right, then a policy of positive sexism cannot be unjust.

A consequentialist foundation for rights thus enables us to distinguish between the justice of traditional and positive sexism. It does so by taking account of the social context in which these different forms of discrimination are practiced, not in order to rectify past injuries but in order to plan the most effective strategy for promoting greater equality in the future. Since traditional sexism discriminates against a group which is already oppressed, its tendency is to reinforce and prolong that oppression. The aim of positive sexism, by contrast, is to alleviate that oppression, at least in one sector of women's lives. In the present circumstances of many capitalist societies, there may therefore be a consequentialist justification for granting women a conventional right to nondiscriminatory treatment while denying the same right to men. Wherever this is so, a program of positive sexism will not treat men unjustly.

NOTES

1. For an account of this covert form of discrimination see Mary Anne Warren, "Secondary Sexism and Quota Hiring," *Philosophy & Public Affairs*, vol. 6, no. 3 (1977).
2. Although goals are often distinguished from quotas, especially in legal arguments, I shall draw no such distinction here. The important differences between alternative policies lie in their administration, not in the terminology we use to characterize their objectives.
3. See, for example, Judith Jarvis Thomson, "Preferential Hiring," *Philosophy & Public Affairs*, vol. 2, no. 4 (1973).
4. The standard objections can be found in Robert Simon, "Preferential Hiring: A Reply to Judith Jarvis Thomson," *Philosophy & Public Affairs*, vol. 3, no. 3 (1974); Alan H. Goldman, *Justice and Reverse Discrimination* (Princeton: Princeton University Press, 1979), ch. 3; and Janet Radcliffe Richards, *The Sceptical Feminist* (Harmondsworth: Penguin Books, 1982), ch. 4.
5. For the best treatment of this issue see Marilyn A. Friedman and Larry May, "Harming Women as a Group," *Social Theory and Practice,* vol. 11, no. 2 (1985).
6. That traditional discrimination is an evil is clearer than why it is. If we say, for instance, that job candidates should always be assessed purely on the basis of merit then we will be barred from taking account of such additional factors as age, nationality, place of residence, seniority, and so on. On the other hand, if we say that the problem lies in assigning some independent weight specifically to gender then we will be forced to conclude that positive sexism is also an evil. A more convincing story will probably condemn traditional discrimination in employment for its assumption of the inferiority of women, or for the way in which it conspires with other oppressive social practices to deny them equal opportunity with men. For a discussion of these issues in the context of race see Ronald Dworkin, *A Matter of Principle* (Cambridge: Harvard University Press, 1985), ch. 14. In Section 3 below, I consider the closely allied question of which rights (if any) are violated by discriminatory practices.
7. It is not essential to this argument that one social group is here disadvantaged in order to benefit another. The same group (broadly defined) may be both victim and beneficiary of positive discrimination. I recall reading some years ago of an inner city housing development in New York which consisted of a black majority and a white minority. Most applicants for flats in the development were black, but experience showed that if the percentage of black residents rose

above some critical point then the phenomenon known as "tipping" occurred and the whites began to leave, leading in the end to the creation of yet another black slum. In order to save the black residents from this fate, a quota had to be established which gave preference to white applicants. Thus in this case (some) blacks were discriminated against in order to prevent even greater discrimination against (other) blacks.

8. For a catalogue of such arguments, see Warren, "Secondary Sexism."

9. In Section 3 below, I consider the claim that the male victims of positive sexism suffer not merely a loss but an injustice, which may not be balanced in this way against the injustices to women which such a policy will avert.

10. Those who wish to pursue them should consult the recent literature on agent-centered restrictions, especially Samuel Scheffler, *The Rejection of Consequentialism* (Oxford: Clarendon Press, 1982), ch. 4; and Thomas Nagel, *The View from Nowhere* (New York and Oxford: Oxford University Press, 1986), ch. 8.

11. Richards, *Sceptical Feminist*, pp. 142–143.

12. See my *The Moral Foundation of Rights* (Oxford: Clarendon Press, 1987).

13. I owe this last suggestion to G. A. Cohen.

QUESTIONS

1. What reasons does L.W. Sumner give for the under-representation of women in some positions? How does this differ from the kind of explanation offered by Jan Narveson regarding under-representation?

2. Do you think that Sumner provides convincing evidence for the claim that merit rankings are "often corrupted by sexist biases"?

3. Sumner argues that a justification of positive or reverse discrimination in terms of compensation or corrective justice arguments are problematic. What does he mean by "corrective justice"? What does he mean by "distributive justice"? Does the notion of distributive justice provide a more adequate tool for dealing with the problem of discrimination? Does his analysis deal effectively with Jan Narveson's objections to the compensation argument?

4. How does Sumner defend quota system hiring? How does he answer the argument that no matter how laudable the goals for eliminating discrimination, using discriminatory means to achieve a state of equality cannot be justified?

EXPANDING THE ROLE OF ROLE MODELLING

Christine M. Koggel

Michel Rosenfeld makes the interesting observation that "the affirmative action debate is not between persons who are 'pro-equality' and others who are 'anti-equality'. Both the most ardent advocates of affirmative action and its most vehement foes loudly proclaim their allegiance to the ideal of equality" (Rosenfeld 1991, 2-3). Theorists defending each of the two main conceptions within the liberal tradition of formal and substantive equality articulate a commitment to equality of opportunity, yet they reach different conclusions about the justifiability of affirmative action. Liberal theorists who defend pure formal equality are critical of affirmative action and see these measures as unjust violations of individual liberty rights of non-interference. They argue that opportunities are equal when all people have the same formal right to compete. Without the legal barriers that once prevented some members from competing, people have an equal opportunity to pursue their goals and the resulting distribution of goods will merely reflect what different people deserve given their natural abilities and their efforts to apply themselves. Ian Hunter, for example, holds that equal opportunity "means that there are no artificial barriers put in the way of a qualified man or a qualified woman." He then adds: "[t]o specifically impose artificial barriers for men, or to create artificial advantages for women, in the name of equality is to debase both logic and language" (Hunter 1991, 204). Yet, liberal substantive theorists certainly view their defence of affirmative action as supporting and promoting equality. They argue that a commitment to equality of opportunity requires positive measures in the form of differential treatment for those whose unequal starting positions result in unfair disadvantages and unequal opportunities. These disagreements amongst liberals make affirmative action an ideal policy issue for testing the adequacy of formal and substantive conceptions of equality.

In this paper, I shall argue that both conceptions limit our understanding of social relations and ultimately constrain attempts to achieve equality. I begin by shifting the focus from identifying what individuals who are members of disadvantaged groups need to assimilate into current structures to the "web of relationships"[1] within which the self-concepts and perceptions of members of disadvantaged groups are formed.[2] I then use insights about the significance of the interactive relationships between members of oppressed groups and those in positions of power and influence to reinterpret and expand traditional role modelling arguments for affirmative action. A relational critique of the liberal understanding of role modelling shows affirmative action to be more subversive, and to lend more support to a radical restructuring of society than is generally thought.

The experiences of those in relationships of oppression and disadvantage can provide vantage points for revealing particular kinds of inequalities not captured by liberal theory. Unless workplace structures and hierarchies are challenged, affirmative action measures may only succeed in perpetuating a status quo in which assimilation is the aim, and different contributions and perspectives that challenge existing structures and ways of thinking are unwelcome and resisted. Switching the focus from individuals to relationships allows us to see that affirmative action is an effective way to create new social relations in which members of disadvantaged groups can act and interact in contexts where they were formerly excluded and are currently underrepresented and thereby challenge stereotypes and begin to change entrenched beliefs about their proper role and function.

I. Liberal Approaches to Affirmative Action

The emphasis on individual freedom and limited state interference makes it difficult for formal equality theorists to defend most sorts of affirmative action programs, which by definition discriminate in favour of some individuals and thereby limit the freedom of others. Robert Sasseen, for example, argues that equal opportunity "does not mean that men are equal at the starting line in the race of life, or that government should attempt to make them so. . . . Equal opportunity consists in, as it arises from, equal treatment under the law"

(Sasseen 1976, 277-278). Most formal equality theorists support anti-discrimination legislation prohibiting employers from deliberately discriminating on the basis of morally irrelevant characteristics such as race, sex, class, ethnic origin, etc. A commitment to equal opportunity means that employers are not free to discriminate against, for example, all but white males. But, they argue, affirmative action measures violate this commitment by using the very same grounds to justify unequal or preferential treatment for those identified on that basis. For those who defend formal equality as sufficient, discrimination is morally wrong whether individuals are singled out because they are women or men, black or white. Affirmative action is unjust discrimination because it singles out individuals for preferential treatment based on an individual's membership in a group. All people have the right to non-discrimination — including white males.

The individual-based approach of the formal equality conception can allow a defence of forms of affirmative action that serve to compensate those who can *prove* they are the victims of direct and deliberate discrimination. Discrimination is dealt with case by case, individual by individual, as backward-looking compensation for proven unjust discrimination. However, individual fault-based accounts of discrimination do not support justifications of compensation based only or mainly on the criterion of membership in a disadvantaged group.[3] Arguments for compensatory justice as redress for individual harm illustrate the limitations of pure formal equality. In practice, the burden is on individuals who were discriminated against and treated unequally to prove discrimination.[4] Unless the discrimination is overt and blatant, it is notoriously difficult for individuals to prove that they lost a competition for a job or a place in an educational institution merely because they belong to a disadvantaged group.[5] In practice, compensation for proven discrimination has also tended to be monetary, an obviously inadequate response to valuing an individual's freedom to pursue interests, projects, and goals.[6] Most importantly, defending strict adherence to proof of deliberate and direct discrimination assumes that accounts of harm to particular persons as a result of unjust discrimination are clearly separable from accounts of harm to all people who are members of disadvantaged groups, an assumption challenged by liberal substantive theorists.

The stronger the commitment to the primacy of individual rights of non-interference, the more vehement the opposition to affirmative action. Libertarians such as Jan Narveson reject the notion basic to most liberal accounts that people have a right to non-discrimination. He formulates an extreme version of mere formal equality and argues that even anti-discrimination legislation is an unjust interference with the freedom of private sector employers to hire, promote, and associate with whomever they choose regardless of their reasons: "Why can't I hire whomever I please? It is useless to respond by saying, 'because you have a duty to treat people equally,' for whether that is so is exactly what's in question here. Moreover, the examples of hands in marriage, handouts to arbitrarily chosen beggars, and any number of others one could readily produce, strongly suggest that it is false. We do *not* have to treat people equally" (Narveson 1995, 249, his emphasis). Not only does Narveson reject the basic tenet of liberal theory that all people ought to be treated with equal concern and respect, he also assumes that moral judgments about unequal treatment are meaningful in any and all contexts in which we discriminate amongst people. Discrimination receives our moral disapproval in social and political contexts in which differences such as race, class, and sex continue to limit the freedom and opportunities of those who are members of these groups.[7] It is precisely these contexts that substantive equality theorists focus on and are concerned about.

Rosenfeld captures the basic problem with the formal equality theorist's understanding of equal opportunity: "It may be that the removal of wrongful legal or quasi-legal obstacles imposed in the past would suffice, and lead to the restoration of the kind of competition envisaged initially. It may also be, however — particularly, if the illicit obstacles have been in place for a long period of time — that the mere removal of such obstacles would not suffice to restore the kinds of conditions that existed (or would have existed) prior to the imposition of such legal or quasi-legal obstacles" (Rosenfeld 1991, 29). Supposing that the mere removal of formal barriers can erase the effects of historically entrenched discrimination assumes that individuals can easily shed discriminatory beliefs and patterns of behaviour. People are embedded in social and historical contexts that perpetuate systems and structures of discrimination even when the rules and practices are legally condemned. While the removal of legal barriers is necessary and can begin to change practices, it is not sufficient for addressing the systemic and systematic effects of a history of entrenched discrimination.

Liberal substantive theorists argue that equality of opportunity requires positive measures for the disadvantaged as a means of equalizing starting positions in the 'race of life'. The more popular kind of liberal substantive defense of affirmative action relies on forward-looking, distributive justice arguments, in which affirmative action measures are viewed as a means justified by its end. Affirmative action admittedly discriminates in 'reverse', but such discrimination is viewed as a temporary evil justified by the end of meaningful equality of opportunity. This consequentialist-type defence of affirmative action is evident in the equality provisions in Section 15 of the *Canadian Charter of Rights and Freedoms*. Implementing the programs described in Section 15(2) as having "as its object the amelioration of conditions of disadvantaged individuals or groups" is viewed as promoting, not violating, the anti-discrimination rights set out in Section 15(1).

To identify those deserving of special consideration, substantive equality theorists turn to statistical data, which show that members of groups discriminated against in the past continue to have a disproportionately small share of the distribution of economic, social and educational benefits. Statistics show that members of traditionally disadvantaged groups are underrepresented in higher-status and higher-paying jobs relative to their numbers in the general population. Moreover, because they are underrepresented relative to their numbers in the qualified pool of applicants, they are underutilized.[8] Substantive equality theorists use the data both as evidence that more subtle forms of systemic or systematic discrimination are still at work and as a yardstick to measure progress towards substantive equality of opportunity. In addition, charges that less qualified or even unqualified candidates are hired through affirmative action practices are addressed by arguing that in a context of historically entrenched discrimination, perceptions of the merits and qualifications of individuals who are members of traditionally disadvantaged groups will be biased by beliefs or stereotypes about these individuals. Affirmative action measures can serve as a means of levelling out the effects of discriminatory attitudes.[9]

Some of these liberal substantive arguments in favour of affirmative action are evident in L.W. Sumner's "Positive Sexism" (included in this chapter). Sumner distinguishes between the morally reprehensible discrimination involved in traditional justifications for unequal treatment for unequals and the discrimination involved in affirmative action measures that have as their goal the elimination of the lingering effects of such discrimination.[10] He defends a version of quota hiring in which he assumes for the sake of argument that it leads to some actual discrimination against men. He then argues that there are two strategies open to proponents of affirmative action for addressing the objection that affirmative action is a violation of anti-discrimination rights: they can admit that affirmative action is discrimination and then distinguish just from unjust discrimination, or they can deny that affirmative action is discrimination and argue that being a member of a disadvantaged group is a qualification for whatever is at stake. Summer rejects the second strategy on the grounds that arguing that affirmative action is not discrimination is too much like trying to revise the meaning of an already established concept. He holds that a settled reaction to affirmative action as discrimination makes it inadvisable to argue that the very same grounds for unjust discrimination (gender, race, etc.) should now be viewed as qualifications in hiring procedures. But I want to show that the kind of consequentialist defence that Summer provides of the first strategy misses descriptive aspects of the effects of affirmative action hiring that can be captured by arguments using the strategy he rejects, defending role modelling. In order to see this, we need to revise the ways in which role modelling and role models have been understood.

II. The Traditional Understanding of Role Modelling

The prevalent understanding of role modelling in the literature on affirmative action is that it provides a consequentialist argument for affirmative action. Charges of unjust discrimination are answered by showing that role models play a positive role in achieving substantive equality of opportunity for two reasons. In the first kind of argument, many defenders of affirmative action focus on the imitative function of role modelling as an explanation for the causal connections between members' seeing others in their group in positions from which they were traditionally excluded and them pursuing the same career paths; thereby having the beneficial consequence of increasing the numbers of members of disadvantaged groups in places where they are underrepresented. Rhode, for example, writes: "[a]lthough positive effects are difficult to quantify, social science research suggests that role models have helped expand women's aspirations" (Rhode 1989, 188). Once we uncover the real reasons for the imitative success of role models, however, the scope and value of the role model begin to expand.

In the second kind of argument, a role model is seen as providing more than a way to increase numbers. Under this reasoning, identifying members of disadvantaged groups for preferential treatment should not be understood as reverse discrimination or even as justified discrimination. Rather, affirmative action hiring is non-discriminatory because a closer affinity and sympathy amongst same group members makes being a member of a disadvantaged group a qualification for certain positions.[11] To see how this argument works, let us examine a particular application of it to the affirmative action hiring of women in philosophy.

In a direct response to Sumner's rejection of the second kind of argument for role modelling, a rejection based on his concern about merely revising the concept "discrimination", Pamela Courtenay Hall argues: "equity hiring is a matter of 'responsive hiring' rather than a matter of justified discrimination in such workplaces as philosophy departments — 'responsive hiring' because it is hiring that is responsive to long-ignored though clearly identifiable responsibilities and needs" (Courtenay Hall 1992, 235). She defends the hiring of women in philosophy departments as a needed response not only because it increases the number of women in philosophy, but also because women have perspectives that can challenge traditional modes of doing philosophy, contribute to new ways of understanding what philosophy is, and provide new theories that begin with the long excluded experiences of women.[12] We can already note that these kinds of contributions are ones that can be applied to any discipline.

Courtenay Hall argues that being a female is a qualification for a teaching job "not because of mere linkage to the generic goal of employment equity, but rather, because it is more deeply an attribute needed for the job that is to be done" (Courtenay Hall 1992, 246). Women are role models that provide an atmosphere sympathetic to women's experiences and conducive to women's self-development. Being able to identify with others and feel welcome in areas traditionally dominated by advantaged white males are phenomena whose value should not be underestimated.[13] Christine Overall points out that as a defence for affirmative action, however, this argument for role modelling raises the following pertinent questions: "why are sensitive and interested males not adequate? Why is a shared interest in and talent for history, let us say, or biology or philosophy, not enough to make a man a good role model for women students?" (Overall 1987, 180).

Michael Martin attempts to answer this kind of question by explaining that while men *can* fill these roles, "women are more likely to be able to teach such a course than men are: they have the insight to do so, not because of some innate ability, but because of their raised consciousness and a special interest brought about in large part by the women's movement" (Martin 1973, 328). He concludes: "[w]omen students need women professors as models, not male professors sensitive to women's problems" (Martin 1973, 331). Courtenay Hall provides a similar answer by pointing out that "given that what is central to feminist philosophy (if anything is) is its starting point in the experiences of women, to look to a male philosopher to provide a standpoint in feminist philosophy would seem to be missing the point" (Courtenay Hall 1992, 238). Finally, Overall provides two possible answers to her own questions:

> the presence of a male as a would-be model fails to fulfil the advertising function which seems so crucial to role models. That is, his presence does not provide evidence to women students that they are welcome in the field and will not be discriminated against. Secondly, it is more difficult to identify with an individual of the other sex than with one of one's own sex. The absence of a common background and experience may make the sharing of perspectives of the male role model and his female students difficult (Overall 1987, 180).

The reasons return us to the two arguments for role modelling with which I began this section: the imitative effect of role modelling increases numbers, and in sharing experiences with female emulators, role models make gender a qualification. Yet there are still problems with the answers given by Martin, Courtenay Hall, and Overall to the question "why women role models?" Not only do the answers fail to capture certain vital aspects of role modelling, but they also raise other questions. The argument that women have a particular perspective or shared experiences falls prey to the tendency to universalize about all women. With respect to an argument for affirmative action, questions are then raised about whether women who do not share these experiences or have this perspective should be hired. Should candidates be screened for their affiliation with the groups to which they are members? Should the selection of candidates be based on traditional stereotypes about what members of those groups are like? We need to take a closer look at how role models function when they are placed in the contexts from which they were traditionally excluded. The common view of the concept of the role model hinders an understanding of role models as moral persons in interactive relationships.

III. Expanding the Role of Role Models

Overall explains that arguments in favour of role modelling are made "without much consideration of the implications of the concept, and of the web of assumptions of which it forms a part" (Overall 1987, 179). She argues that this "web of assumptions" has both isolating and damaging effects on the disadvantaged who are placed in the role of the model. The isolating effects come from raised expectations that a token role model can solve problems of underrepresentation. The damaging effects come from pressures on role models to assimilate into current structures: "feminists should think very carefully about advocating the presence of women as role models, if their presence merely turns out to reinforce existing educational and corporate values, and conventional strategies for personal advancement. The rationale for providing female role models should not be just to help women students conform more readily to traditional pathways to traditionally defined success" (Overall 1987, 183).

Overall is not arguing that women should not be role models, but is instead criticizing the way the concept of the role model is understood.[14] The concept suggests "a one-way relationship between the model and the person who takes her as a model"; "a special status for the model among the largely male majority to whom she is supposed to provide a contrast" (Overall 1987, 182); and "that the model herself is (artificially) playing a role" (Overall 1987, 184). Too often the role model is forced into contexts in which her role is understood to be that of the token representative who will "take care" of those like her. Moreover, "[t]he role model metaphor encourages us to think of the person who is the model as being distinct and isolated from her role as a model . . . instead of as a real person with hopes, needs, struggles, and fears like their own" (Overall 1987, 184). The understanding of the concept encourages a distancing from the person, a person who is viewed as having been hired because she or he is a member of a disadvantaged group. These perceptions of those hired under affirmative action programs risk further stigmatization, disadvantage, and marginalization.

These are genuine worries, ones that emerge from the expectations and assumptions of those who are positioned to judge the capabilities and actions of those who are let into the spheres of influence and power. The assumption is that "the admission of a few women to carefully controlled places, so that they can serve as 'role models' — those cardboard and ephemeral constructs" (Code 1991, 263) can satisfy demands for the greater representation of women while maintaining a status quo of oppressive structures. As Code comments, this way of seeing the function of role models "offers minimal revolutionary promise" (Code 1991, 263). We need to be wary of arguments for role modelling that raise expectations that a few token representatives can serve the function of achieving greater equality and that expect the disadvantaged to accept and assimilate into current structures.

As I see it, the key to answering Overall's worries about the concept "role model" and to retaining the idea that there is something vital and valuable in what role models do is to turn our attention to the "real person with hopes, needs, struggles, and fears". In capturing what it is like to be in that role and treated or viewed in that way, we can begin to reshape our understanding of role modelling. We can begin to see the radical potential of role modelling by shifting the focus from seeing role models as filling a need for the presence of group members with similar experiences to seeing them as beings whose actions and interactions in relationships contribute to new and valuable ways of knowing and of relating to others. When we apply relational insights to the interactive relationships that take place between role models and emulators, for example, we begin to see that the role model will often be a much more radical presence than is usually thought.

Shifting the focus to the "real person" highlights the fact that people serving as role models are not "cardboard and ephemeral constructs"; they are living beings in interactive relationships. To capture this point about the personhood and agency of role models, Code calls for a change in concept: "I refer intentionally to *character* models rather than *role* models in order to emphasise the ontological significance of this point. . . . The point is to show that, unlike roles, these ways of being are not to be assumed and cast aside casually and randomly. Character models are living instances of possible ways of being, for a society" (Code 1986, 58, her emphasis). As "living instances of possible ways of being", character models have an impact and an effect not captured in arguments for role modelling that understand role models as effective ways for achieving proportional representation.[15] Further, those who assume that role models want or need to assimilate to succeed miss the more complex nature and effects of role modelling. Code's concept of the character model comes closer to describing what role models do and are, but it does not yet capture the full impact and implications of the effects of role modelling.

"Character model" still has connotations of separateness and fixity that do not quite capture the significance and importance of interactive relationships. Further, the concept of character model invites moral evaluation. Characters can be observed, described, and judged by others to be good, bad, or flawed characters — models to be emulated or ignored. Affirmative action policies place moral persons, not fixed character roles, into interactive relationships with the dominant and powerful. They are moral agents who through their own complex web of relationships are unique persons as well as members of disadvantaged groups who share self-concepts and identities with other members. As members of disadvantaged groups they can name and claim the social construction of their difference as part of the emancipatory struggle towards reconstructing and reconstituting the perceptions and stereotypes of those identities. As unique persons formed in and through a complex of multiple relationships in various contexts they bring a plurality of perspectives into liberal contexts that endorse inclusion, but practice assimilation. For these reasons, role models, who have particular perspectives that they bring into their interactive relationships with others, are more appropriately referred to as "subjects of difference".

Role modelling is not only about the imitative and supportive functions role models have on members of their group or groups: it is also about the effects they have on all those with whom they interact and relate. The interactive behaviour of the role model does indeed show that the causal connections between the number of role models and emulators "are not simple or unidirectional" (Baker 1991, 14). In describing the interactions between teachers and students, for example, Overall captures the significance of the relationship to a changed understanding: "what must be stressed is . . . the potential for mutual relationships between role models and those for whom they constitute an example. The mentor can learn from her pupil. Furthermore, the pupil can learn to trust in her own competence . . . and in the reliability of her female peers" (Overall 1987, 185). I want to expand this account of interactive relationships even further by emphasizing the effects of the presence of role models in broad relational contexts in which they interact with the dominant and powerful. We shall see that this is one way to extend the reach of subjects of difference from the example of academic settings with which we started to many other areas.

A suggestive example will show that placing that dyadic relationship between teacher and pupil, in which each is affected by the relationship and self-concepts and understandings change, into the broader social and political context of currently valued and entrenched structures has the potential for changing those structures. Suppose that the teacher uses examples of women to illustrate points she makes in her lectures. It is not difficult to see the potential effects on the student: she talks to other students about the teacher, the examples, the fact that this teaching method is rare, or her enthusiasm for learning new perspectives on a traditional discipline. The student may bring this up in class or talk to the teacher about the impact of these different classroom experiences on her. The teacher may learn that this teaching method is rare, that it makes a difference to some of her students, or that it excludes other students. The example shows how the initial impact of the teacher on the student can form the trust and respect Overall discusses, but it also extends the potential effects from the initial relationship to other issues and social contexts. Room is made for raising issues of power and authority in the classroom and of exclusion and marginalization with respect to the material and to others. Room is also made for bringing these issues into students' homes, into parents' workplaces, and into political constituencies. This discussion of potential effects shows how one-to-one relationships can draw in a complex web of relationships in which many more than two people change and are changed.

A relational approach emphasizes that the interdependence and interactions of people have an impact on our understanding of ourselves and others. Viewing interactive relationships as formative of identity and self-concepts emphasizes the ontological significance of relationships and forces us to see role models more as subjects of difference than as "cardboard constructs". Members of disadvantaged groups are not playing roles; nor are those who are affected by them merely modelling those roles. They are persons in a web of relationships and they confront the stereotypes of them by being in the social and political contexts from which they were excluded in the past. The presence of subjects of difference who act and interact in contexts in which they were absent or are underrepresented makes it possible for them to displace and change entrenched perceptions of themselves and of structures that perpetuate disadvantage. The difficulties confronting solitary and isolated members of disadvantaged groups should not be underestimated, however. Fear and isolation may make it impossible to do anything more than fill the expectations of those in power and control. Yet, even here, small openings for change can be created. The example of the multiple effects of the network of relationships arising from the initial impact of the dyadic relationship between teacher and student shows how this can work. Other teachers are placed to reflect on their own teaching methods and its effects on students. Other students are forced to critically examine assumptions about particular disciplines or about fellow students.

We can use the model of the complex web of relationships in which we interact with others to answer the other set of questions raised at the end of the last section about whether affirmative action policies should identify candidates who genuinely represent the group to which they belong. Part of the answer returns us to the greater likelihood that members of disadvantaged groups will be more attentive to issues raised about their difference.[16] Members of disadvantaged groups need to care about the relationships they are in because they are adversely affected by norms and structures that assume their difference is either irrelevant or a justification for discrimination. Another part of the answer is found in the fact that our situatedness in a complex, complicated, and ever-changing network of relationships makes the idea of fixed and static identities difficult to maintain. People do not have a fixed identification and affiliation with one particular group or even with the set of groups to which they are members. The idea that members ought to be hired to represent some identifiable set of interests of their group is untenable.

Social contexts, particular circumstances, and personal relationships are factors that influence levels of disadvantage, commitment to social causes, and identification with same group members. These factors explain how and why some members of disadvantaged groups manage to assimilate all too well and ultimately deny that their difference has been or is relevant to the way they are treated. Finally, even though we are far from reaching this state of affairs, we need to acknowledge that in contexts where affirmative action is legitimated through legislation, where these measures are in place in many areas, and where there are steady increases in the representation of members of disadvantaged groups, it will become more difficult to argue that men, for example, cannot effectively represent or be sympathetic to women's issues or that women represent a united front.[17] The long-term effects of genuine interaction in a network of complex, complicated, and ever-changing relationships would manifest themselves in the enhancement of equal concern and respect for everyone and the proliferation of relationships that are sources of strength, personal growth, and moral development. But we are far from reaching this state of affairs and members of disadvantaged groups continue to provide important perspectives on the structures, perspectives that can and do reveal inequalities and injustices that tend to go unnoticed.

We shall see in the next section that the full force of my argument that affirmative action measures are more subversive than is generally thought, that they hold the promise of "displacing entrenched thought structures", can be captured by taking different perspectives as a starting point for thinking about the treatment of members of disadvantaged groups. Although I will apply this idea to examples most familiar to me, those of the affirmative action hiring of women in academic settings, it has a broader application that supports the case for seeing affirmative action as one way of providing conditions for treating all people with equal concern and respect. Affirmative action legitimates inclusion of the different into current structures of influence and power, enables the reshaping of oppressive structures, and makes the powerful respect the less powerful.

IV. Using Relational Insights to Defend Affirmative Action

Affirmative action measures are generally viewed from the perspective of the powerful, who are in the position of granting special treatment and access to positions of power for those they view as different. From this perspective, the danger of further stigmatization of the disadvantaged becomes very real. Members of disadvantaged groups are allowed in and expected to perform within a structure in which hierarchies and power differentials are accepted and respected. Assuming a neutral and objective perspective from which to judge others perpetuates inequalities for those viewed as different. Taking the perspective of the dominant and powerful as the standard of comparison for assessing all perspectives has several ramifications: it makes it difficult to question existing structures that exclude some members whose differences continue to matter; it places the emphasis on increasing numbers as the means and the measure of achieving substantive equality of opportunity rather than focusing on understanding and including difference; and it misses the more subversive and radical elements of affirmative action measures.

To see the pernicious effects of assuming that there is a neutral perspective for judging others, take the least controversial type of affirmative action, tie-breaking. Suppose an all-male department in a university has a history of selecting males in cases in which male and female candidates are equally qualified. They reason that the male would be more seriously committed to research because he will not take time off to have or care for children.[18] Further, because they only interact with males in the workplace, they also fear that a woman will not fit in and be "one of the boys". They worry, for example, that she will be offended by their "humour" about women, that she will be one of those "uptight" women who takes sexist comments too seriously. Suppose that under pressure to hire women, they now select a woman in tiebreaking case. The point is that she is hired in a context in which she is already perceived as having certain liabilities: she may take time off to have children or she may not like their sexist humour.

Given these background assumptions about child care, and fears about what her difference will mean for their all-male workplace, it is not unreasonable to speculate that if she decides to have children or responds negatively to a sexist comment she will merely reinforce stereotypes of these as liabilities. In the all-male department, perceptions of childbearing and childrearing as activities that get in the way of academic responsibilities not only reinforce stereotypes; they also make it difficult to restructure the workplace to integrate or accommodate caring for children or to see child care responsibilities as an important and valuable social activity. Entrenched assumptions about child care responsibilities may also limit career advancement opportunities for the woman who decides to have children. All of the consequences and effects noted thus far emerge from the way her identity is constructed around perceptions about what her difference means for the all-male department. We need to examine how things look from her perspective to highlight other consequences that are detrimental to her self-respect and self-image and that perpetuate inequalities not addressed by liberal theories of equality.

From her perspective, the world is not as it seems to her colleagues. She knows that child care responsibilities need not be viewed as limitations on self-development and the realization of goals. She sees that excluding child care responsibilities from what is considered to be "work" perpetuates perceptions and stereotypes of "women's work" as less valuable and important. She sees that sexist humour and sexual harassment are not harmless activities but have an impact on self-image and self-confidence when one is the object of this activity. She sees all of the ways in which the effects of the construction of her "difference", her "identity", limit her opportunities to pursue her interests, projects, and goals. When she is told that she should "loosen up" about sexist comments, she may feel that she really cannot fit in unless she becomes silent on these issues. Valuable opportunities to learn new ways of understanding sexism or sexual harassment from her perspective as a woman who experiences these things differently are then closed off. When the dominant and powerful claim to know what her difference means for the workplace and claim to understand what things are like for her, possibilities for challenging settled ways of thinking about equality and justice and for imagining new structures that address the inequalities she experiences are foreclosed. Taking difference seriously means being able to conceive of and be open to the positive contributions that can be made by those whose vantage points or perspectives are different from the dominant and powerful.

In much of the literature, the prevalent response to the problems faced by role models is to fall back on arguments about the importance of achieving a "critical mass" of representatives from disadvantaged groups. Overall, for example, rightly points out that "in practice, the presence of an individual, sole woman is not enough to effect change in an organization" (Overall 1987, 184-185) and adds that "what we should be seeking, as feminists, is the infiltration of massive numbers of women into existing organizations . . . the transformation of those organizations, and the production of new structures. What is important is not just the presence of individuals, but the shoring up of the sex ratio so that women constitute a large percentage of every organization's personnel" (Overall 1987, 184-185). Having a context in which one is not isolated in male dominated structures is vital for developing critical perspectives for understanding and fighting oppression. Within oppressive structures, these critical perspectives expand our understanding of the potentially radical impact of having subjects of difference in places of influence and power. New perspectives can change workplace structures that view the inclusion and incorporation of difference as violations of the injunction to treat equals equally. Only when the perspectives of the disadvantaged are included in current structures can the conditions for equality obtain.

If we examine the relational dynamics of interactions in workplace structures when affirmative action measures are implemented or enforced, we see that we are already undergoing a restructuring in which the inclusion of difference has had and will continue to have an impact.[19] Subjects of difference have an impact not only on other members of the same group, but also on members of other groups. Most importantly, they can and do have an impact on the perceptions that the advantaged have of the traditionally disadvantaged members of society. That impact is felt when stereotypes, formerly entrenched and intransigent, are questioned, and ways of seeing those labelled and viewed as different are challenged and changed. The presence of the woman in the all-male department who encounters a "chilly climate"[20] if she lives her difference forces her male colleagues to confront sexist stereotypes and perceptions; the ways in which they have constructed and understood what her difference means. I would not want to underestimate the difficulty she has in changing perceptions of her difference if she is the only woman in the department. Isolation and marginalization may mean that her relationships with the dominant and powerful result in further damages to her self-concepts, autonomy, and moral development. Further, without a strong affirmative action hiring policy she may remain a solitary representative who has great difficulty being heard and taken seriously. But I would also not want to underestimate the subversive impact of role modelling in its potential to radically transform relationships and workplace structures. Confrontations with stereotypes are more likely in contexts in which the advantaged have to interact with, listen to, and live with those labelled as different.

The radical implications of role modelling also place an onus on subjects of difference to live lives that make a difference. There is a sense in which all members of disadvantaged groups become politicized agents. bell hooks emphasizes that responsibility when she writes: "[t]hough I am not at all into the term 'role model', I know that having many young black women looking at me, not just at my work, but at how I'm living my life — my habits of being, and seeing me as an example, as someone charting the journey, has made me work harder to get my life together. Knowing that they are watching me, seeing what's going on with my psyche, my inner well-being, has changed my priorities. I am less self-indulgent" (hooks 1990, 229). I would add that the responsibility is heightened with the realization that subjects of difference challenge stereotypes and perceptions of difference and make possible the reconstruction and reconstitution of difference and the promotion of equal concern and respect for all people.

Members of disadvantaged groups contribute not only by being a model for members of the same group to imitate, not only because they have histories and experiences shared by same group members, but also because they have experiences and perspectives that can change entrenched social practices and political contexts, the practices and contexts that support the view of difference as inferior and as the basis for unequal treatment. The perspectives and experiences of the disadvantaged become privileged vantage points in the sense that they are "living instances of possible ways of being" (Code 1986, 58). Taking seriously the ways in which identities are structured in relational contexts means that affirmative action measures cannot be seen as merely making the status quo of competition for hierarchical positions more fair. Relational theory demonstrates the impact that affirmative action has on changing the very institutional structures that entrench and perpetuate inequalities. A respect for difference requires that we hear the voices of those whose difference continues to be an obstacle to their self-realization and development. A commitment to equality requires a sustained support of affirmative action as a way of truly including those whose difference continues to matter.

The relational interpretation of the role played by members of disadvantaged groups when affirmative action policies are in place shows that the framework can be restructured from within when these perspectives are validated and valued. A relational approach highlights how genuine interactive relationships between the dominant and powerful and those who are oppressed have the radical potential for changing entrenched structures of thought and practice. When inequalities generated in and through these relationships of oppression and domination are addressed, we see that the project of equalizing starting positions and ensuring genuine equality of opportunity, broadly conceived as the opportunity to pursue interests, projects, and goals, is a much more difficult goal than liberals have thus far imagined. In fact, relational theory suggests that attentiveness to these inequalities could have dramatic social and attitudinal effects and change our understanding of what is needed to achieve equality.*

NOTES

1. Gilligan uses phrases such as web, world, and network repeatedly in her *In A Different Voice* to describe the relational aspects of people's lives (Gilligan 1982, 17; 29; 30; 32; 33; 49; 59; 62; 147; 167).
2. For a detailed account of a relational critique of liberal conceptions of equality that I develop by expanding on insights from Gilligan's work and from what has come to be known as relational feminism, see my *A Relational Theory of Equality* (Koggel 1995).
3. The American literature on affirmative action has many examples of arguments on both sides of the issue concerning whether or not compensation to all members of disadvantaged groups can be justified. On the side of those who defend strict compensation to individuals and not groups, see Goldman (1975a; 1975b); Newton (1973); Blackstone (1975); Sher (1975; 1977); Gross (1975); Simon (1974; 1978; 1979); Levin (1980; 1981); and Lee (1985). On the side of those who defend compensation to groups, see Jaggar's reply to Goldman's objections (1977); Brooks

* I am grateful to Christine Sypnowich, Christine Overall, J.E. Bickenbach, Andrew Brook, Kathleen Okruhlik and the participants at the C-SWIP 1993 conference in Calgary for providing useful comments and criticisms. I would also like to acknowledge financial support from the Social Sciences and Humanities Research Council of Canada.

(1983); Boxill (1978); Nickel (1974); and America (1986). Judith Jarvis Thomson argues that all individuals who are members of disadvantaged groups suffer the detrimental effects of "lack of self-confidence, and lack of self-respect" through discrimination (Thomson 1973, 381) and that this justifies compensating all members of disadvantaged groups. A similar argument is provided by Minas (1977).

4. Viewing justice in terms of compensation for discriminatory actions also raises questions about the burden placed on innocent white males. Here again, the literature provides arguments on both sides of the issue. Examples of those who defend the burdens placed on all white males include Pluhar (1981); Fried (1973); and Thomson (1973). Examples of those who do not think the burden on white males can be justified include Carr (1981); Groarke (1983; 1990); Brooks (1983); and Gross (1975).

5. Hawkesworth views the retributive and compensatory models of justice as "grounded in individualist assumptions that undermine cross-generational claims of justice for groups" (Hawkesworth 1990, 107). She adds:

    That women have suffered discrimination at determinate points in history can be proven; but identifying the particular men responsible for that situation is often far more difficult. The model of compensation underlying this conception of justice requires identification of specific parties in specific instances. Absent such identification, no rectification is possible. Thus, the retributive conception of justice cannot support feminist claims for compensation to contemporary women for a legacy of historical injustices (Hawkesworth 1990, 107).

6. Thomson argues that "the nature of the wrongs done is such as to make jobs the best and most suitable form of compensation. What blacks and women were denied was full membership in the community; and nothing can more appropriately make amends for that wrong than precisely what will make them feel they now finally have it" (Thomson 1973, 383).

7. Linda Nicholson provides an extensive account of the sorts of external and internal barriers that limit the opportunities of members of disadvantaged groups (Nicholson 1983).

8. There is unnecessary confusion about underrepresentation and underutilization in the literature. Jan Narveson, for example, misrepresents proponents of affirmative action as advocating hiring 50% women with no attention to the context of the kind of job or the number of women in the qualified pool of applicants (Narveson 1995, 255-257). Mary Hawkesworth clears up the confusion by distinguishing underutilization from underrepresentation:

    Underutilization involves a comparison of the number of women in particular career positions with the number of women in the labor force who possess all the relevant qualifications for the job. Studies of underutilization compare, for example, the number of women faculty hired in specific disciplines with the number of women Ph.D.s in that discipline who are on the job market in a given year. What investigations of underutilization seek to explain is not the dearth of women professionals or women in skilled craft positions per se, but the dearth of women in these fields given the availability of qualified women candidates (Hawkesworth 1990, 53).

    See a similar discussion of underutilization by Ezorsky (1977).

9. There is an extensive literature defending affirmative action as a means of levelling out the effects of biased perceptions: Sumner (1987); Warren (1977); Purdy (1984); Minas (1977); Wendell (1980); and Nicholson (1983).

10. Also see arguments by Beauchamp (1979); Wasserstrom (1976; 1978); Thalberg (1972; 1973); Nagel (1989); and Vanterpool (1989) in favour of utilitarian justifications for affirmative action as justified discrimination.

11. Michael Davis argues that affirmative action is not discriminatory and that race, in the United States, is a qualification for jobs (Davis 1983).

12. For discussions of what women can contribute in the way of different perspectives and methodologies to a discipline, see Boddington (1988); Moulton (1989); and Sherwin (1987).

13. My own experiences as a lecturer in introductory philosophy courses testify to the importance of female students' being able to observe that others "like them" can do philosophy. Female students repeatedly tell me that having a female instructor makes a difference. When I press them to tell me why, they say that most of their philosophy courses make them feel unwelcome because the syllabus is dominated by male authors, there is an aggressiveness in the way that philosophical debates are conducted that makes them feel uncomfortable, and there is a

sometimes not so subtle rejection of their comments when they attempt to introduce female contributors into the discussion. These reasons are elements of systemic discrimination and are more difficult to identify and address than overt and blatant discrimination. In a 1991 report by the Canadian Philosophical Association on the notorious underrepresentation of women in Philosophy, the authors not only give data of underrepresentation, but provide reasons for the underrepresentation that corresponded closely to the kind of reasons given by Courtenay Hall and my female students (Baker et al 1991). The data are corroborated by Statistics Canada, whose figures for female faculty show that Philosophy runs a close second to Religion as the discipline in the Arts and Social Sciences with the fewest number of women (Statistics Canada. *Teachers in Universities*, 81-241; *Universities: Enrolment and Degrees*, 81-204). See also the report by Symons (1984) for statistical data on university hiring and promotion. A controversial interpretation of the data is offered by Irvine (1996), who argues that relative to their numbers in the pool of applicants women have been preferentially hired in universities for the last three decades. Articles by Burns (1994) and Sumner (1996) reinterpret and challenge Irvine's approach.

14. See an interesting discussion by Jeanne Speizer, who argues that the concept of role model, being fairly new, needs further definition and study and not quick conclusions about the effects on numbers of the presence of role models in institutions (Speizer 1981).

15. Rhode calls the focus on greater proportional representation "a 'body count' approach to affirmative action" (Rhode 1989, 189). Yet, when it comes to defending affirmative action, she herself justifies it in terms of increasing numbers.

16. In an uncompromising argument in favour of strong affirmative action policies that will give women an equal representation in public offices, Hawkesworth argues that "[w]hat could reasonably be expected is that women in office would be sensitive to forms of disadvantage that uniquely affect women and that they would take such problems seriously. Thus, sex parity in office would function as a procedural mechanism designed to ensure that the relevance of sex in any particular policy instance would remain an open question" (Hawkesworth 1990, 184).

17. In the context of her argument for equal representation of women in public office, Hawkesworth writes: "[b]ecause individual women are as different from one another as they are from men, it would be a mistake to expect a univocal stance from women in office. Because the pressures upon legislators from constituents, lobbyists, political parties, colleagues, committee responsibilities, personal loyalties, and individual expertise and conscience all play a role in determining officials' policy stances, it would be absurd to expect women in office to form a unified and invariant voting bloc" (Hawkesworth 1990, 183).

18. Mary Anne Warren labels some of these unarticulated perceptions "secondary sexism" (Warren 1977, 11). It needs to be noted that a lot happens before the candidates are determined to be equally qualified. More overt perceptions such as that her philosophical interests are not mainstream or that she is less aggressive in philosophical debates or that she is too aggressive about feminism are factors that may prevent her from ever getting as far as the tie-breaking situation.

19. Some of these changes are evident in my own experiences in the university setting. When I was an M.A. student over a decade ago, experiences of sexist humour, sexual harassment, and marginalization in the classroom were, more often than not, internalized as personal problems and taken as indications of having provoked the comments or harassment and of not measuring up intellectually. With so few other women students and faculty, these issues were just not discussed. Changes began with an increase in women's representation at the faculty and student level. Women started speaking about their experiences and discovered that other women shared those experiences. More than a decade later, I see in female students a heightened awareness about what counts as discrimination and of the subtle forms it can take. And along with some resentments and bitterness about changes, I also see male faculty who can and do listen to women's experiences as valid entry points to a better understanding of difference.

20. For discussions of the effects of a chilly climate, see Backhouse (1990); Finn (1989); Caplan (1993); and the important collection of essays in *Breaking Anonymity: The Chilly Climate for Women Faculty* (Chilly Collective 1995).

BIBLIOGRAPHY

America, Richard F. (1986). Affirmative action and redistributive ethics. *Journal of Business Ethics*, 5 (February).

Backhouse, Constance. (1990). Women faculty at the University of Western Ontario: reflections on the Employment Equity Award. *Canadian Journal of Women and the Law*, 4 (1).

Baker, Brenda et al. (1991). *Report to the Canadian Philosophical Association from the Committee to Study Hiring Policies Affecting Women*. Ottawa: Canadian Philosophical Association.

Beauchamp, Tom L. (1979). Blackstone and the problem of reverse discrimination. *Social Theory and Practice*, 5 (Spring).

Blackstone, William T. (1975). Reverse discrimination and compensatory justice. *Social Theory and Practice*, 3 (3).

Boddington, Paula Ruth. (1988). The issue of women's philosophy. In *Feminist Perspectives in Philosophy*, ed. Morwenna Griffiths & Margaret Whitford. Bloomington: Indiana University Press.

Boxill, Bernard R. (1978). The morality of preferential hiring. *Philosophy & Public Affairs*, 7 (3).

Brooks, D. H. M. (1983). Why reverse discrimination is especially wrong. *Journal of Value Inquiry*, v. 17.

Burns, Steven. (1994). The Canadian Philosophical Association decision on employment equity. *Deutsche Zeitschrift für Philosophie*, 42 (3). Published in German translation.

Caplan, Paula J. (1993). *Lifting a Ton of Feathers: A Woman's Guide for Surviving in the Academic World*. Toronto: University of Toronto Press.

Carr, C. R. (1982). Unfair sacrifice-reply to Pluhar's 'Preferential Hiring and Unjust Sacrifice'. *Philosophical Forum (Boston)*, 14 (1).

Chilly Collective (eds.) (1995). *Breaking Anonymity: The Chilly Climate for Women Faculty*. Waterloo: Wilfrid Laurier University Press.

Code, Lorraine. (1986). Simple equality is not enough. *Australasian Journal of Philosophy Supplement*, 64 (June).

— (1991). *What Can She Know? Feminist Theory and the Construction of Knowledge*. Ithaca, N.Y.: Cornell University Press.

Courtenay Hall, Pamela. (1992). From justified discrimination to responsive hiring: the role model argument and female equity hiring in philosophy. In *Contemporary Moral Issues*, ed. Wesley Cragg. 3rd edition. Toronto: McGraw-Hill Ryerson.

Davis, Michael. (1983). Race as merit. *Mind*, 92 (July).

Ezorsky, Gertrude. (1977). Hiring women faculty. *Philosophy & Public Affairs*, 7 (1).

Finn, Geraldine. (1989). On the oppression of women in philosophy — or whatever happened to objectivity? In *Feminism: From Pressure to Politics*, ed. Angela Miles & Geraldine Finn. Montreal: Black Rose Books.

Fried, Marlene Gerber. (1973). In defense of preferential hiring. *Philosophical Forum (Boston)*, 5 (2).

Gilligan, Carol. (1982). *In a Different Voice: Psychological Theory and Women's Development*. Cambridge, Mass.: Harvard University Press.

Goldman, Alan H. (1975a). Limits to the justification of reverse discrimination. *Social Theory and Practice*, 3 (2).

— (1975b). Reparations to individuals or groups? *Analysis*, 35 (5).

Groarke, Leo. (1983). Beyond affirmative action. Atlantis, 9 (1).

— (1990). Affirmative action as a form of restitution. *Journal of Business Ethics*, v. 9.

— (1996). What's in a number? Consequentialism and employment equity in Hall, Hurka, Sumner and Baker et al. *Dialogue: Canadian Philosophical Review*, XXXV (2).

Gross, Barry R. (1975). Is turn about fair play? *Journal of Critical Analysis*, 5 (4).

Hawkesworth, Mary E. (1990). *Beyond Oppression: Feminist Theory and Political Strategy*. New York: Continuum.

hooks, bell. (1990). *Yearning: Race, Gender, and Cultural Politics*. Toronto: Between the Lines.

Hunter, Ian. (1992). When human rights become wrongs. In *Contemporary Moral Issues*, ed. Wesley Cragg. 3rd edition. Toronto: McGraw-Hill Ryerson.

Irvine, A.D. (1996). Jack & Jill & employment equity. *Dialogue: Canadian Philosophical Review*, XXXV (2).

Jaggar, Alison M. (1977). Relaxing the limits on preferential treatment. *Social Theory and Practice*, 4 (2).

Koggel, Christine. (1995). *A Relational Theory of Equality*. Dissertation (PhD) Queen's University, Kingston, Ontario.

Lee, Sander H. (1985). Reverse discrimination and social justice. *Philosophy Research Archives*, 11 (March).

Levin, Michael E. (1980). Reverse discrimination, shackled runners, and personal identity. *Philosophical Studies*, 37 (Fall).

— (1981). Is racial discrimination special? *Journal of Value Inquiry*, v. 15.

Martin, Michael. (1973). Pedagogical arguments for preferential hiring and tenuring of women teachers in the university. *Philosophical Forum (Boston)*, 5 (2).

Minas, Anne C. (1977). How reverse discrimination compensates women. *Ethics*, 88 (October).

Moulton, Janice. (1989). A paradigm of philosophy: the adversary method. In *Women, Knowledge, and Reality: Explorations in Feminist Philosophy*, ed. Ann Garry & Marilyn Pearsall. Boston: Unwin Hyman.

Nagel, Thomas. (1989). A defense of affirmative action. In *Moral Choices: Ethical Theories and Problems*, ed. Joseph Grcic. St. Paul, Minn.: West Publishing Company.

Narveson, Jan. (1991). Have we a right to non-discrimination? In *Business Ethics in Canada*, ed. Deborah C. Poff & Wilfred J. Waluchow. 2nd edition. Scarborough, Ont.: Prentice-Hall Canada.

— (1995). *Moral Matters*. Peterborough: Broadview Press.

Newton, Lisa. (1973). Reverse discrimination as unjustified. *Ethics*, 83 (4).

Nicholson, Linda J. (1983). Affirmative action, education, and social class. *Philosophy of Education: Proceedings*, v. 39.

Nickel, James W. (1974). Should reparations be to individuals or to groups? *Analysis*, 34 (5).

Overall, Christine. (1987). Role models: a critique. In *Women: Isolation and Bonding: the Ecology of Gender*, ed. Kathleen Storrie. Toronto: Methuen.

Pluhar, Evelyn B. (1981). Preferential hiring and unjust sacrifice. *Philosophical Forum (Boston)*, 12 (3) (Spring).

Purdy, Laura M. (1984). In defense of hiring apparently less qualified women. *Journal of Social Philosophy*, 15 (Summer).

Rhode, Deborah L. (1989). *Justice and Gender: Sex Discrimination and the Law*. England: Harvard University Press.

Rosenfeld, Michel. (1991). *Affirmative Action and Justice: A Philosophical and Constitutional Inquiry*. New Haven: Yale University Press.

Sasseen, Robert F. (1976). Affirmative action and the principle of equality. *Studies in Philosophy and Education*, 9 (Spring).

Sher, George. (1975). Justifying reverse discrimination in employment. *Philosophy & Public Affairs*, 4 (2).

— (1977). Groups and justice. *Ethics*, 87 (January).

Sherwin, Susan. (1987). Feminist ethics and in vitro fertilization. In *Science, Morality & Feminist Theory*, ed. Marsha Hanen & Kai Nielsen. Calgary: The University of Calgary Press.

Simon, Robert L. (1974). Preferential hiring: a reply to Judith Jarvis Thompson. *Philosophy & Public Affairs*, 3 (3).

— (1978). Preferential treatment: for groups or for individuals? *National Forum*, 58 (Winter).

— (1979). Individual rights and 'Benign' discrimination. *Ethics*, 90 (October).

Speizer, Jeanne J. (1981). Role models, mentors, and sponsors: the elusive concepts. *Signs: Journal of Women in Culture and Society*, 6 (4).

Statistics Canada. *Teachers in Universities*, Catalogue no. 81-7241. Ottawa: Minister of Supply & Services.

Statistics Canada. *Universities: Enrolment and Degrees*, Catalogue no. 81-204. Ottawa: Minister of Supply & Services.

Sumner, L. W. (1987). Positive sexism. *Social Philosophy and Policy*, 5 (1).

— (1996). Why the numbers count. *Dialogue: Canadian Philosophical Review*, XXXV (2).

Symons, Thomas H.B. & Page, James E. (1984). *Some Questions of Balance: Human Resources, Higher Education and Canadian Studies*. Ottawa: Association of Universities and Colleges of Canada.

Thalberg, Irving. (1972). Justification of institutional racism. *Philosophical Forum (Boston)*, 3 (Winter).

— (1973). Reverse discrimination and the future. *Philosophical Forum (Boston)*, 5 (2) (Fall/Winter).

Thomson, Judith Jarvis. (1973). Preferential hiring. *Philosophy & Public Affairs*, 2 (4).

Vanterpool, Rudolph V. (1989). Affirmative action revisited: justice and public policy considerations. *Public Affairs Quarterly*, 3 (4) (October).

Warren, Mary Anne. (1977). Secondary sexism and quota hiring. *Philosophy & Public Affairs*, 6 (3).

Wasserstrom, Richard. (1976). The university and the case for preferential treatment. *American Philosophical Quarterly*, 13 (April).

— (1978). A defense of programs of preferential treatment. *National Forum*, 58 (1).

Wendell, Susan. (1980). Discrimination, sex prejudice and affirmative action. *Atlantis*, 6 (1).

QUESTIONS

1. According to Christine Koggel, what are some of the shortcomings of both the formal and substantive approaches to equality within the liberal tradition?
2. Why, according to Koggel, is it helpful to examine the issue of affirmative action by moving the focus from individuals to the "web of relationships"? How does this approach differ from those offered by the other contributors to this chapter?
3. What reasons does Koggel provide for questioning Narveson's analysis of compensation?
4. Do you think that the examples Koggel provides of the changes that result from a greater representation of disadvantaged group members in workplace settings supports the case for strengthening affirmative action programs?

➜ ⬅

SUGGESTIONS FOR FURTHER READING

Court Cases

- Supreme Court of Canada. *Action Travail des Femmes v. Canadian National Railway Co. et al. Dominion Law Reports* 40 D.L.R. (4th), 1987. A case that ruled it was within the jurisdiction of the Canadian Human Rights Tribunal to order CN to instate quotas for the hiring of women.
- Ontario Board of Inquiry. *Roberts v. Ontario Ministry of Health. Canadian Human Rights Reporter*, 10 C.H.R.R., Decision 948, October 1989. This case provides summaries of arguments for and against affirmative action and excerpts of federal and provincial legislation relevant to affirmative action.

Canadian Government Reports

- Canada. Royal Commission on Equality in Employment. *Report of the Commission on Equality in Employment* (Ottawa: Supply and Services Canada, 1984). This final report of a commission chaired by Judge Rosalie S. Abella as well as the background papers, *Research Studies of the Commission on Equality in Employment*, provides an introduction to equality theory in the context of an examination of the disadvantages and inequalities experienced in Canada by visible minorities, people with disabilities, women, and native people.

Books

- *Canadian Women Studies*, vol. 6, no. 4 (Winter 1985). A special issue devoted to articles on affirmative action that presents a number of perspectives on various workplace contexts in which affirmative action programs have been implemented.
- Marshall Cohen, Thomas Nagel, and Thomas Scanlon, eds., *Equality and Preferential Treatment* (Princeton: Princeton University Press, 1977) . This collection contains notable articles on affirmative action by such authors as Ronald Dworkin, Owen Fiss, Alan Goldman, Thomas Nagel, George Sher, Robert Simon, and Judith Jarvis Thomson. Most of these articles focus on compensation and justice issues in the arguments for affirmative action.

- Fraser Institute. *Discrimination, Affirmative Action and Equal Opportunity* (Vancouver: Fraser Institute, 1982). A collection of readings that defends free market theory and argues against affirmative action programs as a violation of individual freedom. The reading in this chapter by Michael Walker refers to this book.
- Steven M. Cahn. *Affirmative Action and the University: A Philosophical Inquiry* (Philadelphia: Temple University Press, 1993). The articles in this collection use the university setting to examine various arguments for and against affirmative action.
- Gertrude Ezorsky. *Racism & Justice: The Case for Affirmative Action*. Ithaca: Cornell University Press, 1991. As the title suggests, Ezorsky focuses on the particular case of blacks and argues that a history of "murderous racism" in the States justifies affirmative action on both practical and moral grounds.
- Baker, Brenda et al. *Report to the Canadian Philosophical Association from the Committee to Study Hiring Policies Affecting Women*. Ottawa: Canadian Philosophical Association, 1991. This report provides statistical data regarding the under-representation

of women in the discipline of philosophy. As well as suggesting ways of changing the climate for women in philosophy, it formulates an affirmative action policy and recommends that it be adopted by philosophy departments in Canada.

Articles

• A.D. Irvine, "Jack and Jill and Employment Equity," *Dialogue: Canadian Philosophical Review*, v. 35, no. 2 (Spring 1996). This article sets out in summary form the main arguments that people have used to support affirmative action in university hiring and then looks to see whether the factual assumptions underlying those arguments are well founded. Using Statistics Canada figures, the author argues that there is in fact no evidence of systemic discrimination against women in university hiring practices over the past two decades. To the contrary, universities in Canada have been giving systematic preference to female candidates over better-qualified male applicants since the early 1970s. This evidence supports the view that affirmative action does lead to lower standards in university hiring, he argues. Three other articles in the same issue of *Dialogue* pick up this discussion of the statistical evidence regarding discrimination in university hiring. Leo Groarke provides additional support for Irvine by criticizing the sort of arguments given by Thomas Hurka, L.W. Sumner, and Baker et al (see report cited above) that defend the consequentialist view that the goal of achieving proportional representation justifies using affirmative action as a means for achieving that goal. If, as Irvine suggests, the numbers do not point to discrimination in hiring in recent years, then, Groarke argues, the consequentialist argument is weakened. A reply by L.W. Sumner, "Why the Numbers Count," and a counter response by Groarke are also included in this volume.

• Mary Hawkesworth, "The Affirmative Action Debate and Conflicting Conceptions of Individuality," *Women's Studies International Forum*, v. 7, no. 5 (1984). Hawkesworth argues that the arguments provided by proponents and opponents of affirmative action each operate with assumptions about what people are like. While arguments opposing affirmative action rely on a conception of persons as individualistic, competitive, and atomistic, those that support affirmative action "tacitly adopt a conception of 'socialized individualism' which emphasizes the impact of cultural norms and group practices upon the development of individual identity."

• Laura M. Purdy, "In Defense of Hiring Apparently Less Qualified Women," *Journal of Social Philosophy*, v. 15 (Summer 1984). This article mounts an argument for the hiring of women who are apparently less qualified than their male competitors based on evidence that women are perceived to be less qualified.

A fairly comprehensive bibliography of material dealing specifically with affirmative action as well as material covering court decisions, government reports, and legal discussions of the Charter is available upon request from Christine M. Koggel.

Chapter 7

Aboriginal Rights

Introduction

Moral issues often focus on individuals. Euthanasia, abortion, and capital punishment are examples of issues of this kind. Is it morally acceptable for members of the medical profession to assist those who want to die to do so? Is abortion a matter appropriately left to a woman and her doctor? Is a society morally justified in executing people who commit the most serious crimes — like murder?

Moral issues can also be generated by the interaction of individuals who are members of particular groups with other individuals or groups. This adds a degree of complexity, as we saw in our discussion of pornography, discrimination, and affirmative action. The issue with pornography is whether allowing it to circulate is likely to harm individuals exposed to it or indirectly affected by its use or to people by their membership in groups — namely women. Both discrimination and affirmative action take as their focus individuals identified by group membership: race, creed, sex, and so on.

A third focus for moral issues is the relationship of groups to other groups. Each of us is affected in significant ways by our membership in groups. Families are an example. So are the communities we are a part of. In many ways, our identity as individuals is shaped by the culture in which we are raised. It is also shaped by the way in which the groups, communities, or culture we are a part of are regarded by other groups, communities, or cultures. Working out appropriate relationships between and among groups is therefore extremely important. It is also very complex. The relationship between Canadians generally and the aboriginal peoples whose history in this part of the world predates European settlement in Canada is a good example.

Background Considerations

The relationship of the native peoples with the dominant Canadian majority has been an uneasy one virtually from the point of first contact. Substantially different views of the land are one reason for this. From the time Europeans first discovered North America, they regarded the land as unoccupied. They had no qualms about using it for their own purposes, settling on it, and claiming it for the countries from which they had come.

However, this view had an odd quality to it. For the land was occupied by people with well-developed and effective though largely informal political and legal systems. Land and "ownership" played a part in their social system but a part quite different from that assigned to it by the Europeans who landed on their shores. In their view, land was not something that could be owned by individuals or by groups as European law defined ownership. It could only be used and shared. And so it was shared with the first settlers and later through the medium of treaties with the governments they brought with them or formed after their arrival.

One result of these differing attitudes was that the treaties signed by native peoples and their representatives with British and Canadian governments were interpreted in different and often incompatible ways by those involved. The European view was that the treaties involved agreements to surrender ownership of the land in return for reservations on which the native peoples involved could live, together with whatever other considerations were included in the treaties. Yet how could the native peoples surrender land that in their view they did not own? The result has been conflicting views of what the signatories to the various treaties were in fact agreeing to. And where no treaties were signed, serious conflicts have developed about the status of the original inhabitants who continue to occupy the land.

Because they are a relatively insignificant percentage of the Canadian population, the native peoples have been largely unsuccessful in obtaining political solutions to the disputes that have arisen with the dominant culture. As a result, until recently they have had to rely on the courts to resolve outstanding disagreements. This has been particularly true of land claims that have arisen in areas of the country where treaties have never been signed. Consequently, serious disputes have generally been resolved in the context of legal principles that are essentially foreign to the native outlook.

The Current Situation

The status of Canada's native peoples is today very much in flux. That there have been significant and permanent changes in their legal status is hard to deny. The Constitution Act of 1982 which recognized and affirmed the existing aboriginal and treaty rights of Canada's aboriginal people has been decisive. In effect, this Act has entrenched significant, special collective aboriginal rights in Canadian law. The Royal Commission on Aboriginal Peoples has argued that one of these special collective rights is the right to self-government. Without question, legal developments have also altered how the courts and the federal and provincial governments have approached land claim issues in recent years. At the same time, aboriginal/government relations continue to be marked by conflict, hostility, and controversy. As a symbol of conflict and hostility, events at Oka in the summer of 1990 continue to influence relations between radical elements of native communities and local populations and the police. This is clearly reflected in armed confrontations which have since taken place in Ontario and British Columbia.

At the political level, anger over the failure of political leaders to include native concerns in the Meech Lake constitutional negotiations played a decisive role in the defeat of that accord when Elijah Harper, a native member of the Manitoba legislature, refused to give his agreement to a ratification process which required unanimous consent in the Manitoba legislature and the unanimous agreement of all ten provinces. In contrast, the Charlottetown agreement did acknowledge self-government demands on the part of prominent native leaders, a fact which was subsequently appealed to by those urging the Canadian people to endorse the agreement in the referendum vote which followed. The Charlottetown accord, however, was not endorsed by popular vote. Without that additional constitutional backing, governments have turned to local provincial and regional negotiations.

These initiatives have not been without results. In Manitoba, for example, significant steps have been taken toward self-government. A ground-breaking agreement has been reached by the federal and provincial governments with the Nisga'a people of Northern British Columbia. And finally, the Department of Native Affairs in Ottawa, long a symbol of entrenched colonial and paternalistic attitudes, is being phased out as an instrument of policy and administration.

It remains the case, however, that we are a long way from consensus on resolving long-standing problems and disagreements. Recent changes in the political climate have resulted in provincial governments committed to reducing both expenditures and the size and role of government. Statements by some influential political leaders suggest that the position articulated by Pierre Elliot Trudeau on behalf of the federal government in 1969 continues to have considerable appeal to large segments of the Canadian population. At the same time, statistics show that on virtually every available measure of social welfare, income, employment, housing, infant mortality, longevity, and health people of native descent are much the least favoured of Canadians. Hence, the issues raised in the chapter are significant and continue to attract attention and debate as we move toward the millennium.

The Readings

We begin with Section 35 of the Constitution Act of 1982. This is followed by two contrasting views of how to approach the righting of past wrongs suffered by Canada's aboriginal peoples. Pierre Elliot Trudeau, speaking from the perspective of government policy in the 1960s, argues that the most effective way to confront the "native issue" is to move from special status toward full integration into the political and legal life of the country. George Erasmus, a distinguished aboriginal leader, and Joe Sanders then present quite a different understanding to the issues being raised in this chapter. Michael McDonald then examines from a philosophical perspective a range of arguments that have been used in public debate to try to determine the nature and extent of native rights. He concludes that aboriginal rights are grounded on land rights, which in turn derive from the fact that native peoples are the original inhabitants of what is now known as Canada. His conclusions are critically examined by David Gauthier, defender of a contrasting position.

The focus of the readings then shift to the issue of self-government. The case for self-government is made by Fred Plain. The implications of recent legal developments for self-government are then set out in a selection drawn from the work of the Royal Commission on Aboriginal Peoples. Finally, Jack Stevenson asks whether there is a moral principle that has broad cultural acceptance and acceptability by reference to which the issues in question can be evaluated and resolved. He argues that there is such a principle, calling it "the personal security principle." Applying this principle specifically to the issue of land ownership leads him to conclude that the basic claims of Canada's native peoples are well founded, and further, that just resolution will require that the demand for self-government be recognized.

RIGHTS OF THE ABORIGINAL PEOPLES OF CANADA

The Constitution Act of 1982: Section 35

35. (1) The existing aboriginal and treaty rights of the aboriginal peoples of Canada are hereby recognized and affirmed.

(2) In this Act, "aboriginal peoples of Canada" includes the Indian, Inuit and Métis peoples of Canada.

REMARKS ON INDIAN ABORIGINAL AND TREATY RIGHTS

[Part of a speech given August 8, 1969, in Vancouver, British Columbia]

Prime Minister P.E. Trudeau

I think Canadians are not too proud about their past in the way in which they treated the Indian population of Canada and I don't think we have very great cause to be proud.

We have set the Indians apart as a race. We've set them apart in our laws. We've set them apart in the ways the governments will deal with them. They're not citizens of the province as the rest of us are. They are wards of the federal government. They get their services from the federal government rather than from the provincial or municipal governments. They have been set apart in law. They have been set apart in the relations with government and they've been set apart socially too.

So this year we came up with a proposal. It's a policy paper on the Indian problem. It proposes a set of solutions. It doesn't impose them on anybody. It proposes them — not only to the Indians but to all Canadians — not only to their federal representatives but to the provincial representatives too and it says we're at the crossroads. We can go on treating the Indians as having a special status. We can go on adding bricks of discrimination around the ghetto in which they live and at the same time perhaps helping them preserve certain cultural traits and certain ancestral rights. Or we can say you're at a crossroads — the time is now to decide whether the Indians will be a race apart in Canada or whether it will be Canadians of full status. And this is a difficult choice. It must be a very agonizing choice to the Indian peoples themselves because, on the other hand, they realize that if they come into the society as total citizens they will be equal under the law but they risk losing certain of their traditions, certain aspects of a culture and perhaps even certain of their basic rights and this is a very difficult choice for them to make and I don't think we want to try and force the pace on them any more than we can force it on the rest of Canadians but here again is a choice which is in our minds whether Canadians as a whole want to continue treating the Indian populations as something outside, a group of Canadians with which we have treaties, a group of Canadians who have as the Indians, many of them claim, aboriginal rights, or whether we will say well forget the past and begin today and this is a tremendously difficult choice because, if — well, one of the things the Indian bands often refer to are their aboriginal rights and in our policy, the way we propose it, we say we won't recognize aboriginal rights. We will recognize treaty rights. We will recognize forms of contract which have been made with the Indian people by the Crown and we will try to bring justice in the area and this will mean that perhaps the treaties shouldn't go on forever. It's inconceivable, I think, that in a given society one section of the society have a treaty with the other section of the society. We must be all equal under the laws and we must not sign treaties amongst ourselves and many of these treaties, indeed, would have less and less significance in the future anyhow but things that in the past were covered by the treaties like things like so much twine or so much gun powder and which haven't been paid, this must be paid. But I don't think that we should encourage the Indians to feel that their treaties should last forever within Canada so that they be able to receive their twine or their gun powder. They should become Canadians as all other Canadians and if they are prosperous and wealthy they will be treated like the prosperous and wealthy and they will be paying taxes for the other Canadians who are not so prosperous and not so wealthy whether they be Indians or English Canadians or French or Maritimers and this is the only basis on which I see our society can develop as equals. But aboriginal rights, this really means saying, "We were here before you. You came and you took the land from us and perhaps you cheated us by giving us some worthless things in return for vast expanses of land and we want to re-open this question. We want you to preserve our aboriginal rights and to restore them to us." And our answer — it may not be the right one and may not be one which is accepted but it will be up to all of our people to make your minds up and to choose for or against it and to discuss with the Indians — our answer is "no."

If we think of restoring aboriginal rights to the Indians, well, what about the French who were defeated at the Plains of Abraham? Shouldn't we restore rights to them? And what about the Acadians who were deported — shouldn't we compensate for this? And what about the other Canadians, the immigrants? What about the Japanese Canadians who were so badly treated at the end of or during the last war? What can we do to redeem the past? I can only say as President Kennedy said when he was asked about what he would do to compensate for the injustices that the Negroes had received in American society. We will be just in our time. This is all we can do. We must be just today.

QUESTIONS

1. Does it matter that the native peoples were the first people in Canada?
2. If we restore rights to the native peoples, must we then restore rights to other groups in Canada who feel a grievance? Are the native peoples a special case?

CANADIAN HISTORY: AN ABORIGINAL PERSPECTIVE

Georges Erasmus and Joe Sanders

Aboriginal Sovereignty

When non-native people first came to this continent some five hundred years ago, indigenous peoples lived all across the Americas. It is a matter of historical record that before the arrival of Europeans, these First Nations possessed and exercised absolute sovereignty over what is now called the North American continent. Hundreds of tribal communities, made up of a variety of nations and representing at least ten linguistic groups, lived in what is now known as Canada, from Newfoundland to Vancouver Island.

It was not possible to find "empty" land in the Americas. All the land was being used by the First Nations. Our people decided their own citizenship. They had a wide variety and diversity of governmental systems, almost all of them regulating their activities and the relations among their members with a degree of formality. The way they dealt with the Europeans is ample proof of their capacity to enter into relations with foreign powers: they made a number of treaties with the French and British Crowns, and many of the colonies survived because of the assistance First Nations gave to the European settlers.

Our people knew how to survive in this part of the world. They knew all of their valleys and mountains and rivers. They had names in their own languages for all of these places. They believed that all things had their place, from even the smallest insect and the smallest leaf. And they were taught to respect life and all living things. Our people were living lives that must have been of a much higher quality than people now live in Canada.

It was unfortunate that early Christian leaders believed that our people did not understand why human beings were here on earth. Our people did not think there were gods in every leaf. But they did think that everything around was given by the Creator. They believed that there was one supreme being, that there was purpose in all of this, and that the purpose did not end when we died.

Our people were not a war-like people, but they did defend their interests. Our territorial boundaries were clearly defined. Although First Nations had many disputes with neighbours in their history, they eventually arrived at peaceful arrangements with one another.

Our people understood what the non-native people were after when they came amongst our people and wanted to treaty with them, because they had done that many times amongst themselves. They recognized that a nation-to-nation agreement, defining the specific terms of peaceful coexistence, was being arranged.

Broken Agreements

When our people treated with another nation, each nation's interests, its pride, and its word were at stake. The word of the agreement, the treaty, was given in a very sacred way. And it was not very easily broken.

So it was quite amazing to our people — and it took them a long, long time to realize — that they could sit with other people whose religious leaders were present, and who would

From Nation to Nation: Aboriginal Sovereignty and the Future of Canada, *edited by Diane Engels and John Bird. Reprinted by permission of Stoddart Publishing Co. Ltd., Don Mills, Ont.*

be virtually lying to our people as they were executing the treaty. Even before the document reached London or Paris or Ottawa, they were already forgetting the solemn promises they had made. That never happened on the side of the indigenous people.

It didn't help that the European interpretation of a treaty, often differing radically from the First Nation's interpretation or understanding, significantly altered the intent of the original agreement. For example, ownership of land in the Anglo-Canadian "fee simple" sense of title was foreign to the thinking and systems of First Nations. Land was revered as a mother from which life came, and was to be preserved for future generations as it had been from time immemorial. Land was used for common benefit, with no individual having a right to any more of it than another. A nation's traditional hunting grounds were recognized by its neighbours as "belonging" to that nation, but this was different from the idea of private ownership. For the most part, the boundaries were not delineated, although some nations in British Columbia had systems of identifying their boundaries and passing on custodial responsibilities. First Nations peoples, then and now, believe that they live *with* the land, not simply on it.

As our people understood it, they had agreed to allow peaceful settlement by non-native people in large parts of their valleys and mountains and on rivers, but at the same time native people would retain large tracts of land on which they would govern themselves; on which our institutions would continue to survive; where we would nurture our children; where our languages and our culture would flourish; where we could continue our lives; where we could hunt if we wished, plant crops if we wished, fish if we wished. And where, if we wanted to, we could also be educated in a formal way to become doctors, lawyers or whatever we wished.

The history of the settlement of Canada shows that non-native people, represented by federal, provincial and local governments, have continued to break the original agreements. Hunting, fishing, trapping and gathering sections of treaties that were to protect the aboriginal way of life have continued to be changed by Canadian government policies, regulations and legislation. The original land base agreed to at treaty time has continued to be expropriated for bridges, municipal expansion, military exercises and railway and highway right-of-ways, generally without compensation. In many cases, First Nations are still waiting to have the land entitlement of one-hundred-year-old treaties fulfilled.

Rewriting History

Non-native people have even distorted history. It is very difficult to find a history textbook in any province of this country that accurately tells the story of how our two peoples came together. Instead, there are books in which we are still being called pagans and savages, without an accurate reflection of the solemn agreements that were made and which indicate that indigenous people were to continue to govern themselves.

Native people have the enormous job of tapping people on the shoulder and saying, "This is not the way it's supposed to be. This is not the way we are supposed to be coexisting. We aren't supposed to be the poorest of the poor in our land." Our people have an understanding of the early agreements that the school books usually ignore.

In 1763, three years after the French and British resolved their differences in Canada and recognized Britain as the European power here, the Crown of Great Britain laid down a process in the Royal Proclamation that set forth the Crown's policy on land negotiations. That policy has never been revoked. In the Royal Proclamation, the Crown recognized that any lands possessed by First Nations in what was then British North America, would be reserved for them, unless, or until, they ceded that land to the Crown.

The Proclamation could be regarded as the first major legal link between First Nations and the British Crown. And by virtue of that Proclamation, it can be said that First Nations became protected states of the British, while being recognized as sovereign nations competent to maintain the relations of peace and war and capable of governing themselves under that protection. Under international law, a weaker power does not surrender its right to self-government merely by associating with a stronger power and taking its protection.

Between 1781 and Canadian Confederation in 1867, some First Nations signed treaties with the Crown under which they ceded rights and privileges to certain lands. In return, they were to obtain certain treaty rights. These treaties represented further legal links between those nations and the Crown. But again, there is no evidence that sovereignty was surrendered.

Canadian courts, since the latter part of the nineteenth century, have relegated the First Nations' treaties with the Crown almost to the level of private law contracts, thereby denying their status as treaties in the sense of international law. Yet the Supreme Court of Canada repeated in the *R. v. Simon* case that First Nations' treaties are unique and share some of the features of international treaties. If the agreements were "treaties among sovereign nations" in the eighteenth and nineteenth centuries, how could their status be changed without the consent of First Nations?

In 1867, the British North America Act (later renamed the Constitution Act 1867) provided for internal self-government in Canada by European settlers. First Nations were not a party to the Confederation that was established, nor to the drafting of the British North America Act. Nevertheless, subsection 91(24) provided that the federal Parliament would have the authority to legislate for "Indians and lands reserved for the Indians" to the exclusion of the provincial legislatures. By virtue of that subsection, the First Nations were placed under the legislative power of the federal government as agent of the Crown, but not under its territorial jurisdiction.

Certain other treaties were executed between some of the First. Nations and the Crown after Confederation. In many cases it is evident that treaties were imposed upon First Nations and that their leaders had little choice but to consent. The treaties were written in English and the Crown's negotiators often misrepresented the contents.

Today it may be argued that many of those treaties are "unequal" or "unconscionable" or "unfair" in both substance and procedure. Even so, First Nations did not perceive the treaties as being a surrender of sovereignty.

The Indian Act

In 1876, the federal government passed its first Indian Act, "the first consolidation of the laws pertaining to Indians." The Indian Act was passed by the federal government because it had exclusive legislative responsibility for Indians and lands reserved for Indians, but First Nations themselves had no input into it. Neither did First Nations' citizens have any part in electing the politicians who legislated the Indian Acts, since native people were not allowed to vote federally until 1960.

In the early days of European settlement, it is likely that native self-government continued for some time because First Nations had the numbers and the strength at that time to warrant recognition. But as time went on, that changed. During the first sixty years of this century, our people were in the most despicable, colonizing, racist situation imaginable. Under the control of Indian agents, they could not leave their reserves without passes. They were not legally in charge of a single thing that happened on their land.

The same Department of Indian Affairs that controlled our lives through Indian agents until only recently still exists today. It has 4000 civil servants, and its primary function is to maintain control over native people.

The Indian Act still controls every facet of our lives. It allows a certain amount of local self-government, but there is not a single thing on which we can make a law that does not have to go to a department official. That official is usually a bureaucrat whose face we've never seen and who has never seen the community. And yet he has total power to determine whether he is going to pass a dog law, a local development law, a garbage law or any law requiring departmental approval. He doesn't have to give a reason; he can just deny it. No other municipal government in this country is up against that kind of control. Surely it only exists in parts of the world where an occupying army wants to ensure that the population is completely submissive.

Today, every time we see a movement beginning among indigenous people somewhere in this country, the Department of Indian Affairs finds some way to divide those people — discredit their organization, discredit their leadership, create an opposition group, fund an opposition group.

Some day the Department of Indian Affairs should vanish off the face of the earth. There must be a time when the kind of colonial, dictatorial control that is ruining our lives comes to an end. We must have freedom at some point.

Retaining Our Rights: The Ongoing Saga

Despite all of this, the Royal Proclamation of 1763 is still alive and well. That means that where there are no treaties the land belongs to the First Nations, and no Canadian government — whether provincial or federal — should be developing our resources and extracting royalties and taxes from them. There should be indigenous governments and institutions for aboriginal people.

In some cases in this country, we have treaties over a hundred years old by which, very clearly, original land was to have been set aside for native people. After a hundred years and more, the land still hasn't been put aside. Meanwhile, governments have repeatedly invited people from all over the world to come cut down our trees and get a square mile . . . two square miles . . . ten square miles of land. Although everyone agrees that our people have lived here for thousands of years, because the federal government has not recognized First Nations' title, there is not a square centimetre that is recognized as indigenous territory.

First Nations regularly confront governments with their claims to entitlement, and the governments can't deny the validity of such claims. But instead of recognizing land as indigenous territory, they seek to "settle" claims by exchanging historic rights for "fee simple" ownership, so the land can be treated like every other piece of private property in Canada.

Take, for example, the territory we call Denendeh, otherwise known as the western Northwest Territories. The Dene know they have always owned this land, but the federal government refuses to acknowledge our indigenous title. Recently the smallest group of Dene, the Gwitch'in, negotiated an agreement with the federal government to get property title to a portion of the land in exchange for extinguishing historic claims. Outside of this one agreement, no Dene land has ever been surrendered. Yet there is not even a small piece of the vast remaining territory that a Dene can use to build a home. Instead, our people must use a foreign system of government to obtain a building permit.

At the same time, it is clear that the Canadian public has always been on the side of some kind of just, equitable recognition and implementation of both aboriginal rights and treaty rights.

Despite the irony of this state of affairs, First Nations were not even party to the drafting of the renewed Constitution of 1982. The governments did agree, however, that First Nations leaders should be invited to participate in subsequent constitutional conferences to identify and define their rights for inclusion in the Canadian Constitution.

That was the first time in their relationship with the Crown that First Nations were consulted about the Constitution, albeit only to a very limited degree. They were, in effect, merely invited to establish and defend their rights. If First Nations had not participated, it is conceivable that non-native governments would have unilaterally identified and defined those rights.

Finding a Genuine Solution

What is it that our people are after? Simply this: We want to sit down across the table from the leaders of this country and come up with a genuine solution that will be acceptable both to indigenous nations and to the people who have come here from elsewhere.

We think there are sufficient land and resources in this country to allow First Nations to retain enough of their original territory where their own institutions can be sovereign.

We don't want to scare Canadians with our terminology. No one is scared in this country by the fact that Ontario or Manitoba can make laws in education and not a single power in the world can do anything about it. They are sovereign in their area of jurisdiction. We, likewise, want to have clear powers over our territories.

Canada is already set up for it, because we have a confederation that lends itself very easily to what our people are asking for. We have the federal government, we have federal powers. We have provinces, we have provincial powers. We have some areas where the two overlap. We could easily have a third list of First Nation powers.

We are prepared to negotiate. But we definitely need enough control over our lives that we can grow, we can flourish, we can prosper. Our people no longer want to be in a situation where you can have a mine right outside your door but the resources from that mine go to somebody else, the employers come from somewhere else, the employees come from somewhere else, the caterers come from somewhere else, and the decision as to *when* that mine is going to be developed is made somewhere else. This kind of development leads to social disruption. The mobile out-of-town workforce, continuing high unemployment, racism, pollution and the disturbance of hunting, fishing and trapping grounds all take their toll when we don't have the power to make decisions affecting our people.

There has to be a peaceful way to share. And if we can't do it in Canada, with the few people we have here, how will any other parts of the world ever be able to settle their situations?

But native people are losing their patience. It's very clear that our people are not going to sit back and take the treatment we have had to take in the past. That much is guaranteed.

The Canadian people must continue to push their governments to sit down with First Nations and negotiate a just and acceptable solution, to reflect what the Canadian polls say

Canadian people want. Native people by themselves, it is obvious, are not going to get the Canadian government to take that step.

QUESTIONS

1. Compare and contrast the vision of Canada set out in this reading with that implied by Trudeau's 1969 policy statement.
2. In light of this reading of Canadian history, are natives who become frustrated with the slow pace of discussions on resolving long-standing grievances justified in resorting to violence to accomplish the goal of self-government, as some have in recent years? If not, at what point would violence become justifiable? Is there a morally sound answer to this question?

ABORIGINAL RIGHTS

Michael McDonald

How would you respond to the question "What sorts of treatment do the native peoples of Canada deserve?"

Since native peoples are amongst the most underprivileged Canadians, you might respond on the basis of your attitude to the poor. Thus, if you believe that Canadians should have welfare rights, then you would claim that Indians like other Canadians should not be allowed to fall below some national standard of minimum welfare. You may believe that this is best done through providing a guaranteed annual income or through the provision of various goods (such as food and housing) and various services (such as medical care and job training). You would then find yourself in agreement with Prime Minister Trudeau who in 1969 said that native people

> . . . should become Canadians as all other Canadians and if they are prosperous and wealthy they will be treated like the prosperous and wealthy and they will be paying taxes for the other Canadians who are not so prosperous and not so wealthy whether they be Indians of English Canadians or French or Maritimers and this is the only basis on which I see our society can develop as equals.

On the other hand, another person might make a libertarian response and deny that anyone has a right to welfare. He might argue that no one deserves "free passage" — that everyone should work his own way. The debate would then be joined over a whole set of familiar issues. What are the relative merits of free enterprise and planned economies? What does "equal opportunity" involve? How much may the government interfere in citizens' lives? And so the argument will wend its way over time-worn paths until one or both of you get tired and change the subject.

Reprinted from Contemporary Issues in Political Philosophy, *ed. William Shea and John King-Farlow, Academic Publications Inc., New York.*

A very effective way of changing the subject is changing it so that you both wind up on opposite sides of the original question with you arguing against any special treatment for "the poor Indians" and your libertarian opponent demanding that they receive significant advantages from white society. I think this reversal is likely to happen if you shift the topic from welfare rights to aboriginal rights. Topic shifts of this sort, those which get the attacker and defender of a particular *status quo* to change places, very often provide interesting material for the political philosopher. Such is the case with aboriginal rights.

I. Entitlement Theory

What is the reason for this reversal in position?

I would suggest that there is something different about the ways in which we ground welfare and aboriginal rights. That is, when we argue for someone's having a welfare right we usually base our arguments on quite different sorts of premises than when we argue for aboriginal rights. The initial problem is then to characterize these sorts of differences.

Fortunately, this task has been made easier by the recent publication of *Anarchy, State, and Utopia* (New York, 1974) by Robert Nozick, who defends Locke's libertarian political philosophy. He argues that neither more nor less than the minimum or night watchman state of *laissez-faire* economics can be justified. In the course of this argument, he has to explain how people may legitimately have the exclusive use of various things, i.e., how they may come to own things. It is this discussion of "justice in holdings" that sheds light on the salient differences between welfare and aboriginal rights.

According to Nozick there are two primary ways in which I can have a just holding. If the object is unowned, I may under certain conditions come to own it; this is called "justice in the original acquisition of holdings." If the object is owned, then its owner may under certain conditions transfer it to me; this is called "justice in the transfer of holdings." Thus, for example, if you want to find out if the Atlantic salmon in my freezer is mine, you would want to know how I came to have the fish in my freezer: if I caught it, stole it, bought it, received it as a gift, etc. In short, you would ask for a history of ownership. The fish is mine if its original acquisition was just, and all subsequent transfers, if any, are also just. Insofar as you can trace this history, you can determine if I have *clear* title. To the extent that you cannot trace this history, it is not clearly mine, e.g., if all you know is that a friend gave it to me but you have no way of knowing how he got it, you can't say for certain that it really is mine.

If you get a clear history and then find that the original acquisition or one of the subsequent transfers was unjust, then you or someone else has the problem of deciding how to rectify this injustice in holdings. The rectification of injustice in holdings is the third part of Nozick's theory of just ownership. Thus, if you find out that my generous friend stole the salmon from a seafood store, you'll have to decide whether or not you should tell me to return it.

Now let us imagine that you decide to settle the question of my ownership of the salmon by using welfare principles solely. Let us assume that whatever welfare criterion you intend to use will only apply to the two of us in this case. First, you appeal to "need." You say that you are hungry and desperately short of protein, while I am not; since needs should be satisfied, you should have the fish. Say that I ignore that plea, so you try a hedonic appeal: you claim that you will enjoy eating the salmon much more than I will; hence, by the greatest happiness principle, you should have the salmon. It is not difficult in either appeal to imagine how I would have to respond to prove that I have a better title to the fish according to the criterion used. I would argue that I am needier than you or that I would really enjoy it more than you. Further it is not difficult to imagine the two criteria coming into conflict: you need the protein, but I would enjoy the dinner more. Then we would have to sort out which criterion takes precedence, e.g., that needs take precedence over wants. It is also not difficult to foresee some of the problems we might have in applying these considerations: how can I compare my need or enjoyment with yours, how can we properly take into account the effects of giving the fish to you or to me on each of our future needs or enjoyments, how do we know what counts as a "need" as opposed to what counts as a "want"? These are all problems which make up the bulk of philosophical debate about utilitarianism.

In our argument about who has the better welfare claim to the fish we proceed in a quite different way than we did earlier in trying to decide if the fish was a just holding of mine. Then we asked if the salmon had been justly acquired by me or justly transferred to me; in short, we looked backwards in time to see how the fish came into my possession. In the second case, we applied welfare criteria by looking to our present and future conditions to decide the issue according to our relative positions on the scale of need or enjoyment. Two major differences in the determination of ownership stand out in these cases: these are different attitudes to (a) the past and the future, and (b) the characteristics of the affected parties. Both (a) and (b) require some further explanation.

Regarding (a), we have seen that what mattered in determining justice in holdings were the acquisitions and transfers of the object; that is to say, the principle for the determination of ownership was *historical*. In the use of welfare criteria, we looked only at present and future considerations, viz. the relative degrees to which my or your having the fish would meet present and future needs or yield present and future enjoyment. Here we decided who owned the salmon on the basis of *end-results*. Our approach in the second case was *a*historical.

Regarding (b), you will recall that in the application of the welfare criteria we were concerned with the degree to which each of us had or lacked certain characteristics: if you were needier or would enjoy it more, then the fish should be yours. We were concerned in this case with the resulting *patterns* of the alternative distributions. In the first case, however, we proceeded without reference to patterns. There were no characteristics (such as need) which I might or might not have that would be determinative of the question of my ownership. It mattered not why I caught the fish (e.g., that I was trying to satisfy my hunger or pass the time of day) or even what I would do with it (e.g., eat it, throw it back in the stream, or use it for fertilizer). Nor did it matter why someone transferred it to me (e.g., because I paid for it, because I am his son, or because he simply felt like it). In fact it doesn't even matter if I have a freezer full of Atlantic salmon and you have none or even no food at all. Justice in holdings is *unpatterned* in that there is no natural dimension (what I call a "characteristic") or set of dimensions according to which the distribution of goods should take place.

II. Aboriginal Rights

We can now see how Nozick's approach to justice in holdings, which he calls "entitlement theory," ties in with the topic of aboriginal rights. Aboriginal rights are none other than original acquisition rights which haven't been transferred to anyone else. To defend the aboriginal rights of Canada's native peoples necessarily involves us in presenting a theory of original acquisition. Moreover, we must be willing to defend our theory of original acquisition against not only rival theories of original acquisition, but also against non-entitlement theories of ownership.

At the beginning of this paper, the argument about providing help to native people was carried on between a person who held a non-entitlement theory of the distribution of goods and one who held an entitlement theory. As you recall, one argued that native people should be helped on the basis of need. This, we have just seen, is an argument based on end-results and patterns. The other disputant argued that native people were not entitled to help. This argument is essentially historical and unpatterned.

Introducing aboriginal rights into the argument forced a change in the disputants' positions because it introduced a historical and unpatterned basis for the native people's entitlement. Now it was possible for the libertarian defender of property rights to argue that the natives had been dealt a historic injustice which stands in need of rectification. The defender of welfare rights must reject this approach, not because native people shouldn't receive significant benefits, but because in his view the only true basis for the reception of benefits is need. That is, he was arguing that benefits should be distributed in a patterned way with a view to the end-results achievable.

Now it is important to realize that we cannot simply let the disputants "agree to disagree." In practical terms, we are talking about claims to at least half of Canada. According to Peter Cumming and Neil Mickenberg in the second edition of *Native Rights in Canada* (Toronto, 1972), aboriginal claims have been superseded by treaties for less than one half of Canada. This would leave standing aboriginal claims to British Columbia, Quebec, the Maritimes, the Yukon, and parts of the Northwest Territories. Think of what this means to established settlements and to plans for Northern development. Remember, too, that "the natives are restless": they have been pressing their claims in the courts (in 1973 the Supreme Court of Canada split four to three against admitting an aboriginal claim), over the bargaining table (in Quebec native people have received a large cash and land settlement for allowing the James Bay Project to proceed in a scaled down form), at the barricades (in British Columbia), and before a royal commission (Mr. Justice Berger is carrying out an investigation of the effect of the proposed Mackenzie Valley Pipeline on native peoples). The questions of aboriginal rights is a real, not an ivory-tower, question.

In my examination of this question, I do not intend to say much more about non-entitlement theories except by way of contrast to entitlement theories. I shall instead focus on various problems that I see in the application of Nozickian and Lockean entitlement theories to the question of aboriginal rights in Canada. I will argue that some of the problems anticipated in such an application of entitlement theory can be adequately handled, but that other problems — particularly those at the core — are much more difficult and may well be insurmountable.

I shall proceed by presenting a number of objections to an entitlement defence of aboriginal rights. I shall first state the objection in the broad and general way it occurs in non-philosophical discussion. Here I have tried to draw upon statements made by politicians, lawyers, and native people, as well as from discussions I've had with students and colleagues. This response will consist, first, in sorting out various objections that have been confused and run together in the non-philosophical context. After that, I shall see what kind of reply can be made within an entitlement theory. I have tried to give each objection a

name which suggests the sort of objection made and renders the arguments easier to remember. This mnemonic aid is important because the arguments are often interrelated and
used together for or against aboriginal rights.

A. The Vandals Argument

This is the kind of argument that Trudeau has used:

> If we think of restoring aboriginal rights to the Indians, well, what about the French
> who were defeated at the Plains of Abraham? Shouldn't we restore rights to them?
> What about the Acadians who were deported — shouldn't we compensate for this?
> And what about the other Canadians, the immigrants? What about the Japanese Cana-
> dians who were so badly treated at the end [of] or during the last war?

A similar position was taken by many Americans in response to James Forman's demand
that American churches and synagogues pay $500 million as reparations for years of slav-
ery. In his book, *The Case for Black Reparations* (New York, 1973), Yale law professor
Boris Bittker cites the *New York Times* response to Forman: "There is neither wealth nor
wisdom enough in the world to compensate for all the wrongs in history."

An objector might ask if the descendants of the Roman victims of the Vandals' sack of
Rome in 453 A.D. should be able to sue the Vandals' descendants? Here, however, we see
the need to distinguish two separate objections. The first is what I shall call "Historical
Disentanglement," and the second "Arbitrariness."

A.1. Historical Disentanglement. The first objection rests on practical difficulties in sorting
out historical issues. The problem is to find out who is a descendant of the victims of an
injustice and who is a descendant of the perpetrators of that injustice. In the Vandals' case
the problems seem well-nigh insuperable. Even if some sorting out is possible, there will
probably be enough intermarriage to confuse most cases thoroughly. Intermarriage has been
alleged a serious barrier to reparations to blacks in the United States.

In the case we are considering, however, — that of native Canadians — we can get some
powerful assistance from the facts. A quarter of a million Indians are registered under the
Indian Act of 1951 as members of recognized bands. While we may have problems with the
fairness of some of the provisions of that Act (e.g., Indian women who marry non-Indian
males are deregistered and non-Indian females who marry Indian males are automatically
registered), the fact remains that we have an accurate, though somewhat incomplete, record
of many descendants of the purported victims of injustice. The cases of the unregistered
Indians and of the Metis are more difficult, but we have two important facts which will help
disentangle matters. First, these people have regarded themselves as native people. And
secondly, they have been regarded by white Canadians as natives insofar as they have been
objects of the same informal extra-legal distinctions (including racial prejudices) as those
under the Indian Act. It should not prove to be too difficult to arrive at a consensus on who
is or is not a native person amongst the Metis and other unregistered claimants of this
status.

This, of course, leaves the question of tracing the descendants of those purported to have
violated aboriginal title. Here again the facts help us — in this case it is the legal fact that
only the Crown could seize land. In the case of New France, we can regard the Crown as
the inheritor of whatever title France had to aboriginal lands.

It is also possible that we might in hard cases make use of a test Nozick suggests for determining the descendants of victims and perpetrators on the grounds that *persistent* inequalities are most likely a result of historical injustice. (While Nozick does not suggest "persistency" as a criterion here, I think it might make his suggestion more plausible.)

A.2. Arbitrariness. The second distinct element in the Vandals Argument is that suggestion that the defender of aboriginal rights wants to make an arbitrary and invidious distinction between rectifying the injustices done to aboriginal peoples and the injustices done to non-aboriginal Canadians. This is, I think, what Trudeau was asking, namely, how could we defend rectifying the injustices done to the Indians and ignore the injustices done by our nation to the French, the Acadians, and Japanese?

Trudeau goes on to say that we cannot "redeem the past"; we can only be "just in our time." This seems to let us argue that if we can't wholly rectify all the injustices we have ever done, then we needn't rectify any. The most favourable interpretation that I can put on Trudeau's conclusion is that we may have to face a multiplicity of competing claims of all sorts including a number of competing claims for the rectification of past injustices. We may then not be able to do everything that we ought ideally to do; in an imperfect world we may have to pay our most morally pressing debts in full and make only token payments on the remainder. There need be no arbitrariness in the recognition of aboriginal rights, for we can still recognise other past and present injustices. We may not be able to fully satisfy all the claims for rectification, but that isn't arbitrary either — there is no obligation to do more than one can.

B. The Forefathers Argument

There is another way of taking Trudeau's conclusion that we cannot redeem the past, and that is to say that we are only responsible for our sins and not for the sins of our fathers. How can I be blamed for what my French-Canadian ancestors did to the Indians of New French? How can anyone do more than be just in his own time?

Let's sort out this argument.

B.1 Backwards Causation. The first thing to clarify is whether saying that I ought to rectify injustice X involves saying that I am one of X's causes. If my children ruin my neighbor's prize roses, may I not have an obligation to make reparations? If I do, it needn't be the case that in so doing I am admitting that it was I who tramped through the roses. I may not even have to admit that it was somehow my fault that my children were in the garden. I may have told my children to stay out of the garden. Moreover, I may have done the best I can to instill in them a sense of respect for others' property. Then there is nothing more I should have done. (After all, there are outward bounds like child abuse for determining how far a parent can go in instructing his children.) Indeed my children may not have acted deliberately, purposely, or even intentionally; it was an accident pure and simple, for which even they are not to blame. But there it is: the roses are ruined, and I am the one who should set it right.

The point is that "responsibility" can be used in a variety of ways. Sometimes it is used to indicate causality, in which case contemporaneousness or precedence in time is essential. But in the rose garden case, it was used to indicate who was *liable* for damages. The concept of liability is most highly developed within the law, but we do use it outside the law in our ordinary attributions or moral responsibility. The question then is whether anyone today has liability for the past violations (if any) of aboriginal rights.

There is a further confusion in this argument. This is to claim that backwards causation must be involved because I can only have obligations of my own making. Thus, I could have an obligation to contemporary native peoples respecting aboriginal rights only if I had undertaken to respect these rights, i.e., if I made a promise to or contract with their ancestors. It will take only a moment's reflection, however, to see that many obligations we have are not entered into voluntarily (or involuntarily either), e.g., not to kill, to express gratitude for favours received, to be kind, and to be honest.

B.2. Benefits Received. In (B.1) I didn't really so much respond to the Forefathers Argument as clear the way for a response to it. That liability-responsibility is different from causal-responsibility is important; nevertheless, it does not tell us if Canadians today have liability-responsibility for violations of aboriginal title. Neither does knowing that all obligations are not of our own making tell us if the rectification of this putative injustice is our responsibility.

A much more telling response is an analogy with the receipt of stolen goods. If person *A* steals person *B*'s watch and then makes a present of it to *C*, do we think that *C* has an obligation to return it to *B* even though he had no idea that he was in receipt of stolen goods when he accepted the watch? Surely, the answer is "Yes!" We might go on to say that *A* owes *C* something (an apology at minimum) for inconveniencing and embarrassing him. We would, I think, give the same answer even if the thief *A* can't recompense *C* (say that *A* is now dead). It is worth noting here that no one is blaming *C* for *A*'s stealing *B*'s watch or even for unwittingly accepting stolen property. *C* needn't feel any guilt about either of these matters. He should, however, feel guilt if he doesn't return the watch to *B*. I see no reason to change our views about returning the watch if instead of talking about *B* and *C* we talk about their heirs. I would not extend this to *A*'s heirs, however, who presumably have not benefitted either from *A*'s theft, itself, or the gift of the watch to *C*.

The parallels with the case of aboriginal rights should be fairly obvious. Non-Indians have in Canada benefitted (albeit in very unequal degrees) from the noncompensated supersession of aboriginal title. This is not to say that non-Indians *today* refused to compensate native people for the loss of aboriginal rights *during* the last and preceding centuries. These non-Indians certainly can't be held responsible for being born into this society or for immigrating to it. In this respect, breast-beating over what has been done to the "poor native" is neither due nor appropriate. Guilt is appropriate only if nothing is done to remedy injustices in the treatment of native people including, in particular, the rectification of past injustices.

Of course, the case for reparations becomes more difficult if we change the analogy somewhat. For example, what, if anything, does *C* owe *B* if after *C* receives the watch he loses it? It would be different if *C* were keeping *B*'s watch in trust for *B*, for then he could well be responsible for not losing it. This problem posed by lost or ruined articles seems quite likely to occur with the passage of significant periods of time. If we are talking about *C*'s and *B*'s great-grandchildren, the odds are that by this time the watch has been lost or no longer works.

That is, I think, the kind of thing that Bittker has in mind when he says that there would be no case for reparations to blacks if in the period since the Civil War there had been an unbroken ascent up to a present state of genuine equality. That is, the argument here is that reparations are not due if the relative advantage seized by the act of injustice gets lost or equalized in the course of history, so that it no longer makes any difference. It is *not* crucial to this argument that *both* the benefits accruing to the oppressors and their heirs and the evils suffered by the victims and their heirs no longer remain. It is enough to have the first without the second.

B.3. Inheritance. There is a way of taking the Forefathers Argument that avoids the reply just advanced (B-2.). There I argued that if you can inherit benefits, you can inherit burdens chargeable against those benefits. This is like having to pay estate taxes and creditors before receiving an inheritance. As we have just seen, if you inherit nothing, you do not have any obligation (save, perhaps, "a debt of honour") to pay any debts chargeable against the estate. This suggests that there would be no aboriginal rights if there were no rights to make bequests; that is, aboriginal rights disappear if no one may rightfully inherit anything.

Native people could use this as an effective *ad hominem* argument in pressing their case. They could say to the rich and powerful in our society that Indians and Inuit will give up their claims to aboriginal rights if the rich and powerful will surrender all the property that they have inherited. This would not mean the end of private property but only the aspect of it — which I call "bequeathability." Other aspects of private property would remain (viz. rights of alienability, exclusive use, security, management, income, and so forth) but these "standard incidents" of property would be limited to the life of the holder. (To make this suggestion effective, we would have to set a limit to the life of corporations, for under our laws these "artificial persons" can be immortal.)

C. The Double Wrong Argument

The objection here is that to rectify one injustice another will have to be done, so that in rectifying the injustice done to the native people an injustice will have to be done to non-native Canadians by taking away from them land or the profit therefrom which they have in good faith purchased and improved. Moreover, the settlement of aboriginal claims will impose an enormous burden on those who in some cases are already disadvantaged.

The main response to this has already been made in the Forefathers Argument (B.2.). No one has a right to receive and retain what is not another's to give. "Good faith" here excuses one from complicity in the original theft: one is not to blame for the theft, so one needn't feel guilty about it. It does not excuse one from returning the stolen goods or the equivalent. Remember that we are working within the context of entitlement theory; justice in holding demands, justice in acquisition, and transfers. To give weight to the claims of those who have unjust holdings is just the sort of thing end-result theorists would do.

Nevertheless, the entitlement theorist can reduce the practical force of this objection by pointing out that third party beneficiaries (here, non-Indian and non-Inuit property owners) must return what remains of that which was wrongfully transferred to them. Given the ravages of time, one may not have to surrender any of one's own goods in making this reparation because nothing of value remains. I say "may not" because among the benefits received from the stolen property is that there is less drain on one's own resources. Thus, in the watch analogy, *C* or his heirs may benefit from not having to purchase watches of their own because they have the use of the watch stolen from *B*. So if the watch breaks after a few years while in *C*'s possession, *B* might ask for rent for the use of his watch over the years before it broke. If *C* is now bankrupt, there may be little *B* can get (unless it is the case that entitlement theory would demand that *C* work the rent off). If it is the case that in addition to bankruptcy *C* also dies, then *B* cannot demand that *C*'s would-be heirs pay for it out of their own justly acquired resources (including working the debt off). Death without the transmission of a benefice would seem on the entitlement theory to end the case for repayment simply because the unjust holding no longer exists. Presumably, in this wealthy nation, most of the benefit has been transmitted to us.

A final remark on the plight of the small property holder. According to the principles of rectification of injustice in holdings, it surely must be the case that those who have benefitted most from unjust holdings owe more than those who have benefitted least. Keeping in mind the complications about inheritance discussed earlier, it should be the case that in a society like ours, in which most wealth — especially capital — remains concentrated in a few families, the wealthiest would have the most to lose by the recognition of aboriginal rights. Here I would think especially of those who have benefitted most from the exploitation of natural resources (like gas, oil, and minerals) in the areas in question, particularly Alberta, the North, and B.C. Of course, it has already been argued (B.3.) that these same people have the most to lose by denying aboriginal claims for they would thereby undermine their own claims to inherited wealth.

D. The Sovereignty Argument

In an article in *The Globe and Mail* (21 February 1973), Cumming has suggested that one possible reason for the Government's reluctance to recognise aboriginal rights is the fear that in so doing there would be a recognition of aboriginal sovereignty over the lands in question, to wit, Trudeau's reference to the Plains of Abraham. This is evident, too, in the same speech when Trudeau says, "It's inconceivable, I think, that in a given society one section of society have a treaty with another section of society." Trudeau is not the only politician in Canada's history to express concern about holding the country together; this is a country which has been plagued by threats of separatism — from Quebec, the West, and the Maritimes.

If it is the case that the recognition of aboriginal rights would necessarily involve a recognition of a separate aboriginal nation or nations then it is not clear what an entitlement theorist like Nozick would say. Nozick's invisible hand explanation of the emergence of a dominant protection agency as the (minimal) state never comes to grips with the fact that there is more than one nation in this complicated world. The fact of nationalism should also have some effect on Nozick's proposal for utopia — allowing diverse experiments in types of communities *within* a single nation. Are nationalists entirely wrong when they think that they must have control over the state and not just over the community? Another interesting way of putting this question is to ask what sorts of self-determination (determination particularly of a group's identity) are not possible in a libertarian society. Leaving aside these complex and difficult questions, it is possible to argue that if sovereignty is an issue here, then surely we must talk about more than justice in holdings.

The simplest way of dealing with this objection is to deny, as Cumming does, that sovereignty and property rights are connected except in an indirect way. In ordinary disputes over land ownership, neither claimant is trying to set up an independent nation. The adjudication usually follows the laws of the nation in which the property is situated. Although in a few difficult cases there can be arguments about which of two nation's laws are applicable, the dispute is primarily about ownership and only secondarily about sovereignty. It should be pointed out that no less an entitlement theorist like Locke claimed that rights to property are quite independent of rights to rule, for he maintained that property rights should survive changes in government including violent changes brought about by war.

E. The Litigation Argument

The general argument here is that claims to aboriginal title are unlike ordinary property claims. They are not amenable to the usual sorts of tests used by the courts to decide property rights. In particular many aboriginal claims are such as to deny courts the use of a most effective procedure for deciding between rival claims in cases where due to the passage of time both records are missing and memories are uncertain, namely, "prescription" which is "the operation of time as a vestitive fact." If this is correct, then how can anyone maintain that aboriginal claims can be settled in the same way as ordinary disputes about ownership? Indeed, how can anyone maintain that they are property rights at all?

This argument can be taken in part as a necessary corrective to the oversimplified reply that I just advanced against the Sovereignty Argument. There I argued that sovereignty and property were different kinds of rights. This may have left the impression that all property rights are alike and that aboriginal rights are like other property-rights. Neither of these contentions is true.

I agree with A.M. Honore that "property" is probably best thought of in terms of a list of "the standard incidents of ownership." This would be a list of the rights which a property owner has in the standard, full-blown case. It would include rights of physical possession, use, derivation of profit and capital, security, management, and so forth. One would probably also have to say something about the duties of ownership as well, in particular the prohibition of harmful use. If some of these incidents are missing in a particular case, we could still talk about "property-rights." In fact all the Indian treaties deny Indians the liberty of converting their reserves into capital, i.e., they may not alienate their lands, only the Crown may. In this sense, reserves could be seen as belonging to a particular people in perpetuity, not just to its present-day occupants; thus, future generations would have patrimonial rights. Aboriginal land claims involve the same kind of arrangement. (I should add here that if a whole people, conceived as a group extending across time into the future, can have property rights, then such right might well play havoc with many of the positions that Nozick defends on the basis of actions in a free market).

So part of my reply to this argument is that while aboriginal titles may lack some of the standard incidents of property it may well be possible to still think of them as property rights. To properly establish this reply would require a great deal more space than I presently have. I think more needs to be said, however, about this argument along somewhat different lines.

First, there is the issue of "prescription." In the law it is the case that the passage of time can extinguish or establish ownership. This is determined by time limits established by custom or statute. For example, in some jurisdictions if you have made use of part of someone else's land as a right-of-way for twenty years, then the courts will uphold your right to continue to do so and thus bar the landowner from preventing your passage. Thus time has given you a right you formerly did not have and extinguished a property-right that the landowner had. The point of prescription is quite straightforward: the passage of time is used as a conclusive evidence because it simplifies the work of the courts in determining ownership. Thus, the jurist Savigny said, "All property is founded in adverse possession ripened by prescription."

The problem for aboriginal claims is that in many cases the land claimed is not now and has not been occupied by the claimants at all or on an exclusive basis for many years more than the limits set by law for the extinguishment of title. Yet it seems unfair therefore to deny title even though it is fair to do so in ordinary cases. In ordinary cases the law protects the property-owner's exercise of his property-rights before the period of prescription has elapsed. That is, if he wants to prevent his title from lapsing, he need only take action. Thus, in the right-of-way case, the property-owner can put up a "no trespassing" sign before the twenty years are out; this completely extinguishes your claim to a legally guaranteed right-of-way. If it is illegal to post the sign, then using the passage of time to effect a transfer of title would be unfair. The parallel here is that native peoples have not been given an opportunity to present their aboriginal claims, either through the courts or directly to government.

Secondly, the Litigation Argument does raise important doubts about the appropriate *forum* for the determination of the value and extent of various aboriginal claims. Cumming says that "the court is by far the least appropriate forum for dealing with aboriginal rights" because "litigation is expensive, time-consuming, and abounds with technical difficulties." He proposes instead that there be direct negotiations between the government and native people. Thus, this is essentially a practical, not an in-principle concern.

Thirdly, the Litigation Argument hints at a problem which will concern us in the next and final section. The problem, as seen from the perspective of this Argument, concerns the relationship between particular property-rights and the existing legal system. One way of finding the general area of difficulty is to ask if there can be property without laws. If there cannot be property without laws (as has been argued by generations of contractarians, Kant among them), then is property merely a creature of law? If property-rights can only be created and destroyed by law, what must be said about the entitlement theorists' claim that we have a natural right to "estate" in addition to "life and liberty"? In the next section I will consider some of these questions.

F. The Acquisition Arguments

Thus far, in all the objections and replies, I have tried to apply entitlement theory to the question of aboriginal rights. If I am right, then a number of interesting and plausible objections to entitlement theory and its application can be answered. In neither the objections nor the replies have I asked if native people actually have a claim to these lands on the basis of just original acquisition; for the sake of argument I have assumed that they do, and then gone to ask whether such claims should be recognised. Obviously, if native people in general or in particular did *not* make a just original acquisition of the land, the whole case for aboriginal rights fails. This would now show that all the native people's claims to land ownership are null and void, but it would remove the most important and the largest claims.

There is more than this practical issue at stake here. The whole entitlement theory rests on original acquisition. If the justice of an original acquisition is called into question then so also, Nozick says, are all subsequent transfers. If *all* original acquisitions can be called into question, then, perhaps, all claims to property rights are challengeable. One way of calling all aboriginal acquisitions into question is to deny that sense can be made of the concept of "original acquisition." Another way would be to deny that original acquisition as imagined by entitlement theorists can be a basis for rightful ownership.

So now I will turn to the "keystone" issue. I should say that some of the sharpest criticisms of the original acquisition doctrine come from Nozick himself. He writes in an almost ironic, or shall I say, "contrapuntal" way that involves the reader and enlivens debate. I will present four objections and responses. The responses, I should indicate, are partial and do not, I think, save entitlement theory (though, curiously enough, they save aboriginal rights).

F.1. The Jus Tertii Argument. One way of challenging aboriginal rights *within* the framework of entitlement theory is to deny that the Indians and Inuit had made original and just acquisition. This could be denied on the grounds that Indians and Inuit weren't the first human beings in Canada and that Indians and Inuit acquired the northern half of this continent by force. In any event, given the lack of records of property acquisition, it could be claimed that no one can know for certain if the native people's ancestors acquired the lands justly as either first possessors or as a result of just transfer. This would at the very least make aboriginal claims suspect.

The argument presented here rests on a claim like the following: if Bill's acquisition of Blackacres from Alice is unjust, then Chuck's acquisition of the land from Bill need not follow the rules of just transfer in order to get as good, or better, title than Bill has to Blackacres. The underlying contention is that if title is, so to speak, "spoiled" at any point the property is simply up for grabs. Here I am assuming that the just owner Alice is not laying claim to Blackacres and that Chuck is in no way acting on behalf of Alice. The question is not, then, one of Chuck's rectifying an injustice done to Alice by Bill. The objection rests on the contention that given Alice's not laying or transferring her claim to another, Bill's act of injustice returns Blackacres to an ownerless situation from which Chuck may claim it.

Before questioning this contention, I would note that even accepting this reasoning there still is a difference between showing that Bill's title is spoiled and raising a suspicion that it may not be clear. In some cases, it simply is impossible for a possessor to prove that he has clear title; however, this does not mean that others can prove that he does not. Surely the burden of proof rests on those who charge wrongful possession.

Now as to the argument itself, it is worth noting that the practice under common law is not to establish ownership *absolutely* but *only relatively*, i.e., to decide who has a *better* right to possess. It would, I believe, be the case that a court would hold that Bill has a better title to Blackacres than Chuck and Alice has a better title to Blackacres than Bill. Regardless of the court's decision, it is certainly more convenient for a court to decide matters in this relative way (adjudicating only between the rival claims presented to it) rather than trying to do this once and for all (which would involve ruling on every conceivable claim). In this case, the court would settle the dispute between Bill and Chuck leaving it to others such as Alice to bring suit separately.

Which approach should an entitlement theorist adopt — that unjust acquisition or transfer returns the object to an ownerless condition or that it simply "weakens" the possessor's title? I wonder if in answering this question we will have to fall back on utilitarian considerations, e.g., about which procedure would be the most orderly and least disruptive for a given society. I am not sure how this question would be decided on purely entitlement grounds. That is, I don't know what *natural* rights to the ownership of Blackacres are held by Bill as opposed to Chuck. I would suspect that this cannot be determined without a *policy* decision about the rules governing property. Entitlement theory does not say which is the appropriate way of deciding ownership in this case. If this is right then it indicates an important gap in entitlement theory, for it means that the theory of justice in holdings has to be patched up by resorting to utilitarianism.

Apropos the question of aboriginal rights, it would seem that if we proceed on the basis of who has better title rather than on the basis of who has absolute title, then native people's claims would seem to be stronger than those of successive possessors.

F.2 The Spoilage Argument. In *The Second Treatise of Government*, Locke presents an objection to his view of justice in original acquisition:

> That if gathering the Acorns, or other Fruits of the Earth, & c. makes a right to them, then any one may *ingross* as much as he will.

Locke says that this is not so; one may take "as much as one can make use of to any advantage of life before it spoils . . . Whatever is beyond this, is more than his share and belongs to others." Locke grounds this limitation of original acquisition on God's will: "Nothing was made by God for Man to spoil or destroy." Yet it is clear that God's will is not capricious, for as Locke says earlier:

> God, who hath given the World to Men in common, hath also given them reason to make use of it to the best advantage of Life and convenience.

Men then have a right to self-preservation which entitles them to take the means thereto, viz. by acquiring the necessaries of life. Self-preservation grounds appropriation and sets limits to it.

Now it could be argued that the spoilage provision sets the limits too widely in that it allows me to refuse to share my bounty with my starving neighbours so long as I can use that bounty for "the best advantage of [my] Life and convenience." Matters are weighted heavily in favour of the propertied and against those without property. But let us for the sake of argument accept spoilage as an outward limit of just original acquisition. We can then ask whether native peoples violated the spoilage principle in acquiring these lands. If they did and if the Europeans who came here could make use of the wasted portions, then aboriginal claims may be defensible on the grounds of wastage.

If this question is answerable, it would have to be on the basis of historical evidence; however, it is fair for the philosopher to ask about the determination of the criteria for wastage and spoilage: by what marks do we identify something as waste? Here it is tempting to ask if the thing in question is used for anyone's benefit. But will any minute amount of incremental benefit suffice to justify ownership or must there be some standard margin of benefit for this use to count here for title? Must there also be standards of efficient use? Would there be a combined standard, e.g., "Makes the best use of X for the greatest benefit"? Any benefit or efficiency standard would seem to be hopelessly utilitarian and redistributivist. On the other hand, having no standards at all would effectively deny a right of self-preservation to those without property and the correlative duty to share for the propertied.

If we try to fix on some mid-point (i.e., having a spoilage provision which is compatible with entitlement theory), then the question is how to justify our selection of standards on an entitlement basis. This is a particularly troublesome question in the case of aboriginal rights. In many cases an advanced agricultural and industrialised economy came into contact with a hunting, fishing, and gathering economy. The patterns of resource use were bound to be different. What would appear as under-utilisation in one economy might appear as over-utilisation in the other. Clearly Canada's native peoples made ingenious use of the often harsh environment, but their uses could not support the numbers of people that present-day uses can. (In this paper I am being deliberately silent about how much longer we can continue our use-patterns.) However, if we move in the direction of giving title to the Europeans rather than the native peoples, then we would have to surrender our ownership claims to any society which could support more people here more efficiently. This seems quite obviously in direct opposition to the whole thrust of an *entitlement* theory: if I am entitled to something, if it's *mine*, then I should within the limit of non-harmfulness be able to use it as efficiently or as inefficiently as I wish for whosoever's advantage I choose. This would accord with Nozick's slogan: "From each as they choose, to each as they are chosen."

Tentatively, then, if we are willing to deny the right of self-preservation and more especially the correlative duty of sharing when necessary to provide it, then we can still hold the entitlement theory and so avoid the conceptual difficulties posed by the spoilage principle.

F.3. The "Proviso" Argument. Spoilage is not the only limit Locke sets to original acquisition; he also suggests what Nozick calls "the Lockean Proviso," namely that there be "enough and as good left in common for others." This Nozick says, "is meant to ensure that the position of others is not worsened." Thus, we can imagine a parallel argument to the Spoilage Argument being advanced against aboriginal rights on the grounds that aboriginal possession violated the enough-and-as-good proviso.

Factually, this is going to be a tricky argument to work out for not only must it be shown that the native people did not leave enough and as good to the immigrants, but also that the immigrants have taken just enough to rectify this violation of the proviso. This will be very hard to prove, given the relative wealth of natives and immigrants. At present, indeed, native people could justifiably argue that the immigrants haven't left enough and as good to them.

Here, as in the Spoilage Argument, there are serious conceptual problems in determining the appropriate criteria. Nozick advances two interpretations of the Proviso:

> Someone may be made worse off by another's appropriation in two ways: first by losing the opportunity to improve his situation by a particular appropriation or any one, and second, by no longer being able to use freely (without appropriation) what he previously could.

Nozick accepts the second or "weaker requirement" and not the first or "the stringent requirement." The difference between the two seems to be between characterizing the proviso as applying to appropriation (ownership) or to use. But then it must be remembered that earlier Nozick says that the central core of the notion of a property right in X is "the right to determine what shall be done with X." If I have a right to use X, then would I not have a property right in X?

Be that as it may, Nozick argues that those who are unable to appropriate (because everything is now owned) are likely to be compensated for this restriction on their liberty by having their prospects increased by a system which allows (virtually unlimited) private acquisition. Nozick says the free market will make up for their loss of acquisition and/or use rights. The point is to compensate these people enough for not being able to appropriate or use what they could have had they been born earlier. Nozick suggests that the level of compensation can be determined by getting "an estimate of the general economic importance of appropriation."

But this, I suggest, won't do for several reasons. First, if this isn't forcing on someone a kind of compensation that he doesn't want, then in the case of those who really want to make acquisitions the state will have to take something away from various property-owners. Secondly, as my colleague Jan Narveson has argued, the level of compensation will probably have to be set high enough to amount to a tidy guaranteed annual income. Thirdly, it isn't clear how much compensation is to be given to any particular propertyless person. Does he get as much as he would have been likely to get if he were in the position of the last person who acquired property or as much as if he were the first person to acquire property? In either case, the primary basis for distribution (his acquisitiveness) seems suspiciously patterned. Fourth, if the benefits of a free market economy really do provide enough compensation, then why does it seem so unlikely that anyone who has more than a little property, e.g., E.P. Taylor, would want to change places with one of these people who can't acquire any property because everything is owned?

All of which suggests that on a *pure* entitlement theory — one which is based on historical entitlement — there would be no room for the Proviso. On a pure entitlement theory if you are born after all the accessible and useful unowned objects have been taken up by your predecessors, you are simply out of luck. The denial of the Proviso would also seem to be in agreement with Nozick's criticisms of Rawls' contention that a system of natural liberties allows distribution on morally arbitrary grounds — that the distribution of natural talents is not on the basis of desert leads Rawls to design the social system to compensate for this "arbitrariness" by favouring (other things being equal) the least talented in the distribution of goods. Nozick criticises this is a "manna-from-heaven" model that totally ignores who has made these goods, i.e., Rawls ignores the crucial fact of historical entitlement. Similarly, the Proviso seems to ignore the crucial fact of appropriation.

Finally, as in the Spoilage Argument, we can ask what it is to leave "enough and as good"? If the standard is *usability*, then do we adopt the native peoples' idea of what is usable or the non-native immigrants? If we defend the latter, then in effect we are denying native peoples their ways of life. According to the Proviso, this would seem to demand that we compensate the native peoples for that loss. Yet is that something for which adequate compensation is possible other than allowing them to maintain their standards of use and so their way of life? Would not "the base line for comparison" be very high indeed then?

F.4. The Invalid Acquisition Arguments. In both the Spoilage and Proviso Arguments, aboriginal title was challenged on the grounds that Indians and Inuit had acquired too much, i.e., more than they were entitled to acquire. It is possible to raise a different objection by claiming that they failed to acquire anything or scarcely anything at all. The heart of this contention is that native peoples did not perform the appropriate acquisitive acts. We get a variety of objections of this kind based on different views of what is an appropriate act of acquisition, that is depending on what sorts of human actions bring things out of a state of ownerlessness into a state of property. Before trying to get this argument off the ground, it is worth noting that both Nozick and Locke start with the assumption that before individual acquisition things are in an ownerless condition (the *res nullis* doctrine); there is another school of thought that assumes that before private acquisition takes place, things are held in common by all men (the *res communae* doctrine).

The major problem in raising this objection is fixing on some kind(s) of action that can be plausibly regarded as acts of original acquisition, i.e., upon the *rites* that generate property *rights*. Nozick raises very serious problems about Locke's criterion for ownership, namely that one owns that with which one has mixed one's labour. He asks about the boundaries of such an acquisition:

If a private astronaut clears a place on Mars, has he mixed his labour with (so that he comes to own) the whole planet, the whole uninhabited universe, or just a particular plot?

Nozick also asks why mixing one's labour with something isn't simply throwing one's labour away, and if it isn't, then why should one have title to more than the value (if any) added by one's labour? If "mixing labour" is the acquisitive act, then surely these and related questions must be convincingly answered if entitlement theory is to proceed.

We have already seen that if usage is made the standard there are serious problems in determining whose standard of use should prevail. In fact, it would seem that an entitlement theorist should shy away from recognising usage as the acquisitive action, for anyone could take your title to X away from you by finding a better use of X (if you are already using it) or putting it to use for the first time (if you haven't used it yet). I would think that an entitlement theorist should say that it is solely up to X's owner whether and to what use X shall be put. Yet it is Locke who denies that the Indians of America have any ownership rights beyond what they use for food and clothing; English settlers have rights to the land itself because they till it. In short, Locke denies aboriginal rights because the Indians don't use the land in the same way as the English immigrants.

Perhaps, then, it will be suggested that acquisitive actions are *conventional* — literally consisting in the conventions (customs or laws) of a particular people. Thus in one society you own only what you actually have in hand or on your person at the moment, while in another you own whatever bears your mark, and in still another society you own only those things entered in the central ownership registry. Of course, there will be problems when societies with different ownership conventions each want to make exclusive use of the same objects. Each society (assuming no overlap in conventions) can say that the other society's people haven't really acquired the goods in question because of a failure to follow the appropriate conventions. I do not see how an entitlement theorist can say which set of conventions (in part, presumably, adopted for non-arbitrary reasons having to do with different patterns of usage) should prevail on the basis of entitlement theory; it seems to me that he must resort to patterned and, in the end, possibly redistributivist considerations. I think it is on the basis of these considerations that our society will have to deal with the contention (if it can be proven) that the Indian treaties are invalid because the whites and the Indians had totally different conceptions of ownership.

Conclusions

First, I hope to have shown in my consideration of entitlement theory that a number of plausible objections to it (A) through (E), can be answered. These are essentially peripheral objections. Once we get to the core of the theory, however, serious and, I would maintain, insurmountable problems arise. The entitlement theory of original acquisition cannot be maintained without resort to non-entitlement considerations — patterns, end-results, and pure conventions. To cleanse entitlement theory of these additions will make it so unattractive that it cannot be accepted as a theory of justice in holdings.

Secondly, and somewhat surprisingly, I think that I have made out the case for aboriginal rights. I claim that this country ought to recognise aboriginal rights *on the basis of original acquisition*. Of course, this conclusion depends on the validity of my claim that the only rationale that is advanced and is plausible for the present system of holdings in Canada is entitlement theory. I contend that it is on the basis of entitlement theory alone, that we could ever hope to justify the way in which most holdings are distributed in Canada. Just because entitlement theory won't work does not mean that our society won't proceed as if it does. The argument for aboriginal rights is provisional. But it ought to obtain until we are willing to redistribute holdings in this country on a truly just basis.

QUESTIONS

1. If we grant Canada's original peoples aboriginal rights, does it follow from Michael McDonald's argument that we cease to have any obligations to provide welfare?
2. McDonald's arguments about property rights are based on a concept of property derived from Western European thought. Yet the native peoples reject the idea (so important to our way of thinking) that land can be owned or acquired as property. Does this affect McDonald's argument?
3. If entitlement theory won't work, should our society proceed as though it were a valid theory? Do we need to create a new theory?

ABORIGINAL RIGHTS AND THE PROBLEMS OF OWNERSHIP

David Gauthier

McDonald begins with the question, "What sorts of treatment do the native peoples of Canada deserve?" He mentions two very different answers: (i) "Canadians should have welfare rights . . . [so] Indians . . . should not be allowed to fall below some national standard of minimum welfare"; (ii) "no one deserves 'free passage' . . . everyone should work his own way" (p. 27). McDonald then proposes to "shift the topic from welfare rights to aboriginal rights" (ibid.), suggesting that those who defend special welfare rights for Indians (because of their endemic poverty) will reject special aboriginal rights, whereas those who reject special welfare rights (because they reject all such rights) will find that they must defend aboriginal rights.

It is the second part of this reversal which primarily concerns McDonald. Those who reject welfare rights usually defend rights of appropriation. Everyone has a right to what he justly appropriates or justly acquires by transfer, and since this effectively exhausts rights to things, there can be no further welfare rights. But the native peoples were the original appropriators of Canada. Therefore. . . .

McDonald then considers a number of objections to this entitlement theory, which derives from the work of Nozick. His conclusion is that "The entitlement theory of original acquisition cannot be maintained without resort to non-entitlement considerations . . . [However] it is on basis [sic] of entitlement theory alone, that we could ever hope to justify the way in which most holdings are distributed in Canada. Just because entitlement theory won't work does not mean that our society won't proceed as if it does" (pp. 47–48). And so

_____

From a review in Dialogue *of Michael McDonald's "Aboriginal Rights."*

proceeding, "this country ought to recognise aboriginal rights *on the basis of original acquisition*" (p. 47).

My concern with this ingenious argument will be restricted here to McDonald's discussion of objections to the supposition that native peoples did indeed acquire Canada. In particular, referring to the Lockean basis of Nozick's theory, he discusses the *spoilage argument* and the *"proviso" argument.*

Rightful acquisition is limited by spoilage; one may not waste what one acquires. Did the natives, then, waste North America? Were Europeans entitled to appropriate the wasted portions, so that aboriginal rights were not violated by such appropriation?

McDonald argues that it is unclear how the condition of spoilage is to be specified. ". . . by what marks do we identify something as waste? Here it is tempting to ask if the thing in question is used for anyone's benefit. But will any minute amount of incremental benefit suffice to justify ownership or must there be some standard margin of benefit for this use to count here for title? Must there also be standards of efficient use? . . . Any benefit or efficiency standard would seem to be hopelessly utilitarian and redistributivist. On the other hand, having no standards at all would effectively deny a right of self-preservation to those without property and the correlative duty to share for the propertied."

This issue is particularly vexed in the sphere of aboriginal rights, where the native pattern of use differs significantly from the newcomers' pattern. "Clearly Canada's native peoples made ingenious use of the often harsh environment, but their uses could not support the numbers of people that present-day use can . . . However, if we move in the direction of giving title to the Europeans rather than the native peoples, then we would have to surrender our ownership claims to any society which could support more people here more efficiently. This seems quite obviously in direct opposition to the whole thrust of an *entitlement* theory . . ."(pp. 43–44). Hence — despite the harsh consequence of rejecting a right of self-preservation — the native claim to aboriginal acquisition can, McDonald holds, be defended against the spoilage objection.

Against McDonald, I should urge the following form of the spoilage objection. Let us grant that, in the state of nature, a group of persons, *A,* is entitled to appropriate as much land as its members are able to use in any way at all. However, should another group, *B*, of would-be appropriators appear on the scene, and should this group possess a superior technology to *A*, then *B* would be entitled to appropriate, from *A*, as much as would leave *A* with land sufficient, using *B*'s superior technology, to maintain at least as many persons as before, with at least as rich an assortment of material goods, and at least as wide a range of opportunities (though perhaps a different range), *provided B* makes its technology effectively available to *A*.

The rationale for my version of the spoilage objection brings us to the "proviso" argument. Rightful appropriation is limited by leaving, in Locke's word, "enough and as good for others"; this Nozick entitles the Lockean proviso. McDonald supposes the objector to argue that Indian appropriation violates this proviso, in not leaving enough land and as good for the Europeans. I do not think that this can be made to work (nor does McDonald). However, I do hold that the Europeans can justify their appropriation of much of North America by an appeal to the proviso. For in a state of nature, one is entitled to appropriate as much as does not worsen the situation of others, even if one takes from others what they previously, and legitimately, appropriated. In a state of nature, one's title is good *only* against actions which would worsen one's situation. Only under the conventional agreement which constitutes society can there be a stronger title.

The spoilage argument may be understood as a form of the "proviso" argument. To waste what one appropriates is to leave others worse off than if what one wasted had been left free for others to appropriate. The original inhabitants of North America did not appropriate wastefully, given their technology, and so the Europeans could take most of North America from its original inhabitants without violating the Lockean proviso.

Summarily, then, my account is this. The Indians and Eskimo appropriated North America, and their appropriation did not in itself worsen the situation of anyone else. Hence it was legitimate. However, it was not indefeasible, for it could be overridden, in the state of nature, by any group which could leave the original inhabitants better off then they were under their initial appropriation. The Europeans, who were in a state of nature with respect to the Indians and Eskimo, by making available their superior technology, were in a position to make such an overriding appropriation, not of all of North America, but of so much as to leave the original inhabitants with a combination of land and technology superior to their initial combination.

This will put aboriginal rights into a manageable framework. It will not extinguish them, but will severely limit them. McDonald's position would require us to recognize aboriginal rights to all of Canada, with the exception (probably empty) of those rights which have been legitimately exchanged in an agreement not based on force or fraud. My account will instead require us to recognize only such rights as will leave the original inhabitants better off than prior to our coming. Since, of course, we did not provide the Indians and Eskimo with effective access to our technology, and since we did not ensure that they were left sufficient land so that they would be as well off as before our coming, we shall not find the recognition of aboriginal rights costless. But the cost is one that we may realistically consider ourselves able and willing to pay, and one that can be defended by a non-arbitrary application of the Lockean proviso to questions of appropriation in a state of nature.

QUESTIONS

1. David Gauthier concludes that Locke's approach to property rights is sound and can be applied to problems of aboriginal rights. How does Gauthier reach this conclusion?
2. Has Gauthier found a sound set of reasons for the view that we can treat the native peoples justly without taking the radical step urged by Michael McDonald?

A TREATISE ON THE RIGHTS OF THE ABORIGINAL PEOPLES OF THE CONTINENT OF NORTH AMERICA

Fred Plain

I want to deal in this paper with our understanding of the meaning of "aboriginal rights." First of all, I want to quote from a paper produced by the Union of Ontario Indians in 1970. I was president of the union at that time, and I authorized the following statement, which was presented to a special committee dealing with the constitution of Canada.

From Menno Boldt et at., The Quest for Justice: Aboriginal Peoples and Aboriginal Rights *(1985). By permission of The University of Toronto Press Incorporated.*

As Indian people we will always see our special status and our legal right as flowing from the original sovereignty of our nations. The colonial legal system to a large degree denied that sovereignty, but they never denied the existence of rights based on the aboriginal possession of tribal territories. It was the unauthorized violation of these rights that led to the unrest which prompted the Royal Proclamation of 1763.

That document, the first written constitutional document for British North America, recognized the existence of Indians' territorial rights, and established legal procedures for the surrender of these rights. The lands which today comprise Ontario were Indian lands. In the words of the Proclamation, they had not been ceded to or purchased by the colonial power. The procedures established by the Royal Proclamation for ceding Indian lands remain in force today. The last treaty signed under these procedures was in 1956, the Soto adhesion to Treaty #6.

Areas remain today in Ontario for which no valid treaty or surrender exists. Therefore, the procedures of the Royal Proclamation are still of practical consequence even in Ontario. Section 91.24 of the British North America Act of 1867 gave jurisdiction over Indians and lands reserved for the Indians to the Federal Government. This was not enacted as seems popularly believed out of a paternalistic concern for Native peoples.

It was enacted to make clear the power of the Federal Government to engage in colonial expansion in the West. The phrase "land reserved for Indians" included lands not ceded by treaty as of 1867, which for Ontario comprised by far the greater part of the present territory of this Province. If the Indians and their lands had not been crucial to the opening of the West, it would have been more logical to place Indians under Provincial jurisdictions as somewhat different terms of Indian policy developed in each colony of 1867.

Following the surrender of the Hudson's Bay Company Charter in 1869/70, the Governor General, exercising prerogative power in compliance with the procedures established by the Royal Proclamation, began negotiating a series of treaties with the Indian nations in Ontario and the Northwest. The treaties were constitutional documents. They were seen by both sides as establishing basic patterns of interrelationship for the future. They were based on the idea of mutual consent and the understanding that the Indians had legal rights in their patrimony. To violate these documents is to compromise the integrity of the Canadian legal system. The Migratory Birds Convention Act, and the decisions in Regina vs. Sekina in 1964, and in Regina vs. George in 1966, and Daniels vs. White and the Queen in 1968, to Indian people represent violations of basic legal commitments.

The basic rights of the Indian peoples are of constitutional significance. Yet, these rights have not been uniformly safeguarded under the present constitutional structure. This should change.

What Are Aboriginal Rights?

In white society there has always been confusion as to what actually is meant by the term "aboriginal rights." In 1970, for example, Prime Minister Pierre Trudeau was reported to have said that the concept of aboriginal rights is so complicated as to be unworkable. But to us, the Nishnawbe-Aski, the concept is basic, simple, and unambiguous. Our definition of aboriginal rights can be summed up in one phrase: "the right of independence through self-government." When we say that our right to self-government, our right to self-determination, our right to nationhood must be recognized in any new Canadian constitution, we are defining aboriginal rights. This is the goal of the Nishnawbe-Aski as outlined in the Declaration of Nishnawbe-Aski of 1977.

Aboriginal rights defined in this way include the right to develop our own life-style and our own economy, and to protect and encourage the practice of our sacred traditions as we know them. We, the Nishnawbe-Aski, have the inherent right to determine what our future will be. We shall determine the destiny of our land. We want to see the continued development of our people under their own governing systems. Aboriginal rights were a mere concept of Prime Minister Trudeau's mind, but to my people they are a reality. We have the inherent right to develop and grow under our own system, and our own system will flow from our own people, who will develop our own constitution. Our Indian constitutions have every right to be recognized in any new Canadian constitution. This is the true meaning of aboriginal rights.

What Is an Aborigine?

The aborigines are the indigenous inhabitants of a country. For instance, the people that we know as the Indian nations of North and South America are the aborigines of these two continents. They were the first people to live in this part of the world.

Because we were the first people to live here we have a claim to certain rights. These rights include human rights — that is, the basic right to life claimed by all people. However, when we talk about aboriginal rights, we are also talking about the inherent right to self-determination that applies to all aborigines.

What Is Civilization?

To understand aboriginal rights we must understand the meaning of civilization. Civilization is the accumulation of the traditions and culture of a people: their ability to express themselves in a variety of ways — in dance, music, art, law, religion, the telling of stories, the writing of books, and so on. The aboriginal people of North and South America constituted a number of different civilizations.

Aboriginal rights guarantee each indigenous nation the right to develop its own traditions and culture — its own civilization. Each aboriginal nation has the inherent right to seek happiness and a comfortable way of living, and to develop itself at its own pace. This was the right of each aboriginal nation from its beginning, and it exists today. Each nation exercised aboriginal rights within its own lands and boundaries and under its own sovereignty.

To recognize that the aboriginal people were a civilization long before the white man came to North America is to acknowledge that as an aboriginal people we exercised our aboriginal right to govern ourselves. Conversely, to acknowledge that we have aboriginal rights is to recognize that these rights flow from our long-standing civilization.

Aboriginal and European Attitudes Toward the Land

Nishnawbe-Aski means "the people and the land." Our links with the earth are sacred links that no man can ever sever. We are one with the earth, and the earth is one with us. The Nishnawbe-Aski Declaration states that we have the right to govern and control our own people in our own land, and the right to remedy our own situations. The efforts that are made to meet our needs must come from our own people.

As nations of people we made laws to govern ourselves. Among the laws that we made were laws governing our use of the land and its resources. But our attitude toward the land and its use was and still is very different from the European attitude. We aboriginal people believe that no individual or group owns the land, that the land was given to us collectively by the Creator to use, not to own, and that we have a sacred obligation to protect the land and use its resources wisely. For the Europeans, the idea that land can be owned by a person or persons and exploited for profit is basic to the system. The European political and legal systems have been developed to reflect this concept of the land.

Many European and Canadian laws have to do with regulating private property in one form or another and with governing relations among people with respect to private property. The sovereign government has created laws to govern the distribution of the scarce resource of property. The most basic form of property, other than one's own body, is land.

The idea that land can be bought and sold, or that you can exercise some rights but not others in the land, is absolutely foreign to the Nishnawbe-Aski way of thinking. Yet this is the basis for all legislation that has been enacted since the coming of the Europeans to North America.

Legislation Affecting Aboriginal Rights

The Royal Proclamation of 1763 was passed in the British Parliament because of the struggles between Indians and Europeans over the land. This document recognized the existence of Indians' territorial rights and established the legal procedures for the giving up of those rights.

The Constitution Act, 1867, established Canada as a nation. The act sets out the division of power between the provinces and the federal government. Section 91(24) of the act gives jurisdiction over Indians and lands reserved for Indians to the federal government.

The act was intended to make clear the power of the federal government to engage in colonial expansion in the west. This was done because we Indians and our lands were crucial to the opening of the west, and the federal government wanted to be able to control us and our land in order to consolidate its power over the country.

After the royal proclamation, and until as recently as 1956, treaties were signed between the government and the Indian nations. These treaties were seen by both sides as establishing basic patterns of future interrelationships. They were based on the idea of mutual consent and on the understanding that Indians had legal rights in and control of the land.

The treaties were a recognition by colonial law that we Indian people had sovereignty in our land. In fact, there was a widespread acknowledgment that the aboriginal occupants of the land had certain legal claims because of their historical sovereignty over the land. The English legal system developed a theory that those claims were limited in certain ways, but the aboriginal tribes had the legal right to posses their tribal territories. Under the English legal system if the lands passed into non-Indian hands, then the Indian claims had to be extinguished by a formal treaty and by some form of compensation.

The treaties were negotiated sometimes before white settlement, sometimes after. The effect of the treaties was to extinguish many aboriginal rights; to preserve some residual rights, such as hunting, fishing, and trapping; and to create some new rights, such as schooling, medical care, and annuity payments.

While the treaties have not been totally in our favour, the law has never denied that the aboriginal tribes have legal rights to possess their tribal territories.

What Does It Mean to Be a Nation?

Our aboriginal right allows us to determine our future as the Nishnawbe-Aski Nation. What does it mean to be a nation? In 1977, an international conference on discrimination against indigenous populations of the Americas put forward a declaration of principles aimed at gaining recognition for indigenous or aboriginal peoples as nations under international law. The criteria for recognition as a nation are: that the people have a permanent population; that they have a defined territory; that they have a government; that they have the ability to enter into relations with other states. We can assure Canada and the international community that using these criteria we can define ourselves as a nation. We have a population that is permanent; we have always existed and we are not going to die out or fade into oblivion. We have a defined territory stretching from James Bay and Hudson Bay west to the Manitoba boundary; from Hudson Bay and James Bay southward to the height of land known as the Arctic watershed and east to the borders of Quebec. We have a democratic government given to us by the Creator. The Royal Proclamation of 1763 refers to our sovereignty, and the government of Canada approaches us as a nation to enter into a treaty with them. We continue to have the right to enter into relations with other states.

Under these criteria, the Nishnawbe-Aski have a solid basis for claiming our aboriginal right to determine what our future will be and to determine how we are going to attain our goals.

Do the Indian People Have a System of Government?

When the white man first came to America, there were systems of government in operation in this new land. The democratic system employed by the great Six Nations Confederacy was studied by the Europeans, and was picked up and incorporated into their governing systems. Democracy was already flourishing in North America before the white man came. The right to govern one's people, the right to govern one's destiny, the right to determine the paths that a nation will follow to reach its objectives must be recognized as sovereign and aboriginal rights.

We had a government. The government has been dormant because of the influx of federal law, particularly the Indian Act and its administrators, the Department of Indian Affairs. Our government has remained hidden in the hearts of our people, but it has never died. Our government will come forth under the careful guidance and leadership of the Nishnawbe-Aski Commission. We will be prepared to put the constitution of the Nishnawbe-Aski on paper, if that is what is required. Our government is a reality.

We must draw out from our people what they want to see developed in their community with regard to their own governing structure. Only then can we begin to educate our people in the traditional ways of living, traditional Indian government, and the traditional right to determine our future.

What Does It Mean to Be Independent?

When the Nishnawbe-Aski made their declaration in 1977, they stressed that their objective was to see the full development of cultural, economic, spiritual, and political independence.

We think that we have to come to grips with the fact that cultural independence and economic independence cannot be divorced. One cannot exist without the other.

At the time the white man came here, our educational system was complete. The educational system and the political development of the various Indian nations in Canada determined the life-style of the particular tribe in whatever area of America they lived in. For instance, the economy of the Ojibway and the Cree living in this part of North America was based on the presence of animal, fish, bird, and plant life destined to give sustenance to the people. Hunting, fishing and trapping, and gathering were not separate issues to be dealt with at a political level by certain components of the government; they were part of the socio-economic system of our people, and they are included in the overall definition of aboriginal rights. Before the white man came, all Indian nations were independent and exercised their aboriginal rights within their own lands.

The Nishnawbe-Aski and the Constitution

We did not question the statement of Prime Minister Pierre Trudeau that the people of this country have a right to their own constitution. We support the principle of patriation; Canadians have a right to determine the instrument by which government is going to make laws that apply to them.

When the constitutional negotiations became an issue, we told the British parliamentarians that we were not fighting the patriation of the constitution to Canada. We felt that the Canadian people had a right to their own constitution, but we also believed that the Nishnawbe-Aski Nation, which existed before the Europeans came to North America, have a right to their own constitution, and that they must not be deprived of the right to make their own laws and determine their own destiny through their own governing system. Because the Canadian government was unwilling to recognize our right to our own constitution, we challenged the patriation of the British North America Act.

We, the aboriginal people, must clearly spell out the true aboriginal rights that must be recognized in any Canadian constitution. These rights are non-negotiable. But we must take a united stand, or we will find it difficult to persuade Canada's first ministers to heed our claims.

What the Canadian Government Wants from the Aboriginal People

We are in the heat of a tremendous battle, a battle that is focused on jurisdiction. The premiers of the provinces and the prime minister are trying to reduce the aboriginal rights question to a series of legal issues that they can contest or disregard. At the same time, they attempt to placate the Indian people by saying, "We will look after you; we will improve your conditions; we will accommodate your needs." But ultimately they will try to consolidate their jurisdiction over our land and our resources. The first ministers have only one goal in mind in the constitutional negotiations: they hope to gain complete control over all Indian lands and resources. This is what the constitutional process is all about.

The Canadian Government's Attitude to Aboriginal Rights

The Honourable Jean Chrétien had these words to say about aboriginal and treaty rights: "We will honour our lawful obligations to the aboriginal people." Precisely what did he mean? He meant that Canada has obligations to native people only if such obligations will stand the test of the law. If the law decrees that certain obligations must be met, and if those obligations are defined in such a manner that the government can accept the definition, then they will be honoured. But what does the term "law" mean? Law, in the modern liberal state, is the creation of an autonomous and general legal system composed of: private parties; a legitimate legal sovereignty and its administrative agencies (the governor-in-council or Parliament, or the government of Canada, and its cabinet and various departments); and the independent judiciary.

When the explorers from the European nations came to America, they found a land with people and law. The Europeans had no right to come and trample that system of laws underfoot and impose a new legal system in North America. But this fact is not readily going to be recognized and acknowledged by the people who in the first instance denied the existence of the aboriginal system of law. They will fight any attempt to bring truth to bear. Let us go back to the quotation from the Nishnawbe-Aski declaration. In the minds of our people who hunt, trap, and fish the forests, lakes, and rivers of Nishnawbe-Aski land, there is a clear concept of what our land tenure is. However, according to the government of Canada, which makes the laws, aboriginal rights are to be determined by a court interpretation. As far as the courts are concerned aboriginal rights are conceptual rights only; that is to say, they are a concept that exists only in the mind until drafted into some kind of law that makes sense in a legal system. The government makes the law defining aboriginal rights, and the government appoints judges who interpret the law dealing with aboriginal rights. If the government of Canada has its way, the white man's law and the white man's courts will determine how the concept of land tenure is defined in practice.

Who Will Decide What Our Aboriginal Rights Are?

Court cases have never solved the riddle of aboriginal rights. The *Baker Lake* case is a prime instance of what happens when the dominant governing society, through its enacted laws and its judicial system, decides what constitutes aboriginal rights. In the *Baker Lake* case, the court said that the Inuit do have aboriginal rights because they have been here from time immemorial. Because of that one basic fact, the court recognized that aboriginal rights do exist. However, the Supreme Court of Canada took it upon itself to define what the aboriginal right is not. The judgment states that the aboriginal right is not a proprietary right. In other words, the right of the aboriginal people does not relate to the land, and therefore the land is open to those exploiters who want to extract the gas and the oil, destroy the environment, and then move out. The indigenous population is then left with evil consequences that greatly outweigh any potential benefits that might come to them from the resource exploitation.

In the communities of the Nishnawbe-Aski Nation, our fishermen, our trappers, our hunters, our schoolchildren, and our women who maintain our homes understand what our aboriginal rights are. Aboriginal rights are a riddle only to those who do not want to hear or face the truth, who do not want their taking of the land interfered with by the aboriginal owners of this continent.

The aboriginal people have a clear concept of land tenure in their minds; therefore our chiefs, our elders, our people, our children, should define our aboriginal rights — not the federal government, the provinces, or the Canadian courts. It is we who must protect our aboriginal right to self-determination as a nation and our right to develop and use the resources of the land free of interference and intimidation. We have an obligation to preserve the rights granted to us by the Creator. We have that right now. We have always had that right. We are determined to have that right in the future. We don't have to beg the prime minister of Canada and the provincial premiers to recognize that we have certain basic human and aboriginal rights.

Conclusion

I close this paper with a prayer. Great Grandfather, our hearts and our minds are jointed together. We rejoice to know that our right to live and enjoy the beauty of this great land was given to us, not by any foreign government, but by yourself. Great Grandfather, you gave us the land and its resources; you made us one with the birds, the animal life, the fish life; you made us one with nature itself. This is our aboriginal right. It is a right that no government can interpret for us.

Because you gave it to us, no man has a right to take it away from us. Many times, our hearts have been made heavy when we have seen the devastation of our land by those who seek only to mine it for its wealth and then leave it. Our hearts have been made heavy because other powers have come in and made laws that have restricted our free movement of spirit. Yet you have put it in our hearts this day to stand upon our feet once again, and boldly claim that our aboriginal right is forever.

Breathe upon us with your spirit of life, and give us greater determination to press for this right to be fully restored to us and recognized by all people. Great Grandfather, be with us in all of our deliberations, for without your leadership and guidance we are weak and helpless. Cause the sound of the drum to be loud and clear to our hearts and minds in this crucial hour.

QUESTIONS

1. Plain defines aboriginal rights to mean "the right to independence through self-government." What might this mean for the native people and for Canada as it now exists?
2. The native view of land is substantially different from our own, as is pointed out in the introduction to the chapter and in this contribution. That being the case, which of the two incompatible views should prevail when land claims are under consideration? Which view would prevail in our courts?

THE CHARACTER OF ABORIGINAL GOVERNMENTAL RIGHTS

Royal Commission on Aboriginal Peoples

Let us consider first the nature and scope of the Aboriginal right of self-government under section 35. It follows from what we have already said that the right is *inherent* in its source,

From Partners In Confederation: Aboriginal People, Self-Government, and the Constitution. *Ottawa: Supply and Services, 1993. Reprinted by permission of the Royal Commission on Aboriginal Peoples.*

in the sense that it finds its origins within Aboriginal communities, as a residue of the powers they originally held as autonomous nations. It does not stem from constitutional grant; that is, it is not a *derivative* right. The distinction between an inherent and a derivative right is not a mere matter of symbolism. It speaks to the basic issue of how Canada emerged and what it stands for. According to the 'derivative' viewpoint, Aboriginal peoples have no rights of government other than those that the written Constitution creates or that the federal and provincial governments choose to delegate. By contrast under the 'inherent' doctrine, Aboriginal peoples are the bearers of ancient and enduring powers of government that they carried with them into Confederation and retain today. Under the first theory, Aboriginal governments are newcomers on the constitutional scene, mere neophytes among governments in Canada. Under the second doctrine, Aboriginal governments provide the Constitution with its deepest and most resilient roots in the Canadian soil.

The Aboriginal right of self-government is recognized by the Canadian legal system, both under the constitutional common law of Canada and under section 35. So, while the section 35 right is inherent in point of origin, as a matter of current status it is a right held in Canadian law. The implication is that, although Aboriginal peoples have the inherent legal right to govern themselves under section 35, this constitutional right is exercisable only within the framework of Confederation. Section 35 does not warrant a claim to unlimited governmental powers or to complete sovereignty, such as independent states are commonly thought to possess. Aboriginal governments are in the same position as the federal and provincial governments: their powers operate within a sphere defined by the Constitution. In short, the Aboriginal right of self-government in section 35 involves *circumscribed* rather than *unlimited* powers.

Within their sphere of jurisdiction, however, Aboriginal governments possess authority that is not subject to indiscriminate federal or provincial override. This conclusion flows from the *Sparrow* decision,[127] where Aboriginal rights and treaty rights were treated as presumptively resilient to legislative inroads, except where a high constitutional standard could be satisfied. According to this view, Aboriginal governments are not *subordinate* to the actions of other governments; neither are they entirely *supreme*. They occupy an intermediate position. In cases of conflict between Aboriginal laws and external legislation, Aboriginal laws will generally prevail, except in cases where the external laws can be justified under the *Sparrow* standard. This viewpoint recognizes a considerable degree of Aboriginal autonomy and yet allows for the paramount operation of external legislation in matters of transcending importance.

How may the Aboriginal right of self-government in section 35(1) be implemented? Here it is helpful to distinguish between two opposing viewpoints. According to the first view, the right of self-government is merely a *potential* right, which needs to be particularized and adapted to the needs of a specific Aboriginal people before it can be implemented. The latter process requires negotiation and agreement between an Aboriginal people and the Crown or, alternatively, the invocation of arbitral procedures sanctioned by the courts. In either case, the right could not be implemented unilaterally by an Aboriginal group. By contrast, according to the second view, the right of self-government is *actual* rather than potential. As such, it can be implemented immediately to its fullest extent by unilateral Aboriginal initiatives, even in the absence of self-government agreements or court sanction.

In our view, neither of these options is entirely satisfactory. To hold, on the one hand, that the right of self-government cannot be exercised at all without the agreement of the Crown or the permission of the courts appears inconsistent with the fact that the right is inherent. On the other hand, to hold that Aboriginal peoples can unilaterally implement the right to its fullest extent seems to read too much into section 35(1). It appears likely that the true position lies somewhere between these two extremes.

Let us consider briefly a solution that attempts to strike a middle path. According to this view, the right of self-government recognized in section 35(1) should be viewed as *organic*, in a sense similar to that explained in a recent First Nations constitutional report:

> Self-government is not a machine to be turned on or off. It is an organic process, growing out of the people as a tree grows from the earth, shaped by their circumstances and responsive to their needs. Like a tree growing, it cannot be rushed or twisted to fit a particular mould.[129]

We might add that, whereas Aboriginal peoples were once like trees growing in relative isolation on an open plain, they are now more like trees in a grove, coexisting with others in a complex ecological system. So, while the ancient pine of Aboriginal governance is still rooted in the same soil, from which it draws its sustenance, it is now linked in various intricate ways with neighbouring governments.

According to the organic model, the right of self-government would include an *actual* right to exercise jurisdiction over certain core subject-matters, without the need for court sanction or agreements with the Crown. The core areas would include matters of vital concern to the life and welfare of the community that, at the same time, do not have a major impact on adjacent jurisdictions and do not rise to the level of overriding national or regional concern. The organic right of self-government also includes a *potential* right to deal with a wider range of matters that lie beyond the core area and extend to the outer periphery of potential Aboriginal jurisdiction. However, this potential right needs to be adapted to the particular needs of the Aboriginal community or communities in question, either by agreement with the Crown or perhaps by arbitral mechanisms established under judicial supervision.

Under the organic model, the right of self-government is an inherent right when it operates within both the core and the outlying areas of Aboriginal jurisdiction. In neither case is the right a delegated one. The effect of agreements with the Crown is to particularize the inherent right, not to create it. So, for example, where an Aboriginal group concludes a self-government agreement with federal and provincial authorities, the group's governmental authority is inherent throughout the full extent of its jurisdiction, in relation to matters in both the core and the periphery.

At this stage, two related questions arise: (1) what are the potential outer limits of Aboriginal jurisdiction, including both core and periphery, and (2) how does Aboriginal jurisdiction interact with the powers of the federal and provincial governments? These are complex and difficult matters, which will ultimately need to be resolved on a case-by-case basis through co-operative governmental action, as supervised by the courts. Nevertheless, one approach to the matter merits serious consideration. This holds that the subject is governed by three guiding principles.[130]

First, the potential Aboriginal sphere of authority under section 35(1), including both core and outlying areas, has roughly the same scope as the federal head of power over "Indians, and Lands reserved for the Indians" recognized in section 91(24) of the *Constitution Act, 1867*. Within this sphere, Aboriginal governments and the federal government have concurrent legislative powers; that is, they have independent but overlapping powers to legislate. This approach assumes that, in the interests of constitutional rationality and harmony, the word Indians in section 91(24) carries the same meaning as the term Aboriginal peoples in section 35; that is, it extends not only to 'Indians' in the narrow sense of the word, but also to the Inuit and Métis peoples of Canada.[131]

Second, where a conflict arises between an Aboriginal law and a federal law, and both laws are otherwise valid, Aboriginal laws will take priority, except where the federal laws meet the standard laid down in the *Sparrow* case.* Under this standard, federal laws will prevail where the need for federal action can be shown to be compelling and substantial and the legislation is consistent with the Crown's basic trust responsibilities to Aboriginal peoples.[132]

Third, the interaction between Aboriginal and provincial laws is regulated by rules similar to those that govern the interaction of federal and provincial laws in this area. Prior to 1982, provincial authority in relation to Aboriginal peoples was limited by the federal head of power in section 91(24), and the courts had developed a complex set of rules to define the respective Jurisdictions of the two orders of government.[133] This situation did not, of course, change in 1982. However, in this view, there was one new factor. Under section 35(1), Aboriginal governments were recognized as holding concurrent jurisdiction with the federal government over section 91(24) matters. It can be argued that the constitutional rules governing the interaction of federal and provincial laws in this area extend, with relevant adaptations, to the interaction of Aboriginal and provincial laws.[134]

What application does the *Canadian Charter of Rights and Freedoms* have with respect to Aboriginal governments? This is a complex question with important constitutional ramifications.[135] One possible answer, which merits close attention, involves two basic propositions.[136] First, the Aboriginal right of self-government as such is shielded from Charter review because it is protected by section 25 of the document, which states that the Charter shall not be interpreted so as to abrogate or derogate from any Aboriginal, treaty or other rights or freedoms held by Aboriginal peoples.[137] Second, individual members of Aboriginal groups enjoy the protection of Charter provisions in their relations with Aboriginal governments.

This approach distinguishes between the *right* of self-government proper and the *exercise* of governmental powers flowing from that right.[138] Insofar as the right of self-government is an Aboriginal right, section 25 protects it from suppression or amputation at the hands of the Charter. However, individual members of Aboriginal groups, like other Canadians, enjoy Charter rights in their relations with governments, and this protection extends to Aboriginal governments.[139] In this view, then, the Charter regulates the manner in which Aboriginal governments exercise their powers, but it does not have the effect of abrogating the right of self-government proper.

Moreover, section 35(4) contains a provision ensuring sexual equality in the exercise of the right of self-government. This states:

> Notwithstanding any other provision of this Act, the aboriginal and treaty rights referred to in subsection (1) are guaranteed equally to male and female persons.

Insofar as the right of self-government is an Aboriginal or treaty-protected right referred to in section 35(1), it is clearly covered by this guarantee.

It should be remembered that First Peoples are no strangers to the doctrines of freedom and equality that animate the Charter. Early European visitors to North America were struck by the egalitarian nature of most Aboriginal societies and the remarkable degree of personal freedom and responsibility enjoyed by their members.[140] As the French historian, Charlevoix, observed in 1744:

> Born free and independent, they have a horror of the least shadow of a despotic power, but they stray rarely from certain usages and principles founded on good sense. . . . In this country all Humanity believes itself equally men, and in Man what they most esteem is Man. No distinction of birth, no prerogative of rank.[141]

By comparison, many European societies of the seventeenth and eighteenth centuries were highly stratified and authoritarian, with little in the way of democratic freedoms, and servitude a feature of everyday life. According to one school of thought, the example of Indigenous American societies had a significant (and underrated) impact on European political thought and contributed to the formation of the ideals that led to the American and French revolutions.[142] As the chiefs of the Iroquois Confederacy have affirmed:

> European people left our council fires and journeyed forth into the world to spread principles of justice and democracy which they learned from us and which have had profound effects upon the evolution of the Modern World.[143]

The principles that animate the *Canadian Charter of Rights and Freedoms* arguably have multiple roots, then, spreading deep into both Aboriginal and non-Aboriginal societies. To some extent at least, these principles can be viewed as the product of cultural fusion, stemming from inter-societal contacts in the villages and forests of North America, with effects that rippled outward into the salons and marketplaces of pre-revolutionary Europe. In interpreting and applying the Charter, we would do well to keep in mind the complementary ideals of freedom and responsibility that have informed Aboriginal outlooks from ancient times, ideals that have continuing relevance to Canadian society today.

To summarize, the Aboriginal right of self-government has a substantial basis in existing Canadian law, even in the absence of explicit constitutional clauses of the kind proposed in the Charlottetown Accord of 1992. The original basis for this right was the autonomous status of Aboriginal nations at the time they entered into association with the French and British Crowns. The right of Aboriginal nations to govern their own affairs was acknowledged in inter-societal practice and formed a tacit premise of many treaties. The right became part of the common law doctrine of Aboriginal rights, which emerged during the seventeenth and eighteenth centuries as a body of fundamental law governing relations between Aboriginal peoples and incoming European nations. There are persuasive grounds for concluding that the right of self-government continues to exist today as a matter of constitutional common law and qualifies as an existing Aboriginal or treaty-protected right under section 35(1) of the *Constitution Act, 1982*. The right is organic in nature and may be implemented by Aboriginal initiatives within the core areas of Aboriginal jurisdiction. However, implementation in the outlying areas of this jurisdiction likely requires agreements with other relevant orders of government.

NOTES

127. The Sparrow standard is set out earlier in the report in a passage that reads:
    The decision of the Supreme Court in the *Sparrow* case laid down broad guidelines governing

the scope and effect of section 35(1), guidelines that will no doubt be clarified by the Court over the next several decades. Thus far, it is clear that the section gives constitutional protection to a range of special rights enjoyed by Aboriginal peoples, shielding these rights from the adverse effects of legislation and other governmental acts, except where a rigorous standard of justification can be met [p. 31.]

128. R. V. Sparrow, [1990] 1 Supreme Court Reports 1075.

129. Rosie Mosquito and Konrad Sioui, *To the Source: First Nations Circle on the Constitution. Commissioners' Report* (Ottawa: Assembly of First Nations, 1992), p. 21.

130. For a parallel approach, see Slattery, "First Nations and the Constitution", (1992) 71 *Canadian Bar Review* 261 at pp. 282–87.

131. In *Re Term "Indians"*, [1939] Supreme Court Reports 104, the Supreme Court of Canada ruled that section 91(24) applied to the Inuit (or 'Eskimo') peoples. The Supreme Court has not yet decided whether the section also covers the Métis people. A leading constitutional authority, Professor Peter Hogg, offers the view that the Métis are probably included within the section; see Hogg, *Constitutional Law of Canada*, 3rd ed., note 66, pp. 665–66. For background and discussion, see Catherine Bell, "Who Are the Métis People in Section 35(2)?", (1991) 29 Alberta Law Review 351; Clem Chartier, "'Indian': An Analysis of the Term as Used in Section 91(24) of the British North America Act, 1867", (1978-79) 43 Saskatchewan Law Review 37; Paul L.A.H. Chartrand, "Aboriginal Rights: The Dispossession of the Métis", (1991) 29 Osgoode Hall Law Journal 457; Chartrand, *Manitoba's Métis Settlement Scheme*, note 95; Richard I. Hardy, "Metis Rights in the Mackenzie River District of the Northwest Territories", [1980] 1 Canadian Native Law Reporter 1; Cumming and Mickenberg, *Native Rights in Canada*, note 46, pp. 6–9, 200–04; William F. Pentney, *The Aboriginal Rights Provisions in the Constitution Act, 1982* (Saskatoon, Sask.: University of Saskatchewan Native Law Centre, 1987), chap.4; Schwartz, *First Principles, Second Thoughts*, note 11, pp. 213–47; Woodward, *Native Law*, note 66, pp. 53–59.

132. See *R. v. Sparrow*, note 2, at pp. 1113–14. The Supreme Court held that the proposed standards of "reasonableness" and "in the public interest" were not sufficiently stringent; see pp. 1113, 1118–1119.

133. For discussion of these rules, see G.-A. Beaudoin, *La Constitution du Canada* (Montreal: Wilson & Lafleur, 1990), chap. 15; Hogg, *Constitutional Law of Canada*, 3rd ed., note 66, pp. 664–79; Patricia Hughes, "Indians and Lands Reserved for the Indians: Off-Limits to the Provinces?", (1983) 21 Osgoode Hall Law Journal 82; Kenneth M. Lysyk, "The Unique Constitutional Position of the Canadian Indian", (1967) 45 Canadian Bar Review 513; Kenneth M. Lysyk, "Constitutional Developments relating to Indians and Indian Lands: An Overview", in *The Constitution and the Future of Canada, Special Lectures of the Law Society of Upper Canada* (Toronto: Richard de Boo Ltd., 1978), 201; Micheline Patenaude, *Le droit provincial et les terres indiennes* (Montreal: Éditions Yvon Blais, 1986), chap. II; Douglas Sanders, "Prior Claims: Aboriginal People in the Constitution of Canada", in Stanley M. Beck and Ivan Bernier, ed., *Canada and the New Constitution* (Montreal: Institute for Research on Public Policy, 1983), Vol. I, p. 225; Slattery, "Understanding Aboriginal Rights", note 66, pp. 774–81; Woodward, *Native Law*, note 66, pp. 87–131.

134. See discussion in Slattery, "First Nations and the Constitution", note 130, pp. 283–86.

135. For discussion of the question of cultural perspective, see Mary Ellen Turpel, "Aboriginal Peoples and the Canadian *Charter*: Interpretive Monopolies, Cultural Differences", (1989–90) 6 Canadian Human Rights Yearbook 3.

136. Compare Slattery, "First Nations and the Constitution", note 130, at pp. 286–87.

137. Section 25 provides in part: "The guarantee in this Charter of certain rights and freedoms shall not be construed so as to abrogate or derogate from any aboriginal, treaty or other rights or freedoms that pertain to the aboriginal peoples of Canada. . . ."

138. For the distinction between the Charter's effects on the existence of a constitutional power and the exercise of that power, see *Re: An Act to Amend the Education Act*, [1987] 1 Supreme Court Reports 1148, *per* Estey, J. at pp. 1206–07; *Re Provincial Electoral Boundaries (Sask.)*, [1991] 2 Supreme Court Reports 158, *per* McLachlin J. at p. 179; *Donahoe v. Canadian Broadcasting Corp.*, note 125, *per* McLachlin J. at pp. 30–34 (typescript), *per* Cory J. at pp. 8–10 (typescript).

139. While Aboriginal governments are not specifically mentioned in section 32(1) of the Charter, which lists governmental authorities to which the Charter applies, this list does not seem to be comprehensive. In the case of *R.W.D.S.U. v. Dolphin Delivery Ltd.* [1986] 2 Supreme Court Reports 573, the Supreme Court of Canada held that the Charter does not apply in litigation between private parties and that section 32 was conclusive on this point; see McIntyre, J. at p. 597. Justice McIntyre went on to state at p. 598: "It is my view that s. 32 of the *Charter* specifies the actors to whom the *Charter* will apply. They are the legislative, executive and administrative branches of government." This holding suggests that the purpose of section 32 is to draw the dividing line between private and governmental actors, rather than to list in a comprehensive fashion the governmental bodies to which the Charter applies.

140. There is a large literature on the subject. Among recent works, see especially William Brandon, *New Worlds for Old: Reports from the New World and Their Effect on the Development of Social Thought in Europe, 1500–1800* (Athens, Ohio: Ohio University Press, 1986); Denys Delâge, "L'influence des Amérindiens sur les Canadiens et les Français au temps de la Nouvelle-France", (1992) 2 Lekton (No. 2) 103, esp. at pp. 163–91.

141. P.-F.-X. Charlevoix, *Histoire et description générale de la Nouvelle France*. 3 vols. (Paris: Ganeau 1744), Vol. 3, at pages 341–42; quoted in Brandon, *New Worlds for Old*, previous note, at p. 106. On the cultivation of the ideal of autonomous responsibility among the Iroquois, see Anthony F.C. Wallace, *The Death and Rebirth of the Seneca* (New York: Vintage Books, 1972), pp. 34–39.

142. The thesis is argued in Grinde and Johansen, *Exemplar of Liberty: Native America and the Evolution of Democracy*, note 65. For more modulated assessments, see Brandon, *New Worlds for Old*, note 140, and Delâge, "L'influence des Amérindiens", note 140.

143. "Haudenosaunee Statement to the World", Akwesasne Notes 11 (May 1979): 7; quoted in Grinde and Johansen, *Exemplar of Liberty*, note 65, at p. 235.

QUESTIONS

1. One of the issues that has given rise to intense controversy is whether recognizing the right of aboriginal peoples to self-government is consistent with requiring that aboriginal governments respect the Charter of Rights and Freedoms. Thus, some aboriginal leaders have argued that the Charter is an expression of Western individualistically oriented values that are quite incompatible with the traditional, group-oriented, collectivist values of aboriginal societies. The Royal Commission addresses this issue. In your view, is their proposal in this regard persuasive? Is recognizing the right to self-government compatible with requiring that the Charter rights of natives be respected?

ABORIGINAL LAND RIGHTS IN NORTHERN CANADA

J.T. Stevenson

Introduction

I believe that the usual approach to aboriginal land claims in Canada is profoundly misguided. We have imposed our political and legal system on the native peoples and have
forced them to argue for their rights in terms of our current culture. In so doing, we have
ignored their point of view and not addressed some fundamental issues.

Canada's Constitution Act 1982, fortunately, requires (Part IV, S. 37[2]) a constitutional
conference, which is to discuss "the identification and definition of the rights" of aboriginal
peoples. We thus have the opportunity, indeed the duty, to look at the whole question of
land claims philosophically, in a manner broader and deeper than usual.

A Standard Approach

According to the political/legal system that developed in the course of the industrial revolution, land is treated as property, as something that can be owned, as something alien to us
but over which we have dominion. In this liberal tradition, the owner of a property has, on
the face of it, the sole and despotic right to do whatsoever he wills with it. Land is also
treated as a commodity, as something that can be bought and sold and that has value
determined by its market price. There is an elaborate legal system for determining who
owns what, for settling disputes, and for regulating the use of property. The state may,
exercising its ultimate power of sovereignty, expropriate land and give as compensation
other commodities (money, goods, services) equal to the market value of the land.

Within this framework, we argue whether or not native peoples really own the land
where they reside. Some say they do because of the right of first possession. They thus
confer on the native peoples despotic powers over the land that the native peoples never
exercised, never even conceived themselves as possessing, and do not (if they can keep
their own ways) want. Others say that they do not own it because, as the judicial Committee
of the British Privy Council put it in the eighteenth century, the inhabitants were "so low on
the scale of social organization that their usages and conceptions are not to be reconciled
with the institutions and legal ideas of a civilized society." In similar fashion, some have
recently argued that the natives may "own" the land but that we can simply take it from
them because they have a technologically inferior culture — provided we offer them,
whether they want it or not, our superior culture. A third position, sometimes taken by our
courts, is that the natives have a limited ownership in the form of usufruct rights. This
means, roughly, that ultimate ownership resides with the Crown but, because of traditional
usage and customs, the natives have the right, say, to hunt and fish on certain lands. Much
debate has revolved around the issue of compensation for land claims, which presupposes
that the aboriginal peoples have some sort of legal entitlement to their lands but that the
Crown in right of Canada, being sovereign, can expropriate land and determine an adequate
form of compensation.

Why Wrong

All this, I say, is misguided. It proceeds on the assumptions of a particular culture and its political/economic legal regime, when the issue is cross-cultural and concerns the adequacy of that regime. What rarely gets a serious hearing is the native point of view.[1] The native peoples did not traditionally regard their land as something over which they had sovereign dominion, as something they owned and could do with as they pleased. The land and its other inhabitants were regarded, according to their laws, as something essential to their well-being, as something to be used with respect, care, and moderation, as something to be shared and preserved for future generations of all living things. In our terms, we might say that they regarded themselves, in a fashion, as stewards of the land with not only rights but obligations respecting it. They believed they had a very special relation with the land, which we may call religious, spiritual, or philosophical, but which, in any case, was expressed by them in myth, legend, symbol, and ceremony. Their land was not a property and commodity. It may be particularly hard for us to understand how and why the native peoples feel that their individual, personal identity is intimately connected to their relation to the land. Yet, to treat them fairly, it is vital that we make an effort to do so.

Purpose and Plan of Discussion

Because we tend to dismiss their view as primitive, mytho-poetical, or mystical rather than civilized, scientific, and rational, I shall try to explain or translate it into rational and scientific terms, the terms of philosophy, anthropology, and psychology. Some things, especially the experiential dimension, get lost in this translation, but, one hopes, the translation will provide a small bridge of understanding and sympathy.

Thus I shall present an argument designed not only to support certain conclusions, but to serve as a thread tying together a set of considerations usually overlooked in discussing aboriginal land claims. It will tie individual identity and a personal security right, on the one hand, to group rights to culture and land, on the other.

I make three background assumptions: (1) that natural justice requires that we first listen to the voices of the claimants, the native peoples, in their own terms rather than assume that we know best what is good for them; (2) that we should appeal to moral principles that are cross-cultural and find as much other common ground as possible; (3) that in tracing the consequences of our actions we should appeal to the most realistic and well-evidenced scientific theories available.

My discussion focusses on land claims in the Yukon and Northwest Territories because of the special opportunities and dangers faced by people there: on the one hand, they have not yet suffered as much disruption as native peoples in the South; on the other hand, they face severe threats because of the rush to exploit the nonrenewable resources of the northern frontier and have made specific claims on us. While the experiences of the southern aboriginals will be used as evidence in the empirical steps in the argument, a solution to the problems of southern Amerindians and Metis will be particularly difficult and I say nothing directly on the question. I hope, however, that the discussion will indirectly illuminate some aspects of their problems and those of other cultural minorities.

The discussion proceeds as follows. In the second section the problem is presented as it is understood and expressed by native peoples themselves. The claims are then interpreted and summarized in terms that may be more familiar to us so that we can have a common understanding of the problem. In the third section I set out and interpret a widely accepted, cross-cultural moral principle, so that discussion can proceed on a common normative basis. The fourth section outlines a difficult empirical step in the argument: it attempts to express, in terms of theories from anthropology and psychology, the central native view that their individual identity and hence personal security is tied up with their relation to their land. It turns out, I believe, that once again we can find common ground. In the fifth section the argument is restated briefly and certain conclusions, both positive and negative, are drawn. Note that much of the basic evidence has had to be relegated to footnotes.

Native Voices

Let us listen attentively to a carefully chosen but representative selection of native voices in the North that present the problems as *they* see them.

A. To the Indian people our land really is our life. Without our land we cannot — we could no longer exist as people. [Note: "as people" not "as a people."] If our land is destroyed, we too are destroyed. If you people ever take our land you will be taking our life. (Richard Nerysoo)

Every time the white people come to the North or come to our land and start tearing up the land, I feel as if they are cutting up our own flesh because that is the way we feel about our land. It is our flesh. (Georgina Tobac)

B. Ever since they came in I couldn't make a living out of the country. This is my trouble now. There is all kinds of money made around me with the oil, and they don't give me anything. They don't think that I am a person living there. (Johnny Klondike)

C. [They suggest] that we give up our land and resources to the richest nation [the U.S.A. which wanted a pipeline built] in the world; not the poorest. We are threatened with genocide only so the rich and powerful can become more rich and more powerful.
I suggest, in any man's view, that is immoral. If our Indian nation is being destroyed so that poor people of our world might get a chance to share this world's riches, then as Indian people, I am sure we would seriously consider giving up our resources. But do you really expect us to give up our life and our lands so that those few people who are the richest and most powerful in the world today can maintain and defend their own immoral position of privilege?
That is not our way. (Phillip Blake)

D. For myself, I find it very hard to identify with anybody because I have nobody to turn to. My people don't accept me any more because I got an education, and the white people won't accept me because I am not the right colour. So like, a lot of people keep saying, "O.K., we've got to educate these young native people, so that they can become something." But what good is it if a person has no identity? I can't really identify with anybody and I'm lost. I'm just sort of a person hanging in the middle of two cultures and doesn't know which way to go. (Roy Fabian)

E. The Dene have the right to recognition, self-determination, and on-going growth and development as a People and a Nation.

The Dene, as aboriginal people, have a special status under the Constitution of Canada.

The Dene, as aboriginal people, have the right to retain so much of their traditional lands, and under such terms, as to ensure their independence and self-reliance, traditionally, economically and socially.

There will, therefore, be within Confederation, a Dene Government with jurisdiction over a geographical area and over subject matters now within the jurisdiction of either the Government of Canada or the Government of the Northwest Territories. (Proposed by the Dene as an "Agreement in Principle between the Dene Nation and Her Majesty the Queen in Right of Canada.")[2]

Interpretation

Taking into account the cultural context, we can translate these statements into our terms as follows. A: The people believe that they live in a complex, symbiotic relation with the land and its ecosystems; that is, their environment, culture, and personal identity are closely interwoven in a balanced system. B: They believe they are being economically marginalized and treated as non-persons. C: They believe that they are being treated unjustly, that their vital interests are being sacrificed for the less important or trivial interests of those already well-off. D: They believe the form of the enculturation process into white society that is imposed on them prevents or destroys a healthy personality integration. E: They believe they need and have the right to some forms of political and social self-determination. This, in summary but I believe fair fashion, is the native position. My argument will try to elucidate, in particular, A and D.

Let us try to find common ground, both morally and intellectually.

The Personal-Security Principle

One cross-cultural and widely accepted normative principle that is relevant is stated in the UN Charter of Human Rights (1948) — often called "the conscience of mankind" — to which Canada is a subscriber. It says (Article 3): "Everyone has the right to life, liberty and the security of person." Of course, like other abstract legal and moral principles, it must be interpreted to be applied; and its application clarifies and enriches its meaning. I shall focus on the personal-security aspect of this right — Everyone has the right to personal security — and I shall spell out what this means.[3]

Content of Right

We would agree that arbitrary, capricious killing, such as indulged in by Idi Amin in Uganda, would violate this right; as similarly would the more systematic holocaust of the Nazi regime in Germany. Hacking off a person's limbs or reducing him to slavery while keeping him alive would also be clearly prohibited. Of course the right is defeasible. That is to say, it can be overridden: we can kill in self-defence; the criminal can lose his liberty; the surgeon who mutilates a cancer patient to save his life does not violate the patient's security right. So some thought is required in applying the principle.

Such thought, I believe, will lead us to recognize that the right to the security of our person extends beyond life and limb to matters affecting basic personality structure. Many modern states, alas, practise forms of torture that leave a person alive and unmutilated but nevertheless personally destroyed. A person may, for instance, be subjected to sensory deprivation, electro-shock, and hallucinogenic drugs. As a result, he may be prey to chronic anxiety, feelings of guilt and worthlessness, and alternating passivity and rage; he may be unable to function economically and socially; he may suffer from anomie — a state in which normative standards of conduct and belief are weak or lacking, a state that is characterized by disorientation, anxiety, and isolation; he may lack purpose or meaning in his life and be unable to persevere in projects and establish normal social relations; he may lapse into alcoholism and chronic delinquency; he may be so overwhelmed by anxiety and depression that he commits suicide. In short, he may be turned into a human derelict.

Such can be the effects of torture. But, as we shall see, similar effects can be produced unintentionally by other methods and can be observed on reserves and in urban centres throughout Canada. I suggest that the personal security right protects us not only against physical death, mutilation and enslavement, but against such psychic destruction and mutilation.

Qualifications

To avoid controversy as much as possible, let us put a construction on the personal-security right. (1) The right obliges us to acts of omission rather than commission. We may not have to help or enhance a person's security, but we are required to refrain from positive acts that harm personal security. (2) These harms must be serious and substantial. In the myriad of social interactions we engage in, we daily harm other people, intentionally or otherwise: we inflict, for instance, little blows on their pride and self-esteem. But here we speak only of those major blows or the death of a thousand cuts, which strike at the core of personality, which sap our capacity to cope, which in a strong sense destroy and mutilate us. (3) The forbidden harms to be culpable or blameworthy must be foreseeable and avoidable. When we act, we sometimes "know not what we do" or "can't help what we do." We act in ignorance or unintentionally or we produce effects by accident or we couldn't have done otherwise. We speak here, however, only of what a reasonable person in the light of currently available knowledge would expect as the probable consequences of his actions where there is a genuine choice available. Of course, people who are educated or in responsible positions with special access to information and with powers to act will be less able than others to plead ignorance or unavoidability. (4) Since personal security is so important, the onus of proof should be on the agent, but the burden of proof is on me to assure that I am not violating the personal security of those affected by my act. To reverse the onus would mean that the patient or potential victim would have to calculate the consequences of other people's actions and prevent or avoid consequences which would harm his, the victim's, personal security. Second, instead of setting as the level of proof required — what might be reasonable given the importance of the matter — that I refrain from acting unless it is beyond a reasonable doubt that I am harming no one's personal security, let us be conservative and impose a weaker test. I should not act unless the balance of probabilities indicates that I will not be harming someone's personal security. (5) There will be, for psychic personal security as for physical security, defeasibility conditions that prevent absurd applications of the right. Thus, for example, if I am a paedophile whose personality is integrated around my desire to sexually molest children, you do not violate my personal security right if you prevent me from acting on this desire and thereby drastically upset my personality. The personal security rights of children in those circumstances override those of paedophiles.

The problem now is to indicate how, in certain circumstances, it is possible to violate psychic personal security by disrupting a person's relationship to his environment and way of life.

The Evidence of Science

Political and ethical arguments in philosophy usually rely, in part, on views about human nature and society. Often they are theories from the seventeenth and eighteenth centuries; for instance, the psychology of Thomas Hobbes or the anthropology of Jean-Jacques Rousseau. I have thought it wiser to appeal to the much better evidence theories of the twentieth century. And from the plethora of available opinion I have made choices that I cannot here defend in the space available. I can only invite the reader to do what the writer has done: immerse himself in the literature, examine the evidence and try to make a judicious choice; one that avoids as much as possible ideological prejudices.

Systems Analysis

We have become accustomed to the idea of applying systems analysis to our environment, to regarding it as an ecosystem: a set of elements (land, air, water, plants, and animals) connected by a complex web of interdependencies and feedback loops which maintain the system in a delicate balance. For example, a lake, with its water quality, plants, fish, and aquatic animals, may form such a system. The system may absorb some shocks and regain its balance: the lake may, after over-fishing, regenerate the fish stock. But sometimes a shock will be catastrophic: the flow of nutrients into the lake may so increase (more sewage, detergents, and so on) that an algae bloom occurs, oxygen is depleted, the fish die, and we have a eutrophied lake with different forms of life in it. It is not always easy to tell which shocks will be catastrophic. For example, the human body can recover from massive bleeding and many broken bones (as in a car accident) but completely succumb to the administration of enough white powder to cover a pinhead (say the powder is strychnine). If we want to act on a system without destroying it, we need to understand its critical elements and relations, how it will respond to changed conditions and how it may adapt.

It is important to note at this point that the native belief that the natural world forms a complex, interdependent system of which the native peoples are an integral part should not be dismissed as mere primitive or magical thought. It is a view they forged in the struggle for existence and it is based on thousands of years of experience and empirical observation. Although not expressed in our theoretical terms and differing in many details, the general approach is consistent with our most advanced biological science. In their own way, the native peoples got there first.

I suggest that this common ground of a systems mode of thought can be extended from biology to our understanding of society, culture, and the development of personal identity. Two main points will be made. First, a physical and biological environment, a culture and social system in which people earn a living, and the way in which human beings grow and are nurtured into mature personalities in that culture — all three — should be regarded as one system. Second, the personal security of native peoples has been attacked by European settlers at two critical points — in their livelihood from the land and in the nurturance of their children. Let us see how.

Anthropology

The culture of a human society is an integrated pattern of behaviour that includes thought, speech, action, and artifacts, and depends on our capacity for learning and transmitting knowledge to succeeding generations. According to anthropologist Marvin Harris, we may distinguish those broad elements of culture that interact in important ways.[4]

Harris distinguishes an infrastructure, which consists of modes of production and reproduction. The mode of production, Harris says, is "The technology and practices employed for expanding or limiting basic subsistence production, especially the production of food and other forms of energy, given the restrictions and opportunities provided by a specific technology interacting with a specific habitat." The mode of reproduction is "The technology and the practices employed for expanding, limiting and maintaining population size." Harris notes a structure of a domestic and political economy: "the organization of reproduction, production, exchange, and consumption within and between bands, villages, chiefdoms, states, and empires." He also defines a superstructure: "the conscious and unconscious cognitive goals, categories, rules, plans, values, philosophies and beliefs" that are expressed in behaviour generally and often particularly in rituals, religion, art, music, dance, games, literature, and so on.

These interacting elements form a cultural system that can be stable or unstable, concordant or discordant, that can grow or decline, live or die. Some shocks to the system will be easily absorbed; others will produce dramatic changes and be catastrophic.

Harris has advanced a fruitful approach to anthropology, which he calls the "research program of cultural materialism." It says, very roughly: look first to infrastructural elements when attempting to explain the riddles of culture. A disruption in the infrastructure of a culture, for example, a major change in the way land is used, can have dramatic impacts on its other elements, such as its belief and value system and the way it nurtures its offspring into persons. I believe Harris has demonstrated in certain cases the fruitfulness of this approach. I have in mind, for instance, his elegant, plausible, and powerful analysis of the sacred cow taboo in India, which explains a wide range of facts (such as different sex ratios amongst adult cattle in different regions of India) but which other theories leave inexplicable and puzzling.

I am relying on his approach in stressing the importance of land use to the question of a personal-security right. A sudden and drastic disruption of the relation between a people and its environment can reverberate, through elements of its culture, to the very foundations of human personality. But to see how this can be so, we need to add a theory from psychology to the one from anthropology, in order to connect culture and personality development. My views on this are drawn largely from the work of Erik Erikson, Jean Piaget, and Bruno Bettelheim.[5] Each general point made will be followed by an illustration.

Psychology

Persons, in an important sense, are made not born.[6] We know that without some decent system of training and nurturing — the systems can vary within certain broad limits — biological human beings will not develop the cognitive, emotional, and social capacities for personhood at all or will have severe personality disorders. Our practices may be unconscious (based on habit and tradition) but even apparently trivial details can have deep effects on personality structure. A proper understanding of the phenomena requires an integrated approach to personality development.

We are speaking of three processes, the somatic process, the ego process, and the societal process. In the history of science these three processes have belonged to three different scientific disciplines — biology, psychology, and the social sciences — each of which studied what it could isolate, count, and dissect: single organisms, individual minds, and social aggregates. . . . Unfortunately this knowledge is tied to the conditions under which it was secured: the organism undergoing dissection or examination; the mind surrendered to experiment or interrogation; social aggregates spread out on statistical tables. In all of these cases, then, a scientific discipline prejudiced the matter under observation by actively dissolving its total living situation in order to be able to make an isolated section of it amenable to a set of instruments or concepts.[7]

We now know more and can do better. We know something about how culture — the mode of reproduction, the domestic economy, and elements of the superstructure such as myths and legends — plays an important role in the development of personality. Thus anthropology is linked to psychology. We can also recognize the existence of normal pathways of development and critical stages in those paths such that an event which would be relatively harmless at most stages may have profound consequences at a critical stage. We also know something of the importance of systemic consistency and appropriateness: two methods of child-rearing, each separately successful, may, when combined, produce a severely conflicted personality; a method that produces a personality successful in one culture may not be appropriate for producing the type of personality required for success in another culture. Finally, let us note that the destruction or mutilation of personality can occur after childhood. Indeed, Erikson's work on the so-called identity-crisis of early adulthood was triggered by clinical observations of young men suffering from war-induced psychoneuroses and led to his investigations of the developmental stages and crises of the whole human life cycle.

So, in the clinical investigation of individual pathology we need to take into account differences rooted in biology (genetics), critical stages and events in personality development, and the social-cultural-historical setting in which they take place.

Let us now return to the native question. First, contrary to common European belief — which vacillated between regarding Indians as noble, untutored children of nature and regarding them as depraved, untutored savages — native peoples have elaborate child-rearing systems that have produced integrated personalities well-adapted to their culture.

Up to recent decades child training has been an anthropological no man's land. Even anthropologists living for years among aboriginal tribes failed to see that these tribes trained their children in some systematic way. Rather, the experts tacitly assumed with the general public that savages had no child training at all and that primitives grew up "like little animals" — an idea which in the overtrained members of our culture arouses either angry contempt or romantic elation.

The discovery of primitive child-training systems makes it clear that primitive societies are neither infantile stages of mankind nor arrested deviations from the proud progressive norms which we represent: they are a complete form of mature human living, often of a homogeneity and simple integrity which we at times might well envy.[8]

Application

Let me illustrate now the foregoing general discussion. Erikson was asked to investigate the causes of widespread behavioural and personality disorders amongst Dakota Indian children in U.S. government schools.[9] He found that in the first years of their lives they were brought up in a way which, through traditional techniques of child transport, breastfeeding, weaning, and so on, was well suited to produce personalities adapted to a culture based on the buffalo hunt. Then the children were thrust into schools well suited to produce, as personalities, the factory workers needed in an industrial society. The Indian children were deeply conflicted cognitively (e.g., in their structuring of space and time) and emotionally. Moreover, neither form of training was suited to the actual economic basis of their society. The reserves on which they were confined would support neither a hunting culture nor an industrial one. The inconsistency and inappropriateness of their upbringing left them with identity confusions, expressed in their feelings and behaviour. (Recall the statement of Roy Fabian.) Their prospects were poverty and the cycle of the welfare syndrome. The trouble started when their cultural infrastructure was destroyed — the buffalo wiped out and their lands seized — and was compounded by the efforts made to enculturate the children into white society.

Similar stories can be told about Indian bands across Canada. It was once thought that a solution could be found in residential schools, where native children would be separated from the influence of their families and thoroughly indoctrinated in the fundamentals of white society. Little was understood about the importance of critical stages of development and the effects of experiences in infancy; little regard was given to the milieu to which the children would return. The result was a catastrophe for several generations of aboriginal peoples.

If you want a recipe for the destruction of personality, one such would be this: destroy the material basis of a culture; force the people into an environment which provides little means for economic activity; foster the culture of poverty and dependency by means of minimal handouts; make ignorant and racist attacks on the structure and superstructure of what remains of the culture; as the adults disintegrate from these shocks, experiment blindly with their children.

I have sketched an integrated theory from anthropology and psychology which enables us to trace and understand some of the effects of our actions. Is it consistent with the native view of the matter? I believe so. When a native women says that interfering with her land is "cutting up our own flesh," this should not be dismissed as the far-fetched, special pleading of an ignorant primitive. She may well be expressing, metaphorically, what we may express using scientific jargon. And the grounds of the belief may not be altogether different from ours: she may be expressing the native belief in the complex dependencies of the individual/social/environmental system, as well as the results of her own observations of shocks to that system.

In any case the facts must be explained. There is massive evidence of widespread personal pathology amongst Southern Canadian aboriginal peoples.[10] It can be seen with the naked eye on reserves and in urban ghettos; it is described in personal accounts by those affected; it shows up in the statistics on poverty, anomie, school failures, alcoholism, family breakdown, crime, and suicide. How are these changes in individual human lives to be explained?

Many Euro-Canadians and other whites give a racist explanation: somehow the aboriginals are genetically inferior, lacking in intelligence and adaptability. (Winnipeg magistrate Isaac Rice: "There is something in their blood. I don't know what it is but an Indian and alcohol just don't mix . . . I have never come across a married Indian couple.")[11] The facts do not bear them out.

Even those racists who offer the evidence of IQ testing to support (however inadequately) their claims that blacks are genetically inferior have been unable to make similar claims about the aboriginal population. And it is the case that, historically, the Amerindian and Inuit peoples have shown a high degree of adaptability and cultural variation.[12]

The plain fact is that the aboriginal peoples of the Americas have been subjected to a long series of massive assaults equivalent to genocide. Sometimes it has been the genocide (in the strict sense) of politicians, generals, and settlers who conducted campaigns — still going on in the jungles of the Amazon — of slaughter and germ warfare.[13] Sometimes it has been the unexpected effect of well-intentioned efforts by politicians, economists, missionaries, and educators.

We need to be warned particularly against the latter: the politicians who, to preserve traditional life-styles, have deported Indians to reservations which cannot support that life-style or any other decent one; the economists who, under the aegis of the crude doctrines of their dismal science, turn all rights into commodities to be bought and sold at market evaluation and try to force natives into marginal positions in the wage economy; the Christians who, not understanding their meaning and spiritual significance, ban the Potlatch, the Sun-dance, the White Dog Feast as superstitious and barbarous, and replace them with a ceremony in which the body and blood of a man/god is consumed; the teachers who, to civilize and educate, transport little children hundreds of miles from their families and communities and whip them for speaking their native tongues; the philosophers who, in their ignorance, settle Indian land claims by means of *a priori* quibbles amongst themselves. As for you and me, have we ever thought to help the native peoples by offering them as a compensation for their lands the blessings of our philosophy, religion, political theory, economics, technology, and education? And to what effect?

Conclusions

Argument Summarized

So far I have argued (a) that the widely recognized personal-security right protects us against psychic destruction and mutilation; (b) that there are well attested scientific theories in anthropology and psychology that can explain how the disruption of a culture's infrastructure (particularly land use) and other key sectors can produce personal pathology; (c) that there is abundant evidence that such pathology is widespread amongst Southern native peoples who have been subjected to massive cultural assaults; and (d) that racist and genetic explanations of the facts are implausible. It follows, then, that the personal security rights of Southern native peoples have probably been violated by the political, economic and other cultural arrangements — particularly those affecting their relation to the land — that we have forced upon them. This conclusion is in general agreement with what the native peoples themselves claim. Because of ignorance, our past wrongs may not be culpable; but, since we should now know better, future ones of the same sort would be.

First Conclusion

We can draw, then, a negative conclusion concerning aboriginal land rights in Northern Canada: namely, we must not impose a settlement that would violate the personal security rights of the peoples of those territories. This rules out certain types of proposals. For example, it rules out the radical proposals of the Liberals' 1969 White Paper, "Statement of the Government of Canada on Indian Policy."[14]

The 1969 White Paper, in the name of enlightened liberalism and perhaps in fear of Québécois separatism, proposed to abolish all forms of special status for aboriginal peoples and to force a quick-march enculturalization into industrial civilization. Those who couldn't adapt would be left to the tender mercies of provincial welfare legislation. Although the White Paper, as such, was shelved after a storm of protest, the underlying ideology and attitudes are still very much alive. They must be resisted and the implications for federalism accepted.

To be fair to the native people, we will have to give up some of our passion for symmetry and homogenization in political arrangements: a province is a province and all must be treated the same; all must have the same legal and social system; every Canadian must have exactly the same rights and must be able to move anywhere in the country without changing status. In a confederation allowing for various forms and degrees of special status for ethnic groups — whether aboriginals, Québécois or Newfoundlanders — it may seem that we are giving group rights priority over individual rights. But we are not really faced with a choice between individualism and collectivism. For as I tried to show in the case of the native peoples — a primary right to personal security can require, for its implementation, the recognition of certain group rights to land and culture. To violate the latter is, in certain circumstances, to violate the former.

Second Conclusion

Does this negative conclusion imply a *status quo* policy that would freeze development and prohibit change? Would it imply that Northern aboriginals be hived off in wilderness ghettos (reminiscent of the Bantustans of South Africa) and left to fend for themselves? No. The implication is only a modest conservatism which rules out certain kinds of forced change, change of the sort imposed on natives in the past.

Northern natives have already made changes from their traditional ways. They made a swift and successful adaptation from a nomadic/hunting/gathering culture to a nomadic/hunting/trading one, two or three hundred years ago. They desire further change now.

The nature and pacing of cultural change, however, must not be too drastic and swift for successful adaptation. Basic economic change should centrally and positively involve native skills and knowledge — as did the swift adaptation to the fur-trade economy — rather than something like the social and economic marginalization of natives in the later agricultural and industrial changes in the South. The changes should allow for the forms of personal and group autonomy required for successful adaptation and the development of healthy personalities.

These principles of successful change suggest a positive conclusion. The form of land settlement demanded by native peoples in the North is reasonable and consistent with their personal security rights. They want some form of self-determination within Confederation, perhaps through the creation of two new provinces, Denedeh and Nunavut, with their own special rules for land ownership and use. They want a mixed economy based principally on renewable resources which they can manage, with controlled and limited exploitation of non-renewable resources. They want control over education and other cultural institutions so that these can be made amenable to their changing needs and traditions.

In short, they believe that without balanced, carefully timed changes — changes over which they have a large measure of control — in the infrastructure, structure, and superstructure of their culture, they will be destroyed, not only as a people, but as people, not only as a group but as individuals. And, as I have tried to show, they are probably right.

NOTES

1. I am particularly indebted to E. Newbery and J. Dumont of the Native Studies Department of Laurentian University for providing me with reading materials used in their course, "North American Native People: Tradition and Culture." These were most useful in gaining some insight into the native perspective. A standard ethnographic work is Diamond Jenness, *The Indians of Canada*, 4th ed., Ottawa: National Museum of Canada, 1958. See also Dennis and Barbara Tedlock, *Teachings from the American Earth: Indian Religion and Philosophy*, New York: Liveright, 1975. A classic account of shamanism on the world scale is Mircea Eliade, *Shamanism: Archaic Techniques of Ecstasy*, Princeton: Princeton University Press, 1964. For a more personal attempt to understand the phenomena, see James Dumont, "Journey to Day-light Land — Through Ojibway Eyes," *Laurentian Review*, Vol. VIII, No. 2, 1976.

2. The quotation from Phillip Blake and the Dene Proposed Agreement are taken from *Dene Nation: The Colony Within*, ed. by Mel Watkins, Toronto: University of Toronto Press, 1977. The other native voices are from Mr. Justice Thomas R. Berger, *Northern Frontier, Northern Homeland: the Report of the Mackenzie Valley Pipeline Inquiry*. Vol. 1, Ottawa: Ministry of Supply and Services Canada, 1977. The latter in particular is highly recommended for its comprehensiveness, insight, and compassion.

3. For a massive compendium of international work on human rights since World War II, see Louis B. Sohn and Thomas Buergenthal, *International Protection of Human Rights*, Indianapolis: The Bobbs-Merril Co. Inc., 1973. For accounts of torture in the modern world, see the bulletins of Amnesty International. For a set of case studies and an insightful theoretical account of forms of psychological torture, see Robert Jay Lifton, *Thought Reform and the Psychology of Totalism: A Study of "Brainwashing" in China*, New York: W.W. Norton and Company, 1969.

4. For an argumentative survey of anthropological theories, see Marvin Harris, *The Rise of Anthropological Theory: A History of Theories of Culture*, New York: Harper & Row, 1968. For a popular, accessible survey of anthropology, see Peter Farb, *Humankind*, Boston: Houghton Mifflin Co., 1978. The position in the text is drawn from Harris's *Cultural Materialism: the Struggle for a Science of Culture*, New York: Random House, 1979. For a study of the sacred cow taboo and other case studies, see the latter and the more popular works, *Cows, Pigs, Wars and Witches: The Riddles of Culture*, New York: Vintage Books, 1978 and *Cannibals and Kings: The Origins of Cultures*, New York: Vintage Books, 1978. Harris's position bears some marked similarities with and departures from orthodox Marxist accounts of culture and social change. The present writer, while relying heavily on Harris, (a) finds important technical difficulties with the epistemology of his emic/etic distinction and (b) deplores the absence of a sophisticated psychological theory — whence the emphasis on (a) the significance of "native voices" and (b) developmental psychology in my account.

5. See Erik Erikson's seminal work, drawing upon but extending in important ways the Freudian revolution in psychology, *Childhood and Society*, 2nd ed., New York: W.W. Norton and Company, Inc., 1963, especially Part Two: "Childhood in Two American Indian Tribes." See also: *Insight and Responsibility*, New York: W.W. Norton and Company, Inc., 1964 and *Identity: Youth and Crisis*, New York: W.W. Norton and Company, Inc., 1968. An accessible survey of Piaget's theory can be found in *Piaget's Theory of Intellectual Development* by Herbet Ginsburg and Sylvia Opper, Englewood Cliffs: Prentice-Hall Inc., 1969. Some insights into the importance of myths and legends in child-nurturing among Amerindians were drawn from Hyemeyohsts Storm, *Seven Arrows*, New York: Harper & Row, 1972 and backed up by the child psychiatrist Bruno Bettelheim's *The Uses of Enchantment: The Meaning and Importance of Fairy Tales*, New York: Vintage Books, 1977. See also his *Love Is Not Enough*, New York: Avon Books, 1971 and *The Informed Heart*, New York: Avon Books, 1971.

6. I do not attempt to unravel here the complex relations amongst personhood, personal identity, and personality. But, as noted, I am drawing on the work of psychologists in personality theory. I am also assuming that certain human beings who have not developed into "full persons" — or who have declined from that state and become human derelicts — still have rights.

7. *Childhood and Society*, p. 36.

8. *Ibid.*, p. 111.

9. *Ibid.*, Part Two.

10. For a brutally frank, first-hand account of conditions on some Indian reserves, see Heather Robertson, *Reservations Are for Indians*, Toronto: James Lewis & Samuel, 1970. For statistics and an indication of the relation between personal pathology (in the form of alcoholism) and crime see Douglas A. Schmeiser et al., *The Native Offender and the Law*, prepared for the Law Reform Commission of Canada, 1974. See also the Hawthorn Committee Report, *A Survey of the Contemporary Indians of Canada*, 1967. It would be grossly unfair to those whom I have described as "human derelicts" produced by culture shock to leave the impression that they are without hope. The "powerful, baffling, cunning" disease of alcoholism, the chief form of personal pathology amongst native peoples, can be successfully fought through the cross-cultural program of Alcoholics Anonymous. A multi-faceted approach is required, but key elements seem to be a rediscovery of cultural roots and a form of spiritual growth. For theoretical perspectives, see Herbert Fingarette, *The Self in Transformation*, New York: Harper & Row, 1965 and Erik Erikson's *Young Man Luther, New York: W.W. Norton & Co., Inc., 1962, and Gandhi's Truth*, New York: W.W. Norton & Co., Inc., 1969. For relevant personal perspectives, see Lame Deer/ Richard Endoes, *Lame Deer: Seeker of Visions*, New York: Simon & Schuster, 1972, and Maria Campbell, *Halfbreed*, Toronto: McClelland and Stewart-Bantam Ltd., 1979. The creativity that can flourish amidst personal and cultural chaos is illustrated in the life of Norval Morrisseau: see his *Legends of My People: The Great Ojibway* (illustrated and told by Morrisseau, ed. by Selwyn Dewdney), Toronto: McGraw-Hill Ryerson Ltd., 1965, and Lister Sinclair and Jack Pollock, *The Art of Norval Morrisseau*, Toronto: Methuen, 1979.

11. The remarks of Magistrate Rice are quoted in James Burke, *Paper Tomahawks: From Red Tape to Red Power*, Winnipeg: Queenston House Publishing Inc., 1976.

12. For an account of Amerindian adaptability and cultural evolution see Peter Farb, *Man's Rise to Civilization, as Shown by the Indians of North America from Primeval Times to the Coming of the Industrial State*, New York: Avon Books, 1971. An antidote to Hollywood glamorization of European settlements is the revisionist history, *Bury My Heart at Wounded Knee: An Indian History of the American West*, by Dee Brown, New York: Bantam Books, 1972.

13. Perhaps the first commission of deliberate germ warfare was by the British general Lord Jeffrey Amherst in 1763 when he had smallpox-infested blankets and handkerchiefs distributed to his Indian enemies. (See Farb, p. 298).

14. For an Indian reaction to the 1969 White Paper, see Harold Cardinal, *The Unjust Society*, Edmonton: M.G. Hurtig Ltd., 1969.

QUESTIONS

1. Is there a right to personal security? Is it a universal right? How would you relate the personal-security principle to the protection-of-life or the avoidance-of-suffering principles that were introduced in earlier chapters?

2. Do J.T. Stevenson's arguments apply only to those native groups who have not signed treaties?

3. Do you think Stevenson has provided convincing reasons for rejecting the position outlined by Trudeau?

4. Does respect for the personal-security principle imply acceptance of some form of self-government on the part of Canada's native peoples?

➡ ⬅

SUGGESTIONS FOR FURTHER READING

- Because the matter of land claims has, throughout our history, been treated as a legal matter, much of the background discussion of the issues involved has been developed by our courts. In turn, commentary by legal scholars attempting to interpret and evaluate legal decisions has influenced social and political debate in significant ways. For that reason, the bibliography that follows has three sections. The first lists a number of cases that have had an important impact on the way in which our ideas about the moral foundation of land and self-government claims have been articulated. In this section, D.L.R. refers to the *Dominion Law Reports*. S.C.C. refers to a series of reports that set out the findings of the Supreme Court of Canada. Both series can be found in law libraries and often in other libraries as well; both D.L.R. and S.C.C. references are provided in each case. The second group identifies legal commentaries that provide insight into the legal and social dimensions of the issues involved. The third group is drawn from nonlegal sources including the writing of philosophers on the subject.

Important Cases

- *Calder v. Attorney-General of British Columbia* (1973), 34 D.L.R. (3D) 145 (S.C.C.) This case dealt with a land claim by the Nishga people in northern British Columbia. The decision proved to be significant in its acceptance of aboriginal land rights even though the court split evenly on the question. The Nishga people did have a legitimate claim to the land for which they were seeking title.
- *Delgamuukw v. The Queen* (1991), 79 D.L.R. (4th) 185 (B.C.S.C.) This judgement reflects a traditional form of reasoning with regard to native land claims that has its roots in Privy Council judgements of the last century.
- *Guerin v. The Queen* (1984), 13 D.L.R. (4th) 321 (S.C.C.) The court decided that the government had a trustlike responsibility to use its powers respecting native lands in a manner that reflected native interests and concerns.
- *Simon v. The Queen* (1984), 13 D.L.R. (4th) 390 (S.C.C.) This case had to do with a treaty signed with aboriginal peoples in the 1750s. The court ruled that the treaty was still valid and blocked the application of provincial game laws in the area concerned.
- *R. v. Sioui* (1990), 70 D.L.R. (4th) 427 (S.C.C.) In this case, the court was asked to consider whether Huron customary law continued to have authority given a treaty signed with incoming British forces in the eighteenth century. The court upheld the treaty, said its provisions were still valid, and gave Huron customary law precedence over provincial law in the matter at issue.
- *R. v. Sparrow* (1990), 70 D.L.R. (4th) 385 (S.C.C.) This case provided the Supreme Court with its first opportunity to interpret Section 35 of the Constitution Act of 1982, which recognizes existing aboriginal and treaty rights. The Court held that this section guarantees protection to any aboriginal or treaty right that had not been completely extinguished prior to 1982 even if the exercise of the right had been narrowly constrained. What this meant was that the court could then review the way in which exercise of the right had been regulated and decide whether the restrictions were justifiable.

Books and Articles

- Michael Asch, *Home and Native Land: Aboriginal Rights and the Canadian Constitution* (Toronto: Methuen, 1984). Writing from an anthropological point of view, this writer explores the idea of aboriginal self-government and argues for its acceptability.

- Leroy Little Bear, Menno Bolt, and J. Anthony Log, eds., *Pathways to Self-Determination: Canadian Indians and the Canadian State* (Toronto: University of Toronto Press, 1985). This is an anthology with native and non-native contributors on the topic of self-determination and self-government.
- Menno Bolt and J. Anthony Long, eds., *The Quest for Justice: Aboriginal People and Aboriginal Rights* (Toronto: University of Toronto Press, 1985). This book is an anthology that takes up a variety of issues arising from the idea of aboriginal rights.
- Hugh Brody, *Maps and Dreams: Indians and the British Columbia Frontier* (Toronto: Penguin, 1983). The chapters in this book alternate between accounts of personal experiences with natives and their culture and thematic discussions of the issues raised by those experiences.
- Diane Engelstad and John Bird, eds., *Nation to Nation: Aboriginal Sovereignty and the Future of Canada* (Concord, Ontario: Anansi Press, 1992). This is a book which attempts to tell the story of aboriginal/Canadian relations down through the years from the perspective of both aboriginal and non-aboriginal authors. It has three parts. In the first, authors describe the pursuit of sovereignty to the 1990s. Part II describes how aboriginal people have been working out their visions of sovereignty and self-determination within the realities of their own communities. Part III looks at the non-native support for aboriginal rights.
- Kent McNeil, *Common Law Aboriginal Title* (Oxford: Clarendon Press, 1989). The author's purpose in this book is to argue that aboriginal land title can be grounded in English common law.
- Dennis McPherson and Doug Rabb, *Indian from the Inside* (Lakehead, Ontario: Lakehead University, 1991). This book, which is available from Lakehead University, was prepared by Doug Rabb, a philosopher teaching at that university, and Dennis McPherson, a native social worker and graduate of Lakehead University, for use in a philosophy course entitled "Native Canadian World Views." It attempts to construct an understanding of native thinking on a wide range of issues.
- J.R. Miller, *Skyscrapers Hide the Heavens: A History of Indian-White Relations in Canada* (Toronto: University of Toronto Press, 1989). The title of this book explains its content.
- Anastasia M. Shkilnky, *A Poison Stronger Than Love: The Destruction of an Ojibwa Community* (New Haven: Yale University Press, 1985). The author describes the effect on an Ojibwa community of a move from traditional lands to a new reserve. The move was necessitated by mercury pollution in the rivers on which the community depended.
- Brian Slattery, "Aboriginal Sovereignty and Imperial Claims: Reconstructing North American History," *Osgoode Hall Law Journal*, vol. 29, no. 4 (1991). In this paper, the author examines and rejects the thesis central to the approach of European law that aboriginal America was vacant territory when first discovered by Europeans. He then attempts to identify basic principles of justice that could provide the reference points for fair settlement of aboriginal land and sovereignty claims.
- — "The Hidden Constitution: Aboriginal Rights in Canada," *American Journal of Comparative Law*, vol. 32 (1984): 361. Most analyses of native rights start from assumptions central to European political and legal traditions. Brian Slattery argues in this paper that an adequate view of aboriginal rights in Canada cannot be grounded on those assumptions alone. In this paper, he examines the history of diplomatic relations between the imperial powers who, for a wide variety of reasons, found it necessary to negotiate with the native people to secure their imperial objectives and constructs from his study a view

of aboriginal rights based on the character of the diplomatic relations that resulted.

- —, "The Organic Constitution: Aboriginal Peoples and the Evolution of Canada," *Osgoode Hall Law Journal* (publication pending). In this article, Slattery argues that despite recent advances in the law of aboriginal rights, most Canadian lawyers still tacitly view the Constitution as the outgrowth of European legal traditions transplanted into North America. The paper identifies the main features of this model of the Constitution and proposes a more appropriate model to replace it. The alternative focuses on the Constitution's deep roots in Canadian history and traditions, and acknowledges the distinctive contributions of aboriginal peoples and their long-standing relations with the Crown.

- "Symposium on Aboriginal Land Rights," *Australian Journal of Philosophy,* vol. 68, no. 3 (September 1990). This issue of the journal carries two articles, "Land Rights and Aboriginal Sovereignty" and "Land, Well-Being and Compensation," that explore the issue of aboriginal rights from an Australian perspective. These articles have the virtue of examining the range of issues faced by Canadians as they have arisen in the Australian context and provide a good basis for comparing the development of land claims and self-government questions in the two countries.

- Mary Ellen Turpel, "Aboriginal Peoples and the Canadian Charter: Interpretive Monopolies, Cultural Differences," *Canadian Human Rights Yearbook*, vol. 6 (1989–90): 3. The theme of this book is that because of significant cultural differences, Canadian courts should take into consideration the native point of view in interpreting the Constitution and its bearing on aboriginal rights.

Chapter 8

Poverty

Introduction

It may not be clear to everyone who reads this book that the topic of poverty properly belongs in a book about contemporary moral issues. That is not to say that poverty does not pose a serious social problem. Clearly it does. However, if it is an issue, it has some quite distinctive characteristics. To begin with, unlike abortion or euthanasia or affirmative action or any of the other topics discussed in these pages, poverty is not the obvious or intended consequence of individual or government decision making. It is clearly not a problem that can be solved by individuals acting alone. It is not even clear that it is a problem that can be solved by national governments, since poverty is not just a local but also a global phenomenon. Like wars and famines in other parts of the world, poverty outside our national borders is something widely regretted, but for which responsibility is not readily assumed or easily assigned.

Seen from a moral perspective, poverty is also in many respects a hidden or disguised problem. There seem to be two reasons for this. First, none of us can be certain we will not face the reality of a painful death. No one with an extended network of family or friends can be sure that people who are close to them will not be touched directly or indirectly by an unwanted pregnancy. Native land claims are a political issue that we cannot avoid as Canadians. Environmental degradation is no respecter of persons. But many of us seem to believe that whatever else life might have in store for us, poverty, at least, is something we can guard carefully against.

This last observation points to a second factor that does play a role, sometimes hidden, sometimes explicit, when the topic is under discussion. Because we tend to think of poverty as a condition that we can avoid with planning and hard work, it is not unusual for us to assume that others should be able to do so as well. As a consequence, poverty carries with it a kind of social stigma. People who find themselves gripped by poverty are frequently ashamed of their condition. For many, poverty is a morally blameworthy condition, one which it is rather easy to assume could be avoided by hard work. And if most of us can avoid it, why cannot the rest do so as well?

These are not thoughts easily set aside. Yet they deserve careful evaluation. For the issue of poverty, though distinctive in many respects, does intersect with each of the principles that have guided our introductory discussions throughout this book. Poverty is life threatening. The mortality rates of infants and children born into poverty is much higher than is the case generally where poverty is not a factor. Those who are poor are much less able to ward off life-threatening illness, or to recover from serious and even not-so-serious accidents than are those with a reasonable income. Hence, it is difficult to avoid the conclusion that we have an obligation to protect life, and thus an obligation to respond to the causes of poverty.

Suffering and poverty are also frequent companions because of poor health care, inadequate shelter, limited educational opportunities, and so on. If there is a general obligation to attempt to alleviate suffering, then surely there is an obligation to seek to alleviate suffering brought on by poverty. The same would appear to apply to the moral autonomy principle. Poverty clearly impedes the ability of those afflicted by it to direct their own lives in accordance with values of their own choosing.

Finally, it is widely thought that poverty is a condition that both invites and attracts discrimination. If this claim is true, then the equal worth principle also has application to this issue.

The difficulty, however, is to work out what application the principles do have in this case and what they generate by way of rights and obligations. For reasons already set out, this task is not an easy one.

Background Considerations

Human beings are interdependent. As individuals, all of us at some points in our lives depend on a support structure for our survival and our well-being. As infants and children in old age, when ill or injured, in the face of natural calamities, for example, crop failures or floods or earthquakes, we can become utterly dependent on the support of others to see us through.

Poverty also illustrates human interdependence. And it is something to which throughout human history human beings have felt an obligation to respond. They have done so in a variety of ways. Many societies have assigned the responsibility to lend a helping hand to families. Some societies have understood responses to poverty to be a religious obligation often associated with tithing, the giving of alms, or charitable donations. Indeed, European societies have relied heavily throughout their history on religious and charitable institutions in dealing with the poor. This pattern continues to be an influential one in our society today as evidenced by soup kitchens, food banks, clothing drives and a plethora of charitable organizations that are supported by donations from private citizens.

Increasingly, however, dealing with poverty has come to be seen as a government responsibility. In Canada, the impetus for this development can be traced to the Great Depression of the 1930s. Faced with social devastation resulting from the collapse of the economy, populist political movements took shape with a view to persuading the country that the pursuit of social justice should be accepted as a government responsibility. Rooted most firmly on the prairies in the first instance, this movement led to the creation of a new party, the CCF (the Cooperative Commonwealth Federation), which won office in Saskatchewan in 1944. The result was, among other things, the first provincial public health insurance program, which then served as the model for the Canadian public heath insurance program, today providing a high standard of medical services to all Canadians regardless of ability to pay. This development was accompanied by federal and provincial legislation creating a comprehensive social welfare safety net whose goal has been, among other things, to alleviate the effects of poverty in its various forms.

Although the focus of increasing debate and controversy, the social safety net put in place in the 1950s and 60s continues to constitute this country's principle response to the problem of poverty. Publicly funded social welfare, though varying in form from country to country, is today the basic response to poverty in Western industrialized societies.

At the international level, the picture is a good deal less clear. A fundamental social response in first world countries takes the form of donations on the part of individuals to international aid and famine relief agencies like the Red Cross and Save the Children. Western governments have also created publicly funded agencies like the Canadian International Development Agency, more commonly known as CIDA, much of whose work has been designed to eliminate poverty by fostering conditions of economic development. Finally, international organizations like the United Nations have attempted to focus world attention on poverty and to stimulate and coordinate efforts to alleviate it.

The Current Situation

Canadians are on the whole a fortunate people. Canada has been judged by the United Nations *Human Development Report* for the fourth year running as the best place in the world to live measured by reference to health, education, and income. In spite of this ranking, however, there are great disparities in the distribution of income in this country. If we accept Statistics Canada low-income cut-offs as the definition of poverty, then in 1994 over 16 percent of Canadians were living below the poverty line. Again in 1994, using Statistics Canada low-income cut-offs, 57 percent of single-parent mothers under the age 65 with children under the age of 18, 89 percent of single mothers under the age of 25 and 1.3 million or 19.1 percent of Canadian children lived in poverty. In the same year, a total of 226,000 families and 367,000 unattached people had incomes that amounted to less than half what the National Council of Welfare describes as the poverty line. (For a detailed analysis, see the National Council of Welfare *Poverty Profile, 1994,* referenced in the attached bibliography.)

Neither is poverty particularly easy to escape in Canada. The unemployment rate has remained in excess of 9 percent for several years. Many of those who are employed have part-time jobs that pay the minimum wage and have no benefits. Many of those living below what the National Welfare Council has defined as the poverty line are what have come to be called the working poor. Equally important, with cutbacks in government spending and private sector downsizing, people who once thought they had secure, well-paying jobs are now finding themselves unemployed, with very uncertain job prospects.

All of this is accompanied today by austerity budgets and significant reductions in social welfare programs, unemployment insurance, and other social safety net provisions.

Poverty is clearly a matter of concern for Canadians. However, it is a problem of much greater proportions internationally. According to the United Nations *Human Development Report*, the income of the poorest 20 percent of the world's population has been declining steadily over the past fifteen years. Their share of the world's income is now only 1.4 percent, while the richest 20 percent of the world's population now receive 85 percent of the world's income. Disparities between rich and poor are enormous. As an illustration, the combined assets of the world's 358 billionaires is now reported to exceed the total annual income of 2.3 billion people at the bottom end of the income scale, or 45 percent of the world's population. Set out in human terms, what these disparities in income signal is a world in which great wealth coexists with great poverty.

The Moral Dimension

The fact of poverty raises two questions from a moral perspective. Do individuals who are relatively speaking well off have an individual or a collective moral obligation to seek to alleviate poverty? If the answer to this question is yes, then what is the nature of those responsibilities? Posed this way, these questions appear simple. Yet they hide a complex range of moral perplexities. As individuals and as a society, if we decide that pornography is immoral and should not be allowed, we can refuse to consume it and we can support government measures designed to render it illegal. The same could be said of the other issues addressed elsewhere in this book. Responding to the phenomenon of poverty is another matter. It is true that individuals can choose to share their wealth with the poor. Indeed, many do.

However, charity raises moral quandaries. It can be demeaning, however well intentioned. It can create dependence as well as the illusion that problems are being solved, when in fact they are not. Further, taken by itself, it is unlikely that the problem of poverty in today's world can be effectively addressed by private generosity, however important such gestures might be as acts of social solidarity.

Government intervention is an obvious alternative response to poverty. Furthermore, whatever else might be said for or against it, legislative responses can be effective. For example, the poverty rate in Canada of those older than 65 has been dropping steadily since the 1960s and now stands at about 17.2 percent (though this trend may well be reversing itself in response to changing government policies). These changes are clearly the result of the introduction of such things as public medical insurance and government-financed old age pensions. At the same time, legislatively imposed transfers of wealth from one group to another inevitably raise issues of justice, efficiency, and effectiveness.

The problems are even more acute at the international level, where legislative tools are mostly non-existent. Here the favoured tool is international aid. At this level, the pursuit of social justice and charity seem once more to converge with implications and consequences that are notoriously difficult both to predict and assess.

Even assuming the existence of policy instruments adequate to the task, we are faced with determining how much is enough. When it comes to alleviating poverty, how far do the obligations of individuals and states extend?

None of these questions are easily addressed. All of them are touched on in one form or another in the readings that follow.

The Readings

We begin with selected articles from the *International Covenant on Economic, Social and Cultural Rights*. The covenant is significant because it specifies what its signatories concur are universal rights, and the obligations of governments that follow from their recognition. The second reading is an extract from the 1995 United Nations *Human Development Report*. The extract chosen points to both the progress that has been made globally in this century in human development and the problems that yet remain.

The next reading by Trudy Govier looks at three different views of the responsibilities of a modern state confronted with the issue of poverty. She ties the discussion of welfare to basic moral principles and rights like the right to life and argues that supportive welfare systems are justified as preconditions for the exercise of important human rights. Amartya Sen then evaluates and supports the thesis that human beings have a right not to be hungry. Finally, Alistair Macleod examines one of the most common arguments for inequality in the distribution of resources, the need for incentives. He argues that standard justifications of incentives leading to inequality in the distribution of resources are not persuasive.

INTERNATIONAL COVENANT ON ECONOMIC, SOCIAL AND CULTURAL RIGHTS

[Published by The United Nations]

PREAMBLE

The States Parties to this Convention,

Considering that, in accordance with the principles proclaimed in the Charter of the United Nations, recognition of the inherent dignity and of the equal and inalienable rights of all members of the human family is the foundation of freedom, justice and peace in the world,

Recognizing that these rights derive from the inherent dignity of the human person,

Recognizing that, in accordance with the Universal Declaration of Human Rights, the ideal of free human beings enjoying freedom from fear and want can only be achieved if conditions are created whereby everyone may enjoy his economic, social and cultural rights, as well as his civil and political rights,

Considering the obligation of States under the Charter of the United Nations to promote universal respect for, and observance of, human rights and freedoms,

Realizing that the individual, having duties to other individuals and to the community to which he belongs, is under a responsibility to strive for the promotion and observance of the rights recognized in the present Covenant,

Agree upon the following articles:

PART I

Article 1

1. All peoples have the right of self-determination. By virtue of that right they freely determine their political status and freely pursue their economic, social and cultural development.

2. All peoples may, for their own ends, freely dispose of their natural wealth and resources without prejudice to any obligations arising out of international economic cooperation,

based upon the principle of mutual benefit, and international law. In no case may a people be deprived of its own means of subsistence.

PART II

Article 2

1. Each State Party to the present Covenant undertakes to take steps, individually and through international assistance and co-operation, especially economic and technical, to the maximum of its available resources, with a view to achieving progressively the full realization of the rights recognized in the present Covenant by all appropriate means, including particularly the adoption of legislative measures.

2. The States Parties to the present Covenant undertake to guarantee that the rights enunciated in the present Covenant will be exercised without discrimination of any kind as to race, colour, sex, language, religion, political or other opinion, national or social origin, property, birth or other status.

Article 3

The States Parties to the present Covenant undertake to ensure the equal right of men and women to the enjoyment of all economic, social and cultural rights set forth in the present Covenant.

Article 4

The States Parties to the present Covenant recognize that, in the enjoyment of those rights provided by the State in conformity with the present Covenant, the State may subject such rights only to such limitations as are determined by law only in so far as this may be compatible with the nature of these rights and solely for the purpose of promoting the general welfare in a democratic society.

Part III

Article 6

1. The States Parties to the present Covenant recognize the right to work, which includes the right of everyone to the opportunity to gain his living by work which he freely chooses or accepts, and will take appropriate steps to safeguard this right.

2. The steps to be taken by a State Party to the present Covenant to achieve the full realization of this right shall include technical and vocational guidance and training programmes, policies and techniques to achieve steady economic, social and cultural development and full and productive employment under conditions safeguarding fundamental political and economic freedoms to the individual.

Article 7

The States Parties to the present Covenant recognize the right of everyone to the enjoyment of just and favourable conditions of work which ensure, in particular:

(a) Remuneration which provides all workers, as a minimum, with:

(i) Fair wages and equal remuneration for work of equal value without distinction of any kind, in particular women being guaranteed conditions of work not inferior to those enjoyed by men, with equal pay for equal work;

(ii) A decent living for themselves and their families in accordance with the provisions of the present Covenant;

(b) Safe and healthy working conditions;

(c) Equal opportunity for everyone to be promoted in his employment to an appropriate higher level, subject to no considerations other than those of seniority and competence;

(d) Rest, leisure and reasonable limitation of working hours and periodic holidays with pay, as well as remuneration for public holidays.

Article 9

The States Parties to the present Covenant recognize the right of everyone to social security, including social insurance.

Article 11

1. The States Parties to the present Covenant recognize the right of everyone to an adequate standard of living for himself and his family, including adequate food, clothing and housing, and to the continuous improvement of living conditions. The States Parties will take appropriate steps to ensure the realization of this right, recognizing to this effect the essential importance of international co-operation based on free consent.

2. The States Parties to the present Covenant, recognizing the fundamental right of everyone to be free from hunger, shall take, individually and through international cooperation, the measures, including specific programmes, which are needed:

(a) To improve methods of production, conservation and distribution of food by making full use of technical and scientific knowledge, by disseminating knowledge of the principles of nutrition and by developing or reforming agrarian systems in such a way as to achieve the most efficient development and utilization of natural resources;

(b) Taking into account the problems of both food-importing and food-exporting countries, to ensure an equitable distribution of world food supplies in relation to need.

Article 12

1. The States Parties to the present Covenant recognize the right of everyone to the enjoyment of the highest attainable standard of physical and mental health.

Article 13

1. The States Parties to the present Covenant recognize the right of everyone to education.
They agree that education shall be directed to the full development of the human personality and the sense of its dignity, and shall strengthen the respect for human rights and
fundamental freedoms. They further agree that education shall enable all persons to participate effectively in a free society, promote understanding, tolerance and friendship among all
nations and all racial, ethnic or religious groups, and further the activities of the United
Nations for the maintenance of peace.

THE STATE OF HUMAN DEVELOPMENT

The real wealth of a nation is its people — both women and men. And the purpose of
development is to create an enabling environment for people to enjoy long, healthy and
creative lives. This simple but powerful truth is too often forgotten in the pursuit of material
and financial wealth.

Concept and Measurement Revisited

Human development is a process of enlarging people's choices. In principle, these choices
can be infinite and can change over time. But at all levels of development, the three
essential ones are for people to lead a long and healthy life, to acquire knowledge and to
have access to the resources needed for a decent standard of living. If these essential
choices are not available, many other opportunities remain inaccessible.

But human development does not end there. Additional choices, highly valued by many
people, range from political, economic and social freedom to opportunities for being creative and productive and enjoying personal self-respect and guaranteed human rights.

Human development thus has two sides. One is the formation of human capabilities —
such as improved health, knowledge and skills. The other is the use people make of their
acquired capabilities — for productive purposes, for leisure or for being active in cultural,

social and political affairs. If the scales of human development do not finely balance the two sides, much human frustration can result.

According to the concept of human development, income clearly is only one option that people would like to have, though certainly an important one. But it is not the sum-total of their lives. The purpose of development is to enlarge all human choices, not just income.

The concept of human development is much broader than the conventional theories of economic development. Economic growth models deal with expanding GNP rather than enhancing the quality of human lives. Human resource development treats human beings primarily as an input in the production process — a means rather than an end. Welfare approaches look at human beings as beneficiaries and not as agents of change in the development process. The basic needs approach focuses on providing material goods and services to deprived population groups rather than on enlarging human choices in all fields.

Human development, by contrast, brings together the production and distribution of commodities and the expansion and use of human capabilities. Encompassing these earlier concerns, human development goes beyond them. It analyses all issues in society — whether economic growth, trade, employment, political freedom or cultural values — from the perspective of people. It thus focuses on enlarging human choices — and it applies equally to developing and industrial countries.

Human development also encompasses elements that constitute the critical issues of gender and development. There are four major elements in the concept of human development — productivity, equity, sustainability and empowerment (box 1.1). Through enhanced capabilities, the creativity and productivity of people must be increased so that they become effective agents of growth. Economic growth must be combined with equitable distribution of its benefits. Equitable opportunities must be available both to present and to future generations. And all people, women and men, must be empowered to participate in the design and implementation of key decisions that shape their lives.

Human development is impossible without gender equality. As long as women are excluded from the development process, development will remain weak and lopsided. Sustainable human development implies engendering the development paradigm.

BOX 1.1

FOUR ESSENTIAL COMPONENTS OF THE HUMAN DEVELOPMENT PARADIGM

The human development paradigm contains four main components:

- *Productivity.* People must be enabled to increase their productivity and to participate fully in the process of income generation and remunerative employment. Economic growth is, therefore, a subset of human development models.

- *Equity.* People must have access to equal opportunities. All barriers to economic and political opportunities must be eliminated so that people can participate in, and benefit from, these opportunities.

- *Sustainability.* Access to opportunities must be ensured not only for the present generations but for future generations as well. All forms of capital — physical, human, environmental — should be replenished.

- *Empowerment.* Development must be by people, not only *for* them. People must participate fully in the decisions and processes that shape their lives.

The human development index was constructed to reflect the most important dimensions of human development. A composite index, the HDI contains three indicators: life expectancy, representing a long and healthy life; educational attainment, representing knowledge; and real GDP (in purchasing power parity dollars), representing a decent standard of living. . . . .

The concept of human development has gone beyond its basic premises to emphasize the sustainability of the development process. It not only puts people at the centre of development. It also advocates protecting the life opportunities of future generations as well as present generations and respecting the natural systems on which all life depends.

Sustainable human development addresses both equity within generations and equity among generations — enabling all generations, present and future, to make the best use of their capabilities. It brings the development process within the carrying capacity of nature, giving the highest priority to environmental regeneration — to protect the opportunities of future generations.

This issue of sustainability has many dimensions: capacity, environment and institutions. If the development process does not create institutions fully supportive of people's rights, it cannot be sustainable in the long run. Human development thus emphasizes strengthening the institutions of both government and civil society so that the entire development process becomes internally sustainable.

State of Human Progress

An objective review of the state of human affairs reveals that humanity has advanced on several critical fronts in the past 50 years:

- Most states are now independent.
- With the end of the cold war, the world has been made increasingly safe from the threat of nuclear holocaust. And with the reduction of global military spending, there is a potential peace dividend that can be mobilized for human development.
- The speed of human development has been unprecedented, with developing countries setting a pace three times faster than that of the industrial countries a century ago.
- Human ingenuity has led to many technological breakthroughs, particularly in information, communication, medicine and space exploration.
- An irrepressible wave of human freedom is sweeping across many lands — and the human spirit, long suppressed, is beginning to find its voice.

Despite this progress, a long agenda of human deprivation still awaits:

- We still live in a world characterized by hunger, poverty and increasing disparities.
- We also live in a world of disturbing contrasts — with hunger in some lands and waste of food in others, and with the disparity between rich and poor nations widening constantly.
- Poor nations as well as rich are afflicted by growing human distress — in the form of a weakening social fabric, threats to personal security and a spreading sense of individual isolation.
- The threats to human security are no longer personal or local or national. They are global — with drugs, HIV/AIDS, terrorism and pollution roaming the world.

- There are now more conflicts within nations than between nations, and the social and political fabric of several nations is beginning to disintegrate.
- The basic question of human survival on an environmentally fragile planet has gained urgency.

What is the nature of the world we live in? What are the broader trends in the political, social and economic arenas? A better understanding of these issues can help put the trends of human progress and human deprivation in a clearer perspective.

Political and Social Change

- Today, between two-thirds and three-quarters of the world's people live under relatively pluralistic and democratic regimes. In 1993 alone, elections were held in 43 countries — in some for the first time.
- The end of apartheid and the emergence of a free independent South Africa in the 1990s mark a turning point for humanity. More than half of the African states are now undertaking democratic reforms and renewing civil society.
- While the democratic transition has raised human hopes in many lands, there has also been a disturbing revival of ethnic conflicts. These conflicts are mainly internal, among people, rather than external, among countries — and more than 90% of the casualties are civilians.
- Today, one in 200 people in the world is a refugee or a displaced person. Between 1970 and 1994, the number of refugees in the world increased ninefold, from 3 million to 27 million.

Globalization of Economies

- The world has become a global financial village. During 1965–90, world merchandise trade tripled, and trade in services increased more than fourteenfold.
- But the poorest 20% of the world's people have benefited little from the increased globalization of economies. In world trade, their share is only 1% — and in world commercial lending, a scant 0.2%.
- Private investment flows to developing countries increased from $5 billion to nearly $160 billion during 1970–93. But three-fourths of these flows went to ten countries, mostly in East Asia and Latin America. At the same time, the external debt of developing countries in 1993 amounted to more than $1.8 trillion, and their debt service rose to 22% of export earnings.

Economic Growth and Structure

- The world today is richer than it was in 1950. During 1950–92, world income increased from $4 trillion to $23 trillion, and in per capita terms it more than tripled, with important implications for the environment and sustainability.
- More than three-fourths of the world's people live in developing countries, but they enjoy only 16% of the world's income — while the richest 20% have 85% of global income.
- The structure of global production has changed significantly. The contribution of agriculture to GDP in both low-income and middle-income countries has fallen by a third in the past three decades — while the share of industry in GDP increased by nearly a third in low-income countries.

Labour Force and Employment

- More than one-fourth of the labour force in developing countries and more than two-thirds of that in industrial countries are now in services. But in developing countries, nearly 60% of the labour force is still in agriculture.
- During the past three decades, employment has consistently lagged behind economic growth in some regions. And today, the world is facing a large shortage of jobs — with about 35 million job-seekers in industrial countries and a need for one billion new jobs in developing countries during the next decade.
- In developing countries, the informal sector is growing almost everywhere. In Latin America, more than 30% of all nonagricultural workers were in the informal sector at the end of the 1980s. In 1990, the informal sector in Sub-Saharan Africa employed more than 60% of the urban workforce — more than twice the share of the modern sector.

Technological Progress

- Rapid technological progress has revolutionized people's lives. Today, a network of 19 satellites provides public service channels in 180 countries.
- Computer technology has gone through more than four phases in the span of one person's lifetime. In 1993, world sales of computer terminals exceeded 12 million units.
- Basic immunization saves the lives of three million children every year in developing countries.

Environment

- Environmental degradation poses a major threat to human security. As many as 70,000 square kilometres of farmland are abandoned each year as a result of degradation, and about 4 million hectares of rain-fed cropland are lost annually to soil erosion.
- In Europe, 475,000 square kilometres of forest area, an area larger than Germany, have been damaged by air pollution. The resulting economic loss is about $35 billion a year, equal to Hungary's GDP.

Four Conclusions

An arresting picture of hope and fear, of unprecedented human progress and unspeakable human misery — that is what emerges from two simple balance sheets of human progress and deprivation over the past three decades for developing and industrial countries (boxes 1.2 and 1.3).

With human advances on some fronts and retreats on several others, the following conclusions can be drawn from a complex maze of data:

1. The developing world has witnessed unprecedented improvement in human development in the past 30 years. It has covered as much distance during those 30 years as the industrial world did in a century. Life expectancy is now 17 years longer than it was in 1960. Infant mortality has been more than halved. The combined enrolment in primary and secondary school is nearly 1.5 times higher. The human development disparities between the North and the South have diminished sharply. Even though the South has a per capita GNP that is a mere 6% of the North's, it now has a life expectancy that is 85%, and nutritional levels and adult literacy that are 81%, of those in the North.

2. Despite this progress, considerable human deprivation remains in both the developing and the industrial world. In developing countries, one person in three lives in poverty. Even basic social services — primary health care, basic education, safe water and adequate nutrition — are not available to more than one billion people. About 90% of the 17 million people infected with HIV are in developing countries. In the industrial world, about 100 million people are still below the official poverty line, though social safety nets help protect them. And many people are insecure — with threats coming from drugs, homelessness, unemployment, pollution, AIDS and crime.

3. Rapid human progress is possible, development cooperation works, and much more can be done by focusing national and international energy on essential targets. That is what the experience of the past 30 years shows. It also shows that a lack of resources is often an excuse for a lack of proper priorities. Sufficient resources can be generated for the essential human agenda by cutting excessive military spending, privatizing inefficient public enterprises and realigning development priorities.

4. The key human development challenges for the next century will require global compacts. These challenges include reducing population growth, providing basic social services to all deprived people, accelerating job-led growth, creating an external environment conducive to growth, particularly by dismantling trade and investment barriers, and making global compacts for alleviating poverty and improving the physical environment.

BOX 1.2

Balance sheet of human development — developing countries

PROGRESS	DEPRIVATION
HEALTH	
• During 1960–92, average life expectancy increased by more than a third. By now, 30 countries have achieved a life expectancy of more than 70 years. • Over the past three decades, the population with access to safe water almost doubled, from 36% to 70%.	• About 17 million people die every year from infectious and parasitic diseases, such as diarrhoea, malaria and tuberculosis. • More than 90% of the 17 million HIV-infected people live in developing countries.
EDUCATION	
• Net enrolment at the primary level increased by nearly two-thirds during the past 30 years, from 48% in 1960 to 77% in 1991.	• About 130 million children at the primary level and more than 275 million at the secondary level are out of school.
FOOD AND NUTRITION	
• Despite rapid population growth, per capita food production rose by more than 20% during the past decade.	• Nearly 800 million people do not get enough food, and about 500 million people are chronically malnourished.

PROGRESS	DEPRIVATION

INCOME AND POVERTY

• During the past decade, both agriculture and industry expanded at an annual rate of more than 3% in developing countries.	• Almost a third of the population, about 1.3 billion people, live below the poverty line.

WOMEN

• The combined primary and secondary enrolment of girls increased from 38% to 68% during the past two decades. • During the past two decades, fertility rates declined by more than a third.	• Maternal mortality in developing countries, at 350 per 100,000 live births, is about nine times higher than that in OECD countries. • Women hold about 10% of parliamentary seats.

CHILDREN

• In 1960–92, the infant mortality rate was more than halved, from 149 per thousand live births to 70. • During the past two decades, the lives of about three million children were saved every year through the extension of basic immunization.	• More than a third of children are malnourished and underweight. • The under-five mortality rate, at 100 per thousand live births, is still nearly seven times higher than that in industrial countries.

ENVIRONMENT

• Developing countries' contribution to global emissions is less than a fourth that of industrial countries, even though their population is 3.5 times larger.	• About 200 million people are severely affected by desertification. • Every year, some 20 million hectares of tropical forest are cleared outright or grossly degraded.

POLITICS AND CONFLICTS

• More than two-thirds of the population in developing countries live under relatively pluralistic and democratic regimes.	• At the end of 1993, there were more than 13 million refugees in the developing world.

BOX 1.3

Balance sheet of human development — industrial countries

PROGRESS	DEPRIVATION

HEALTH

• By 1992, 24 industrial countries had achieved a life expectancy of more than 75 years.	• More than 1.5 million people are infected with HIV.

EDUCATION

- The tertiary enrolment ratio more than doubled between 1960 and 1991, from 15% to 40%.

- More than a third of adults have less than an upper-secondary education.

INCOME AND EMPLOYMENT

- Between 1972 and 1992, real per capita GNP grew by 46%.
- The annual rate of inflation is now less than 4%.

- The total unemployment rate is more than 8%, and the rate among youths nearly 15%. More than 35 million people are seeking jobs.
- The poorest 40% of households get only 18% of total income.

WOMEN

- In science and technology at the tertiary level, the number of girls per 100 boys has more than doubled, from 25 in 1970 to 67 in 1990.
- Women now make up more than 40% of the labour force and hold about 28% of administrative and managerial positions.

- Women's non-agricultural wage rate is still only three-fourths of men's.
- Women hold only 12% of parliamentary seats.

SOCIAL SECURITY

- Social security expenditures account for about 16% of GDP.

- About 100 million people live below the poverty line.
- More than five million people are homeless.

SOCIAL FABRIC

- There are more than five library books and one radio for every person, one TV set for every two people. One in three people reads a newspaper.

- More than a third of marriages end in divorce, and about 7% of households are headed by a single female parent.
- Nearly 130,000 rapes are reported annually in the age group 15–59.

ENVIRONMENT

- Between 1965 and 1991, energy use per $10 of GDP was cut dramatically, from 168 kilograms of oil equivalent to 25 kilograms, through aggressive conservation measures and more appropriate pricing policies.

- Each year, damage to forests due to air pollution leads to economic losses of about $35 billion in Europe alone — equivalent to Hungary's GDP.
- People in industrial countries constitute a little more than a fifth of the world's population but consume nearly nine times more commercial energy per capita than people in developing countries.

Note: In the balance sheets, *industrial countries* excludes countries in Eastern Europe and the Commonwealth of Independent States (CIS).

QUESTIONS

1. The *Human Development Report* identifies three indicators of human development. What are those indicators? Do they have the importance that the authors of the report ascribe to them?
2. In your view, is it a matter of moral concern that the gap between rich and poor in the world today is growing?
3. Among the concerns the report raises, are environmental issues central or peripheral?
4. Should we as human beings recognize a universal human right not to be hungry?

THE RIGHT TO EAT AND THE DUTY TO WORK

Trudy Govier

Although the topic of welfare is not one with which philosophers have often concerned themselves, it is a topic which gives rise to many complex and fascinating questions — some in the area of political philosophy, some in the area of ethics, and some of a more practical kind. The variety of issues related to the subject of welfare makes it particularly necessary to be clear just which issue one is examining in a discussion of welfare. In a recent book on the subject, Nicholas Rescher asks:

> In what respects and to what extent is society, working through the instrumentality of the state, responsible for the welfare of its members? What demands for the promotion of his welfare can an individual reasonably make upon his society? These are questions to which no answer can be given in terms of some *a priori* approach with reference to universal ultimates. Whatever answer can appropriately be given will depend, in the final analysis, on what the society decides it should be.[1]

Rescher raises this question only to avoid it. His response to his own question is that a society has all and only those responsibilities for its members that it thinks it has. Although this claim is trivially true as regards legal responsibilities, it is inadequate from a moral perspective. If one imagines the case of an affluent society which leaves the blind, the disabled, and the needy to die of starvation, the incompleteness of Rescher's account becomes obvious. In this imagined case one is naturally led to raise the question as to whether those in power ought to supply those in need with the necessities of life. Though the needy have no legal right to welfare benefits of any kind, one might very well say that they ought to have such a right. It is this claim which I propose to discuss here.[2]

I shall approach this issue by examining three positions which may be adopted in response to it. These are:

> *1. The Individualist Position:* Even in an affluent society, one ought not to have any legal right to state-supplied welfare benefits.

From Philosophy of Human Sciences, *v. 5 (1975), pp. 125–43. Reprinted by permission of Sage Publications.*

2. *The Permissive Position:* In a society with sufficient resources, one ought to have an unconditional legal right to receive state-supplied welfare benefits. (That is, one's right to receive such benefits ought not to depend on one's behaviour; it should be guaranteed).

3. *The Puritan Position:* In a society with sufficient resources one ought to have a legal right to state-supplied welfare benefits; this right ought to be conditional, however, on one's willingness to work.

But before we examine these positions, some preliminary clarification must be attempted. . . .

Welfare systems are state-supported systems which supply benefits, usually in the form of cash income, to those who are in need. Welfare systems thus exist in the sort of social context where there is some private ownership of property. If no one owned anything individually (except possibly his own body), and all goods were considered to be the joint property of everyone, then this type of welfare system could not exist. A state might take on the responsibility for the welfare of its citizens, but it could not meet this responsibility by distributing a level of cash income which such citizens would spend to purchase the goods essential for life. The welfare systems which exist in the western world do exist against the background of extensive private ownership of property. It is in this context that I propose to discuss moral questions about having a right to welfare benefits. By setting out my questions in this way, I do not intend to endorse the institution of private property, but only to discuss questions which many people find real and difficult in the context of the social organization which they actually do experience. The present analysis of welfare is intended to apply to societies which *(a)* have the institution of private property, if not for means of production, at least for some basic good; and *(b)* possess sufficient resources so that it is at least possible for every member of the society to be supplied with the necessities of life.

The Individualist View

It might be maintained that a person in need has no legitimate moral claim on those around him and that the hypothetical inattentive society which left its blind citizens to beg or starve cannot rightly be censured for doing so. This view, which is dramatically at odds with most of contemporary social thinking, lives on in the writings of Ayn Rand and her followers.[3] The Individualist sets a high value on uncoerced personal choice. He sees each person as a responsible agent who is able to make his own decisions and to plan his own life. He insists that with the freedom to make decisions goes responsibility for the consequences of those decisions. A person has every right, for example, to spend ten years of his life studying Sanskrit — but if, as a result of this choice, he is unemployable, he ought not to expect others to labour on his behalf. No one has a proper claim on the labour of another, or on the income ensuing from that labour, unless he can repay the labourer in a way acceptable to that labourer himself. Government welfare schemes provide benefits from funds gained largely by taxing earned income. One cannot "opt out" of such schemes. To the Individualist, this means that a person is forced to work part of his time for others.

Suppose that a man works forty hours and earns two hundred dollars. Under modern-day taxation, it may well be that he can spend only two-thirds of that money as he chooses. The rest is taken by government and goes to support programs which the working individual may not himself endorse. The beneficiaries of such programs — those beneficiaries who do not work themselves — are as though they have slaves working for them. Backed by the force which government authorities can command, they are able to exist on the earnings of others. Those who support them do not do so voluntarily, out of charity; they do so on government command.

> Someone across the street is unemployed. Should you be taxed extra to pay for his expenses? Not at all. You have not injured him, you are not responsible for the fact that he is unemployed (unless you are a senator or bureaucrat who agitated for further curtailing of business which legislation passed, with the result that your neighbour was laid off by the curtailed business). You may voluntarily wish to help him out, or better still, try to get him a job to put him on his feet again; but since you have initiated no aggressive act against him, and neither purposefully nor accidentally injured him in any way, you should not be legally penalized for the fact of his unemployment.[4]

The Individualist need not lack concern for those in need. He may give generously to charity; he might give more generously still, if his whole income were his to use, as he would like it to be. He may also believe that, as a matter of empirical fact, existing government programs do not actually help the poor. They support a cumbersome bureaucracy and they use financial resources which, if untaxed, might be used by those with initiative to pursue job-creating endeavours. The thrust of the Individualist's position is that each person owns his own body and his own labour; thus each person is taken to have a virtually unconditional right to the income which that labour can earn him in a free market place.[5] For anyone to pre-empt part of a worker's earnings without that worker's voluntary consent is tantamount to robbery. And the fact that the government is the intermediary through which this deed is committed does not change its moral status one iota.

On an Individualist's view, those in need should be cared for by charities or through other schemes to which contributions are voluntary. Many people may wish to insure themselves against unforeseen calamities and they should be free to do so. But there is no justification for non-optional government schemes financed by taxpayers' money. . . .

The Permissive View

Directly contrary to the Individualist view of welfare is what I have termed the Permissive view. According to this view, in a society which has sufficient resources so that everyone could be supplied with the necessities of life, every individual ought to be given the legal right to social security, and this right ought not to be conditional in any way upon an individual's behavior. *Ex hypothesi* the society which we are discussing has sufficient goods to provide everyone with food, clothing, shelter and other necessities. Someone who does without these basic goods is scarcely living at all, and a society which takes no steps to change this state of affairs implies by its inaction that the life of such a person is without value. It does not execute him; but it may allow him to die. It does not put him in prison; but it may leave him with a life of lower quality than that of some prison inmates. A society which can rectify these circumstances and does not can justly be accused of imposing upon the needy either death or lifelong deprivation. And those characteristics which make a person needy — whether they be illness, old age, insanity, feeblemindedness, inability to find work, or even poor moral character — are insufficient to make him deserve the fate to which an inactive society would in effect condemn him. One would not be executed for inability or failure to find work; neither should one be allowed to die for this misfortune or failing.

A person who cannot or does not find his own means of social security does not thereby forfeit his status as a human being. If other human beings, with physical, mental and moral qualities different from his, are regarded as having the right to life and to the means of life, then so too should he be regarded. A society which does not accept the responsibilities for supplying such a person with the basic necessities of life is, in effect, endorsing a difference between its members which is without moral justification. . . .

The adoption of a Permissive view of welfare would have significant practical implications. If there were a legal right, unconditional upon behaviour, to a specified level of state-supplied benefits, then state investigation of the prospective welfare recipient could be kept to a minimum. Why he is in need, whether he can work, whether he is willing to work, and what he does while receiving welfare benefits are on this view quite irrelevant to his right to receive those benefits. A welfare recipient is a person who claims from his society that to which he is legally entitled under a morally based welfare scheme. The fact that he makes this claim licenses no special state or societal interference with his behaviour. If the Permissive view of welfare were widely believed, then there would be no social stigma attached to being on welfare. There is such a stigma, and many long-term welfare recipients are considerably demoralized by their dependent status.[6] These facts suggest that the Permissive view of welfare is not widely held in our society.

The Puritan View

This view of welfare rather naturally emerges when we consider that no one can have a right to something without someone else's, or some group of other persons', having responsibilities correlative to this right. In the case in which the right in question is a legal right to social security, the correlative responsibilities may be rather extensive. They have been deemed responsibilities of "the state." The state will require resources and funds to meet these responsibilities, and these do not emerge from the sky miraculously, or zip into existence as a consequence of virtually effortless acts of will. They are taken by the state from its citizens, often in the form of taxation on earned income. The funds given to the welfare recipient and many of the goods which he purchases with these funds are produced by other members of society, many of whom give a considerable portion of their time and their energy to this end. If a state has the moral responsibility to ensure the social security of its citizens then all the citizens of that state have the responsibility to provide state agencies with the means to carry out their duties. This responsibility, in our present contingent circumstances, seems to generate an obligation to *work*.

A person who works helps to produce the goods which all use in daily living and, when paid, contributes through taxation to government endeavours. The person who does not work, even though able to work, does not make his contribution to social efforts towards obtaining the means of life. He is not entitled to a share of the goods produced by others if he chooses not to take part in their labours. Unless he can show that there is a moral justification for his not making the sacrifice of time and energy which others make, he has no legitimate claim to welfare benefits. If he is disabled or unable to obtain work, he cannot work; hence he has no need to justify his failure to work. But if does choose not to work, he would have to justify his choice by saying "others should sacrifice their time and energy for me; I have no need to sacrifice time and energy for them." This principle, a version of what Rawls refers to as a **freerider's principle**, simply will not stand up to criticism.[7] To deliberately avoid working and benefit from the labours of others is morally indefensible.

Within a welfare system erected on these principles, the right to welfare is conditional upon one's satisfactorily accounting for his failure to obtain the necessities of life by his own efforts. Someone who is severely disabled mentally or physically, or who for some other reason cannot work, is morally entitled to receive welfare benefits. Someone who chooses not to work is not. The Puritan view of welfare is a kind of compromise between the Individualist view and the Permissive view. . . .

The Puritan view of welfare, based as it is on the inter-relation between welfare and work, provides a rationale for two connected principles which those establishing welfare schemes in Canada and in the United States seem to endorse. First of all, those on welfare should never receive a higher income than the working poor. Secondly, a welfare scheme should, in some way or other, incorporate incentives to work. These principles, which presuppose that it is better to work than not to work, emerge rather naturally from the contingency which is at the basis of the Puritan view: the goods essential for social security are products of the labour of some members of society. If we wish to have a continued supply of such goods, we must encourage those who work to produce them. . . .

Appraisal of Policies: Social Consequences and Social Justice

In approaching the appraisal of prospective welfare policies under these two aspects I am, of course, making some assumptions about the moral appraisal of suggested social policies. Although these cannot possibly be justified here, it may be helpful to articulate them, at least in a rough way.

Appraisal of social policies is in part teleological. To the extent that a policy, P, increases the total human welfare more than does an alternative policy, P', P is a better social policy than P'. Or, if P leaves the total human welfare as it is, while P' diminishes it, then to that extent, P is a better social policy than P'. Even this skeletal formulation of the teleological aspect of appraisal cannot be entirely teleological. We consider total consequences — effects upon the total of "human well-being" in a society. But this total is a summation of consequences on different individuals. It includes no judgements as to how far we allow one individual's well-being to decrease while another's increases, under the same policy. Judgements relating to the latter problems are judgements about social justice.

In appraising social policies we have to weigh up considerations of total well-being against considerations of justice. Just how this is to be done, precisely, I would not pretend to know. However, the absence of precise methods does not mean that we should relinquish attempts at appraisal: some problems are already with us, and thought which is necessarily tentative and imprecise is still preferable to no thought at all.

Consequences of Welfare Schemes

First, let us consider the consequences of the non-scheme advocated by the Individualist. He would have us abolish all non-optional government programs which have as their goal the improvement of anyone's personal welfare. This rejection extends to health schemes, pension plans and education, as well as to welfare and unemployment insurance. So following the Individualist would lead to very sweeping changes.

The Individualist will claim (as do Hospers and Ayn Rand) that on the whole his non-scheme will bring beneficial consequences. He will admit, as he must, that there are people who would suffer tremendously if welfare and other social security programs were simply terminated. Some would even die as a result. We cannot assume that spontaneously developing charities would cover every case of dire need. Nevertheless the Individualist wants to point to benefits which would accrue to businessmen and to working people and their families if taxation were drastically cut. It is his claim that consumption would rise, hence production would rise, job opportunities would be extended, and there would be an economic boom, if people could only spend all their earned income as they wished. This boom would benefit both rich and poor.

There are significant omissions which are necessary in order to render the Individualist's optimism plausible. Either workers and businessmen would have insurance of various kinds, or they would be insecure in their prosperity. If they did have insurance to cover health problems, old age and possible job loss, then they would not be spending their whole earned income on consumer goods. Those who run the insurance schemes could, of course, put this money back into the economy — but government schemes already do this. The economic boom under Individualism would not be loud as originally expected. Furthermore the goal of increased productivity must be questioned from an ecological viewpoint: many necessary materials are only available in limited quantities.

Finally, a word about charity. It is not to be expected that those who are at the mercy of charities will benefit from this state, either materially or psychologically. Those who prosper will be able to choose between giving a great deal to charity and suffering from the very real insecurity and guilt which would accompany the existence of starvation and grim poverty outside their padlocked doors. It is to be hoped that they would opt for the first alternative. But, if they did, this might be every bit as expensive for them as government-supported benefit schemes are now. If they did not give generously to charity, violence might result. However one looked at it, the consequences of Individualism are unlikely to be good.

Welfare schemes operating in Canada today are almost without exception based upon the principles of the Puritan view. To see the consequences of that type of welfare scheme we have only to look at the results of our own welfare programs. Taxation to support such schemes is high, but not so intolerably so as to have led to widescale resentment among taxpayers. Canadian welfare programs are attended by complicated and often cumbersome bureaucracy, some of which results from the interlocking of municipal, provincial and federal governments in the administration and financing of welfare programs. The cost of the programs is no doubt increased by this bureaucracy; not all the tax money directed to welfare programs goes to those in need. Puritan welfare schemes do not result in social catastrophe or in significant business stagnation — this much we know, because we already live with such schemes. Their adverse consequences, if any, are felt primarily not by society generally, nor by businessmen and the working segment of the public, but rather by recipients of welfare.

Both the Special Senate Committee Report on Poverty and the Real Poverty Report criticize our present system of welfare for its demoralization of recipients, who often must deal with several levels of government and are vulnerable to arbitrary interference on the part of administering officials. Welfare officials have the power to check on welfare recipients and to cut off or limit their benefits under a large number of circumstances. The dangers to welfare recipients in terms of anxiety, threats to privacy and loss of dignity are obvious. According to the Senate Report, the single aspect shared by all Canada's welfare systems is "a record of failure and insufficiency, of bureaucratic rigidities that often result in the degradation, humiliation and alienation of recipients."[8] The writers of this report cite many instances of humiliation, leaving the impression that these are too easily found to be "incidental aberrations."[9] Concern that a welfare recipient either be unable to work or be willing to work (if unemployed) can easily turn into concern about how he spends the income supplied him, what his plans for the future are, where he lives, how many children he has. And the rationale underlying the Puritan scheme makes the degradation of welfare recipients a natural consequence of welfare institutions. Work is valued and only he who works is thought to contribute to society. Welfare recipients are regarded as parasites and spongers — so when they are treated as such, this is only what we should have expected. Being on welfare in a society which thinks and acts in this fashion can be psychologically debilitating. Welfare recipients who are demoralized by their downgraded status and relative lack of personal freedom can be expected to be made less capable of self-sufficiency. To the extent that this is so, welfare systems erected on Puritan principles may defeat their own purposes.

In fairness, it must be noted here that bureaucratic checks and controls are not a feature only of Puritan welfare systems. To a limited extent, Permissive systems would have to incorporate them too. Within those systems, welfare benefits would be given only to those whose income was inadequate to meet basic needs. However, there would be no checks on "willingness to work," and there would be no need for welfare workers to evaluate the merits of the daily activities of recipients. If a Permissive guaranteed income system were administered through income tax returns, everyone receiving the basic income and those not needing it paying it back in taxes, then the special status of welfare recipients would fade. They would no longer be singled out as a special group within the population. It is to be expected that living solely on government-supplied benefits would be psychologically easier in that type of situation.

Thus it can be argued that for the recipients of welfare, a Permissive scheme has more advantages than a Puritan one. This is not a very surprising conclusion. The Puritan scheme is relatively disadvantageous to recipients, and Puritans would acknowledge this point; they will argue that the overall consequences of Permissive schemes are negative in that these schemes benefit some at too great a cost to others. (Remember, we are not yet concerned with the *justice* of welfare policies, but solely with their consequences as regards *total* human well-being within the society in question.) The concern which most people have regarding the Permissive scheme relates to its costs and its dangers to the "work ethic." It is commonly thought that people work only because they have to work to survive in a tolerable style. If a guaranteed income scheme were adopted by the government, this incentive to work would disappear. No one would be faced with the choice between a nasty and boring job and starvation. Who would do the nasty and boring jobs then? Many of them are not eliminable and they have to be done somehow, by someone. Puritans fear that a great many people — even some with relatively pleasant jobs — might simply cease to work if they could receive non-stigmatized government money to live on. If this were to happen, the permissive society would simply grind to a halt.

In addressing these anxieties about the consequences of Permissive welfare schemes, we must recall that welfare benefits are set to ensure only that those who do not work have a bearable existence, with an income sufficient for basic needs, and that they have this income regardless of why they fail to work. Welfare benefits will not finance luxury living for a family of five! If jobs are adequately paid so that workers receive more than the minimum welfare income in an earned salary, then there will still be a financial incentive to take jobs. What guaranteed income schemes will do is to raise the salary floor. This change will benefit the many non-unionized workers in service and clerical occupations.

Furthermore it is unlikely that people work solely due to (i) the desire for money and the things it can buy and (ii) belief in the Puritan work ethic. There are many other reasons for working, some of which would persist in a society which had adopted a Permissive welfare system. Most people are happier when their time is structured in some way, when they are active outside their own homes, when they feel themselves part of an endeavour whose purposes transcend their particular egoistic ones. Women often choose to work outside the home for these reasons as much as for financial ones. With these and other factors operating I cannot see that the adoption of a Permissive welfare scheme would be followed by a level of slothfulness which would jeopardize human well-being.

Another worry about the Permissive scheme concerns cost. It is difficult to comment on this in a general way, since it would vary so much from case to case. Of Canada at the present it has been said that a guaranteed income scheme administered through income tax would cost even less than social security payments administered through the present bureaucracies. It is thought that this saving would result from a drastic cut in administrative costs. The matter of the work ethic is also relevant to the question of costs. Within a Puritan framework it is very important to have a high level of employment and there is a tendency to resist any reorganization which results in there being fewer jobs available. Some of these proposed reorganizations would save money; strictly speaking we should count the cost of keeping jobs which are objectively unnecessary as part of the cost of Puritanism regarding welfare.

In summary, we can appraise Individualism, Puritanism and Permissivism with respect to their anticipated consequences, as follows: Individualism is unacceptable; Puritanism is tolerable, but has some undesirable consequences for welfare recipients; Permissivism appears to be the winner. Worries about bad effects which Permissive welfare schemes might have due to high costs and (alleged) reduced work-incentives appear to be without solid basis.

Social Justice Under Proposed Welfare Schemes

We must now try to consider the merits of Individualism, Puritanism and Permissivism with regard to their impact on the distribution of the goods necessary for well-being. [Robert] Nozick has argued against the whole conception of a distributive justice on the grounds that it presupposes that goods are like manna from heaven: we simply get them and then have a problem — to whom to give them. According to Nozick we know where things come from and we do not have the problem of to whom to give them. There is not really a problem of distributive justice, for there is no central distributor giving out manna from heaven! It is necessary to counter Nozick on this point since his reaction to the (purported) problems of distributive justice would undercut much of what follows.[10]

There is a level at which Nozick's point is obviously valid. If A discovers a cure for cancer, then it is A and not B or C who is responsible for this discovery. On Nozick's view this is taken to imply that A should reap any monetary profits which are forthcoming; other people will benefit from the cure itself. Now although it cannot be doubted that A is a bright and hardworking person, neither can it be denied that A and his circumstances are the product of many co-operative endeavours: schools and laboratories, for instance. Because this is so, I find Nozick's claim that "we know where things come from" unconvincing at a deeper level. Since achievements like A's presuppose extensive social co-operation, it is morally permissible to regard even the monetary profits accruing from them as shareable by the "owner" and society at large.

Laws support existing income levels in many ways. Governments specify taxation so as to further determine net income. Property ownership is a legal matter. In all these ways people's incomes and possibilities for obtaining income are affected by deliberate state action. It is always possible to raise questions about the moral desirability of actual conventional arrangements. Should university professors earn less than lawyers? More than waitresses? Why? Why not? Anyone who gives an account of distributive justice is trying to specify principles which will make it possible to answer questions such as these, and nothing in Nozick's argument suffices to show that the questions are meaningless or unimportant.

Any human distribution of anything is unjust insofar as differences exist for no good reason. If goods did come like manna from heaven and the Central Distributor gave A ten times more goods than B, we should want to know why. The skewed distribution might be deemed a just one if A's needs were objectively ten times greater than B's, or if B refused to accept more than his small portion of goods. But if no reason at all could be given for it, or if only an irrelevant reason could be given (e.g., A is blue-eyed and B is not), then it is an unjust distribution. All the views we have expounded concerning welfare permit differences in income level. Some philosophers would say that such differences are never just, although they may be necessary, for historical or utilitarian reasons. Whether or not this is so, it is admittedly very difficult to say just what would constitute a good reason for giving A a higher income than B. Level of need, degree of responsibility, amount of training, unpleasantness of work — all these have been proposed and all have some plausibility. We do not need to tackle all this larger problem in order to consider justice under proposed welfare systems. For we can deal here solely with the question of whether everyone should receive a floor level of income; decisions on this matter are independent of decisions on overall equality or principles of variation among incomes above the floor. The Permissivist contends that all should receive at least the floor income; the Individualist and the Puritan deny this. All would claim justice for their side.

The Individualist attempts to justify extreme variations in income, with some people below the level where they can fulfill their basic needs, with reference to the fact of people's actual accomplishments. This approach to the question is open to the same objections as those which have already been raised against Nozick's non-manna-from-heaven argument, and I shall not repeat them here. Let us move on to the Puritan account. It is because goods emerge from human efforts that the Puritan advances his view of welfare. He stresses the unfairness of a system which would permit some people to take advantage of others. A Permissive welfare system would do this, as it makes no attempt to distinguish between those who choose not to work and those who cannot work. No one should be able to take advantage of another under the auspices of a government institution. The Puritan scheme seeks to eliminate this possibility, and for that reason, Puritans would allege, it is a more just scheme than the Permissive one.

Permissivists can best reply to this contention by acknowledging that any instance of free-riding would be an instance where those working were done an injustice, but by showing that any justice which the Puritan preserves by eliminating free-riding is outweighed by *injustice* perpetrated elsewhere. Consider the children of the Puritan's free-riders. They will suffer greatly for the "sins" of their parents. Within the institution of the family, the Puritan cannot suitably hurt the guilty without cruelly depriving the innocent.

There is a sense, too, in which Puritanism does injustice to the many people on welfare who are not free-riders. It perpetuates the opinion that they are non-contributors to society and this doctrine, which is over-simplified if not downright false, has a harmful effect upon welfare recipients.

Social justice is not simply a matter of the distribution of goods, or the income with which goods are to be purchased. It is also a matter of the protection of rights. Western societies claim to give their citizens equal rights in political and legal contexts; they also claim to endorse the larger conception of a right to life. Now it is possible to interpret these rights in a limited and formalistic way, so that the duties correlative to them are minimal. On the limited, or negative, interpretation, to say that A has a right to life is simply to say that others have a duty not to interfere with A's attempts to keep himself alive. This interpretation of the right to life is compatible with Individualism as well as with Puritanism. But it is an inadequate interpretation of the right to life and of other rights. A right to vote is meaningless if one is starving and unable to get to the polls; a right to equality before the law is meaningless if one cannot afford to hire a lawyer. And so on.

Even a Permissive welfare scheme will go only a very small way towards protecting people's rights. It will amount to a meaningful acknowledgement of a right to life, by ensuring income adequate to purchase food, clothing and shelter — at the very least. These minimum necessities are presupposed by all other rights a society may endorse in that their possession is a precondition of being able to exercise these other rights. Because it protects the rights of all within a society better than do Puritanism and Individualism, the Permissive view can rightly claim superiority over the others with regard to justice.

NOTES

1. Nichols Rescher, *Welfare: Social Issues in Philosophical Perspective*, p. 114.
2. One might wish to discuss moral questions concerning welfare in the context of **natural rights** doctrines. Indeed, Article 22 of the United Nations Declaration of Human Rights states, "Everyone, as a member of society, has the right to social security and is entitled, through national effort and international cooperation and in accordance with the organization and resources of each State, to the economic, social and cultural rights indispensable for his dignity and the free development of his personality." I make no attempt to defend the right to welfare as a **natural right**. Granting that rights imply responsibilities or duties and that "ought" implies "can," it would only be intelligible to regard the right to social security as a natural right if all states were able to ensure the minimum well-being of their citizens. This is not the case. And a natural right is one which is by definition supposed to belong to all human beings. The analysis given here in the permissive view is compatible with the claim that all human beings have a *prima facie* natural right to social security. It is not, however, compatible with the claim that all human beings have a natural right to social security if this right is regarded as one which is so absolute as to be inviolable under any and all conditions.
3. See, for example, Ayn Rand's *Atlas Shrugged, The Virtue of Selfishness,* and *Capitalism: The Unknown Ideal.*
4. John Hospers, *Libertarianism: A Political Philosophy for Tomorrow,* p. 67.
5. I say virtually unconditional, because an Individualist such as John Hospers sees a legitimate moral role for government in preventing the use of force by some citizens against others. Since this is the case, I presume that he would also regard as legitimate such taxation as was necessary to support this function. Presumably that taxation would be seen as consented to by all, on the grounds that all "really want" government protection.
6. Ian Adams, William Cameron, Brian Hill, and Peter Penz, *The Real Poverty Report*, pp. 167–187.
7. See *A Theory of Justice*, pp. 124, 136. Rawls defines the free-rider as one who relies on the principle "everyone is to act justly except for myself, if I choose not to," and says that his position is a version of egoism which is eliminated as a morally acceptable principle by formal

constraints. This conclusion regarding the tenability of egoism is one which I accept and which is taken for granted in the present context.

8. *Senate Report on Poverty*, p. 73.
9. The Hamilton Public Welfare Department takes automobile licence plates from recipients, making them available again only to those whose needs meet with the Department's approval. (*Real Poverty Report*, p. 186.) The *Globe and Mail* for 12 January 1974 reported that welfare recipients in the city of Toronto are to be subjected to computerized budgeting. In the summer of 1973, the two young daughters of an Alabama man on welfare were sterilized against their own wishes and without their parents' informed consent. (See *Time*, 23 July, 1973.)
10. Robert Nozick, "Distributive Justice," *Philosophy and Public Affairs*, Fall 1973.

QUESTIONS

1. Trudy Govier distinguishes between and among three different views of the collective responsibility of a society to respond to human need. What are the salient features of these three views?
2. Evaluate workfare from the perspective of "individualist," "puritan," and "permissive" views as set out in this reading.
3. Do considerations of justice militate for or against permissive welfare systems as a response to the reality of poverty?

PROPERTY AND HUNGER

Amartya Sen

In an interesting letter to Anna George, the daughter of Henry George Bernard Shaw wrote: "Your father found me a literary dilettante and militant rationalist in religion, and a barren rascal at that. By turning my mind to economics he made a man of me." I am not able to determine what making a man of Bernard Shaw would exactly consist of, but it is clear that the kind of moral and social problems with which Shaw was deeply concerned could not be sensibly pursued without examining their economic aspects. For example, the claims of property rights, which some would defend and some (including Shaw) would dispute, are not just matters of basic moral belief that could not possibly be influenced one way or the other by any empirical arguments. They call for sensitive moral analysis responsive to empirical realities, including economic ones.

Moral claims based on intrinsically valuable rights are often used in political and social arguments. Rights related to ownership have been invoked for ages. But there are also other types of rights which have been seen as "inherent and inalienable," and the American Declaration of Independence refers to "certain unalienable rights," among which are "life, liberty and the pursuit of happiness." The Indian constitution talks even of "the right to an adequate means of livelihood." The "right not to be hungry" has often been invoked in recent discussions on the obligation to help the famished.

From Economics and Philosophy, *v. 4 (1988), pp. 57–68. Reprinted by permission of Amartya Sen and Cambridge University Press.*

Rights: Instruments, Constraints, or Goals?

Rights can be taken to be morally important in three different ways. First, they can be considered to be valuable *instruments* to achieve other goals. This is the "instrumental view," and is well illustrated by the utilitarian approach to rights. Rights are, in that view, of no intrinsic importance. Violation of rights is not in itself a bad thing, nor fulfillment intrinsically good. But the acceptance of rights promotes, in this view, things that are ultimately important, to wit, utility. Jeremy Bentham rejected "natural rights" as "simple nonsense," and "natural and imprescriptible rights" as "rhetorical nonsense, nonsense upon stilts." But he attached great importance to rights as instruments valuable to the promotion of a good society, and devoted much energy to the attempt to reform appropriately the actual system of rights.

The second view may be called the "constraint view," and it takes the form of seeing rights as *constraints* on what others can or cannot do. In this view rights are intrinsically important. However, they don't figure in moral accounting as goals to be generally promoted, but only as constraints that others must obey. As Robert Nozick has put it in a powerful exposition of this "constraint view": "Individuals have rights, and there are things no person or group may do to them (without violating their rights)." Rights "set the constraints within which a social choice is made, by excluding certain alternatives, fixing others, and so on."

The third approach is to see fulfillments of rights as goals to be pursued. This "goal view" differs from the instrumental view in regarding rights to be intrinsically important, and it differs from the constraint view in seeing the fulfillment of rights as goals to be generally promoted, rather than taking them as demanding only (and exactly) that we refrain from violating the rights of others. In the "constraint view" there is no duty to help anyone with his or her rights (merely not to hinder), and also in the "instrumental view" there is no duty, in fact, to help unless the right fulfillment will also promote some other goal such as utility. The "goal view" integrates the valuation of rights — their fulfillment and violation — in overall moral accounting and yields a wider sphere of influence of rights in morality.

I have argued elsewhere that the goal view has advantages that the other two approaches do not share, in particular, the ability to accommodate integrated moral accounting including inter alia the intrinsic importance of a class of fundamental rights. I shall not repeat that argument here. But there is an interesting question, of dual roles of rights in the sense that some rights may be *both* intrinsically important and instrumentally valuable. For example, the right to be free from hunger could — not implausibly — be regarded as being valuable in itself as well as serving as a good instrument to promote other goals such as security, longevity or utility. If so, both the goal view and the instrumental view would have to be simultaneously deployed to get a comprehensive assessment of such a right. This problem of comprehensiveness is a particularly important issue in the context of Henry George's discussion of rights, since he gave many rights significant dual roles.

The instrumental aspect is an inescapable feature of every right, since irrespective of whether a certain right is intrinsically valuable or not, its acceptance will certainly have other consequences as well, and these, too, have to be assessed along with the intrinsic value of rights (if any). A right that is regarded as quite valuable in itself may nevertheless be judged to be morally rejectable if it leads to disastrous consequences. This is a case of the rights playing a *negative* instrumental role. It is, of course, also possible that the instrumental argument will *bolster* the intrinsic claims of a right to be taken seriously. I shall presently argue that such is the case in George's analysis with the right of labor to its produce.

There are two general conclusions to draw, at this stage, from this very preliminary discussion. First, we must distinguish between (1) the intrinsic value of a right, and (2) the overall value of a right taking note inter alia of its intrinsic importance (if any). The acceptance of the intrinsic importance of any right is no guarantee that its overall moral valuation must be favorable. Second, no moral assessment of a right can be independent of its likely consequences. The need for empirical assessment of the effects of accepting any right cannot be escaped. Empirical arguments are quite central to moral philosophy.

Property and Deprivation

The right to hold, use and bequeath property that one has legitimately acquired is often taken to be inherently valuable. In fact, however, many of its defenses seem to be actually of the instrumental type, e.g., arguing that property rights make people more free to choose one kind of a life rather than another. Even the traditional attempt at founding "natural property rights" on the principles of "natural liberty" (with or without John Locke's proviso) has some instrumental features. But even if we do accept that property rights may have some intrinsic value, this does not in any way amount to an overall justification of property rights, since property rights may have consequences which themselves will require assessment. Indeed, the causation of hunger as well as its prevention may materially depend on how property rights are structured. If a set of property rights leads, say, to starvation, as it well might, then the moral approval of these rights would certainly be compromised severely. In general, the need for consequential analysis of property rights is inescapable whether or not such rights are seen as having any intrinsic value.

Consider Henry George's formula of giving "the product to the producer." This is, of course, an ambiguous rule, since the division of the credits for production to different causal influences (e.g., according to "marginal productivities" in neoclassical theory, or according to human efforts in classical labor theory) is inevitably somewhat arbitrary, and full of problems involving internal tensions. But no matter how the ambiguities are resolved, it is clear that this rule would give no part of the socially produced output to one who is unemployed since he or she is producing nothing. Also, a person whose productive contribution happens to be tiny, according to *whichever* procedure of such accounting we use, can expect to get very little based on this so-called "natural law." Thus, hunger and starvation are compatible with this system of rights. George thought that this would not occur, since the economic reforms he proposed (including the abolition of land rights) would eliminate unemployment, and provision for the disabled would be made through the sympathetic support of others. These are empirical matters. If these empirical generalizations do not hold, then the outlined system of rights would yield a serious conflict. The property rights to one's product (however defined) might be of some intrinsic moral importance, but we clearly must also take note of the moral disvalue of human misery (such as suffering due to hunger and nutrition-related diseases). The latter could very plausibly be seen as having more moral force than the former. A positive intrinsic value of the right to one's product can go with an overall negative value, taking everything into account.

I have tried to argue elsewhere — not in the context of disputing these moral theories but in trying to understand the causation of famines in the modern world — that famines are, in fact, best explained in terms of failures of entitlement systems. The entitlements here refer, of course, to legal rights and to practical possibilities, rather than to moral status, but the laws and actual operation of private ownership economies have many features in common with the moral system of entitlements analyzed by Nozick and others.

The entitlement approach to famines need not, of course, be confined to private owner-ship economies, and entitlement failures of other systems can also be fruitfully studied to examine famines and hunger. In the specific context of private ownership economies, the entitlements are substantially analyzable in terms, respectively, of what may be called "endowments" and "exchange entitlements." A person's endowment refers to what he or she initially owns (including the person's own labor power), and the exchange entitlement mapping tells us what the person can obtain through exchanging what he or she owns, either by production (exchange with nature), or by trade (exchange with others), or a mixture of the two. A person has to starve if neither the endowments, nor what can be obtained through exchange, yields an adequate amount of food.

If starvation and hunger are seen in terms of failures of entitlements, then it becomes immediately clear that the total availability of food in a country is only one of several variables that are relevant. Many famines occur without any decline in the availability of food. For example, in the Great Bengal famine of 1943, the total food availability in Bengal was not particularly bad (considerably higher than two years earlier when there was no famine), and yet three million people died, in a famine mainly affecting the rural areas, through rather violent shifts in the relative purchasing powers of different groups, hitting the rural laborers the hardest. The Ethiopian famine of 1973 took place in a year of average per capita food availability, but the cultivators and other occupation groups in the province of Wollo had lost their means of subsistence (through loss of crops and a decline of economic activity, related to a local drought) and had no means of commanding food from elsewhere in the country. Indeed, some food moved *out* of Wollo to more prosperous people in other parts of Ethiopia, repeating a pattern of contrary movement of food that was widely observed during the Irish famines of the 1840s (with food moving out of famine-stricken Ireland to prosperous England which had greater power in the battle for entitlements). The Bangladesh famine of 1974 took place in a year of *peak* food availability, but several occupation groups had lost their entitlement to food through loss of employment and other economic changes (including inflationary pressures causing prices to outrun wages). Other examples of famines without significant (or any) decline in food availability can be found, and there is nothing particularly surprising about this fact once it is recognized that the availability of food is only one influence among many on the entitlement of each occupa-tion group. Even when a famine *is* associated with a decline of food availability, the entitlement changes have to be studied to understand the particular nature of the famine, e.g., why one occupation group is hit but not another. The causation of starvation can be sensibly sought in failures of entitlements of the respective groups.

The causal analysis of famines in terms of entitlements also points to possible public policies of prevention. The main economic strategy would have to take the form of increas-ing the entitlements of the deprived groups, and in general, of guaranteeing minimum entitlements for everyone, paying particular attention to the vulnerable groups. This can, in the long run, be done in many different ways, involving both economic growth (including growth of food output) and distributional adjustments. Some of these policies may, how-ever, require that the property rights and the corresponding entitlements of the more pros-perous groups be violated. The problem, in fact, is particularly acute in the short run, since it may not be possible to engineer rapid economic growth instantly. Then the burden of raising entitlements of the groups in distress would largely have to fall on reducing the entitlements of others more favorably placed. Transfers of income or commodities through various public policies may well be effective in quashing a famine (as the experience of famine relief in different countries has shown), but it may require substantial government intervention in the entitlements of the more prosperous groups.

There is, however, no great moral dilemma in this if property rights are treated as purely *instrumental*. If the goals of relief of hunger and poverty are sufficiently powerful, then it would be just right to violate whatever property rights come in the way, since — in this view — property rights have no intrinsic status. On the other hand, if property rights are taken to be morally inviolable irrespective of their consequences, then it will follow that these policies cannot be morally acceptable even though they might save thousands, or even millions, from dying. The inflexible moral "constraint" of respecting people's legitimately acquired entitlements would rule out such policies.

In fact this type of problem presents a reductio ad absurdum of the moral validity of constraint-based entitlement systems. However, while the conclusions to be derived from that approach might well be "absurd," the situation postulated is not an imaginary one at all. It is based on studies of actual famines and the role of entitlement failures in the causation of mass starvation. If there is an embarrassment here, it belongs solidly to the consequence-independent way of seeing rights.

I should add that this dilemma does not arise from regarding property rights to be of intrinsic value, which can be criticized on other grounds, but not this one. Even if property rights *are* of intrinsic value, their violation may be justified on grounds of the favorable consequences of that violation. A right, as was mentioned earlier, may be intrinsically valuable and still be justly violated taking everything into account. The "absurdum" does not belong to attaching intrinsic value to property rights, but to regarding these rights as simply acceptable, regardless of their consequences. A moral system that values both property rights and other goals — such as avoiding famines and starvation, or fulfilling people's right not to be hungry — can, on the one hand, give property rights intrinsic importance, and on the other, recommend the violation of property rights when that leads to better overall consequences (*including* the disvalue of rights violation).

The issue here is not the valuing of property rights, but their alleged inviolability. There is no dilemma here either for the purely instrumental view of property rights or for treating the fulfillment of property rights as one goal among many, but specifically for consequence-independent assertions of property rights and for the corresponding constraint-based approaches to moral entitlement of ownership.

That property and hunger are closely related cannot possibly come as a great surprise. Hunger is primarily associated with not owning enough food and thus property rights over food are immediately and directly involved. Fights over that property right can be a major part of the reality of a poor country, and any system of moral assessment has to take note of that phenomenon. The tendency to see hunger in purely technocratic terms of food output and availability may help to hide the crucial role of entitlements in the genesis of hunger, but a fuller economic analysis cannot overlook that crucial role. Since property rights over food are derived from property rights over other goods and resources (through production and trade), the entire system of rights of acquisition and transfer is implicated in the emergence and survival of hunger and starvation.

The Right Not to Be Hungry

Property rights have been championed for a long time. In contrast, the assertion of "the right not to be hungry" is a comparatively recent phenomenon. While this right is much invoked in political debates, there is a good deal of skepticism about treating this as truly a right in any substantial way. It is often asserted that this concept of "right not to be hungry" stands essentially for nothing at all ("simple nonsense," as Bentham called "natural rights" in general). That piece of sophisticated cynicism reveals not so much a penetrating insight into the practical affairs of the world, but a refusal to investigate what people mean when they assert the existence of rights that, for the bulk of humanity, are not in fact guaranteed by the existing institutional arrangements.

The right not to be hungry is not asserted as a recognition of an institutional right that already exists, as the right to property typically is. The assertion is primarily a moral claim as to what should be valued, and what institutional structure we should aim for, and try to guarantee if feasible. It can also be seen in terms of Ronald Dworkin's category of "background rights" — rights that provide a justification for political decisions by society in abstract. This interpretation serves as the basis for a reason to change the existing institutional structure and state policy.

It is broadly in this form that the right to "an adequate means of livelihood" is referred to in the Constitution of India: "The state shall, in particular, direct its policy towards securing . . . that the citizens, men and women equally, have the right to an adequate means of livelihood." This does not, of course, offer to each citizen a guaranteed right to an adequate livelihood, but the state is asked to take steps such that this right could become realizable for all.

In fact, this right has often been invoked in political debates in India. The electoral politics of India does indeed give particular scope for such use of what are seen as background rights. It is, of course, not altogether clear whether the reference to this right in the Indian constitution has in fact materially influenced the political debates. The constitutional statement is often cited, but very likely this issue would have figured in any case in these debates, given the nature of the moral and political concern. But whatever the constitutional contribution, it is interesting to ask whether the implicit acceptance of the value of the right to freedom from hunger makes any difference to actual policy.

It can be argued that the general acceptance of the right of freedom from acute hunger as a major goal has played quite a substantial role in preventing famines in India. The last real famine in India was in 1943, and while food availability per head in India has risen only rather slowly (even now the food availability per head is no higher than in many sub-Saharan countries stricken by recurrent famines), the country has not experienced any famine since independence in 1947. The main cause of that success is a policy of public intervention. Whenever a famine has threatened (e.g., in Bihar in 1967–68, in Maharashtra in 1971–73, in West Bengal in 1978–79), a public policy of intervention and relief has offered minimum entitlements to the potential famine victims, and thus have the threatening famines been averted. It can be argued that the quickness of the response of the respective governments (both state and central) reflects a political necessity, given the Indian electoral system and the importance attached by the public to the prevention of starvation. Political pressures from opposition groups and the news media have kept the respective governments on their toes, and the right to be free from acute hunger and starvation has been achieved largely because it has been seen as a valuable right. Thus the recognition of the intrinsic moral importance of this right, which has been widely invoked in public discussions, has served as a powerful political instrument as well.

On the other hand, this process has been far from effective in tackling pervasive and persistent undernourishment in India. There has been no famine in post-independence India, but perhaps a third of India's rural population is perennially undernourished. So long as hunger remains non-acute and starvation deaths are avoided (even though morbidity and mortality rates are enhanced by undernourishment), the need for a policy response is neither much discussed by the news media, nor forcefully demanded even by opposition parties. The elimination of famines coexists with the survival of widespread "regular hunger." The right to "adequate means" of *nourishment* does not at all seem to arouse political concern in a way that the right to "adequate means" to *avoid starvation* does.

The contrast can be due to one of several different reasons. It could, of course, simply be that the ability to avoid undernourishment is not socially accepted as very important. This could be so, though what is socially accepted and what is not is also partly a matter of how clearly the questions are posed. It is, in fact, quite possible that the freedom in question would be regarded as a morally important right if the question were posed in a transparent way, but this does not happen because of the nature of Indian electoral politics and that of news coverage. The issue is certainly not "dramatic" in the way in which starvation deaths and threatening famines are. Continued low-key misery may be too familiar a phenomenon to make it worthwhile for political leaders to get some mileage out of it in practical politics. The news media may also find little profit in emphasizing a non-spectacular phenomenon — the quiet survival of disciplined, non-acute hunger.

If this is indeed the case, then the implications for action of the goal of eliminating hunger, or guaranteeing to all the means for achieving this, may be quite complex. The political case for making the quiet hunger less quiet and more troublesome for governments in power is certainly relevant. Aggressive political journalism might prove to have an instrumental moral value if it were able to go beyond reporting the horrors of visible starvation and to portray the pervasive, non-acute hunger in a more dramatic and telling way. This is obviously not the place to discuss the instrumentalities of practical politics, but the endorsement of the moral right to be free from hunger — both acute and non-acute — would in fact raise pointed questions about the means which might be used to pursue such a goal.

Moral Assessment and Social Relations

. . . If there is one thing that emerges sharply from the discussion I have tried to present in this paper, it is the importance of factual analysis for moral assessment, including moral scrutiny of the acceptability and pursuit of specific rights. This is so even when the right in question is acknowledged to have intrinsic moral value, since valuing a right is not the same thing as accepting it. To affirm acceptability independently of consequences can be peculiarly untenable, as was discussed in analyzing entitlements and hunger. In assessing the claims of property rights, of the right not to be hungry, the examination cannot be confined to issues of basic valuation only, and much of the challenge of assessment lies in the empirical analysis of causes and effects. In the world in which we live — full of hunger as well as wealth — these empirical investigations can be both complex and quite extraordinarily important. The big moral questions are frequently also deeply economic, social, or political.

QUESTIONS

1. What is the difference between rights seen as instruments, rights seen as constraints, and rights seen as goals? Which of these three accounts of the nature of rights does Amartya Sen advocate?
2. Sen argues that hunger is typically the result of an inadequate distribution of entitlements rather than an inadequate supply of food. Explain his views in this regard.
3. What is a property right? What bearing do property rights have on the problem of hunger?
4. In Sen's view, which should take priority, property rights or what he describes as the moral disvalue of human misery?
5. In Sen's view, do human beings have a right not to be hungry?
6. Amartya Sen concludes that "if there is one thing that emerges sharply from the discussion I have tried to present in this paper, it is the importance of factual analysis for moral assessment." What leads him to this conclusion? Do you agree?

ECONOMIC INEQUALITY: JUSTICE AND INCENTIVES

Alistair M. Macleod

Schemes that are designed to provide people with economic incentives, whether for the purpose of increasing productivity in the workplace, for example, or (somewhat differently) for the purpose of encouraging investment, typically contribute to economic inequality in society. This is partly because the potential beneficiaries of such schemes generally belong to (often quite small) sub-classes of the community and partly because the members of these subclasses will in any case not benefit to the same extent by what they do in response to the offered inducements. The question I want to discuss is whether incentive-providing economic differences can be justified on grounds of justice. Since the assumption is sometimes made that *economic* inequalities — including those associated with the provision of incentives — need occasion no concern from the standpoint of justice, my first task is to try to show that the project of differentiating sharply between economic and noneconomic versions of the ideal of equality is bound to fail.

After a brief exploration of certain common but confused attitudes toward economic inequality, I argue that there is a presumption on fairness grounds in favor of equality in the distribution of economic resources, both because the most persuasive argument for the view that the members of a just society must be assured of equality in legal, political, educational, and employment contexts can be invoked in condemnation of certain common forms of economic inequality, and because it is impossible in any case to provide effective protection for these ostensibly noneconomic equalities without endorsing measures to reduce economic inequality. I will consider the question whether there are broader *rational* grounds

From Economic Justice: Private Rights and Public Interests, *edited by K. Kipnis and D. Meyers. New Jersey: Rowman and Allanheld, 1985, pp. 176–189. Reprinted by permission of Rowman and Littlefield Publishers Inc.*

too for this presumption in favor of equal distribution of economic resources. Finally, I take up the question whether incentive-providing economic differences can be justified on grounds of justice. I review several commonly touted ways of trying to bring incentive schemes under the 'umbrella' of a theory of distributive justice and conclude that this is a forlorn hope, since it is only *per accidens* that just economic inequalities will coincide with incentive-providing inequalities.

I begin with the fact of economic inequality, inequality within and between societies. By economic inequality I understand not only inequality in income or in wealth but also inequality in ease of access to, and in opportunity for enjoyment of, a wide range of goods and services in both the public and private sectors. In short, I have in mind all those differences among people that show up as differences in their standard of living. It is, of course, a complicated technical question how precisely 'economic inequality' is to be defined and how thereafter it is to be measured — if 'measurement' is not too ominously quantitative an expression. For present purposes, however, these complications do not matter, provided it can be taken for granted both that there is a broadly shared understanding or the kinds of differences among people which go to constitute economic inequality in the sense indicated, and that there is a great deal of economic inequality of this sort both within particular societies (including the most affluent) and between societies.

Is the fact of economic inequality, especially in its more dramatic forms, a disturbing fact? Should the fact that some people are well off and others not so well off and yet others are hardly able to eke out a precarious existence occasion concern?

Before identifying a number of distinct grounds, prudential and moral, for an affirmative answer to this question, let me describe briefly three occasionally heard responses on the other side. First, there are people who seem to suppose that economic inequality need not concern us much or at all in practice because by and large we cannot do much about it. The New Testament prediction "The poor ye shall always have with you" has been a perennial source of comfort and reassurance to the rich, offsetting to some extent the unease generated by the pronouncement that "it is easier for a camel to go through the eye of a needle than for a rich man to enter the kingdom of heaven." According to views of this sort, measures to help the poor are bound to be unavailing in the long run, unavailing "because . . ." — with some story supplied after the "because" purporting to show why economic inequality of the sort(s) often thought to be morally troublesome cannot be eliminated in any permanent way.

It is tempting to respond to such defeatist explanations by painting out that since successful attempts to reduce economic inequality in its more problematic forms have in fact been made, any explanatory story according to which it is impossible to reduce economic inequality in significant and permanent ways must, on that score alone, be rejected out of hand.

A second argument for the view that economic inequality ought not to occasion serious concern is that the poor are themselves to blame for their poverty and that consequently those who could help them are under no obligation to do so. The obvious rejoinders are two: (1) that no informed explanation of the major differences in standards of living that exist can trace these differences to the laziness or shiftlessness or the poor; and (2) that in any case there may well be an obligation, both prudential and moral, to assist even the so-called "undeserving" poor.

A third reason sometimes heard for not adopting practical measures to reduce economic inequality is that those who are well placed to underwrite such measures are generally not personally responsible for the plight of the poor and therefore have no obligation to enlist as foot soldiers in the war against poverty. Whereas the second argument places responsibility for poverty on the shoulders of the poor, according to this third argument, if the poor are not to blame for their plight, neither are the rich. The short answer to this argument is that even if the rich are not to blame (even indirectly) for the poverty of the poor, they may well have an obligation, both prudential and moral, to play their part in efforts, individual and collective, to diminish economic inequality. By no means all the obligations generated by the fact of injustice in society are obligations that fall upon those who can be reliably identified as having perpetrated the injustices in question: There can, after all, be injustice even when there is no villain in sight.

What, then, is the case for an affirmative answer to the question with which we began: whether the existence of economic inequality is the sort of fact that ought to occasion practical concern?

I have referred more than once to the prudential obligation the rich might be thought to have to help in the battle against economic inequality. What I have in mind is that it is to the advantage of the rich, certainly in the long run and sometimes also in the short run, to take practical steps to remedy the grievances of the economically disadvantaged. One of the clearer lessons of history, confirmed daily by newspaper headlines, is that people with economic grievances are often prepared to resort to socially disruptive measures if they have to. It is a commonplace of criminology, for example, that there is a disturbing correlation between economic deprivation and certain sorts of criminal behavior. Again, the dramatic upheavals associated with war or with civil strife in its various forms or with terrorist activity — all can be seen, at least in part, as attempts to secure economic betterment by violent means. Even from a narrowly prudential standpoint, then, rich nations and individuals have good reason to respond in practical ways to the demands of the poor. When Alexander Haig during his brief tenure at the State Department announced in a U.N. speech that it was "unrealistic" to expect the developed countries to make larger economic transfers to developing countries, he was expressing a profoundly foolish view given the stake the former have in maintaining peaceful relations with the latter.

The moral case for policies aimed at diminishing economic inequality is sometimes thought to require appeal to principles of common humanity. It is immaterial on this view whether the beneficiaries of such policies can be said either to deserve or to have a right to economic assistance. What matters is that they need it and that sympathetic concern for their predicament is often sufficient to motivate people to provide them with assistance. While this sort of benevolently motivated economic aid should not be looked at askance, it provides a very fragile basis for systematic action to eliminate undesirable forms of economic inequality. For one thing there may be too few people with the requisite feelings of sympathy to match the need for assistance. Moreover, it is demeaning to the recipients of such aid to be beholden to their benefactors, especially if the needs to be met are basic economic needs, and if the needy are in need through no fault of their own.

II

The question, then, is whether there are reasons of *justice* for supposing that economic inequality in at least some of its forms is something we ought to seek to diminish. I begin with a view that purports to take justice seriously — and which concedes the closeness of the connection there has traditionally been assumed to be between justice and equality — but which nevertheless contrives to deny that the fact of economic inequality is a source of legitimate concern on grounds of justice. On this view, a sharp distinction is drawn between economic inequality and various other kinds of inequality — inequality under the law, inequality in educational opportunity, inequality in job opportunity, and political inequality: And it is to these noneconomic inequalities alone that there is thought to be any objection from the standpoint of justice.

There are at least two reasons for doubting the feasibility of this kind or surgery on the equality ideal. The first and most obvious is that economic inequality is often itself a serious obstacle to satisfactory implementation of the ideals of equality under the law, equality of opportunity, and political equality. Thus full equality under the law may be unattainable in societies in which there is continuing substantial inequality in income or wealth: The resources of the legal system can be tapped more frequently and effectively by citizens with ample means than by those who cannot afford the best legal advice. Again, it is notoriously difficult to eliminate the many kinds of economic barriers there can be to proper achievement of the ideal of equality of opportunity in education and employment: Children from poor families typically have worse educational and employment prospects than children from more affluent homes even if they are entitled to attend the same schools and apply for the same jobs. And as for political equality, it is something of a commonplace that the right to participate in political decision-making processes cannot be satisfactorily secured for all the members of professedly democratic societies unless fairly far-reaching efforts are made either to eliminate certain kinds of economic inequalities or to neutralize the advantages of wealth in the political marketplace.

There is a second — and perhaps more interesting — reason for the inherent instability of attempts to combine principled commitment to the ideals of equality under the law, equality of opportunity, and political equality with indifference to the question whether economic resources are equally or unequally distributed in society. When it comes to the question *why* we should attach importance to bringing about equality of the favored kinds — and the question cannot be evaded, especially when it is recognized that justice requires equality of certain sorts only — the most plausible answer involves an appeal to the idea that the individual members of a society have an equal stake in being provided with the conditions for the living of a satisfactory life. In the absence of equality under the law, some people will have better prospects than others both of steering clear of the clutches of the law and of availing themselves of the resources of the legal system; and this means that they will be being provided — unfairly — with better general conditions for the living of their lives. Similarly, without equality of educational and employment opportunity, it will be much more difficult for some people than for others — and for reasons outside their control — to give effect over time to the life-plans they favor.

Finally, if political power is unequally distributed, those with little or no political clout run a greater risk of finding that the institutional framework within which they must seek to live out their lives is inimical to the achievement of their most deeply cherished aims. But if the right of the members of society to the conditions for the living of a satisfactory life underlies sponsorship of the ostensibly noneconomic versions of the equality ideal, it provides a plausible basis for concern about the justice of at least certain sorts of economic inequality. When economic resources are unequally distributed among the members of a society, those who are adversely affected by this distribution are arguably at an unfair disadvantage vis-a-vis those who are benefited by it — especially if the individuals in question cannot be said to deserve their good or bad fortune and if there is little they can do as individuals to alter the distribution.

Those who enjoy a larger than average share of economic resources have a much better chance than those with a smaller share of successfully implementing the life-plans they favor. In these circumstances, economic inequality must be seen to be as grave an obstacle to equalization of the conditions for the living of a satisfactory life as legal inequality or inequality of opportunity or political inequality. Would-be defenders of the various noneconomic equality ideals are thus confronted by an awkward dilemma: Either they must jettison the most persuasive defense available for the ideals of which they approve, or they must concede that certain kinds of economic inequality are as objectionable from the standpoint of justice as the inequalities that violate these ideals.

III

If the fundamental requirement of justice is that all the members of a society — and all equally — must be afforded the opportunity to live a satisfactory life, and if this means that there is a presumption on fairness grounds in favor of equal distribution of economic resources no less than of legal protection or of educational and employment opportunity or of political power, it is worth asking whether this presumption can be bolstered by appeal to broader considerations of rationality. Is there a rational presumption in favor of equal distribution of economic resources, or is there apt to be a more or less systematic conflict between the distribution that would be presumptively just and the distribution that would be presumptively rational?

I shall try to sketch an argument for the view that equality has a strong claim to recognition as a principle of rational decision making in situations in which the interests of the members of a society are in potential conflict. The argument is in three parts. In the first, an attempt is made to explain briefly why the principle of self-interest is a nonstarter as a principle for the making of rational allocative decisions when the interests of competing claimants to resources are at odds. In the second, I claim that it is doctrinaire (and question-begging) to assume that there can be no rational solution to the problem of rational allocation once the principle of self-interest peters out. In the final part, I argue that the principle of equality is the natural successor to the principle of self-interest once the latter, despite its appeal as a principle of rational decision making, is seen not to have any interesting application to the problem posed by the conflicting interests or claimants to resources.

(1) The first point to be established, then, is that in situations in which resources are scarce — that is, in situations in which it is impossible to provide all the members of a society with all the resources they would ideally require in order to give full effect to the schemes of life it is in their interest to seek to implement — the rationality of allocative decisions cannot be grounded in the principle of self-interest. The explanation is alarmingly simple. The principle of self-interest can be applied to determine what it would be rational to do only if the individual whose interests are to be promoted is specified, yet there seems to be no nonarbitrary way of providing the requisite specification that will yield a single, consistent answer to the rational distribution question. Let A, B, and C be three typical members of a society in which resources are not plentiful enough to provide all three with all they need for the implementation of the ideally advantageous life-plan. From whose point of view is the principle of self-interest to be applied for the purpose of determining what would constitute a rational distribution of resources among A, B, and C?

One possibility is to adopt A's standpoint as a self-interested agent and to represent as rational the distribution that would be maximally advantageous to A, no matter how disadvantageous it proved to be for B and C. Yet it is entirely arbitrary — and thus in the present context not at all rational — to single out A for specialty favored treatment: A solution to the distribution problem just as determinate — and one having the same formal structure, moreover — could have been reached by applying the principle of self-interest from B's point of view as a self-interested agent, or for that matter from C's.

Can we, then, eliminate the taint or arbitrariness from solutions that assign privileged status to the point of view of just one of A, B, and C by applying the principle of self-interest from A's standpoint *and* from B's standpoint *and* from C's and thereafter trying to amalgamate the resulting judgments? The trouble with this strategy, of course, is that it yields either three mutually contradictory judgments about what would constitute a rational distribution or three judgments which, while not mutually contradictory, nevertheless say nothing about what it would be rational to do, all things considered. The latter will be the case if each of the judgments to be amalgamated incorporates a reference to the point of view from which a given distribution would have to be said to be rational. The judgment that distribution D1 is the rational one from A's point of view is clearly quite compatible with the judgment that D2 is the rational distribution from B's point of view (or D3 from C's), yet none of these judgments tells us which of D1, D2, and D3 it would be rational to bring about, *all things considered.*

However, if we eliminate the phrases "from A's point of view," "from B's point of view," and "from C's point of view" from the judgments purporting to tell us what distribution it would be rational to effect, the three judgments are mutually contradictory. While each of them does indeed now identify some determinate distribution of resources among A, B, and C as rational *period* — and not simply as rational *from A's point of view* (of from B's or C's) — it is not the same distribution for all three, yet the rational distribution *period* cannot be the distribution that is maximally advantageous to A (viz. D1) *and* the distribution that is maximally advantageous to B (viz. D2) *and* the distribution that is maximally advantageous to C (viz. D3).

It seems, then, that the attempt to apply the principle of self-interest to our distribution problem by amalgamating into a single comprehensive judgment the judgments made from the standpoints of each of the three members of our hypothetical society cannot give us what we need: Either the component judgments are mutually compatible but unhelpful, or they are judgments that, while individually informative, cancel one another out. Can this stalemate be avoided? Only, it would seem, by transforming the situation in which A, B, and C are at odds with one another about what the answer is to the question what distribution of resources among them it would be *rational* to effect into one in which they are prepared to negotiate a deal with one another that reflects not only their sense of what would be advantageous to them as individuals whose interests conflict but also their sense of their relative power to secure for themselves more than an equal share through issuance of threats and counter threats. Thus if there is a shared recognition of the fact that B and C would be no match for A if it came to a fight for resources, and if it would be advantageous all around for the fight not to take place, there is a clear enough sense in which determinate distribution D4 — a distribution of resources markedly more advantageous to A than to B or C — might have to be said to be the distribution required in these circumstances by the principle of self-interest.

It is true that on this reconstruction of the situation — and of what is involved in the application of the principle of self-interest to the resolution of the conflicting claims of A, B, and C — we do not get the kind of stalemate we got earlier. But the price is high. For without acknowledgment, we are now permitting a nonrational criterion — viz. the relative power of the claimants to make a successful grab for more than an equal share — to play a crucial part in determining what distribution of resources it would be rational to try to bring about. The only reason why D4 furnishes the favored solution is that B and C are known to be no match for A in a knock-down fight. That the *rationality* of a judgment about the distribution of resources to be aimed at should be thought to be a function of the relative power of the individuals whose interests are in conflict runs counter, however, to the idea that appeals to *reason* must be contrasted in these contexts with appeals (however cunningly veiled or disguised) to *force*.

(2) The failure of the principle of self-interest to provide a rational basis for adjudication of the competing claims to scarce resources of A, B, and C ought not to be taken as evidence that there is *no* rational basis. That would be to assume that the principle of self-interest is the only available principle for the making of rational decisions — which is precisely what is at issue. It is not an a priori truth that self-interest is the only possible principle of practical rationality, and the shape of the resource-allocation problem posed by the fact that the interests of the members of society are often at odds with one another itself strongly suggests that appeal to considerations of self-interest will not suffice. It is, after all, precisely because we know that the shares it would be to the advantage of the competing claimants to receive cannot be made available to them that we face the problem about what distribution of resources it would be rational to aim at.

(3) Is there, then, any rational solution to the problem of conflicting interests if the principle of self-interest provides no satisfactory basis for rational decision making in such contexts? Consider the following argument. Importance attaches from A's point of view to the protection and promotion of A's interests, as the principle of self-interest itself clearly presupposes. Importance must also be held to attach (and for the same reason) to protection and promotion of B's — and indeed of C's — interests. It would be arbitrary (and thus not rational) to give systematic precedence to A's interests when they are in conflict with the interests of B or of C without providing reasons for doing so. But reasons of self-interest (the only reasons so far in sight) cannot be supplied for doing so that could not as easily be offered in support of giving systematic precedence to the interests of B or C. Is it therefore reasonable to conclude that equal importance must be held to attach to protection and promotion of interests of A *and* B *and* C? It is, in short, presumptively rational for the distribution problem posed by the conflicting claims of A, B, and C to be solved by allocating an equal share of the resources in question to each of A, B, and C.

It should be observed that the principle of equality has a claim to be recognized as the natural successor to the principle of self-interest once the latter is seen to be not even a contender as a principle for the rational adjudication of conflicts of interest. After all, it takes seriously the assumption that importance attaches to protection and promotion of A's interests (which is built into the view that it is rational for A to do what will serve to protect and promote his own interests), and the assumption that importance attaches to protection and promotion of B's interests (which is implicit in the view that B acts rationally when he does what will serve to protect and promote his own interests), and the assumption that importance attaches to protection and promotion of C's interests (which is part and parcel of the view that C acts rationally when he does what is in his own interest.) All that the principle of equality as a putative successor principle adds is a recognition that if importance is to be held to attach to the securing of the interests of A *and* B *and* C, then in situations in which these interests are in conflict, the rational assumption for any would-be adjudicator to make is that *equal* importance attaches to protection and promotion of the interests of A and B and C.

IV

Even if there is a presumption in favor of the fairness of equal distribution of resources — a presumption, moreover, which is not at all at odds with the sort of distribution it might be thought to be *rational* to try to effect — it is, of course, a rebuttable presumption. I want to examine briefly the view that the requisite rebuttal can take the form of demonstrating that unequal distribution is sometimes necessary for the provision of incentives.

It should be noted to begin with that incentive arguments are often difficult to get off the ground for reasons unrelated to the question whether incentive-providing economic differentials are *fair*. It is often no small feat to establish that this or that determinate inequality in the distribution of resources is in fact needed in given circumstances for the provision of incentives. Suppose A is an individual who — according to the sponsor of an incentive argument — must be supplied with a larger than equal share of resources to ensure that he engages in activity 'a'. For the argument to be in the running for recognition, three things will have to be established: (1) that A will not in fact engage in activity 'a' if no incentive is offered him to do so; (2) that A will engage in activity 'a' if he is guaranteed extra resources of the sort contemplated in the incentive scheme; and (3) that he cannot be induced to engage in activity 'a' if he is offered any smaller share of the resources available for distribution than that envisaged in the scheme. Where the first condition is not met — because there is good reason to believe that A fully intends to engage in activity 'a' *anyway* — giving additional resources to A cannot even be described without linguistic impropriety as a matter of providing him with an incentive to engage in activity 'a', so the question whether it would be justified on incentive grounds does not arise.

Where (2) is not substantiated, we have no evidence yet that the determinate share of the available resources earmarked for A under the proposed scheme will suffice to induce him to engage in activity 'a'; and we do not even know whether the needed incentive could be supplied by his being offered some larger — perhaps much larger — share. It is simply false that every man has his price: It may be impossible to induce A to engage in activity 'a' no matter how large a share of resources he is promised. Where condition (3) is not satisfied, there is clearly no reason to accept the claim that the sort of unequal allocation of resources envisaged under the scheme is justified on incentive grounds. If a smaller share for A would suffice, what we have is at best an argument for a less dramatic inequality. ("The bigger the bonus, the greater the incentive" is a seductive falsehood.)

At least three additional hurdles must be surmounted if an incentive argument is to be constructed in rebuttal of the presumption in favor of the fairness of equal distribution of resources. First, any doubt there may be about the desirability in principle of activity 'a' — or about the propriety of offering A economic inducements to engage in it — must be laid to rest. Second, the 'payoff' to those who stand to benefit from the doing of 'a' must be examined to determine whether there is a prima facie case for preferring the situation where A is induced to engage in 'a' at the cost to others of the 'extra' resources he needs to motivate him to the situation where others hang on to these resources but lose out on whatever benefit would have come their way had A engaged in activity 'a'. For example, it may cost an employer so much to provide a reluctant employee with the incentive to carry out some workplace task that he may conclude that the bonus would not be worth paying. It might be clearly preferable from the employer's point of view for the task to be left unperformed than for A to be given the kind of extra payment it might take to persuade him to undertake it. While in this case the verdict on the incentive scheme is one the employer reaches on the basis of a review of the benefits and costs to *him* of (a) setting up and (b) not setting up an incentive scheme, it is clear that the 'payoff' issue might call for examination of the benefits and costs associated with incentive schemes for all who are likely to be affected by them, whether favorably or unfavorably. Equally clearly, the broader the investigation, the smaller the likelihood becomes of our being able to plot with any confidence all the advantages and disadvantages associated with an incentive scheme, let alone to determine where the balance of advantage lies.

The final hurdle — and much the most difficult to surmount — has to do with the fairness of the inequalities generated, perpetuated, or accentuated by incentive schemes. If the presumption in favor of the fairness of equal distribution of resources is successfully to be rebutted on the basis of an argument about the need for incentives, it must be shown how incentive-providing differentials are fair, or at any rate not unfair. Can this be shown?

I can only sketch, without much discussion, a number of possible answers. The upshot will be (at best) the highlighting of one part of the problem of trying to give recognition to incentive-providing differentials within the framework of a theory of economic justice. First, a rather bald formulation of the views in question.

(a) According to utilitarians, economic inequalities associated with incentive-providing schemes can be said to be just (or at any rate not unjust) if and only if they serve to maximize the net benefit to society as a whole.

(b) According to Rawls, economic inequalities generated by incentive schemes are just provided they serve to maximize the benefit for the worst-off members of society.

(c) According to one kind of desert theory, incentive-providing differentials are just because and so far as they contribute to a distribution of resources that reflects the deserts or merits of the individual members of society.

(d) According to another sort of desert theory — one that accents the notion of fair compensation — incentive-providing inequalities are just if and so far as they serve to compensate individuals for the unusual burdensomeness (dangerousness, unpleasantness) of the work they do.

What, if anything, is wrong with these arguments?

The first two — that is, the arguments sponsored by utilitarians and by Rawls — reflect a sound grasp of the structure of incentive arguments and attempt to provide "space" for them within the framework of a theory of justice. They do this by imposing a stringent condition on the 'pay-off' associated with incentive schemes. This means that such schemes can be highly beneficial — conferring benefit perhaps on a great many people who were not among their intended beneficiaries — and yet fail to satisfy this condition. Thus the utilitarian is prepared to represent an incentive-providing inequality as just (or not unjust) only if it will serve to maximize the benefit to society as a whole. Tough though this condition is to meet, it is arguably the wrong sort of condition: Even if on some rare occasion the distribution to which an incentive scheme contributed could be said to be both just and benefit-maximizing, it is about as implausible to suppose that a distribution is just *because* it is benefit-maximizing as it would be to claim that conduct is courageous *because* it serves to maximize the benefit for society as a whole.

There is a somewhat similar confusion in Rawls's position when he contrives to represent as just (or not unjust) any incentive-providing inequality that will serve to maximize the benefit to the worst-off. Incentive schemes that measure up to the demanding requirement embedded in Rawls's Difference Principle cannot be said *on that account* to be just. To suppose that they can would be to suppose that we can represent as fair, for example, the exorbitant demands of people who happen to have socially valuable and comparatively rare skills, even where the fact that they press these demands more relentlessly than others with roughly similar competences is principally a reflection of their greater greed or obstinacy in the negotiations that determine the distribution of resources. The lion's share such people are sometimes able to secure for themselves must on Rawls's view be said to be their fair share of the resources at society's disposal — provided, of course, his maximum condition is met — even though their success in securing this share is traceable to their willingness to drive a hard bargain. Yet it offends our sense of what is fair to suppose that ruthless pursuit of one's own interests at the bargaining table can be even a partial determinant of what one's fair share of society's resources is going to have to be said to be.

With the other two views, the trouble is that while the principles to which they appeal are plausibly representable as principles of fair distribution, it is unclear how precisely they serve to constrain acceptance of incentive-providing schemes. Thus it is plausible to argue that it is not unfair to pay A more than B if A has worked longer hours than B. It is only fair, we might say, for A's share of resources (in this case in the form of earnings) to be larger than B's: A, we might say, deserves a larger share. But how does this sort of argument — even if we are disposed to accept it — tell us when we should and when we should not endorse incentive schemes that will contribute to unequal distribution of resources as between A and B? What is at issue is the forging of a connection between desert-reflecting differences in remuneration and incentive-providing differences. These are clearly differences of different kinds. It is one thing to skew rates of pay in A's favor in order to induce him to work longer hours, and quite another to pay him more because he has in fact worked longer hours. Nor are these differences necessarily connected — with the one being a forward-looking and the other a backward-looking version of one and the same position on the question whether A and B should or should not receive the same income. For the evidence may be that A is in fact prepared to work longer hours than B *whether or not* he receives extra pay for doing so. This will be fatal to the incentive argument, yet the desert argument will be unaffected.

Similarly, to turn to the compensation argument, it is plausible to hold that people who work at unusually dangerous or unpleasant or otherwise arduous jobs ought in fairness to be paid more than those who work at safe, pleasant, less arduous jobs, with extra pay being designed to compensate them for the additional burdens they are required to carry. But how does this argument, even if we are disposed to accept it, help us determine when we should and when we should not accept incentive-providing differences in the levels of remuneration proposed for A and B? What is at issue is the forging of a connection between incentive-providing differences in pay and differences in pay designed to provide compensation for unpleasant features of job-related tasks. These are clearly differences of different kinds. It is one thing to pay A more than B in order to induce A to take on the dirty and hazardous job of coal miner; it is quite another to pay him more in order to compensate him for the difficulties and dangers associated with working two miles underground. Moreover, there is a merely contingent connection between remuneration strategies designed to provide employees with incentives and remuneration strategies designed to compensate them for the burdensomeness of the tasks they perform. Thus if it is known to be the case in a remote mining community hard hit by unemployment that local residents are in fact prepared to work underground at rates no higher than those paid workers doing roughly comparable work in a pleasanter and safer environment, the argument that they should be offered extra pay on incentive grounds will be a nonstarter, yet the argument that they ought to be given premium pay to compensate them for the unpleasantness of having to work two miles underground will retain its force.

The general conclusion to be drawn is that the presumption in favor of the fairness of equal distribution or resources cannot easily be rebutted by arguing that economic inequality is necessary for the provision of incentives. There may, of course, be a case for permitting certain inequalities for this purpose. What is questionable is whether the case can be argued on fairness grounds.

There is one obvious enough way in which there may be a direct connection between fair economic differentials and incentive-providing differentials, though it is a connection very different from the sort needed to remedy the deficiencies in incentive arguments noted above. Suppose it would be fair (or at any rate not unfair) for A to receive a larger salary than B, perhaps because this reflects their relative deserts (since A regularly works longer hours than B, say), or because on compensatory grounds it is appropriate for the rate of remuneration for the kind of work A does to be higher than that for the kind of work B does. Suppose too that there is a recognition of this on A's part: Suppose that A firmly believes that he ought in fairness to be paid more than B. And suppose, finally, that A is unprepared to perform job-related tasks — or unprepared to perform them diligently or conscientiously — unless he is fairly remunerated. Under these conditions, arranging fair remuneration for A (paying him more than B) may hold the key to inducing him to continue working, or at any rate to continue working diligently. There would, in short, be a direct connection between giving recognition to principles of fair remuneration in the vetting of income differentials and providing employees like A with an incentive to go on working reasonably diligently.

Two things should be noted, however, about this way of trying to forge a link between incentive-related economic inequalities and just economic inequalities. First, it is a link mediated by the merely contingent fact that people are sometimes motivated to accept or reject proposed remuneration schedules on the basis of the degree to which these conform to their sense of what would be fair in the way of income differentials. It is a nice empirical question as to how far a sense of what is fair in matters of remuneration in fact plays in motivating people. Second, even when the rather special conditions in our example are satisfied, the question of whether economic inequalities are defensible on fairness grounds is clearly logically independent of the question of whether acceptance of such inequalities is defensible on incentive grounds. No matter what the basis of A's belief that it would be fair for him to receive more than an equal share of economic resources, it clearly has nothing to do with his asking himself whether or not he will lack the incentive to undertake job-related tasks if he receives less. The fact that once he has reached the conclusion — on ground quite independent of incentive considerations — that a larger share would be fair, he will be unprepared to undertake job-related tasks unless he receives this share is a contingent fact about him, a fact that does nothing to show that there is any *essential* connection between principles of fair remuneration and principles that accord recognition to incentive-providing economic inequalities.

NOTES

Part of the preliminary work on this paper was begun while I was a Visiting Fellow at the Institute for Advanced Studies in the Humanities at the University of Edinburgh. An earlier version was presented at the AMINTAPHIL conference on Economic Justice held in January 1983 at the University of Florida in Gainesville. A travel grant provided by the School of Graduate Studies and Research at Queen's University made it possible for me to take part in the conference.

BIBLIOGRAPHY

Amartya, K. Sen. *On Economic Inequality*. Oxford: Oxford University Press, 1973.

Atkinson, A. B. *The Economics of Inequality*. Oxford: Oxford University Press, 1975.

Barry, Brian. *A Liberal Theory of Justice*, chap. 15, "Economics." Oxford: Oxford University Press. 1973.

Clegg, Hugh. *How to Run an Incomes Policy and Why We Made Such a Mess of the Last One*. chaps. IV and V. London: Heinmann, 1971.

Nagel, Thomas. "Equality." In Nagel, *Mortal Questions*. Cambridge: Cambridge University Press, 1979.

QUESTIONS

1. How is the issue of economic incentives related to evaluating the moral significance of disparities in income or the problem of poverty?

2. In Macleod's view, is the existence of economic inequality something that should occasion practical concern? Should it occasion moral concern? Are these two kinds of concern related?

3. Why in the end does Macleod conclude that the argument from the need for economic incentives is not a persuasive justification of economic disparities?

SUGGESTIONS FOR FURTHER READING

- As Amartya Sen points out in his contribution to this chapter, facts are of crucial importance in building a critical understanding of an issue like poverty. The facts about poverty, however, are constantly being updated. What is needed to keep abreast of current information is not specific publications but rather reliable sources of information. There are many such sources. What follows are just a few that are readily accessible.

- The Canadian Council on Social Development publishes an annual fact book on poverty which includes information about the changing face of poverty, comparisons with poverty in other countries, and poverty data for the provinces and large cities. These reports are available from CCSD, 441 MacLaren St., 4th Floor, Ottawa ON K2P 2H3, tel: 613-236-8977/fax:236-2750.

- Citizens for Public Justice is a non-partisan national Christian organization of citizens which promotes justice in Canadian public affairs. It has a strong research wing that studies and reports from an ethical perspective on public issues including the issue of poverty. It is located in Toronto at #311, 229 College St., M5T 1RA, tel: 416-979-2443, email: cjp@web.apc.org.

- *Human Development Reports* are published by the United Nations Development Program (UNDP). The United Nations began preparing these reports in 1990. They are published annually and can be found in the public documents sections of libraries, from United Nations bookstores which are found in a number of cities across the country, or from the United Nations itself. They provide a wealth of information about human development in all parts of the world.
- The National Council of Welfare, referred to in the introduction of this chapter, publishes annual *Poverty Profiles*, the latest of which reports on 1994. These reports are available from the Council (2nd floor, 1010 Somerset St. W., Ottawa ON K1A 0J9, tel: 613-957-2961).
- The National Anti-Poverty Organization has a wealth of material on the subject of poverty. One of their reports is included as a reading in this chapter. They can be reached at: 316-256 King Edward Ave., Ottawa ON K1N 7M1, tel: 613-789-0242, e-mail: NAPO@web.apc.org.

Books and Articles

- Nigel Dower, "World Poverty," in *A Companion to Ethics*, edited by Peter Singer (Cambridge: Cambridge University Press, 1991). This article argues that there is an obligation to relieve world poverty "though not a relentless, overburdening one."
- Garrett Hardin, "Living on a Lifeboat," is found in many moral issues texts including *Ethical Issues*, edited by Eldon Soifer (Peterborough: Broadview Press, 1992). In this well-known article, Harding argues against the view that the wealthy nations of the world have an obligation to help nations that are poor.
- Susan James, "The Duty to Relieve Suffering," *Ethics* 93, October 1982. The author argues that our duty to prevent harm is greater than people usually are prepared to admit. The way to persuade people of this fact is to take existing beliefs seriously and to help people to understand their implications for responding to suffering. Appealing to moral theory is not likely to achieve the same results.
- Peter Marin, "Helping and Hating the Homeless," in *Harpers Magazine*, January 1987. This is an insightful exploration of the nature of poverty and the people in its grip. The author describes who the poor are and where they come from, their reasons and motives for living in poverty and the paradoxes and challenges they pose for modern America.
- Kai Nielsen, "Arguing for Equality," in *Philosophic Exchange* 1986 published by the Centre for Philosophic Exchange, State University of New York. In this paper, Kai Nielsen defends the thesis that for there to be a free society there must be an extensive equality of living conditions across that society. Large disparities in wealth and income are not compatible with freedom, contrary to the widely held opposing view.
- *Policy Options* is a periodical which is published ten times a year by the Institute for Research on Public Policy. Its July-August 1996 issue is devoted to a discussion by several contributors from several points of view of welfare and unemployment in Canada.
- Christopher Sarlo, *Poverty in Canada* (2nd ed.) (Vancouver: The Fraser Institute, 1996). This is an updated version of the same book which was published in 1994. It challenges the definition of poverty widely used by organizations such as those referred to above and then undertakes a detailed analysis of the extent of poverty in light of its own definition. The author argues that poverty is considerably less prevalent in Canada than is widely reported by the media.

- Peter Singer, "Rich and Poor," from *Practical Ethics*, edited by the same author (Cambridge: Cambridge University Press, 1979). This is another widely read article in which Peter Singer argues the very strong view that those who are well off have an obligation to share their wealth with the poor — to the point where to do so would make them less well off than those they are helping.

Chapter 9

Environmental Ethics

Introduction

In this final chapter, we turn to an area unique among the topics considered to this point To begin with, the matters of previous chapters have been the subject of discussion for centuries, and in some cases for much of human history. In contrast, environmental issues have emerged as the focus of a sustained public ethical discussion and debate only recently. One of the challenges of this chapter is understanding why this is so. Second, the focus of discussion in previous chapters has been on articulating the values and principles that should guide human interaction. With this chapter, we look to see whether the principles that have emerged from our discussion apply or ought to apply to our interaction with other sentient creatures, and with the environment generally.

Background Considerations

Until relatively recently, environmental issues have not been the subject of sustained or widespread ethical scrutiny. Why this is so is itself a matter of considerable controversy and debate, some of which is addressed directly or alluded to in the readings which follow. Two factors, however, seem uncontroversially relevant. First, until this century, the human population has expanded, if only quite slowly. There are, no doubt, many complex reasons for this; however, exposure to disease and limitations on the capacity to produce and distribute food are important factors. In the twentieth century, these limiting conditions have witnessed radical alteration. The explosion in medical knowledge has brought the eradication of communicable diseases like smallpox, dramatic improvements in public health standards, and the capacity to control infections through the use of antibiotics. From this has come declining rates of infant mortality and a significantly increased lifespan for much of the world.

A second factor, and one related to the first, has been the explosion of knowledge in science and technology. Human beings can now quite literally move mountains, change the direction of the flow of water across continents, produce energy cheaply in response to exponentially increasing demand, and create new technologies, new products, new chemicals, and now new life forms at a speed unique in human history.

The result is a rapidly increasing human population and an increasingly more powerful capacity to change the natural world in environmentally significant ways.

The Current Situation

Today, we find ourselves faced with a situation unique in human history. Our numbers are growing rapidly. The green revolution made possible by scientific advances in the field of agriculture has allowed the increased agricultural production needed to feed a rapidly expanding human population. However, the changes that have made this possible have not been without significant environmental impact. One of the most important impingements is that of soil depletion resulting from an agro-economy based on new technologies. A second is the impact of chemicals on human and other life forms, of which the history of DDT is a good illustration. It is not irrelevant that in spite of remarkable advances in agriculture and the ability to distribute food from one part of the world to another, starvation is not uncommon, and many people today simply do not have enough to eat, as our discussion of poverty in an earlier chapter illustrates.

Equally important is the fact that advances in scientific technology have opened the door to industrial activity, the byproducts of which have caused far-reaching and damaging environmental impacts. The most dramatic evidence of this is global warming. Just the suggestion that modern industrial activity has the capacity to alter climates globally illustrates the kind of changes that have brought to environmental issues an urgent ethical dimension.

Global warming, however, is just one of the many significant environmental issues we face today. Others include the pollution of land and water, deforestation, soil depletion, the extinction of species, the impact of new farming technologies on the welfare of animals, the disposal of waste in all its forms, including radioactive wastes resulting from the production of nuclear energy, energy consumption (Canadians consume more energy per person than almost any other country in the world) and so on.

One of the concepts that has emerged from the discussion of these issues is that of sustainable development. Popularized by the Brundtland Commission, this notion is now central to environment debates. In the words of the Commission, development is sustainable if it "meets the needs of the present without compromising the ability of future generations to meet their own needs." In spite of its broad appeal, the notion of sustainable development has been vigorously challenged by many environmentalists who have concluded that the capacity of the earth to absorb further development has now been exhausted. Environmental protection or conservation, they argue, requires nothing less than a dramatic change in the way particularly those in the advanced industrial countries live, as well as the way in which we as human beings understand our place in nature.

A final important component of this picture is the role of government in responding to what many see as a developing environmental crisis. This is essentially a public policy issue having to do with environmental regulation. Throughout much of the second half of this century, there has been increasing momentum in the industrialized world toward increasingly strict environmental regulation. The result is that it is not uncommon to have environmental assessments precede the launch of large industrial projects. Recent changes in the political coloration of provincial and federal governments in Canada, however, are now leading to a reassessment of this trend. Hence, the role of governments in addressing environmental concerns has itself become a matter of ethical analysis and debate.

The Moral Dimension

What, then, are the moral dimensions of these wide-ranging environmental concerns? As it turns out, this is not an easy question to answer, for reasons that attach to all moral analysis but are particularly acute where environmental issues are under discussion.

The first hurdle to be overcome is simply getting the facts straight. Thought of in abstract terms, this may not seem a particularly challenging problem. After all, getting one's facts right is an important first step in resolving any moral issue. There are particular difficulties, however, where environmental issues are concerned. This is because the factual component of environmental issues is complex and often contested. As a consequence, expertise is highly valued. The result, frequently, is that the relevant facts are usually assembled by scientists and communicated in technical language that non-scientists have a good deal of trouble understanding. The debates that environmental concerns generate are frequently dominated by experts, and this has led some to believe that the real problems are technical or scientific. Hence, ethical concerns are frequently shunted aside.

Faced with these complexities, the ethical analysis of environmental issues can be challenging. First, it requires some technical expertise. Second, the ethical dimensions of the issues must be carefully analyzed. This, in turn, leads to a second important consideration, best set out by comparing the ethical character of environmental issues with the treatment we have given the issues examined in earlier chapters of this book.

To this point in the book, our focus has been more or less exclusively on the obligations we have as human beings to other human beings thought of individually or collectively. Environmental ethics challenges that focus. In particular, it requires that we think carefully about whether our obligations as human beings extend only to other human beings, or whether the kinds of principles we have been articulating — the protection of life principle, the avoidance of suffering principle, the moral autonomy principle, and the equal worth principle — apply also to other sentient creatures and perhaps also to the environment. For example, ensuring the preservation of wild fur-bearing animals is of obvious importance for anyone whose life depends on trapping. But if it could be established that no human beings were likely to be affected by their disappearance, would protecting these animals have moral significance? This kind of question is central to the emerging field of environmental ethics.

A second important dimension of environmental ethics is captured by notions like sustainable development. What is central to the debate is not simply the welfare of currently existing people and other morally significant entities. Crucially important, as well, are our obligations to future generations. Do we have obligations to the future? If so, are these obligations similar to those we have to the present? Finally, how are our obligations to the future, assuming we have such obligations, to be balanced against those we have to the present?

These questions are not of purely academic interest. The answers we give to them could have significant implications for the way in which we currently live, eat, work, and play.

The Readings

In the discussions that follow, environmental issues are explored from a variety of perspectives. Northrop Frye sets out some of the historical and intellectual dimensions of traditional Canadian attitudes to the environment. The second reading, a case study, explores the cultural and moral dimensions of the concept of sustainable development. In the third reading, Mary Midgley in "Duties Concerning Islands" criticizes theories that ignore the social and cultural dimensions of morality and treat individuals as though they were "social atoms" whose moral obligations extend only to other human beings who are in a position to hinder or help them as they pursue their individual interests. Rather, she argues, human beings have a much broader range of obligations or duties of care and responsibility to a wide range of people and things not in a position to help or harm them. This includes the duty not to be gratuitously destructive even where it cannot be shown to have harmful implications for other human beings.

The focus then shifts to an evaluation of deep ecology, a environmental philosophy that has attempted to set out in a systematic and holistic way a comprehensive understanding of our relation and responsibility as human beings to the environment. It is a view that implies that the protection of life, avoidance of suffering, moral autonomy, and equal worth principles do have moral force in describing our obligations to the environment. Tom Regan explores the claims of deep ecology sympathetically but ultimately rejects them. He argues, nevertheless, that animals, being sentient, do have rights that human beings ought to respect. Jan Narveson then questions Regan's position, arguing against Regan and Midgley for a view of morality that roots moral obligations in contractual relations between and among existing human beings. Finally, Andrew Brook examines the ethics of waste disposal using nuclear waste as a test case. Central to his discussion are our obligations to future generations.

CANADA: NEW WORLD WITHOUT REVOLUTION

Northrop Frye

Canada, with four million square miles and only four centuries of documented history, has naturally been a country more preoccupied with space than with time, with environment rather than tradition. The older generation, to which I have finally become assigned, was brought up to think of Canada as a land of unlimited natural resources, an unloving but rich earth-mother bulging with endless supplies of nickel and asbestos, or, in her softer parts, with the kind of soil that would allow of huge grain and lumber surpluses. The result of such assumptions is that many of our major social problems are those of ecology, the extinction of animal species, the plundering of forests and mines, the pollution of water, as the hundreds of millions of years that nature took to build up our supplies of coal and oil are cancelled out in a generation or two. The archaeologists who explore royal tombs in Egypt and Mesopotamia find they are almost always anticipated by grave robbers, people who got there first because they had better reasons for doing so than the acquisition of knowledge. We are the grave robbers of our own resources, and posterity will not be grateful to us. There is, however, a growing understanding that our situation is not simply one of people against planes, or whatever the current issue may be, but of soil and trees and water against concrete and tarmac.

From Divisions on a Ground: Essays on Canadian Culture *(Toronto: House of Anansi Press, 1982). Reprinted by permission of Stoddart Publishing Co. Ltd.*

These spatial and environmental problems have a temporal dimension as well. Our history began in the seventeenth century, the age of Baroque expansion in Europe, where the countries advancing most rapidly into the future were those on the Atlantic seaboard. Rapid advance is usually followed either by rapid decline or by a rapid change in some other direction: even by then Spain and Portugal had passed their meridian of growth, and France soon turned back to its European preoccupations. If the French had held Canada they might well have sold it, as they did Louisiana. What is important is not nationality but cultural assumptions. The Baroque age was an age of intense belief in the supremacy of human consciousness over nature. It had discovered something of the technological potential of mathematics, once mathematics had become attached to a powerful social organization. It was not an age of individualism, as is often said, but an age of relatively enlightened despotism, and in some ways very like the dawn of civilization in the Near East, when the pyramids of Egypt and the ziggurats of Babylon emerged as dramatic witness to what men could do when united under a sufficiently strong social will. Both then and in the Baroque period, mathematics, and the appearance of geometrical patterns in the human environment, was a symbol of aggressiveness, of imperialistic domination. We can see the results all over our country, in the grid patterns of our cities, the concession lines that divide up the farmland into squares, the railways and highways that emphasize direction through land-scape rather than accommodation to it. Improvement in such communications always means a wider and straighter path through nature, and a corresponding decline of interest in it. With the coming of the aeroplane, even the sense of passing through a natural environment disappears. Our attitude to nature is reflected in our social environment, the kind we build ourselves. Washington was a city designed for automobiles rather than pedestrians long before there were any automobiles: Los Angeles, a city never designed at all, seems to have broken through the control even of the automobile. It was, after all, named after angels, who traditionally do not travel through space but simply manifest themselves elsewhere.

The religion that the British and French brought to the New World was not a natural monotheism, like the Algonquin worship of a Great Spirit, nor an imperial monotheism like that of the Stoics, but a revolutionary monotheism, with a God who took an active and partisan role in history; and like all revolutionary movements, including Marxism in our time, it equipped itself with a canon of sacred books and a dialectical habit of mind, a mental attitude in which the neighboring heresy is much more bitterly hated than the total rejection of the faith. The dialectical habit of mind produced the conception of the false god, a conception hardly intelligible to an educated pagan. All false gods, in the Christian view, were idols, and all idolatry came ultimately from the belief that there was something numinous in nature. The Christian teaching was that there were no gods in nature; that nature was a fellow-creature of man, and that all the gods that had been discovered in it were devils. We have derived many benefits from this attitude, but it had a more sinister side: it tended to assume that nature, not being inhabited or protected by gods or potentially dangerous spirits, was simply something available for human exploitation. Everywhere we look today, we see the conquest of nature by an intelligence that does not love it, that feels no part of it, that splits its own consciousness off from it and looks at it as an object. The sense of the absolute and unquestionable rightness of man's conquest over nature extended to other cultures regarded as being in a "state of nature." The primary principle of white settlement in this country, in practice if not always in theory, was that the indigenous cultures should be destroyed, not preserved or continued or even set apart.

The spokesman for the Baroque phase of this attitude is Descartes, whose fundamental axiom, "I think, therefore I am," rested on a desire to derive human existence from human consciousness, and to see that consciousness as being in a different world from the nature which for Descartes was pure extension in space. This attitude, in itself a logical development from the traditional Christian view of nature, got so far away from idolatry that it became a kind of idolatry in reverse, the idol this time being human consciousness itself, separated from nature. We live today in a social environment which is a triumph of Cartesian consciousness; an abstract and autonomous world of interlocking co-ordinates, in which most of our imagination is focussed not on nature but on the geometrical shapes that we have imposed on nature. My own few childhood memories of big cities are full of a kind of genial clutter: crowds of people on streets, shops with their doors open, theatres with glittering lights; and certainly the exhilaration of this had much to do with the attractiveness of cities for those in smaller centres a generation or two ago. Much of it of course remains, but it is becoming clearer that each advance of technology is accompanied by an advance in introversion, and less sense of public use. Many of the streets now in these same cities, with their deserted sidewalks and cars whizzing up and down the road past scowling fortress-like buildings, show us the kind of anti-community symbolized for me by University Avenue in Toronto and by the areas in Los Angeles where pedestrians are regarded as vagrants. The amount of mental distress caused by living in an environment which expresses indifference or contempt for the perspectives of the human body is very little studied: one might call it proportion pollution.

My own university is in the middle of a big industrial city: this means great masses of box-lunch students, who commute in and out from distant suburbs and take their courses with little experience of a real university community, of the kind that Cardinal Newman regarded as the "idea" of the university. The surrounding streets keep steadily turning into anonymous masses of buildings that look eyeless in spite of being practically all windows. Many of them seem to have had no architect, but appear to have sprung out of their excavations like vast toadstools. City planners speak of the law of conserving the plan, meaning that Bloor Street in Toronto or Sherbrooke Street in Montreal are still where those streets originally were even though there has been a total metamorphosis of the buildings on them. But even this law, which seems at first sight like a concession to a sense of tradition, is really a means of confining change to the inorganic. And as we shuttle from a pigeon-hole in a high-rise apartment to another pigeon-hole in an office, a sense of futility and humiliation takes possession of us that we can now perhaps see in its historical dimension.

As civilization has "progressed" from ax to bulldozer, the growing withdrawal from nature paralyzes something natural in ourselves. A friend of my wife's, an interior decorator, remarked that she had a group of neurotic clients whom it seemed impossible either to please or to get rid of, and she suddenly realized that they had something in common: they all lived in high-rise apartments at a level above the trees. A withdrawal from nature extends into a growing withdrawal from human society itself. I mentioned the increasing introversion that technology brings with it: the aeroplane is more introverted than the train; the super-highway, where there is a danger of falling asleep, more introverted than the most unfrequented country road. The international airport, completely insulated even from the country it is in, is perhaps the most eloquent symbol of this, and is parodied in Stanley Kubrick's movie *2001*, where the hero lands on the moon, dependent on human processing even for the air he breathes, and finds nothing to do there except to phone his wife back on earth, who is out.

A revolutionary habit of mind, being founded on the sense of a crucial break in time at some point, the Exodus from Egypt, the Incarnation of Christ, the flight of Mohammed, the October Revolution in Russia, has a hostility to continuous tradition built into it. In Moslem countries everything that happened before Mohammed's time is part of the age of ignorance. Guides in developing countries, especially Marxist ones, want to show tourists the achievements of their own regime, and often get angry or contemptuous when the tourists want to see the cultural products of the old exploiting days. Similarly with our own culture. The Puritans in Massachusetts were in communion with the Puritans in Norwich who petitioned the Cromwellian government to pull down a useless and cumbersome cathedral which was a mere relic of superstition. Even the Jesuit missionaries, for all their zeal and devotion, still assumed that the Indians, so long as they were heathen, were a part of subconscious nature, and that only Christianity could incorporate them into a fully human society. A cultural sense thus got started which was still operative until quite recently. My late friend Charles Currelly, the founder of the Archaeological Museum in Toronto, was horrified by the indifference with which the authorities of his day regarded the British Columbia totem poles, and by the eagerness with which they were ready to sell them off to anyone whom they thought would be fool enough to want them. What we are now beginning to see is that an original belief in the rightness of destroying or ignoring a so-called "savage" culture develops toward a contempt for our own. In Margaret Atwood's very ironic novel *Surfacing*, the heroine, trying to get back to an original identity represented by the Quebec forests, finds that she has to destroy everything cultural that she possesses, or, as she says: "everything from history must be eliminated."

The revolutionary aspect of white settlement extended from religion into economics, as entrepreneur capitalism developed. Every technological change brought with it a large-scale shift in population centres. The skyline of Toronto sixty years ago was dominated by the spires of the great churches: now the churches are points of depression within the skyline. My moral is not the shift of interest from spiritual to financial administration: my moral is rather that the churches themselves are now largely without parishes, the population, at least the church-going part of it, having moved elsewhere. Similarly Canada is a land of ruins to an extent that the less spacious countries of Europe would not dare to be: ghost towns at exhausted mines or the divisional points of old railways remind us how quickly our economy can scrap not merely a building but an entire city. As Earle Birney remarks, the country is haunted by its lack of ghosts, for a ghost town has no ghosts: it is only one of the rubbish heaps that spring up in an economy of waste. We may remember Sam Slick on the beauties of Niagara Falls:

> "It would be a grand speck to get up a jint stock company for factory purposes, for such another place for mills ain't to be found atween the poles. Oh dear!" said I, "only think of the cardin' mills, fullin' mills, cotton mills, grain mills, saw mills, plaster mills, and gracious knows what sort o' mills might be put up there . . . and yet them goneys the British let all run away to waste."

For Sam Slick the ideal thriving mill town of this sort was Lowell in Massachusetts, where my father started in business, and it was a sad day for both of us when I took him there as an old man, after all the mills had been moved to the south, and he saw only the empty shell of the town he once knew. One question that such events raise is obviously: what can or should be preserved of what is no longer functional, and has little interest in itself apart from being a part of our past?

Whatever the answer, our social environment is a revolutionary one in which the main forces are indiscriminately destructive. This has to some extent always been true. Once there was a great city called Nineveh, so great that, according to the Book of Jonah, it took three days to journey across it. Then, quite suddenly, Nineveh disappeared under the sand, where it remained for nearly three thousand years. This kind of destruction from enemy action without is a greater danger now, as hydrogen bombs would leave nothing for the sand to preserve; but along with it is the even more insidious sense of destruction from within, destruction that proceeds from the very nature of technology itself, not impossibly inspired by some death wish in ourselves. The only possible economic alternative to capitalism, we feel, is socialism, but if capitalism is a destroyer, socialism is even more of one, because more committed to technology. In ancient Egypt one of the first things a new Pharaoh often did was to deface his predecessor's monuments: this is still our rhythm of life, but it is largely an unconscious one, except when rationalized as progress.

The violence of our almost unmanageable cities is bringing about another great population shift, as people move out of them and back to smaller centres. We are beginning to see a very large cycle of history turning here, and with this is slowly growing another social vision. Ecology, the sense of the need for conserving natural resources, is not a matter of letting the environment go back to the wilderness, but of finding some kind of working balance between man and nature founded on a respect for nature and its inner economies. As part of natural ecology, we are also developing some sense of the need for a kind of human ecology, of conserving not only our natural but our cultural and imaginative resources. Again, this is not simply a matter of leaving alone everything that is old: it is a way of life that grows out of a sense of balance between our present and our past. In relation to the natural environment, there are two kinds of people: those who think that nature is simply there to be used by man, and those who realize that man is himself a part of nature and will destroy himself if he destroys it. In relation to time and human history, there are also two kinds of people: those who think that the past is dead, and those who realize that the past is still alive in us. A dead past left to bury its dead ends in a dead present, a society of sleepwalkers, and a society without a memory is as senile as an individual in the same plight.

QUESTIONS

1. Northrop Frye suggests that "our attitude toward nature is reflected in our social environment." What evidence does he provide in support of this view? Is it convincing? Can you find evidence in your social environment that would support this claim?
2. Frye sees a relationship between natural ecology (conserving natural resources) and "human ecology" (conserving cultural and imaginative resources). Do you think that a good case can be made for the existence of such a relationship?

SUSTAINABILITY AND HISTORICAL INJUSTICE: LESSONS FROM THE MOOSE RIVER BASIN[1]

Wesley Cragg and Mark Schwartz[2]

Introduction

Sustainable development is about environmentally friendly economic growth and the elimination of poverty through equitable distribution of economic wealth. Thought of this way, sustainable development is about the future. It is also about the past — or perhaps more accurately about escaping a past in which economic growth was more often than not environmentally destructive and distributively unjust. Finally, the idea of sustainability, as articulated by the Brundtland Commission and the increasingly converted business community, is inherently optimistic.

It is this optimism that sustainable economic growth remains a genuine possibility at this stage of human economic history that is most frequently questioned by critics. Can we find in nature the resources and the capacity to support the growth that will be required if the grinding poverty in which much of the world now lives is to be overcome? And can we find in ourselves the political and moral resources required to ensure that wealth is fairly distributed?

These questions offer profound challenges in their own right. Yet they appear to leave unaddressed some central environmental and social problems whose focus is not so much the future as the past. Indeed much of the current sustainable development rhetoric implicitly suggests a posture popularized by Prime Minister Trudeau in his first term of office when he argued, faced with aboriginal discontent, that a political system could only be held responsible for its own actions. It should not be asked to correct historical injustices for two reasons. First, history could not be changed and those harmed could not be compensated. Second, to require those now living to bear costs for which they are not responsible would be unfair.

Trudeau's position on this question was subsequently rejected by his government. It is now widely recognized that creating the conditions in which poverty and social inequity can be addressed requires that we face not just the future, but also the historical grievance-generating events which have shaped the present.[3]

Is there a lesson here for discussions of sustainable development? If so, what attention should be paid to historical injustices in the pursuit of sustainable development? Looked at globally, the legacy of injustice seems so complex that it defies analysis, let alone resolution. Discrete examples, on the other hand, may not have that character. A good example is Ontario Hydro's proposal for restructuring and developing the hydroelectric potential of the Mattagami River in northeastern Ontario. The Mattagami River north of Kapuskasing was first harnessed in 1928 to provide power for a pulp mill which in turn gave life to the northern community of Kapuskasing. The same part of the river was redeveloped in the 1960's by Ontario Hydro to assist in meeting peak power demands of a rapidly growing industrial economy. Those developments had a significantly positive impact on the developing economy of the north and a significantly negative impact on the river itself and the subsistence economies of the original inhabitants of the river basin.

From Journal of Canadian Studies, vol. 31, no. 1 (Spring 1996). Reprinted by permission of the Journal of Canadian Studies.

In the last decade, faced with what were then thought to be accelerating demands for energy, Ontario Hydro proposed a redevelopment of what has come to be known as the Mattagami Complex. Although most other aspects of Hydro planning have been shelved in response to greatly reduced growth in Ontario's economy, this particular proposal is still under active study. Blocking the development have been Native grievances linked directly to the environmentally damaging impacts of the original development.

What is at issue then is the meaning of sustainability in a setting in which there is strong support for resource development juxtaposed with deeply felt historically grounded grievances connected with previous exploitation of natural resources. Added to this are serious concerns about the environmental impacts of both the current complex and its redevelopment for the river and the river basin.

This article will look at the Mattagami project from an economic and ethical perspective. In particular, we will examine three approaches to resolving both past and present issues raised by the project. The first was developed by Ontario Hydro in the context of its now shelved twenty-five year plan, which aimed at what might be called compensatory justice based on economic analysis. The First Nations in the area are calling for a recognition of their right to self-government followed by co-planning and co-management of resource development. The Ontario Government is advocating a process-oriented solution based on equitable participation in the decision making process.

We begin with the case itself. The second section of the article examines the case from the perspective of distributive justice and sustainable development. We turn in section three to a description and evaluation of the three alternatives outlined in the preceding paragraph, and then draw some lessons on the moral structure of the concept of sustainability. We conclude with some observations about the nature of the exercise and a postscript describing how the case has evolved over the period of our study.

Part One — The Case[4]

The Moose River Basin is an area larger in size than Ireland. The Mattagami is one of three rivers that empty into James Bay via the Moose River. The ecosystems of the region, in common with other boreal and sub-arctic areas, are fragile and easily damaged. The Ontario Hydro complex which is the focus of our study consists of four dams on the Mattagami River 60 to 100 km north of Kapuskasing. Vegetation in the vicinity of the four dams consists mainly of boreal forests. The Basin's wildlife population includes moose, bear, beaver, fox, otter and numerous species of birds, amphibians, and fish.

Aboriginal settlement would appear to date back as much as 5,000 years. European settlement dates to 1776 when the Hudson's Bay Company opened a post on Moose Factory Island. In the early 1900's railway lines opened up the area to agriculture, mining, and lumbering. In the following years, private hydroelectric developments were established in the Basin to provide power to new resource industries.

In 1922, the "model" town of Kapuskasing was built around a pulp and paper mill which was operated by the Spruce Falls Pulp and Paper Company and owned by Kimberly Clark and The New York Times. The first of four dams in the complex, the Smoky Falls station, was built by Spruce Falls in 1928 to supply inexpensive hydroelectric power to the mill. This dam destroyed a beautiful natural waterfall and did cause long term environmental damage, but not on the scale of later hydroelectric developments. In the 1960's Ontario Hydro added three more dams: Little Long (1963), Harmon (1965), and Kipling (1966).

Unlike the Smoky Falls station, however, these were "peaking" stations, operating only 5 hours per day and requiring "headponds" whose water levels were to fluctuate up to 3 metres each day. Also required was a spillway which would operate during the spring runoff. The spillway was created by diverting water into Adam Creek, a small natural water course adjacent to the river itself. The resulting erosion has created river banks 20 to 30 metres in height and washed millions of cubic metres of soil down the river.

The hydroelectric developments of the 1960's have had a significant impact on the Basin's ecology and its aboriginal inhabitants. Construction of the dams provided employment for some aboriginals. Connecting the communities of Moose Factory and Moosonee to the Ontario power grid has resulted in important improvements for the communities affected. These developments have also been accompanied by deterioration in water quality; fluctuating water levels leading to trapped fish, sandbars, and silted-over spawning beds; erosion; significant flooding; a loss of food and habitat for beavers and other animals; and the destruction of historic Cree settlement sites, historic portages, fur trade sites, and cemeteries. Aboriginal inhabitants have also linked noise from generators to declining birds, otter, mink, and fox in the area of the dams and complained of deterioration in the quality of the fur from beaver, muskrat, and otter. The dams' construction roads have improved access for non-native hunters generating competition for resources, and provided greater access for logging companies whose cutting activities have also had a negative impact on fur-bearing mammals and fish. Finally, the use of the rivers for transportation has been seriously affected by the fluctuating river levels.

All of these impacts have taken a toll on the traditional way of life of the Basin's aboriginal inhabitants and appear to have been accompanied throughout by an absence of consultation, mitigation, or compensation by Ontario Hydro.

In 1990, Ontario Hydro submitted to the Ontario government an environmental assessment for a redevelopment of the four dams to increase the hydroelectric generation capacity of the Mattagami River. Additional generating units were proposed for the Little Long, Harmon, and Kipling stations. The base load Smoky Falls station was to be retired, and a new peaking power station constructed adjacent to it. The goal was to optimize energy production from the river by building a new "in-step" operation which Ontario Hydro projected would provide enough new energy to supply the demand of electricity for 150,000 homes. In its environmental assessment, Ontario Hydro predicted that the redevelopment would cause little new damage while reducing environmental impacts on the part of the existing operations.

In 1991, the owners of Spruce Falls Pulp and Paper Company, having failed to find a buyer for an increasingly uneconomic operation, announced their decision to shut down most of the Kapuskasing mill operation with the possible loss of 1,200 direct and 6,200 indirect jobs in a town of 11,000. The resulting political crisis caused the Ontario government to intervene. As a result, the company was sold by Kimberly Clark and The New York Times to its employees. As part of the package, the Smoky Falls station was sold to Ontario Hydro on the condition that the environmental assessment process found the redevelopment proposal acceptable. Alternatively, the Ontario government would be required to pay Ontario Hydro $247 million.[5] The focus of this article is the debates and proposals generated by the ensuing environmental assessment process. The project's stakeholders include:

Ontario Hydro, the proponent of the Mattagami extension proposal. Although the urgency for finding new sources of power has now vanished, the project has until recently been regarded as an efficient way of providing inexpensive hydroelectric power to the Ontario grid.

The aboriginal people now living in the Moose River Basin. Most affected by the dams in question are the aboriginal residents of Moosonee, about 900 in number, and Moose Factory, a community of about 2,200 aboriginal inhabitants. In total there are about 10,000 aboriginal inhabitants in the Basin area. For these people, on-going land claims and their traditional way of life is of deep significance.

The Ontario government with political, economic and financial interests in discussions and negotiations that have accompanied the environmental assessment process.

The non-aboriginal residents of surrounding communities where unemployment is high and opportunities for economic development have been warmly welcomed. Other stakeholders include the more distant municipalities, labour unions, independent power producers, tourist operators, and environmental groups.

Part Two: The Structure of Injustice

1) Distributive Justice and the Concept of Sustainable Development

Ontario Hydro's proposed Mattagami Complex extension poses a complex challenge to the application of the notion of sustainable development. That complexity derives in large measure from the nature of the environmental impacts of earlier developments set against the likely benefits of further development. Economic analysis suggests, as we have already pointed out, that redevelopment of the complex would bring substantial benefits to the town of Kapuskasing, to the economy of the northeastern region of the province and to Ontario Hydro consumers. Analysis also suggests that the proposed development would have beneficial environmental impacts. This of course is a significant component of Ontario Hydro's case for development. If we focus exclusively on the future, the proposal might therefore seem to be sustainable. Nevertheless, it has generated considerable controversy and deep opposition, particularly from the Native population. It is virtually impossible to understand that opposition without exploring the links between sustainability and distributive justice.

The idea of sustainable development has been reformulated by critics of the Brundtland Commission definition in numerous ways. Criticism, however, has not managed to undermine the importance of the role the idea continues to have in the thinking of those concerned with the impact of modern industrial development on the world's environment. It has continued to play this role in part, we suggest, because of the way in which the idea of sustainable development has helped to bring environmental concerns into dialogue with economic ones.

Under-riding that dialogue is a set of moral imperatives. This is evidenced by two things. First, sustainable development is at its most fundamental level about sharing the planet's resources with the future in equitable ways. Second, underlying the concept is a conviction that unsustainable development carries with it morally significant costs that are cumulative and will be passed as costs to future generations. The harnessing of the great rivers draining the Canadian Shield illustrates these points; discussions of future developments unavoidably confront them.

What then is the moral structure of sustainable development?[6] We propose that it must include the principle that: *The costs of resource development should be born by those who will reap its benefits.*[7] This principle is clearly a principle of distributive justice. Failure to respect it, we propose, must unavoidably lead to injustice, the imposition of morally significant costs unbalanced by benefits to those on whom they are imposed. We shall argue that sustainable resource development which is insensitive to this principle may be possible. However, in those cases where it occurs it will be by accident and not design.

2) Cost Benefit Analysis and the Problem of Externalities

For much of the century, Ontario Hydro, a publicly owned provincial public utility, has studied and exploited the hydraulic potential of the great rivers draining the Canadian Shield. The Province of Ontario has been the direct beneficiary of hydroelectric development undertaken by Ontario Hydro in pursuit of this mandate.

Even a cursory survey of the evidence shows that hydroelectric development in the north has not been constrained or guided by principles of sustainable development in the past. The dams constructed on northern rivers turbines have diverted and altered the flow of rivers in environmentally significant ways, resulting in the creation of huge new reservoirs needed to ensure reliable energy delivery over long time periods in response to fluctuating demand. The resulting energy has been delivered at relatively low monetary cost to the residents of Ontario with considerable economic benefit. On the other hand, substantial costs have been imposed on Native communities in the absence of meaningful consultation and countervailing benefits recognizable as such by those affected.

The legacy of these developments is reflected in an acute sense of grievance which now dominates discussion of northern Ontario resource use. It is reflected as well in substantial environmental problems that now confront Native and non-Native communities in the north.[8]

What is the source or origin of the injustice that has been imposed on Native communities in the north? A first clear candidate is moral insensitivity on the part of planners, developers and the Crown corporation itself. The histories that are now being collected and the accounts of the Native people that are now being assembled in defence of self-government claims suggest that much of the development has taken place in an environment in which the fact that the land was occupied and under use by an indigenous population was simply ignored.[9] A second candidate is the Friedmanite character of modern economic activity. The task of business, Friedman has argued, is to operate as profitably as possible within the constraints set by law. So long as they work within the law, managers are not responsible for monitoring or compensating costs that have no direct impact on profits. Responding to inequities resulting from economic activities is more properly the responsibility of governments.[10] Finally, it might be argued that the injustice resulting from northern hydro development is a direct consequence of the structure of the planning process that guided the development of the hydraulic potential of the north of Ontario.

It is this third explanation that holds the key to the problems of injustice on the one hand and unsustainability on the other. Ontario Hydro's mandate is an economic one. Ontario Hydro is directed by law to maximize economic benefits and minimize costs which must be passed on to consumers. In the past, where hydroelectric installations were concerned, the costs Ontario Hydro could not avoid passing on to consumers were those costs resulting from construction, transmission and maintenance of its northern generating facilities as well as whatever compensation the law required be paid to those with a legal right to compensation, private property owners for example. Legally speaking, Ontario Hydro was entitled to regard all other costs as externalities and therefore not its responsibility. For the most part, this was the path Ontario Hydro chose to follow. Given its mandate, the approach taken is hardly surprising.

Ontario Hydro's past approach to the development of Ontario's northern rivers is best characterized as "least cost" planning. It is an approach to planning that Litchfield argues has dominated energy planning by utilities throughout North America until very recently.[11] It reflects a Friedmanite approach to the issue of corporate social responsibility. Finally, it is an approach which taken by itself in the absence of alternative noncorporate responses to environmental and human impacts is obviously open to the charge of moral insensitivity. In the case under consideration, no adequate strategies for dealing with external (to Ontario Hydro) costs were put in place by the government. As a consequence, the full burden of carrying those costs was shifted to the indigenous residents of the north and their communities.

It is this legacy which underlies the conflicts which Ontario Hydro's proposals for the redevelopment of the Mattagami Complex have generated. It remains a legacy in spite of the fact that all of the parties to the conflict acknowledge the inadequacies of past planning and development and have committed themselves to the idea of sustainable development in planning and assessing new projects. The central dilemma is to determine what role that legacy should play in creating a sustainable development strategy for the Mattagami River.

Part Three: The Structure of Environmental Conflict

1) Economic Analysis and Compensatory Justice

Ontario Hydro's proposal for redeveloping the Mattagami Complex derives from its mandate "to provide a reliable supply of electrical power and energy to the people of Ontario, at the lowest long-term feasible cost."[12] Its proposal is designed to assist it to meet its obligations by expanding the four existing sites so as to extract the greatest possible energy potential of the river with the least possible adverse environmental effects.

It is clear from both the *Environmental Assessment Summary and The Demand Supply Plan Report* that the proposed extensions are designed to increase the peak energy capacity of Ontario Hydro. Its case for the project rests on "least-cost" planning that incorporate all (but only) those costs to be "borne directly by Hydro."[13] Ontario Hydro acknowledges that "(c)osts and benefits for the Ontario community beyond these direct costs are not factored into cost comparisons."[14] In this respect the approach used in developing the current proposal is no different from that which Hydro has used in developing all its hydraulic sites in northern Ontario in this century.

In spite of the similarities with past planning methods, however, the approach used to plan the Mattagami extension represents important differences. Among other things, it incorporates a commitment to take into account social and environmental as well as the economic impacts in the planning process. This change is clearly significant. Given a commitment to "least cost" planning, how is it to be accounted for?

The answer lies in two places. First Ontario's *Environmental Assessment Act*[15] which aims at "the betterment of the people of Ontario by providing for the protection, conservation and wise management in Ontario of the environment".[16] That act defines the environment broadly to include the natural environment as well as "the social, economic and cultural conditions that influence the life of man or a community".[17] This Act has meant significant changes to the regulatory environment in which energy planning must now take place in Ontario. As a result, in planning the Mattagami extension, Ontario Hydro has been required by law to take into account costs which previously it had externalized.

It is clear from the *DSP Environmental Analysis* offered in justification of the Mattagami extension, however, that not only the law but also Ontario Hydro's own thinking has undergone significant changes since the 1960's. Respect for principles of sustainable development is now Ontario Hydro policy.[18] This has been interpreted to mean that project planning must consider environmental protection and conservation, regional economic stability, recreation, health, heritage protection and aboriginal concerns. More striking for our purposes, however, is recognition that sustainable development carries the moral implication that:

Generally, it is preferable that those who bear the risks also share equitably in the benefits.[19] To be committed to sustainable development is thus understood to require qualified respect for the principle of distributive justice already identified.

The planning and internal environmental assessment process which appears to have emerged as a result of these changes can be summarized in the following way:

1. Meet the electrical power needs of the province in the most sustainable manner possible;
2. Integrate environmental as well as economic costs in all cost calculations;
3. Inform and consult with the public in identifying benefits and costs;
4. Mitigate all adverse impacts where economically feasible;
5. For all residual impacts, provide substitute off-setting benefits for losses where economically feasible;
6. Compensate fairly for all adverse residual impacts where mitigation or substitution is not possible.

Ontario Hydro's own assessment has led it to conclude that tested against these criteria the Mattagami Extension represents the lowest cost option available to it and that the criteria constitute a fair basis for responding to the concerns of all those likely to benefit or suffer as a result of the development. The redevelopment will allow a more efficient and productive use of the hydraulic potential of the river than the present installations allow. The construction phase will provide jobs. Permitting the redevelopment will justify the purchase of the Smoky Falls station from the Spruce Falls Pulp and Paper Company, saving tax dollars and indirectly strengthening the economic viability of the mill and consequently of Kapuskasing by contributing to the continued provision of low cost power through the Ontario grid. These economic benefits are to be accompanied by minimal environmental damage and the potential for certain environmental improvements.[20] For example, there will be little impact on soil, vegetation, wildlife, and aquatic habitat. There will be a reduction in shoreline erosion in headponds, downstream erosion in Adam Creek, and in the passage of fish through the Adam Creek control structure.

Ontario Hydro does acknowledge that negative environmental impacts may occur as a result of the redevelopment that it is proposing. However, those that do occur will be mitigated. For example, although there may be additional angling and hunting pressure on fish and wildlife populations from the construction workforce, measures will be taken to both restrict and discourage excessive hunting and angling activities during the construction period.[21] Although the peaking operations will increase the water level fluctuation downstream of the Kipling station, Hydro proposes to maintain minimal water levels to prevent the dewatering of aquatic habitat. A new spawning habitat will be created in the Smoky

Falls tailrace[22] to compensate for the loss of spawning grounds as a result of the redevelopment.[23] Ontario Hydro's environmental assessment also acknowledges that there will be some residual impacts. For example, Hydro proposes to "co-operate with trappers to identify yields before the project and compensate financial losses resulting from project activities".[24] It has also offered to compensate for impacts on aboriginal harvesting activities. Thus:

> . . . Ontario Hydro will seek to provide fair compensation for all subsistence users and licensed trappers in the project area, for any losses that may result from the undertaking. With their co-operation, funding will be provided to area First Nations to define both pre- and post-development levels of aboriginal harvesting.[25]

Furthermore:

> Should impacts be identified, options such as financial compensation, replacement of losses in kind (eg., provision of fish, fowl, etc. from other sources) or other equivalent impact management measures (e.g., to establish new trap lines, relocate cabins, etc.) will be offered.[26]

The commitment to inform and consult is reflected in "public information and feedback" which "were the cornerstones of the public involvement program for the Mattagami River Extensions Environmental Assessment Study".[27] And although Hydro's relationship with the Nishnawbe-Aski First Nations is acknowledged as strained,[28] attempts have been made to rectify the situation including the appointment of a Corporate Aboriginal Affairs Coordinator.[29]

Finally, Ontario Hydro has undertaken to deal with the grievances to which the earlier developments on the river have given rise. However, at the time of the original environmental assessment, it rejected the view that settling those grievances is or should be an element in any environmental assessment carried out under the *Environmental Assessment Act.*

Ontario Hydro's position on the Mattagami Extension represents an attempt to achieve important economic goals within a sustainable development framework. However, the resulting development model has failed to win agreement particularly on the part of Native stakeholders. Seen from a Native perspective, Ontario Hydro's approach, which, Ontario Hydro acknowledges, was implemented without substantial Native input on consultation, has two defects. First is its fundamentally utilitarian structure. The overriding objective is the provision of adequate supplies of reliable, low cost electricity for the people of Ontario. The key to the exercise is identifying low cost or lowest cost options. Achieving this goal, however, becomes extremely difficult unless the monetary value of costs and benefits can be accurately determined.

Herein lies the difficulty for many of the participants.[30] For example, Hydro's environmental assessment identifies as priorities: low cost reliable electric power, efficient use of water resources, environmental protection, conservation, regional economic stability, recreation, health, heritage protection and aboriginal concerns. If we probe the documents assembled in response to the *Demand/Supply Plan*, we discover as aboriginal concerns: a deep sense of obligation to the land or "mother earth"; treaty rights; control over those land areas on which they have relied for subsistence, and finally a profound sense of obligation to the Creator, their traditional way of life, and aboriginal rights. It is not at all clear how one would seek to cost environmental impacts from the perspective of this set of concerns.[31]

The importance of the ability to cost impacts is further emphasized by the way this approach to planning relies on substitution of off-setting benefits for costs incurred and, failing that, on compensation. Values readily quantified can be easily assimilated to this approach. The risk, however, is that values that cannot be quantified will be ignored just because the methodology has no way of dealing with them.[32] In short, the problem in using a mitigation and compensation approach is that it appears to call for what has been described as the commodification of values. It is perhaps not surprising that the methodology and its application have given rise to both offence and criticism. Aboriginal reaction to Ontario Hydro's plans reflects that kind of judgment. To propose financial compensation for polluted water, or poisoned fish, or the loss of traditional hunting grounds, or flooded grave sites is from a Native perspective to misunderstand in a profound way the nature of the losses for which compensation is being offered.

Second, lying at the heart of the First Nations' refusal to cooperate is a deep sense of historical grievance, grounded not simply in the costs that have been imposed as a result of hydroelectric development. Rather it is a reaction to the contempt for Native values, and the way of life in which they have traditionally been enshrined, implied by the way development in the north has typically taken place. It is unlikely that a planning and assessment process, which assumes that adequate mitigation, substitution and compensation are in principle available for all unavoidable negative impacts, could respond to that sense of injustice. These sentiments are captured by the alternative solution to the conflict proposed by First Nation leaders.

2) Respecting Rights: The Self-Government Option

The First Nations' response to the Mattagami extension proposal has three components. First is a commitment to sustainable development, which the Native People's Circle on Environment and Development suggests has always has been a guiding concept for Native people. This commitment, they go on to say, is reflected in the view that "the land and its resources be preserved for the benefit of past, present, and future generations".[33]

As with Ontario Hydro, sustainability is closely linked to economic well-being. What separates the two views, however, is how best to achieve that goal. As Randy Kapashesit, Chief of the MoCreebec First Nation, points out:

> Ontario Hydro's notion of economic development is not supportive of the kind of economy that is reflective of our own culture, values, traditions and environment.[34]

For Hydro, the land is a resource to be used. From a Native perspective, the land is something deserving great respect, a source of cultural, aesthetic, spiritual as well as economic values. The land is seen as of great value in its own right. Its health is viewed as directly linked to their well-being.[35]

The implications of these two perspectives for dealing with the concept of sustainability are striking. What for Ontario Hydro are impacts properly discussed with a view to substitution and providing financial compensation raise questions for the aboriginal people about their capacity to sustain a way of life. In short, from an aboriginal perspective, sustainability is impossible in the absence of respect for the land. Unavoidably, therefore, sustainability raises the issue of historical grievances, the second component in the aboriginal perspective on the Mattagami extensions.

Why is this so? The aboriginal position on grievances is succinctly set out by Chief Kapashesit in a statement to the Environmental Assessment Board which was created to evaluate Ontario Hydro's twenty-five year *Demand/Supply Plan,* who argues that:

> Justice requires that . . . past grievances be settled before future projects are even considered. It is immoral for Ontario Hydro to be talking about future projects when they have not entered settlements to compensate for the damage they inflicted by past projects.[36]

At first glance this stance may appear paradoxical. If, as we have been suggesting, the objectionable character of Ontario Hydro's proposal for resolving conflicts over the Mattagami Extension rest in part in the suggestion that the way to deal with residual impacts of the development it is proposing is through compensation, how is it possible that Native leaders should propose that serious grievances be resolved through compensation?

The question is important. It is also relatively easily answered. Those historical grievances now hold enormous symbolic value for the Native people of the north. They represent the failure on the part of an alien and insensitive culture to give to the land slated for development as well as the life dependent on it the profound respect which is its due. The Native inhabitants' response to this failure is analogous to the outrage which would greet a proposal to burn the contents of Canada's libraries to heat the city of Toronto, or the art hanging on the walls of the Louvre to light the city of Paris.

To understand the analogy requires seeing books and paintings as renewable resources, which in a sense they are. There is no shortage of either authors or painters to renew our libraries or art galleries. But to see books and paintings in this light would be clearly unacceptable, indeed offensive for many people raised in a European culture. Native people regard the western response to water as a renewable natural resource in a similar way. At issue in both cases is an implied disrespect for things of great value and, by implication, for the people who value them.

What then could count as compensation? Or more properly, what is the role of compensation in cases such as this? Compensation cannot replace valued items with things of equal value. What compensation can do is restore a sense of respect or acknowledge in a significant way the nature of the offence which has been given.[37] It is unlikely that a people so offended could accept as sincere a commitment to change that offered nothing by way of restitution for activities said now to be regretted and not to be repeated.

The third component of the aboriginal position on the proposed Mattagami Extension is the demand that there be no further development until the rights of the First Nation communities to self-government have been recognized. Recognition is to include control over the development of natural resources in areas of Native jurisdiction. The logic of this demand flows directly from the importance to the traditional native way of life of sustainability and the failure on the part of those developing the north to respect values of central importance to the Native communities affected. Control over the land and uses imposed would ensure that future development was appropriately responsive to those values.

As with the Ontario Hydro proposal for the Mattagami Complex, this solution to the current impasse has clear strengths. If we accept that sustainability is a fundamental value in aboriginal culture as Native leaders have claimed, it would move environmental values to a much more significant place in the evaluation of development proposals than has been the case previously. It would ensure respect for the interests of a minority who have been required historically to carry substantially more than their fair share of the costs of development.

The idea of a veto for aboriginal or local communities over development proposals in areas like northern Ontario has been advanced in a number of formats and contexts and is not unique to the aboriginal people of northeastern Ontario. For example, the environmental assessment *Guidelines for the Great Whale River Hydroelectric Project* require that "the proposed (Great Whale) project must . . . respect the rights of local communities to determine their future and their own societal objectives".[38] But is this proposal consistent with the moral principle that those who benefit from an activity should carry the costs it generates? To satisfy this principle requires a careful accounting of the interests of all those who have a stake in any decisions about the future of, for example, the Mattagami Complex. What is being proposed would appear simply to shift control over development from one stakeholder, Ontario Hydro, to another. It is not obvious that the effect of such a shift would be a fair sharing of the costs and benefits of decisions affecting the use of nature's resources.

There are two immediate objections to this interpretation of this second option seen from a northeastern Ontario aboriginal perspective. What First Nation stakeholders are calling for in this case is co-planning and co-management of resources;[39] surely a demand of this nature is not inconsistent with principles of distributive justice. Further, the demand for self-government is a rights claim. It is not based on an appeal to principles of distributive justice or sustainable development. As such it might well be argued that it is immune to moral arguments seeking to balance costs and benefits of actions and policy decision for those affected.

These are important considerations. What they seem to point to is a weakness in the analysis of the moral underpinnings of the idea of sustainable development. The principle that those who reap the benefits of a development project should bear the costs can be operationalized acceptably only where there is substantial agreement on what is to count as a cost or a benefit. However the concepts of cost and benefit are culturally sensitive. One form of moral insensitivity is insensitivity to this fact. Historical injustice is frequently the result. When it occurs, it undermines trust on the part of its victims in the willingness of its perpetrators to change their ways. The demand for self-government can be seen as a response to that breakdown in trust.

Whether the idea of self-government, accompanied as it almost always is with a desire to exercise control over natural resources, is an acceptable response to the fact of historical injustice is too large a question for this paper.[40] Seen from the perspective of sustainable development and its moral underpinnings, however, it raises an instructive point. If we accept that individuals themselves are usually the best judges of their own interests, then it is unlikely in practice that a principle like the one we have highlighted will find morally acceptable implementation in the absence of equitable participation in decision making by those likely to be affected.[41] And while acknowledging this point does raise significant difficulties for shaping decision making so that it reflects adequately the interests of future generations, it does point to the need to add a principle of equitable participation as a practical requirement for sustainable development.

It is considerations of this sort which lead to the third option presented by stakeholders for resolving the conflict generated by the Mattagami extension proposal.

3) Operationalizing the Principle of Equitable Participation

As the stakeholder analysis in Part One indicates, the Ontario Government had a substantial financial, economic and political interest in resolving the conflict that emerged in response to the Mattagami Extension proposal. In response to a report it commissioned in July 1991 and extensive informal negotiations with First Nation representatives, the provincial government undertook to create two consultative processes. Both were designed to resolve conflict over the Mattagami Extension proposal while laying the framework for constructive resolution of the longer term resource use planning issues. Both processes reflected an acknowledgement that the short term and longer term issues could not be resolved unless both non-Native concerns about the economic future of the region and aboriginal concerns about the right to equitable participation in resource development and resource management were addressed.

First, the Ontario government undertook to create a "technical group" whose mandate was to review "how the design and/or operation of the (Mattagami Complex) Project could be modified to achieve the primary objective of environmental enhancement as well as the production of energy." The government proposed that the group have four members, two appointed by the government and two by the Moose River James Bay (Aboriginal) Coalition and/or its members, on behalf of Moose Factory, New Post, and MoCreebec First Nations. In proposing this group, the government committed itself to providing the financial and technical resources the group would need to assess the Mattagami extension project, consult broadly and report back to the government and the elected chiefs and councils of the New Post, Moose Factory and MoCreebec First Nations.[42]

The intention was to bring the environmental assessment process to a successful conclusion while recognizing the importance of First Nation self-government concerns by appointing an advisory group with an equal number of Native and non-Native members. Further, the technical group was to be given a mandate to report with recommendations to the appropriate bodies on any issues of concern identified in the consultative process. In proposing the committee, the Minister implied a willingness to be guided in his decisions on the project by a consensus report that won First Nation approval.

The second element in the government proposal was the creation of a baseline data collection project, given the task of describing the existing biophysical, social, cultural and economic environmental conditions in the Moose River Basin. These data could then be used to identify a base line against which the cumulative impacts of resource development in the basin could be measured.[43] The government also proposed that "traditional knowledge" as well as data gathered using the techniques of modern science should be included in the data base.

Here, the government was responding to a fundamental Native environmental concern, namely, that the environment should be looked at holistically. In responding to resource development proposals, Native spokespeople argued that what matters is not the aggregate environmental impact of any particular development looked at in isolation but the cumulative impact of resource development in the Moose River Basin looked at together. Native groups also argued that cumulative impacts could only be calculated against pre-established environmental benchmarks. Identifying such benchmarks for the Moose River Basin before further development was approved was therefore a fundamental First Nation demand.

The proposals advanced by the Ontario government which were accepted by the Moose Cree First Nation as a single package focus on matters of process. They assume that, if a fair dispute resolution process can be established, sound environmental and economic decisions will be forthcoming. As such, the Ontario government proposals are not derived directly from a commitment to sustainable development or to the equitable sharing of the costs and the benefits of resource development. The option proposed does seem to rest on a moral principle, however, namely the principle of equitable participation.[44] Are there important connections between these two principles? As a matter of practice, the answer is surely yes.

We have already suggested that the deep sense of grievance that Native leaders have carried into the Mattagami extension debate can be understood as a legitimate moral response to the lack of respect exhibited in the past for their peoples' values by resource developments. It is at least arguable that the Native people of northern Ontario would not have been treated as they were had they been granted the right to equitable participation. It is equally difficult to see how in practice distributive justice or sustainable development could be guiding principles of resource development where equitable participation on the part of those likely to be adversely affected was denied.

Part Four: The Moral Structure of Sustainability

What lessons can be learned from the debate that has been generated by Ontario Hydro's Mattagami Extension proposals? There would seem to be several.

1. Commitment to sustainable development by itself is not likely to lead to consensus on environmentally acceptable development unless we are able to unpack carefully the moral structure of that idea. This need may not be obvious in morally homogeneous cultural settings. But where the moral underpinnings of the idea are not carefully considered, consensus may reflect little more than a pervasive cultural bias. It was not the presence of Native people in northern Ontario that made hydraulic development of northern rivers unsustainable. What their presence has done, though all too slowly and at great cost, is to make the unsustainable character of that development visible.

2. Distributive justice is an important component of sustainable development. The relevant principle of distributive justice is that those who benefit from resource development should bear the costs it generates. Injustice results when significant costs are externalized. Hence, externalizing costs is simply incompatible with a commitment to distributive justice and hence to sustainable development.[45]

3. The identification, measurement and sharing of costs and benefits of development is a key element in assessing sustainability. This process, however, is culturally sensitive. That is to say, what counts as a cost and a benefit will be a function of the values and patterns of life of those affected. Because of this, moral insensitivity is both a significant obstacle to assessments of sustainability and a source of injustice.

4. One form of moral insensitivity to which least cost planning seems particularly prone is the monetization of costs. Monetizing all costs assumes the homogeneity of values. But more importantly, it assumes that everything valued, particularly anything which is a part of the natural environment, can be instrumentalized in monetary terms. What our study suggests is that this view clashes with the need for cultural sensitivity in identifying, assessing and sharing costs and benefits. The issue here is not whether in some cultures at least there are things which are so valuable they cannot be given up whatever the circumstances. Rather the issue is how the cost or perhaps the loss of things of that sort is to be assessed.

5. In practice ensuring equitable participation in processes which are directed toward the identification, measurement or sharing of costs is a requirement of sustainable development. This is not because it is in principle impossible for people to identify and measure impacts from the perspective of those with a different cultural background. Rather it is because: first, it is reasonable to assume that adults are the best judges of the value of things seen from their own perspective; and second, overcoming moral insensitivity in practice is a difficult challenge and one which is likely to be met only imperfectly much of the time in the absence of the active cooperation and participation of those whose perspective is in question.

6. Finally, while historical injustice is not an infallible indicator of unsustainability, it does stand as a powerful symbol of moral insensitivity. Moral sensitivity is not a necessary condition of sustainable development. However, where it is absent, sustainability can only be realized by accident, not by design.

Part Five: Final Observations and a Concluding Postscript

This paper is an exercise in applied ethics. Our purpose in writing it has been to identify the moral values that underpin the pursuit of sustainability, values that must be respected if it is to be achieved. The argument of this paper is designed to support two conclusions in this regard. First, sustainable development does indeed have a moral structure. Second, the moral structure of sustainability has three components. The first two are principles of distributive justice: *those who benefit from resource development should bear all its costs; costs and benefits of resource development should be distributed fairly.* The third is a practical corollary of the first two: *equitable participation in planning and management of resource developments on the part of those on whom a particular development is likely to have an impact is in practice necessary if moral insensitivity in identifying and "costing" costs and benefits likely to accrue from development and injustice in the distribution of costs and benefits is to be avoided.*

Our analysis has not outlined a strategy for eradicating historical injustice in this or any of its many manifestations, although the article does purport to identify the political, legal, economic, or social roots of historical injustice. Neither does it make substantive recommendations about policies, procedures or initiatives required if sustainable development is to be achieved in social environments in which historical injustice is a seriously complicating factor. Ethical analysis alone cannot provide answers to these questions. It can help to expose the moral structure of historical grievances. It can also help to identify morally necessary conditions for their resolution. However, the task of rectifying those injustices requires a depth and breadth of practical wisdom only one part of which is moral insight. Also needed will be depth of cultural knowledge, practical political skills, political and economic analysis and so on.

For some, this conclusion will appear a counsel of despair. In our view, however, it is a simple acknowledgement that moral values are only one of the keys to unlocking sustainable futures.

A Concluding Postscript

In 1994, the Ontario government gave approval for the Mattagami Complex project, thus avoiding the $247 million payment. A condition of that approval, however, is a proviso that any future Mattagami complex redevelopment will be overseen by a "Mattagami Extensions Coordinating Council" consisting of equal representation from the First Nations and the Ontario government. This uniting of aboriginal and provincial interests appears to be unprecedented for Ontario's environmental assessment process.

Whether the complex will be redeveloped in the future is now a moot point. However, in 1995, Ontario Hydro signed an agreement for the settlement of past grievances with one aboriginal First Nation, and is currently in negotiations with several others. Such actions appear to reflect a new direction for Ontario Hydro, based on recommendations made by its Task Force on Sustainable Energy Development such as securing greater stakeholder involvement and strengthening partnerships with First Nation and aboriginal communities.[46] Also in 1995, the Ministry of Natural Resources launched the "Environmental Information Partnership" for the Moose River Basin consisting of First Nations, the federal government, and the Ontario government, a continuation of the original Baseline Data Collection Project. The goal of the partnership is to develop an information management system for the Moose River Basin that will assist in the identification and evaluation of potential cumulative effects of any planned developments within the Basin. Integral to that information management agreement is recognition that aboriginal environmental knowledge has a legitimate place along with modern science in that identification process.

Meanwhile discussions on aboriginal self-government are still pending amongst the First Nation, federal and Ontario governments.[47] Based on these recent developments, it appears to be the case that several of the "lessons" to be learned from the conflict are beginning to be put into practice. Whether or not a complete resolution to the conflict which is morally satisfactory to the major stakeholders, remains to be seen.

NOTES

1. The authors acknowledge funding support for this research on the part of the Social Sciences and Humanities Research Council (Strategic Grants Program), York University's Haub Program in Business and the Environment and York University's Faculty of Administrative Studies Small Research Grants Program.
2. This paper is a product of an interdisciplinary environmental ethics research project which is studying four resource use proposals for northeastern Ontario and northern British Columbia. We wish to acknowledge the contribution of Maria Radford, who did much of the original document research. David Pearson, a project coinvestigator, Ralph Wheeler of the Ministry of Natural Resources who are project partners, Mario Durepos from Ontario Hydro who are project partners, and Paul Wilkinson and Associates all have provided assistance at various stages in our research. The Ontario Aboriginal Research Coalition, created to direct research into the effects on Ontario's First Nations of Ontario Hydro's Twenty-five Year Plan, financed the collection of oral histories assembled to which we refer in a number of places. Chief Ernest Beck and David Fletcher of the Moosecree Factory First Nation, Chief Randy Kapashesit of the MoCreebec First Nation, and John Turner of the Mushkegowuk Tribal Council provided guidance and site visit assistance. David Fletcher has been of continuing assistance throughout the research process. Ontario Hydro arranged a site visit to the Mattagami Complex. Without the assistance of all of these people, this research would not have been possible.
3. For a statement of Trudeau's position and a discussion of the issues raised by it, see A.W. Cragg, *Contemporary Moral Issues* — Third Edition (Toronto: McGraw-Hill, 1992), Chapter 5, "Native Rights".
4. The information in the following case is based on Ontario Hydro's *Environmental Assessment*, Aboriginal Witness Statements (Adams, Conway, Roderique, J. Sutherland, P. Sutherland), and an exhibit from J. Morrison used during the DSP Environmental Assessment Hearing.
5. Noble, K. "Kapuskasing Deal Best for Everybody," *The Globe and Mail*, B4.

6. For an attempt to identify cross-cultural moral principles appropriate for resource development decisions which goes beyond a discussion of the moral principles imbedded in the concept of sustainable development, see Michael McDonald, Jack T. Stevenson and Wesley Cragg, "Finding a Balance of Values: An Ethical Assessment of Ontario Hydro's Demand/Supply Plan" Report to the Aboriginal Research Coalition of Ontario (1992), and Wesley Cragg, Michael McDonald and Jack T. Stevenson, "The Demand/Supply Plan and the Moose River Basin" (unpublished). These reports are complementary ethical analyses of the Ontario Hydro 25 Year Demand/Supply Plan. The analysis is a direct moral evaluation which alludes to the concept of sustainable development but is not based on it. For a discussion that illustrates the need for value based analysis see Litchfield et al., "Integrated Resource Planning and the Great Whale Public Review" Background Paper, No. 7, Great Whale Environmental Assessment (Great Whale Environmental Public Review Office, 1994. Further references will be made to these reports in what follows.

7. It might be argued that a fuller and wider application of this principle than what we propose here might require that it be qualified by phrases like: "In the absence of genuinely voluntary agreement to the contrary, the costs, etc." This caveat is ignored in this study since it is clear that introducing it would not modify the argument which we propose to advance in what follows. The principle itself is defended by Andy Brook in "Obligations to Future Generations: A case study," *Contemporary Moral Issues*, e.d. A.W. Cragg (Toronto: McGraw/Hill Ryerson, 1993), 359. Brook ties this principle to two others:
    Liberty: Our actions must not result in preventable and foreseeable restriction of others' opportunities (which disease, pain, mutation or costs of avoiding these would do).
    Freedom from pain: Our actions must not result in preventable and foreseeable pain (or discomfort or diminution of ability) in others.
    Brook ties these three principles in turn to a fourth which he claims under-rides all three:
    Prior to considerations of individual distinguishing qualities of moral relevance, each person has the same value as any other.
    For the purposes of the discussion in this paper, the distributive justice principle is the key one. What Brook's account offers is a defence of the use of that principle and proposals for others that a full examination of the ethics of resource extraction would want to explore.

8. For the purpose of this discussion we propose to use as our definition of the term "environment", the meaning set out in by Ontario statute in the *Environmental Assessment Act*:
    i)   air, land or water,
    ii) plant and animal life, including man,
    iii) the social, economic and cultural conditions that influence the life of man or a community,
    iv) any building, structure, machine or other device or thing made by man,
    v)   any solid, liquid, gas, odour, heat, sound, vibration or radiation resulting directly or indirectly from the activities of man, or
    vi) any part or combination of the foregoing and the interrelationships between any two or more or them.
    (Revised Statutes of Ontario, 1980, s. 1(c))

9. See Aboriginal Witness Statements, DSP Environmental Assessment Hearing, Exhibits: 829–886, 947–951, 1018–1019.

10. See for example M. Friedman, "The Social Responsibility of Business is to Increase its Profits," *The New York Times Magazine*, September, 1970.

11. Litchfield et al., "Integrating Resource Planning . . .," 1994.

12. Ontario Hydro, *Environmental Assessment: Hydroelectric Generation Station Extensions Mattagami River*, October 1990, 2–1.

13. Litchfield et al., "Integrated Resource Planning . . .," 4, describe this as the traditional planning model for utilities in North America in this century.

14. Ontario Hydro, *Demand/Supply Plan Report*, DSP Environmental Assessment Hearing, Exhibit #3, December 1989, 6–13.

15. Presently the *Environmental Assessment Act* R.S.O. 1990, c.E. 18.

16. Ibid., s.2.

17. Ibid. s. 1(c).

18. Ontario Hydro, *Demand Supply Plan Environmental Analysis*, DSP Environmental Assessment Hearing, Exhibit #4, December 1989, 3–3.
19. Ibid., 3–5.
20. Ontario Hydro, *Environmental Assessment Summary: Hydroelectric Generation Station Extensions Mattagami River*, October 1990, 18.
21. Ibid., 23.
22. A channel which carries away water which has passed through the generating station.
23. Ontario Hydro, *Environmental Assessment Summary*, 24–25.
24. Ibid., 6–13.
25. Ibid., 6–48.
26. Ibid., 6–48.
27. Ibid., 8–11.
28. The First Nations in the Moose River Basin refused to cooperate with Ontario Hydro's environmental assessment.
29. Ontario Hydro, *Environmental Assessment Summary*, 8–11.
30. These difficulties are subject of ongoing debate among economists and others. An accessible (to the lay person) discussion is offered in Litchfield et al., "Integrated Resource Planning …". For a more detailed examination of the limitations of cost/benefit analysis from the perspective of distributive justice see McDonald, Stevenson and Cragg, "Finding a Balance of Values".
31. This conclusion is not unique to the authors of this paper. Two recent attempts by major utilities, Ontario Hydro in its Twenty-five Year Plan and Quebec Hydro with regard to the Great Whale project, at costing impacts relevant to these concerns have seemed to have led to the same conclusion. Ontario Hydro put off assessing these costs to the formal environmental assessment process which of course was never completed. What they appear to have concluded was that costing would have to be arrived at through some process of negotiation after the developments they were seeking had been approved in principle. Quebec Hydro's environmental assessment from "Grande-Baleine Complex: Feasibility Study", Hydro Québec, August 1993, is worth quoting in this regard:

    > The financial evaluation of sociocultural impacts is . . . difficult. Many believe economists do not have the right to put a price tag on goods or values for which it is difficult, if not impossible, to imagine a market. Such people may find it reprehensible that economists perform economic assessments of certain aspects of Native culture.

    Further:

    > In the case of other externalities, which are generally social or cultural, an approach aimed at establishing an economic value appears neither appropriate nor possible. (Part 2, Book 8, p. 37.)

32. For a discussion of this point see Litchfield et al., "Integrated Resource Planning . . .".
33. Native People's Circle on Environmental and Development, Report prepared for the Ontario Round Table on Environment and Economy, 1992, 4.
34. R. Kapashesit, "Evidence in Chief," DSP Environmental Assessment Hearing, Exhibit #1019, January 4, 1993, 7.
35. Native People's Circle, Report, 4.
36. Kapashesit, "Evidence in Chief," 7.
37. There are no relevant studies that we know of in environmental ethics that probes this perspective. However, there are relevant studies in other areas. Philosophy of law and punishment is a good example. Punishment of offenders is often seen as a form of compensation for offensive actions. This theme is explored at length by Jean Hampton and Jeffrey Murphy in their book *Forgiveness and Mercy* (Cambridge: Cambridge University Press, 1988). H.L.A Hart explores a similar theme in Punishment and Responsibility (Oxford: Claredon Press, 1963), particularly "Punishment and the Elimination of Responsibility", 183. See also A.W. Cragg, *The Practice of Punishment: Toward a Theory of Restorative Justice* (London: Routledge, 1993).

    A further note is appropriate here. Paul Wilkinson, whose contribution to this paper is acknowledged elsewhere, has pointed out in private correspondence that compensation of the sort to which Chief Kapashesit refers need not be thought of in purely financial terms. He points out that "compensation might take a symbolic form such as the erection of a monument, a public apology, environmental remediation, economic development to replace lost opportunities, or many other forms." He also points out that acceptance of financial compensation should not be construed as a recognition by concerned First Nations of its appropriateness given the nature of the harms experienced.

38. *Guidelines for the Great Whale River Hydroelectric Project*, #113.
39. D. DeLauney, "Report of the Provincial Representative: Moose River Basin Consultations," prepared for the Ministry of Natural Resources, April 1992, 7.
40. Will Kymlicka goes some distance in that direction in a recent article (unpublished) entitled "Concepts of Community and Social Justice" prepared for a conference on "Global Environmental Change and Social Justice" at Cornell University, September 1993. In that paper, Kymlicka explores the interplay of the right to self-determination of minorities and with principles of distributive justice concerned with a fair distribution and use of natural resources.
41. The idea of equitable participation has been most carefully examined in the context of medical ethics, where it is now widely accepted that it is the competent patient's judgement of his or her own interests which should guide treatment and not that of the health care provider. Beauchamp T. and Childress, J., *Principles of Biomedical Ethics* (New York: Oxford University Press, 1979), p. 62 and p. 153, and Edmund Pellegrino, "Trust and Distrust in Professional Ethics," *Trust and the Professions: Philosophical and Cultural Aspects* (Washington, DC: Georgetown University Press, date) 81.
42. Ministry of Natural Resources, "Draft Terms of Reference/Work Plan for the Technical Group," July 28, 1993, 1.
43. Ministry of Natural Resources, "Moose River Basin Baseline Data Collection Project, Background Report," August 1993, 2.
44. Cragg, McDonald, and Stevenson, "Finding a Balance . . .," 20.
45. It does not follow, of course, that any project with externalized costs is unsustainable. It does follow on the other hand that to externalize costs for which there are inadequate compensating benefits recognizable as such by those on whom the costs are imposed is unjust.
46. Ontario Hydro, *Report of the Task Force on Sustainable Energy Development: A Strategy for Sustainable Energy Development and Use for Ontario Hydro*, October 18, 1993, 32-35.
47. The members of the research team of which this project is a part consist of: Wesley Cragg, Principal Investigator, and co-investigators John Lewko, David Pearson and Craig Summers (Laurentian University). For further information about the project please write: Wesley Cragg, Faculty of Administrative Studies, York University, 4700 Keele St., North York, Ontario (M3J 1P3); E-mail wcragg@mail.fas.yorku.ca.

BIBLIOGRAPHY

Adams, T. "Witness Statement," DSP Environmental Assessment Hearing, Exhibit #855, December, 1992.

Allen, G. "Ontario Backs Mill Buyout Plan," *The Globe and Mail*, June 20, 1991, a. 4.

Bay and Basin Bulletin: The Moose River Basin Project Newsletter, Vol. 1, No. 2, January, 1995.

Beauchamp, T. and Childress, J. *Principles of Biomedical Ethics.* (New York: Oxford University Press), 1979.

Bennett, Kearon. "Small Hydro Research Summary Report," Appendix G, DSP Environmental Assessment Hearing, Exhibit #926, November, 1992.

Brook, A. "Obligations to Future Generations: A Case Study," *Contemporary Moral Issues* (Toronto: McGraw-Hill Ryerson, 1993) p. 359.

Brundtland Commission. *Our Common Future* (Oxford: Oxford University Press), 1987.

Cheena, G. "Witness Statement," DSP Environmental Assessment Hearing, Exhibit #883, December, 1992.

Conway, T. "Impacts of Prior Development," DSP Environmental Assessment Hearing, Exhibit #890, December, 1992.

Cragg, A.W. *Contemporary Moral Issues* (Toronto: McGraw-Hill Ryerson), 1992.

Cragg, A.W. *The Practice of Punishment: Toward a Theory of Restorative Justice* (London: Routledge) 1993.

Cragg, A.W., McDonald and Stevenson. "Finding a Balance of Values: An Ethical Assessment of Ontario Hydro's Demand/Supply Plan," November, 1992.

DeLauney, D. "Report of the Provincial Representative: Moose River Basin Consultations," prepared for the Ministry of Natural Resources, April, 1992.

Environmental Assessment Act, R.S.O. 1980, c. 140.

Environmental Assessment Act, R.S.O. 1990, c.E. 18.

ESSA (Environmental and Social Systems Analysts Ltd.). "Hypotheses of Effects of Development in the Moose River Basin Workshop Summary — Final Report," DSP Environmental Assessment Hearing, Exhibit #719, March, 1992.

Faries, B. "Witness Statement," DSP Environmental Assessment Hearing, Exhibit #876, December, 1992.

Fowlie, L. "Town That Refused To Die," *Financial Post*, December 28-30, 1991, p. 16.

Friedman, M. "The Social Responsibility of Business is to Increase Its Profits," *The New York Times Magazine*, September 13, 1970.

"Guidelines: Environmental Impact Statement for the Proposed Great Whale River Hydroelectric Project", Evaluating Committee, Kativik Environmental Quality Commission, Federal Review Committee North of the 55th Parallel, Federal Environmental Assessment Review Panel, published by Great Whale Public Review Support Office, 1155 Sherbrooke St. West, Suite 1603, Montreal, Quebec (H3A 2N3).

Hampton, J. and Murphy, J. *Forgiveness and Mercy* (Cambridge: Cambridge University Press) 1988.

Hart, H.L.A. *Punishment and Responsibility* (Oxford: Clarendon Press) 1963.

Jones, I. "Witness Statement," DSP Environmental Assessment Hearing, Exhibit #950, December, 1992.

Kapashesit, R. "Evidence in Chief," DSP Environmental Assessment Hearing, Exhibit #1019,

Keir, A. "Socio-Economic Impact Assessment: Reference Document of Hydroelectric Generating Station Extensions Mattagami River," prepared for Ontario Hydro Corporate Relations Branch, Volumes 1 & 2, January, 1991.

Kymlicka, W. "Concepts of Community and Social Justice". Unpublished. Presented at "Global Environmental Change and Social Justice" conference at Cornell University, September, 1993.

Linklater, M. "Witness Statement," DSP Environmental Assessment Hearing, Exhibit #877, December, 1992.

Litchfield, James; Hemmingway, Leroy and Raphals, Philip. "Integrated Resource Planning and the Great Whale Public Review", Background Paper No. 7, Great Whale Environmental Assessment, Great Whale Public Review Office, 1994.

MacDonald, R. "Witness Statement," DSP Environmental Assessment Hearing, Exhibit #852, December, 1992.

Mackie, R. "Can't Afford Mill Bailout, Premier Says," *Globe and Mail*, July 15, 1991, Section A, 8.

Ministry of Natural Resources. "Draft Terms of Reference/Work Plan for the Technical Group," July 28, 1993.

Ministry of Natural Resources. "Moose River Basin Baseline Data Collection Project, Background Report," August, 1993.

Mittelstaedt M. "Hydro Looking To End Environmental Hearing," *Globe and Mail*, November 13, 1992, a.5.

Mittelstaedt, M. "Ontario Gives Hydro Project Go-Ahead," *Globe and Mail*, October 6, 1994, b. 10.

Morrison, J. "Colonization, Resource Extraction and Hydroelectric Development in the Moose River Basin: A Preliminary History of the Implications For Aboriginal People," DSP Environmental Assessment Hearing, Exhibit #869 November, 1992.

Mugiskan, Chief W. "Witness Statement," DSP Environmental Assessment Hearing, Exhibit #866, December, 1992.

Nation K. and Noble K. "U.S. Firm Rejects Newsprint Mill Deal," *Globe and Mail*, June 29, 1991, b.1 & b.4.

Native People's Circle on Environment and Development, Report prepared for the Ontario Round Table on Environment and Economy, 1992.

Noble, K. "Kapuskasing Deal Best For Everybody," *Globe and Mail*, August 15, 1991, Section B 1 & 4.

Ontario Hydro, *Demand/Supply Plan Report*, DSP Environmental Assessment Hearing, Exhibit #3, December, 1989.

Ontario Hydro, *Demand Supply Plan Environmental Analysis*, DSP Environmental Assessment Hearing, Exhibit #4, December, 1989.

Ontario Hydro, *Environmental Assessment: Hydroelectric Generating Station Extensions Mattagami River*, October, 1990.

Ontario Hydro, *Environmental Assessment Summary: Hydroelectric Generating Station Extensions Mattagami River*, February, 1991.

Ontario Hydro, *Report of the Task Force on Sustainable Energy Development: A Strategy For Sustainable Energy Development and Use For Ontario Hydro*, October 18, 1993.

Pellegrino, Edmund. "Trust and Distrust in Professional Ethics." Ethics, *Trust and the Professions Philosophical and Cultural Aspects* (Washington D.C.: Georgetown University Press).

Philp, M. "Spruce Falls Mill May Close," *Globe and Mail*, March 20, 1991, b. 3.

Roderique, J. "Witness Statement," DSP Environmental Assessment Hearing, Exhibit #875, December, 1992.

Sears, S.K. and Paterson, M. "Integrated Ecosystem-Based Planning for Hydroelectric Generation Development in a Remote Northern Ontario River Basin," DSP Environmental Assessment Hearing, Exhibit #382, May, 1991.

Submission Letters re: Review of Environmental Assessment for the Proposed Hydroelectric Generating Station Extensions on the Mattagami River. 1992, Ministry of the Environment, Environmental Assessment Branch, 1992.

Sutherland, J. "Witness Statement," DSP Environmental Assessment Hearing, Exhibit #873, December, 1992.

Sutherland, P. "Witness Statement," DSP Environmental Assessment Hearing, Exhibit #874, December, 1992.

QUESTIONS

1. Does Ontario Hydro's development of the Moose River Basin illustrate ingrained attitudes toward nature of a sort that Northrop Frye identifies and then criticizes?

2. Does this case serve to confirm or refute the view implied by Trudeau in commenting on

aboriginal rights that the best way to respond to injustice of the past is to build a more just future?

3. What is involved in "the externalization of costs"? What costs did Ontario Hydro externalize in building dams on the Mattagami River? Why would a mandate "to provide a reliable supply of electrical power to the people of Ontario at the lowest feasible long-term cost" encourage externalization of costs? What are the moral objections to externalization of costs of the sort described in this case?

4. Is financial compensation as a way of dealing with the unavoidable environmental impacts of projects that can be shown otherwise to have economic benefits an acceptable way in principle of dealing with harmful impacts that cannot be mitigated? What reasons are offered for thinking that it is objectionable in this case? Are the reasons given convincing in your view?

5. What is distributive justice? How is it related to sustainable development?

6. Is the concept of sustainable development the tool we need to overcome the ecological blind spots that Frye describes as characterizing our culture?

DUTIES CONCERNING ISLANDS

Mary Midgley

Had Robinson Crusoe any duties?

When I was a philosophy student, this used to be a familiar conundrum, which was supposed to pose a very simple question; namely, can you have duties to yourself? Mill, they correctly told us, said no. "The term duty to oneself, when it means anything more than prudence, means self-respect or self-development, and for none of these is anyone accountable to his fellow-creatures."[1] Kant, on the other hand, said yes. "Duties to ourselves are of primary importance and should have pride of place . . . nothing can be expected of a man who dishonours his own person."[2] There is a serious disagreement here, not to be sneezed away just by saying, "It depends on what you mean by duty." Much bigger issues are involved — quite how big has, I think, not yet been fully realized. To grasp this, I suggest that we rewrite a part of Crusoe's story, in order to bring in sight a different range of concerns.

> 19 Sept. 1685. This day I set aside to devastate my island. My pinnace being now ready on the shore, and all things prepared for my departure, Friday's people also expecting me, and the wind blowing fresh away from my little harbour, I had a mind to see how all would burn. So then, setting sparks and powder craftily among certain dry spinneys which I had chosen, I soon had it ablaze, nor was there left, by the next down, any green stick among the ruins. . . .

From Environmental Philosophy, *eds. Robert Elliot and Aaran Gare, published by University of Queensland Press, 1983. Reprinted by permission of University of Queensland Press.*

Now, work on the style how you will, you cannot make that into a convincing paragraph. Crusoe was not the most scrupulous of men, but he would have felt an invincible objection to this senseless destruction. So would the rest of us. Yet the language of our moral tradition has tended strongly, ever since the Enlightenment, to make that objection unstateable. All the terms which express that an obligation is serious or binding — duty, right, law, morality, obligation, justice — have been deliberately narrowed in their use so as to apply only in the framework of contract, to describe only relations holding between free and rational agents. Since it has been decided *a priori* that rationality admits of no degrees and that cetaceans are not rational, it follows that, unless you take either religion or science fiction seriously, we can only have duties to humans, and sane, adult, responsible humans at that. Now the morality we live by certainly does not accept this restriction. In common life we recognize many other duties as serious and binding, though of course not necessarily overriding. If philosophers want to call these something else instead of duties, they must justify their move.

We have here one of those clashes between the language of common morality (which is of course always to some extent confused and inarticulate) and an intellectual scheme which arose in the first place from a part of that morality, but has now taken off on its own claims of authority to correct other parts of its source. There are always real difficulties here. As ordinary citizens, we have to guard against dismissing such intellectual schemes too casually; we have to do justice to the point of them. But, as philosophers, we have to resist the opposite temptation of taking the intellectual scheme as decisive, just because it is elegant and satisfying, or because the moral insight which is its starting point is specially familiar to us. Today, this intellectualist bias is often expressed by calling the insights of common morality mere "intuitions." This is quite misleading, since it gives the impression that they have been reached without thought, and that there is, by contrast, a scientific solution somewhere else to which they ought to bow — as there might be if we were contrasting common sense "intuitions" about the physical world with physics or astronomy. Even without that word, philosophers often manage to give the impression that whenever our moral views clash with any simple, convenient scheme, it is our *duty* to abandon them. Thus, Grice states:

> It is an inescapable consequence of the thesis presented in these pages that certain classes cannot have natural rights: animals, the human embryo, future generations, lunatics and children under the age of, say, ten. In the case of young children at least, my experience is that this consequence is found hard to accept. But it is a consequence of the theory; it is, I believe, true; and I think we should be willing to accept it. At first sight it seems a harsh conclusion, but it is not nearly so harsh as it appears.[3]

But it is in fact extremely harsh, since what he is saying is that the treatment of children ought not to be determined by their interests but by the interests of the surrounding adults capable of contract, which, of course, can easily conflict with them. In our society, he explains, this does not actually make much difference, because parents here are so benevolent that they positively want to benefit their children, and accordingly here "the interests of children are reflected in the interests of their parents." But this, he adds, is just a contingent fact about us. "It is easy to imagine a society where this is not so," where, that is, parents are entirely exploitative. "In this circumstance, the morally correct treatment of children would no doubt be harsher than it is in our society. But the conclusion has to be accepted."

Grice demands that we withdraw our objections to harshness, in deference to theoretical consistency. But "harsh" here does not mean just "brisk and bracing," like cold baths and a plain diet. (There might well be more of those where parents do feel bound to consider their children's interests.) It means "unjust." Our objection to unbridled parental selfishness is not a mere matter of tone or taste; it is a moral one. It therefore requires a moral answer, an explanation of the contrary *value* which the contrary theory expresses. Grice, and those who argue like him, take the ascetic, disapproving tone of those who have already displayed such a value, and who are met by a slovenly reluctance to rise to it. But they have not displayed that value. The ascetic tone cannot be justified merely by an appeal to consistency. An ethical theory, which, when consistently followed through, has iniquitous consequences, is a bad theory and must be changed. Certainly we can ask whether these consequences really are iniquitous, but this question must be handled seriously. We cannot directly conclude that the consequences cease to stink the moment they are seen to follow from our theory.

The theoretical model which has spread blight in this area is, of course, that of social contract, and, to suit it, that whole cluster of essential moral terms — right, duty, justice and the rest — has been progressively narrowed. This model shows human society as a spread of standard social atoms, originally distinct and independent, each of which combines with others only at its own choice and in its own private interest. This model is drawn from physics, and from seventeenth-century physics, at that, where the ultimate particles of matter were conceived as hard, impenetrable, homogeneous little billiard balls, with no hooks or internal structure. To see how such atoms could combine at all was very hard. Physics, accordingly, moved on from this notion to one which treats atoms and other particles as complex items, describable mainly in terms of forces, and those the same kind of forces which operate outside them. It has abandoned the notion of ultimate, solitary, independent individuals. Social-contract theory, however, retains it.

On this physical — or archaeo-physical — model, all significant moral relations between individuals are the symmetrical ones expressed by contract. If, on the other hand, we use a biological or "organic" model, we can talk also of a variety of asymmetrical relations found within a whole. Leaves relate not only to other leaves, but to fruit, twigs, branches and the whole tree. People appear not only as individuals, but as members of their groups, families, tribes, species, ecosystems and biosphere, and have moral relations as part to these wholes. The choice between these two ways of thinking is not, of course, a simple once-and-for-all affair. Different models are useful for different purposes. We can, however, reasonably point out, firstly, that the old physical pattern does make all attempts to explain combination extremely difficult; and, secondly, that since human beings actually are living creatures, not crystals or galaxies, it is reasonable to expect that biological ways of thinking will be useful in understanding them.

In its own sphere, the social contract model has of course been of enormous value. Where we deal with clashes of interest between free and rational agents already in existence, and particularly where we want to disentangle some of them from some larger group that really does not suit them, it is indispensable. And for certain political purposes during the last three centuries these clashes have been vitally important. An obsession with contractual thinking, and a conviction that it is a cure-all, are therefore understandable. But the trouble with such obsessions is that they distort the whole shape of thought and language in a way which makes them self-perpetuating, and constantly extends their empire. Terms come to be defined in a way which leaves only certain moral views expressible. This can happen without any clear intention on the part of those propagating them, and even contrary to their occasional declarations, simply from mental inertia. Thus, John Rawls, having devoted most of his long book to his very subtle and exhaustive contractual view of justice, remarks without any special emphasis near the end that "we should recall here the limits of a theory of justice. Not only are many aspects of morality left aside, but no account can be given of right conduct in regard to animals and the rest of nature."[4] He concedes that these are serious matters. "Certainly it is wrong to be cruel to animals and the destruction of a whole species can be a great evil. The capacity for feelings of pleasure and pain and for the forms of life of which animals are capable clearly impose duties of compassion and human-ity in their case." All this is important, he says, and it calls for a wider metaphysical enquiry, but it is not his subject. Earlier in the same passage he touches on the question of permanently irrational human beings, and remarks that it "may present a difficulty. I cannot examine this problem here, but I assume that the account of equality would not be materi-ally affected."[5] Won't it though? It is a strange project to examine a single virtue — justice — without at least sketching in one's view of the vast background of general morality which determines its shape and meaning, including, of course, such awkward and noncon-tractual virtues as "compassion and humanity." It isolates the duties which people owe each other *merely as thinkers* from those deeper and more general ones which they owe each other as beings who feel. It cannot, therefore, fail both to split a man's nature and to isolate him from the rest of the creation to which he belongs.

Such an account may not be *Hamlet* without the prince, but it is *Hamlet* with half the cast missing, and without the state of Denmark. More exactly, it is like a history of Poland which regards Russia, Germany, Europe and the Roman Church as not part of its subject. I am not attacking Rawls' account on its own ground. I am simply pointing out what the history of ethics shows all too clearly — how much our thinking is shaped by what our sages *omit* to mention. The Greek philosophers never really raised the problem of slavery till towards the end of their speech, and then few of them did so with conviction. This happened even though it lay right in the path of their enquiries into political justice and the value of the individual soul. Christianity did raise that problem, because its class back-ground was different and because the world in the Christian era was already in turmoil, so that men were not presented with the narcotic of a happy stability. But Christianity itself did not, until quite recently, raise the problem of the morality of punishment, and particularly of eternal punishment. This failure to raise central questions was not, in either case, complete. One can find very intelligent and penetrating criticisms of slavery occurring from time to time in Greek writings — even in Aristotle's defence of that institution.[6] But they are mostly like Rawls' remark here. They conclude that "this should be investigated some day." The same thing happens with Christian writings concerning punishment, except that the consideration, "this is a great mystery," acts as an even more powerful paralytic to thought. Not much more powerful, however. Natural inertia, when it coincides with vested interest or the illusion of vested interest, is as strong as gravitation.

It is important that Rawls does not, like Grice, demand that we toe the line which would make certain important moral views impossible. Like Hume, who similarly excluded ani-mals from justice, he simply leaves them out of his discussion. This move ought in principle to be harmless. But when it is combined with an intense concentration of discussion on contractual justice, and a corresponding neglect of compassion and humanity, it inevitably suggests that the excluded problems are relatively unimportant. This suggestion is still more strongly conveyed by rulings which exclude the nonhuman world from rights, duties and morality. Words like "rights" and "duties" are awkward because they do indeed have narrow senses approximating to the legal, but they also have much wider ones in which they cover the whole moral sphere. To say "they do not have rights," or "you do not have duties to them" conveys to any ordinary hearer a very simple message; namely, "they do not matter." This is an absolution, a removal of blame for ill treatment of "them," whoever they may be.

To see how strong this informal, moral usage of "rights" is, we need only look at the history of that powerful notion, the "rights of man." These rights were not supposed to be ones conferred by law, since the whole point of appealing to them was to change laws so as to embody them. They were vague, but vast. They did not arise, as rights are often said do, only within a community, since they were taken to apply in principle everywhere. The immense, and on the whole coherent, use which has been made of this idea by reform movements shows plainly that the tension between the formal and the informal idea of "right" is part of the word's meaning, a fruitful connection of thought, not just a mistake. It is therefore hard to adopt effectively the compromise which some philosophers now favour, of saying that it is indeed wrong to treat animals in certain ways, but that we have no duties to them or that they have no rights.[7] "Animal rights" may be hard to formulate, as indeed are the rights of humans. But "no rights" will not do. The word may need to be dropped entirely. The compromise is still harder with the word "duty," which is rather more informal, and is more closely wedded to a private rather than political use.

Where the realm of right and duty stops, there, to ordinary thinking, begins the realm of the optional. What is not a duty may be a matter of taste, style or feeling, of aesthetic sensibility, of habit and nostalgia, of etiquette and local custom, but it cannot be something which demands our attention whether we like it or not. When claims get into this area, they can scarcely be taken seriously. This becomes clear when Kant tries to straddle the border. He says that we have no direct duties to animals, because they are not rational, but that we should treat them properly all the same because of "indirect" duties which are really duties to our own humanity.[8] This means that ill-treating them (a) might lead us to ill-treat humans, and (b) is a sign of a bad or inhumane disposition. The whole issue thus becomes a contingent one of spiritual style or training, like contemplative exercises, intellectual practice or, indeed, refined manners.[9] Some might need practice of this kind to make them kind to people, others might not, and, indeed, might get on better without it. (Working off one's ill-temper on animals might make one treat people *better*.) But the question of cruelty to animals cannot be like this, because it is of the essence to such training exercises that they are internal. Anything that affects some other being is not just practice, it is real action. Anyone who refrained from cruelty *merely* from a wish not to sully his own character, without any direct consideration for the possible victims, would be frivolous and narcissistic.

A similar trivialization follows where theorists admit duties of compassion and humanity to noncontractors, but deny duties of justice. Hume and Rawls, in making this move, do not explicitly subordinate these other duties, or say that they are less binding. But because they make the contract element so central to morality, this effect appears to follow. The priority of justice is expressed in such everyday proverbs as "be just before you're generous." We are therefore rather easily persuaded to think that compassion, humanity and so forth are perhaps emotional luxuries, to be indulged only after all debts are paid. A moment's thought will show that this is wrong. Someone who receives simultaneously a request to pay a debt and another to comfort somebody bereaved or on their death bed is not as a matter of course under obligation to treat the debt as the more urgent. He has to look at circumstances on both sides, but in general we should probably expect the other duties to have priority. This is still more true if, on his way to pay the debt, he encounters a stranger in real straits, drowning or lying on the road. To give the debt priority, we probably need to think of his creditor as also being in serious trouble — which brings compassion and humanity in on both sides of the case.

What makes it so hard to give justice a different clientele from the other virtues, as Hume and Rawls do, is simply the fact that justice is such a pervading virtue. In general, all serious cases of cruelty, meanness, inhumanity and the like are also cases of injustice. If we are told that a certain set of these cases does not involve injustice, our natural thought is that these cases must be *trivial*. Officially, Hume's and Rawls' restriction is not supposed to mean this. What, however, is it supposed to mean? It is forty years since I first read Hume's text, and I find his thought as obscure now as I did then. I well remember double-taking then, going back over the paragraph for a point which, I took it, I must have missed. Can anyone see it?

> Were there a species of creatures intermingled with men, which, though rational, were possessed of such inferior strength, both of body and mind, that they were incapable of all resistance, and could never, upon the highest provocation, make us feel the effects of their resentment; the necessary consequence, I think, is that we should be bound by the laws of humanity to give gentle usage to these creatures, but should not, properly speaking, lie under any restraint of justice with regard to them, nor could they possess any right or property, exclusive of such arbitrary lords. Our intercourse with them could not be called society, which supposes a degree of equality, but absolute command on one side and servile obedience on the other. . . . This is plainly the situation of men with regard to animals.[10]

I still think that the word "justice," so defined, has lost its normal meaning. In ordinary life we think that duties of justice become *more* pressing, not less so, when we are dealing with the weak and inarticulate, who cannot argue back. It is the boundaries of prudence which depend on power, not those of justice. Historically, Hume's position becomes more understandable when one sees its place in the development of social-contract thinking. The doubtful credit for confining justice to the human species seems to belong to Grotius, who finally managed to ditch the Roman notion of *jus naturale*, natural right or law, common to all species. I cannot here discuss his remarkably unimpressive arguments for this.[11] The point I want to make here is simply in reference to the effect of these restrictive definitions of terms like "justice" on people's view of the sheer size of the problems raised by what falls outside them.

Writers who treat morality as primarily contractual tend to discuss noncontractual cases briefly, casually and parenthetically, as though they were rather rare. Rawls' comments on the problem of mental defectives are entirely typical here. We have succeeded, they say, in laying most of the carpet; why are you making this fuss about those little wrinkles behind the sofa? This treatment confirms a view, already suggested by certain aspects of current politics in the United States, that those who fail to clock in as normal rational agents and make their contracts are just occasional exceptions, constituting one more "minority" group — worrying, no doubt, to the scrupulous, but not a central concern of any society. Let us, then, glance briefly at their scope, by roughly listing some cases which seem to involve us in noncontractual duties. (The order is purely provisional and the numbers are added just for convenience.)

Human Sector	1. The dead
	2. Posterity
	3. Children
	4. The senile
	5. The temporarily insane
	6. The permanently insane
	7. Defectives, ranging down to "human vegetables"
	8. Embryos, human and otherwise
Animal Sector	9. Sentient animals
	10. Nonsentient animals
Inanimate Sector	11. Plants of all kinds
	12. Artefacts, including works of art
	13. Inanimate but structured objects — crystals, rivers, rocks, etc.
Comprehensive	14. Unchosen groups of all kinds, including families and species
	15. Ecosystems, landscapes, villages, warrens, cities, etc.
	16. Countries
	17. The Biosphere
Miscellaneous	18. Oneself
	19. God

No doubt I have missed a few, but that will do to go on with. The point is this; if we look only at a few of these groupings, and without giving them full attention, it is easy to think that we can include one or two as honorary contracting members by a slight stretch of our conceptual scheme, and find arguments for excluding the others from serious concern entirely. But if we keep our eye on the size of the range, this stops being plausible. As far as sheer numbers go, this is no minority of the beings with whom we have to deal. We are a small minority of them. As far as importance goes, it is certainly possible to argue that some of these sorts of beings should concern us more and others less: we need a priority system. But, to build it, *moral* arguments are required. The various kinds of claims have to be understood and compared, not written off in advance. We cannot rule that those who, in our own and other cultures, suppose that there is a direct objection to injuring or destroying some of them, are always just confused, and mean only, in fact, that this item will be needed for rational human consumption.[12]

The blank antithesis which Kant made between rational persons (having value) and mere things (having none) will not serve us to map out this vast continuum. And the idea that, starting at some given point on this list, we have a general licence for destruction, is itself a moral view which would have to be justified. Western culture differs from most others in the breadth of destructive licence which it allows itself, and, since the seventeenth century, that licence has been greatly extended. Scruples about rapine have been continually dismissed as irrational, but it is not always clear with what rational principles they are supposed to conflict. Western destructiveness has not in fact developed in response to a new set of disinterested intellectual principles demonstrating the need for more people and less redwoods, but mainly as a by-product of greed and increasing commercial confidence. Humanistic hostility to superstition has played some part in the process, because respect for the nonhuman items on our list is often taken to be religious. It does not have to be. Many scientists who are card-carrying atheists can still see the point of preserving the biosphere. So can the rest of us, religious or otherwise. It is the whole of which we are parts, and its other parts concern us for that reason.

But the language of rights is rather ill-suited to expressing this, because it has been developed mainly for the protection of people who, though perhaps oppressed, are in principle articulate. This makes it quite reasonable for theorists to say that rights belong only to those who understand them and can claim them. When confronted with the "human sector" of our list, these theorists can either dig themselves in, like Grice, and exclude the lot, or stretch the scheme, like Rawls, by including the hypothetical rational choices which these honorary members *would* make if they were not unfortunately prevented. Since many of these people seem less rational than many animals, zoophiles have, then, a good case for calling this second device arbitrary or specious, and extending rights to the border of sentience. Here, however, the meaning of the term "rights" does become thin, and when we reach the inanimate area, usage will scarcely cover it. (It is worth noticing that long before this, when dealing merely with the "rights of man," the term often seems obscure, because to list and specify these rights is so much harder than to shout for them. The word is probably of more use as a slogan, indicating a general direction, than as a detailed conceptual tool.) There may be a point in campaigning to extend usage. But to me it seems wiser on the whole not to waste energy on this verbal point, but instead to insist on the immense variety of kinds of beings with which we have to deal. Once we grasp this, we ought not to be surprised that we are involved in many different kinds of claim or duty. The dictum that "rights and duties are correlative" is misleading, because the two words keep rather different company, and one may be narrowed without affecting the other.

What, then, about duties? I believe that this term can properly be used over the whole range. We have quite simply got many kinds of duties to animals,[13] to plants and to the biosphere. But to speak in this way we must free the term once and for all from its restrictive contractual use, or irrelevant doubts will still haunt us. If we cannot do this, we shall have to exclude the word "duty," along with "rights" from all detailed discussion, using wider words like "wrong," "right" and "ought" instead. This gymnastic would be possible but inconvenient. The issue about duty becomes clear as soon as we look at the controversy from which I started, between Kant's and Mill's views on duties to oneself. What do we think about this? Are there duties of integrity, autonomy, self-knowledge, self-respect? It seems that there are. Mill is right, of course, to point out that they are not duties to someone in the ordinary sense. The divided self is a metaphor. It is as natural and necessary a metaphor here as it is over, say, self-deception or self-control, but it certainly is not literal truth. The form of the requirement is different. Rights, for instance, certainly do not seem to come in here as they often would with duties to other persons; we would scarcely say, "I have a right to my own respect." And the *kind* of things which we can owe ourselves are distinctive. It is not just chance who they are owed to. You cannot owe it to somebody else, as you can to yourself, to force him to act freely or with integrity. He owes that to himself, the rest of us can only remove outside difficulties. As Kant justly said, our business is to promote our own perfection and the happiness of others; the perfection of others is an aim which belongs to them.[14] Respect, indeed, we owe both to ourselves and to others, but Kant may well be right to say that self-respect is really a different and deeper requirement, something without which all outward duties would become meaningless. (This may explain the paralyzing effect of depression.)

Duties to oneself, in fact, are duties with a different *form*. They are far less close than outward duties to the literal model of debt, especially monetary debt. Money is a thing which can be owed in principle to anybody, it is the same whoever you owe it to, and if by chance you come to owe it to yourself, the debt vanishes. Not many of our duties are really of this impersonal kind; the attempt to commute other sorts of duties into money is a notorious form of evasion. Utilitarianism however wants to make all duties as homogeneous as possible. And that is the point of Mill's position. He views all our self-concerning motives as parts of the desire for happiness. Therefore he places all duty, indeed all morality, on the outside world, as socially required restrictions of that desire — an expression, that is, of other people's desire for happiness.

> We do not call anything wrong, unless we mean that a person ought to be punished in some way or another for doing it; if not by law, by the opinion of his fellow-creatures; if not by opinion, by the reproaches of his own conscience. This seems the real turning point of the distinction between morality and simple expedience. It is a part of the notion of Duty in every one of its forms, that a person may rightly be compelled to fulfil it. Duty is a thing which may be *exacted* from a person, as one exacts a debt.[15]

To make the notion of wrongness depend on punishment and public opinion in this way instead of the other way round is a bold step. Mill did not mind falling flat on his face from time to time in trying out a new notion for the public good. He did it for us, and we should, I think, take proper advantage of his generosity, and accept the impossibility which he demonstrates. The concepts cannot be connected this way round. Unless you think of certain acts as wrong, it makes no sense to talk of punishment. "Punishing" alcoholics with aversion therapy or experimental rats with electric shocks is not really punishing at all; it is just deterrence. This "punishment" will not make their previous actions wrong, nor has it anything to do with morality. The real point of morality returns to Mill's scheme in the Trojan horse of "reproaches of his own conscience." Why do *they* matter? Unless the conscience is talking sense — that is, on Utilitarian principles, unless it is delivering the judgment of society — it should surely be silenced. Mill, himself a man of enormous integrity, deeply concerned about autonomy, would never have agreed to silence it. But, unless we do so, we shall have to complicate his scheme. It may well be true that, in the last resort and at the deepest level, conscience and the desire for happiness converge. But in ordinary life and at the everyday level they can diverge amazingly. We do want to be honest but we do not want to be put out. What we know we ought to do is often most unwelcome to us, which is why we call it duty. And whole sections of that duty do not concern other people directly at all. A good example is the situation in Huxley's *Brave New World*, where a few dissident citizens have grasped the possibility of a fuller and freer life. Nobody else wants this. Happiness is already assured. The primary duty of change here seems to be that of each to himself. True, they may feel bound also to help others to change, but hardly in a way which those others would *exact*. In fact, we may do better here by dropping the awkward second party altogether and saying that they have a duty *of* living differently — one which will affect both themselves and others, but which does not require, as a debt does, a named person or people *to* whom it must be paid. Wider models like "the whole duty of man" may be more relevant.

This one example from my list will, I hope, be enough to explain the point. I cannot go through all of them, nor ought it to be necessary. Duties need *not* be quasi-contractual relations between symmetrical pairs of rational human agents. There are all kinds of other obligations holding between asymmetrical pairs, or involving, as in this case, no outside beings at all. To speak of duties to things in the inanimate and comprehensive sectors of my list is not necessarily to personify them superstitiously, or to indulge in chatter about the "secret life of plants."[16] It expresses merely that there are suitable and unsuitable ways of behaving in given situations. People have duties *as* farmers, parents, consumers, forest dwellers, colonists, species members, shipwrecked mariners, tourists, potential ancestors and actual descendants, etc. As such, it is the business of each not to forget his transitory and dependent position, the rich gifts which he has received, and the tiny part he plays in a vast, irreplaceable and fragile whole.

It is remarkable that we now have to state this obvious truth as if it were new, and invent the word "ecological" to describe a whole vast class of duties. Most peoples are used to the idea. In stating it, and getting back into the centre of our moral stage, we meet various difficulties, of which the most insidious is possibly the temptation to feed this issue as fuel to long-standing controversies about religion. Is concern for the nonhuman aspects of our biosphere necessarily superstitious and therefore to be resisted tooth and nail? I have pointed out that it need not be religious. Certified rejectors of all known religions can share it. No doubt, however, there is a wider sense in which any deep and impersonal concern can be called religious — one in which Marxism is a religion. No doubt, too, all such deep concerns have their dangers, but certainly the complete absence of them has worse dangers. Moreover, anyone wishing above all to avoid the religious dimension should consider that the intense individualism which has focused our attention exclusively on the social contract model is itself thoroughly mystical. It has glorified the individual human soul as an object having infinite and transcendent value; has hailed it as the only real creator; and bestowed on it much of the panoply of God. Nietzsche, who was responsible for much of this new theology,[17] took over from the old theology (which he plundered extensively) the assumption that all the rest of creation mattered only as a frame for humankind. This is not an impression which any disinterested observer would get from looking around at it, nor do we need it in order to take our destiny sufficiently seriously.

Crusoe then, I conclude, did have duties concerning this island, and with the caution just given we can reasonably call them duties *to* it. They were not very exacting, and were mostly negative. They differed, of course, from those which a long standing inhabitant of a country has. Here the language of *fatherland* and *motherland*, which is so widely employed, indicates rightly a duty of care and responsibility which can go very deep, and which long-settled people commonly feel strongly. To insist that it is really only a duty to the exploiting human beings is not consistent with the emphasis often given to reverence for the actual trees, mountains, lakes, rivers and the like which are found there. A decision to inhibit all this rich area of human love is a special manoeuvre for which reasons would need to be given, not a dispassionate analysis of existing duties and feelings. What happens, however, when you are shipwrecked on an entirely strange island? As the history of colonization shows, there is a tendency for people so placed to drop any reverence and become more exploitative. But it is not irresistible. Raiders who settle down can quite soon begin to feel at home, as the Vikings did in East Anglia, and can, after a while, become as possessive, proud and protective towards their new land as the old inhabitants. Crusoe himself does, from time to time, show this pride rather touchingly, and it would, I think, certainly have inhibited any moderate temptation, such as that which I mentioned, to have a good bonfire. What keeps him sane through his stay is in fact his duty to God. If that had been absent, I should rather suppose that sanity would depend on a stronger and more positive attachment to the island itself and its creatures. It is interesting, however, that Crusoe's story played its part in developing that same icy individualism which has gone so far towards making both sorts of attachment seem corrupt or impossible. Rousseau delighted in *Robinson Crusoe*, and praised it as the only book fit to be given to a child, *not* because it showed a man in his true relation to animal and vegetable life, but because it was the bible of individualism. "The surest way to raise him [the child] above prejudice and to base his judgments on the true relations of things, is to put him in the place of a solitary man, and to judge all things as they would be judged by such a man in relation to their own utility. . . . So long as only bodily needs are recognized, man is self-sufficing . . . the child knows no other happiness but food and freedom."[18] That false atomic notion of human psychology — a prejudice above which nobody ever raised Rousseau — is the flaw in all social-contract thinking. If he were right, every member of the human race would need a separate island—and what, then, would our ecological problems be? Perhaps, after all, we had better count our blessings.

NOTES

1. John Stuart Mill, *Essay on Liberty* (London: Dent, Everyman's Library, 1910), chap. 4, p. 135.
2. Immanuel Kant, "Duties to Oneself," in *Lectures on Ethics*, trans. Louis Infield (London: Methuen, 1930), p. 118.
3. G.R. Grice, *Grounds for Moral Sentiments* (Cambridge: Cambridge University Press, 1967), pp. 147–149.
4. John Rawls, *A Theory of Justice* (Oxford: Oxford University Press, 1972), p. 512.
5. Ibid., p. 510.
6. Aristotle, Politics 1. 3–8; cf., idem, *Nicomachean Ethics* 7, 2.
7. For example, John Passmore, *Man's Responsibility for Nature* (London: Duckworth, 1974), pp. 116–117, H.J. McCloskey, "Rights," *Philosophical Quarterly* 15 (1965).
8. Nor will it help for philosophers to say "it is not the case that they have rights." Such pompous locutions have either no meaning at all, or the obvious one.
9. Immanual Kant, "Duties towards Animals and Spirits," in *Lectures on Ethics*, p. 240.
10. David Hume, "An Enquiry concerning the Principles of Morals," in *Hume's Moral and Political Philosophy*, ed. H.E. Aiben (New York: Hafner, 1949), app. 3, pp. 190–191.
11. A point well discussed by Stephen R.L. Clark, *The Moral Status of Animals* (Oxford: Clarendon Press, 1977), pp. 12–13.
12. For details, see John Rodman, "Animal Justice: The Counter-Revolution in Natural Right and Law," *Inquiry* 22, nos. 1–2 (Summer 1979).
13. A case first made by Jeremy Bentham, *An Introduction of the Principles of Moral and Legislation*, chap. 17, and well worked out by Peter Singer, *Animal Liberation* (New York: Avon, 1975), Chaps. 1, 5 and 6.
14. Immanuel Kant, *Preface to the Metaphysical Elements of Ethics*, section "Introduction to Ethics," 4 and 5.
15. John Stuart Mill, *Utilitarianism* (London: Dent, Everyman's Library, 1910), chap. 5, p. 45.
16. P. Thompkins and C. Bird, *The Secret Life of Plants* (New York: Harper and Row, 1973), claimed to show, by various experiments involving electrical apparatus, that plants can feel. Attempts to duplicate their experiments have, however, totally failed to produce any similar results. (See A.W. Galston and C.L. Slayman, "The Secret Life of Plants," *American Scientist* 67 [1973]: 337. It seems possible that the original results were due to a fault in the electrical apparatus. The attempt shows, I think, one of the confusions which continually arise from insisting that all duties must be of the same form. We do not need to prove that plants are animals in order to have reason to spare them. The point is well discussed by Marian Dawkins in her book *Animal Suffering* (London: Chapman and Hall, 1981), pp. 117–119.
17. See particularly, Friedrich Nietzsche, *Thus Spake Zarathustra* 3, section "Of Old and New Tables"; and *The Joyful Wisdom* (otherwise called *The Gay Science*), p. 125 (the Madman's

Speech). I have discussed this rather mysterious appointment of man to succeed God in a paper called "Creation and Originality," *Heart & Mind: The Varieties of Moral Experience* (Brighton: The Harvester Press, 1981).

18. Barbara Foxley, trans., *Emile* (London: Dent, Everyman's Library, 1966), pp. 147–148.

QUESTIONS

1. What is it about social contract theory that leads Midgley to say that it is excessively individualistic in orientation? Is she right to suggest that one indication social contract theory is not sound is that it is based on a physical rather than a biological model of the ways in which individuals relate?
2. If my friend has no right to ask me for help, does it follow that I have no duty or obligation to offer it?
3. What do you think of Hume's claim about the nature of justice (see pp. 351–53)? What would such a view imply for issues like abortion, euthanasia, or war? Does Midgley offer convincing reasons for thinking that Hume was mistaken?
4. Did Crusoe have a duty not to destroy his island once it was of no further use to him? Would the situation change if it could be shown to be of no further use to anyone?

HONEY DRIBBLES DOWN YOUR FUR

Tom Regan

For Dogen, the others who are "none other than myself" include mountains, rivers, and the great earth. When one thinks like a mountain, one thinks also like the black bear and this is a step . . . to deep ecology which requires openness to the black bear, becoming truly intimate with the black bear, so that honey dribbles down your fur as you catch the bus to work.

> Robert Aitken, Roshi "Gandhi, Dogen and Deep Ecology" quoted by John Seed, "Anthropocentrism Questioned," *Ecophilosophy V,* George Sessions and Bill Devall, eds., p. 14.

I imagine there would be more on my mind than the honey dribbling down my fur if I were to become truly intimate with the black bear as I caught the bus to work. I imagine I would be terrified by the sights and sounds of urban life. And the smells. There would be nothing inviting about the interior of the bus — or its dreaded occupants — unless the bear with whom I was truly intimate was a cute fellow, near domestication from human contact. But then my sympathetic participation in his form of life, however episodic, would be less of a step to deep ecology. A more or less tame bear is more or less the shadow of a bear.

From Environmental Ethics: Philosophical and Policy Perspectives, *edited by Philip P. Hanson. Burnaby: Institute for the Humanities/SPU Publications, 1986, pp. 99–113. Reprinted by permission of the Institute for the Humanities.*

Perhaps, though, I am to think like a bear, not in my urban environment, but in his wild one. The honey dribbling down my fur is the remains of a recent adventure. With him I remember the dense fragrance of wildflowers, sweet to the nose; somewhere, nearby, the source, hidden from the careless eye. But it was found, and, amid the buzzing protestations of the bees, we had drunk the heavy liquid, chewed the catacombed interior, and now, with honey dribbling down my fur, I am setting out in search of new satisfaction — a fish from the nearby stream, a drink from the spring.

Though not easy, this imaginary participation in a bear's life is intelligible. Because we share a common fund of experience with the black bear, we can project ourselves into his life, at least to a limited, perhaps evanescent, extent, whether we imagine ourselves as a bear in his, or in our, environment. If we have the time and inclination, we can — or so I believe — feel his pain, grow thirsty and hungry with him, take pleasure in the presence of companions, taste the honey. Our sympathetic participation in his life will — or can — make us more sensitive to his needs, less willing to unthinkingly frighten him or destroy the wilderness that is his home. Thinking like a bear, in a word, can raise our ursine conscious-ness. To drink honey like a bear is a step to becoming less self-centered, indeed, less species-centered, in our thinking. And it is in this respect that it is a step to deep ecology.

"Deep ecology" is the name now commonly given to a constellation of views about our proper relationship to the natural order. First introduced by the Norwegian philosopher Arne Naess[1], the name marks the distinction between

1) views that assess the morality of our interactions with nature and its inhabitants exclusively in terms of human interests (what here will be called "anthropocentric environmental ethics" or "anthropocentrism"); and

2) views that assess the morality of our interactions in ways that are not wholly anthropocentric ("nonanthropocentric environmental ethics" or "nonanthropocen-trism"). Views of the former type are more or less 'shallow'; those of the latter type, more or less 'deep.'

The "more-or-less" of this contrast in many ways is as important as the basic contrast itself. In the shallow camp, for example, we find those who think that our obligations, as they involve the nonhuman world, are to be fixed exclusively in terms of the interests of the present generation of human beings; but we also find those who would include the interests of generations not yet born.[2] And among a view of either sort there are those who compute human interests exclusively in terms of economic criteria (for example, the criterion of willingness-to-pay), while others deny that our aesthetic and political values, for example, are reducible to units in, or are adequately reflected by, even the most refined economic theory.[3] The class of anthropocentric environmental ethics, in short, is anything but a theo-retical monolith. It is home to great diversity.

The same is true of the 'deep' side of the distinction. There are some who allow the relevance of the interests of individual human beings in determining the ethics of our dealings with nature; others are openly hostile to what humans want or prefer, stridently misanthropic.[4] Some think that species *as such* have value, while others (often called "holists") think right and wrong are to be fixed by weighing the effects of what we do for *ecosystems*, possibly even the whole biosphere.[5]

We do not as yet have a full typology of the two major classes of environmental ethics — anthropocentric and nonanthropocentric. Already we know enough, however, to under-stand why the differences between theories belonging to the same class are no less important than their similarities. We also know why thinking like a bear is, or at least can be, a step to deep ecology. To the extent that our imagining-our-way-into-the-bear's-skin raises our ursine consciousness, makes us less species-centered in thinking about how we should act when it comes to our sometimes fatal interactions with the natural order, to that extent we are moved away from an exclusively anthropocentric environmental ethic. Not just human interests, but also the interests of the black bear must somehow find a place in our moral deliberation and judgement. And not only the interests of the black bear. Our imaginative penetration of the bear's way of life will not have taught us much if the lives of other, relevantly similar animals, whether domestic or wild, are ignored. If we can feel the honey dribbling down our fur, we can also taste the salt with the cow at the lick, smell the blood of the wounded caribou with the wolf, and, with the dog, hear the familiar tread of the master on the stairs.

I think any ethical theory laying claim to our rational assent must be at least this deep — must, that is, recognize the independent moral status, the direct moral relevance, of animals such as these. It is not clear how, or whether, one can 'prove' that this is so; it is not clear how, or whether, one can 'prove' any moral belief of this sort.[6] What one can do is consider the assumptions and implications of anthropocentrism and ask how rationally and morally satisfactory they are. For example, if a given theory considers *human* pain and suffering morally relevant but denies the moral relevance of the pain and suffering of the black bear, then it seems to be rationally defective. For pain is pain, and pain is in itself undesirable, to whomsoever it may occur, whether beast or human.[7] Or if a theory assumes that moral principles are the rules self-interested agents agree to have imposed on everyone's behavior, and claims that one has duties directly *only* to those individuals who are capable of entering into such agreements (or *contracts*), then one wants to protest, I think, that the theory's implications are morally skewed.[8] A young child, for example, lacks the abilities necessary for contracting; the theory implies, therefore, that we can do no wrong directly to the child, that we have no direct duties in this case, and so *do no wrong to the child* if, for example, we spend an evening's amusement torturing her. But if, as I assume, thoughtful people will agree that we *owe it to the child* not to torture her, despite her inability to contract, then it cannot be rational to deny that we owe it to a dog not to torture him, because *he* lacks the abilities required to contract. For these reasons, then, though not only for these, I do not myself believe that any version of anthropocentrism is rationally or morally satisfactory.

These sketchy objections to anthropocentric environmental ethics must face serious problems of their own. One does not offer a sound objection to a moral theory unless the objection is *of a kind* that is both relevant and fair. How moral theories *are* to be fairly and relevantly assessed, however, is a highly divisive issue, one that cannot be even *superficially* examined on this occasion.[9] As is always true in philosophy, questions outnumber answers. If those of us involved in this conference are to make any progress in our attempt to answer some of our questions about environmental ethics, we must assume that we can agree on how we should answer others. So let us assume, for the sake of argument — and this is a large assumption, certainly — that I am right: No version of anthropocentrism is adequate. Some form of nonanthropocentric environmental ethic, some specimen of a (more or less) deep ecology, must be where the truth lies. Our question then becomes, Which one? Or, alternatively, How deep?

One answer is: Deeper than you've gone so far. And one way to suggest the depth others would have us plumb is to recall the passage quoted at the outset. For Dogen, it will be recalled, not only became "truly intimate" with the black bear; he also "thought as a mountain." So, to understand our moral place in nature's scheme of things, the passage suggests, we must not only enter imaginatively into the lives of nonhuman animals; we must also enter imaginatively into the mute majesty of mountains — and, by implication, of oceans, stars, rocks, forests, or, in a word, *all* that dwell therein. To think like a black bear, on this view, is a step to deep ecology, but it is only a step, failing by itself to complete the journey of a thousand miles to the true environmental ethic.

What shall we make of the injunction to think like a mountain? Peter Singer gives part of the correct answer, I think, when he states that "such imagining yields a perfect blank."[10] Unlike the case of the black bear, with whom we share a real, even if comparatively small, family of experiences, a mountain is not a conscious individual and so has no experiences in common with us. This is why, were I to attempt to imagine being a mountain, the result would be "a perfect blank" — that is, no awareness. Thus, if, in order to demonstrate the need for an environmental ethic that is deeper than one that requires consideration of what benefits and harms nonhuman animals, we must first think the thoughts of a mountain, and given, as seems obvious, that the attempt to do this yields *no thoughts at all*, then the need for a deeper environmental ethic has not been demonstrated.

Singer and many others believe the lesson to be learned from this exercise is simple: the boundary of morality is sentience, where by "sentience" is meant the capacity to experience pleasure and pain. When that capacity is present, then there is something to take into account, something of direct moral importance; when it is absent, then there is nothing of direct moral relevance to consider. Black bears are in; Black Mountain is out. Let us call this view *sentientism*. Is this as far, as deep, as we can or should go in our search for a nonanthropocentric environmental ethic?

If the only theory of value that required our serious consideration was one that reduces value to certain mental states or feelings, or, more particularly, if the only view of this sort worthy of our assent was hedonism (pleasant mental states have positive, painful mental states have negative, value), then we wouldn't have a serious choice. Sentientism would win hands down. But philosophical plots are never this simple. There are important theories of value that differ from, and are inconsistent with, any unqualified version of a mental state theory, including hedonism. Of particular relevance in the present context is a view of the sort we find in Kant, where it is individuals, not their mental states, that are said to have a distinctive kind of value, what we'll call *inherent value*. Kant, it is true, offers his vision of inherent value in the course of developing a very famous anthropocentric theory,[11] so the relevance of his ideas to nonanthropocentric environmental ethical theories needs to be approached indirectly. But let us set out some of the important features of the idea of inherent value as this applies to individual human beings, as, on Kant's view, it does; then we will be able to understand what it would mean to apply this idea to those who are not human.[12]

A large part of the characterization of inherent value, or what Kant refers to as "end in itself", is negative. Among the defining characteristics are the following.

1. The inherent value of an individual human being is not reducible to, and is incommensurate with, the value of that individual's mental states. A normally happy person, for example, is not of greater inherent value than someone who is chronically depressed. Our inherent value does not wax or wane with changes in the hedonic tone of our lives.

2. The inherent value of an individual human being is not reducible to, nor does it vary with, the individual's usefulness relative to the interests of others. A surgeon,

for example, has no greater inherent value, even assuming her greater utility, than a dishwasher.

3. The inherent value of an individual human being is not reducible to, nor does it vary according to the possession of, the individual's skills or other virtues, including moral virtues. Wayne Gretzky is neither more nor less inherently valuable than the substitute right wing on the company hockey team, and Sister Theresa has no greater inherent value than a woman doing time for child abuse.

4. An individual human being's inherent value is not dependent on, and is not reducible to, the attitudes and beliefs others have toward, or about, him. Those who are loved and idolized are no more valuable, inherently, than those who are hated and despised, and persons who belong to 'lower' classes are not less inherently valuable than those who belong to 'higher' classes (e.g., Untouchables and Brahmins in India).

Though not complete, the foregoing remarks about inherent value at least should suggest how the idea offers something on which to pin our (presumed) egalitarian hopes. If, as the idea allows, all who have inherent value have it equally, then the noble vision of the equality among 'all men' may have found a home in theory. For differ though we do in many ways — in terms of our skills, for example, or our moral character and usefulness to others — we are all the same, all equal, when it comes to possessing this fundamental value, inherent value. Each of us is, in Kant's terminology, an end in himself or herself, and no one of us who is, is so to a lesser or greater degree than anyone else. Moreover, if this much is true, then we can glimpse both the spirit and the letter of Kant's proscription against treating one another "as means merely." This I do, for example, whenever I treat you as if your value as an individual is reducible to your usefulness to me or, less self-centeredly, to some group, even the public at large. To treat you thus is to treat you as if you were a thing, a tool, a mere resource, whose purpose for being is to advance the interests of others.

Now, types of value, like entities generally, ought not to be multiplied beyond necessity. Why, then, introduce a second, quite different, kind of value (inherent value) if one kind of value (the value of mental states, such as pleasure) is enough? The short answer some philosophers give is that value of this latter kind just isn't enough. Unless our individual, equal inherent value is postulated, these thinkers believe — (and Kant is one member of this group, I believe) — the moral theory we will be left holding will be unequal to the task of providing a fully adequate account of moral right and wrong. In particular, such a theory will allow, possibly encourage, us to treat the individual *merely as a means* to some supposedly desirable end (for example, the general welfare). To the extent that such treatment of the individual is wrong, and assuming that any and all theories that fail to recognize our equal inherent value imply that it is not, to that extent we have good reason to deny their validity as theories and postulate our equal inherent value.

That this value is postulated in our case is not unimportant. Kant, for example, makes it abundantly clear that our value as ends-in-ourselves is not observed by the senses, nor 'intuited' by the intellect in its *a priori* exercise. The status of inherent value in our moral theorizing, he implies, is analogous to the status of electrons in our theorizing in physics. In the latter case, we postulate that there are electrons in order both to unify and explain what we know, or what we think we know, about the physical order; analogously, then, we postulate inherent value in order to unify and explain what we know, or think we know, about the moral order. We know — or at least many of us think we know — that it is wrong to treat any human person merely as a means, regardless of race, sex, age, intellect, virtue, economic standing, etc.; and it is only by postulating our equal inherent value, or so some moral philosophers believe, that we are able to explain why this is wrong and bring unity to other, related beliefs about the wrongful treatment of the individual (for example, that it is wrong to execute a native youth known to be innocent of a crime in order to avert a race riot in the community).

The concept of inherent value, then, has important uses in anthropocentric ethical views. But it also holds promise for views that are nonanthropocentric. It has been argued, for example — and convincingly, to my mind[13] — that possession of inherent value rationally cannot be limited only to human persons but instead must be attributed to nonhuman animals like the black bear — to animals, that is, who, like human persons, are the experiencing subjects of a life that matters to them as individuals, independently of their usefulness to others. Indeed, the grounds for postulating inherent value in the case of these animals are the same as those we have for doing so in the case of human persons — namely, in order to unify and explain what we know, or think we know, at least on reflection, about the moral ties that bind us to these animals. Thus, though the notion of inherent value or its equivalent (e.g., Kant's concept of "end in itself") historically has been a major theme of anthropocentrism in ethics, there is no reason why it cannot play a leading role in nonanthropocentric theories.

Like sentientism, theories that are built on the notion of inherent value ("inheritism," if this verbal barbarism will be forgiven me) can move us in the direction of a deep ecology. How deep? Here we encounter an enormously important difference between the two kinds of theory. *By definition* sentientism limits those individuals of direct moral concern to those who have *mental states*, to those who are conscious. Everything else, whether individual, group, or system, fails to possess what is of direct moral significance, so that nonsentient nature in general is consigned, in John Rodman's graphic phrase, to "to the realm of thinghood."[14] Mountains, rivers, deserts, prairies, wetlands — all wilderness, wherever it may be, lacks what it takes to be of direct moral relevance. So long as we do not embrace panpsychism, everything lacking consciousness remains beyond the moral pale.

Inheritism, by contrast, is theoretically open-minded at this point. Notwithstanding the fact that theories of both human and animal rights deploy this notion, and despite the fact that both the humans and animals in question are conscious, it remains true that *there is nothing in the notion of inherent value itself that necessarily limits its possession to what is capable of having mental states, to what is conscious. Anything* that has a value that is not reducible to its utility for others, or to how others feel about it, or to its virtues, or to how happy or miserable it is, to that extent *can* have inherent value. Whether a strong case can be made for believing that it *actually* has such value will depend on our showing more than that these negative tests are passed, but there is nothing in the nature of these tests themselves that entails that something lacking consciousness cannot possess value of this kind.

Once this much is seen, we should not be surprised that a variety of theories on the nonanthropocentric side affirm that a variety of things are inherently valuable. Indeed, one measure of the "depth" of nonanthropocentric theories is how much they depart from the Kantian model, where such value is limited to individual human persons (at least amongst terrestrial beings). A version of inheritism that includes individual animals like the black bear is deeper than Kant's theory, but still like it in limiting such value to individuals. A deeper theory would be one that recognized the inherent value of *species as such*, for example, or one that attributed such value to *ecosystems*, and, in either case, denied that individuals have the sort of independent value that inherent value is. The theoretical limit, perhaps, is a theory that affirms the inherent value of the *biosphere itself* and sees the value of the individual as mythological, a product, perhaps, of a bankrupt individualistic paradigm in Western metaphysics. If we think of the best environmental ethical theory as the key with which we open the full range of our ethical questions as these relate to the natural order, the task before us is to decide what version of nonanthropocentric theory this is, how deep we go in parting company both with the Kantian and the sentientist tradition in ethics.

How shall we rationally decide this? How can we? One way is to follow Singer and refuse to go beyond sentientism. When, in the spirit of Dogen, Singer is asked to "think like a mountain," he finds, we know, "a perfect blank" and concludes that there is nothing to consider: Since there is nothing that matters experientially to the mountain, there is nothing of direct moral importance that can matter to us. Such is the provocative ambiguity of the invitation to 'think like a mountain,' however, that one might reach a very different conclusion. *Of course* one draws a "perfect blank" when one attempts to put oneself in a mountain's shoes. *Of course* there is nothing that matters experientially to the mountain, nothing that gives it pleasure or causes it pain, for example. To realize these truths is, one might say, the whole point of the exercise. Well, not quite the whole point since a truth half understood is misunderstood, and the other half of the truth, the half that Singer and other sentientists fail to understand, is that we carry prejudicial baggage with us if we assume that the moral status of the mountain depends on whether it can *experience* anything, pleasure and pain in particular. Isn't this assumption simply an unrecognized vestige of the anthropocentrism Singer and other sentientists triumphantly think they have put behind them? For consider: A mountain doesn't have to be one of us, be human, given the sentientist's views, to be of direct moral relevance; it just has to be *sufficiently like us*, be sentient, to count. Isn't that so close to anthropocentrism as to make us wonder how far we've gone beyond it? To reply that one draws 'a perfect blank' whenever one tries to 'think like a mountain' assumes that a clear and compelling answer has been given to this question. It does not give it. It is not difficult to imagine Dogen's tolerant smile over the sentientist's treatment of this question.

I think Dogen would be right to insist on the need for more from sentientists at this juncture, and right too (if Dogen took this step) to argue that the 'blank' state of mind we encounter when we 'think like a mountain' is not the answer some sentientists evidently think it is. Right on both points, however, Dogenites have their work cut out for them if, short of a preemptive appeal to an unarguable mysticism, they are to move us, rationally, to a deeper environmental ethic. The need for argument is not peculiar to sentientists, so that if, as seems to me, there is good reason to believe that standard sentientist arguments are weak,[15] it in no way follows that those who follow Dogen win by default. How, then, by way of positive argument, can an environmental ethic deeper than sentientism, deeper even than a version of inheritism that extends to the black bear and other individual animals — how can the case for a deeper theory proceed?

Among the possibilities that have been explored, three merit our attention. The first is cut from familiar theoretical cloth. Inherent value is postulated in the case of something (for example, species, ecosystems, the biosphere) to illuminate and unify our considered beliefs about right and wrong; theories that attempt to avoid postulating inherent value, we are to suppose, fail to offer the desirable illumination and unity. By way of example: Some have argued[16] that species *as such* must be viewed as having inherent value because (a) thoughtful people agree that it is wrong to render any species extinct and because (b) the only satisfactory way to account for this belief is by postulating independent, inherent value for species in and of themselves.

This approach cannot be any stronger than the success proponents have in convincing us that both (a) and (b) are true. Success is not easy to come by in either case. Although many people are enthusiastic about the immorality of destroying some species (for example, the great blue whale, the African elephant, and the Siberian tiger), moral vigor wanes in the case of obscure species of plants or species of lethal viruses. Comparatively few people are of the opinion that we would do something wrong if we killed the last four remaining specimens of *Phacelia argilaceae* (all of which are enclosed by a fence in an inhospitable region of Utah), and even fewer believe it would be wrong to destroy, *absolutely*, every trace of the smallpox virus *(Poxvirus variolae)*; most people, it seems, would happily consign that species to utter oblivion. So it is, at best, an unstable platform, this attempt to argue for the inherent value of species *as such* because otherwise we will be unable to unify and illuminate the moral beliefs thoughtful people have about the extinction of species. Whether right or wrong, most people, even thoughtful ones, seem to be selective when it comes to the species they think ought to be saved.

Or consider variations of the so-called "last man argument."[17] You are the last human being on earth. None will come after you, and you know it. You have the means to blow the earth to smithereens before you die; or you can leave it be, to work out its future destiny on its own, so to speak. What ought you to do? Some there are who think that thoughtful people will speak with one voice: Don't blow it up. There is room for robust skepticism on this point, however, and a skepticism that is dwarfed by the one that surrounds the suggestion that the *only* or *best* way to account for this presumed belief about the desirability of saving the earth is by attributing inherent value to it. Equally plausible, it seems, is the suggestion that destroying it when this is avoidable would be singularly ungrateful, like smashing the dinner plates after the host has dropped dead of a heart attack. Just as I owe the host, even when deceased, behaviour that displays my thanks for the opportunity to dine, so I owe the earth something like a debt of gratitude for my past life. Or so it may be argued. It is more in the nature of a leap of faith than a reasoned argument to conclude that we *must* attribute inherent value to the earth if we are to have any reason, as the last man, not to blow it to kingdom come.

A second possibility for deeper theories is to resurrect naturalism in ethics. Where we find certain *facts* (for example, facts of the form X-is-alive), there we also find *values* (of the form, say, X-is-inherently-good), and, once values take up independent lodging in the world, obligation cannot be far behind. From "X is inherently good" more than a few have derived "X ought not to be destroyed". But naturalism is a vision ill-suited to the dominant temper of the times, where the shadows of both Hume and Moore are still cast across the thought of most of their philosophical descendants. Even in the case of the most promising work among the new naturalists — Paul Taylor's ethic of respect for nature[18] — the centuries old doubts do not go away. With Taylor we can, I think, agree that living things are teleological centers of life, all 'striving' to realize their individual potential — their good, if you like, a good they have independently of their usefulness to us. But the good we find here seems an inadequate sort of good on which to erect human obligations. An oak tree that fully actualizes its natural propensities is, let us agree, a better oak tree than one that does not — is better *as an oak tree*, better *of its kind*. That something is good-of-its-kind, however, creates no obligation to preserve or protect it. Otherwise we would be obliged to rally round and save Henry Lee Lucas, who, as the confessed murderer of over

150 people, is the best of his kind, the most prolific murderer, we have yet encountered. If, in reply, we are told that it is exemplars of *natural* kinds that we are to preserve and protect, the case seems just as counterintuitive. A specimen of belladonna is good of its kind if it has the power to kill off the unwary hiker. Must we, therefore, act to save the most virulent strains, out of respect for their value? I do not think it unfair to give a negative answer to this question in particular and to resist in general the suggestion that living things that are good of their kind ought to be respected and preserved. This sort of goodness (good of its kind), which is, I think, naturalistic, is not equal to the theoretical task of grounding human obligations. Morally significant values, ones on which our duties are based, are not facts in the way naturalism assumes or requires. Or so it seems to me.

The third possibility worthy of consideration has mystical markings. Rooted in the awareness of the interconnectedness of all things (my body, for example, in all likelihood contains atoms from a long dead brontosaurus, from an even older dead star, from the body of Julius Caesar) — rooted in this awareness, a mystical environmental ethic transports us beyond the illusoriness of separateness, including the myth of the separateness of our own individual being, and replaces this pedestrian vision of the self and world with a more or less ineffable vision of the unity or sameness of all that is. Where, before, we took comfort in the ignorant sound of two hands clapping, we now listen to the wise timbre of the solitary hand.

It would be nice — or so many will suppose — if unbridled monism could be summarily dismissed. But it is both too old and too new for that, and the names and life-ways associated are too noble to allow a breezy rejection to count. "Merely to list the variations on [the] theme," writes Theodore Roszak,[19] himself an ardent supporter, "would fill a book. Lao Tzu teaching 'the great Tao flows everywhere' . . . the Vedic wisdom which can say of all things the eye may light upon '*tat tuam asi* — that's *you*! . . . the Avatamsaka Sutra that transfigures the universe into the Buddha's sacred body of light . . . the night Hermetic Uroborus inscribed 'One is All' . . . the *Wakan-Tanka* of the American Indians, whose presence made every object holy, as much the stone as man . . . Blake summoning us 'To see a world in a grain of sand' . . . Dylan Thomas discovering that 'The force that through the green fuse drives the flower drives my blood' . . .". A recent addition to this list, John Seed, the Australian environmentalist, expresses the unitary vision in these terms.[20]

> When humans investigate and see through their layers of anthropocentric self-cherishing, a most profound change in consciousness begins to take place. Alienation subsides. The human is no longer an outsider, apart. Your humaneness is then recognized as being merely the most recent stage of your existence, and as you stop identifying exclusively with this chapter, you start to get in touch with yourself as mammal, as vertebrate, as a species only recently emerged from the rain forest. As the fog of amnesia disperses, there is a transformation in your relationship to other species, and in your commitment to them . . . "I am protecting the rain forest" develops into "I am that part of the rain forest recently emerged into thinking." What a relief then: The thousands of years of (imagined) separation are over and we begin to recall our true nature. That is, the change is a spiritual one, thinking like a mountain, sometimes referred to as deep ecology.

As your memory improves, as the implications of the sciences of evolution and ecology are internalised and replace the outmoded anthropocentric structures in your mind, there is identification with all life. There follows the realisation that the distinction between 'life' and 'lifeless' is a human construct. Every atom in this body existed before organic life emerged 4,000 million years ago. Remember your own childhood as minerals, as lava, as rocks? Rocks contain the potentiality to weave themselves into such stuff as this. We are the rocks dancing. Why do we look down on them with such a condescending air? It is they that are the immortal part of us.

It is hard to decide what to say of the stuff of which the unitary vision is made. It is tempting to dismiss it, not because the arguments are bad (more often than not, there are no arguments, good or bad), but because most of it is unintelligible to the outsider. On the other hand, it is tempting to be tempted, to give in to the pull of union-with-nature which, I assume, all of us feel at times in our life. (I do, in any event.) If the power and existence of the feeling were the marks of its truth, we would know where to stand. But feelings, alas, do not wear their veracity on their sleeve, so that we must, if we are to show respect for the ordinary canons of reason, think about, not merely experience, the unitary vision, test its mettle by critical reflection, not accept its validity on the grounds that it is psychologically compelling or because ancient sages and noble peoples have believed it. And here's the rub. For the noble vision does not fare well when subjected to tests which, administered in other quarters to other views, are fair.

For example: There are problems enough in making sense of my *identity* over time as a human person, if we accept a worldview that has human persons in it. How much more difficult must it be, therefore, to tie my identity to the rain forest or to 4 billion year old atoms. What can be the criterion of identity, given such a view? If I am the same as a rock because we both contain some of the same atoms of a more ancient bit of matter, what is it that makes this atom, now, the same as the atom it was then? I do not think we have any easy, or possibly any intelligible, answers ready to hand. It is not clear to me whether, in the end, it is the sound rather than the substance of the ideas that attracts us — their novelty, their psychological resonance, their romance. But not their truth.

Most proponents of the unitary vision are aware of the difficulties others find; nor are they short on replies. The limits of both time and my own knowledge make it impossible for me even to attempt to do justice to this debate here. The perennial philosophy does not lend itself to simple confirmation. Or disconfirmation. (Or, possibly, to neither!) I hope it is not unfair to note, however, that the gaze of the unitary vision seems not so much to avoid, as to raise to a different environment, the problems that plague more pedestrian accounts of the world and our place in it. If, for example, naturalism is not a credible theory of value given our ordinary, non-unitary vision, it is difficult to understand how the case is any different if, in place of natural facts, we have mystical ones. It is, that is, not clear to me how we can infer that something *is good*, in any morally significant sense of "good", simply from our knowledge of realization that something *is*. If, in reply, we are told that mystical knowledge of value is immediate, not inferential, so that in knowing the true nature of what is we also know, immediately, the truth about what is good and ought to be, then we ought, I think, to test this ice *very* carefully before skating on it. To advance a position that builds in its own immunity from criticism runs the risk of permitting nonsense to pass for truth. And the greater the possible truth, the greater the actual risk.

Some will view this reluctance to take such risks as a symptom of a deeper, more sinister uneducability. George Sessions, whose influential work I commend to your attention, may have this in mind when he voices his "fear that many western philosophers and other intellectuals are so thoroughly entrenched in their Western academic training and methodologies and narrow specialities that they are going to be of very little help toward, and might actually constitute a reactionary hindrance to, the development of an ecological paradigm"[21] of the sort we find articulated, for example, by John Seed. Well, perhaps. But perhaps these "reactionaries," if not on the side of the angels, at least are on the side of what is true. The veracity of the unitary vision, the "new ecological paradigm," if accepted by enough of us, would move us to an environmental ethic deeper than the one I would personally endorse, the one that knows the feel and taste of honey dribbling down our fur. To go any deeper than this, to my mind at least, is to get in way over our heads when we can, and rationally should, avoid it.

NOTES

1. Arne Naess, "The Shallow and the Deep Long-Range Ecology Movements", *Inquiry*, Vol. 16 (1973), pp. 95–100.
2. As representative of the former view, see Gregory Kavka, "The Futurity Problem," in R.I. Skora and Brian Barry, eds. *Obligations to Future Generations* (Philadelphia: Temple University Press, 1978) 186-203. The latter position finds expression in, for example, Annette Baier, "For the Sake of Future Generations," in Tom Regan, ed., *Earthbound: New Introductory Essays in Environmental Ethics* (New York: Random House, 1983). Additional references are found in Baier's "Suggestions for Further Reading."
3. As representative of the former view, see William Baxter, *People or Penguins: The Case for Optimal Pollution*, (New York: Columbia University Press, 1974). The latter position finds expression in, for example, Mark Sagoff, "Ethics and Economics in Environmental Law," in Tom Regan, ed., *Earthbound, op. cit.* Additional references are found in Sagoff's "Suggestions for Further Reading."
4. As representative of the former view, see William Aiken, "Ethical Issues in Agriculture," in Tom Regan, ed., *Earthbound, op. cit.* The latter position finds expression in, for example, J. Baird Callicott, "Animal Liberation: A Triangular Affair," *Environmental Ethics* 2, no. 4 (Winter 1980), 311–38. Additional references are found in Sagoff's "Suggestions for Further Reading."
5. As representative of the former view, see Alastaire Gunn, "Why Preserve Rare Species?" in Tom Regan, ed., *Earthbound, op. cit.* The latter position finds expression in, for example, Callicott's "Animal Liberation: A Triangular Affair," *op. cit.* Additional references are found in Gunn's "Suggestions for Further Reading."
6. These issues are pursued more fully in my *The Case For Animal Rights* (Berkeley: University of California Press, 1983), Chapter 4.
7. The point is made forcefully by both Bentham and Mill, for example. See their respective selections in Tom Regan and Peter Singer, eds., *Animal Rights and Human Obligations* (Englewood Cliffs: Prentice-Hall, 1976).
8. The point is pursued at length in my *The Case For Animal Rights, op. cit.*, Chapter 5.
9. See *The Case for Animal Rights*, Chapter 4, for a discussion of these issues.
10. Peter Singer, *Practical Ethics* (New York: Oxford University Press, 1982), p. 92. Singer refers to a weed, not a mountain, in the passage cited. The philosophical point remains the same.
11. See, for example, Immanuel Kant, *The Fundamental Principles of the Metaphysic of Morals*, many editions.
12. A fuller discussion is offered in Chapter 7 of *The Case for Animal Rights, op. cit.*
13. *Ibid.*
14. John Rodman, "The Liberation of Nature," *Inquiry*, 20 (1977), 83–131.
15. I argue this in, for example, "The Nature and Possibility of an Environmental Ethic," *Environmental Ethics*, 3 (1981), 19–34; reprinted in Tom Regan, *All That Dwell Therein: Essays on Animal Rights and Environmental Ethics* (Berkeley: University of California Press, 1982), 184–205.
16. See, for example, the essay by Callicott cited above.
17. For a full discussion, see Robert Elliot, *An Environmental Ethic* (Ph. D. Dissertation, Queensland University).

18. Paul Taylor, "The Ethics of Respect for Nature," *Environmental Ethics*, 3, no. 3 (1981). Taylor's views are much deeper and more subtle than I am able to suggest here.
19. Theodore Roszak, *Where the Wasteland Ends* (New York: Doubleday Books, 1973), p. 398.
20. John Seed, "Anthropocentrism Questioned," in George Sessions and Bill Devall, eds., *Ecophilosophy V*, pp. 11–12.
21. George Sessions, *ibid*., p. 7. Session's address is Sierra College, Rocklin, California 95677.

QUESTIONS

1. Contrast anthropocentric environmental ethics with deep ecology.
2. Why does Regan reject a deep ecology approach to explaining and justifying animal rights? What justification does he put in its place?
3. What is the "mental states" theory of value and why do its proponents believe that it justifies the view that animals have rights? Kantians object to grounding morality on mental states or feelings. Why? Kantians have traditionally thought that only human beings have inherent moral value. Why? What are Regan's reasons for thinking that they are mistaken in this regard?
4. Why does Regan think that things lacking consciousness cannot possess inherent value?

AGAINST ANIMAL RIGHTS*

Jan Narveson

Professor Regan distinguishes three levels, as we might call them, of theoretical involvement with the environment:

1) the Anthropocentric, which views all such problems from the strictly human viewpoint;
2) the Sentientistic, which views them from the standpoint of all sentient creatures, not just humans; and
3) the Deep Ecologistic, which views them from the standpoint of the entire natural environment, including nonsentient entities.

In his paper, Regan rejects the first, accepts the second, and expresses rather more sympathy for the third than I think it deserves, although he does reject it as well. In the present comments, I shall be concerned with the way in which he argues for the position he holds, and supply some arguments for staying at the first level — not quite all of that either, in fact! I shall also supplement his arguments against the third level, and make a specific criticism, one that will be seen to be crucial for purposes of environmental ethics, of *his* level-two position. (Not all level-two positions would be susceptible of this criticism, but those that did not would, I think, succumb to our combined criticisms of the third-level position.)

Let us begin by contemplating, for a moment, the subject of 'inherent value' as described by Regan. Following Kant, he suggests that this "type" of value is not reducible to "the

From Environmental Ethics: Philosophical and Policy Perspectives, *edited by Philip P. Hanson. Burnaby: Institute for the Humanities/SPU Publications, 1986, pp. 119–123. Reprinted by permission of the Institute for the Humanities.*

value of that individual's mental states", nor with his usefulness to others or their attitudes to or beliefs about him, nor with any of his skills or "other virtues, including moral virtues"; and he suggests that "there is nothing in the notion of inherent value itself that necessarily limits its possession to what is capable of having mental states . . ." Is this right? Well, here we must make a distinction, at least. No doubt this may seem an academic point, but as a matter of fact *Kant's* notion of 'inherent value' was such that it certainly would *not* be possible for anything but minded entities to have it. In fact, Kant didn't think animals had it either, so far as that goes. The reason is that, on this concept of inherent value, to 'have' inherent value is to be a subject with values in a strong sense of the term "values" such that one must have a rational will to have them. People have 'inherent' dignity and moral worth by virtue of being moral beings, centres of moral decision-making. It is easy enough to see why the term "inherent value" is appropriate here: for beings of this kind are 'centres' of value — one is tempted to say 'originators' of value; and so nobody *else* needs to be on the scene in order for them to be subjects of value, since, so to speak, they already are. Nothing of this sort makes any sense regarding mountains, however.

But there is another sense of "inherent value" in which non-minded entities may be said to have it (sometimes). Consider, as perhaps the outstanding category of cases in question, the notion of aesthetic value. When we say that a certain musical performance is a fine one, or a certain painting a great one, we are making a judgement that does not call for completion along the lines of specifying the purpose to which the performance or painting in question contributes. It is not the point of a painting to be a means to some further, distinct state of affairs in the world. Mechanical devices, say, are good (or bad) 'for' something, but not works of art. Nevertheless, it would be absurd to say of a painting that its value is necessarily equal in all things that have any of it at all. Nor, in a sense, is its value "not dependent on . . . the attitudes and beliefs others have toward, or about" it. Of course it is a debatable issue whether beauty is 'in the eye of the beholder', but it would be absurd to claim that the eye of the beholder had absolutely nothing to do with it. We build museums and symphony halls in order that *we* may enjoy the experiences which great works of art afford us. We do *not* build them in order that the works of art *themselves* may get their just rewards for being great! I am sure that it is a matter of the most utter indifference to a painting where or how it happens to be lodged, or even whether it 'lives' or 'dies'! In the case of entities with Kantian-type 'inherent' value, on the other hand, it at least makes sense to suppose that they can be owed duties in their own right, and perhaps even that their existence constrains us independently of our own end, which is what Kant thought.

Having made this distinction, we can see that 'Deep Ecology' derives no benefit from the notion of inherent value. On the one hand, it makes no sense to attribute Kantian-type inherent value to the environment, so that road, together with Kantian conclusions about treating it as an end-in-itself, is out; and if our valuing of the environment is aesthetic, then it is at least not true that we ought to regard mountains and whatnot as having *rights*. Rather, our question would then be whether the beauty of various things in the environment outweighs the value of various alterations that would diminish that beauty. And that seems to me exactly the right sort of question to ask, as a matter of fact. But beauty is one of *our* interests, and that is how it enters the picture — i.e., *not* as 'inherent' in Regan's sense.

As an additional point, I would like to urge that the whole idea of Deep Ecology is hopeless for a different reason. The trouble with Nature is that everything is a part of it, including ourselves. *No matter what we do to it*, this will still be true. Should we blow up as much of our environment as we can with hydrogen bombs, the smithereens into which we blow it will be just as 'natural', just as much 'whole system', as it is now or ever was. It is, then, useless to try to do anything to 'preserve' Nature: anything you can conceivably do to it will leave it just as much Nature as ever. When we are concerned about our environment, then, what makes this concern coherent is precisely that it is *our* environment, and that so viewed, we are better off if it is in some conditions rather than others: it looks nicer, smells better, leaves us in a better state of health, affords us with more of the things we want. To imagine that Nature in its own right has interests conflicting with ours, and interests which take precedence over or are even equal to ours, is simply to go off a conceptual deep end. 'Deep' Ecology is too deep — indeed, a bottomless pit.

Next, we need to observe something about the character of Regan's concern with animals. On his view, animals are people, as it were: that is, we have duties to them as individuals, duties not to kill or harm them, to sustain them in good health, and so on. Even if we have any such duties at all, in general — which I doubt — I don't accept Regan's reasons for thinking that we have them. But rather than arguing about that here, I just wish to point out that this is not the kind of moral relation to animals that will capture one of the concerns many or most people do have regarding the animal part of our environment. That concern is for the preservation of *species*, not individuals. It is environmental and ecological, rather than personal. A given species exists and is preserved if it has members — *any* members. And it flourishes at some optimal size, which can be either fallen short of *or* exceeded. In the latter case, it might be environmentally sound to declare open season for awhile and thin down the population. In the former, it might be well to capture a few sound specimens and have them breed in safe captivity for awhile. But this is not the sort of treatment that John Q. Bear should get if he literally has *rights*. We can't shoot a few million Chinese or Indians just because there are too many of them. And on the other hand, we do not owe it to anybody that we, for instance, capture a few females and shack him and them up together in a motel for a few years until they restore the right population density to their particular biological variety of *Homo sapiens*.

For similar reasons, the whole idea of doing environmental ethics by positing rights on the part of the things we are concerned to protect is completely misguided. Forests, mountains, species — these simply aren't the sort of things that can sensibly be thought to have rights. And while particular animals can, perhaps, be alleged without actual self-contradiction to have rights, I am very far from persuaded that they do, and in any case it is quite clear that the preservation or protection of individual animals as such simply isn't where the action is when it comes to environmental ethics.

Let us return to the Reganian position, that animals have rights in their own right. His arguments for this, mainly, are two: first, that we are required to acknowledge such rights when we consider such cases as those of the senile, the feeble-minded, or infant humans. And second, that we can sympathize with sentient beings, because we are sentient ourselves, and if our own claims to good treatment are based on our own sentience, then we must extend those to all sentient creatures, in consistency. I reject both of these arguments. The fact that one can sympathize with another entity, come to realize that it has a point of view, does not rationally commit one to giving it rights, including those one wants in those same respects on one's own behalf. Something more is needed: to wit, the capacity to act in such a way as to make it in our interest to extend those rights. We do sympathize strongly with marginal humans, and more especially do those who are near and dear to them. This, I think, is sufficient basis to extend the rights it clearly is in our interest to extend to all normal humans to marginal cases as well; but that basis is clearly lacking for animals.[1] But

I cannot here develop this more robust theory of rights.[2] I just don't think that rights are as easily come by as Regan thinks!

But rights certainly do come into these questions: not rights of animals or plants or mountains, but rights of plain old people such as ourselves. Where they come into it — and in a very big way — is in the possibility that certain humans have the right to do things to the environment that certain *other* humans don't like. In these possibilities lie, I think, all of the problems of environmental ethics currently exercising responsible people. That's quite enough, in my judgment, without going further and taking on the problems of animals for their own sakes, or of trees or canyons for theirs.

One can view certain questions about the treatment of animals in this light. Suppose you wish to mistreat an animal, in my view of how animals should be treated: e.g., to whip it, or to stick electrodes into it, or to eat it. If it is *my* animal, there is no conceptual problem: I then have the right to insist that you refrain from doing those things to it. But what if it is yours? Then, it would seem, I do not. I have only the right to request that you refrain, and to attempt to persuade you to my point of view. That is not enough to satisfy enthusiasts for animal rights, however. They want recognition of a right on the part of the animal itself. But there is another possibility to consider. What if they have the right to an environment in which animals do not suffer? Perhaps that would be like the right to clean air. Armed with such a right, if we have it, we can insist that others clean up their air-polluting acts on our accounts. I am inclined to think that we do have such a right, but in this commentary cannot develop the case for it.

But would a right to an environment free of suffering animals be enough like a right to clean air so that I could act similarly against a torturer of animals? This is problematic. We need to ask what the right to clean air would be based on, if we have one. Is it the right to health, so that others may not do what is injurious to my health, such as to insert smoke into my lungs? I don't think so. It doesn't negatively affect my health if you put your hand gently but firmly against my chest, thus preventing my further progress in that direction. But unless it is a direction I have no right to go in, you don't have the right to do that. I can insist that you get your hands off me just because the body you are putting them on is mine. However, with others' pains, things are different. It may well not be bad for my *health* at all if my environment is full of suffering animals (or people, for that matter). And if it isn't then the snag is that I do not obviously *own* the parts of my environment that are negatively affected, in my view, when the animals in it suffer. While I also do not own those parts of the environment that are immediately affected by pollution, I do own the body which is eventually visited with those bad effects. What sort of claim is available here? So long as tastes differ at all, we logically *cannot all* have the right to any sort of environment we like: what is an improvement to you is then a deterioration to me.

We do in fact agree to a very substantial extent on some aspects of these problems. Being sympathetic creatures, we don't like the pains of others, even when those others are animals. And most of us would classify grime-covered slums as eyesores, and the Place Des Arts as attractive. Yet we don't have the right to require a slum-dweller to clean up his act at the slum-dweller's expense; nor, I think, have we the right to prevent sealers from clubbing small seals for the sake of their valuable hides, even though nearly all of us, including probably the sealer, would rather that those animals not undergo such a fate. Even substantial identity of tastes doesn't solve all problems here; and in fact there is substantial diversity in the case of many of the issues of environmental ethics. Since we have a truly common interest in health, further information linking these issues to issues of human health is likely to be of enormous assistance in solving them, but I do not suppose that all of them will succumb to that treatment.

NOTES

* This commentary is not a transcript of my adlibbed remarks on the occasion of my response to Tom Regan at the environmental ethics workshop. I am dealing more fully with some aspects of his paper, and develop much less than I did on that occasion the alternative position on these matters that I am partial to.
1. See my "Animals Rights Revisited", in Harlan Miller and William Williams, eds., *Ethics and Animals* (Clifton, New Jersey: Humana Press, 1983).
2. The fundamentals of my current views are to be found in "Human Rights: Which, if Any, There Are", in *NOMOS XXIII: Human Rights* (New York University Press, 1981); edited by J. Roland Pennock & John W. Chapman.

QUESTIONS

1. Narveson gives an alternate reading of Kant from that of Regan. What are the main points of difference? Are these two readings as important to the issue of animal rights as Narveson makes out? Why or why not?
2. Narveson argues that things like mountains can have inherent value. Why does he think this view is consistent with rejecting deep ecology?
3. Narveson seems to suggest that a central concern of environmental ethics, namely the preservation of species, is not addressed by a focus on animal rights. Is he right about this?
4. Do all of the problems of environmental ethics currently exercising responsible people flow from the possibility that certain human beings have the right to do things to the environment that certain other human beings don't like, as Narveson claims?

ETHICS OF WASTES: THE CASE OF THE NUCLEAR FUEL CYCLE

Andrew Brook

In Canada and the United States, we consume a huge amount of energy and other goods relative to other parts of the world and are totally dependent on large industries. Among the problems created by this way of life, the vast quantity of often dangerous wastes we produce is among the more difficult. A particularly interesting case study for the ethics of wastes and their management is the nuclear power industry. It presents some major waste management problems, problems that will require enormous amounts of money and labour to solve.

What to do about nuclear wastes is a policy question; policy questions always have moral questions at their heart. Those posed by nuclear energy tax the full resources of

Reprinted by permission of Andrew Brook.

modern moral philosophy. In a classic study of two decades ago, Arthur Porter put it this way:

> . . . an assessment of the value of nuclear power . . . ultimately requires an examination of the acceptability to society of the risk and benefits of the technology, relative to other options. This process is, by definition, extremely difficult since value judgments of a particularly complex kind, transcending nuclear power per se, are clearly involved. Indeed, whose values are to be judged worthy and how this assessment is to be accomplished with justice are pertinent questions.[1]

All this is just as true today as it was when Porter wrote it. Of the wide range of cost/risk/benefit issues to which Porter alludes, we will concentrate on those resulting from the wastes created by nuclear power. The major wastes in the nuclear industry are the wastes from the mining and milling process used to create uranium fuel and the wastes left behind when this fuel is used to generate electricity in a reactor. We will focus on what are called high level wastes, the wastes created by burning fuel in a reactor. Our aim is to determine the values that should govern policy questions about these wastes and how to apply these values in a variety of contexts. The most central ethical question concerns our obligations to future generations.

Ethical decisions always underlie policy decisions. The former are often made in an analytic vacuum that we would not begin to accept for making design decisions or investment decisions. Similarly, cost/benefit assessments are often carried out with very narrow notions of what can properly be classed as costs or benefits. Here is how an ideal method for settling ethical issues in policy contexts might work. First we would collect the relevant facts: what are the problems, what are the possible solutions? We would next identify basic ethical principles such as fairness in the distribution of costs, risks and benefits over populations and times and liberty for the people concerned, and so on. Then we would lay out criteria for setting costs against costs, benefits against benefits, etc., both considered broadly enough to include full social costs and benefits, direct and indirect. Finally, we would apply the principles and criteria to the facts. We will carry this method out as fully as a short paper allows. We will sketch the relevant facts about the nuclear fuel cycle, identify relevant values, and lay out some of the relevant costs and benefits.

High-Level Reactor Wastes

The best known wastes in the nuclear industry are the high level wastes produced by nuclear reactors. In Canada, nuclear reactors are concentrated in Ontario, where they generate about 50% of the province's electricity. Quebec and New Brunswick also have reactors. Nuclear reactors generate electricity by setting up a controlled chain reaction in the radioactive component of uranium fuel, uranium 235. This fuel is manufactured into pellets held in tubes tied together into circular bundles and these bundles are inserted into long tubes inside the reactor. The chain reaction in this fuel generates an enormous amount of heat. This heat is used to superheat steam, which then powers turbines connected to electrical generators. In the course of the uranium being 'burned', the industry term for the chain reaction, a number of highly radioactive materials come into existence inside the fuel bundles — radioactive strontium, cesium, americium, and so on — and the metal holding the pellets also becomes radioactive.

One important new mineral is plutonium, which is dangerous radiologically and also chemically — the radiation from a minute amount on the inside of the lungs can cause lung cancer. Plutonium is more toxic chemically than almost any other material. Plutonium also poses a security risk; it can be refined into bomb grade material. Of the two atomic bombs dropped on Japan by the United States, one used refined plutonium, the other heavily enriched uranium 235.[2]

The radioactivity in spent fuel increases many orders of magnitude when burned.[3] Natural processes of radioactive decay restore the spent fuel to something like the radioactivity it once had but that takes 300 to 800 years (after about 500 years, the radioactivity of the fuel has decreased 200,000 times[4]). Different radioactive materials decay at rates that vary by orders of magnitude; plutonium, for example, has a halflife of about 24,000 years, which make wastes in which it occurs particularly long lived.[5]

Compared to the amounts of wastes produced by other industrial processes, the volume of high level wastes produced by a reactor is quite small, however. A pellet of fuel roughly the size of a large marble produces enough electricity to power an average house for a year. By comparison, it would take many *tons* of coal producing many *tons* of CO_2 and a large amount of fly ash to produce the same amount of electricity. By comparison, all the high level wastes ever produced in Canada weigh less than 25,000 tons. In fact, all the high level waste produced by Canadian reactors in a history that is now about forty five years long is still stored onsite, first in large pools of water for six years or so, then in thick concrete containers as the fuel becomes less active. This form of storage is adequate to ensure that there is almost no release of radioactivity to the atmosphere so long as nothing goes wrong. The proviso, 'so long as nothing goes wrong', is important, however; these methods need constant monitoring and maintenance. They are thus the very opposite of being a passive, permanent solution requiring no further human intervention.

Mine/Mill Wastes

To make the fuel burned in reactors, uranium ore is mined and milled to extract the uranium and then fabricated into fuel. This process produces large quantities of low level wastes. The amounts of these wastes are huge — well over 150 million tonnes of these wastes now exist in Canada alone — and they may lead to more exposure to radiation than any other part of the fuel cycle.[6] Because the volumes are so huge, and also because much of the waste is fluid, these 'low level' wastes may well be a more intractable problem than high level wastes. Currently, no good scheme for managing them has ever been devised. Thus they eminently deserve to be studied from the ethical point of view. In this paper, however, we will focus on high level wastes. One reason is that a promising scheme has been devised for dealing with these wastes and it is in need of careful ethical assessment.[7]

Long-Term Management of High-Level Wastes

High level wastes are contained in highly corrosion-resistance structures. Thus, they will not disperse for a long period of time, though still well before the radioactive materials in them decay to insignificant levels. Release via a massive uncontained explosion and fire on the model of the Chernobyl disaster is unlikely in Canada or the United States. What exploded in Chernobyl was active fuel in which a chain reaction was taking place within a reactor. All reactors outside the former Soviet countries have massive reinforced concrete containment shells. When the fuel is spent and removed from the reactor, there is no longer a chain reaction. The dangers become heat and extremely high levels of radioactivity. And the major risk is over the long term. Over time, the risk that the active monitoring of water tanks and concrete containers needed to ensure safety will decrease or even cease altogether obviously increases. If the monitoring and necessary repairs, etc., ceased, living beings could spend dangerous amounts of time around the concrete containers. Further, in the medium term any spent fuel not in containers, and in the long term these containers themselves, would deteriorate, allowing the spent fuel to dissipate.

A method for permanent disposal of spent fuel has been undergoing research and development for a couple of decades now. The method involves sinking mine shafts into stable, waterproof structures of plutonic rock in the Canadian Shield.[8] The spent fuel, which is itself highly resistant to corrosion, would be put into lead containers. These containers would be placed in cavities lined with clay at the bottom of the shaft (clay lined to prevent any possible moisture penetration.) The shafts would then be backfilled with clay or concrete, effectively isolating the wastes from the environment and making any contact between them and living beings highly unlikely. The aim is to achieve a level of isolation such that there would not be more than one chance in a million per year that a maximally exposed creature would develop a fatal cancer or serious genetic defect, and that this isolation be assured for at least 10,000 years without active intervention. We receive much more radiation than this every year from the radium found in all rock, concrete and soil, from X-rays, from air travel, and so on.

Everything to do with nuclear power is contentious, but nuclear wastes have one feature that distinguishes them from other nuclear issues: they are already with us. Thus there is no longer any question about whether to bring them into existence. This means that many of the ethical issues that are central to decisions about nuclear power, issues arising from such questions as whether to build more reactors or phase out the ones we already have, do not arise. The principal ethical issue that remains is this: are we obliged to assume the costs of disposing of these wastes, and as permanently as possible, or is it permissible for us to pass at least some of the costs of dealing with them on to future generations? This issues breaks into two questions:

1. What are our obligations? and,
2. To what beings: just human beings, or all creatures, ecosystems, and the biosphere as a whole?

Values for the Facts

Our task now is to identify values appropriate to the facts about wastes from the nuclear fuel cycle. Nuclear wastes have two useful features as a test case for ethical issues of waste management:

1. Nobody currently alive and nobody for a number of generations is going to benefit much from finding a more permanent solution to them; the current solution will protect us and a number of generations to come quite adequately. (Spent fuel does have one possible near benefit, but exploiting it is actually made more difficult by long term disposal, a point to which we will return.) Thus managing them does not give rise to difficult questions about distribution of benefits: who should get, or be allowed to use, how much of what, when and

how?, and similar questions of distributive justice. Wastes raise primarily cost questions: given that they have to be managed for many thousands of years, who is obliged to assume the costs of doing so? This simplifies the ethical situation.

2. Because nobody alive now or for some time is going to benefit much from finding a more permanent solution than the one already in place, finding a more permanent solution will not be motivated by self-interest. Thus, the arguments in its favour have to be moral ones alone.

What are our obligations with respect to nuclear wastes? A number of issues need to be distinguished:

1. *Principles.* What are the general principles that should guide our ethical thinking about the disposal of nuclear wastes?

2. *Scope.* Are our obligations restricted to humans or do they extend to other creatures? To the environment? To the biosphere as a whole? To future generations as well as to the current one? Only to people, animals and ecologies close to us or over the whole surface of the planet?

   1. and 2. cover the two issues identified at the end of the last subsection. Other partly moral, partly conceptual issues are also highly relevant:

3. *Discounting.* Are creatures of other kinds or far distant future generations of our own kind worth less morally than people existing now?

4. *Cost/risk/benefit.* Given that better solutions to a waste management problem tend to cost more money, what, all aspects of risk, cost and benefit considered, is the optimal expenditure on this problem versus other social problems and demands?

5. *Moral assessment and risk assessment.* How should risk assessments shape our moral assessment?

6. *Uncertainty.* Given that we can never be certain about any outcome in a complex industrial system and given that the further we project into the future, the more uncertain we become, how can we reach ethical conclusions in the face of such uncertainty?

7. *Reducing risk vs. retaining benefits.* What is the appropriate balance between reducing the risks contained in high level wastes and leaving open the possibility of exploiting the very considerable economic potential that the fuel rods still contain?

8. *Procedural issues.* What procedures would allow us to arrive at fair and democratic decisions, and who should have what roles in them?

1. Principles What principles should govern our ethical thinking about deep disposal?[9] One is a principle of distributional equity: costs, risks and benefits must be distributed equitably, at a time and across time. A second is that liberty is a particularly central good (benefit), at least for members of the human species, and any reduction of liberty requires particularly powerful justification. We need to narrow both notions down.

The part of the principle of distributional equity of relevance here is this:

A. *Fairness.* Those who benefit should bear the costs.

It follows from this principle that, since the people now alive have reaped most of the benefits of the activities that have created the high level wastes we are considering, we have an obligation to bear the costs of disposing of them, and disposing of them permanently. I do not think that there is any way around this.

That may appear to settle the matter and so far as identifying our obligations on *this* issue, it does. But obligations can be overridden if there are conflicting obligations that are even stronger. We will take up this issue in 4. below. Furthermore, even if A. settles our intergenerational obligations, there is also a tricky interregional issue. Most of the beneficiaries of nuclear power live in or near large centres; people in the outlying regions have reaped few benefits. Yet any long term solution to the wastes will inevitably be constructed in some outlying region; that's where the appropriate rock structures are found and there is room to build a large mine complex.

To see our way to the most ethical solution here, I think the word 'inevitably' is important: if any long term disposal facility must be built in the hinterland, then there are only two choices: construction in the hinterland or forego a long term solution and continue the short term procedures now in place. If so, then disposal in the hinterland is the fair*est* long term solution possible, even if it is not entirely fair. If we adopted it, we would still be obliged, of course, to ensure that the costs to present and future beings in the area selected are kept as low as feasible, that benefits be maximized, and that any differential in costs is accompanied by fair compensation. The secure, well paid jobs that go with a waste disposal facility would be one compensatory benefit.

The aspect of the ethics of liberty of relevance to nuclear wastes is this:

> B. *Liberty.* Our actions must infringe on the lives of other beings to the smallest extent reasonably possible.

This principle applies particularly obviously to human beings but it may well apply to many other beings, too, as we will see below. Here are some of the ways in which the management, or perhaps more accurately *mis*management, of high level wastes could restrict liberty: causing pain; damaging bodies; harming abilities; imposing significant protection costs; spoiling ecosystems; reducing opportunities; and so on. Some of the examples I just gave concerned freedom *from* (freedom from unnecessary pain, unnecessary costs, etc.) and some concerned freedom *to* (not harming the field of opportunities available). With this distinction, we can spell out the demand of liberty this way:

> B'. We must choose the solution to the disposal of high level wastes that will reduce future beings' freedom from costs and harms and limit their freedom to pursue their life as they would live it to the minimum extent reasonably possible.

Note that even this longer version of the principle of liberty is weaker than some would argue it should be. It says nothing about *enhancing* freedom from or freedom to.

Of course, protecting the liberty of future beings requires that we restrict our own liberty in certain ways. In particular, the liberty to spend the resources needed to dispose of nuclear wastes permanently on things of immediate benefit to us must go. Thus, the demands of fairness and the liberty of future beings are in conflict with enhancing our own liberty. To resolve this conflict, we have to look deeper.

Here is a principle that can start to resolve the conflict:

> C. *Equal worth.* Prior to considerations of morally relevant distinguishing qualities, each person has the same value as any other.

The argument for it is a general principle of rationality: unless we treat similar things as similar, it would be impossible to make general, comparative judgments about them at all.

If so, it would be irrational to assign two relevantly similar people different moral value. This argument grounds the ethical principle of equal *prima facie* worth on a general consideration about what is required for rationality as a whole.

To be sure, discriminatory assignments of value can be justified — so long as there is a morally relevant difference. And we could be quite generous about what such differences might be.[10] Other kinds of partiality might also be allowable. For example, only a few people (including myself) are within my control; partiality toward these people will increase the chances of my doing what I can to procure and distribute things of value in this world. Similarly, special bonds of affection may justify special concern, if the loss of those bonds would seriously undermine my life having any point or purpose in my eyes, seriously undercut my self-confidence, and so on. All these would reduce my chances of doing something of value. (Williams has explored arguments for partiality to some people and also for partiality to humans over other beings, an issue directly related to Scope below.[11])

Some differences are not morally relevant, however. Self-interest, maximizing (or a desire to maximize) one's own benefits and minimizing one's costs simply because the benefits and costs would accrue to me, is not, for example. Here there is no relevant difference between me and anyone else; as the nineteenth century philosopher Henry Sidgwick put it, mere numerical difference makes no moral difference. Similarly, the collective self-interest of one's own generation is not by itself a morally relevant difference between one's own generation and future generations. In general, no one person (even if he is me) and no one generation (even if it is mine) have features that justify giving that person or generation preferential treatment in the distribution of costs and benefits.

Since we are the ones enjoying the benefits of nuclear energy, any passing on of the costs of the activities involved would constitute just such a discriminatory assignment of costs and benefits. From this we can conclude that we have a moral obligation to find a permanent, passive solution to the problem of nuclear wastes. If we were passing on additional benefits as large as the benefits we are enjoying and if we were also assuming half the costs of these benefits, the conclusion would not hold. But it seems unlikely that we are doing so. Of course, the principles of fairness is just an instantiation of the equal worth principle. But it is possible to argue for the latter in ways not open to the former, not directly.

It seems to me that the conclusion of the discussion above is clear: we have an ethical obligation to find a permanent, passive solution to the problem of radioactive waste management. A true ethical sceptic or someone with a strong interest in ignoring the problem of nuclear wastes might still try to wiggle out, but to refuse to accept such arguments as ethically binding would be pretty much to get out of the business of justifying courses of action, finding good and sufficient reasons for what we do, altogether. Moreover, we do care about these principles — they are deeply embedded in our view of how interpersonal relations ought to be governed, and therefore in our notions of self-respect and sense of decency.

Return now to the suggestion that liberty is a distinctively human good and therefore that the analysis above applies only to human beings. We take up the general issue of obligations to the nonhuman in the next section but on this specific issue, I think we can say the following: 1. Animals do care about their own liberty; think of how animals suffer when caged. 2. Disease, radioactive poisoning, etc., limit the liberty of animals just as much as of humans.

2. Scope Questions of scope come in a number of dimensions. To how many kinds of creatures do our obligations extend, just to humans or also to other creatures, the various ecologies, and the biosphere as a whole? Over what space — to people, animals and ecologies close to us or across the whole planet? And over what span of time — just to us or to future generations, too? We are most apt to reach ethical judgments that can be defended if we take the widest possible scope: All beings, not just humans; everywhere on the planet, not just in our own communities; and at all times, not just now and in the immediate future. If something has the capacity to be harmed, it has interests, and if it has interests, the principle of equal worth can be applied, *mutatis mutandis*, to argue that it would be unfair to load a discriminatory mix of costs and benefits on it. Quantifying 'discriminatory' over members of various species, the species themselves, their ecosystems, etc., will be a difficult task but it will be an unavoidable one if we wish our waste management decisions to be ethical over the scope of the whole biosphere.[12]

3. Discounting Even if we do consider everything everywhere and at all times, does it all have to be given *equal* consideration? This is the difficult issue of discounting. In economics, discounting is clearly justified. An economic benefit in the distant future is worth less to me now than one immediately available to me. Is there anything comparable in ethics? Is it ever ethical to value far distant beings, beings far in the future, beings very different from us (earth worms, say, or bacteria) less than we value ourselves and the human beings immediately around us?

This issue tends to break down into two subissues. One concerns *human* beings far distant from us in space or time, the other concerns *all other* beings. In connection with the first, I cannot see any ethical justification for valuing one human being less than another, no matter where or when that human being may live. By contrast, we might be able to make a case for valuing some forms of life less than others: even if we want to keep plentiful *examples* of each kind of life, even down to bacteria, etc., it is far less clear that each *individual* in many lifeforms deserves the same concern as we extend to human individuals.

All this raises a number of difficulties for the principles enunciated earlier. For beings where preservation of genetic material may be more important than protection of the well-being or even the existence of individuals, liberty is at most a far smaller concern. Likewise, with such beings we switch from the worth of individuals to the worth of types, something anathema to the ethics of human beings. And so on. When one combines these complications with the uncertainties that still infect the notion of discounting for the future in general, I think we rapidly find ourselves completely at sea. For these reasons, I will restrict my discussion of discounting to human beings.

For distant human beings, especially human beings distant in time, we might try to use the economist's notion of discounting to justify extending less concern to them than we extend to human beings living now. It would argue that future generations, like other things in the future, are worth less than the equivalent things right now. This is the principle that a bird in the hand is worth two in the bush. In financial contexts it can be argued for on a number of bases: uncertainties or probabilities, rates of return on present wealth, and so on. The economist's notion probably has no relevance to moral questions. One discounts the economic value of the future on the basis of its value for us (now); one considers the moral worth of future generations on the basis of their value, period — their value for anyone, including themselves.

There are, however, other discounting principles. Some people might argue that far distant people, just by being so far distant, are worth less per head than people currently alive. While this does not seem a morally relevant difference, being mere location in time, two other discounting principles are perhaps more plausible.

1. *Nature of future persons.* The farther we move into the future, the greater the probability that persons alive then will be different from us in one or another of a number of relevant ways: they may be immune to radiological damage and chemical poisoning; though still at risk, such risks may no longer affect their interests; their forms of social life may be so different from ours that their moral worth is reduced; they may be such moral monsters that they would not merit our moral concern. These all seem to be very remote possibilities.

2. *Existence of future persons.* The farther we move into the future, the greater the probability that no persons will exist at all. This claim is sound but ignores the fact (as does the first) that significant damage from nuclear wastes could occur within a few hundred years if nothing more is done, a period short enough to reduce the probability considerably.

To see the real moral force of these discounting principles, it is essential to distinguish between *epistemic possibility* ('It may, I just don't know') and *real probability* ('It may; reliable calculation reveals a chance of . . ., which is more than insignificant'). If we just don't know, we can ensure that we have met our obligations (though we don't, of course, know that we have them either) only by acting as though there will, in the future, be people, and people relevantly like us. And even if we do know that there is some real probability that there won't be, this probability must, I think, be fairly high before our obligation to act as though there will be is significantly reduced — though this point is controversial. So long as there is any significant probability that there will be relevantly similar people, there is a probability that we have obligations. Thus any discounting principle of which I am aware seems to have only a negligible effect on our obligations to future generations.

In addition to the question of temporal scope and discounting, there is an important ethical issue that arises with spatial scope and consideration of beings elsewhere on the planet. Canada is not the only country with nuclear waste disposal problems. Indeed, compared to the problems faced by the United States, Russia or any other bomb producing country, our problems are pretty small. Both the United States and Russia have literally hundreds of times as much high level waste in storage as we do. If we can find a passive, permanent solution to our own high level wastes, do we have an obligation to use it to help other countries deal with theirs?

The issues here are practical and political as well as ethical. On the practical side, there is the issue of transportation and the dangers inherent in moving highly toxic wastes such long distances. On the political side, there is the fact that both the United States and Russia have been massively less responsible in their management of high level wastes than Canadians have been, Russia in particular. Nevertheless, a question does arise about whether we have obligations to peoples in other parts of the world as they face their nuclear waste problems.

4. Cost/Risk/Benefit   Earlier we looked at the implications of principles of fairness and protection of liberty for the management of nuclear wastes. Another principle is also important, indeed can overrule the demands of fairness and liberty in some contexts. It is the broadly utilitarian principle that we should strive to get the maximum benefit, that is to say, to do the greatest good, for each expenditure of resources and incurring of risk. The argument for this principle is very simple: anything else wastes resources. The mechanism for applying it is cost/risk/benefit analysis.

Cost/risk/benefit analysis is the activity of assessing the benefits of a proposal, the costs of achieving those benefits, and the risks involved. More precisely, it consists of analyzing financial risks — financial costs times probability of incurring them; nonfinancial risks — harms times probably of incurring them and costs of rectifying them —; and both the probability and the size of the benefits that would accrue.

Sometimes benefits are so great or costs relative to a benefit so high that neither an analysis nor additional moral judgment is needed to decide what should be done. For example, no competent cost/risk/benefit analysis of hospitals is going to question whether we should keep them — though there can certainly be disagreement about how many we need, what kind, and where, as we are seeing! We view health as a benefit that can be traded off against other things only down to a certain level (though that level may be falling right now). At the other extreme, no competent public authority would allocate $1m to fix a few potholes. But benefits and/or costs are often not so clear.

In particular, better management of wastes is a benefit that we have historically viewed as readily tradeable for other benefits, lower debt loads for example. For this reason, we tend to make decisions about waste management on a comparative basis: for a given expenditure, what is the greatest benefit we can attain, and at what overall cost of resources and harms? I think that this is the right approach and that we should do it on the widest possible basis. In considering radiological wastes, we should take into account, for example, the fact that nonradiological toxins have no halflife. In considering an expenditure of resources to dispose of radioactive wastes, we should consider what else we could accomplish for the same money. And not just for us; also for people elsewhere and well into the future, and for beings of other kinds. (We are part of the 5% of the population of the world that uses 40% of the world's resources; we can afford to be generous.)

Here is one central issue: for a given cost, at a given probability or risk level, what is the greatest obtainable benefit? To meet our obligations to future generations with respect to the hazards in radioactive wastes would cost a lot. Would the benefit conferred on living things as a whole from expending resources on these wastes be as great as the benefits we could confer by expending the resources in some other way?

Some answers to this question might well cancel obligations arising from application of the principles of fairness and liberty. Suppose that the answer to the above question is no, that achieving a permanent solution to nuclear wastes would not be a benefit as great as we could achieve by expending the same resources in other ways. Suppose further that the greater benefit can be secured with as much fairness and protection of liberty across species, space, and time as would be true of a permanent disposition of nuclear wastes. In this situation, our obligations with respect to nuclear wastes would either be cancelled or greatly reduced. Resources can be expended only once, and we can obtain a greater benefit with as much fairness, etc., by expending them another way. Therefore, we are obliged to expend them the other way. If we have spent them some other way, we cannot expend them on nuclear wastes. But ought implies can. Therefore, our obligation to expend the resources on nuclear wastes is either cancelled or at least greatly reduced.

Whether the answer is no is a complicated, partly philosophical, partly factual question: philosophical to the extent that we would need criteria for comparing costs and ranking benefits; factual for reasons that are perfectly obvious. A couple of examples of possible alternative expenditures of the relevant resources may serve to highlight not only the complexity but also the practical reality of both the philosophical and the factual issues. There is increasing evidence that one unhappy byproduct of modern medicine is what one might call pollution of the human gene pool. The exponential increase and spread of diabetes is one example. Certainly passing on a sound gene pool would be a great benefit to future generations. An even simpler example is CO_2 and other 'greenhouse gas' emissions; all fossil fuel power generation releases vast quantities of CO_2 and also SO_2, as well as fly ash, particulate carbon and even radiation. (Some authorities suggest that the radon and other radioactive materials released when some coal is burned in a normal operation exceed the amount of radioactivity likely to be released from a nuclear power plant during the most seriously likely breakdown or accident.) Or what about the benefits of winding 'big energy' options such as nuclear, fossil and hydro generation down and substituting 'small' options such as conservation and solar and wind generation?

Would the benefit of improvements in the gene pool or in levels of greenhouse gas and other emissions or in conversion to small energy options be as great as the benefit of freedom from the dangers of radioactive poisoning from reactor wastes or uranium tailings? And could they be secured for a similar expenditure of resources? I doubt that anyone knows the answer to these questions. But the questions must be asked. As Bodde has put it, "our duty is to create solutions to the disposal of radioactive wastes in the context of other threats to human existence, rather than in isolation" — and not just to human existence![13] Rational public policy requires answers to thousands of similar questions. Ask yourself: What *would* the balance be if the comparison were with renewable energy? And what would it be if the comparison were with heavy metal contamination? (Heavy metals have no halflife and retain their toxicity forever.)

These hypothetical cost/benefit questions are still artificially simplistic. The real cost/benefit questions (and hence the real moral questions) also include:

1. When we allocate resources to create a new benefit, how should the new benefits in turn be used? For example, should we use it to expand wealth or to enhance health, safety or make other gains in liberty?
2. Then distributional questions arise: additional wealth or liberty for what beings, over what space and what time? We are clearly permitted to consume some benefits, but it is equally clear that if we are to honour the principles of the equal worth of every person and the worth of all that lives, we cannot consume as much as we like unless we can leave others with the same largesse. Within these parameters, however, lies an enormous range of options, both with respect to us and others alive now, us and future generations, and us and other kinds of being.
3. Technical questions, such as whether the principle of equal worth can be realized in equal cost/benefit *ratios*, or whether equal cost/benefit *distributions* (so that everyone gets the same amount of each, and not just the same ratio) are required. This question too needs to be asked for nonhuman as well as human beings.[14]

And so on, almost without limit. Public policy that is rational from the cost/benefit point of view (and therefore public policy that meets even the necessary conditions of moral soundness) is extraordinarily complicated — something that will come as no surprise to those familiar with the deep and sometimes unavoidable vacuum in which many policy decisions are taken.[15]

It is perhaps worth noting, before we leave this topic, that cost/benefit issues may also be relevant to our previous discussion of probability and obligations. There I argued that the probability of there not being relevantly similar people, or people at all, must be determinate and fairly high before our obligations are significantly reduced. This argument may have to be modified in the following way. If the costs of meeting these obligations are high enough that great benefits could otherwise be achieved, our obligations may fall faster than would otherwise be the case. The same might be argued, *mutatis mutandis*, for other creatures, ecological systems, etc.

5. Moral Assessment and Risk Assessment   Costs and benefits and other aspects of resource utilization always have risks attached: there is a risk that expending resources will not achieve the targeted benefit, that something in the process will have unintended side effects, and so on. How should assessment of risks guide our ethical assessments? In my view, no matter how well technological risk assessment based in probability calculations is done, it never settles the ethical questions. Of course, this does not imply that risk assessments have no role to play. Even if we should always do a separate ethical assessment, we must also ground it in the best knowledge of the facts available. This is what the regime of risk assessment can provide. Nevertheless, after all the facts are in, we still have to apply our ethical principles and make an independent determination of what we ought to do.

Here is an easy example to demonstrate that level of risk and level of ethical seriousness are not the same thing. Consider the spate of children run over by school buses every year. With these accidents, increased moral acceptability is not linear with decreasing risk. Reducing the frequency of such accidents would not be enough to make the ones that remain morally acceptable. No such accidents are acceptable. That implies that the only acceptable level of risk in this case is the lowest level we can attain. In short, risk and moral acceptability are not in a linear relationship.

Here is another way in which risk assessment does not settle the ethical questions. In Canada, we generate electricity primarily in three ways: nuclear fission, burning fossil fuels (coal, oil or natural gas), and hydro power. Compare nuclear to fossil fuel generation. These technologies clearly have very different harm/probability profiles. The harms that nuclear power can inflict are catastrophically severe, as Chernobyl demonstrated, but the probability of incurring them is generally thought to be quite low, at least in Canada. By contrast, with fossil fuel, we are virtually certain to incur the harms they can produce, harms such as the CO_2 and SO_2 emissions and release of radium and other radioactive and/or toxic elements already mentioned and also depletion of a nonrenewable resource. But these harms are generally considered less significant than those that a nuclear disaster can inflict. Whether we are right to consider the harms inflicted by burning fossil fuels relatively less significant might be debated, but the point I want to make here is this. Only by a separate ethical assessment in the light of our various visions of the good life for ourselves and other kinds of being can one assess the high harm/low probability risks of nuclear power against low harm/high probability risks such as we find with fossil fuels.

Other philosophically difficult questions arise about risks, too. For example, how does diminishing level of risk work, or rather, how should it work, as a discounter of costs? It is quite clear that it does do so: in connection with the nuclear industry we have been able to accept some potential costs that would be quite horrendous because we have been able to convince ourselves that the risk of having to pay them is quite low. Since we cannot avoid running some low risks of high costs in whatever we do, it seems clear that some discount factor must be morally acceptable. But how much a cost can be discounted as the probability of risk moves to very small figures is totally unclear. It is an important question in connection with the nuclear industry generally and in connection with our relation to future generations in particular. The principle of equal worth is unlikely to be able to help us with it.

Second, is there such a thing as an absolutely unacceptable cost, however low the risk and whatever the benefit? Given the Doomsday aura that surrounds certain aspects of the nuclear industry, this is a question that some people have asked. Even the principles, let alone the criteria and facts, for an adequate answer probably do not exist.

A third starts from the idea that the depletion of nonrenewable resources is itself a cost being imposed on future generations. Classical economic cost/benefit analysis does not seem well suited to thinking about this kind of cost, there being no possible benefit that could compensate for it. Criteria for assigning cost values to questions of depletion are needed, and might be difficult to find.

6. Uncertainty   We can never be certain about any outcome in a complex industrial system and the further we move into the future, the more uncertain we become. How can we reach ethical conclusions in the face of such uncertainty?

One of the most ethically vexing aspects of the nuclear industry or any other big, technologically complex system flows from the limits of knowledge. Though I have spoken about many factual issues above as though the relevant facts are known with a high degree of certainty, in fact that is not always the case. It would have taken many detailed qualifications to identify even the most important limits to certainty but that does not mean that they do not exist. This compounds the problem of risk assessment: not only must we try to assess the level of risk in each relevant context, risk being a matter of the size of a danger times the probability of it occurring, we must also recognize that there are uncertainties built into these calculations so large that our conclusions could be seriously in error.

There is probably no good ethical way to take account of this limitation. The best we can do from the moral point of view is to err on the side of caution. Where we are dealing with the health and safety of large numbers of humans and other living things over large ecologies and geological periods of time, we can be sure that we have met our obligations in the face of uncertainty only if we build the worst outcomes that are at all likely into our analyses at all relevant points.

7. Reducing Risk Vs. Retaining Benefits   As well as posing very serious risks of radiological and chemical poisoning, spent nuclear fuel also houses a huge potential benefit. As was noted earlier, one of the results of fissioning uranium is an even heavier and more fissionable metal, plutonium. Plutonium does not exist in nature but substantial amounts of it are contained in spent reactor fuel. Since it is just as good a reactor fuel as uranium, it would generate enormous amounts of additional energy if it were to be 'burned' in its own controlled chain reaction. This gives rise to a tricky ethical question.

On the one hand, we want to protect future generations from the risks posed by spent fuel — unprotected contact and diversion for weapons. On the other hand, we do not want to cut them off from a potentially huge benefit. What is the optimal balance between reducing these hazards over a geological time frame and leaving this potential benefit available to future generations? In the light of the diversion risk, should we make it impossible for future generations to use this resource at all? It does have potential to be used to make bombs — it could diverted and purified into weapons grade material.

8. Procedural Issues   My comments on procedural ethics will be very sketchy; the topic requires a paper of its own. In connection with the management of nuclear wastes, a number of important ethical issues arise that have to do with procedures. Who should make the decisions? What procedures will allow all stakeholders to have a fair say? What procedures will generate the best decisions? (These are not necessarily the same.) How can we prevent the majority from tyrannizing minorities; should communities have veto power, for example, over the location of a facility in their area? (This is a basic problem of all democratic decision making.) Can compensation justify overruling a community's or an individual's objections? And how should the wishes of people with views very different from ourselves be taken into account?

This last question is pressing with respect to the geological deep disposal proposal. The facility is likely to be built in northern Ontario. If it is, aboriginal people will be far more affected by the facility than by any other aspect of the nuclear fuel cycle. Yet, not only have they not received many benefits from the power thus generated, they tend to view the world and our place in it in a way that is quite antithetical to big power or any other system that imposes heavy environmental demands. How should these people enter the decision making process, in particular the process of choosing a site?

The Current Proposal

We have now discussed the eight considerations introduced earlier: principle; scope; discounting; cost/risk/benefit; moral assessment and risk assessment; uncertainty; reducing risk vs. retaining benefits; and procedures. Let us now ask how well the current proposal to bury spent fuel in plutons in the Canadian Shield does when assessed against these desiderata.

1. Deep geological disposal of high level wastes probably achieves fairness and protects future liberty better than any other proposal.
2. Deep disposal seems likely to provide protection of the widest scope compared to other concepts, in all three dimensions, that is, kind of being, time, and place.
3. Because of its long time frame, deep disposal discounts future generations of people and other living things less than any other concept.
4. Concerning costs and benefit, the deep disposal concept clearly forces those who benefit to assume the costs. On the issue of achieving the greatest benefit for a given cost, however, I wonder if the deep disposal concept may not be less than optimal. I suspect that greater social and ecological goods could be attained by building a less secure facility and expending some of the funds in other ways. I have in mind things such as other protections for ecosystems, population control, and of course the perennial demands of feeding the hungry, helping people find sustainable ways to provide for themselves, and achieving a fairer distribution of resources.
5. Because deep disposal reduces risk as far as is reasonably achievable, given current knowledge, it does as well at satisfying our moral demands for risk reduction as any concept is likely to do.
6. At least half a billion dollars worth of research has been done in connection with the deep disposal concept. Thus this proposal probably reduces the uncertainties in our knowledge farther than other concepts.
7. Recovering the plutonium contained in spent fuel buried in plutonic rock would be expensive but not impossible. So a balance is struck between minimization of harm and retrievability of possible benefits, though one favouring minimization of harm.

8. Since most of the important procedural issues will arise as the proposal is considered in the public arena and decisions are made about commencement, site, etc., it is too early to say how the proposal stacks up procedurally.

Application to Other Issues

The methodology we have used for determining our obligations in connection with nuclear wastes could be applied to many other issues, too. Within the nuclear industry, some nonenvironmental issues to which it could be applied include: uranium mining and an economy based on exploitation of natural resources; marketing nuclear technology; terrorism and the weapons risk; consumption vs. conservation in industrial economies; the creation of a technological 'priesthood' having esoteric knowledge not possessed by the rest of us and having a lot of power in society by virtue of their control of large industrial complexes; and other industrial and social structure issues.

The moral analysis offered above can be applied to other social and environmental issues. I have used it, for example, in connection with land use policy in British Columbia. The issues such as soil depletion, biomass depletion, and diversion of land from agriculture to housing, transportation and industry have essentially the same moral structure as the issue of nuclear wastes. They are all situations in which gaining a benefit for ourselves now will impose large costs on future generations of humans and other beings with little by way of compensating benefits unless we do something. Yet the costs of doing anything effective would be quite high and yield little if any direct benefit to us. The moral issue is also the same: Do we have an obligation to assume costs of our current activities such as these, saving future generations from having to do so?

More analyses are needed before definitive moral conclusions can be reached about nuclear energy and the environment, both factual and criterial analyses. Much has been done — a number of fairly well founded standards now exist, for example, and a promising proposal for a high level waste disposal facility is under consideration. But more remains to be done and we still do not have an integrated ethical framework within which to think about the industry and what surrounds it as a whole.

The biggest problem may not be the lack of a clear ethical framework, however. In many areas of social policy, what we are obliged to do is actually quite clear. The problem is to muster the personal and political will and the resources to do it. I think that we know what we should do about nuclear wastes: find the most permanent, passive solution to them that comes at a reasonable cost, given the costs of other potential benefits, and that will not make future exploitation of the fuel impossible. How do we marshall the will and the resources to do it?[16]

NOTES

1. Royal Commission on Electric Power Planning, *A Race Against Time* (known as the Porter Commission Report after the Chair of the Commission, Arthur Porter) Toronto: Queen's Printer, 1978, p. 153.
2. Here is what is meant by saying that uranium is enriched. In nature, more than 99% of uranium is of the isotope 238, less than 1% is 235, the fissionable material. In bombs, enough of the 238 is removed to raise the portion of 235 to roughly 70% of the total. The fuel in most reactors is enriched, too, but the ratio of 235 is increased only to about 7%, not to 70% or more as in bombs. Candu reactors use unenriched fuel, in which the fissionable 235 makes up only about

.7% of the total. Among other things, this makes Candu fuel more difficult to use as raw material for bombs.

3. An order of magnitude is ten times larger or smaller than the initial amount. So if X is two orders of magnitude larger than Y, then X is 100 times (10x10) larger than Y.

4. "300 to 800 years": see the report of the Advisory Panel on Tailings of the Atomic Energy Control Board, "An Appraisal of Current Practices for the Management of Uranium Mill Tailings" (AECB 1156). '200,000 times less': *Environmental Impact Statement on the Concept for the Disposal of Canada's Nuclear Fuel Wastes* Atomic Energy of Canada Ltd 10721, COG-93–11, 1994. Unless otherwise noted, facts cited concerning high level wastes are taken from this document.

5. A half-life is the time it takes the radioactivity in a material to diminish by one half. Thus plutonium is half as radioactive after 24,000 years, one quarter as radioactive after 48,000 years, one eighth as radioactive after 72,000 years, and so on.

6. American Physical Society, "Report to the American Physical Society by the Study Croup on Nuclear Fuel Cycles and Waste Management," *Review of Modern Physics* 50 (January 1978), pp. 1–186.

7. There is an article on the ethics of managing low level uranium mine/mill waste by the same author in earlier editions of *Contemporary Moral Issues*.

8. Unlike most rock, plutonic rock has few cracks or fissures and is highly impermeable. Over one thousand possibly suitable structures have been identified.

9. At this point, some ethicists would introduce the leading metaethical positions such as libertarianism, contractarianism, utilitarianism, and various egalitarian and deontological approaches. An interesting example is contained in Ch. 6 of the first reference document for *Environmental Impact Statement on the Concept for the Disposal of Canada's Nuclear Fuel Wastes,* Atomic Energy of Canada Ltd 10721, COG-93-11, 1994. The background document is entitled *The Disposal of Canada's Nuclear Fuel Waste: Public Involvement and Social Aspects*, M. Greber et al., AECL 10712, COG-93-2, 1994. Some of this moral background can also be found in R. Gaizauskas, "A Philosophical Examination of Our Responsibility to Future Generations." Project for the AECB (AECB: Ottawa, 1977). I have adopted a different strategy.*

10. We could even go so far as to weigh personal attributes differentially without violating the principle, though many would consider these morally *ir*relevant: for some people and in some contexts, having Beethoven's powers may make him more valuable than John Smith. Likewise for other kinds of genius, sensitivity, and maybe even personal beauty, grace or charm.

11. Williams, B. *Ethics and the Limits of Philosophy* Cambridge, MA: Harvard University Press 1985, see esp. Ch. 6.

12. Holmes Rolston mounts an argument along these lines connecting interests to moral worth in *Environmental Ethics,*

    An argument diametrically opposed to the thrust of his and my analysis has enjoyed some currency in libertarian and contractarian circles. It urges that we have no obligations to future generations, to other creatures, or even to many contemporary persons, as follows:

    1. We have obligations only where someone has rights; rights are conferred by explicit or implicit agreement of others.
    2. Only actual, not possible, persons can enter into agreements and thereby gain rights. Very few even of them have entered any such agreements with me or people with whom I share rights.
    3. In particular, no future person could enter agreements or have rights; to contract, you have to be alive.
    4. Hence no future person can have rights now.
    5. Hence we have no obligation now to future persons.
    6. Likewise, *mutatis mutandis,* for other species, most other people alive now, and so on.
        Even if we accept 1. to 3., however, 4. does not follow. First, a person's rights may extend further in time than the person does. Thus *any* actual person, no matter at what time he or she is actual, may well have rights now. Second, the argument as a whole assumes that we have no obligations to people and other beings that are not conferred by agreement. Against this view, a powerful argument can be mounted that people and other beings have *intrinsic* value, value that does not depend on whether others acknowledge it or bind themselves by agreement to respect it.

13. Bodde, D. L. Radioactive wastes: pragmatic strategies and ethical perspectives. In D. Maclean and P. G. Brown, eds. *Energy and the Future* Totowa NJ: Rowman and Littlefield 1983, p. 121.

14. To some extent, this is merely an academic question. Some level of cost is unavoidable to any being who has to service a body, so any strict adherence even to the ratio interpretation will achieve at least some measure of distributional equity.

15. In some contexts, at least three further cost/benefit questions would have to be addressed. Fortunately, they do not affect our obligations with respect to nuclear wastes. (i) Are total benefits of an activity greater than minimum total costs? With respect to nuclear wastes, the answer is almost certainly yes. (ii) Are sufficient total resources available at all? The answer is again yes, though the real question here is whether sufficient resources can reasonably be made available; and were the answer not yes, we would have to go into that very difficult question in a serious way. (iii) Will future generations be able to secure the same benefits for themselves much more cheaply than we can? Although the answer is probably no, the whole question can be rejected, if my earlier argument is sound, because it is we who are reaping the benefits of nuclear power and so there is no sound moral reason in general that future generations should be made to assume any of the costs.

16. I would like to thank Christine Koggel and especially Wesley Cragg for very helpful comments and suggestions.

* Editor's Note: The AECB studies may be obtained by writing to: Atomic Energy Control Board, 280 Slater St., P.O. Box 1046, Ottawa K1P 5S9. Atomic Energy of Canada Ltd. documents can be obtained from: AECL Research, Whiteshell Laboratories, Pinawa, Manitoba R0E 1L0. The material you wish to obtain should be identified by name and date or number as indicated above.

QUESTIONS

1. Andrew Brook sets out three principles that he suggests should guide our thinking about the disposal of nuclear wastes. What are those principles? Are they similar to or different from the principles that the authors/editors of this book have articulated in the introductions to the chapters of this book?

2. Do we have obligations to future generations? What are Brook's views on this subject? Does he present convincing arguments to support his view?

3. Brook identifies eight issues that ought to guide our thinking about the disposal of nuclear waster. Do you agree with this list? Can the issues be given an order of priority?

4. Is Brook right in thinking that Canadians have a moral obligation to endorse and finance the deep disposal proposal for nuclear wastes that he describes in his paper?

SUGGESTIONS FOR FURTHER READING

• Susan J. Armstrong and Richard Botzler, eds., *Environmental Ethics: Divergence and Convergence* (New York: McGraw-Hill, 1993). This is an excellent anthology covering a wide range of issues. Intended as a text, the book is also an excellent though challenging introduction to the topic of environmental ethics.

• Raymond Bradley and Stephen Duguid, eds., *Environmental Ethics: Philosophical and Policy Perspectives* (Vancouver: University of British Columbia Press, 1988). See previous note.

• G.H. Brundtland, *Our Common Future* (Oxford: Oxford University Press, 1987). This is the report of the World Commission on Environment and Development referred to often as the Brundtland Report. Its impact was felt around the world when it was published and it continues to shape the debate over environmental concerns.

- Conrad G. Brunk, Lawrence Haworth and Brenda Lee, *Value Assumptions in Risk Assessment: A Case Study of the Alachlor Controversy* (Waterloo: Wilfrid Laurier University Press, 1991). This is an excellent study of the role of values in risk assessment built on a detailed analysis of the a risk analysis of agricultural chemical alachlor.

- Alex Davidson and Michael Dence, eds., *The Brundtland Challenge and the Cost of Inaction* (The Institute for Research on Public Policy, P.O. Box 3670 South Halifax, Nova Scotia, 1988). This is a report on two workshops on environmental issues held in 1988 in Hull, Quebec, and at the University of Waterloo. The workshops were sponsored by the Institute and the Royal Society of Canada. The report identifies the issues that participants at the workshop regarded as pressing and the recommendations that resulted.

- Robert Elliot and Arran Gare, eds., *Environmental Philosophy* (Queensland: University of Queensland Press, 1983). This is another valuable collection on the general topic of environmental ethics. Contributors are drawn from Canada, the United States, Great Britain and Australia.

- Al Gore, *Earth in the Balance* (Boston, New York and London: Houghton Mifflin Company, 1992). Written prior to Gore's election as vice-president of the United States, this book is an appeal to government, business, and the public at large to take notice of approaching environmental crises caused by abusive development and ecological insensitivity.

- Philip Hanson, ed., *Environmental Ethics: Philosophical and Policy Perspectives* (Vancouver, Simon Fraser Publications, 1986). This book and the next one are anthologies resulting from seminars held in the 1980s in British Columbia. They introduce the concerns of a variety of authors who are prominent in the field.

- Arne Naess, *Ecology, Community and Lifestyle* (Cambridge: Cambridge University Press, 1989). In this book the father of deep ecology traces the deep ecology movement and outlines his environmental philosophy, which is described as ecosophy.

- Ernest Partridge, ed., *Responsibilities to Future Generations: Environmental Ethics* (Buffalo: Prometheus Books, 1981). This collection includes many contributions on the subject of our obligations to posterity. It is helpful because of both the variety of discussions of the issues and the way it traces the development of a variety of themes in the last decade.

- John Passmore, *Man's Responsibility for Nature* (London: Duckworth, 1974). This book, now regarded as something of a classic in the field, evaluates a variety of views of nature found in western literature and concludes by formulating a conservation ethic.

- Peter Singer, *Animal Liberation* (New York: Random House, 1990). This is the second edition of a book that has had a great influence in shifting attitudes on the part of many people toward animals. In it the author argues that animals do have rights that should be respected and seeks to understand the implications for our relationship to them of that finding.

- Alex Wellington, Alan Greenbaum and Wesley Cragg, eds., *Canadian Issues in Applied Environmental Ethics* (Peterborough: Broadview Press, 1997). This book is an anthology of articles published for the first time in this collection. Topics include the environment and the economy, ethical issues relating to non-human animals, mining, fishing, and native hunting.

Chapter 10

Tools and Theories

Introduction

The goal of contributors to a book like this one is to provide answers to questions about how we determine as individuals and as a society the morally appropriate solutions to difficult practical issues. The fact that the issues are contemporary and the readings for the most part current may mislead us into thinking that reflections on morality are a recent phenomenon. While it is true that critical reflections on practical moral issues of the sort we have examined in this book are fairly recent, for thousands of years philosophers have been concerned with providing theories that explain the role of morality in daily life. Many of these theories have been at the level of generalized accounts of what morality is and of how we come to know what we ought to do. In this chapter, we provide a selection of some of these moral theories and consider some of the connections between those theories and the resolution of moral issues.

Moral philosophers have always been concerned to connect theory and practice. Philosophers such as Plato, Aristotle, Kant, Hume, and Mill provided general theories about how we ought to live at the same time as they examined practical issues such as capital punishment, poverty, sexuality, and the treatment of animals, for example. In this century, however, positivism and analytical philosophy have directed attention away from the resolution of issues, now considered not the proper domain of philosophy, to an examination of the use and function of the language of morality. Many moral philosophers became convinced that their proper job was linguistic and conceptual analysis.

In the second half of this century, however, this trend has been reversed. Two publications in particular illustrate that change. John Rawls's *A Theory of Justice* and the journal *Philosophy & Public Affairs* came out in 1971 and succeeded in once again legitimizing the examination of practical issues. By providing a theory of justice and generating principles that were to form the background structure of a just society, Rawls's highly influential work turned attention back to applying theory to practice. Rawls's theory is examined by several authors in this book, including Annette Baier in this chapter. Judith Jarvis Thomson's article on abortion in the first issue of *Philosophy & Public Affairs* (included in the readings for that chapter) is also regarded by many as signalling a decisive shift back toward the examination of practical issues.

Technology has also played a role in directing attention back to practical problems. With technological advances have come new moral dilemmas with respect to issues such as abortion, euthanasia, pornography, and environmental ethics. These developments not only demand our immediate attention, but highlight the need for critical tools that allow us to evaluate the complex and multiple dimensions of these practical issues. These technological advances have also breathed new life into the project of using insights from the kind of theories presented in this chapter as critical tools for evaluating moral issues. This development is reflected in a number of contributors to this book whose conclusions on the moral issues they are examining are derived from the application of specific moral theories.

The resurgence of practical ethics has also brought with it, however, close critical examination of traditional moral theories themselves. This has been stimulated at least in part by growing awareness of the entrenched character of discrimination in both modern and traditional societies, widespread resistance to its eradication and the apparent insensitivity of traditional moral theorists to its pervasiveness and importance. Issues such as discrimination, affirmative action, aboriginal rights, and poverty focus attention on these concerns, although there continues to be deep disagreement about where and how principles of equality are appropriately applied.

How might we distinguish what we do when we critically examine practical moral issues and what we do when we provide theories of morally right action? As a first attempt, we can say that any human activity can be approached at two levels. We might call the first the level of participation and the second the level of reflection. Thus, for example, we can participate in a game like hockey or chess. Or we can stand back and reflect on the nature of the game and how it is played.

Resolving moral issues can be thought of as an activity. And, as with any human activity, we can, if we wish, participate by becoming involved in discussions aimed at resolving particular issues. Or we can stand back and reflect on the nature of morality and how moral problems are solved. As with most activities, of course, serious reflection pre-supposes some direct experience with the activity itself. That is one of the reasons the approach to moral issues that has dominated this book has been that of participant in the activity of resolving concrete moral issues. However, participation in the resolution of concrete moral issues pre-supposes certain commitments to particular principles and theoretical foundations. It also raises questions that are genuinely interesting in their own right, questions that can be approached only by reflecting on our own attempts, as well as the attempts of others, to resolve particular moral problems.

What kinds of questions are suggested by discussion and argument in previous chapters? We shall highlight just two. First, one of the striking features of the readings collected in this anthology is the extent to which those who have made serious efforts to develop and support positions on particular issues disagree. What are we to conclude from this? One possible response is simply to throw up our hands in frustration and go on to some more "productive" activity. But this response has serious implications. The issues we have been examining are important and virtually unavoidable. If we cannot resolve them through rational discussion, how are they going to be resolved? Some would argue (as, for example, in the capital punishment or pornography debate) that the position of the majority should prevail. But this, too, has worrisome implications that require careful exploration. It would seem, on reflection, that there is no "easy" way to escape the fact that well-intentioned people do disagree on moral questions. Why is this so? Does it tell us something of importance about the nature of morality?

Asking whether moral issues can be resolved would seem to lead to further questions: is the resolution of moral issues a general responsibility? Or is it a task that can be or ought to be assigned to experts? There is one sense in which responsibility for resolving moral problems clearly cannot be assigned to others. If I am faced with a request by an ill person that she be helped in terminating her life, then I must respond to the request. No one else can do it for me. In this sense, we cannot assign responsibility for our own behaviour to others. But it is always possible to seek advice in deciding what to do. We might then rephrase our question by asking whether moral philosophers are a good source of advice for those who are faced with difficult moral problems.

Consideration of all these questions has given rise to a number of positions, many of which are reflected in the readings in previous chapters. Faced with disagreement on moral questions, some philosophers have opted for a position of moral relativism (discussed in this chapter by David Wong). Others reject this view. An alternative position might be that not all moral disputes are alike. In some cases, agreement can be achieved, and in some cases, it cannot. Finally, some have argued that there are basic principles that no agent could rationally reject. If moral argument is built on those principles, agreement should be possible. This view would seem to be implied by Andrew Brook in his discussion of our obligation to future generations (Chapter 9) and by J.T. Stevenson in his discussion of aboriginal rights (Chapter 7).

Further reflection on the features of moral argument and the nature of morality reveals another dimension to the activity of examining moral issues, one that is less visible because it operates at the level of assumptions about the nature of human beings and social relations. The readings in this chapter explore this dimension of morality and provide us with various views about the nature of human beings, morality, and social relations.

The Readings

Immanuel Kant takes the human capacity to reason to be the basis for describing human beings as "ends in themselves" and as having "absolute worth." This capacity, he argues, distinguishes us from non-human animals in that it enables people to deliberate and make decisions about what they ought to do, decisions that are an obvious vital part of morality. Kant formulates what he calls the categorical imperative, "act only on that maxim whereby thou canst at the same time will that it should become a universal law," as the basis for determining morally right action.

The reading by Ayn Rand assumes a conception of the nature of morality very different from that defended by Kant. While Rand agrees that rationality is a unique and valuable human capacity, she argues that the purpose of morality is to tell us how to survive and flourish. To that end, nature equips us with the capacities for pleasure and pain and the capacity to use this information to reason about what is in our own best interests. She defends what she calls an "objectivist ethics," a morality of rational self-interest.

In the third reading by John Stuart Mill, we get a different view of how to interpret the importance of pleasure and pain in human life. Mill agrees with Rand that "pleasure, and freedom from pain, are the only things desirable as ends" and that a calculation of pleasure should form the basis for morality. However, his utilitarian account departs from Rand's brand of egoism in one major respect. Mill argues that everyone's interests count equally; there is no justification for giving more value to one's own interests than to the interests of anyone else affected by one's actions. The greatest happiness principle dictates that morally right action is that which produces the greatest happiness for the greatest number of people.

The fourth reading by David Wong presents an approach that is sceptical of the project in which each of the authors thus far have been engaged, the project of determining morally right action on the basis of a formula that holds for all people in all places and at all times.

By providing examples of deep disagreements about moral practices in various cultures, Wong sounds a warning against complacency in a belief that we can formulate universal principles that dictate duties that are absolutely without exception. This belief, he argues, has and can result in a disrespect for people from different cultures. Wong defends a form of relativism that he sees as occupying the middle ground between universalism and the extreme version of relativism that holds that all moralities are equally true.

In the fifth and final reading, Annette Baier also reflects on the tendency in traditional moral theory to formulate universal principles. However, Baier focuses attention on both the contexts within which the theories were formulated and the assumptions about people and social relations underlying these theories. She distinguishes two sorts of approaches to thinking about morality, one that sees justice as a primary virtue and values individual rights and one that emphasizes our interdependency and values relationships and responsibilities to others. Like other theorists defending the second approach of care, Baier connects this way of thinking about morality to people who have been and continue to be disadvantaged and argues that this approach offers important insights that can and should be incorporated by the justice approach, which has dominated moral and political theory.

THE CATEGORICAL IMPERATIVE

Immanuel Kant

Nothing can possibly be conceived in the world, or even out of it, which can be called good without qualification, except a *good will.* Intelligence, wit, judgment, and the other *talents* of the mind, however they may be named, or courage, resolution, perseverance, as qualities of temperament, are undoubtedly good and desirable in many respects; but these gifts of nature may also become extremely bad and mischievous if the will which is to make use of them, and which, therefore, constitutes what is called *character*, is not good. It is the same with the *gifts of fortune.* Power, riches, honor, even health, and the general well-being and contentment with one's condition, which is called *happiness*, inspire pride, and often presumption, if there is not a good will to correct the influence of these on the mind, and with this also to rectify the whole principle of acting, and adapt it to its end. The sight of a being who is not adorned with a single feature of a pure and good will, enjoying unbroken prosperity, can never give pleasure to an impartial rational spectator. Thus a good will appears to constitute the indispensable condition even of being worthy of happiness.

* * * * * * *

An action done from duty derives its moral worth, *not from the purpose* which is to be attained by it, but from the maxim by which it is determined, and therefore does not depend on the realization of the object of the action, but merely on the *principle of volition* by which the action has taken place, without regard to any object of desire. It is clear from

---

From Fundamental Principles of the Metaphysics of Morals *(1785), translated by T.K. Abbott.*

what precedes that the purposes which we may have in view in our actions, or their effects regarded as ends and springs of the will, cannot give to actions any unconditional or moral worth. In what, then, can their worth lie if it is not to consist in the will and in reference to its expected effect? It cannot lie anywhere but in the *principle of the will* without regard to the ends which can be attained by the action. For the will stands between its *a priori** principle, which is formal, and its *a posteriori*† spring, which is material, as between two roads, and as it must be determined by something, it follows that it must be determined by the formal principle of volition when an action is done from duty, in which case every material principle has been withdrawn from it.

The third proposition, which is a consequence of the two preceding, I would express thus: *Duty is the necessity of acting from respect for the law.* I may have *inclination* for an object as the effect of my proposed action, but I cannot have *respect* for it just for this reason that it is an effect and not an energy of will. Similarly, I cannot have respect for inclination, whether my own or another's; I can at most, if my own, approve it; if another's, sometimes even love it, that is, look on it as favorable to my own interest. It is only what is connected with my will as a principle, by no means as an effect — what does not subserve my inclination, but overpowers it, or at least in case of choice excludes it from its calcula-tion — in other words, simply the law of itself, which can be an object of respect, and hence a command. Now an action done from duty must wholly exclude the influence of inclination, and with it every object of the will, so that nothing remains which can deter-mine the will except objectively the *law*, and subjectively *pure respect* for this practical law, and consequently the maxim that I should follow this law even to the thwarting of all of my inclinations.

Thus the moral worth of an action does not lie in the effect expected from it, nor in any principle of action which requires to borrow its motive from this expected effect. For all these effects — agreeableness of one's condition, and even the promotion of the happiness of others — could have been also brought about by other causes, so that for this there would have been no need of the will of a rational being; whereas it is in this alone that the supreme and unconditional good can be found. The pre-eminent good which we call moral can therefore consist in nothing else than *the conception of law* in itself, *which certainly is only possible in a rational being*, in so far as this conception, and not the expected effect, determines the will. This is a good which is already present in the person who acts accord-ingly, and we have not to wait for it to appear first in the result.

* * * * * * *

The conception of an objective principle, in so far as it is obligatory for a will, is called a command (of reason), and the formula of the command is called an Imperative.

All imperatives are expressed by the word *ought* [or *shall*], and thereby indicate the relation of an objective law of reason to a will which from its subjective constitution is not necessarily determined by it (an obligation). They say that something would be good to do or to forbear, but they say it to a will which does not always do a thing because it is conceived to be good to do it. That is practically *good*, however, which determines the will by means of the conceptions of reason, and consequently not from subjective causes, but objectively, that is, on principles which are valid for every rational being as such. It is

---

*   *a priori:* known prior to sense experience
†   *a posteriori:* known as the result of sense experience

distinguished from the *pleasant* as that which influences the will only by means of sensation from merely subjective causes, valid only for the sense of this or that one, and not as a principle of reason which holds for every one.

A perfectly good will would therefore be equally subject to objective laws (viz., laws of good), but could not be conceived as *obliged* thereby to act lawfully, because of itself from its subjective constitution it can only be determined by the conception of good. Therefore no imperatives hold for the Divine will, or in general for a *holy* will; *ought* is here out of place because the volition is already of itself necessarily in unison with the law. Therefore imperatives are only formulae to express the relation of objective laws of all volition to the subjective imperfection of the will of this or that rational being, for example, the human will.

Finally, there is an imperative which commands a certain conduct immediately, without having as its condition any other purpose to be attained by it. This imperative is *categorical*. It concerns not the matter of the action, or its intended result, but its form and the principle of which it is itself a result; and what is essentially good in it consists in the mental disposition, let the consequence be what it may. This imperative may be called that of *morality*.

* * * * * * *

There is therefore but one categorical imperative, namely, this: *Act only on that maxim whereby thou canst at the same time will that it should become a universal law.*

Now if all imperatives of duty can be deduced from this one imperative as from their principle, then, although it should remain undecided whether what is called duty is not merely a vain notion, yet at least we shall be able to show what we understand by it and what this notion means.

Since the universality of the law according to which effects are produced constitutes what is properly called *nature* in the most general sense (as to form) — that is, the existence of things so far as it is determined by general laws — the imperative of duty may be expressed thus: *Act as if the maxim of thy action were to become by thy will a universal law of nature.*

We will now enumerate a few duties, adopting the usual division of them into duties to ourselves and to others, and into perfect and imperfect duties.

1. A man reduced to despair by a series of misfortunes feels wearied of life, but is still so far in possession of his reason that he can ask himself whether it would not be contrary to his duty to himself to take his own life. Now he inquires whether the maxim of his action could become a universal law of nature. His maxim is: From self-love I adopt it as a principle to shorten my life when its longer duration is likely to bring more evil than satisfaction. It is asked then simply whether this principle founded on self-love can become a universal law of nature. Now we see at once that a system of nature of which it should be a law to destroy life by means of the very feeling whose special nature it is to impel to the improvement of life would contradict itself, and therefore could not exist as a system of nature; hence that maxim cannot possibly exist as a universal law of nature, and consequently would be wholly inconsistent with the supreme principle of all duty.

2. Another finds himself forced by necessity to borrow money. He knows that he will not be able to repay it, but sees also that nothing will be lent to him unless he promises stoutly to repay it in a definite time. He desires to make this promise, but he has still so much

conscience as to ask himself: Is it not unlawful and inconsistent with duty to get out of a difficulty in this way? Suppose, however, that he resolves to do so, then the maxim of his action would be expressed thus: When I think myself in want of money, I will borrow money and promise to repay it, although I know that I never can do so. Now this principle of self-love or of one's own advantage may perhaps be consistent with my whole future welfare; but the question now is, Is it right? I change then the suggestion of self-love into a universal law, and state the question thus: How would it be if my maxim were a universal law? Then I see at once that it could never hold as a universal law of nature, but would necessarily contradict itself. For supposing it to be a universal law that everyone when he thinks himself in a difficulty should be able to promise whatever he pleases, with the purpose of not keeping his promise, the promise itself would become impossible, as well as the end that one might have in view in it, since no one would consider that anything was promised to him, but would ridicule all such statements as vain pretenses.

3. A third finds in himself a talent which with the help of some culture might make him a useful man in many respects. But he finds himself in comfortable circumstances and prefers to indulge in pleasure rather than to take pains in enlarging and improving his happy, natural capacities. He asks, however, whether his maxim of neglect of his natural gifts, besides agreeing with his inclination to indulgence, agrees also with what is called duty. He sees then that a system of nature could indeed subsist with such a universal law, although men (like the South Sea islanders) should let their talents rest and resolve to devote their lives merely to idleness, amusement, and propagation of their species — in a word, to enjoyment; but he cannot possibly *will* that this should be a universal law of nature, or be implanted in us as such by a natural instinct. For, as a rational being, he necessarily wills that his faculties be developed, since they serve him, and have been given him, for all sorts of possible purposes.

4. A fourth, who is in prosperity, while he sees that others have to contend with great wretchedness and that he could help them, thinks: What concern is it of mine? Let everyone be as happy as Heaven pleases, or as he can make himself; I will take nothing from him nor even envy him, only I do not wish to contribute anything to his welfare or to his assistance in distress! Now no doubt, if such a mode of thinking were a universal law, the human race might very well subsist, and doubtless even better than in a state in which everyone talks of sympathy and good-will, or even takes care occasionally to put it into practice, but, on the other side, also cheats when he can, betrays the rights of men, or otherwise violates them. But although it is possible that a universal law of nature might exist in accordance with that maxim, it is impossible to *will* that such a principle should have the universal validity of a law of nature. For a will which resolved this would contradict itself, inasmuch as many cases might occur in which one would have need of the love and sympathy of others, and in which, by such a law of nature, sprung from his own will, he would deprive himself of all hope of the aid he desires.

These are a few of the many actual duties, or at least what we regard as such, which obviously fall into two classes on the one principle that we have laid down. We must be *able to will* that a maxim of our action should be a universal law. This is the canon of the moral appreciation of the action generally. Some actions are of such a character that their maxim cannot without contradiction be even *conceived* as a universal law of nature, far from it being possible that we should *will* that it *should* be so. In others, this intrinsic impossibility is not found, but still it is impossible to *will* that their maxim should be raised to the universality of a law of nature, since such a will would contradict itself. It is easily seen that the former violate strict or rigorous (inflexible) duty; the latter only laxer (meritorious) duty. Thus it has been completely shown by these examples how all duties depend as regards the nature of the obligation (not the object of the action) on the same principle.

If now we attend to ourselves on occasion of any transgression of duty, we shall find that we in fact do not will that our maxim should be a universal law, for that is impossible for us; on the contrary, we will that the opposite should remain a universal law, only we assume the liberty of making an *exception* in our own favor or (just for this time only) in favor of our inclination. Consequently, if we considered all cases from one and the same point of view, namely, that of reason, we should find a contradiction in our own will, namely, that a certain principle should be objectively necessary as a universal law, and yet subjectively should not be universal, but admit of exceptions. As, however, we at one moment regard our action from the point of view of a will wholly conformed to reason, and then again look at the same action from the point of view of a will affected by inclination, there is not really any contradiction, but an antagonism of inclination to the precept of reason, whereby the universality of the principle is changed into a mere generality, so that the practical principle of reason shall meet the maxim half way. Now, although this cannot be justified in our own impartial judgment, yet it proves that we do really recognize the validity of the categorical imperative and (with all respect for it) only allow ourselves a few exceptions which we think unimportant and forced from us.

* * * * * *

Supposing, however, that there were something *whose existence* has *in itself* an absolute worth, something which, being *an end in itself*, could be a source of definite laws, then in this and this alone would lie the source of a possible categorical imperative, that is, a practical law.

Now I say: Man and generally any rational being *exists* as an end in himself, *not merely as a means* to be arbitrarily used by this or that will, but in all his actions, whether they concern himself or other rational beings, must be always regarded at the same time as an end. All objects of the inclinations have only a conditional worth; for if the inclinations and the wants founded on them did not exist, then their object would be without value. But the inclinations themselves, being sources of want, are so far from having an absolute worth for which they should be desired that, on the contrary, it must be the universal wish of every rational being to be wholly free from them. Thus the worth of any object which is *to be acquired* by our action is always conditional. Beings whose existence depends not on our will but on nature's, have nevertheless, if they are rational beings, only a relative value as means, and are therefore called things; rational beings, on the contrary, are called *persons*, because their very nature points them out as ends in themselves, that is, as something which must not be used merely as means, and so far therefore restricts freedom of action (and is an object of respect). These, therefore, are not merely subjective ends whose existence has a worth *for us* as an effect of our action, but *objective ends*, that is, things whose existence is an end in itself — an end, moreover, for which no other can be substituted, which they should subserve *merely* as means, for otherwise nothing whatever would possess *absolute worth*; but if all worth were conditioned and therefore contingent, then there would be no supreme practical principle of reason whatever.

If then there is a supreme practical principle or, in respect of the human will, a categorical imperative, it must be one which, being drawn from the conception of that which is necessarily an end for everyone because it is *an end in itself*, constitutes an *objective* principle of will, and can therefore serve as a universal practical law. The foundation of this principle is: *rational nature exists as an end in itself*. Man necessarily conceives his own existence as being so; so far then this is a *subjective* principle of human actions. But every other rational being regards its existence similarly, just on the same rational principle that holds for me, so that it is at the same time an objective principle from which as a supreme practical law all laws of the will must be capable of being deduced. Accordingly the practical imperative will be as follows: *So act as to treat humanity, whether in thine own person or in that of any other, in every case as an end withal, never as means only*. We will now inquire whether this can be practically carried out.

To abide by the previous examples:

First, under the head of necessary duty to oneself: He who contemplates suicide should ask himself whether his action can be consistent with the idea of humanity *as an end in itself*. If he destroys himself in order to escape from painful circumstances, he uses a person merely as a *mean* to maintain a tolerable condition up to the end of life. But a man is not a thing, that is to say, something which can be used merely as means, but must in all his actions be always considered as an end in himself. I cannot, therefore, dispose in any way of a man in my own person so as to mutilate him, to damage or kill him. (It belongs to ethics proper to define this principle more precisely, so as to avoid all misunderstanding, for example, as to the amputation of the limbs in order to preserve myself, as to exposing my life to danger with a view to preserve it, etc. This question is therefore omitted here.)

Secondly, as regards necessary duties, or those of strict obligation, towards others: He who is thinking of making a lying promise to others will see at once that he would be using another man *merely as a means*, without the latter containing at the same time the end in himself. For he whom I propose by such a promise to use for my own purposes cannot possibly assent to my mode of acting towards him, and therefore cannot himself contain the end of this action. This violation of the principle of humanity in other men is more obvious if we take in examples of attacks on the freedom and property of others. For then it is clear that he who transgresses the rights of men intends to use the person of others merely as means, without considering that as rational beings they ought always to be esteemed also as ends, that is, as beings who must be capable of containing in themselves the end of the very same action.

Thirdly, as regards contingent (meritorious) duties to oneself: It is not enough that the action does not violate humanity in our own person as an end in itself, it must also *harmonize with* it. Now there are in humanity capacities of greater perfection which belong to the end that nature has in view in regard to humanity in ourselves as the subject; to neglect these might perhaps be consistent with the *maintenance* of humanity as an end in itself, but not with the *advancement* of this end.

Fourthly, as regards meritorious duties towards others: The natural end which all men have is their own happiness. Now humanity might indeed subsist although no one should contribute anything to the happiness of others, provided he did not intentionally withdraw anything from it; but after all, this would only harmonize negatively, not positively, with *humanity as an end in itself*, if everyone does not also endeavor, as far as in him lies, to forward the ends of others. For the ends of any subject which is an end in himself ought as far as possible to be *my* ends also, if that conception is to have its *full* effect with me.

This principle that humanity and generally every rational nature is *an end in itself* (which is the supreme limiting condition of every man's freedom of action), is not borrowed from experience *first*, because it is universal, applying as it does to all rational beings whatever, and experience is not capable of determining anything about them; *secondly* because it does not present humanity as an end to men (subjectively), that is, as an object which men do of themselves actually adopt as an end; but as an objective end which must as a law constitute the supreme limiting condition of all our subjective ends, let them be what we will; it must therefore spring from pure reason. In fact the objective principle of all practical legislation lies (according to the first principle) in *the rule* and its form of universality which makes it capable of being a law (say, for example, a law of nature); but the *subjective* principle is in the *end*; now by the second principle, the subject of all ends is each rational being inasmuch as it is an end in itself. Hence follows the third practical principle of the will, which is the ultimate condition of its harmony with the universal practical reason, viz., the idea of *the will of every rational being as a universally legislative will.*

On this principle all maxims are rejected which are inconsistent with the will being itself universal legislator. Thus the will is not subject to the law, but so subject that it must be regarded *as itself giving the law*, and on this ground only subject to the law (of which it can regard itself as the author).

QUESTIONS

1. According to Immanuel Kant, how do I determine what actions are morally right?
2. Kant tells us to treat people "as ends and never as means only." What does he mean by this? What is the relevance of this precept for the categorical imperative?
3. Why, according to Kant, do I have a duty not to take my own life?
4. Using the example of lying, illustrate how Kant would have us decide if lying can be morally permissable. Is Kant's answer satisfactory? If not, is this a good reason to reject Kant's formulation of the categorical imperative?

➜ ⬅

THE VIRTUE OF SELFISHNESS

Ayn Rand

The title of this book may evoke the kind of question that I hear once in a while: "Why do you use the word 'selfishness' to denote virtuous qualities of character, when that word antagonizes so many people to whom it does not mean the things you mean?"

To those who ask it, my answer is: "For the reason that makes you afraid of it."

But there are others, who would not ask that question, sensing the moral cowardice it implies, yet who are unable to formulate my actual reason or to identify the profound moral issue involved. It is to them that I will give a more explicit answer.

It is not a mere semantic issue nor a matter of arbitrary choice. The meaning ascribed in popular usage to the word "selfishness" is not merely wrong: it represents a devastating intellectual "package-deal," which is responsible, more than any other single factor, for the arrested moral development of mankind.

In popular usage, the word "selfishness" is a synonym of evil; the image it conjures is of a murderous brute who tramples over piles of corpses to achieve his own ends, who cares for no living being and pursues nothing but the gratification of the mindless whims of any immediate moment.

Yet the exact meaning and dictionary definition of the word "selfishness" is: *concern with one's own interests.*

This concept does not include a moral evaluation; it does not tell us whether concern with one's own interests is good or evil; nor does it tell us what constitutes man's actual interests. It is the task of ethics to answer such questions.

The ethics of altruism has created the image of the brute, as its answer, in order to make men accept two inhuman tenets: (a) that any concern with one's own interests is evil, regardless of what these interests might be, and (b) that the brute's activities are *in fact* to one's own interest (which altruism enjoins man to renounce for the sake of his neighbors). . . .

There are two moral questions which altruism lumps together into one "package-deal": (1) What are values? (2) Who should be the beneficiary of values? Altruism substitutes the second for the first; it evades the task of defining a code of moral values, thus leaving man, in fact, without moral guidance.

Altruism declares that any action taken for the benefit of others is good, and any action taken for one's own benefit is evil. Thus the *beneficiary* of an action is the only criterion of moral value — and so long as that beneficiary is anybody other than oneself, anything goes.

Hence the appalling immorality, the chronic injustice, the grotesque double standards, the insoluble conflicts and contradictions that have characterized human relationships and human societies throughout history, under all the variants of the altruist ethics.

Observe the indecency of what passes for moral judgments today. An industrialist who produces a fortune, and a gangster who robs a bank are regarded as equally immoral, since they both sought wealth for their own "selfish" benefit. A young man who gives up his career in order to support his parents and never rises beyond the rank of grocery clerk is regarded as morally superior to the young man who endures an excruciating struggle and achieves his personal ambition. A dictator is regarded as moral, since the unspeakable atrocities he committed were intended to benefit "the people," not himself.

Observe what this beneficiary-criterion of morality does to a man's life. The first thing he learns is that morality is his enemy: he has nothing to gain from it, he can only lose; self-inflicted loss, self-inflicted pain and the gray, debilitating pall of an incomprehensible duty is all that he can expect. He may hope that others might occasionally sacrifice themselves for his benefit, as he grudgingly sacrifices himself for theirs, but he knows that the relationship will bring mutual resentment, not pleasure — and that, morally, their pursuit of values will be like an exchange of unwanted, unchosen Christmas presents, which neither is morally permitted to buy for himself. Apart from such times as he manages to perform some act of self-sacrifice, he possesses no moral significance: morality takes no cognizance of him and has nothing to say to him for guidance in the crucial issues of his life; it is only his own personal, private, "selfish" life and, as such, it is regarded either as evil or, at best, *amoral.*

Since nature does not provide man with an automatic form of survival, since he has to support his life by his own effort, the doctrine that concern with one's own interests is evil means that man's desire to live is evil — that man's life, as such, is evil. No doctrine could be more evil than that.

Yet that is the meaning of altruism, implicit in such examples as the equation of an industrialist with a robber. There is a fundamental moral difference between a man who sees his self-interest in production and a man who sees it in robbery. The evil of a robber does *not* lie in the fact that he pursues his own interests, but in *what* he regards as to his own interest; *not* in the fact that he pursues his values, but in *what* he choses to value; *not* in the fact that he wants to live, but in the fact that he wants to live on a subhuman level.

If it is true that what I mean by "selfishness" is not what is meant conventionally, then *this* is one of the worst indictments of altruism: it means that altruism *permits no concept* of a self-respecting, self-supporting man — a man who supports his life by his own effort and neither sacrifices himself nor others. It means that altruism permits no view of men except as sacrificial animals and profiteers-on-sacrifice, as victims and parasites — that it permits no concept of a benevolent coexistence among men — that it permits no concept of *justice*.

If you wonder about the reasons behind the ugly mixture of cynicism and guilt in which most men spend their lives, these are the reasons: cynicism, because they neither practice nor accept the altruist morality — guilt, because they dare not reject it.

To rebel against so devastating an evil, one has to rebel against its basic premise. To redeem both man and morality, it is the concept of *"selfishness"* that one has to redeem.

The first step is to assert *man's right to a moral existence* — that is: to recognize his need of a moral code to guide the course and the fulfillment of his own life.

. . . The reasons why man needs a moral code will tell you that the purpose of morality is to define man's proper values and interests, that *concern with his own interests* is the essence of a moral existence, and that *man must be the beneficiary of his own moral actions*.

Since all values have to be gained and/or kept by men's actions, any breach between actor and beneficiary necessitates an injustice: the sacrifice of some men to others, of the actors to the nonactors, of the moral to the immoral. Nothing could ever justify such a breach, and no one ever has.

The choice of the beneficiary of moral values is merely a preliminary or introductory issue in the field of morality. It is not a substitute for morality nor a criterion of moral value, as altruism has made it. Neither is it a moral *primary*: it has to be derived from and validated by the fundamental premises of a moral system.

The Objectivist ethics holds that the actor must always be the beneficiary of his action and that man must act for his own *rational* self-interest. But his right to do so is derived from his nature as man and from the function of moral values in human life — and, therefore, is applicable *only* in the context of a rational, objectively demonstrated and validated code of moral principles which define and determine his actual self-interest. It is not a license "to do as he pleases" and it is not applicable to the altruists' image of a "selfish" brute nor to any man motivated by irrational emotions, feelings, urges, wishes or whims.

This is said as a warning against the kind of "Nietzschean egoists" who, in fact, are a product of the altruist morality and represent the other side of the altruist coin: the men who believe that any action, regardless of its nature, is good if it is intended for one's own benefit. Just as the satisfaction of the irrational desires of others is *not* a criterion of moral value, neither is the satisfaction of one's own irrational desires. Morality is not a contest of whims. . . .

A similar type of error is committed by the man who declares that since man must be guided by his own independent judgment, any action he chooses to take is moral if *he* chooses it. One's own independent judgment is the *means* by which one must choose one's actions, but it is not a moral criterion nor a moral validation: only reference to a demonstrable principle can validate one's choices.

Just as man cannot survive by any random means, but must discover and practice the principles which his survival requires, so man's self-interest cannot be determined by blind desires or random whims, but must be discovered and achieved by the guidance of rational principles. This is why the Objectivist ethics is a morality of *rational* self-interest — or of *rational selfishness.*

Since selfishness is "concern with one's own interests," the Objectivist ethics uses that concept in its exact and purest sense. It is not a concept that one can surrender to man's enemies, nor to the unthinking misconceptions, distortions, prejudices and fears of the ignorant and the irrational. The attack on "selfishness" is an attack on man's self-esteem; to surrender one, is to surrender the other.

QUESTIONS

1. How does Ayn Rand define "selfishness"? What does Rand mean by the "ethics of altruism"? Do you think Rand's accounts of each are accurate and fair?
2. Do you agree with Rand that "concern with his own interests is the essence of a moral existence, and that man must be the beneficiary of his own moral actions"?
3. What does Rand mean by "rational" self-interest? Outline her account of an "objectivist ethics."

UTILITARIANISM

John Stuart Mill
Chapter II. What Utilitarianism Is

. . . The creed which accepts as the foundation of morals, Utility, or the Greatest Happiness Principle, holds that actions are right in proportion as they tend to promote happiness, wrong as they tend to produce the reverse of happiness. By happiness is intended pleasure, and the absence of pain; by unhappiness, pain, and the privation of pleasure. To give a clear view of the moral standard set up by the theory, much more requires to be said; in particular, what things it includes in the ideas of pain and pleasure; and to what extent this is left an open question. But these supplementary explanations do not affect the theory of life on which this theory of morality is grounded — namely, that pleasure, and freedom from pain, are the only things desirable as ends; and that all desirable things (which are as numerous in the utilitarian as in any other scheme) are desirable either for the pleasure inherent in themselves, or as means to the promotion of pleasure and the prevention of pain.

Now, such a theory of life excites in many minds, and among them in some of the most estimable in feeling and purpose, inveterate dislike. To suppose that life has (as they express it) no higher end than pleasure — no better and nobler object of desire and pursuit — they designate as utterly mean and grovelling; as a doctrine worthy only of swine, to whom the followers of Epicurus were, at a very early period, contemptuously likened; and modern

From Utilitarianism *(1861).*

holders of the doctrine are occasionally made the subject of equally polite comparisons by its German, French, and English assailants.

When thus attacked, the Epicureans have always answered, that it is not they, but their accusers, who represent human nature in a degrading light; since the accusation supposes human beings to be capable of no pleasures except those of which swine are capable. If this supposition were true, the charge could not be gainsaid, but would then be no longer an imputation; for if the sources of pleasure were precisely the same to human beings and to swine, the rule of life which is good enough for the one would be good enough for the other. The comparison of the Epicurean life to that of beasts is felt as degrading, precisely because a beast's pleasures do not satisfy a human being's conceptions of happiness. Human beings have faculties more elevated than the animal appetites, and when once made conscious of them, do not regard anything as happiness which does not include their gratification. I do not, indeed, consider the Epicureans to have been by any means faultless in drawing out their scheme of consequences from the utilitarian principle. To do this in any sufficient manner, many Stoic, as well as Christian elements require to be included. But there is no known Epicurean theory of life which does not assign to the pleasures of the intellect, of the feelings and imagination, and of the moral sentiments, a much higher value as pleasures than to those of mere sensation. It must be admitted, however, that utilitarian writers in general have placed the superiority of mental over bodily pleasures chiefly in the greater permanency, safety, uncostliness, & c., of the former — that is, in their circumstantial advantages rather than in their intrinsic nature. And on all these points utilitarians have fully proved their case; but they might have taken the other, and, as it may be called, higher ground, with entire consistency. It is quite compatible with the principle of utility to recognise the fact, that some *kinds* of pleasure are more desirable and more valuable than others. It would be absurd that while, in estimating all other things, quality is considered as well as quantity, the estimation of pleasures should be supposed to depend on quantity alone.

If I am asked, what I mean by difference of quality in pleasures, or what makes one pleasure more valuable than another, merely as a pleasure, except its being greater in amount, there is but one possible answer. Of two pleasures, if there be one to which all or almost all who have experience of both give a decided preference, irrespective of any feeling of moral obligation to prefer it, that is the more desirable pleasure. If one of the two is, by those who are completely acquainted with both, placed so far above the other that they prefer it, even though knowing it to be attended with a greater amount of discontent, and would not resign it for any quantity of the other pleasure which their nature is capable of, we are justified in ascribing to the preferred enjoyment a superiority in quality, so far outweighing quantity as to render it, in comparison, of small account.

Now it is an unquestionable fact that those who are equally acquainted with, and equally capable of appreciating and enjoying, both, do give a most marked preference to the manner of existence which employs their higher faculties. Few human creatures would consent to be changed into any of the lower animals, for a promise of the fullest allowance of a beast's pleasures; no intelligent human being would consent to be a fool, no instructed person would be an ignoramus, no person of feeling and conscience would be selfish and base, even though they should be persuaded that the fool, the dunce, or the rascal is better satisfied with his lot than they are with theirs. They would not resign what they possess more than he, for the most complete satisfaction of all the desires which they have in common with him. If they ever fancy they would, it is only in cases of unhappiness so extreme, that to escape from it they would exchange their lot for almost any other, however undesirable in their own eyes. A being of higher faculties requires more to make him happy, is capable probably of more acute suffering, and is certainly accessible to it at more points, than one of an inferior type; but in spite of these liabilities, he can never really wish to sink into what he feels to be a lower grade of existence. We may give what explanation we please of this unwillingness; we may attribute it to pride, a name which is given indiscriminately to some of the most and to some of the least estimable feelings of which mankind are capable; we may refer it to the love of liberty and personal independence, an appeal to which was with the Stoics one of the most effective means for the inculcation of it; to the love of power, or to the love of excitement, both of which do really enter into and contribute to it: but its most appropriate appellation is a sense of dignity, which all human beings possess in one form or other, and in some, though by no means in exact, proportion to their higher faculties, and which is so essential a part of the happiness of those in whom it is strong, that nothing which conflicts with it could be, otherwise than momentarily, an object of desire to them. Whoever supposes that this preference takes place at a sacrifice of happiness — that the superior being, in anything like the equal circumstances, is not happier than the inferior — confounds the two very different ideas, of happiness, and content. It is indisputable that the being whose capacities of enjoyment are low, has the greatest chance of having them fully satisfied; and a highly-endowed being will always feel that any happiness which he can look for, as the world is constituted, is imperfect. But he can learn to bear its imperfections, if they are at all bearable; and they will not make him envy the being who is indeed unconscious of the imperfections, but only because he feels not at all the good which those imperfections qualify. It is better to be a human being dissatisfied than a pig satisfied; better to be Socrates dissatisfied than a fool satisfied. And if the fool, or the pig, is of a different opinion, it is because they only know their own side of the question. The other party to the comparison knows both sides.

It may be objected, that many who are capable of the higher pleasures, occasionally, under the influence of temptation, postpone them to the lower. But this is quite compatible with a full appreciation of the intrinsic superiority of the higher. Men often, from infirmity of character, make their election for the nearer good, though they know it to be the less valuable; and this no less when the choice is between two bodily pleasures, than when it is between bodily and mental. They pursue sensual indulgences to the injury of health, though perfectly aware that health is the greater good. It may be further objected, that many who begin with youthful enthusiasm for everything noble, as they advance in years sink into indolence and selfishness. But I do not believe that those who undergo this very common change, voluntarily choose the lower description of pleasures in preference to the higher. I believe that before they devote themselves exclusively to the one, they have already become incapable of the other. Capacity for the nobler feelings is in most natures a very tender plant, easily killed, not only by hostile influences, but by mere want of sustenance; and in the majority of young persons it speedily dies away if the occupations to which their position in life has devoted them, and the society into which it has thrown them, are not favourable to keeping that higher capacity in exercise. Men lose their high aspirations as they lose their intellectual tastes, because they have not time or opportunity for indulging them; and they addict themselves to inferior pleasures, not because they deliberately prefer them, but because they are either the only ones to which they have access, or the only ones which they are any longer capable of enjoying. It may be questioned whether any one who has remained equally susceptible to both classes of pleasures, ever knowingly and calmly preferred the lower, though many, in all ages, have broken down in an ineffectual attempt to combine both.

From this verdict of the only competent judges, I apprehend there can be no appeal. On a question which is the best worth having of two pleasures, or which of two modes of existence is the most grateful to the feelings, apart from its moral attributes and from it consequences, the judgment of those who are qualified by knowledge of both, or, if they differ, that of the majority among them, must be admitted as final. And there needs be the less hesitation to accept this judgment respecting the quality of pleasures, since there is no other tribunal to be referred to even on the question of quantity. What means are there of determining which is the acutest of two pains, or the intensest of two pleasurable sensations, except the general suffrage of those who are familiar with both? Neither pains nor pleasures are homogeneous, and pain is always heterogeneous with pleasure. What is there to decide whether a particular pleasure is worth purchasing at the cost of a particular pain, except the feelings and judgment of the experienced? When, therefore, those feelings and judgment declare the pleasures derived from the higher faculties to be preferable *in kind*, apart from the question of intensity, to those of which the animal nature, disjoined from the higher faculties, is susceptible, they are entitled on this subject to the same regard.

I have dwelt on this point, as being a necessary part of a perfectly just conception of Utility or Happiness, considered as the directive rule of human conduct. But it is by no means an indispensable condition to the acceptance of the utilitarian standard; for that standard is not the agent's own greatest happiness, but the greatest amount of happiness altogether; and if it may possibly be doubted whether a noble character is always the happier for its nobleness, there can be no doubt that it makes other people happier, and that the world in general is immensely a gainer by it. Utilitarianism, therefore, could only attain its end by the general cultivation of nobleness of character, even if each individual were only benefitted by the nobleness of others, and his own, so far as happiness is concerned, were a sheer deduction from the benefit. But the bare enunciation of such an absurdity as this last, renders refutation superfluous.

According to the Greatest Happiness Principle, as above explained, the ultimate end, with reference to and for the sake of which all other things are desirable (whether we are considering our own good or that of other people), is an existence exempt as far as possible from pain, and as rich as possible in enjoyments, both in point of quantity and quality; the test of quality, and the rule for measuring it against quantity, being the preference felt by those who, in their opportunities of experience, to which must be added their habits of self-consciousness and self-observation, are best furnished with the means of comparison. This, being, according to the utilitarian opinion, the end of human action, is necessarily also the standard of morality; which may accordingly be defined, the rules and precepts for human conduct, by the observance of which an existence such as has been described might be, to the greatest extent possible, secured to all mankind; and not to them only, but, so far as the nature of things admits, to the whole sentient creation. . . .

I must again repeat, what the assailants of utilitarianism seldom have the justice to acknowledge, that the happiness which forms the Utilitarian standard of what is right in conduct, is not the agent's own happiness, but that of all concerned. As between his own happiness and that of others, utilitarianism requires him to be as strictly impartial as a disinterested and benevolent spectator. In the golden rule of Jesus of Nazareth, we read the complete spirit of the ethics of utility. To do as one would be done by, and to love one's neighbour as oneself, constitute the ideal perfection of utilitarian morality. As the means of making the nearest approach to this ideal, utility would enjoin, first, that laws and social arrangements should place the happiness, or (as speaking practically it may be called) the interest, of every individual, as nearly as possible in harmony with the interest of the whole; and secondly, that education and opinion, which have so vast a power over human character, should so use that power as to establish in the mind of every individual an indissoluble association between his own happiness and the good of the whole; especially between his own happiness and the practice of such modes of conduct, negative and positive, as regard for the universal happiness prescribes: so that not only he may be unable to conceive the possibility of happiness to himself, consistently with conduct opposed to the general good, but also that a direct impulse to promote the general good may be in every individual one of the habitual motives of action, and the sentiments connected therewith may fill a large and prominent place in every human being's sentient existence. If the impugners of the utilitarian morality represented it to their own minds in this its true character, I know not what recommendation possessed by any other morality they could possibly affirm to be wanting to it: what more beautiful or more exalted developments of human nature any other ethical system can be supposed to foster, or what springs of action, not accessible to the utilitarian, such systems rely on for giving effect to their mandates.

. . . .

Chapter IV. Of What Sort of Proof the Principle of Utility Is Susceptible

It has already been remarked, that questions of ultimate ends do not admit of proof, in the ordinary acceptation of the term. To be incapable of proof by reasoning is common to all first principles; to the first premises of our knowledge, as well as to those of our conduct. But the former, being matters of fact, may be the subject of a direct appeal to the faculties which judge of fact — namely, our senses, and our internal consciousness. Can an appeal be made to the same faculties on questions of practical ends? Or by what other faculty is cognizance taken of them?

Questions about ends are, in other words, questions about what things are desirable. The utilitarian doctrine is, that happiness is desirable, and the only thing desirable, as an end; all other things being only desirable as means to that end. What ought to be required of this doctrine — what conditions is it requisite that the doctrine should fulfil — to make good its claim to be believed?

The only proof capable of being given that an object is visible, is that people actually see it. The only proof that a sound is audible, is that people hear it: and so of the other sources of our experience. In like manner, I apprehend, the sole evidence it is possible to produce that anything is desirable, is that people do actually desire it. If the end which the utilitarian doctrine proposes to itself were not, in theory and in practice, acknowledged to be an end, nothing could ever convince any person that it was so. No reason can be given why the general happiness is desirable, except that each person, so far as he believes it to be attainable, desires his own happiness. This, however, being a fact, we have not only all the proof which the case admits of, but all which it is possible to require, that happiness is a good: that each person's happiness is a good to that person, and the general happiness, therefore, a good to the aggregate of all persons. Happiness has made out its title as *one* of the ends of conduct, and consequently one of the criteria of morality.

But it has not, by this alone, proved itself to be the sole criterion. To do that, it would seem, by the same rule, necessary to show, not only that people desire happiness, but that they never desire anything else. Now it is palpable that they do desire things which, in common language, are decidedly distinguished from happiness. They desire, for example, virtue, and the absence of vice, no less really than pleasure and the absence of pain. The desire of virtue is not as universal, but it is as authentic a fact, as the desire of happiness. And hence the opponents of the utilitarian standard deem that they have a right to infer that there are other ends of human action besides happiness, and that happiness is not the standard of approbation and disapprobation.

But does the utilitarian doctrine deny that people desire virtue, or maintain that virtue is not a thing to be desired? The very reverse. It maintains not only that virtue is to be desired, but that it is to be desired disinterestedly, for itself. Whatever may be the opinion of utilitarian moralists as to the original conditions by which virtue is made virtue; however they may believe (as they do) that actions and dispositions are only virtuous because they promote another end than virtue; yet this being granted, and it having been decided, from considerations of this description, what *is* virtuous, they not only place virtue at the very head of the things which are good as means to the ultimate end, but they also recognise as a psychological fact the possibility of its being, to the individual, a good in itself, without looking to any end beyond it; and hold, that the mind is not in a right state, not in a state comfortable to Utility, not in the state most conducive to the general happiness, unless it does love virtue in this manner — as a thing desirable in itself, even although, in the individual instance, it should not produce those other desirable consequences which it tends to produce, and on account of which it is held to be virtue. This opinion is not, in the smallest degree, a departure from the Happiness principle. The ingredients of happiness are very various, and each of them is desirable in itself, and not merely when considered as swelling an aggregate. The principle of utility does not mean that any given pleasure, as music, for instance, or any given exemption from pain, as for example health, are to be looked upon as a means to a collective something termed happiness, and to be desired on that account. They are desired and desirable in and for themselves; besides being means, they are a part of the end. Virtue, according to the utilitarian doctrine, is not naturally and originally part of the end, but it is capable of becoming so; and in those who love it disinterestedly it has become so, and is desired and cherished, not as a means to happiness, but as a part of their happiness.

To illustrate this farther, we may remember that virtue is not the only thing, originally a means, and which if it were not a means to anything else, would be and remain indifferent, but which by association with what it is a means to, comes to be desired for itself, and that too with the utmost intensity. What, for example, shall we say of the love of money? There is nothing originally more desirable about money than about any heap of glittering pebbles. Its worth is solely that of the things which it will buy; the desires for other things than itself, which it is a means of gratifying. Yet the love of money is not only one of the strongest moving forces of human life, but money is, in many cases, desired in and for itself; the desire to possess it is often stronger than the desire to use it, and goes on increasing when all the desires which point to ends beyond it, to be encompassed by it, are falling off. It may be then said truly, that money is desired not for the sake of an end, but as part of the end. From being a means to happiness, it has come to be itself a principal ingredient of the individual's conception of happiness. The same may be said of the majority of the great objects of human life — power, for example, or fame; except that to each of these there is a certain amount of immediate pleasure annexed, which has at least the semblance of being naturally inherent in them; a thing which cannot be said of money. Still, however, the strongest natural attraction, both of power and of fame, is the immense aid they give to the attainment of our other wishes; and it is the strong association thus generated between them and all our objects of desire, which gives to the direct desire of them the intensity it often assumes, so as in some characters to surpass in strength all other desires. In these cases the means have become a part of the end, and a more important part of it than any of the things which they are means to. What was once desired as an instrument for the attainment of happiness, has come to be desired for its own sake. In being desired for its own sake it is, however, desired as *part* of happiness. The person is made, or thinks he would be made, happy by its mere possession; and is made unhappy by failure to obtain it. The desire of it is not a different thing from the desire of happiness, any more than the love of music, or the desire of health. They are included in happiness. They are some of the elements of which the desire of happiness is made up. Happiness is not an abstract idea, but a concrete whole; and these are some of its parts. And the utilitarian standard sanctions and approves their being so. Life would be a poor thing, very ill provided with sources of happiness, if there were not this provision of nature, by which things originally indifferent, but conducive to, or otherwise associated with, the satisfaction of our primitive desires, become in themselves sources of pleasure more valuable than the primitive pleasures, both in permanency, in the space of human existence that they are capable of covering, and even in intensity.

Virtue, according to the utilitarian conception, is a good of this description. There was no original desire of it, or motive to it, save its conduciveness to pleasure, and especially to protection from pain. But through the association thus formed, it may be felt a good in itself, and desired as such with as great intensity as any other good; and with this difference between it and the love of money, of power, or of fame, that all of these may, and often do, render the individual noxious to the other members of the society to which he belongs, whereas there is nothing which makes him so much a blessing to them as the cultivation of the disinterested love of virtue. And consequently, the utilitarian standard, while it tolerates and approves those other acquired desires, up to the point beyond which they would be more injurious to the general happiness than promotive of it, enjoins and requires the cultivation of the love of virtue up to the greatest strength possible, as being above all things important to the general happiness.

It results from the preceding considerations, that there is in reality nothing desired except happiness. Whatever is desired otherwise than as a means to some end beyond itself, and ultimately to happiness, is desired as itself part of happiness, and is not desired for itself until it has become so.

QUESTIONS

1. How does John Stuart Mill's claim that "pleasure, and freedom from pain, are the only things desirable as ends" differ from Rand's statement that the ground for morality is rational self-interest?
2. What is the Utilitarian formula for determining morally right action and how does this differ from Rand's account of morality?
3. What does Mill mean when he says that "it is better to be a human being dissatisfied than a pig satisfied; better to be Socrates dissatisfied than a fool satisfied"?
4. What is the Greatest Happiness Principle? Do you think that a theory of morality should be based on a calculation of happiness?

➡ ⬅

RELATIVISM

David Wong

i Introduction

Moral relativism is a common response to the deepest conflicts we face in our ethical lives. Some of these conflicts are quite public and political, such as the apparently intractable disagreement in the United States over the moral and legal permissibility of abortion. Other conflicts inviting the relativistic response are of a less dramatic but more recurrent nature. This author's experience as a first-generation Chinese American exemplifies a kind of conflict that others have faced: that between inherited values and the values of the adopted country. As a child I had to grapple with the differences between what was expected of me as a good Chinese son and what was expected of my non-Chinese friends. Not only did they seem bound by duties that were much less rigorous in the matter of honouring parents and upholding the family name, but I was supposed to feel superior to them because of that. It added to my confusion that I sometimes felt envy at their freedom.

Moral relativism, as a common response to such conflicts, often takes the form of a denial that any single moral code has universal validity, and an assertion that moral truth and justifiability, if there are any such things, are in some way relative to factors that are culturally and historically contingent. This doctrine is *meta-ethical* relativism, because it is about the relativity of moral truth and justifiability. Another kind of moral relativism, also a common response to deep moral conflict, is a doctrine about how one ought to act toward those who accept values very different from one's own. This *normative* moral relativism holds that it is wrong to pass judgement on others who have substantially different values, or to try to make them conform to one's values, for the reason that their values are as valid as one's own. Another common response to deep moral conflict, however, contradicts moral relativism in its two major forms. It is the universalist or absolutist position that both sides of a moral conflict cannot be equally right, that there can be only one truth about the matter at issue. This position is so common, in fact, that William James was led to call us 'absolutists by instinct' (James, 1948). The term 'universalism' will be used hereafter, because 'absolutism' is used not only to refer to the denial of moral relativism, but also to the view that some moral rules or duties are absolutely without exception.

ii Meta-Ethical Relativism

The debate between moral relativism and universalism accounts for a significant proportion of philosophical reflection in ethics. In ancient Greece at least some of the 'Sophists' defended a version of moral relativism, which Plato attempted to refute. Plato attributes to the first great Sophist, Protagoras, the argument that human custom determines what is fine and ugly, just and unjust. Whatever is communally judged to be the case, the argument goes, actually comes to be the case (*Theaetetus*, 172ab; it is unclear, however, whether the real Protagoras actually argued in this manner). Now the Greeks, through trade, travel, and war, were fully aware of wide variation in customs, and so the argument concludes with the

From A Companion to Ethics, *edited by Peter Singer. From the Blackwell Companions to Philosophy. Oxford: Basil Blackwell Publishers, 1993. Reprinted by permission of Basil Blackwell Publishers.*

relativity of morality. The question with this argument, however, is whether we can accept that custom determines in a strong sense what is fine and ugly, just and unjust. It may influence what people *think* is fine and just. But it is quite another thing for custom to determine what is fine and just. Customs sometimes change under the pressure of moral criticism, and the argument seems to rely on a premise that contradicts this phenomenon.

Another kind of argument given for relativism is premised on the view that the customary ethical beliefs in any given society are functionally necessary for that society. Therefore, the argument concludes, the beliefs are true for that society, but not necessarily in another. The sixteenth-century essayist, Michel de Montaigne, sometimes makes this argument ('Of custom, and not easily changing an accepted law', in Montaigne, 1595), but it has had its greatest acceptance among anthropologists of the twentieth century who emphasize the importance of studying societies as organic wholes of which the parts are functionally interdependent. The problem with the functional argument, however, is that moral beliefs are not justified merely on the grounds that they are necessary for a society's existence in anything like its present form. Even if a society's institutions and practices crucially depend on the acceptance of certain beliefs, the justifiability of those beliefs depends on the moral acceptability of the institutions and practices. To show that certain beliefs are necessary for maintaining a fascist society, for instance, is not to justify those beliefs.

Despite the weaknesses of these arguments for moral relativism, the doctrine has always had its adherents. Its continuing strength has always been rooted in the impressiveness of the variation in ethical belief to be found across human history and culture. In an ancient text (*Dissoi Logoi* or the *Contrasting Arguments*; Robinson, 1979) associated with the Sophists, it is pointed out that for the Lacedaemonians, it was fine for girls to exercise without tunics, and for children not to learn music and letters, while for the Ionians, these things were foul. Montaigne assembled a catalogue of exotic customs, such as male prostitution, cannibalism, women warriors, killing one's father at a certain age as an act of piety, and recites from the Greek historian Herodotus the experiment of Darius. Darius asked Greeks how much they would have to be paid before they would eat the bodies of their deceased fathers. They replied that no sum of money could get them to do such a thing. He then asked certain Indians who customarily ate the bodies of their deceased fathers what they would have to be paid to burn the bodies of their fathers. Amidst loud exclamations, they bade him not to speak of such a thing (Montaigne's 'Of custom' (1595), and Herodotus, *Persian Wars*, Book III, 38).

But while many have been moved by such examples to adopt moral relativism, the argument from diversity does not support relativism in any simple or direct way. As the Socrates of Plato's dialogues observed, we have reason to listen only to the wise among us (*Crito*, 44cd). The simple fact of diversity in belief is no disproof of the possibility that there are some beliefs better to have than the others because they are truer or more justified than the rest. If half the world still believed that the sun, the moon, and the planets revolved around the earth, that would be no disproof of the possibility of a unique truth about the structure of the universe. Diversity in belief, after all, may result from varying degrees of wisdom. Or it may be that different people have their own limited perspectives of the truth, each perspective being distorted in its own way.

It is sometimes thought that the extent and depth of disagreement in ethics indicates that moral judgements are simply not judgements about facts, that they assert nothing true or false about the world but straightforwardly express our own subjective reactions to certain facts and happenings, whether these be collective or individual reactions (e.g. see C. L. Stevenson, *Ethics and Language* 1944). A more complicated view is that moral judgements purport to report objective matters of fact, but that there are no such matters of fact (see J. L. Mackie, *Ethics: Inventing Right and Wrong*, 1977). The success of modern science in producing a remarkable degree of convergence of belief about the basic structure of the physical world probably reinforces these varieties of scepticism about the objectivity of moral judgements. It is hard to deny that there is a significant difference in the degree of convergence of belief in ethics and in science. Yet there are possible explanations for that difference that are compatible with claiming that moral judgements are ultimately about facts in the world. These explanations might stress, for instance, the special difficulties of acquiring knowledge of subjects that pertain to moral knowledge.

An understanding of human nature and human affairs is necessary for formulating an adequate moral code. The enormously difficult and complex task of reaching such an understanding could be a major reason for differences in moral belief. Furthermore, the subject matter of ethics is such that people have the most intense practical interest in what is established as truth about it, and surely this interest engenders the passions that becloud judgement (for a reply in this spirit see Nagel, 1986, pp. 185–88). Universalists could point out that many apparently exotic moral beliefs presuppose certain religious and metaphysical beliefs, and that these beliefs, rather than any difference in fundamental values, explain the apparent strangeness. Consider, for example, the way our view of Darius' Indians would change if we were to attribute to them the belief that eating the body of one's deceased father is a way of preserving his spiritual substance. Finally, some of the striking differences in moral belief across societies may not be rooted in differences in fundamental values but in the fact that these values may have to be implemented in different ways given the varying conditions that obtain across societies. If one society contains many more women than men (say, because men are killing each other off in warfare), it would not be surprising if polygamy were acceptable there, while in another society, where the proportion of women to men is equal, monogamy is required. The difference in accepted marriage practice may come down to that difference in the proportion of women to men, and not to any difference in basic moral ideals of marriage or of the proper relationships between women and men.

The mere existence of deep and wide disagreements in ethics, therefore, does not disprove the possibility that moral judgements can be objectively correct or incorrect judgements about certain facts. Moral relativists must chart some other more complicated path from the existence of diversity to the conclusion that there is no single true or most justified morality. I believe (and have argued, in *Moral Relativity*, 1984) that the relativist argument is best conducted by pointing to particular kinds of differences in moral belief, and then by claiming that these particular differences are best explained under a theory that denies the existence of a single true morality. This would involve denying that the various ways that universalists have for explaining ethical disagreement are sufficient for explaining the particular differences in question. (For another strategy of argument that relies more on an analysis of the meaning of moral judgements, see Harman, 1975.)

One apparent and striking ethical difference that would be a good candidate for this sort of argument concerns the emphasis on individual rights that is embodied in the ethical culture of the modern West and that seems absent in traditional cultures found in Africa, China, Japan and India. The content of duties in such traditional cultures instead seems organized around the central value of a common good that consists in a certain sort of ideal community life, a network of relationships, partially defined by social roles, again, ideal, but imperfectly embodied in ongoing existing practice. The ideal for members is composed of various virtues that enable them, given their place in the network of relationships, to promote and sustain the common good.

Confucianism, for instance, makes the family and kinship groups the models for the common good, with larger social and political units taking on certain of their features, such as benevolent leaders who rule with the aim of cultivating virtue and harmony among their subjects. Moralities centred on such values would seem to differ significantly from ones centred on individual rights to liberty and to other goods, if the basis for attributing such rights to persons does not seem to lie in their conduciveness to the common good of a shared life, but in a moral worth independently attributed to each individual. By contrast a theme frequently found in ethics of the common good is that individuals find their realization as human beings in promoting and sustaining the common good. Given this assumption of the fundamental harmony between the highest good of individuals and the common good, one might expect the constraints on freedom to have greater scope and to be more pervasive when compared to a tradition in which no such fundamental harmony between individual and common goods is assumed.

If the contrast between the two types of morality is real, it raises the question of whether one or the other type is truer or more justified than the other. The argument for a relativistic answer may start with the claim that each type focuses on a good that may reasonably occupy the centre of an ethical ideal for human life. On the one hand, there is the good of belonging to and contributing to a community; on the other, there is the good of respect for the individual apart from any potential contribution to community. It would be surprising, the argument goes, if there were just one justifiable way of setting a priority with respect to the two goods. It should not be surprising, after all, if the range of human goods is simply too rich and diverse to be reconciled in just a single moral ideal.

Such an argument could be supplemented by an explanation of why human beings have such a thing as a morality. Morality serves two universal human needs. It regulates conflicts of interest between people, and it regulates conflicts of interest within the individual born of different desires and drives that cannot all be satisfied at the same time. Ways of dealing with those two kinds of conflict develop in anything recognizable as human society. To the extent that these ways crystallize in the form of rules for conduct and ideals for persons, we have the core of a morality. Now in order to perform its practical functions adequately, it may be that a morality will have to possess certain general features. A relatively enduring and stable system for the resolution of conflict between people, for instance, will not permit the torture of persons at whim.

But given this picture of the origin and functions of morality, it would not be surprising if significantly different moralities were to perform the practical functions equally well, at least according to standards of performance that were common to these moralities. Moralities, on this picture, are social creations that evolve to meet certain needs. The needs place conditions on what could be an adequate morality, and if human nature has a definite structure, one would expect further constraining conditions on an adequate morality to derive from our nature. But the complexity of our nature makes it possible for us to prize a variety of goods and to order them in different ways, and this opens the way for a substantial relativism to be true.

The picture sketched above has the advantage of leaving it open as to how strong a version of relativism is true. That is, it holds that there is no single true morality, yet does not deny that some moralities might be false and inadequate for the functions they all must perform. Almost all polemics against moral relativism are directed at its most extreme versions: those holding that all moralities are equally true (or equally false, or equally lacking in cognitive content). Yet a substantial relativism need not be so radically egalitarian. Besides ruling out moralities that would aggravate interpersonal conflict, such as the one described above, relativists could also recognize that adequate moralities must promote the production of persons capable of considering the interests of others. Such persons would need to have received a certain kind of nurturing and care from others. An adequate morality, then, whatever else its content, would have to prescribe and promote the sorts of upbringing and continuing interpersonal relationships that produce such persons.

A moral relativism that would allow for this kind of constraint on what could be a true or most justified morality might not fit the stereotype of relativism, but would be a reasonable position to hold. One reason, in fact, that not much progress has been made in the debate between relativists and universalists is that each side has tended to define the opponent as holding the most extreme position possible. While this makes the debating easier, it does nothing to shed light on the vast middle ground where the truth indeed may lie. Many of the same conclusions could be drawn about the debate over normative moral relativism: much heat, and frequent identification of the opponent with the most extreme position possible.

iii Normative Relativism

The most extreme possible position for the normative relativist is that no-one should ever pass judgement on others with substantially different values, or try to make them conform to one's own values. Such a definition of normative relativism is usually given by its opponents, because it is an indefensible position. It requires self-condemnation by those who act according to it. If I pass judgement on those who pass judgement, I must condemn myself. I am trying to impose a value of tolerance on everyone, when not everyone has that value, but this is not what I am supposed to be doing under the most extreme version of normative relativism. Philosophers are usually content with such easy dismissals of the most extreme version of normative relativism, but there is reason to consider whether more moderate versions might be more tenable. The reason is that normative relativism is not just a philosophical doctrine but a stance adopted toward morally troubling situations.

Anthropologists are sometimes identified with this stance, and it is instructive to understand how this identification emerged from a historical and sociological context. The birth of cultural anthropology in the late nineteenth century was in part subsidized by colonizing governments needing to know more about the nature and status of 'primitive' peoples. Influenced by Darwinian theory, early anthropological theory tended to arrange the peoples and social institutions of the world in an evolutionary series, from primordial man to the civilized human being of nineteenth-century Europe. Many anthropologists eventually reacted against the imperialism of their governments and to its rationalization supplied by their predecessors. More importantly, they came to see the peoples they studied as intelligent men and women whose lives had meaning and integrity. And this led to questioning the basis for implicit judgements of the inferiority of their ways of life, especially after the spectacle of the civilized nations in brutal struggle with one another in the First World War (see, for example, Ruth Benedict, *Patterns of Culture*, 1934, and more recently, Melville Herskovits, *Cultural Relativism: Perspectives in Cultural Pluralism*, 1972).

The normative relativism of some of the anthropologists of that period, then, was a response to real moral problems concerning the justifiability of colonization and more generally concerning intervention in another society so as to cause major changes in previously accepted values or in people's ability to act on those values. No simple version of normative relativism is the answer to these problems, as was illustrated by the fact that an ethic of non-judgemental tolerance would self-destruct when used to condemn the intolerant. The inadequacy of the simple versions also is illustrated by the swing in anthropology on the question of normative relativism after the Second World War. That war, many realized, was a battle against enormous evil. Such a realization brought vividly to the forefront the necessity of passing judgement at least sometimes and of acting on one's judgement. And accordingly there was a new trend within cultural anthropology toward finding a basis for making judgements that would depend on criteria to be applied to all moral codes.

A more reasonable version of normative relativism would have to permit us to pass judgement on others with substantially different values. Even if these different values are as justified as our own from some neutral perspective, we still are entitled to call bad or evil or monstrous what contradicts our most important values. What we are entitled to do in the light of such judgements, however, is another matter. Many of us who are likely to read this book would be reluctant to intervene in the affairs of others who have values substantially different from ours, when the reason for intervention is the enforcement of our own values, and, when we think that we have no more of an objective case for our moral outlook than the others have for theirs. The source of this reluctance is a feature of our morality. A liberal, contractualist outlook is very much part of our ethical life in the postmodern West, whether we acknowledge it or not. We want to act toward others in such a way that our actions could be seen as justified by them if they were fully reasonable and informed of all relevant facts. If we hold a meta-ethical moral relativism, however, then we must recognize that there will be occasions when some otherwise desirable course of action toward others with different values will violate this feature of our morality.

At that point, there is no general rule that will tell us what to do. It would seem to depend on what other values of ours are at stake. If a practice performed by others were to involve human sacrifice, for example, then the value of tolerance might indeed be outweighed, and we may decide to intervene to prevent it. The disagreement over the legal permissibility of abortion demonstrates how difficult the weighing can be, however. Consider the position of those who believe that abortion is morally wrong because it is the taking of life that has moral status. Within this group some seem undisturbed by the fact that there is deep disagreement over the moral status of the fetus. They wish to prohibit abortion. But others in this group, while holding that abortion is wrong, admit that reasonable persons could disagree with them and that human reason seems unable to resolve the question. For this reason they oppose legal prohibitions of abortion. The former believe that the latter do not take the value of human life seriously, while the latter believe that the former fail to recognize the depth and seriousness of the disagreement between reasonable persons.

Each position has some force, and clearly normative relativism offers no simple solution to the dilemma. What the doctrine provides, however, is a set of reasons for tolerance and non-intervention that must be weighed against other reasons. The doctrine applies not only to proposed interventions by one society in another, but also, as in the case of abortion, to deep moral disagreements within pluralistic societies containing diverse moral traditions. If meta-ethical relativism is true, even if only with respect to a limited set of moral conflicts such as abortion, then our moral condition is immeasurably complicated. We must strive to find what will be for us the right or the best thing to do, and also deal with the feelings of unease caused by the recognition that there is no single right or best thing to do. This task, no matter how difficult, is not the end of moral reflection. It instead may be the beginning of a different sort of reflection that involves on the one hand an effort to reach an understanding with those who have substantially different values, and on the other the effort to stay true to one's own values. Some of those who believe that abortion is the taking of a life with moral status, for instance, have chosen to oppose it by placing their efforts into organizations that aim to lessen the perceived need for abortion, organizations that aid unwed mothers, for example.

One final issue regarding relativism needs addressing. Relativism has a bad name in some quarters because it is associated with a lack of moral conviction, with a tendency toward nihilism. Part of the reason for the bad name may be the identification of relativism with its most extreme forms. If these forms are true, then everything is permitted, on someone's morality. But another reason for the bad name is the assumption that one's moral confidence, one's commitment to act on one's values, is somehow dependent on maintaining the belief that one's morality is the only true or the most justified one. But surely some reflection will reveal that such a belief alone would not guarantee a commitment to act. The commitment to act involves a conception of what one's morality means to the self, whether it be the only true one or not. It involves making a connection between what one desires, what one aspires to, and the substantive content of one's moral values. It is being able to see morality as important to us in these ways that allows us to avoid nihilism. The belief that our morality is the only true or most justified one does not automatically create this kind of importance, nor is it a necessary condition for this kind of importance, because the values I may see as important and part of what makes life most meaningful to me may not have to be values that all reasonable persons would accept or recognize to be true.

Here, as in other matters concerning relativism, the emotion provoked by the mere name tends to muddle the issues and to polarize unnecessarily. When we get through defending and attacking what most people conceive as relativism or what they associate with it, then most of the real work remains to be done. What is left is a moral reality that is quite messy and immune to neat solutions. But why should we have expected anything else?

REFERENCES

Benedict, R.: *Patterns of Culture* (New York: Penguin, 1934).

Harman, G.: 'Moral relativism defended', *Philosophical Review* 84 (1975), 3–22.

Herodotus: *The Persian Wars*, trans. George Rawlinson (New York: Modern Library, 1942).

Herskovits. M.: *Cultural Relativism: Perspectives in Cultural Pluralism* (New York: Vintage, 1972).

James, W.: 'The will to believe', *Essays in Pragmatism*, ed. Aubrey Castell (New York: Hafner, 1948).

Mackie, J.L.: *Ethics: Inventing Right and Wrong* (Harmondsworth: Penguin, 1977).

Montaigne, M. de: *Complete Essays* (1595); trans. Donald M. Frame (Stanford: Stanford University Press, 1973).

Nagel, T.: *The View from Nowhere* (New York: Oxford University Press, 1986).

Plato: *Crito* and *Theaetetus*; trans. E. Hamilton and H. Cairns, *Collected Dialogues of Plato* (Princeton: Princeton University Press, 1961).

Robinson, T. M., trans.: *Contrasting Arguments: an edition of the Dissoi Logoi* (New York: Arno Press, 1979).

Stevenson, C. L.: *Ethics and Language* (New Haven: Yale University Press, 1944).

Wong, D. B.: *Moral Relativity* (Berkeley: University of California Press, 1984).

QUESTIONS

1. What does David Wong mean by the term "meta-ethical" relativism?
2. Do you think that an appropriate response to conflicts and disagreements about morality is to conclude that moral truth and justifiability are "relative to factors that are culturally and historically contingent"?
3. What is the distinction drawn by Wong between "normative" moral relativism and universalism?
4. According to Wong, what prompted the development of normative relativism? What reasons does Wong provide for rejecting the most extreme version of normative relativism?
5. Do you think that Wong's account of a "more reasonable version of normative relativism" addresses the concerns he himself raises about relativism as a theory about morality?

THE NEED FOR MORE THAN JUSTICE

Annette C. Baier

In recent decades in North American social and moral philosophy, alongside the development and discussion of widely influential theories of justice, taken as Rawls takes it as the 'first virtue of social institutions,'[1] there has been a counter-movement gathering strength, one coming from some interesting sources. For some of the most outspoken of the diverse group who have in a variety of ways been challenging the assumed supremacy of justice among the moral and social virtues are members of those sections of society whom one might have expected to be especially aware of the supreme importance of justice, namely blacks and women. Those who have only recently won recognition of their equal rights, who have only recently seen the correction or partial correction of longstanding racist and sexist injustices to their race and sex, are among the philosophers now suggesting that justice is only one virtue among many, and one that may need the presence of the others in order to deliver its own undenied value. Among these philosophers of the philosophical counterculture, as it were — but an increasingly large counterculture — I include Alasdair MacIntyre,[2] Michael Stocker,[3] Lawrence Blum,[4] Michael Slote,[5] Laurence Thomas,[6] Claudia Card,[7] Alison Jaggar,[8] Susan Wolf[9] and a whole group of men and women, myself included,

From the Canadian Journal of Philosophy, *Supplementary Vol. 13, 1987, pp. 41–56. Published by the University of Calgary Press. Reprinted by permission of* Canadian Journal of Philosophy *and Annette C. Baier.*

who have been influenced by the writings of Harvard educational psychologist Carol Gilligan, whose book *In a Different Voice* (Harvard 1982; hereafter D.V.) caused a considerable stir both in the popular press and, more slowly, in the philosophical journals.[10]

Let me say quite clearly at this early point that there is little disagreement that justice is a social value of very great importance, and injustice an evil. Nor would those who have worked on theories of justice want to deny that other things matter besides justice. Rawls, for example, incorporates the value of freedom into his account of justice, so that denial of basic freedoms counts as injustice. Rawls also leaves room for a wider theory of the right, of which the theory of justice is just a part. Still, he does claim that justice is the 'first' virtue of social institutions, and it is only that claim about priority that I think has been challenged. It is easy to exaggerate the differences of view that exist, and I want to avoid that. The differences are as much in emphasis as in substance, or we can say that they are differences in tone of voice. But these differences do tend to make a difference in approaches to a wide range of topics not just in moral theory but in areas like medical ethics, where the discussion used to be conducted in terms of patients' rights, of informed consent, and so on, but now tends to get conducted in an enlarged moral vocabulary, which draws on what Gilligan calls the ethics of *care* as well as that of *justice*.

For 'care' is the new buzz-word. It is not, as Shakespeare's Portia demanded, mercy that is to season justice, but a less authoritarian humanitarian supplement, a felt concern for the good of others and for community with them. The 'cold jealous virtue of justice' (Hume) is found to be too cold, and it is 'warmer' more communitarian virtues and social ideals that are being called in to supplement it. One might say that liberty and equality are being found inadequate without fraternity, except that 'fraternity' will be quite the wrong word, if as Gilligan initially suggested, it is *women* who perceive this value most easily. ('Sorority' will do no better, since it is too exclusive, and English has no gender-neuter word for the mutual concern of siblings.) She has since modified this claim, allowing that there are two perspectives on moral and social issues that we all tend to alternate between, and which are not always easy to combine, one of them what she called the justice perspective, the other the care perspective. It is increasingly obvious that there are many male philosophical spokespersons for the care perspective (Laurence Thomas, Lawrence Blum, Michael Stocker) so that it cannot be the prerogative of women. Nevertheless Gilligan still wants to claim that women are most unlikely to take *only* the justice perspective, as some men are claimed to, at least until some mid-life crisis jolts them into 'bifocal' moral vision (see D.V., ch. 6).

Gilligan in her book did not offer any explanatory theory of why there should be any difference between female and male moral outlook, but she did tend to link the naturalness to women of the care perspective with their role as primary care-takers of young children, that is with their parental and specifically maternal role. She avoided the question of whether it is their biological or their social parental role that is relevant, and some of those who dislike her book are worried precisely by this uncertainty. Some find it retrograde to hail as a special sort of moral wisdom an outlook that may be the product of the socially enforced restriction of women to domestic roles (and the reservation of such roles for them alone). For that might seem to play into the hands of those who still favor such restriction. (Marxists, presumably, will not find it so surprising that moral truths might depend for their initial clear voicing on the social oppression, and memory of it, of those who voice the truths.) Gilligan did in the first chapter of D.V. cite the theory of Nancy Chodorow (as presented in *The Reproduction of Mothering* [Berkeley 1978]) which traces what appears as gender differences in personality to early social development, in particular to the effects of the child's primary caretaker being or not being of the same gender as the child. Later, both in 'The Conquistador and the Dark Continent: Reflections on the Nature of Love' (*Daedalus* [Summer 1984]), and 'The Origins of Morality in Early Childhood' (in press), she develops this explanation. She postulates two evils that any infant may become aware of, the evil of detachment or isolation from others whose love one needs, and the evil of relative power-lessness and weakness. Two dimensions of moral development are thereby set — one aimed at achieving satisfying community with others, the other aiming at autonomy or equality of power. The relative predominance of one over the other development will depend both upon the relative salience of the two evils in early childhood, and on early and later reinforce-ment or discouragement in attempts made to guard against these two evils. This provides the germs of a theory about *why*, given current customs of childrearing, it should be mainly women who are not content with only the moral outlook that she calls the justice perspec-tive, necessary though that was and is seen by them to have been to their hard won liberation from sexist oppression. They, like the blacks, used the language of rights and justice to change their own social position, but nevertheless see limitations in that language, according to Gilligan's findings as a moral psychologist. She reports their discontent with the individualist more or less Kantian moral framework that dominates Western moral theory and which influenced moral psychologists such as Lawrence Kohlberg,[11] to whose conception of moral maturity she seeks an alternative. Since the target of Gilligan's criti-cism is the dominant Kantian tradition, and since that has been the target also of moral philosophers as diverse in their own views as Bernard Williams,[12] Alasdair MacIntyre, Philippa Foot,[13] Susan Wolf, Claudia Card, her book is of interest as much for its attempt to articulate an alternative to the Kantian justice perspective as for its implicit raising of the question of male bias in Western moral theory, especially liberal-democratic theory. For whether the supposed blind spots of that outlook are due to male bias, or to non-parental bias, or to early traumas of powerlessness or to early resignation to 'detachment' from others, we need first to be persuaded that they *are* blind spots before we will have any interest in their cause and cure. Is justice blind to important social values, or at least only one-eyed? What is it that comes into view from the 'care perspective' that is not seen from the 'justice perspective'?

Gilligan's position here is most easily described by contrasting it with that of Kohlberg, against which she developed it. Kohlberg, influenced by Piaget and the Kantian philo-sophical tradition as developed by John Rawls, developed a theory about typical moral development which saw it to progress from a pre-conventional level, where what is seen to matter is pleasing or not offending parental authority-figures, through a conventional level in which the child tries to fit in with a group, such as a school community, and conform to its standards and rules, to a post-conventional critical level, in which such conventional rules are subjected to tests, and where those tests are of a Utilitarian, or, eventually, a Kantian sort — namely ones that require respect for each person's individual rational will, or autonomy, and conformity to any implicit social contract such wills are deemed to have made, or to any hypothetical ones they would make if thinking clearly. What was found when Kohlberg's questionnaires (mostly by verbal response to verbally sketched moral dilemmas) were applied to female as well as male subjects, Gilligan reports, is that the girls and women not only scored generally lower than the boys and men, but tended to *revert* to the lower stage of the conventional level even after briefly (usually in adolescence) attaining the post conventional level. Piaget's finding that girls were deficient in 'the legal sense' was confirmed.

These results led Gilligan to wonder if there might not be a quite different pattern of development to be discerned, at least in female subjects. She therefore conducted interviews designed to elicit not just how far advanced the subjects were towards an appreciation of the nature and importance of Kantian autonomy, but also to find out what the subjects themselves saw as progress or lack of it, what conceptions of moral maturity they came to possess by the time they were adults. She found that although the Kohlberg version of moral maturity as respect for fellow persons, and for their rights as equals (rights including that of free association), did seem shared by many young men, the women tended to speak in a different voice about morality itself and about moral maturity. To quote Gilligan, 'Since the reality of interconnexion is experienced by women as given rather than freely contracted, they arrive at an understanding of life that reflects the limits of autonomy and control. As a result, women's development delineates the path not only to a less violent life but also to a maturity realized by interdependence and taking care' (D.V., 172). She writes that there is evidence that 'women perceive and construe social reality differently from men, and that these differences center around experiences of attachment and separation . . . because women's sense of integrity appears to be intertwined with an ethics of care, so that to see themselves as women is to see themselves in a relationship of connexion, the major changes in women's lives would seem to involve changes in the understanding and activities of care' (D.V., 171). She contrasts this progressive understanding of care, from merely pleasing others to helping and nurturing, with the sort of progression that is involved in Kohlberg's stages, a progression in the understanding, not of mutual care, but of mutual *respect*, where this has its Kantian overtones of distance, even of some fear for the respected, and where personal autonomy and *in*dependence, rather than more satisfactory interdependence, are the paramount values.

This contrast, one cannot but feel, is one which Gilligan might have used the Marxist language of alienation to make. For the main complaint about the Kantian version of a society with its first virtue justice, construed as respect for equal rights to formal goods such as having contracts kept, due process, equal opportunity including opportunity to participate in political activities leading to policy and law-making, to basic liberties of speech, free association and assembly, religious worship, is that none of these goods do much to ensure that the people who have and mutually respect such rights will have any other relationships to one another than the minimal relationship needed to keep such a 'civil society' going. They may well be lonely, driven to suicide, apathetic about their work and about participation in political processes, find their lives meaningless and have no wish to leave offspring to face the same meaningless existence. Their rights, and respect for rights, are quite compatible with very great misery, and misery whose causes are not just individual misfortunes and psychic sickness, but social and moral impoverishment.

What Gilligan's older male subjects complain of is precisely this sort of alienation from some dimly glimpsed better possibility for human beings, some richer sort of network of relationships. As one of Gilligan's male subjects put it, 'People have real emotional needs to be attached to something, and equality does not give you attachment. Equality fractures society and places on every person the burden of standing on his own two feet' (D.V., 167). It is not just the difficulty of self reliance which is complained of, but its socially 'fracturing' effect. Whereas the younger men, in their college years, had seen morality as a matter of reciprocal noninterference, this older man begins to see it as reciprocal attachment. 'Morality is . . . essential . . . for creating the kind of environment, interaction between people, that is a prerequisite to the fulfillment of individual goals. If you want other people not to interfere with your pursuit of whatever you are into, you have to play the game,' says the spokesman for traditional liberalism (D.V. 98). But if what one is 'into' is interconnexion, interdependence rather than an individual autonomy that may involve 'detachment,' such a version of morality will come to seem inadequate. And Gilligan stresses that the interconnexion that her mature women subjects, and some men, wanted to sustain was not merely freely chosen interconnexion, nor interconnexion between equals, but also the sort of interconnexion that can obtain between a child and her unchosen mother and father, or between a child and her unchosen older and younger siblings, or indeed between most workers and their unchosen fellow workers, or most citizens and their unchosen fellow citizens.

A model of a decent community different from the liberal one is involved in the version of moral maturity that Gilligan voices. It has in many ways more in common with the older religion-linked versions of morality and a good society than with the modern Western liberal ideal. That perhaps is why some find it so dangerous and retrograde. Yet it seems clear that it also has much in common with what we can call Hegelian versions of moral maturity and of social health and malaise, both with Marxist versions and with so-called right-Hegelian views.

Let me try to summarize the main differences, as I see them, between on the one hand Gilligan's version of moral maturity and the sort of social structures that would encourage, express and protect it, and on the other the orthodoxy she sees herself to be challenging. I shall from now on be giving my own interpretation of the significance of her challenges, not merely reporting them.[14] The most obvious point is the challenge to the individualism of the Western tradition, to the fairly entrenched belief in the possibility and desirability of each person pursuing his own good in his own way, constrained only by a minimal formal common good, namely a working legal apparatus that enforces contracts and protects individuals from undue interference by others. Gilligan reminds us that noninterference can, especially for the relatively powerless, such as the very young, amount to neglect, and even between equals can be isolating and alienating. On her less individualist version of individuality, it becomes defined by responses to dependency and to patterns of interconnexion, both chosen and unchosen. It is not something a person *has*, and which she then chooses relationships to suit, but something that develops out of a series of dependencies and interdependencies, and responses to them. This conception of individuality is not flatly at odds with, say, Rawls' Kantian one, but there is at least a difference of tone of voice between speaking as Rawls does of each of us having our own rational life plan, which a just society's moral traffic rules will allow us to follow, and which may or may not include close association with other persons, and speaking as Gilligan does of a satisfactory life as involving 'progress of affiliative relationship' (D.V., 170) where 'the concept of identity expands to include the experience of interconnexion' (D.V., 173). Rawls can allow that progress to Gilligan-style moral maturity may be *a* rational life plan, but not a moral constraint on every life-pattern. The trouble is that it will not do just to say 'let this version of morality be an optional extra. Let us agree on the essential minimum, that is on justice and rights, and let whoever wants to go further and cultivate this more demanding ideal of responsibility and care.' For, first, it cannot be satisfactorily cultivated without closer cooperation from others than respect for rights and justice will ensure, and, second, the encouragement of some to cultivate it while others do not could easily lead to exploitation of those who do. It obviously *has* suited some in most societies well enough that others take on the responsibilities of care (for the sick, the helpless, the young) leaving them free to pursue their own less altruistic goods. Volunteer forces of those who accept an ethic of care, operating within a society where the power is exercised and the institutions designed, redesigned, or maintained by those who accept a less communal ethic of minimally constrained self-advancement, will not be the solution. The liberal individualists may be able to 'tolerate' the more communally minded, if they keep the liberals' rules, but it is not so clear that the more communally minded can be content with just those rules, nor be content to be tolerated and possibly exploited.

For the moral tradition which developed the concept of rights, autonomy and justice is the same tradition that provided 'justifications' of the oppression of those whom the primary right-holders depended on to do the sort of work they themselves preferred not to do. The domestic work was left to women and slaves, and the liberal morality for right-holders was surreptitiously supplemented by a different set of demands made on domestic workers. As long as women could be got to assume responsibility for the care of home and children, and to train their children to continue the sexist system, the liberal morality could continue to be the official morality, by turning its eyes away from the contribution made by those it excluded. The long unnoticed moral proletariat were the domestic workers, mostly female. Rights have usually been for the privileged. Talking about laws, and the rights those laws recognize and protect, does not in itself ensure that the group of legislators and rights-holders will not be restricted to some elite. Bills of rights have usually been proclamations of the rights of some in-group, barons, landowners, males, whites, non-foreigners. The 'justice perspective,' and the legal sense that goes with it, are shadowed by their patriarchal past. What did Kant, the great prophet of autonomy, say in his moral theory about women? He said they were incapable of legislation, not fit to vote, that they needed the guidance of more 'rational' males.[15] Autonomy was not for them, only for first class, really rational, persons. It is ironic that Gilligan's original findings in a way confirm Kant's views — it seems that autonomy really may not be for women. Many of them reject that ideal (D.V., 48), and have been found not as good at making rules as are men. But where Kant concludes — 'so much the worse for women,' we can conclude — 'so much the worse for the male fixation on the special skill of drafting legislation, for the bureaucratic mentality of rule worship, and for the male exaggeration of the importance of independence over mutual interdependence.'

It is however also true that the moral theories that made the concept of a person's rights central were not just the instruments for excluding some persons, but also the instruments used by those who demanded that more and more persons be included in the favored group. Abolitionists, reformers, women, used the language of rights to assert their claims to inclusion in the group of full members of a community. The tradition of liberal moral theory has in fact developed so as to include the women it had for so long excluded, to include the poor as well as rich, blacks and whites, and so on. Women like Mary Wollstonecraft used the male moral theories to good purpose. So we should not be wholly ungrateful for those male moral theories, for all their objectionable earlier content. They were undoubtedly patriarchal, but they also contained the seeds of the challenge, or antidote, to this patriarchal poison.

But when we transcend the values of the Kantians, we should not forget the facts of history — that those values were the values of the oppressors of women. The Christian church, whose version of the moral law Aquinas codified, in his very legalistic moral theory, still insists on the maleness of the God it worships, and jealously reserves for males all the most powerful positions in its hierarchy. Its patriarchal prejudice is open and avowed.

In the secular moral theories of men, the sexist patriarchal prejudice is today often less open, not as blatant as it is in Aquinas, in the later natural law tradition, and in Kant and Hegel, but is often still there. No moral theorist today would say that women are unfit to vote, to make laws, or to rule a nation without powerful male advisors (as most queens had), but the old doctrines die hard. In one of the best male theories we have, John Rawls's theory, a key role is played by the idea of the 'head of a household.' It is heads of households who are to deliberate behind a 'veil of ignorance' of historical details, and of details of their own special situation, to arrive at the 'just' constitution for a society. Now of course Rawls does not think or say that these 'heads' are fathers rather than mothers. But if we have really given up the age-old myth of women needing, as Grotius put it, to be under the 'eye' of a more 'rational' male protector and master, then how do families come to have any one 'head,' except by the death or desertion of one parent? They will either be two-headed, or headless. Traces of the old patriarchal poison still remain in even the best contemporary moral theorizing. Few may actually say that women's place is in the home, but there is much muttering, when unemployment figures rise, about how the relatively recent flood of women into the work force complicates the problem, as if it would be a good thing if women just went back home whenever unemployment rises, to leave the available jobs for the men. We still do not really have a wide acceptance of the equal right of women to employment outside the home. Nor do we have wide acceptance of the equal duty of men to perform those domestic tasks which in no way depend on special female anatomy, namely cooking, cleaning, and the care of weaned children. All sorts of stories (maybe true stories), about children's need for one 'primary' parent, who must be the mother if the mother breast feeds the child, shore up the unequal division of domestic responsibility between mothers and fathers, wives and husbands. If we are really to transvalue the values of our patriarchal past, we need to rethink all of those assumptions, really test those psychological theories. And how will men ever develop an understanding of the 'ethics of care' if they continue to be shielded or kept from that experience of caring for a dependent child, which complements the experience we all have had of being cared for as dependent children? These experiences form the natural background for the development of moral maturity as Gilligan's women saw it.

Exploitation aside, why would women, once liberated, not be content to have their version of morality merely tolerated? Why should they not see themselves as voluntarily, for their own reasons, taking on *more* than the liberal rules demand, while having no quarrel with the content of those rules themselves, nor with their remaining the only ones that are expected to be generally obeyed? To see why, we need to move on to three more differences between the Kantian liberals (usually contractarians) and their critics. These concern the relative weight put on relationships between equals, and the relative weight put on freedom of choice, and on the authority of intellect over emotions. It is a typical feature of the dominant moral theories and traditions, since Kant, or perhaps since Hobbes, that relationships between equals or those who are deemed equal in some important sense, have been the relations that morality is concerned primarily to regulate. Relationships between those who are clearly unequal in power, such as parents and children, earlier and later generations in relation to one another, states and citizens, doctors and patients, the well and the ill, large states and small states, have had to be shunted to the bottom of the agenda, and then dealt with by some sort of 'promotion' of the weaker so that an appearance of virtual equality is achieved. Citizens collectively become equal to states, children are treated as adults-to-be, the ill and dying are treated as continuers of their earlier more potent selves, so that their 'rights' could be seen as the rights of equals. This pretence of an equality that is in fact absent may often lead to desirable protection of the weaker, or more dependent. But it somewhat masks the question of what our moral relationships *are* to those who are our superiors or our inferiors in power. A more realistic acceptance of the fact that we begin as helpless children, that at almost every point of our lives we deal with both the more and the less helpless, that equality of power and interdependency, between two persons or groups, is rare and hard to recognize when it does occur, might lead us to a more direct approach to questions concerning the design of institutions structuring these relationships between unequals (families, schools, hospitals, armies) and of the morality of our dealings with the more and the less powerful. One reason why those who agree with the Gilligan version of what morality is about will not want to agree that the liberals' rules are a good minimal set, the only ones we need pressure *everyone* to obey, is that these rules do little to protect the young or the dying or the starving or any of the relatively powerless against neglect, or to ensure an education that will form persons to be *capable* of conforming to an ethics of care and responsibility. Put baldly, and in a way Gilligan certainly has not put it, the liberal morality, if unsupplemented, may *unfit* people to be anything other than what its justifying theories suppose them to be, ones who have no interest in each others' interests. Yet some must take an interest in the next generation's interests. Women's traditional work, of caring for the less powerful, especially for the young, is obviously socially vital. One cannot regard any version of morality that does not ensure that it gets well done as an adequate 'minimal morality,' any more than we could so regard one that left any concern for more distant future generations an optional extra. A moral theory, it can plausibly be claimed, cannot regard concern for new and future persons as an optional charity left for those with a taste for it. If the morality the theory endorses is to sustain itself, it must provide for its own continuers, not just take out a loan on a carefully encouraged maternal instinct or on the enthusiasm of a self-selected group of environmentalists, who make it their business or hobby to be concerned with what we are doing to mother earth.

The recognition of the importance for all parties of relations between those who are and cannot but be unequal, both of these relations in themselves and for their effect on personality formation and so on other relationships, goes along with a recognition of the plain fact that not all morally important relationships can or should be freely chosen. So far I have discussed three reasons women have not to be content to pursue their own values within the framework of the liberal morality. The first was its dubious record. The second was its inattention to relations of inequality or its pretence of equality. The third reason is its exaggeration of the scope of choice, or its inattention to unchosen relations. Showing up the partial myth of equality among actual members of a community, and of the undesirability of trying to pretend that we are treating all of them as equals, tends to go along with an exposure of the companion myth that moral obligations arise from freely *chosen* associations between such equals. Vulnerable future generations do not choose their dependence on earlier generations. The unequal infant does not choose its place in a family or nation, nor is it treated as free to do as it likes until some association is freely entered into. Nor do its parents always choose their parental role, or freely assume their parental responsibilities any more than we choose our power to affect the conditions in which later generations will live. Gilligan's attention to the version of morality and moral maturity found in women, many of whom had faced a choice of whether or not to have an abortion, and who had at some point become mothers, is attention to the perceived inadequacy of the language of rights to help in such choices or to guide them in their parental role. It would not be much of an exaggeration to call the Gilligan 'different voice' the voice of the potential parents. The emphasis on care goes with a recognition of the often unchosen nature of the responsibilities of those who give care, both of children who care for their aged or infirm parents, and of parents who care for the children they in fact have. Contract soon ceases to seem the paradigm source of moral obligation once we attend to parental responsibility, and justice as a virtue of social institutions will come to seem at best only first equal with the virtue, whatever its name, that ensures that each new generation is made appropriately welcome and prepared for their adult lives.

This all constitutes a belated reminder to Western moral theorists of a fact they have always known, that as Adam Ferguson, and David Hume before him emphasized, we are born into families, and the first society we belong to, one that fits or misfits us for later ones, is the small society of parents (or some sort of child-attendants) and children, exhibiting as it may both relationships of near equality and of inequality in power. This simple reminder, with the fairly considerable implications it can have for the plausibility of contractarian moral theory, is at the same time a reminder of the role of human emotions as much as human reason and will in moral development as it actually comes about. The fourth feature of the Gilligan challenge to liberal orthodoxy is a challenge to its typical *rationalism*, or intellectualism, to its assumption that we need not worry what passions persons have, as long as their rational wills can control them. This Kantian picture of a controlling reason dictating to possibly unruly passions also tends to seem less useful when we are led to consider what sort of person we need to fill the role of parent, or indeed want in any close relationship. It might be important for father figures to have rational control over their violent urges to beat to death the children whose screams enrage them, but more than control of such nasty passions seems needed in the mother or primary parent, or parent-substitute, by most psychological theories. They need to love their children, not just to control their irritation. So the emphasis in Kantian theories on rational control of emotions, rather than on cultivating desirable forms of emotion, is challenged by Gilligan, along with the challenge to the assumption of the centrality of autonomy, or relations between equals, and of freely chosen relations.

The same set of challenges to 'orthodox' liberal moral theory has come not just from Gilligan and other women, who are reminding other moral theorists of the role of the family as a social institution and as an influence on the other relationships people want to or are capable of sustaining, but also, as I noted at the start, from an otherwise fairly diverse group of men, ranging from those influenced by both Hegelian and Christian traditions (MacIntyre) to all varieties of other backgrounds. From this group I want to draw attention to the work of one philosopher in particular, namely Laurence Thomas, the author of a fairly remarkable article[16] in which he finds sexism to be a more intractable social evil than racism. In a series of articles, and a forthcoming book,[17] Thomas makes a strong case for the importance of supplementing a concern for justice and respect for rights with an emphasis on equally needed virtues, and on virtues seen as appropriate *emotional* as well as rational capacities. Like Gilligan (and unlike MacIntyre) Thomas gives a lot of attention to the childhood beginnings of moral and social capacities, to the role of parental love in making that possible, and to the emotional as well as the cognitive development we have reason to think both possible and desirable in human persons.

It is clear, I think, that the best moral theory has to be a cooperative product of women and men, has to harmonize justice and care. The morality it theorizes about is after all for all persons, for men and for women, and will need their combined insights. As Gilligan said

(D.V., 174), what we need now is a 'marriage' of the old male and the newly articulated female insights. If she is right about the special moral aptitudes of women, it will most likely be the women who propose the marriage, since they are the ones with more natural empathy, with the better diplomatic skills, the ones more likely to shoulder responsibility and take moral initiative, and the ones who find it easiest to empathize and care about how the other party feels. Then, once there is this union of male and female moral wisdom, we maybe can teach each other the moral skills each gender currently lacks, so that the gender difference in moral outlook that Gilligan found will slowly become less marked.

NOTES

1. John Rawls, *A Theory of Justice* (Harvard University Press)
2. Alasdair MacIntyre, *After Virtue* (Notre Dame: Notre Dame University Press)
3. Michael Stocker, 'The Schizophrenia of Modern Ethical Theories,' *Journal of Philosophy* 73, 14, 453–66, and 'Agent and Other: Against Ethical Universalism,' *Australasian Journal of Philosophy* 54, 206–20
4. Lawrence Blum, *Friendship, Altruism and Morality* (London: Routledge & Kegan Paul 1980)
5. Michael Slote, *Goods and Virtues* (Oxford: Oxford University Press 1983)
6. Laurence Thomas, 'Love and Morality,' in *Epistemology and Sociobiology*, James Fetzer, ed. (1985); and 'Justice, Happiness and Self Knowledge,' *Canadian Journal of Philosophy* (March, 1986). Also 'Beliefs and the Motivation to be Just,' *American Philosophical Quarterly* 22 (4), 347–52
7. Claudia Card, 'Mercy,' *Philosophical Review* 81, 1, and 'Gender and Moral Luck,' forthcoming.
8. Alison Jaggar, *Feminist Politics and Human Nature* (London: Rowman and Allanheld 1983)
9. Susan Wolf, 'Moral Saints,' *Journal of Philosophy* 79 (August, 1982), 419–39
10. For a helpful survey article see Owen Flanagan and Kathryn Jackson, 'Justice, Care & Gender: The Kohlberg-Gilligan Debate Revisited,' *Ethics*
11. Lawrence Kohlberg, *Essays in Moral Development*, vols. I & II (New York: Harper and Row 1981, 1984)
12. Bernard Williams, *Ethics and the Limits of Philosophy* (Cambridge: Cambridge University Press 1985)
13. Philippa Foot, *Virtues and Vices* (Berkeley: University of California Press 1978)
14. I have previously written about the significance of her findings for moral philosophy in 'What Do Women Want in a Moral Theory?' *Nous* 19 (March 1985), 'Trust and Antitrust,' *Ethics* 96 (1986), and in 'Hume the Women's Moral Theorist?' in *Women and Moral Theory*, Kittay and Meyers, ed., forthcoming.
15. Immanuel Kant, *Metaphysics of Morals*, sec. 46
16. Laurence Thomas, 'Sexism and Racism: Some Conceptual Differences,' *Ethics* 90 (1980), 239–50; republished in *Philosophy, Sex and Language*, Vetterling-Braggin, ed. (Totowa, NJ: Littlefield Adams 1980)
17. See articles listed in note 6, above. The forthcoming book has the title *A Psychology of Moral Character*.

QUESTIONS

1. What are some of the differences in the two approaches to morality that Annette Baier outlines in her summary of Carol Gilligan's account of an ethic of care and John Rawls's defence of justice?
2. According to Baier, how does reasoning about moral problems in terms of relationships and an inter-connection with others challenge what she refers to as "the individualism of the Western tradition"?
3. Does the perspective of the ethic of care adopted by those on the margins of society force us to reject the kind of moral theory offered by Kant?

4. Do you think that the approach to morality defended by Baier can be harmonized with a justice approach, as she suggests?

SUGGESTIONS FOR FURTHER READING

There are two ways to proceed in your exploration of the ideas introduced in this chapter. The first is to go directly to the main sources: either to the larger works by the authors in the chapter or to the works referred to in the notes appended to some of the contributions. A second approach is to look for a guide that will provide an overview of the field of moral philosophy as well as suggestions for approaching primary sources. It is with this latter approach in mind that we suggest the first group of readings.

- D.D. Raphael, *Moral Philosophy*, 2nd ed. (Oxford: Oxford University Press, 1994). This book is intended as an introduction to the subject and requires no previous knowledge of philosophy. Written expressly for beginners, it makes a point of showing the connections between abstract ethics and practical problems in law and government and in the social sciences generally.
- James Rachels, *The Elements of Moral Philosophy* (New York: Random House, 1986). In the course of providing a survey of traditional moral theory, Rachels also gives reasons for endorsing or rejecting the "contending ideas, theories, and arguments" in the area of moral philosophy.
- Paul W. Taylor, *Principles of Ethics: An Introduction* (Belmont, California: Wadsworth Publishing Company, 1975). The chief merit of this book as an introduction to moral philosophy is that it discusses some of the most important perennial topics encountered in moral philosophy, topics such as relativism, egoism, and freedom of the will. The book also includes lists of suggested readings that might prove helpful.
- Mary Warnock, *Ethics Since 1900* (Oxford: Oxford University Press, 1978). This, too, is an introductory text. However, its approach is quite different from that used by Taylor. Warnock surveys the development of modern moral philosophy by introducing some of the major moral philosophers and philosophical schools of the twentieth century.
- David Rosenthal and Fadlou Shahadi (eds.), *Applied Ethics and Ethical Theory* (Salt Lake City: University of Utah Press, 1988). A collection of articles by philosophers such as Ruth Macklin, Dale Jamieson, Onora O'Neill, and Frances Kamm, who examine the connections between moral theory and practical issues and address the specific issue of whether we can apply theory to practice.

A Selection of Theoretical Works

- Will Kymlicka, *Contemporary Political Philosophy* (Oxford: Clarendon Press, 1990). This book provides a useful survey of dominant and influential political theorists; in particular, of liberal theorists such as Ronald Dworkin and John Rawls.
- Ronald Dworkin, *Taking Rights Seriously* (London: Duckworth, 1978). Dworkin distinguishes between the formal and substantive approaches to equality, calling the first, "the right to equal treatment" and the second, "the right to treatment as an equal." He applies these approaches to such issues as affirmative action and pornography.

- John Rawls, *A Theory of Justice* (Cambridge, MA: Harvard University Press, 1971). This book has had a big impact on moral and political theory, as is evident in Annette Baier's critique of Rawls's account of justice in her reading in this chapter. Rawls sets forth principles of justice that "free and rational persons would accept in an initial position of equality."
- David Gauthier, *Morals by Agreement* (Oxford: Clarendon Press, 1986). In this book, Gauthier develops a contractarian rationale for moral behaviour. The result is a theory of morality that identifies the moral principles that would emerge from agreement among rational persons, who acknowledge a distinction between what they may and may not do by recognizing a place for mutual constraint.
- Carol Gilligan, *In a Different Voice: Psychological Theory and Women's Development* (Cambridge, Mass.: Harvard University Press, 1982). This is another book that has had a large impact on moral theory in particular. A number of authors in this collection, including Celia Wolf-Devine, Susan Sherwin, Christine Koggel, and Annette Baier, have summarized or made references to Gilligan's work on an ethic of care and its connections to women.
- Alasdair MacIntyre, *After Virtue: A Study in Moral Theory* (London: Duckworth, 1981). Recognized as a controversial re-evaluation of contemporary moral philosophy, this book offers an analysis of various moral theories in the context of an examination of history and tradition.

Notes on the Contributors

Anthony G. Amsterdam is a lawyer in the United States and has represented many clients who have received the death sentence.

Annette Baier teaches philosophy at the University of Pittsburgh. She has numerous publications in moral theory including two books, *Moral Prejudices: Essays on Ethics* (1994) and *Postures of the Mind: Essays on Mind and Morals* (1985).

Jerome E. Bickenbach teaches at Queen's University and is cross-appointed in Philosophy and the Faculty of Law. He is the editor of *Canadian Cases in the Philosophy of Law* (1991) and the author of *Physical Disability and Social Policy* (1993).

Andrew Brook is Professor of Philosophy and Director of the Institute of Interdisciplinary Studies at Carleton University. In addition to work as a consultant for Ontario Hydro, Atomic Energy of Canada Ltd., and the Ministry of Natural Resources of Ontario, he was an expert witness before the Canadian Environmental Assessment Agency panel on the AECL proposal for a geological deep disposal facility for high-level nuclear wastes in northern Ontario.

Alan Brudner is a Hegel Scholar and teaches at the University of Toronto in the Faculty of Law.

Lorenne Clark is a former member of the Department of Philosophy at the University of Toronto, practised law for several years in Nova Scotia, and is now the deputy minister of Justice for the Yukon.

Peter de Carteret Cory is a justice of the Supreme Court of Canada.

Wesley Cragg is the George R. Gardiner Professor of Business Ethics in the Schulich School of Business and a member of the Department of Philosophy at York University.

Jane English, now deceased, taught philosophy at the University of North Carolina, Chapel Hill, at the time the article included was first published.

George Erasmus served as president of the Dene Nation from 1976 to 1983 and was national chief of the Assembly of First Nations from 1985 to 1991. He was co-chair of the Royal Commission on Aboriginal Peoples. Erasmus was appointed to the order of Canada in 1987.

Ezzat A. Fattah teaches criminology at Simon Fraser University. His research on the deterrent effect of capital punishment was presented by the solicitor-general of Canada as background information for those participating in the parliamentary debates on the abolition of capital punishment in the 1970s.

Marilyn Frye is the author of *The Politics of Reality: Essays in Feminist Theory* (1983) and *Willful Virgin: Essays in Feminism* (1992). She teaches for Women's Studies and the Department of Philosophy at Michigan State University.

Northrop Frye, now deceased, is one of Canada's eminent literary scholars. His essays on Canadian culture are collected in a small volume entitled *Divisions on a Ground* (1982).

Raymond D. Gastil works with the Batell Research Centre in Seattle, Washington. One of his most recent works is *Progress: Critical Thinking about Historical Change* (1993).

David Gauthier is a former head of the Department of Philosophy at the University of Toronto. He currently teaches philosophy at the University of Pittsburgh and is the author of *Morals by Agreement* (1986).

Trudy Govier has taught philosophy at Trent University in Peterborough. She is the author of *A Practical Study of Argument*, a book on logic now in its third edition.

George Grant, now deceased, is one of Canada's best-known political thinkers. He is the author of *Lament for a Nation, Philosophy in a Mass Age, Technology and Empire*, and most recently, *English Speaking Justice*.

Sheila Grant is an active participant in the Right to Life movement.

Leo Groarke teaches philosophy at Sir Wilfrid Laurier University.

Colin P. Harrison, now deceased, practised medicine in Vancouver.

Thomas Hurka teaches philosophy at the University of Calgary. He is the author of *Principles: Short Essays on Ethics* (1994), a collection of newspaper columns written for *The Globe and Mail*.

Immanuel Kant was a prominent eighteenth-century German philosopher who made significant contributions in all areas of philosophy. Some of his most important works are *Critique of Pure Reason, Prolegomena to All Future Metaphysics, Critique of Practical Reason*, and *The Principles of the Metaphysics of Morals*.

Edward W. Keyserlingk is a former project research director with the Law Reform Commission of Canada. He is currently the director of the Biomedical Ethics Unit, Faculty of Medicine, McGill University.

Christine Koggel has a PhD in Philosophy from Queen's University. She recently held a SSHRCC post-doctoral fellowship and now teaches philosophy at Bryn Mawr College.

Rt. Hon. Antonio Lamer is chief justice of the Supreme Court of Canada.

Alistair M. Macleod is professor of philosophy and head of the Department of Philosophy at Queen's University. He is the author of articles and book chapters on such topics as rights, distributive justice, equality, rationality, and business ethics.

Michael McDonald is currently the head of the University of British Columbia Centre for Applied Ethics. He is the former editor of *Dialogue*, the official journal of the Canadian Philosophical Association.

Wendy McElroy writes and lectures on political theory and feminism. She is a fellow of the Center for Libertarian Studies and a member of the Association of Libertarian Feminists. In addition to the book *XXX: A Woman's Right to Pornography*, she has edited a collection of essays, *Freedom, Feminism, and the State*.

William R. McIntyre is a former justice of the Supreme Court of Canada.

Beverly McLachlin is a justice of the Supreme Court of Canada.

Mary Midgley, formerly a member of the University of Newcastle, England, is now retired. She is well known for her writing in applied ethics.

John Stuart Mill is best known for his development of utilitarianism from foundations set out by Jeremy Bentham in the early nineteenth century.

Jan Narveson, the editor of *Moral Issues* (1983) and the author of *Moral Matters* (1993), teaches at the University of Waterloo. He is a Fellow of the Royal Society of Canada.

Patrick Nowell-Smith is a former member of the Department of Philosophy at York University. He is now retired and living in Wales.

Fred Plain is a policy analyst on intergovernmental relations for the Nishnawbe-Aski nation. He has served as president of the Union of Ontario Indians and as chief of the Chippewas of Sarnia.

James Rachels teaches philosophy at the University of Alabama at Birmingham. He is the author of *The Elements of Philosophy* (1986) and the editor of *The Right Thing to Do: Basic Readings in Moral Philosophy* (1989).

Ayn Rand, now deceased, is best known for her novels *The Fountainhead* and *Atlas Shrugged*, in which she defends the "virtue of selfishness."

Tom Regan is a member of the Department of Philosophy and Religion at North Carolina State University. He has written numerous articles and books, including *The Case for Animal Rights* (1984).

Joe Sanders, a lawyer and political consultant, was an advisor to the National Indian Brotherhood from 1981 to 1991.

Mark Schwartz has an MBA from the Schulich School of Business at York University and an LLB from Osgoode Hall. He is currently enrolled as a PhD student in business ethics at the Schulich School of Business.

Karen Selick practises law in Belleville, Ontario. She is a columnist for the *Canadian Lawyer* and has done work for the Fraser Institute.

Amartya Sen is the author of numerous publications in economics and political theory. He is a professor of economics and of philosophy at Harvard University.

Susan Sherwin has written extensively on ethical issues from a feminist perspective, work which includes the book *No Longer Patient: Feminist Ethics & Health Care* (1992). She teaches philosophy at Dalhousie University in Halifax.

John Sopinka is a justice with the Supreme Court of Canada.

J.T. Stevenson has written extensively in the field of applied ethics and the history of Canadian political and social thought. He is professor emeritus at the University of Toronto.

L.W. Sumner teaches philosophy at the University of Toronto. He has written extensively on utilitarianism and rights and is the author of *The Moral Foundation of Rights* (1987) and *Abortion and Moral Theory* (1981).

Judith Jarvis Thomson teaches philosophy at the Massachusetts Institute of Technology. She is the author of *The Realm of Rights* (1990) and of *Rights, Restitution and Risk* (1986), a collection of her writings on ethics.

P.E. Trudeau, a former prime minister of Canada, now resides in Montreal.

Michael Walker is executive director of the Fraser Institute and is an author, co-author, and editor of numerous Fraser Institute publications.

Adrian Alex Wellington is a part-time instructor in the Division of Social Science at York University and a doctoral candidate in the Department of Philosophy at York University. She has a previous degree in law.

Cornel West is professor of religion and director of Afro-American studies at Princeton University. He has recently co-edited a five-volume encyclopedia entitled *Encyclopedia of African-American Culture and History* (1996).

Bertha Wilson is a former justice of the Supreme Court of Canada.

Celia Wolf-Devine teaches philosophy at Stonehill College in North Easton, Massachusetts.

David B. Wong is the author of *Moral Relativity* (1984). He is currently the chair of the Philosophy Department at Brandeis University in Massachusetts.

James O. Young teaches philosophy at the University of Victoria in British Columbia.

— — — — — — — — — *cut here* — — — — — — — — — —

STUDENT REPLY CARD

In order to improve future editions, we are seeking your comments on

CONTEMPORARY MORAL ISSUES, Fourth Edition

by Wesley Cragg and Christine M. Koggel

After you have read this text, please answer the following questions and return this form via Business Reply Mail. *Your opinions matter. Thank you in advance for your feedback!*

Name of your college or university: _____

Major program of study: _____

Course title: _____

Were you required to buy this book?　　yes _____　　　no _____

Did you buy this book new or used?　　new _____　　used _____ ($_____)

Do you plan to keep or sell this book?　keep _____　　sell _____

Is the order of topic coverage consistent with what was taught in your course?

— — — — — — — — — *fold here* — — — — — — — — — —

Are there chapters or sections of this text that were not assigned for your course? Please specify:

Were there topics covered in your course that are not included in this text? Please specify:

What did you like most about this text?

What did you like least?

If you would like to say more, we'd love to hear from you. Please write to us at the address shown on the reverse of this card.

- *cut here* - - - - - - - - - - - - - - - - -

- *fold here* - - - - - - - - - - - - - - - - -

Postage will be paid by

0183560299-L1N9B6-BR01

Attn.: Sponsoring Editor
College Division

MCGRAW-HILL RYERSON LIMITED
300 WATER ST
WHITBY ON   L1N 9Z9

cut here